www.brookscole.com

www.brookscole.com is the World Wide Web site for Brooks/Cole and is your direct source to dozens of online resources.

At www.brookscole.com you can find out about supplements, demonstration software, and student resources. You can also send e-mail to many of our authors and preview new publications and exciting new technologies.

www.brookscole.com
Changing the way the world learns®

THIRD EDITION

▲ AT-RISK YOUTH:
A COMPREHENSIVE RESPONSE

FOR COUNSELORS, TEACHERS, PSYCHOLOGISTS, AND HUMAN SERVICE PROFESSIONALS

J. Jeffries McWhirter
Arizona State University

Benedict T. McWhirter
University of Oregon

Ellen Hawley McWhirter
University of Oregon

Robert J. McWhirter
Federal Public Defenders, Phoenix, AZ

THOMSON

™

BROOKS/COLE

Australia • Canada • Mexico • Singapore • Spain
United Kingdom • United States

THOMSON

BROOKS/COLE

Executive Editor: Lisa Gebo
Aquisitions Editor: Julie Martinez
Assistant Editor: Shelley Gesicki
Editorial Assistant: Amy Lam
Technology Project Manager: Barry Connolly
Marketing Manager: Caroline Concilla
Marketing Assistant: Mary Ho
Advertising Project Manager: Tami Strang
Project Manager, Editorial Production: Katy German

Print/Media Buyer: Doreen Suruki
Permissions Editor: Kiely Sexton
Production Service: Carlisle Publishers Services
Copy Editor: Julie Kennedy
Cover Designer: Denise Davidson
Cover Image: Veer
Printer: Webcom

Printed in the Canada
2 3 4 5 6 7 07 06 05 04

For more information about our products,
contact us at:
**Thomson Learning Academic
Resource Center
1-800-423-0563**
For permission to use material from this text,
contact us by:
Phone: 1-800-730-2214
Fax: 1-800-730-2215
Web: http://www.thomsonrights.com

Library of Congress Control Number: 2003103758

ISBN 0-534-54871-7

Brooks/Cole—Thomson Learning
10 Davis Drive
Belmont, CA 94002
USA

Asia
Thomson Learning
5 Shenton Way #01–01
UIC Building
Singapore 068808

Australia/New Zealand
Thomson Learning
102 Dodds Street
Southbank, Victoria 3006
Australia

Canada
Nelson
1120 Birchmount Road
Toronto, Ontario M1K 5G4
Canada

Europe/Middle East/Africa
Thomson Learning
High Holborn House
50/51 Bedford Row
London WC1R 4LR
United Kingdom

Latin America
Thomson Learning
Seneca, 53
Colonia Polanco
11560 Mexico D.F.
Mexico

Spain/Portugal
Paraninfo
Calle/Magallanes, 25
28015 Madrid, Spain

This book is dedicated to the youngest generation of the McWhirter clan: Mary Veronica, Anna Cecilia, Paul John, Mark Thomas, Luke Robert, Monica Clare, Marielena Rose, Joseph Benedict, Jacob Nicholas, Robert Anthony, and Ryan Alexander. May we find ways to prevent them and all children from being at risk. May we find ways to help them and all children grow and develop into healthy, happy adults with people to love and important work to do. Albert Camus wrote, "Without work, all life goes rotten, but when work is soulless, life stifles and dies." And without people to love, nothing much matters anyway.

CONTENTS

CHAPTER **3**

FAMILY PROBLEMS OF AT-RISK CHILDREN AND YOUTH 36

CHAPTER **4**

SCHOOL ISSUES THAT RELATE TO AT-RISK CHILDREN AND YOUTH 57

CHAPTER **5**

INDIVIDUAL CHARACTERISTICS OF HIGH-RISK AND LOW-RISK CHILDREN AND YOUTH   77

PART **2**

AT-RISK CATEGORIES   93

CHAPTER **6**

SCHOOL DROPOUTS   95

CHAPTER **7**

CHAPTER 8

CHAPTER 9

CHAPTER **10**

SCHOOL SHOOTERS 177

CHAPTER **11**

YOUTH SUICIDE 195

PART **3**

PREVENTION, INTERVENTION, AND TREATMENT
APPROACHES   219

CHAPTER **12**

A PREVENTION/EARLY INTERVENTION/TREATMENT FRAMEWORK
AND OTHER ENVIRONMENTAL CONSIDERATIONS   221

CHAPTER **13**

CORE COMPONENTS OF PROGRAMS FOR PREVENTION AND EARLY INTERVENTION   240

CHAPTER **14**

PEER INTERVENTIONS   264

CHAPTER **15**

C H A P T E R **16**

PREFACE

▲ Since 1983, when the National Commission on Excellence in Education issued its report *A Nation at Risk*, educators, counselors, and many other professionals within and outside of the human services began to use the term *at risk* to identify a wide range of social-psychological problems. The term *at risk* can be useful for describing many young people whose potential for becoming responsible and productive adults is limited by challenges within the ecology of their lives. These include problems at home, in schools, in communities; problems with some cultural norms and social messages that contribute to risk in children's lives; and problems within children and adolescents themselves.

Now in its third edition, our goals for this book continue to be to provide the reader with up-to-date information and research on the categories of problems experienced by at-risk youth and to provide the reader with effective interventions for these problems. More specifically, we have completely revised all chapters to reflect the most current information and statistics of each problem presented. We continue to present a unified and consistent conceptual framework that includes discussions of all levels of the ecology of problem development and resolution related to youth at risk. This framework includes discussions of all levels of the ecology of problem development and resolution related to youth at risk. Finally, we present a variety of practical educational, psychological, and counseling interventions for the prevention and treatment of the problems. For this edition, we have expanded our discussion to reflect new intervention trends, especially empirically supported approaches; we have continued our focus on both teens and younger children along with their families and peers.

The information we present and the interventions we suggest can be used by a broad range of professionals, such as counselors, psychologists, social workers, human service professionals, and teachers. We direct our work primarily to graduate students in counseling, social work, education and special education, applied psychology, and other human service disciplines at both the pre- and in-service levels. However, we also write for teachers-in-training, as well as for undergraduate students in psychology, social work, justice studies, nursing, community psychology, and human services. We believe they may find this text useful. Many of the prevention and treatment methods we present here may also be used by school and community health, direct line human service, and mental health personnel—some directly and some with modification—in a wide range of settings, from birth-to-three enrichment programs to juvenile detention to family counseling.

As such, this book is intended as a textbook for courses in education, psychology, social work, special education, and human services. It is appropriate for developmental counseling courses as well, such as principles of counseling, elementary school guidance, and agency counseling interventions. This book also applies to courses related to counseling students with special needs, maladjusted children, and, of course, at-risk children and adolescents. It may also be useful as a supplemental or primary text in courses in child and youth care, case management, child/adolescent behavioral and emotional problem management, educational administration, and community agency administration. Feed-back we have received indicates that school and agency counselors as well as special education teachers find this book very useful.

In many ways this book reflects our belief about pedagogy, which is that three domains are important to learning: cognitive, affective, and behavioral. Whenever we plan a seminar, develop a workshop, or teach a class, we ask ourselves three questions: What is the most important information we want our students to know about the subject? How can we engage our students on an emotional/affective level? What new skills can we help our students learn to use? In this book we attend to the cognitive domain by providing up-to-date facts, research findings, and a theoretical and practical information base to stimulate thinking. We focus on the affective domain by presenting short readings at the beginning of each chapter and by presenting real-life case studies and sidebar stories to describe struggling young people and their families. We also include many specific behavioral strategies throughout the book to provide concrete and specific intervention skills to use with young clients and families. Although in Part II of the book we apply specific interventions to specific problems, nearly all of the interventions presented can be applied to a broad variety of problems and concerns experienced by children and adolescents.

This book may be used in a number of ways. For instance, educators can use the entire text in the standard semester (or quarter) university course such as a graduate counseling course, or they can use parts of it as the basis for modular units elected by students in social sciences, human services, education, and psychology. At the University of Oregon we use this book as the principal text for a quarter-long undergraduate course in the human services. At Arizona State University we have offered several modules on a variety of topics within an upper-division educational psychology course taught by graduate assistants. This text is used in some of the modules, and ten such modules could actually be based on this text alone: an overview of at-risk problems (Chapters 1, 2, 13, and 14); a family module (Chapters 3 and 15); a school issues module (Chapters 4, 6, 10, 13, and 14); a prevention module (Chapters 5, 12, and 13); and six modules based on the at-risk categories—school dropout (Chapter 6), substance use (Chapter 7), teen pregnancy and risky sexual behavior (Chapter 8), juvenile delinquency (Chapter 9), school shooters (Chapter 10), and youth suicide (Chapter 11). The final chapter on legal and ethical issues could be used across all areas. This text is also useful for training workshops and other forms of continuing professional education.

In this third edition, we have supplemented many of the chapters with additional prevention and treatment intervention suggestions. These include but are not limited to: refusal and resistance training; an Adlerian/Dreikurs intervention model; Glasser's Reality Therapy; Miller and Rollnick's Motivational Interviewing; crisis intervention strategies; parent training models; solution-focused interventions; and peer programs (such as cooperative learning, peer support networks, cross-age peer tutoring, and conflict resolution and peer mediation strategies). We have also added a completely new chapter on "school shooters" and suggest school-based prevention strategies, including anger management and anti-bullying programs, for this fairly recent national problem. On the inside of the front cover we provide a chart to help guide the reader in finding the strategies and in conceptualizing when to apply them in working with at-risk children and adolescents.

Based on feedback from instructors and students, we have added several other features to this edition that are available via the Brooks/Cole Web page. In reference to each chapter, we refer to further readings to supplement the information in the text. We have thoroughly updated Appendix A, which provides an extensive list with addresses, phone numbers, and Web page information of national organizations, agencies, and clearinghouses that provide information, technical assistance, and other resources on the problems that face high-risk children, adolescents, and families. Appendix B is a compilation of practical, concrete resources (such as manuals for conducting group interventions) that counselors, teachers, psychologists, and other human service professionals can use with populations of interest. Visit *http://helpingprofs.com.*

The book is divided into three major sections. In Part I we provide information on the factors that contribute to school dropout, substance use, teen pregnancy, delinquency and violence, and youth suicide. We discuss the ecology of children's lives, including the societal, neighborhood, family, school, and individual characteristics that increase risk for children and adolescents. In Part II we present data about the six at-risk categories introduced in Part I and we discuss treatment and prevention approaches for each. In Part III we incorporate more prevention strategies that focus on the family, the school, the peer groups, and the individual. We suggest how and when prevention can be applied to meet the developmental needs of children and families. Finally, we examine legal and ethical concerns important to counselors and other human service professionals when working with at-risk youth.

Throughout the book we have used case studies to highlight, apply, and personalize the information in the text. In the first four chapters we introduce the Andrews, Baker, Carter, and Diaz families. These families represent various ethnic/cultural groups from diverse socioeconomic and educational backgrounds and with different individual attitudes and behaviors. Each of the children in these families presents some risk of problem behavior. The background and circumstances of each family are described, and each family highlights and illustrates environmental, family, and school issues and concerns. The family members introduced in these case studies reappear throughout the book to illustrate specific issues. Readers will also find vignettes throughout the text that help to personalize and exemplify the issues being discussed.

It seems clear that if we do not confront the issues facing our young people and their families that our society will lose nearly a quarter of its youth to lifelong difficulty who might otherwise become productive, successful, and happy adults. We hope that this text increases awareness of the problems youth face and contributes to their solution.

About the Authors

This book is one of many McWhirter family projects that always seem to begin quite innocently around the breakfast bar but often take us far from home as they unfold. Such kitchen conversations led us to spend an intensive and exhilarating year in Turkey and another in Australia, both years as a Fulbright family. In Australia we developed a traveling road show with puppets and poems, music, and skits on learning disabilities, adult-child communication, and family enrichment. These discussions have also led us to pursue other international experiences along the way and most currently to help develop a center for family enrichment in Peñalolen, Santiago, Chile, one of the poorest communities of that great city, where we also annually conduct training workshops in Spanish on family communication, couples conflict resolution/mediation, and strategies for working with young people, families, and groups. This book has not taken us nearly so far geographically, but it has been a richly rewarding process.

Any book with four same-name authors seems bound to arouse curiosity, so perhaps we'd better explain who we are. Jeff is the father of Benedict and Robert, and Ellen and Benedict are married.

Jeff McWhirter holds a diplomate in counseling psychology from the American Board of Professional Psychology (ABPP) and is a fellow of the American Psychological Association (Divisions 17, 51, and 52), the American Psychological Society, the Association for Specialists in Group Work, and the Academy of Counseling Psychology. He is a professor in the Division of Psychology in Education, Arizona State University. A former teacher and school counselor, Jeff received his Ph.D. in Counseling Psychology from the University of Oregon in 1969. He has maintained a small private practice for over 30 years and consults regularly with schools and agencies that work with at-risk individuals. He has published over 120 chapters and articles in refereed journals, over a dozen training manuals, and seven books or monographs. He has been a Fulbright-Hays Senior Scholar to Turkey (1977–78), a Fulbright Senior Scholar to Australia (1984–85), and has taught summer sessions or short courses at 20 other universities in the United States or internationally. In 1989 he received the Arizona State University Distinguished Teacher Award. Most recently, he was selected as a candidate for the Fulbright Senior Specialist Program, a new Fulbright Program. He has been the principal investigator of several externally funded projects including a large Safe and Drug Free School and Community grant and a violence reduction grant for an alternative high school. His other areas of interest include group counseling, family counseling, learning disabilities, international aspects of counseling psychology, and grandchildren—not necessarily in the order listed.

Benedict McWhirter is an associate professor of counseling psychology at the University of Oregon and has served for most of his tenure there as Director of Doctoral Training. While serving as Director of Training, the Counseling Psychology Program received the American Psychological Association 2001 Suinn Minority Achievement Award for its efforts and success in contributing to the training of psychologists of color. Benedict received his Ph.D. in counseling psychology from Arizona State University in 1992. He was on the faculty in the Department of Educational Psychology at the University of Nebraska—Lincoln from 1993–1997, has taught at Arizona State University, and has been a teacher for seventh and eighth grades in Peru. He consults with schools on developing psychoeducational curriculum for high-risk youth. With Ellen, he also regularly conducts workshops with couples and provides counseling services to members of the community of Peñalolen in Santiago, Chile. He has extensively published and presented his scholarship at professional conferences in the areas of prevention for at-risk youth, training practices and multicultural training, college student development, loneliness, and counseling intervention approaches. Benedict received the 2001 University of Oregon Office of Multicultural Affairs Outstanding Faculty Award for his mentoring and support of students of color, and in 2003, he was named a Fulbright Scholar to conduct research and teach in Chile for the year 2004.

Ellen Hawley McWhirter is an associate professor of counseling psychology at the University of Oregon. Between 1993–1997 she was an assistant professor of counseling psychology at the University of Nebraska—Lincoln. Ellen received her Ph.D. in counseling psychology from Arizona State University in 1992. Her dissertation research was funded by a fellowship from the American Association of University Women. Her teaching experience also includes working with Head Start and teaching undergraduate students university academic survival skills. She has also taught and counseled Spanish-speaking children and parents. She has extensively published and presented her research and scholarship at national conventions in the areas of career and vocational counseling, multicultural counseling and training, empowerment, and socioeconomic factors related to mental health. She is the author of *Counseling for Empowerment* (American Counseling Association Press). Ellen was recently awarded the 2001 Fritz and Linn Kuder Early Career Scientist Practitioner Award from the Division of Counseling Psychology of the American Psychological Association. She has been involved in evaluating school-based career exploration courses that include school-to-work transition components, and studies the vocational development of adolescents of color. Ellen was named as a Fulbright Scholar to teach and conduct research in Chile for 2004, and she continues to conduct workshops in Chile with Benedict.

Anna McWhirter served as a co-author on previous editions to this book and is now focusing her attention and commitments on her family; she and her husband John have five young children. We thank Anna for her past efforts and work on this book.

Our son and brother, Robert, J. McWhirter who had written the chapter on legal and ethical issues and assisted with editing the text in past editions, has been added now as a new co-author. Robert has been a practicing attorney with the Federal Public Defender's Office in Phoenix, Arizona, since 1989. He received his Juris Doctorate from Arizona State University in 1988 and clerked with Vice Chief Justice Stanley G. Feldman of the Supreme Court of Arizona until 1989. Robert has developed a specialty in criminal immigration law and teaches it to Criminal Justice Act Panel Attorneys, sponsored by the Administrative Office of the United States Courts. During a sabbatical from the Federal Public Defender's Office in 1998, Robert was a visiting professor of law at Catholic University of Chile and at the University of Chile teaching seminars in Spanish on free speech, privacy, and the Internet and on American criminal procedure. Most recently, Robert travels to Venezuela, Chile, Nicaragua, and Columbia where he teaches trial practice skills to public defenders and judges and where he consults with new public defender offices as part of judicial reform in those countries. Through support from the United States Department of State, Robert has also served as an advisor to the Venezuelan Constitutional Assembly drafting the new Venezuelan constitution. Related to his teaching and consulting, Robert has also published articles in the *Georgetown Immigration Law Review* and the *Criminal Practice Law Reports*. He is also the author of the texts: *The Criminal Lawyer's Guide to Immigration Law: Questions and Answers* (2001; American Bar Association Press), *Criminal Law of Arizona* (2001; State Bar of Arizona Press), and *Strangers in an Even Stranger Land: Aliens and Immigration Law After September 11th* (2002; American Bar Association Press).

Acknowledgments

Although we four are the most visible in this family project, other members of the clan contributed in many ways. We would particularly like to thank our daughter and sister, Dr. Paula McWhirter, another counseling psychologist, who was a source for great ideas and resources, and we thank Mary McWhirter (Jeff's wife and mother to Benedict and Robert) who has been a source of great support over the years and who cares for all the grandchildren so that her own children can write. We also thank Ben and Ellen's two daughters Anna and Marielena for their loving patience and humor.

We are also grateful to our colleagues at Arizona State University and at the University of Oregon. In particular we acknowledge Sheila Saunders and Donna LaGuardia from

ASU. Our friend Reba Wilson at ASU again pulled us out of a tight spot by graciously volunteering much of her own time to assist us with the final stages of text preparation. Several students were also helpful. We are grateful to Katie Millard, graduate student in ASU's nutrition program, who was so helpful that we made her part of the family (well, there may have been other reasons too). Katie is now married to our son/brother Mark, who wrote one of the poems to begin one of the chapters. We thank members of SNOF: Allison Lau, May Lim, Sharilyn Lum, James Lyda, Heather Marshall, Katy Cahill, Carolyn Swearingen, and especially Keith Miller, as well as Colleen Comeau and Jenie Liang from the University of Oregon's Counseling Psychology Program for their wonderful research assistance. Additionally, we would like to thank all of our students, advisees, and members of our doctoral research seminars who have helped us with hours of discussions, questions, and ideas over the years that have helped enrich our thinking and this text; in particular, Alysha Bundy, Adriana Tarazon, Sean Gilboy, Veronica Rodriguez, and Scott Herrmann from ASU, and Jason Burrow-Sanchez, Krista Marie Gragg, Rebecca Hart, Jarrett Horibata, and Saba Rasheed from the University of Oregon. Our thanks to all of you.

We appreciate the useful suggestions and comments offered by all those persons who have reviewed the book. These include: Mary Deck of Western Carolina University, Robert J. Drummond of the University of North Florida, Larry Golden of the University of Texas at San Antonio, Jack Sutton of the University of Southern Maine for the first edition; Marjorie A. Rust, University of Phoenix and Adelaide Santana, Northern Arizona University, for the second edition; and Fred Bemak, University of Wisconsin, Oshkosh; Robin Allen, Boise State University; Trey Fitch, Morehead State University; Bonnie Bowers, Centre College of Kentucky; Robert Coombs, Southern College; David J. Srebalus, West Virginia University-Morgantown; Marjorie Rust; Adelaida Santana Pellicier, Northern Arizona University, Tuscon; Keren M. Humphrey, Texas A&M University-Commerce; John C. Worzbyt, Indiana University of Pennsylvania, who reviewed this third edition. In addition, a number of colleagues who have adopted this book for classes have been generous in their praise and constructive feedback. They are: Judy Daniels and Michael D'Andrea at the University of Hawaii at Manoa; William E. Miller at the University of Maine—Orono; Gary Ross-Reynolds, Nicholls State University; John Romano from the University of Minnesota; and Joanne Curran, SUNY—Oneonta. To them all: Thank you again. You have helped to make this book better. The Brooks/Cole staff, as usual, has been very helpful throughout this process. We are especially grateful to our editor, Julie Martinez, who has always been flexible, professional, and fun to work with.

At-Risk Children and Youth: The Ecology of Problems

▲ Part 1 consists of five chapters. In Chapter 1 we discuss and define the term *at risk* and provide an overview of the book and a metaphor for unifying various aspects of concerns for children and adolescents who are at risk. In the next four chapters we provide overviews of the problems related to children and adolescents. We discuss environmental and societal issues; family, community, and school concerns; and high-risk/low-risk behaviors, attitudes, and skills that young people possess and develop. We also present four family case studies that will be used throughout the rest of the book to illustrate specific problems and issues.

An Introduction to At-Risk Issues: The Tree

▲ *Rather than the hasty tinkering of the mechanic, the nurturing of life requires the patience of the gardener. The fast technological rush of society leads us to be mechanics. We must preserve the long patience of the gardener.*

J. J. McWhirter

Chapter Outline

▲   The well-being of our society depends on our ability to prepare well-adjusted, responsible, well-educated young people to step forward as the older generation passes. Our nation's continuing stability and strength depend on our ability to ensure that our youth are prepared to fill the courtrooms and boardrooms, the classrooms and operating rooms, the high-tech factories and industries of tomorrow. And young people will only be prepared to meet the demands of the future if schools, families, and communities are involved in the project.

Schools must provide an environment that maximizes learning and minimizes conditions that interfere with learning, not simply for middle-class white children, but for those who struggle with poverty, learning problems, and other issues as well. Family life also determines a nation's strength and stability. A family must provide its children and adolescents security and safety, affection and discipline. Young people need to learn appropriate and healthy behaviors to develop responsible attitudes and mutual interdependence. Communities can enhance access to quality child care, education programs, health care, and living wages, and provide young people with opportunities to work for the welfare of others.

In this chapter we highlight the problems that threaten children and youth and consequently society. We present statistics that illuminate the severity of problems and then personalize these statistics by describing one family. Next, we provide an overview of the entire at-risk arena, using the metaphor of a tree as an organizational and pedagogical device. The tree with all its parts—the soil (environment), the roots (family and school issues), the trunk (high-risk versus low-risk attitudes and behaviors), the branches (specific at-risk categories), and the foliage, fruit, and flowers (the individual young people)—together with the gardener who provides pruning and nurturing (intervention techniques), provide a conceptual metaphor that shows the interrelationships of the problems from an ecological perspective.

The Scope of the Problems: An Overview of the Ecology of At-Risk Youth

Unfortunately, too many of our young people are falling by the wayside. In fact, so many are falling away—so many are at risk—that we might conclude that our society itself is at risk. The scope of the problem is enormous. The statistics cited below are discussed in detail in later chapters, but for now they provide a reminder of the problems that confront young people. Professionals who deal with young people know these problems and their pervasiveness.

Facts of an At-Risk Society

- In 2000 11.6 million children lived in poverty and one in three children will live in poverty at some point during their childhood.
- African American and Latino children are disproportionately poor. In 2000, 31% of African American youth and 28% of all Latino children were poor, with children of color under age 6 disproportionately poor.
- The majority of poor children live in families that work. More than three out of four poor children (77%) reside with a family member who worked in the last year.
- In 2000, nearly 40% of children in single-parent households headed by women were poor.
- Violent youth crime occurs most often between 3 P.M. and 6 P.M., when almost 7 million U.S. children are at home alone. A child's chance of being a victim of crime triples after school.
- Surveys consistently find that between 30 and 40% of male youth and 15 and 30% of female youth report having committed a serious violent offense by age 17.
- One in 1,000 children will be killed by guns before they reach age 20.
- In 1999 14% of students reported being in a physical fight on school property and 7 to 8% of ninth through twelfth graders were threatened or injured with a weapon.
- During the 1995–1999 period, teachers were the victims of 635,000 violent crimes in schools.
- The number of youth involved in gangs remains at peak levels, with female gangs a significant social problem, and involvement with gangs remains one of the most powerful predictors of future violence.
- Teen pregnancy rates, although declining, are much higher in the United States than in other developed countries—twice as high as in England, Wales, and Canada, and nine times higher than in the Netherlands or Japan.
- About 30% of young adolescents report having had sexual intercourse by age 15. Fully one-fourth of all adolescents will be infected with a sexually transmitted disease before they graduate from high school.
- A sexually active teen who does not use contraception has a 90% chance of pregnancy, and 78% of teenage pregnancies are unplanned.
- Males born to teen mothers are 13% more likely to end up in prison. Females born to teen mothers are 22% more likely to be teenage moms.
- Two-thirds of all high school seniors have used illegal drugs. Ninety percent of high school seniors have used alcohol.

- Seventy-seven percent of eighth graders report having used alcohol with over 13% of eighth graders and 27% of seniors using alcohol on a regular and heavy basis.
- School vandalism costs our nation over $600 million each year.
- Finally, in 2001 it was estimated that just 3.5% ($65.3 billion) of the federal budget was allocated for education, training, employment, and social services *combined*. In contrast, nearly five times as much ($299 billion, 16.1%) of the federal budget was spent on national defense.

Even though there are hints of some improvement, this gloomy catalog of the problems facing American children and adolescents shows only moderate signs of improvement (Garbarino, 1998; Moore & Hagedorn, 2001). The catalog reflects millions of personal stories, some of which are reported under dramatic headlines about abandoned infants, battered and sexually abused children, suicides, and drug overdoses. The catalog also reflects millions of less "newsworthy" stories of troubled, depressed, and anxious young people: children who suffer at home and at school; young people afraid, bored, or angry; adolescents bewildered by family conflict, divorce, or absentee parents; and young people afraid of violence while at home and at school.

The Use of the Term *At Risk:* Definition Problems

During the past two decades the term *at risk* has appeared frequently in literature on education, psychology, medicine, social work, and economics as well as in the legislation of various states and in federal government reports. Its origins are obscure and its use in various contexts indicates a lack of consensus regarding its meaning. Psychologists, social workers, and counselors use the term to denote individuals who suffer emotional and adjustment problems. Educators use it sometimes to refer to young people who are at risk of dropping out of the educational system, sometimes to refer to youth who are not learning skills to succeed after graduation, and sometimes to refer to children whose current educational mastery makes their future school career problematic. Medical workers use the term to refer to individuals with health problems. Economists and the business community use it to refer to workers who do not have the requisite literacy and numeracy skills to obtain employment or to succeed at their jobs.

Here is one definition of *at risk* as applied to children and adolescents that we believe will be helpful in clarifying the term and construct:

> *At risk* denotes a set of presumed cause-effect dynamics that place an individual child or adolescent in danger of future negative outcomes. *At risk* designates a situation that is not necessarily current (although we sometimes use the term in that sense, too) but that can be anticipated in the absence of intervention.

For example, young people who use tobacco are at risk for alcohol use; young people who use alcohol are at risk for illicit drug use. Children and adolescents who use illicit drugs are at risk for drug abuse. Thus, a specific behavior, attitude, or deficiency provides an initial marker of later problem behavior. Conduct disorders, aggression, and low achievement in elementary school become markers that predict later delinquent and antisocial behavior in adolescence. This is why the term *at risk* does not necessarily designate a situation that is current but that can be anticipated in the absence of intervention.

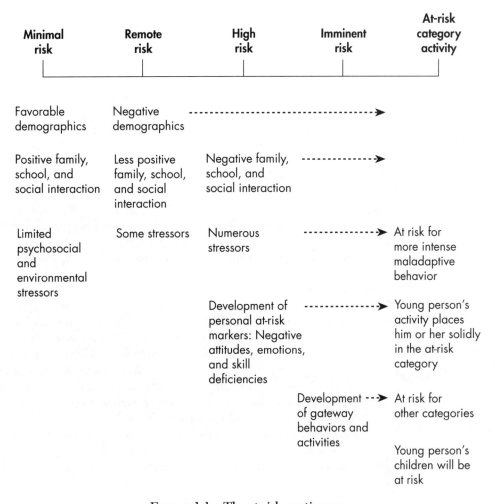

FIGURE 1.1   The at-risk continuum

Perhaps even more important, being at risk must be viewed less as a discrete, unitary diagnostic category than as a series of steps along a continuum. Figure 1.1 illustrates this continuum from minimal and remote risk to personal behavior that anticipates imminent risk and finally precipitates the activities associated with being engaged in one or more types of risky behavior. The following definitions outline some of the descriptive characteristics that correspond to different levels of risk along this continuum. Although not all characteristics in each category are always predictive of outcomes, in general these clusters of risk and protective factors help determine each child's potential level of risk.

Minimal risk.   Young people who are subjected to few psychosocial stressors, who attend good and well-funded schools, who have loving, caring relationships, and whose families are of higher socioeconomic status are generally at minimal risk for future trouble. Because of the complex ecology of stressors that young people face, we do not use the term *no risk*. Young people in all circumstances may have to cope with a death, family discord, incapacity, or unpredictable family factors such as bankruptcy, divorce, or loss of home. Such stressors can appear at any time regardless of existing protective factors. Depending on the young person's age, developmental level, and personal characteristics, the environmental resources available, and a host of other factors, the consequences may or may not be negative in the long term. Further, neither favorable demographics nor "good" families and schools provide invulnerability (Mitchell, 1996). Affluent adolescents may reject positive adult values and norms. Neither money or social status guarantees meaning and purpose in life. Finally, some "perfect" families harbor secrets—alcoholism, incest, depression—that stem from and perpetuate dysfunction.

Remote risk.   The point on the continuum at which risk, although still remote, seems increasingly possible is reached when markers of future problems appear. The demographic characteristics of low socioeconomic status, poor economic opportunity, poor access to good education, and membership in an ethnic minority group are associated with greater dropout rates, teen pregnancy, vulnerability, participation in violence, and other problems. Clearly risk factors do not emerge *due* to a person being a person of color, but membership in an ethnic minority group often suggests experiences of oppression, economic marginalization, and racism that negatively influence children and adolescents. That is, children of color who are poor are overrepresented in the at-risk behavioral categories. Negative interactions and increased psychosocial stressors (such as divorce or death in the immediate family or loss of family income) are also markers of potential problems. Of course, most poor African American, Latino, and Native American young people survive such difficulties and function well. Thus, even though these background factors are important, they are not predictive of risk for an individual child.

It is important to note that risk factors are also multiplicative. A young person who is from an impoverished, dysfunctional family and who attends a poor school in an economically marginalized neighborhood is potentially farther along the at-risk continuum than children who do not experience these conditions, especially if there are additional major psychosocial stressors. This is particularly the case when the individual child demonstrates personal characteristics that place him or her at even greater risk.

High risk.   Although dysfunctional families, poor schools, negative social interactions, and numerous psychosocial stressors nudge a young person toward higher levels of risk, the final push is supplied by the person's own negative attitudes, emotions, and behaviors. Characteristics that suggest a child is at "high-risk" include aggression and conduct problems, impulsivity, anxiety, affective problems such as depression and bipolar disorder, and hopelessness, as well as deficits in social skills and coping behaviors. Of course, these characteristics both emerge from and enhance the negativity of the environment around the child; the causal pathway is dynamic. These personal markers signal the internalization of problems and set the stage for participation in gateway behaviors.

Imminent risk.   Individual high-risk characteristics often find expression in participation in gateway behaviors. Gateway behaviors are mildly or moderately distressing activities, frequently self-destructive, which often progress to increasingly deviant behaviors. A child's aggression toward other children and adults, for example, is a gateway to juvenile delinquency. Cigarette use is a gateway to alcohol and marijuana use, which can be a gateway to use of harder drugs. Although progression through each gate is neither certain nor predictable (for example, some evidence suggests that early use of marijuana among girls is actually a precursor or gateway to chronic cigarette smoking in adulthood and not the other way around), evidence linking gateway behaviors with more serious activities is so strong that such behaviors must be recognized as placing young people at imminent risk.

At-risk category activity.   The final step in the continuum is reached when the young person participates in those activities that define the at-risk categories. Here we confront the conceptual problem with the term *at risk*. Although the literature in this area continues to refer to young people at this level as "at risk," they have already passed beyond risk because they are already engaged in the problems that define the category. Of course, activity in any at-risk category can both escalate as well as generalize to other categories. The young person who uses drugs can begin to abuse them and become addicted. The youthful delinquent can go on to commit violent crimes as a later teen and adult. Category activity by the adolescent can lead to lifelong involvement in self- and other-destructive behavior. Generalization means that individuals who participate in one category activity are at risk for engaging in others. The teen who drops out of school, for example, is at great risk for drug dependence, delinquency, and so forth. Consequently, we continue to apply the term *at risk* to behaviors and characteristics along the entire continuum, using the appropriate points along the way to anchor our discussion.

Assess the Context of Problems, Such as Poverty and Racism

The use of the term *at risk* has generated criticism and debate (Tidwell & Corona Garrett, 1994; Tidwell, 1993; Swadener & Lubeck, 1995). Viewing level of risk as a continuum that denotes future possibilities resolves some of the objections to the term (J. J. McWhirter, B. T. McWhirter, A. M. McWhirter, & E. H. McWhirter, 1995). But Swadener and Lubeck (1995) argue that an emerging ideology of risk emphasizes a deficit model that locates problems and pathology in the victim. The use of the term in the media, in casual conversations, and even by professionals suggests that risk is inherent in individual children and families. As will become abundantly clear (see especially Chapter 2), we place the blame for 14 million children living in poverty firmly in the public domain. Adequate parental leaves, affordable child care, more accessible housing, increased employment opportunities and living wages, full funding of Women, Infants, and Children (WIC) and Head Start initiatives, and accessible health care will go a long way toward reducing risk. Equally problematic is the fact that children labeled "at risk" frequently are children of color from low socioeconomic environments. Rearing children and adolescents in the context of economic disparities, political powerlessness, and a cultural and social milieu steeped in racism provide the soil that nurtures risk.

Behind each of the statistics we have cited are flesh-and-blood children, adolescents, and families. In this first part of the book, we describe several cases that are composites of families. These cases give vivid and personal life to the faceless statistics. In addition, the cases help clarify educational, psychological, and counseling strategies. The first family to be considered is the Andrews family.

CASE STUDY

The Andrews Family

The Andrews family consists of Jack, Alicia, and two children from Alicia's previous marriage. Mr. and Mrs. Andrews have been married for eight years, and this marriage is the second for both. They live in a modest and rundown house in a working-class neighborhood of a major city.

Jack Andrews is a 46-year-old semiskilled laborer who was once employed as a technician in an electronics plant. About five years ago the plant was computerized, and the new technology reduced the labor force by 40%. Jack lost his job and held a series of short-term, part-time jobs since that time. He currently has a part-time position pumping gas at a local service station. Thus, the family income, which was never very high, fell drastically. Jack is an angry, hostile man with limited insight and a blustering, aggressive style in his interactions with his family.

Jack was an only child. He alludes to a stormy relationship with his own father, who apparently was quite strict and harsh. Jack is especially critical of his mother, with whom he had a very poor relationship. When he was 13, his mother had a "nervous breakdown," and he lived with his aunt for about a year because, as he said, "my mother didn't want me." He graduated from high school and served approximately 10 years in the army. He married during this time but divorced a few months later. He maintains no contact with his first wife. He met Alicia about nine years ago and after a brief courtship they married.

Alicia is the third of four children. She lived with her parents until she was six, when they divorced. Her mother could not support the children, so Alicia spent the next two years with her grandparents. She then moved in with her father and his new wife. Alicia dropped out of school after the ninth grade and never finished high school.

Alicia went to work in a factory and married John Steiner at age 18. This marriage was difficult and stormy, beginning with Alicia's almost immediate pregnancy with Allie. John had dropped out of school, was a heavy drinker as a young man, and continued to indulge in periodic drinking binges. The drinking escalated after Paul was born. John physically abused the children and Alicia. When Alicia discovered that he was also sexually abusing Allie, the tensions in the family reached the breaking point and she divorced him. Alicia retained the house as part of their divorce settlement. John was convicted of sexual abuse and served a prison sentence, and neither Alicia nor the children have had any contact with him since the trial. Alicia believes

The Andrews Family *(continued)*

or hopes that Allie has "gotten over" the sexual abuse and forgotten it. Neither one ever brings it up or acknowledges that it happened.

After divorcing John, Alicia worked as a waitress in a coffee shop until she married Jack. She is now 34 years old and works the lunch shift (11–2) at the same coffee shop. Alicia appears shy, unassertive, and somewhat depressed. She seems to be worried about the family interactions and often attempts to mediate family disputes and conflicts.

Mr. and Mrs. Andrews describe their marriage as an average one. They are somewhat hesitant to talk about their marital conflicts, but Jack has expressed his dissatisfaction with Alicia's complaints about his "laziness." Alicia says he is unwilling to do housework and neglects home maintenance, and she voices frustration about his limited income. They believe themselves to be fairly strict parents, and Alicia sometimes fears they are too strict.

Allie Andrews, 16, is in her second year of high school. She is an attractive girl of average ability. About three years ago Allie went through what her mother refers to as a "sudden transformation," changing from an awkward girl into a physically mature young woman. At the age of 14, she expressed a desire to date. Her interest in boys was reciprocated, and she seemed to be popular among the older boys in high school. Her parents reluctantly gave in, but firmly stipulated the time she was to be home, the places she could go, the boys she could go out with, and so forth. During this time her relationship with her parents became increasingly conflictual. Recently she has begun to violate her curfew and hang out with a "bad crowd." When she is grounded, she sometimes sneaks out to join her friends. Her school grades have been dropping, although she continues to pass all her courses. She became a cheerleader this year. Allie is currently dating several different boys, including an African American classmate. She has been expressly forbidden to date African Americans, so she meets him away from home.

Allie is sullen around her stepfather. She believes that Jack blames her for most of the tension in the family, and she shows her hurt by constantly defying him. Days go by without a word between them. Their mutual dislike is a consistent part of their interactions. Jack uses the same harsh, authoritarian child-rearing style that he resented in his own father. He is the unquestioned decision maker and controls the children primarily through shouting, threatening to throw them out of the house, and grounding. Alicia is worried about Allie, blames herself for the sexual abuse that occurred, and wants Allie to be "happy" and have a

CASE STUDY

The Andrews Family *(continued)*

"normal family." Alicia absorbs conflict between the other family members, attempting to mediate and keep everyone calm. Over the past two years, Allie's parents, in particular her stepfather, have become increasingly suspicious and fearful. They suspect that Allie may be sexually active and fear she is not responsible enough to prevent pregnancy. They also suspect that her friends are drug users and fear that she will become addicted. Several times a week these issues erupt into loud arguments between Allie and Jack, or between Alicia and Jack. In the end, Allie, faced with her parents' lack of faith in her, feels hurt and misjudged. She responds with defiance, which invokes even more anger, and Jack tightens the restrictions. Lately she has threatened to run away if Jack doesn't let her choose her own friends, set her own timetable, and quit suspecting her of being a sexually promiscuous drug user.

The most recent confrontation occurred when Jack discovered Allie's dating relationship with her African American friend. This discovery has provoked a family crisis. Jack has threatened to "disown" Allie if she does not break off the relationship. Allie is sulking and threatening to run away. Alicia is frustrated and depressed about the antagonism between the two people to whom she feels most closely connected. Allie feels deeply hurt and sees running away as a means to hurt back. Her stepfather, in his own way, feels deeply hurt that his once compliant stepdaughter is now so unaccepting of his authority and protection. He expresses a strong dislike of his stepdaughter and is quite angry about her behavior.

Paul Andrews, 12, is a short, stocky eighth grader with an air of bravado. Underneath the bravado, however, he appears to be a very depressed and angry child. His parents' main concerns are Paul's dislike of school and his aggressive behavior, although Jack often tries to convince Alicia that Paul's behavior is "how boys are." Paul says he feels very sad at times for no reason. His aggressive behavior is a problem in the classroom, and he is suspected of stealing other children's lunch money. His behavior at home is no better. Two months ago he "accidentally" set fire to one of Alicia's dresses. He shows an intense interest in bloodshed, accidents, fires, and violent crimes. Between the incidents of aggression he seems overly controlled, and unless he gets help now, he may become increasingly violent or self-destructive as a teenager. He is also reaching the stage of development at which questions of personal and sexual identity are assuming some urgency for him. He seeks acceptance while at the same time rejecting pressures to conform. His relationship with both parents fluctuates from lukewarm to cold and back again several times a week.

AT-RISK PROBLEMS AND ISSUES

Cause or Effect?

One of the difficulties in trying to understand at-risk problems is fragmentation of knowledge. School dropout, drug and alcohol abuse, risky sexual activity, juvenile delinquency, youth suicide, and other problems are usually studied separately. In the real world, however, they interact; they reinforce one another; they cluster together. Not only do problems cluster, but so do the young people who have these problems; they tend to live in the same neighborhoods and to be exposed to many of the same influences. The damage that begins in childhood becomes much more visible in adolescence. The problems reverberate within the community and frequently are intergenerational.

Empirical research is a relatively recent development in the study of at-risk behavior. Much of this growing body of research is correlational, and the fact that two factors are correlated do not indicate that one is the cause of the other. Parent depression is correlated with child antisocial behavior but the direction of causality is unclear. Perhaps the child's negative behavior contributes to the parent's depression; or perhaps the underlying depression of the parent results in inconsistent parenting that contributes to the child's predelinquent behavior; or likely both effect each other and are related to other factors as well. Circular or dynamic causality is operating—each problem and risk factor contributes to the other—so our knowledge of families like the Andrews illustrate that at-risk families and at-risk young people influence each other in many ways. In recent years, longitudinal research that tracks individual and contextual factors over time has assisted in answering some questions about "which came first," but overall demonstrates the multidirectional influencing nature of community, school, family, and individual characteristics. In later chapters we identify the relationships between variables that contribute to risk and resilience and consider issues of causality when it is possible to do so.

Vulnerable and Underserved

In addition to issues of cause and effect, particular attention needs to be directed to young people who are especially vulnerable to risk and who receive inadequate intervention. Several reports (e.g., Garbarino, 1998) have suggested that the physical and mental health needs of children and adolescents in general are underserved, and some children are treated even less equitably than others. Two groups of youth are particularly vulnerable and underserved. Children and adolescents of color usually do not receive culturally sensitive, relevant, and appropriate interventions and are more likely to be educationally and economically marginalized. They also often face issues of acculturation, ethnic identity, and language challenges. The second group are gay, lesbian, bisexual, and transgendered youth, who are particularly vulnerable to marginalization and violence.

Children and adolescents of color. Demographics in the United States are changing rapidly. Populations of color are growing at such a pace that by the year 2020 they will be the majority population in the United States. Asian Americans are the fastest growing ethnic group and are a very heterogeneous group. As many as 32 different Asian American ethnic groups are now identified in the United States. Soon the Filipino American population will be the largest Asian group, followed by Chinese, Korean, Vietnamese, Indian, and

Japanese. Nearly 60% of Asians in the United States are foreign-born, often recently immigrated, and represent a serious challenge to educational systems and to mental health professionals (Cheng, 1996). Clearly, the United States is rapidly becoming more and more of a nation of color, with richly diverse cultural groups growing in virtually every region of the country.

The historical and contemporary mistreatment and marginalization of people of color continues an ethos of racism and inequitable opportunity in the United States that has contributed to youth being "at risk." Many of the conditions that predict negative outcomes for youth, such as poor living conditions, poor quality and underfunded schools, and lack of economic opportunity, are correlated with being a child of color and so it is hard to tell where one risk factor ends and another begins. As we examine various frames of the at-risk picture, we need to make prevention, early intervention, and treatment approaches more culturally relevant, sensitive, and accessible to larger numbers of children and adolescents.

Gay, lesbian, bisexual, and transgendered youth.   Although considerably fewer in number than children and adolescents of color, youth who are gay, lesbian, bisexual, and transgendered (GLBT) are particularly vulnerable. Anderson (1994) and Savin-Williams (1995; Savin-Williams & Rodriguez, 1993) argue convincingly that gay and lesbian youth are ignored in most professional writing about children and adolescents. The increased visibility of homosexuality has not been paralleled by attention to the younger members of the lesbian and gay communities. This lack of attention is consequential, because young people who are "sexual minorities" are disproportionately at risk for negative outcomes.

Most GLBT youth experience stress associated with their sexual orientation. They commonly experience disapproval, anger, and rejection from family and peers when they disclose same-sex attraction. And, denial of same-sex attraction directly interferes with self-exploration and ability to form healthy relationships critical to identity formation. "Living a lie" or "passing" can lead to incredible isolation and loneliness.

GLBT young people are particularly vulnerable to alcohol and drug abuse, depression, and a higher rate of suicide than heterosexual youth, as they seek to cope with the isolation and rejection they experience (Sullivan & Wodarski, 2002). Homosexuals are a frequent target of hate crimes (Federal Bureau of Investigation [FBI], 2000). Educators do little to support them or are prohibited from doing so; GLBT youth often leave school before graduation. Although GLBT young people receive services from multiple systems, frequently providers have not addressed their special needs (Mallon, 1998).

THE AT-RISK TREE: A METAPHOR

The cultural anthropologist Becker (1981) once observed that information accumulated in the last half of the twentieth century has become "strewn all over the place, spoken in a thousand competitive voices. Its insignificant fragments are magnified out of all proportion while its major and world historical insights lie around begging for attention" (p. 14). Becker's statement is true today. Information about at-risk children and youth is indeed "strewn all over the place." What is cause and what is effect? How does one situation relate to another? What is the relationship between various aspects of a child's problem? What are the underlying connections? In efforts to solve the problem, intertwined and complex problems are divided into manageable parts. Programs to reduce school failure, for instance, are isolated from efforts to prevent juvenile delinquency. Strategies to ameliorate teen pregnancy may ignore problems of substance abuse. Researchers and policy planners chip away at what remains unknown but often do not identify what is known. We attempt to determine the impact of narrowly defined interventions and strategies and ignore the powerful effects of a broad combination of strategies.

In this book we lay out a systematic framework to guide the reader toward an understanding of the scope and range of problems for which children and adolescents are at risk. We use a metaphor as a conceptual and organizing framework. This metaphor integrates the various at-risk categories and intervention strategies and allows us to pull together information and knowledge that is "strewn all over" and focus on specific at-risk categories in a unifying framework.

We turn to horticulture for our metaphor. The analogy of a tree permits us to consider a range of issues that relate to at-risk children and youth. The soil of this tree is the individual's societal environment. The roots of family, school, and peer group connect the tree to the soil (that is, the environment) to provide some support and nurturance. The trunk serves as the conduit of developing attitudes and behaviors of each individual child that lead to specific at-risk categories, which are the branches of the tree.

The soil.   Various aspects of the environment, such as socioeconomic status, political realities, economic climate, and cultural factors, must be considered if we are fully to understand at-risk issues. The environment/soil also includes the dramatic changes that are occurring in society. Urbanization, the feminization of poverty, the threat of violence and terrorism, and the fantastic changes in technology are part of the soil that nourish or fail to nourish at-risk children and adolescents. The "soil" of the Andrews family is the low socioeconomic status of the family, the limited access to mental health providers, the change of job status because of technological advances, and the racist attitudes expressed by Mr. Andrews; all indicate environmental pressures that mold this family and affect its members. This environment, this soil, potentially contributes to at-risk products—Allie and Paul.

The roots.   The at-risk tree has three primary roots: family, school, and peer groups. Just as the roots provide a network that anchors and nourishes life, so the family and the transmit culture and along with the peer group mediate young people's develop. These primary social institutions and environments provide the structures through w the children assimilate their experiences.

The family is the taproot. In the Andrews family the conflict, friction, and vastly differing parenting styles contribute to Allie's and Paul's dysfunctions. Jack's anger and hostility and Alicia's depression and placating behavior limit the nurturance and support that the children receive. Multi-problem families such as the Andrews present a challenge because of the variety of at-risk issues they represent.

The school is another major root. Society looks to schools for help: to provide a secure environment for children, to foster appropriate learning experiences, and to attend to learning and emotional problems. Increasingly, schools teach essential life skills that families and churches taught in the past. The role of the school in the future of the Andrews children is critical. How the school handles Allie's and Paul's situations will have both short- and long-term effects on their attitudes toward school, learning, and life.

Peers are another major root. Although the peer group influence usually starts later in a child's life—generally by preadolescence—it can be enormously powerful in transmitting culture, values, and norms that influence behavior. Failing to consider peers in understanding and intervening with young people has a high probability of leading to interventions that are ineffective.

The trunk.   The trunk is the support and brace for the tree's branches and the conduit from the soil and roots up to the leaves, blossoms, and fruit. The trunk of the at-risk tree consists of specific behaviors, attitudes, and skills of individual children and adolescents. It represents young people's strengths and weaknesses, talents and disabilities, personal risk and protective factors. These behaviors, attitudes, and skills are also conduits to the branches, because specific characteristics such as inability to delay gratification, depression, anxiety, low self-esteem, and impulsivity lead directly to at-risk behaviors. In the Andrews family, Allie's oppositional and self-defeating behavior and Paul's anxiety, depression, and aggressiveness lead to specific at-risk behaviors.

The branches.   The branches of the tree represent children and youths' adaptation to society. Many young people are doing well. They are healthy and sound; they are integrated into society and preserve their cultural heritage; they will be productive as workers, as parents, as members of the community. Young people with this healthy adaptation contrast strikingly with those who isolate themselves from their cultural heritage, their families, and society through destructive attitudes and behaviors—those who are in specific at-risk categories.

The five branches that produce the most damaged fruit—that is, the five specific at-risk categories that seem most central to our concerns—are school dropout, substance abuse, risky sexual behaviors, delinquency/violence, and suicide. Both Allie and Paul are approaching school dropout. Further, Allie is at risk for teen pregnancy and drug abuse; Paul is at risk for delinquency and violence, and possibly for suicide.

Foliage, fruit, and flowers.   The fruits of the tree are individual and specific young people, such as Allie and Paul Andrews. Some young people are whole and healthy; others are bruised and damaged; still others drop from the tree. Although broken branches sometimes produce good fruit and healthy branches sometimes produce damaged fruit, the fact remains that certain branches—the maladaptive behaviors in the five major at-risk categories—increase the probability that at-risk behavior will escalate. Perhaps even more tragic is the probability that at-risk youths will themselves be the seeds of future generations of at-risk trees.

The gardener.   Like all growing trees, the at-risk tree needs pruning, staking, and trimming; it needs adequate sun, water, and nurturing. Hence, this book is for the gardeners: the counselors and teachers, psychologists and social workers, human service workers and others—those who nurture the Pauls and Allies of our society. Nurturing must be directed sometimes toward the soil, sometimes toward the roots; sometimes toward the trunk or branches; but always the intent is to improve the fruit of the tree. Throughout this text we recommend useful strategies for working with youth that will help you be a better gardener.

▲ Box 1.1
Carrie

Several years ago one of us was asked to work with a distressed, disturbed young girl named Carrie. At the personal level, 13-year-old Carrie was very self-defeating, angry, and fearful. She was obstinate and oppositional—a problem to her family, her school, and herself. Her behaviors and attitudes were more easily understood, however, when one analyzed the shifting ecology of her life.

Carrie had been raised in a rural community by a mother who worked part-time as a waitress and received a modest monthly check for child support from her former husband. The mother was periodically anxious and depressed, and during these episodes Carrie assumed responsibility for herself, for her mother, and for their modest house. The living arrangements provided by both her mother and her other relatives (many of whom lived close by) could best be described as permissive and nonstructured, with a high tolerance for a wide range of behaviors.

Carrie attended the small local school and had known most of her classmates for years. Even though she gave evidence of a specific learning disability, Carrie's schoolwork was generally adequate, perhaps because the school's expectations were not high.

When her mother went through a particularly acute depressive episode, it was determined that Carrie should go to live with her father. Overnight she went from her small home in a peaceful, rural community to her father's huge house in a wealthy suburban neighborhood. Carrie's father, a self-made millionaire, had become successful as the owner and chief executive officer of a chain of drugstores. He worked long hours, drove himself very hard, and had high expectations of everyone with whom he had contact—suppliers, tradespeople, employees, school personnel, and family members.

Carrie suddenly found herself in a household that included her father, his woman friend (who was shortly to become Carrie's stepmother), a housekeeper, and a live-in nanny hired to support, tutor, discipline, and provide companionship for her.

Carrie enrolled in the local public school. Because of the high socioeconomic status of the neighborhood, the academic expectations and achievement norms were high. Her classmates were the sons and daughters of university professors, physicians, and business executives. Most students in this school went on to graduate from college, a large proportion of them from the most prestigious universities in the country.

(continued)

Box 1.1 *(continued)*

Carrie might be considered a very "lucky" girl, rescued from a mother unable to care for her and provided with "every advantage" and a clear pathway to success. Her "ungrateful" behavior might be confusing from a perspective that narrowly focuses on socioeconomics. Considered from an ecological perspective, Carrie's deviant and pathological behaviors are a logical and obvious reaction to her environmental change. Carrie was like a fern that is transplanted from a shaded corner of the garden into the hot, glaring sun. The fern cannot thrive; neither could Carrie.

CONCLUSION

This chapter highlights the severity of the problems that U.S. children and adolescents confront as they progress toward adulthood. The concept of an at-risk continuum is useful to teachers, counselors, psychologists, and human service professionals interested in identifying the nature and level of risk faced by the young people with whom they work. The Andrews family, whom we will meet again in later chapters, demonstrates the complex interrelationships of family, school, and social problems that young people frequently experience. As we indicate in this chapter, this book is intended to clarify the problems of youth at risk and to provide multifaceted, comprehensive, practical, and ethical suggestions for prevention and treatment.

Environmental/Societal Factors That Contribute to Risk

▲ *For the truly humanist educator [counselor and human service professional] and the authentic revolutionary, the object of action is the reality to be transformed by them together with other people.*

Paulo Freire
Pedagogy of the Oppressed

CHAPTER OUTLINE

▲   Heraclitus is credited with saying that "nothing is permanent except change." Perhaps at no time in history has this insight been clearer than it is today. Children and youth face the challenge of growing into mature, responsible, and healthy adults amidst a maelstrom of economic, political, social, and technological change. Technological advances are occurring more rapidly than ever before in history. The resulting highly specialized systems of production and service, communication and transportation, add complexity to lives that are already complex. The World Wide Web, for example, is enormously promising in connecting our world and making it smaller, yet at the same time provides children and adolescents with rapid exposure to information and social influences that are difficult to monitor and sometimes risky. The continuing mobility of the population, the declining influence of the extended family, the movement of industries from the North to the South, and the rapid automation in the workplace make our society one in which nothing seems certain. These societal forces add roadblocks that can turn young people from their chosen path or cut the journey short. Beyond these national issues, international instability, terrorist attacks, and the pervasive awareness of the nuclear capabilities of several nations affect people, especially in this "post–September 11th" era. Our economy is globally interdependent, and the social and economic forces that affect other parts of the world also affect our young people.

 In this chapter we survey environmental influences that are associated with at-risk categories. We briefly review the ecological model as a conceptual framework for understanding the environment and its affect on children's lives. We discuss economic policy trends, with particular attention to poverty. We survey the complex effects of socioeconomic status, ethnicity, and public policy.

THE ECOLOGICAL MODEL

The ecological model is a theory of human development that is a background to our understanding of and suggestions for working with youth at risk. The ecological model articulated by Bronfenbrenner (1979, 1989) posits that individual human development occurs within multiple embedded ecological systems. Bronfenbrenner identified these systems as the micro-, meso-, exo-, macro-, and chronosystems, with the **individual** at the center (see Figure 2.1). The **microsystem** consists of the people with whom an individual comes into direct contact. For example, the family is the child's primary microsystem, and the child's school—including teachers, staff, and classmates—constitutes another. Each microsystem influences the child's development. The **mesosystem** refers to the interconnections between the different microsystems. Mesosystemic influences include the relationships between a child's parent and teacher, and between the child's school and the surrounding neighborhood. The ecological model assumes that an individual's development is enhanced if the mesosystem—that is, the relationships among the microsystems—is consistent and positive (Bronfenbrenner, 1979, 1989). The **exosystem** consists of the interconnections between one or more settings that do not directly involve the individual. Public policy is an excellent example of an exosystemic factor. Public policy decisions regarding educational standards, teacher wages, and health care or school lunch programs

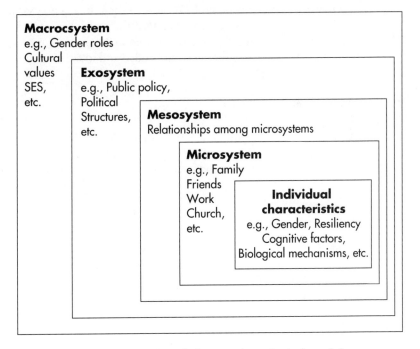

FIGURE 2.1 Bronfenbrenner's ecological model

have an impact on an individual and his/her microsystems (e.g., family, community, and school), but the individual may not be present in the environments in which public policy decisions are made (e.g., city council or state legislative sessions). The **macrosystem** represents a social blueprint: cultural values, belief systems, societal structure, gender-role socialization, race relations, and national and international resources (Bronfenbrenner, 1989). Research that examines the relationship between children's aggressive behavior and exposure to violent television is an example of studying macrosystemic influences on the individual. An additional concept is the **chronosystem,** which is the development of interconnections among individuals and their environments over time.

There are three explicit assumptions of the ecological model (Bronfenbrenner, 1979, 1989). First, the ecological model assumes that an individual and his/her environment are continually interacting and exerting *mutual influence*, and as a result, constantly changing. The environment influences individual development and, in turn, the individual changes the environment. Second, the ecological model assumes that an *individual is an active participant* in his/her development. That is, the individual is not merely acted upon by the environment, but exerts influence on the environment. Third, the ecological model assumes *bidirectionality*, or the idea that changes in one ecological system may influence changes in systems that are more proximal and distal to the individual. For example, public policy decisions impact human development in more immediate or proximal ecological systems. In the same way, individuals, families, and communities in the micro- and mesosystems influence public policy decisions (exosystem) by writing government representatives, speaking at public forums, or protesting. This example illustrates bidirectionality and how factors in every system within the ecology can effect change in another system. Throughout this chapter, as in the entire book, many examples of risk and protective factors are located within these embedded and interacting systems.

THE ECONOMY AND POVERTY

One major exosystemic influence in children's lives is the economy. Economic trends that have the greatest affect on at-risk young people include: (a) increasing poverty, (b) welfare reform, (c) the economic stagnation of the working poor, (d) single mothers, and (e) homeless families.

Poverty

Poverty is the risk factor most closely associated with family stress and highly correlated with school failure (Children's Defense Fund [CDF], 2001a), delinquency (Jarjoura, Triplett, & Brinker, 2002), and other problems, even though some children from poor economic backgrounds fare well. Nearly 16% of American children (11.6 million children) are being raised in poverty in the early 2000s, and one in three children in the United States will live in poverty at some point during their childhood (CDF, 2001a; 2001d). Children of color are disproportionately poor: 28% of all Latino children and more than 31% of all African American children lived in poverty in 2000, compared with 13% of European American children (CDF, 2001a). Children of color under age 6 are even worse off: 33% of African American children and 29% of Latino children under 6, in contrast to 10% of European American children under 6, are poor (CDF, 2001b).

Among the detrimental effects that Garbarino (1998) lists as ingredients for the "social toxicity" of poverty are: increased risk of exposure to violence, racism, unstable care arrangements, economic deprivation, and community insecurity. Some of the by-products of these "toxins" are academic failure, learning disabilities, and child abuse (Garbarino, 1998). Children from poor families begin school developmentally unprepared to succeed in the classroom.

In the 2002 economic downturn, the United States has faced sharp rises in childhood poverty that resemble the increases in child poverty that accompanied recessions in the early 1980s and 1990s. Although the number of children living below the poverty line dropped to a 20-year low of 11.6 million in the year 2000, the number of poor children who live in families with a full-time year-round worker rose to over 4 million children. Despite devoting more time to work, many low-income families remain poor. Promising news of less children living in poverty was an artifact of the late 1990s boom in employment, as the economy weakened and employment fell (CDF, 2001a).

Welfare Reform

From 1995 to 2000 the number of children who lived in extreme poverty yet received no welfare rose 16%, coinciding with a 57% decline in the national welfare caseload. Previously, most extremely poor families received welfare. National welfare legislation passed in 1996 resulted in only one in three extremely poor families receiving such assistance in 2000 (CDF, 2001a).

Meanwhile, research on the effects of the 1996 welfare reform has revealed poor outcomes (e.g., Wycoff et al., 2002). In one study of 700 women moving off of welfare, Fuller and colleagues (2002) found that although mothers' income rose significantly, broader measures of the family's well-being deteriorated. For instance, one-fifth of all mothers had cut the size of meals for their children because they didn't have enough cash to buy sufficient food. Even though a majority of women found jobs, few were able to climb above the poverty line (Fuller et al., 2002). Further, two in every five women (more than twice the national average) suffered from clinical depression, known to have significant detrimental effects on children's development (Fuller et al., 2002). The children displayed more developmental delays by age 3 or 4. Just 30% of the study children could write their first name correctly, compared to 66% in a sample of Head Start children and 70% in a national sample of 4-year-olds (Fuller et al., 2002). So, moving off of welfare into low-wage jobs does not ensure that families or children are better off (Fuller et al., 2002).

Child care also is a major obstacle for mothers moving off of welfare. Two in five mothers reported that they had quit or passed up a job due to the lack of affordable child-care options (Fuller et al., 2002). Although children in day-care centers watched less television than children who were home (Fuller et al., 2002). Many children moved into child-care with low-quality and limited learning materials, a lack of structured or positive interactions with caregivers, and activities that do not contribute to robust child development (Fuller et al., 2002).

Stagnation of the Working Poor

The majority of poor children live with a working parent. In fact, more than 77% of children living in poverty reside with a family member who worked in the last year and over a third live with a full-time year-round worker (CDF, 2001a, 2001b). In 2000, child poverty in families with a full-time worker hit its highest point during the 26 years on record. But, poor families must spend more income for child care than families who are not poor (Smith, 2002). What is problematic about economic recession is that workers who lose their jobs and then are reemployed typically earn 20% less than they had earlier (CDF, 1995).

The economic problems faced by working poor families influence a child's development through parental attitude, disposition, and behavior. For example, parents with financial stress are more tense, irritable, and explosive, and became increasingly arbitrary and punitive in child discipline (Schliebner & Peregoy, 1994). Further, adult mental health is affected by economic problems (McLloyd, 1989). Unemployed parents are more dissatisfied with themselves and with their lives, feel victimized, and are more anxious, depressed, and hostile than employed parents. The incidence of neurosis, psychosis, and suicide is higher among unemployed parents; they have more sleeping, eating, and somatic problems; and they consume more alcohol (Smith, 2002). These changes in attitude, disposition, and behaviors strain family relationships and harm children's development.

In Chapter 1 we introduced the Andrews family. Recall that technological changes resulted in the loss of Jack's electronic technician job and that he now works part-time in a service station. This change in his employment status and income level undoubtedly accounts in large part for his angry, hostile, and aggressive feelings. These feelings cause him to be less nurturing with his stepchildren and more punitive and arbitrary toward them.

Allie Andrews's sullenness and defiance reflect her heightened stress and lowered self-esteem. Her sexual acting out (if indeed her parents' suspicions are correct) can be at least partially explained as a reaction to her stepfather's harsh and abrasive behavior. Similarly, Paul's depression, anger, and low self-esteem are exacerbated by his stepfather's situation. Paul's destructive behavior and poor school adjustment are among the consequences.

In short, the Andrews family is a good illustration of the working poor in the United States. In the case of the Andrews, child care is not a problem because Alicia works only during school hours; however, the low minimum wage and Alicia's and Jack's limited employment opportunities are important factors in this family's problems.

Vulnerable and underserved families.   Families of color have experienced a disproportionate share of income and job loss, primarily because of structural changes in the economy. This has been exacerbated by the shift of manufacturing employment from the cities to outlying areas, including outsourcing to other countries. Because families of color reside in inner-city areas in disproportionate numbers and are overrepresented in the blue-collar jobs that have been disappearing, they are disproportionately affected by displacement and unemployment. The problem is likely to be prolonged as the United States continues its transformation from a goods-producing economy to a service economy.

Families of color also continue to maintain less-skilled jobs. African Americans, for instance, are particularly concentrated in lower ranking occupations in the United States. In 1995, African Americans made up 19.4% of all enlisted military personnel, but only 11.4% of all officers. Similarly, African Americans made up only 4.2% of doctors and 3.7% of dentists; however, they made up 9.3% of registered nurses, 18.7% of licensed practical nurses, and almost 30% of nurses aides, orderlies, and attendants (Goldfield, 1997). This pattern is also seen in the federal workforce. African Americans make up almost 19% of the federal workforce, but fewer than 7% of senior executive service positions (Zorn, 2001).

Poverty rates among African Americans are consistently three times higher than among European Americans; for Latino Americans they are two and one half times higher. Female-headed households with children are particularly vulnerable to poverty; over 39% of those living in such households were poor in 2000. This figure rises to about 50% for Latino American and African American children. Nearly one in three African American children and 16% of all children lived below the poverty line in 2000 (U.S. Census Bureau, 2001). Over 5 million of America's children live in extreme poverty, with family incomes less than 50% of the poverty threshold (National Center for Children in Poverty [NCCP], 2002). Native Americans are generally unaffected by national economic cycles because they consistently suffer high unemployment, which hovers at about 30% on most reservations, and some Plains reservations report unemployment rates of over 70% (La Fromboise, 1988). Furthermore, the national poverty line or "threshold" is extremely low to begin with.

Young families. If Allie Andrews continues her presumed sexual behavior, becomes pregnant (which is probable), and marries the father (which is less probable), and if she keeps her baby (also probable), she is setting herself up for a limited income and a heavy workload. She will assume most of the care for her baby and most of the household chores. She will probably also work outside the home.

Increasing numbers of young unmarried mothers are members of the workforce out of necessity, some because of the decline in real family income. In the United States today the minimum wage is $5.15 an hour. By contrast, in 1968 in current inflation-adjusted dollars, it was $7.67 an hour. Multiple attempts to raise the minimum wage closer to a "living wage" have been stalled in Congress. For workers to escape the federal definition of poverty, the minimum wage would have to be $8.20 an hour (Lind, 2001). In some families both parents must work simply to keep the family out of poverty, and young families are increasingly stressed to provide for their families.

In the Andrews family we see the effects of the first two trends we have discussed: job and income loss leading to economic stagnation, and young families. The Andrews family structure, however, has less bearing on two other areas of concern: single mothers and homeless families. The Baker family knows these problems all too well.

Single Mothers

Young female-headed families are at the greatest risk of poverty and co-occurring problems. Children in families headed by a single parent (teen pregnancy or divorce, separation, or death) are also more likely to be poor. In 2000, 40% of single-parent families with children under 18 headed by women were below the official poverty line. In contrast, 8.2% of dual-parent families with children were poor (CDF, 2001b). At least 20% of working single mothers need assistance, such as food banks, to make ends meet (Kim, Ohls, & Cohen, 2001). Indeed, the economic plight of most families headed by single mothers has steadily worsened in the past 20 years.

CASE STUDY

The Baker Family

Sally Baker is a tall, slender, 28-year-old African American woman. She is still legally married to the father of her 9-year-old son, Tyrone, and her 7-year-old daughter, Daniella, although she has not lived with him for five years. Her 3-year-old son, Jerome, was fathered by a boyfriend whom she has not seen for over a year. During most of her nine years of motherhood Sally's primary means of support has been Aid to Families with Dependent Children (AFDC). For several months she and her children have been residing at the Andre House, a shelter for homeless families.

Sally was born in rural Alabama. She never knew her father but thought that his last name was Johnson. When Sally was 8 she and her mother moved to Dallas with her younger brother. Sally remembers that her mother was not working and that "she couldn't afford to keep me and couldn't afford to send me back." As their situation became increasingly strained, her mother's frustration spilled over into abuse. After several years of intermittent abuse, Sally finally refused to take any more of it and at 14 left home. After living for several weeks in a local park, she was arrested for being out after curfew and was sent to a detention facility for status offenders. From there she went to the first of several foster homes. She reports being sexually abused in this home before she fled it. This became the pattern of her life over the next few years. She lived on the streets for several weeks or months until the police picked her up again and sent her to a detention facility, which placed her in another foster home. From then on, she was in and out of foster homes and girls' homes and detention facilities until she finally met and married George.

Sally's marriage to George was not particularly happy. After several years of conflict, George availed himself of a "poor people's divorce": He walked out and did not return.

In the year before their arrival at Andre House, the Baker family's lifestyle mirrored Sally's earlier life—a chronic pattern of lurching from crisis to crisis. Sally had been living on AFDC in a Housing Authority complex in a small city. Because her unit was subsidized by the Housing Authority, she was paying hundreds of dollars less than she would have had to pay for a private unit, but she had to contend with drug dealers, gang activity, and considerable neighborhood violence. When Tyrone started to wear the "colors" of one of the local gangs, Sally decided to move in with her sister-in-law in a neighboring town. The safety of this new living arrangement was offset by the crowded conditions; there were now two adults and seven children in a two-bedroom

The Baker Family *(continued)*

apartment. Sally was able to stay for three months and saved some money, but not enough to get a place of her own.

Sally and her children moved back to Dallas to live with another sister, who also had a two-bedroom apartment. The sister and her boyfriend slept in one bedroom, the sister's three children slept in the other, and Sally and her three children slept on the living-room floor. Again there were problems. Her sister's boyfriend used and sold crack cocaine. Sally contributed a share of the monthly rent, but a few months later both families were evicted because the boyfriend was not paying the rent.

Sally and her children moved in with a friend, but once again drugs were a problem—this time because friends of the friend were using her apartment to make their deals. The police frequently came to the house because of the drug activity and finally threatened to take Sally's children away from her unless she got them out of the house.

Bit by bit Sally had been saving money from her AFDC checks, but the $100 she had managed to put aside was still too little to pay the first and last months' rent on a place of her own plus a security deposit. In any case, the fruit of her prudence and foresight disappeared when the apartment was robbed by the drug-dealing friends of the woman with whom she was staying. She was beaten, her life was threatened, and even her children were threatened. The elderly couple next door called the paramedics, who took her to a clinic. After all the threats to her life, she was too frightened to let anyone call the police. The counselor at the clinic found a shelter that had room for them and gave her money for the bus. And so the Baker family found themselves at Andre House.

Sally's children reflect the type of chaotic life she has led. Ty especially seems to have been negatively affected by his experiences. His behavior is highly impulsive. His attention shifts rapidly from one object or activity to the next. At school he is an "attention-starved" child. He must be first in line, the one to sit next to the teacher, the first to play with a new toy. At times he hurts other children and is destructive. Sometimes conflict with his mother erupts into aggressive outbursts and he lashes out at his 3-year-old brother.

Daniella, by contrast, has a good relationship with her family. She and Sally talk frequently, and Daniella is able to ask for what she wants and needs. Her calm, sweet disposition endears her to adults and apparently helps her with

CASE STUDY

The Baker Family *(continued)*

both of her brothers, even Tyrone. She is especially helpful in caring for Jerome. Even though this task is sometimes frustrating to her, she is quite responsible and affectionate with him.

Jerome is a shy, passive, sickly child who is fearful of strangers. He prefers to be left alone and makes few demands. He is apathetic and disinterested and when left alone mostly watches television. He seems indifferent to Tyrone's temper outbursts, even when they are directed at him. He tends to cling to Daniella, though, and follows her closely about.

By the year 2000, births to unmarried females reached the highest level ever recorded (Center for Disease Control [SDC], 2001). One in two children will spend part of their childhood in a single-parent home (CDF, 2001d). The children and adolescents living in single-parent families are at greatest risk for poverty and all its co-occurring problems (Dickerson, 1995; Mulroy, 1995). On a more positive note, however, the national birthrate for U.S. *teenagers* declined steadily throughout the 1990s, with an overall drop of 22% (CDC, 2002).

Nevertheless, when young teenage mothers become pregnant and carry their babies to term they tend to not receive prenatal care—placing their child at risk for future problems. In 1996, one in fourteen teenage mothers received no prenatal care or obtained it only in the last trimester. Only two in three received prenatal care during the first trimester (Ventura & Curtin, 1999). Lack of prenatal care influences the child's future health, well-being, and learning ability, and the consequences are borne by our schools and health-care systems. Sally Baker and her children tragically illustrate these problems.

Homeless Families

At the end of 2001, the U.S. Conference of Mayors issued their status report on hunger and homelessness in 27 U.S. cities. In addition to the statistics listed here, all cities forecasted increases for requests for emergency food assistance and for emergency shelter by homeless families (U.S. Conference of Mayors, 2001). The problem of homelessness is widespread and getting worse. Here is a sample of what they reported:

- Requests for food assistance by families with children increased by an average of 19% from the previous year and on average emergency food assistance facilities had to turn away 14% of families in need due to lack of resources.
- Requests for shelter by homeless families increased by 22% between 2000 and 2001, and 52% of requests by homeless families for emergency shelter were estimated to have gone unmet due to a lack of resources.
- In 22% of the cities families have to spend their daytime hours outside of the shelter they use at night. In 52% of the cities, families must separate in order to be sheltered.

- Lack of affordable housing is the most commonly cited cause of homelessness identified by city officials. On average, families with children represent 40% of the homeless population.
- Families must wait an average of 16 months for public housing. The wait for Section 8 certificates is 20 months, for Section 8 vouchers, 22 months. Nineteen percent of the cities have stopped accepting applications for a least one assisted housing program due to the excessive length of the waiting list.
- Barriers to homeless children enrolling and attending school include transportation, lack of official school records, immunization requirements, residency requirements, and providing birth certificates (Office of Elementary and Secondary Education, 2000).

Like poverty, homelessness is often explained at the individual, personal level. Sally Baker must be lazy or imprudent or unlucky. She didn't want to work. She should have put her savings in the bank. These arguments hardly explain her situation and don't come close to explaining away the systemic realities. Homelessness, at the aggregate level, is caused by a lack of low-cost housing, which means many thousands of families will not have access to any housing. In these circumstances, poor people either pay more for housing, move in with friends or family members (Fuller et al., 2002; Office of Elementary and Secondary Education, 2000), or become homeless. Basic arithmetic demonstrates that the Sally Bakers of this country have few, if any, choices.

Research on homeless families shows that they are disproportionately likely to be families of color, to be young, to be composed of parents who are more likely to have been abused as children and battered as adults, and to have limited social support networks (Styron, Hanoff-Bulman, & Davidson, 2000). Additionally, life in shelters for the homeless children and adolescents has been linked to depression, anxiety, behavioral disturbances, and an assortment of educational problems (Quint, 1994). As might be expected, children of homeless families perform poorly in school and have more erratic attendance records (Office of Elementary and Secondary Education, 2000).

Here again the Baker family exemplifies the problems of homelessness. The early physical and sexual abuse, the chaotic and stressful living arrangements, and the lack of purpose and hope place Sally and her children at risk.

SOCIOECONOMIC STATUS

The social and economic environment in which children grow is a significant exosystemic predictor of their overall well-being. Almost all available data support the conclusion that children's education, later employment, future earnings, and health greatly depend on their families' socioeconomic status (SES). Membership in the lowest SES group, that is, families in extreme poverty, is clearly linked to a wide variety of problems among children and adolescents (Garbarino, 1998).

Health Problems and SES

Children and adolescents from impoverished families have an increased risk of health problems. In contrast to middle SES children, they are more likely to have suffered neonatal damage, to have been underweight at birth and malnourished, to have had problems with vision and hearing that were unidentified and uncorrected, and to have experienced untreated childhood illnesses (Garbarino, 1998). Children who come from low SES families usually grow up with highly stressed immediate environments, or microsystems. They live in disorganized and impoverished neighborhoods and their microsystems often involve socially isolated and very young mothers, no fathers, and minimal support from other family members (Garbarino, 1998). Further, low SES status is associated with problems of mental health, impaired parent-child relationships, and a high incidence of child abuse and neglect (CDF, 2001b).

At-Risk Categories and SES

Low SES status coupled with being a person of color is the strongest predictor of school dropout (Entwisle & Alexander, 1992). Low SES status is also related to juvenile delinquency (Jarjoura, Triplett, & Brinker, 2002) and is the strongest predictor of teenage pregnancy (AGI, 1999). We will examine the relationship between SES and each at-risk category behavior more fully in Part II of this book.

THE WIDENING GAP

For many reasons related to the changing economy, most U.S. workers are finding it more and more difficult to meet their financial needs. Meanwhile, they are also losing ground to the wealthy. For example, the income gap—that is, the disparity between the most rich and the most poor—in Manhattan, New York, is worse than it is in Guatemala (Roberts, 1994). The combined wealth of the top 1% of American families is nearly the same as the combined wealth of the entire bottom 95% (Sklar, 1995).

The average family income in the middle and lower brackets has decreased while the income for the wealthiest families has increased. For instance, salaries for major executives jumped 571% between 1990 and 2000. Salaries for CEOs rose even in the year 2000, a year in which the S&P 500 suffered a 10% loss, and CEO salaries increased dramatically even in companies that experienced major layoffs. The explosion in CEO pay over the decade dwarfed the 37% growth in worker pay (Anderson, Cavanagh, Hartman, & Leonard-Wright, 2001). Said another way, if the average annual pay for production workers had grown at the same rate since 1990 as it has for CEOs, their 2000 annual earnings would have been $120,491 instead of $24,668. Likewise, if the minimum wage, which stood at $3.80 an hour in 1990, had grown at the same rate as CEO pay over the decade, it would now be $25.50 an hour, rather than the current $5.15 an hour (Anderson et al., 2001). These income patterns have been accompanied by an increasingly lower standard of living among most workers and an increase in poverty in the United States overall. Because much of the shifting redistribution of wealth upward is based on income-producing assets—bonds, trusts, and business equity—this trend will likely continue.

ENNUI AND PURPOSE

The economic conditions of a major portion of our population contributes greatly to increasing risk factors for children and adolescents. It would be a mistake, however, to conclude that only poverty creates risk. Many young people from affluent backgrounds are also at risk. Affluent children typically spend a great deal of time on their own and often seek peer support and nurturance instead of parental and familial support (consider Carrie in Box 1.1). Among other problems, children and youth without family presence and adult support experience a great deal of "ennui."

Ennui refers to an emotional state of noninvolvement and boredom that comes from a lack of connectedness and a lack of life purpose. Many of our young people suffer from ennui, a lack of connectedness with others, themselves, and/or their own sense of future, which increases the possibility that they will be at risk (Townsend & McWhirter, 2002). Ennui can occur in children from all types of families—rich and poor, blue collar and white collar, working class and professional class, European American families, and families of color. It both causes and is affected by aimlessness, alienation, and lack of direction.

Two areas that are often missing in children's lives but that would help inhibit ennui and support a sense of life purpose among young people are parenting networks and training for life. We consider these two concepts more fully in Chapter 3, which focuses on family problems, and in Chapter 4, which deals with school issues. But because they are also a part of the soil of the problem of at-risk youth, we briefly introduce them here.

Parenting Networks

In earlier generations the majority of children were raised through the collective efforts of a network of extended family relatives, in-laws, and friends who interacted with them throughout childhood and adolescence. Today children have fewer adults to help them develop responsibility, judgment, and self-discipline, even though the task requires more understanding, care, and awareness than ever before. Most young people do not have an extended family network of grandparents, in-laws, aunts, and uncles to support them and their parents. For example, only about 5% of American children see a grandparent on a regular basis (Hamburg, 1995). Among most U.S. families, children often become acquainted with the adult world through television, highlighted by programs that portray casual sex, drinking, gratuitous acts of violence, and self-centered aggrandizement as routine behavior. Through commercials, television also gives negative messages about sacrifice, self-discipline, and patience. Many young people lack skills to promote a sense of bonding and connection with others, lack a sense of being tied emotionally to other people and sharing commitments to common values, and do not see themselves as part of society or contributing members of their communities, their schools, and sometimes even their families. Enhancing family and parenting networks may counter this.

TRAINING FOR LIFE

One of the greatest human needs is to be needed. Too often our society fails to let young people affirm their worth to themselves and others by not providing meaningful roles for young people to assume. By doing too much for children, we destroy their self-confidence and foster low self-esteem. Not infrequently, adults provide children with an environment that demands nothing of them and teaches them nothing. Then we criticize our children for not appreciating the lifestyle or the parents who provided it. In many instances, young people have been progressively denied the opportunity to be engaged in work that is important to others and therefore denied the rewards that such work produces. Children and adolescents who tutor their peers or younger children, who assist people with disabilities, who help to care for young children, who visit with the elderly, and who participate in other programs to help their families, schools, and communities are filling the void that our age of technology and specialization has created in their lives. They are responding to real social needs and they are assuming meaningful roles at the microsystemic and mesosystemic levels. In so doing, they are satisfying their own need to be needed.

MODEST PROPOSALS AND SUGGESTIONS

What can be done? In later chapters we try to provide some of the answers. Here we suggest several measures that may help to nurture the soil. These policy areas focus on child care, skill-building programs, and comprehensive preschool programs.

Child Care

Child care is an issue that affects all families. This task requires the joint efforts of families and communities to provide choices that are healthy and beneficial for children and their parents. The number of children who are cared for by people other than their parents during work hours continues to rise. Access to adequate child care enables parents to work without undue stress and concern for the welfare of their children. Adequate child care prevents parents from missing days of work because arrangements have fallen through, because quality care is not available, or because a child is ill. When both parents work, some of the socioeconomic limitations of their children's environment are likely to be overcome. The benefits of adequate child care are obvious—both by eliminating neglect, abuse, poor nutrition, and poor health that are likely in poorly run facilities, and by providing the stable, consistent child care by providers who promote the healthy development of each child.

Fears and biases about child care have resulted in the failure to develop constructive social policies that ensure affordable, accessible quality child care to people of all economic statuses. Studies that suggest negative effects of child care fail to account for variations in the type of care provided (from in-house caretakers to centers that care for more than 100 children), for the family/home environment (from abusive to highly supportive), and for the qualifications and training of care providers (from minimal attention by untrained caretakers to programmatic enrichment by highly trained child-care professionals). In sum, there is nearly complete consensus among developmental psychologists and early childhood experts that child care per se does not constitute a risk factor in children's lives; rather, poor quality care and poor family environments can together produce poor developmental outcomes (Scarr, Phillips, & McCartney, 1990).

The quality of child care is determined by the ratio of children to caregivers, the number of children cared for in the setting, the caring and responsiveness of caregivers, the stability of caregivers and settings, and the training and experience of caregivers (Gormley, 1995). The low pay and lack of benefits received by the majority of child-care workers result in a high turnover rate for this occupation. Many child-care workers cannot survive on the income that the position provides.

A national policy to shape and direct child-care services would help resolve this problem (Clarke-Stewart, Gruber, & Fitzgerald, 1994). A commitment from workplaces to reevaluate personnel policies that create difficulty for employees with families would also contribute to its solution. Currently, the social values that prevail in the United States generally require families to adjust to the demands of the workplace rather than expecting workplaces to modify policies to meet the realistic demands of families. Teachers and counselors can be effective advocates of parents by informing them of procedures for reaching their legislators. In addition, teachers and counselors might devise ways to facilitate exchanges of information on child care and to link parents interested in sharing child-care arrangements. Currently, many communities have nonprofit organizations that serve as clearinghouses for child-care service information, but even these services involve at least a nominal cost to families.

The lack of adequate day care is a persistent problem particularly for the working poor. Workers with children are often prevented from securing employment because affordable day care is unavailable. Mishel and Bernstein (1995) suggested that mothers out of work due to child-care problems were disproportionately poorly educated, lowering their potential to earn a wage that might have allowed them to purchase the very child care they need. Thus, they are stuck in a vicious cycle. Although the federal government subsidizes some day care through the dependent-care tax credit, Head Start, and Social Service Block Grant programs, the majority of poor people do not benefit from them.

The dependent-care tax credit, for example, is the major federal support for child care. A family may deduct a portion of annual child-care expenses from their federal income tax, up to a maximum of $3000 for one child—but the credit cannot be greater than the family's tax liability. The very poor rarely owe any income tax. Thus, poor and single mothers whose children are at risk and who most need quality child care are least likely to receive any benefit of this policy. The child-care tax credit primarily benefits middle- and upper-income families.

At the same time, poor families with an employed mother who paid for child care spent roughly three times as much of their budget on it than families who were not poor (20% versus 7%) (Smith, 2002). The least well-off families, those with incomes under $15,000, spend nearly 25% of their annual income on child care (Smith, 2002). Additionally, securing safe and affordable child care remains a major obstacle for mothers moving off of welfare (Fuller et al., 2002).

Skill-Building Programs

Although the general level of education has risen in the United States over the decades (Berliner, 2001), a large number of Americans lack basic skills, and these deficits impede gainful employment. About one in four Americans lacks a high school diploma and one in eight is illiterate. Basic competence is essential in today's labor market, even in most entry-level jobs, and low proficiency in these skills is correlated with low educational attainment and low earnings. Basic skill needs have also intensified as our economy becomes increasingly "digital." Additionally, the problem is compounded by the fact that unskilled minimum-wage jobs have less actual purchasing power than at any time in over three decades. And contrary to popular notions, only 31% of minimum-wage workers are teenagers in their first jobs. Nearly half of minimum-wage earners are 25 years old or older, and 28% are heads of households (U.S. Census Bureau, 2001).

More important for children and youth, the difficulties of the unskilled worker are often transferred to the next generation. The proportion of young people from households with low skills and low incomes who do not complete high school is twice that of youth from more affluent families (U.S. Census Bureau, 2001). Thus, children of the unskilled and poor are more likely than children from affluent families to be poorly prepared when they enter the workforce, and their chances of escaping the cycle of poverty are very slim.

Finally, there is growing global competitive pressure for a highly skilled workforce. The United States is facing a tremendous mismatch between the jobs available and the ability of U.S. citizens to perform them. An undereducated and unskilled workforce that cannot keep pace with skill requirements will continue to lose jobs to international labor that meets the knowledge and skill-intensive work requirements. So, forming programs that support and better train our workforce in basic and more advanced skills are highly needed within nearly all of our communities. Vocational education and programs that support the school-to-work transition are needed to assist in breaking cycles of poverty and provide a skilled workforce for the nation.

Comprehensive Preschool Programs

Another means to link family, school, and community is the provision of comprehensive preschool programs for children who are identified as at risk. Evidence suggests that overcoming deficits in skills needs to begin early, and so preschool is extremely important. The following results have been documented as a result of participation in early childhood interventions, including preschool programs such as Head Start: increased cognitive and emotional development, improved parent-child relationships, improved educational outcomes for children, increased economic self-sufficiency for parents and later for the child, decreased criminal activity, and decreased child abuse, substance abuse, and increased maternal reproductive health (Greenwood, 1999). Consultation with the state's economic security or human service agency as well as familiarity with the local human services directory will provide counselors, teachers, and other human service professionals with ample resources and referrals for the families with whom they are in contact. Head Start, a nationwide, federally funded program for economically disadvantaged prekindergarten children, is one comprehensive preschool program (Oden, Schweinhart, & Weikart, 2000). Head Start programs vary from locale to locale, but each provides a classroom-based, multicultural learning experience for 4-year-olds. Through Head Start, children with little structured home stimulation and lack of exposure to the resources of the middle class are given a "head start" on kindergarten. Children have a year to become familiar with school-related vocabulary and behaviors in a nonpressured environment. Children are assessed for a variety of developmental problems and may be provided access to speech therapists, psychologists, and other professionals as the need arises.

Head Start provides enrichment for the rest of the family as well (Oden et al., 2000). By actively participating in the daily events of the classroom and by receiving specific training in parenting, life skills, and health and employment issues, parents become engaged in an empowering process that extends beyond the nine months of the school year (see Box 15.4). Although the success of Head Start varies with the quality of its implementation, Head Start programs have helped children from challenging economic backgrounds to persevere and eventually graduate from high school. Preschool programs generally have had a positive impact on children's cognitive and social development. Overall, both child-care assistance and comprehensive preschool programs have also enabled welfare-to-work programs to succeed (Oden et al., 2000).

The combination of inadequate child care and pervasive deficits in skills contributes to the stagnation of the poor and leaves our children at risk. If Sally Baker had adequate child care for her children, a reasonable wage, and support to enhance her work-related skills, she and her children might escape from their predicament. Unfortunately, the safety net our society provides for Sally and others like her is badly in need of repair.

CONCLUSION

Providing training for life and quality child care for all are only two ways to enhance the potential of youth at risk. Ultimately, preventing and assisting youth at risk may require us all to be active in securing the type of public policy that affects everyone, especially families who are economically struggling and socially marginalized. In this chapter we discussed the problems of poverty, the stagnation of the working poor, the struggles of young families, welfare reform, and how low SES is an important risk factor. We propose that improving social policy and funding around child care, worker skill enhancement, and comprehensive preschool programs are examples of some of the first steps to take to confront the environmental, exosystemic, and macrosystemic problems that place our children and adolescents at risk for future difficulty.

CHAPTER 3

FAMILY PROBLEMS OF AT-RISK CHILDREN AND YOUTH

▲ *Why are some families like bubbling fountains, filling goblets full for thirsty people living there*

While other fountains fill cups with dark, bitter liquid

And yet other fountains are dead-dry—nothing flows and mugs remain empty?

Too many children have either dusty-dry, empty vessels or bitter-brown, sewage-filled ones.

How do we turn on the fountains so that the cold, clear water flows?

J. J. MCWHIRTER

CHAPTER OUTLINE

▲ As we saw in Chapter 2, shifting economic, political, and policy trends have created an often disturbing environment that directly affects the roots of the problems young people face. Nowhere is this more evident than in the family. And because the family is a major influence on individuals, in this chapter we focus on family issues that affect at-risk children and adolescents.

SOCIETAL CHANGES AFFECTING THE FAMILY

The American family has undergone major changes in recent decades. In fact, the American family has changed more during the past 30 years than at any other time in history. Striking family demographic transitions are apparent to all. In Chapter 2 we considered the impact of SES and poverty and noted the increasing numbers of single parents and mothers in paid employment. Here we highlight two related trends that influence modern family life: divorce and the decline of extended-family networks.

Divorce

The marked rise in the divorce rate that characterized the late 1960s and 1970s actually declined (except for teens) during the 1980s and now remains stable. The divorce rate in the United States remains very high and still affects enormous numbers of people. Because divorce is more likely in younger marriages, children are involved in approximately two-thirds of all divorces (Arendell, 1995). Twenty-three percent of American children are now being raised in mother-only families (Riche, 2000) and one in two African American children live in mother-only households (Belsie, 2001). In 2000, two-fifths of single mothers had never been married (Bianchi & Caspar, 2000). Divorce, out-of-wedlock births, and declining marriage rates have significantly altered the composition of the typical family.

Single-parent families are particularly stressed. For example, Hilton, Desrochers, and Devall (2001) conducted a comparison study of child and parent functioning in single-mother, single-father, and intact families. Single fathers had better economic resources than did single mothers; single fathers had more positive parenting than married fathers, and they relied more on friends than did married parents. Single mothers, meanwhile, had less education, less prestigious jobs, lower incomes, and more economic strain. These mothers also had fewer social resources and more parenting difficulty than married parents. Children living with single mothers were found to have more internalized problems, whereas those living with either a single mother or father had more externalized behavior problems (Hilton, Desrochers, & Devall, 2001). Additionally, children living in single-mother homes were more at risk for school dropout (Pong & Ju, 2000).

The Erosion of Extended-Family Networks

Not only is a mother or father more likely to be absent from the home now than at any time in history, but extended-family members are also less likely to be involved in family life. When the extended family is involved in child-rearing, it is typically not adjunctive—that is, supportive of the children's parents—but, in fact, replaces parental roles as primary or even sole caretakers. For example, among the nearly 20 million preschoolers, grandparents are leading child-care providers, taking care of 21% of preschool children (U.S. Department of Commerce, 1997). Years ago the extended family provided a variety of role models, opportunities to anticipate and vicariously experience child-related problems, and individuals available to serve as resources. Today children and their parents have less access to the extended family as they face life crises. The family, once buffered with supports, is now stretched thin. Not infrequently, recreation, spiritual training, and education all take place outside the home.

Divorce and the decline of the extended family do not necessarily result in a reduction of social networks for children and young people. Indeed, the increased complexity of family patterns may actually increase the availability of people who can serve as resources. Consider Lisa, born in 1972. Her father has several children from a previous marriage with whom she interacts when they come for visits. When Lisa is 8 years old, her parents divorce. She lives with her mother but continues to see her father in the summer and on weekends. When Lisa is 13, her mother remarries. Lisa and her stepfather get along well and do many things together. Lisa continues to see her father, although less frequently, because he has now moved to another state and has married a woman with two children. Lisa graduates from high school and enters college. During two of her college years she lives with a man, and soon after graduation she marries another man. She and her husband have a son. After several years, Lisa and her husband divorce and she is awarded custody of her son, who continues to see her ex-husband in the summer and on weekends. Three years later Lisa remarried. She and her second husband have two more children. During Lisa's life so far she has lived in nine families either part-time or full-time.

Lisa's situation is not typical but neither is it unusual. Although the relationships in some of Lisa's families may not have been ideal, in each case there were people she enjoyed doing things with, wanted to continue seeing, and loved. This situation represents a substantial change from the experience of people who grew up several decades ago, when one might have been part of two or three families at the most. Some of these family experiences have the potential of enriching children's lives by providing more adults to serve as role models and by providing a greater variety of experiences. Unfortunately, for many youth these changing patterns and variable family experiences produce alienation, a sense of rootlessness, and anomie.

CHANGES WITHIN THE FAMILY

Even in the absence of structural changes arising from evolving societal conditions, the family normally changes over time. All changes necessitate shifts in the relationships of family members. At each stage the family has specific developmental tasks to accomplish, which lay the foundations for later stages.

The Family Life Cycle

The family life cycle is the name given to stages that a family goes through in its developmental history (Carter & McGoldrick, 1999). The family group begins with each newly married couple even though the couple continues to be a part of their two original family groups. The fact that a new family cycle begins with each new marriage does not cut short the cycles of the families of origin of each partner. The couple continues the family life cycles of their earlier family groups at the same time that they begin their own family life cycle.

Duvall and Miller (1985) proposed an eight-stage model of the traditional family life cycle that holds true today. This framework is appropriate for many families because most progress through certain predictable marker events or phases (such as marriage, the birth of the first child, the onset of adolescence, and so forth). Each stage is determined by the age of the oldest child, and each stage has its own set of tasks for the family to complete before it moves to the next stage. Carter and McGoldrick (1999) have outlined sets of developmental tasks for nontraditional blended families and single-parent families. They also add an initial stage—the unattached young adult—to the family life cycle. The inability of the family to negotiate developmental tasks at any of the stages contributes to the child's problems. Professionals need to be aware of the family developmental tasks and help the family to develop the necessary skills to meet them. The following stages are derived from the works of Duvall and Miller (1985), Carter and McGoldrick (1999), and Norton (1994).

Unattached young adult stage. The young adult must accomplish several developmental tasks at this stage. The young person must develop responsible habits and become established in a work environment. In addition, it is important that the young adult establish close peer relationships and begin to separate from the family of origin through an ongoing process of differentiation.

Establishment stage (married, no children). This stage begins with marriage. The young adult continues to break away from the family of origin. The major task for the couple at this stage is to establish their identity as a new unit. Making rules, defining roles within the marriage, and realigning relationships with friends and family are important components of this stage.

New parent stage (infant to 3 years). When the couple become parents, their duties and roles change. Their relationship as a couple must shift in order to accommodate the infant.

Preschool stage (oldest child 3 to 6 years). Parents continue to develop their work and family roles. The major developmental task at this stage is learning and applying effective parenting skills to help the children learn how to interact positively with others.

School-age stage (oldest child 6 to 12 years). The family becomes more involved with community and school activities as the children grow and develop. Members of the family fulfill assigned roles and must learn to renegotiate boundaries to include the children's peer group.

Teenage stage (oldest child 13 to 20 years). The married couple are required to deal with individual, work, and marital issues along with the developmental tasks of their children and their own aging parents. The adolescents who are going through the individual developmental task of establishing their own identities and independence challenge the boundaries and rules of the family system.

Launching stage (departure of children). Children and parents must separate emotionally and physically from one another. Thus, the primary task of the family at this point is to let go. Other tasks are reestablishment of the marital system as a dyad and negotiation of adult relationships between the parents and the children. Many families must cope with the death of a grandparent.

Two final stages. Two final stages, the post-parental middle years and the aging family, are equally important in the family life cycle, but they do not bear directly on our subject so we will not describe them here.

Cultural variations. Cultural variations influence the nature of the tasks within each stage. In some cultural groups, for example, young people are expected to leave home at age 18 or soon thereafter, whereas other groups expect young adults to live with their parents until they marry, and in some cultures even after they marry. In any assessment of a family's passage through the stages and the completion of tasks, the cultural norms of the family must always be explored.

Normal crises. Families undergo such profound changes as they move from one stage to another that the transitions present all families with normal family developmental crises. Most families negotiate these transitions adequately. Unfortunately, some families have such difficulty with the transitions between stages that they compromise the well-being of their children. Such families can become dysfunctional. If we are to understand dysfunctional families, we have to understand the family as a system. Additionally, helping professionals need to view the cultural, ethnic, and unique aspects of families' backgrounds as resources and strengths that can be fostered and supported for their benefit. This appreciation of diversity is critical. Human service professionals need to develop and maintain an attitude that learning about culture and cross-cultural practice is an essential, ongoing, and ethical process synonymous with professionalism (Sue & Sue, 2003). This appreciation will also assist helping professionals in understanding similarities and differences in family systems across various cultural/ethnic groups.

The Family System

The family is a system consisting of connected components (family members) organized around various functions that interact to maintain balance and a state of equilibrium. Each element is dependent on the functioning of other elements. Among family functions are the giving and receiving of affection, child-rearing, and the division of labor. Families are interdependent in that each member of the system influences and is influenced by each other member.

As they live together from day to day, families develop systematic patterns of behavior that serve to maintain the system in a state of equilibrium. Each family member contributes to this equilibrium or homeostatic balance. Homeostasis is represented by a particular family's ongoing behaviors, habits, expectations, and communication patterns.

To see the family as a homeostatic system, consider a family in which the husband/father is an alcoholic. He serves as a scapegoat and maintains the system by receiving all the blame for the family's problems. Rather than accept the blame, he projects it onto his spouse. She internalizes the blame and enables him to continue his drinking by trying to improve her own behavior and the children's rather than confront his drinking. One child may try to keep the parents from fighting by diverting their attention to his or her own problems through drug use, pregnancy, or truancy. Another child may attempt to dissipate tension by being the family clown. These roles are not conscious attempts to keep the family in balance, however precarious this balance may be, but are patterns maintained at an unconscious level in a manner that is sometimes blatantly obvious and sometimes extremely subtle. When the patterns of behavior that maintain homeostasis are rigid and unyielding, the family system is considered "closed."

A closed system is dysfunctional because it is isolated from the environment, is less receptive to external stimuli, and is unresponsive to change. Because of its impermeable boundaries and nonreceptiveness to change, a closed system tends to move toward increasing disorder. Open systems, by contrast, interact with the environment and so may be capable of both adaptation and flexibility. Adaptation depends on maintaining enough stability to permit the family members to develop coherent, separate identities, as they make the necessary accommodations to environmental changes.

Closed-system families contribute a disproportionate share of troubled children and youth to society because problem behaviors emerge more in closed family systems. Closed family systems typically demonstrate two major types of problems: detachment and enmeshment.

Detachment.   A detached family is one in which the individual members function separately and autonomously, with little family interdependence. When one family member faces a time of stress, the family hardly seems to notice or respond at all. Detached families tend to be unresponsive because each member is isolated within the system. In such families, the boundaries are so rigid that only a high level of individual stress may activate support from other family members. The family members cannot get their social and emotional needs met within the family, nor do they learn appropriate ways to meet the needs of others. It is relatively pointless for such a family to remain together, yet they often do remain together because they seem to have no alternatives. Unfortunately, detached families produce young people who form inadequate or dysfunctional relationships outside the family because they have not learned how to have good relationships within the family. Obviously, such youth are at risk for a variety of problem behaviors.

Enmeshment.   Enmeshed families demonstrate such intensity and closeness in family interactions that the members are overinvolved and overconcerned with each other's lives. In enmeshed families, the children in particular experience a distorted sense of involvement, attachment, and belonging. They fail to develop a secure sense of individuality, separateness, and autonomy. When a member of an enmeshed family encounters a stressful situation, the family is likely to respond by rescuing rather than teaching constructive problem solving. Subsystem boundaries are weak, easily crossed, and poorly differentiated; children may act like parents and parental control may be ineffective. The young person's distorted sense of belonging and attachment interferes with his or her capacity to negotiate developmental tasks successfully. For example, a child may remain isolated from classmates and repeatedly feign illness so as not to "threaten" the mother-child relationship.

The Carter family demonstrates the difficulties of negotiating the family life cycle and illustrates one kind of dysfunctional family. As you read this case study, take a few minutes to reflect on the family life cycle, the family as a social system, and issues of detachment and enmeshment.

The Carter family is at the transition point leading to the teenage stage of the family life cycle. Jason's underlying problems are intensifying precisely because adolescents begin to challenge rules and boundaries as they seek to establish their own identities. As the family is struggling to negotiate this transition, both Mr. and Mrs. Carter are attempting to cope with their own midlife transitional periods.

The Carters illustrate not only the family life cycle but the family as a social system. The presenting problem—behavior difficulties at school—is an extension of Jason's role in his family. His "angelic" younger sister supports this role; his angry and depressed mother maintains it; and his isolated father covertly encourages it. Everyone in the family maintains homeostasis. Even though each of them is in some pain, the unknown (if Jason's position should change) is more anxiety-provoking than the status quo. In other words, although Jason is the catalyst that prompts the Carters to seek an outside helper, the underlying causes of his behavior are embedded within the family's interaction. Each family member maintains equilibrium in the closed circle of the family because each is vulnerable.

The Carter Family

The Carter family came to our attention after Jason, a thin, pale, and intense 13-year-old, got into a particularly vicious fight. The other family members are Jason's parents, Doug and Lois Carter, and his 10-year-old sister, Christie. Jason was referred by his teacher because of fighting and other behavioral difficulties. He frequently disrupted his classes by harassing and fighting other children and by talking back to teachers. His short attention span and apparent inability to sit still were the focus of a subsequent neurological examination, but no neurological impairment was indicated. Next Jason underwent an evaluation at school, consisting of a standard social history and an intake interview.

The findings suggested that poor family communication and ineffective discipline might be the source of Jason's problem behavior. On the basis of this information, family therapy was strongly recommended. Referral to the neurological clinic, contact with school personnel, the social history, and the intake interview were all accomplished by a school social worker assigned to the case. She was also responsible for the family casework and referred Jason and his family to a mental health clinic that provided individual and family therapy.

Lois Carter, a chronically depressed European American woman, was torn by guilt over her perceived failure to rear a child who could function adequately at home and in school. She also seemed to have considerable unspoken anger, which was frequently directed at Jason. Mr. Carter, an engineer, was also a caldron of unexpressed anger. Emotionally locked out by his wife's depression, he seemed to resent Jason and to continually put the child in a double bind by subtly sending the message that his acting out was just a case of "boys will be boys" and at the same time reprimanding him for his behavior. He seemed unwilling or unable to follow through with punishment. In part, this behavior was an acting out of his own angry feelings toward his wife.

Mrs. Carter was the second daughter in her family of origin. She described her parents, who lived close to the Carters, in ambivalent terms. Her father was a chronic drinker, and he physically and emotionally abused his wife and children. He suffered brain damage as a result of drinking and had mellowed considerably in recent years. Mrs. Carter's mother was a passive-aggressive woman who turned to religion for comfort in her later years. Lois had an older sister who had twice married and divorced. After repeated attempts, the sister

The Carter Family *(continued)*

attained a college degree and now worked as an elementary school teacher. Mrs. Carter's two brothers expressed the family dysfunction more obviously. The youngest brother had committed suicide several years earlier. The other brother continued to live with his parents. At 30 he was unemployed and unmarried, and existed on a small payment for service-connected emotional disability.

Doug Carter, of English and French descent, was the older of two brothers. His father, a bookkeeper for a small manufacturing firm, was a harsh, critical, and sarcastic parent. His mother was a pleasant though ineffectual woman who "adored" Mr. Carter's younger brother. A paternal grandmother, now deceased, lived in the home while Mr. Carter was growing up, and she tended to favor him. Mr. Carter and his brother had been very competitive as children and now had no contact. His parents resided in another state and contact with them was infrequent.

Both Jason and Christie Carter had been adopted as infants. Jason was considered the identified problem (patient) and Christie was regarded as a perfect little angel.

A counselor saw the family weekly for therapy that focused on their style of communication. During the first six sessions, the family discussed the setting of limits and the need for more direct communication. They reached an impasse, however, because the family members refused to listen to one another. Jason frequently pointed out, for instance, that his sister instigated many situations by teasing him. His parents refused to acknowledge that Christie could possibly do such a thing and reprimanded Jason for not listening to them and for trying to get his sister in trouble. Christie sat quietly and primly, in silent agreement with her parents. At the end of six sessions, the counselor felt that she was making little headway in helping the parents listen to Jason or to each other. Christie indicated little willingness to modify her secure position in the family structure. Jason continued to disrupt his classes and behave outrageously at school, in the neighborhood, and at home.

Christie is vulnerable because she builds her self-esteem on being the model child. If things shift, she may become the bad one—the "devil"—in the family. She appears to be enmeshed in the family system. Mrs. Carter is vulnerable because if she loses the reasons for her depression, she might need to feel more guilty and be self-punitive to maintain her depression. Jason provides her with a scapegoat on which to vent her emotions.

She would also have to develop a new relationship with both Christie and her husband, and any change appears threatening. Mr. Carter might have to confront directly his anger and resentment toward his wife. He might also have to redefine Christie's role and change his behavior toward Jason. Jason is vulnerable because if his role changes he might have to improve in school and he will have fewer excuses for acting out. These shifts in perception, roles, and behavior are inevitably threatening. Thus, each family member has a vested interest in maintaining his or her current functioning.

Families of Color

Family life cycle and family system theories are useful constructs in understanding family dynamics. Although useful in understanding and helping many families, the framework must be adapted to families of color. The professional helper's multicultural knowledge, awareness, and skills in working with people from diverse backgrounds is critical.

A specific example is the concept of enmeshment. What is enmeshment in dominant culture may be collective sharing and interdependence in families of color. We must be cautious in relying on stereotypes to guide us; often families of color rely on a larger social base and extended-family support than typical European American families. Among African American families, for example, extended family and friends are central. Arnold (1995) reports that most African American mothers in her study had a large and supportive social network of family and friends with the mean number of social contacts to be 15.6 people for single women and 18.1 people for married women. The role of the church community also provides a rich network of support for many African American families. Among Native American families, the extended kinship system—including uncles, aunts, cousins, and grandparents—are central in children's lives, and multiple households that include non-blood-related individuals are often incorporated into the kinship circle. Many American Indian groups even have formal rituals to induct significant individuals into the family system. Asian American families often have close-knit and hierarchical family structures with particular authority being invested in the father and elders. Often, Asian American relatives participate in family life and in family decisions. And for traditional Latino families, the family structure is extended by formalized kinship relationships to the godparents. Also, the term *cousin* includes many people—often same-age peers who are from non-blood-related families. With many families of color, loyalty to family and to extended family often takes priority over other social demands and dominant culture expectations. Clearly, there are cultural variations, group differences within ethnic groups, and individual differences within families of color as well as within European American families.

Families of Gay, Lesbian, Bisexual, and Transgendered Youth

For many youth who are gay, lesbian, bisexual, or transgendered (GLBT), family life is not a very safe life. Significant numbers of GLBT young people report that they have been verbally and physically assaulted at home (Sullivan & Wodarski, 2002). Many youth are rejected and become the focus of the family's dysfunction. In fact, the process of "coming out" is a major developmental task of homosexual youth, and GLBT youth often have a difficult time finding appropriate strategies for the coming-out process (Sullivan & Wodarski, 2002).

Even more problematic is that lack of support and acceptance at home usually leads to other problems. Many GLBT youth run away; others are thrown out of the home when their sexual orientation is revealed. With life on the street, problems get worse. Young people on the streets are not attending school; many are also using alcohol and drugs; many youth become prostitutes. Among runaways, GLBT youth have higher levels of early onset of sex and drug use, and are at exceptionally high risk for HIV infection (Moon, McFarland, Kellogg, Baxter, Katz, MacKellar, & Valleroy, 2000). Interventions within the family need to be sensitive to sexual orientation.

Family Problems and Problem Families

A focus on societal change, stages and transitions in the family life cycle, and the family as a system helps us identify stressors that may contribute to problems for young people. Specific family problems also contribute to the development of risky behaviors. Here we examine some family situations that may place all family members, but especially children, at risk.

Families That Are Stressed

As we saw in Chapter 2, single-parent and poor families experience considerable stress. Two other kinds of families that are subject to stress, especially the children, are blended families and latchkey families.

Blended families.   Blended families (or reconstituted or stepparent families), are families in which the remarried partners bring children into the relationship. Because divorce and remarriage are increasingly common, blended families are becoming more and more numerous. Children in such families face an unfamiliar network of relationships, particularly with an adult with whom they have not fallen in love. They often suffer some degree of discomfort. These children may have few resources to draw upon in their attempts to cope with a new parent, new grandparents, possible new stepsiblings, and a new family lifestyle. As the new couple shapes and ritualizes their lives, the young people face a whole new set of expectations, procedures, and interactions. Further, these children are struggling to adjust to their new conditions while the most significant people in their lives— their parents—are themselves adjusting and are consistently less available to them.

Viewed in the context of the family life cycle, the newlyweds must negotiate the establishment stage—a complex task in itself—at the same time that they must adopt a satisfactory and consistent system of child parenting and disciplining. The needs of the children are unlikely to coincide with those of the parents. Obviously, this situation causes problems and may be a major factor in the fragility of second marriages, which are more likely than first marriages to end in divorce.

Latchkey families.   Latchkey families are those in which the parents are unavailable to the children before or after school and on school holidays. Because 74% of mothers with children over 1 year old are in the workforce, around 7 million children are latchkey children (CDF, 2001c; U.S. Census Bureau, 2002). Twenty-six percent of 11- to 13-year-olds and 5% of 5- to 10-year-olds take care of themselves either before and/or after school (National Center for Education Statistics, 2001). Many latchkey children suffer from fear, boredom, and loneliness and are also more susceptible to accidents. They may also engage in acts of vandalism or delinquency (Dishion et al., 2001). Not surprisingly, violent youth crime is most common between 3 and 6 o'clock in the afternoon and a child's chance of being a victim of crime triples after school (CDF, 2001c).

Families with Dysfunction

All dysfunctional families subject children to stresses that may lead to risky behavior. Substance abuse by the adult caretaker, interpersonal violence, child abuse/neglect, and parental psychopathology are among those most likely to result in problems for young people. Most adults in such families experienced the same problems in their own families of origin and, as is common, perpetuate the same problems for their children.

Families experiencing substance abuse.   Children of alcoholic (or drug-using) parents are at risk for neglect and abuse. But even without overt neglect or abuse, parental alcoholism inflicts emotional damage on children. Such children may be predisposed to become alcoholic themselves or to enter into relationships with alcoholics (Wilens, Biederman, Bredin, Hahesy, Abrantes, Neft, Millstein, & Spencer, 2002). Children are at high risk for emotional and social adjustment problems, including hyperactivity, relationship difficulties, aggression, depression, school absenteeism, and drug use (Watkins & Durant, 1996). The expanding literature on adult children of alcoholics documents the comprehensive and long-term impact that substance-abusing parents have on their children.

Families experiencing violence.   Interpersonal violence is strongly correlated with children's problems. Of course, violence signals general marital discord, which is also associated with problematic behavior in children. Even when the child is not a direct target of family violence, exposure to adults who verbally abuse each other and who are not in control of their explosive anger can have long-lasting repercussions (Fincham, 1994; Fincham, Grych, & Osborne, 1994). The effect of family violence around the child is wholly negative and violence exposure can destroy the child's self-esteem and confidence (Straus, 1994). Such children are more vulnerable to stress disorders and other psychological disturbances. Violence also begets more violence. As violence in the family increases, it also increases the likelihood that the child will grow up to engage in violent and abusive behavior (American Psychological Association, 1996).

Families with child abuse.   As another form of violence, child abuse occurs in many forms: physical violence, emotional abuse, psychological abuse, neglect, and sexual abuse. *Physical violence* is any physically harmful action against a child, from hair-pulling and slapping to beating and burning. *Emotional abuse* occurs when children are subjected to harsh criticism, ridicule such as name-calling, irrational punishment, and inconsistent expectations. *Psychological abuse* occurs when parents manipulate children by withholding of affection, giving inconsistent verbal and nonverbal messages, threatening suicide in front of children, and isolating children from peer contact, including making the home environment miserable so that peers never want to come over and play. *Neglect* occurs when a parent fails to safeguard the health, well-being, and safety of the child.

Children who are not fed and bathed regularly, who are left unattended, or are consistently ignored are victims of neglect. *Sexual abuse* is any form of sexual behavior with a child, including molestation, incest, and rape, as well as systematic and consistent exposure to explicit sexual material. Children who grow up in such families find themselves at risk for future problems. For example, the correlation of child abuse to teenage pregnancy and to later sexual victimization via unwanted sexual experiences is well documented (Kellog, Hoffman, & Taylor, 1999; Smith, 1996). The age of first pregnancy is also linked with the presence of a family member with a drinking problem and with early physical and/or sexual abuse in the family (Kellog et al., 1999).

Families with parental psychopathology. Many young people are at risk because of parental psychopathology. Schizophrenia, bipolar disorders, and depression in adult caretakers seem to be particularly debilitating to young people (e.g., Radke-Yarrow, Nottelmann, Belmont, & Welsh, 1993). Usually the family is characterized by poor marital adjustment with a low level of parent solidarity, warmth, and support. The parents' mental illness contributes to disturbed parent-child interaction, which leads to limited cognitive, emotional, and social development in the child. Teenagers in these families frequently have poor emotional and behavioral control and school adjustment problems. They may become easily upset, may disturb the class with unusual behavior, and have consistent discipline problems. These young people are at risk both for possible psychopathology themselves and for at-risk behaviors.

In reality, the various types of dysfunctional families often overlap. Interpersonal violence, for example, is closely associated with alcohol use (60% of spouse batterers abuse alcohol), drug use (32% of spouse batterers use drugs), or both (22%) (Walker, 1996). Violence between spouses is often accompanied by violence toward children; parent alcohol and drug use are associated with child neglect and physical abuse (Walker, 1996). Alcoholic fathers, for example, are eight times more likely and alcoholic mothers three times more likely to abuse or neglect their children than parents who are not alcoholic (American Psychological Association, 1996).

When a child or adolescent exhibits at-risk behavior, it is important to consider the family in which the individual is being raised. The behavior of concern may be a reasonable—even if disturbing or dangerous—response to the stress of living in a dysfunctional family. The problems of the parents are sad and distressing; their effects on the children are tragic.

CHILD-REARING PRACTICES: THREE DIMENSIONS OF CHILD-REARING

Over the years, researchers have reached a remarkable degree of agreement on the existence of three basic dimensions of child-rearing despite the diversity of instruments, methodologies, and samples brought to bear on the subject. Researchers examining the basic factors involved in child-rearing have consistently found three fundamental bipolar dimensions, although the names assigned to them vary (e.g., Arnold, O'Leary, Wolff, & Acker, 1993; Baumrind, 1995; Carlson, Grossbart, & Stuenkel, 1992; Vickers, 1994). These dimensions appear to provide an accurate description of parent-child interactions.

The *permissiveness/restrictiveness* dimension incorporates the constructs of control and power; permissiveness refers to low control and low power in parents' behaviors, whereas restrictiveness refers to high control and high power. The *hostility/warmth* dimension ranges from low to high levels of affection. The *anxious, emotional involvement/calm detachment* continuum ranges from high anxiety to low anxiety and reflects the emotional engagement or connectedness of the parent. These three dimensions appear to be relatively independent of each other and provide a key to understanding child-rearing.

Figure 3.1 illustrates the three dimensions of child-rearing in three-dimensional space. Note that the two end points of each dimension represent the extremes of parental behavior. The behavior of most parents tends to fall near the middle rather than the extremes on most dimensions. That is, a father is not likely to be either completely hostile or overwhelmingly warm; most mothers neither permit nor restrict everything their children want to do. It is typically parents with either extreme or inconsistent behaviors that place their children at greater risk.

Parental Inconsistency

The at-risk child's family life is often characterized by parental inconsistency as well as by the extreme behaviors. We know that consistent behavior by parents increases the child's ability to predict the environment and leads to more stable behavior patterns. Inconsistency has negative effects on children and may take various forms:

- Certain behaviors are permitted at one time but not at another, unpredictably: because of another child's behavior; because the parent's mood changes; because the parent is paying attention or not paying attention.
- What the child is told to do is inconsistent with what the child sees other family members doing, is rewarded for doing, or is punished for doing or for not doing.
- Patterns of rewards and punishments are inconsistent. The parent punishes a behavior at one time and does nothing the next time, rewards a behavior at one time and punishes it at another, threatens punishment and does not follow through, or promises a reward and does not give it.
- The degree of consistency the parent practices varies. One parent may be consistent in the overt goals set for the child but behaves in ways that subvert them; another may be so rigidly and literally consistent that the result is ludicrous; another may gradually relax restrictive rules over time as the child approaches adolescence.

Research findings on the effects of parental inconsistency have been limited because of variations in inconsistency. Nevertheless, clear evidence of the deleterious effects of inconsistency emerges from the research literature on delinquency, which has repeatedly demonstrated a strong connection between inconsistent and erratic discipline (both between parents and within an individual parent) and a youth's antisocial behavior (Dishion & Bullock, 2002; Patterson, Reid, & Dishion, 1998). A related concern is the unstable home, or a home characterized by overstimulation and capricious discipline. Children may be teased, taunted, and encouraged to play rough, for instance, and then punished for their boisterous behavior. Such unstable families produce children who lack social

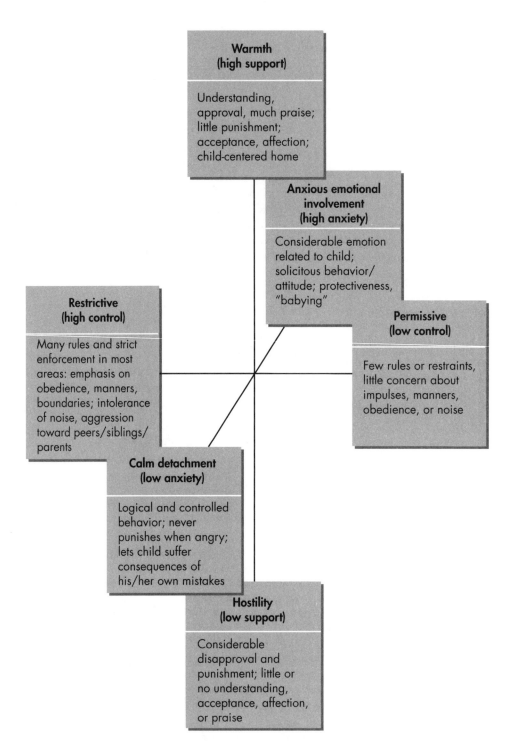

**Warmth
(high support)**

Understanding, approval, much praise; little punishment; acceptance, affection; child-centered home

**Anxious emotional involvement
(high anxiety)**

Considerable emotion related to child; solicitous behavior/ attitude; protectiveness, "babying"

**Restrictive
(high control)**

Many rules and strict enforcement in most areas: emphasis on obedience, manners, boundaries; intolerance of noise, aggression toward peers/siblings/ parents

**Permissive
(low control)**

Few rules or restraints, little concern about impulses, manners, obedience, or noise

**Calm detachment
(low anxiety)**

Logical and controlled behavior; never punishes when angry; lets child suffer consequences of his/her own mistakes

**Hostility
(low support)**

Considerable disapproval and punishment; little or no understanding, acceptance, affection, or praise

FIGURE 3.1   Dimensions of child-rearing practices

responsibility and display a low degree of conscientiousness. Capricious discipline contributes to conflict, aggression, and maladjustment (Dishion & Bullock, 2002; Patterson et al., 1998).

Clusters of Child-Rearing Behaviors

To illustrate the interrelationships among the three dimensions of child-rearing, we have transformed Figure 3.1 into a cubic model. Figure 3.2 depicts the resultant "parenting cube," which is made up of eight sections or clusters of parenting attitudes and behaviors. Sections 2, 4, 6, and 8, on the right, represent degrees of permissive parenting behavior, and sections 1, 3, 5, and 7, on the left, represent degrees of restrictive behavior. Sections 5 to 8, on the back half of the cube, represent anxious, emotional behavior, whereas the four in front, 1 to 4, represent calm detachment. The four cubes on the top, 1, 2, 5, and 6, reflect highly supportive, warm parental behavior; the four on the bottom, 3, 4, 7, and 8, reflect hostility or low support.

The parenting cube.   Each of the eight sections of the parenting cube represents a cluster of child-rearing practices that incorporate the three dimensions we discussed earlier.

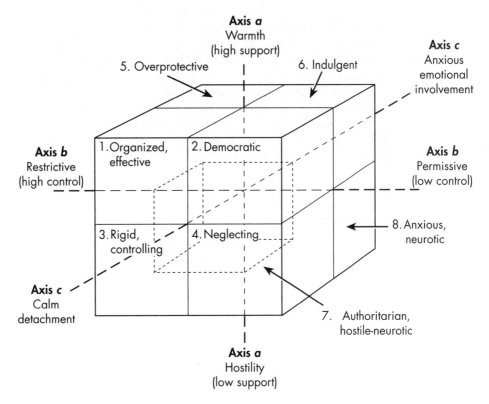

FIGURE 3.2   **A cubic model of child-rearing practices**

The eight sections have been labeled with descriptive phrases that provide a rough generalization of the parenting behavior within sections. We consider each one in turn.

Section 1. Organized, effective behavior (restrictiveness, warmth, calm detachment). Parents who occupy this extreme position tend to control, shape, and evaluate the behavior of the child according to a high standard of conduct. The parents are positively involved with the child and use rewards, praise, and encouragement to engage the child. They discuss issues, values, and behavior without emotional turmoil.

Section 2. Democratic behavior (permissiveness, warmth, calm detachment). Parents who occupy this section usually encourage or permit discussion of family rules and regulations and tolerate a fairly wide range of behavior. The home environment is generally positive; the parents logically discuss the reasons why a behavior is unacceptable.

Section 3. Rigid, controlling behavior (restrictiveness, hostility, calm detachment). Parents in this category appear cruel in their interactions with their children. They generally have a large number of rules and regulations that they enforce in a cold, rigid, sometimes precise manner. The parents sometimes appear to relish punishing their children for misbehavior.

Section 4. Neglecting behavior (permissiveness, hostility, calm detachment). These parents allow their children to run free with few or no regulations. In extreme cases, the child's basic needs are not met because the parent is so uninvolved or hostile that the child is rejected and neglected.

Section 5. Overprotective behavior (restrictiveness, warmth, anxious emotional involvement). Parents in this cell offer consistent support along with many rules and regulations, but they do so with inappropriate emotional involvement and high levels of anxiety. They are often described as a mother bear (or father bear) protecting the young against a hostile environment.

Section 6. Indulgent behavior (permissiveness, warmth, anxious emotional involvement). The parents occupying this area can be said to spoil their children. The children have few rules, break those that they do have with few consequences, and tend to control the emotions and behavior of the parents.

Section 7. Authoritarian, hostile-neurotic behavior (restrictiveness, hostility, anxious emotional involvement). These parents establish many rules and regulations and rigidly enforce them, often with much anger, shouting, and physical punishment. Extreme behaviors in this cell may constitute child abuse.

Section 8. Anxious, neurotic behavior (permissiveness, hostility, anxious emotional involvement). The parents in this category are also potential child batterers and in most cases they tend to exert little control over their children and exhibit little care for them. They tend to direct a lot of anger at their children (and others). These parents may do a great deal of ineffectual nagging and emotional battering with little expectation of modifying the child's behavior.

These eight categories of parenting styles affect child development. Some categories are likely to result in more at-risk behaviors than others. All have consequences for children's and adolescents' behavior.

Consequences of parenting styles. These eight clusters of child-rearing styles provide a reasonable model of the complex relationships between parents and their children. But the efficiency of the model is offset by a lack of comprehensiveness: Some parental behaviors are not reflected in these clusters. Many factors influence the consequences of these parenting styles in the behavior of children and adolescents. The age of the child, the personality and constitution of the child, and the degree and duration of the unhealthy (or healthy) relationship with the parents all are of influence. Other factors include the child's perception of the interaction, the family setting, and other ecological factors. Nevertheless, there are some consistent consequences of each of these parenting styles on children and youth:

Section 1. Organized, effective parents = high-achieving conformers. These youth tend to be highly socialized and conforming. Often model children and adolescents, they may experience some internal conflict and may be timid and withdrawn but are rarely a problem to society. Children in this category are high in compliance, dependency, responsibility, leadership, and conscience. They are rarely referred for counseling, although intrapersonal stress sometimes forces them to seek treatment.

Section 2. Democratic parents = friendly, achieving bohemians. These children and adolescents tend to be active, socially outgoing, and friendly. Often they take an aggressive stance on social issues and assume adult role-taking behavior quite early. They are often creative, independent individuals who achieve when and if they decide it is important to do so.

Section 3. Rigidly controlling parents = delinquent runaways. These children often exhibit considerable fear and rejection of authority figures. Outwardly conforming, they may develop a repertoire of manipulative behaviors that passively express their aggression. Ultimately the child may explode into highly delinquent behavior or escape by running away.

Section 4. Neglecting parents = neglected children. These children are poorly equipped to take on adult roles and may eventually reject society's standards. They may develop self-punitive and self-defeating behaviors, becoming isolated and socially withdrawn.

Section 5. Overprotective parents = conforming, dependent children. These children are likely to show high compliance. They follow rules closely and with some anxiety. They may also be submissive, dependent, withdrawn, and timid. They frequently have a difficult time becoming independent.

Section 6. Indulgent parents = spoiled children. Children whose parents occupy this section tend to be pampered and spoiled. Often independent and creative, they can be disobedient, impudent, demanding, and "bratty." As they get older, they may develop antisocial, aggressive, or narcissistic behavior and then expect to be protected from the consequences.

Section 7. Authoritarian, hostile-neurotic parents = abused/aggressive children. Children in this category are fearful and angry, and may eventually vent their rage against society. Often their rebellion takes the form of highly aggressive, delinquent, acting-out behavior. Some of these children run away.

Section 8. Anxious-neurotic parents = emotionally disturbed children. Children in this cell tend to be neurotic and disturbed. Often socially withdrawn, they may have poor peer-group attachment characterized by shyness and quarreling. They are likely to be unable to assume adult roles and to have poor self-esteem.

These profiles are based on professional observation, descriptive reports in the literature, and a review of research studies. Although much needs to be done to expand knowledge in this area, some common parenting patterns have been identified with enough certainty to enable us to characterize the parenting styles seen in families. These patterns are crucial to the family environment and to the overall personal development of children.

Parenting styles in the Andrews family. Let us consider Allie Andrews, whom we met in Chapter 1. It would be helpful at this point to review Allie's case. Recall that she and her stepfather were in open conflict regarding family rules and regulations and that their relationship had deteriorated.

Although the Andrews case study does not provide a great deal of information about Jack and Alicia's parenting styles, it does tell us enough to permit us to offer some tentative hypotheses about the family interaction and make a preliminary evaluation of the Andrews' parenting styles. This situation is not an atypical one. Indeed, one of the major problems for teachers and counselors is the difficulty of gaining access to the total picture. One is called upon to teach and counsel, to make judgments and evaluations, to provide treatment plans, and to respond to conflict and pain in the young person without knowing the full background and thus without completely understanding the life situation of the individual. Effective and competent counselors, teachers, and others are always working with hunches and tentative hypotheses.

When we review Allie's situation, several issues stand out. First, we find descriptions of parental behavior that represent each one of the three dimensions of child-rearing practices. Jack appears to be highly controlling and restricting. He sets firm, perhaps harsh rules and upholds them with punishment. He also seems to provide little warmth and low support for Allie. His apparent dislike for Allie and his punishments reflect a hostile style of interaction. Finally, his emotional involvement is negative and extreme—he is hurt, fearful, and angry, as well as suspicious and mistrustful.

We find less information on the parenting behavior of Allie's mother. We do know that she has assumed the role of the family mediator, however, and that she occasionally has absorbed some of the conflict. Her parenting style appears to differ from her husband's in the area of emotional involvement. And so we come to the second issue: inconsistency. Even though the mother's emotional response may have a calming and placating effect, Allie may view it as encouragement to act out. This inconsistency may be a strong clue to the dysfunction within the family system.

The third issue that emerges from the case study is the intensity of the father's engagement in his parenting of Allie. On each of the three continuums, his behavior is extreme. That is, he is quite restrictive and provides Allie very low support. He is obviously very emotionally involved with her. This behavior places him in Section 7: He is authoritarian and hostile-neurotic. Needless to say, Allie's stepfather is a major negative influence on her at this point. Figure 3.3 summarizes the behaviors that are involved in Allie's parenting.

The parenting issues raised in Allie's case suggest possible intervention strategies. The family system is already under considerable stress at this time and might be amenable to intervention. It is obvious that Allie's stepfather is a major influence in her life. This observation leads to several questions that may eventually need to be addressed. Should Jack be included in any treatment plans that are developed? Should Jack or the family as a whole be considered for intervention? Should school programs be arranged to provide Allie with a more reasonable limit-setting model? Possible answers to these questions will be provided in later chapters.

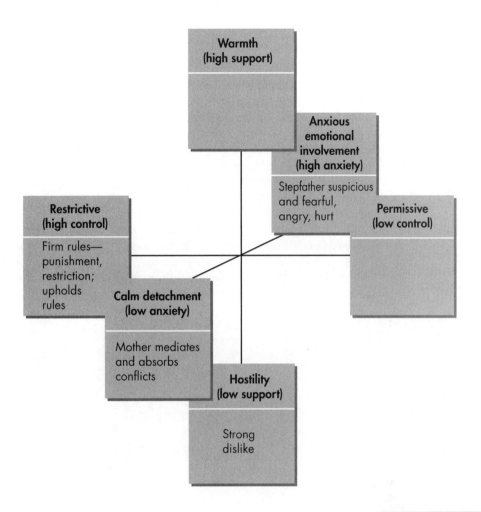

Comments: Allie's stepfather, Jack, operates out of Section 7 of the parenting cube and has become more reactive and violent as Allie has reached adolescence. Mother's parenting style is different (calm detachment), but the case study does not provide enough data to locate her precisely in the cube.

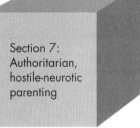

Section 7: Authoritarian, hostile-neurotic parenting

FIGURE 3.3 Parenting behaviors (the case of Allie)

CONCLUSION

In this chapter we considered social changes that affect today's families and the rapid changes that occur within families in response to them. Helping professionals need to understand and appreciate cultural differences in families rather than impose dominant culture assumptions. Many families are characterized by detachment, enmeshment, poor parenting practices, or are dysfunctional in other ways. The Carter family illustrates a fairly common family dysfunction. As families progress through developmental periods, or stages of the family life cycle, some of the interaction patterns that developed early, such as parenting styles, must adapt to the changing needs of the children. When they do not, young people are often at risk for engaging in maladaptive and self-defeating behaviors. The conceptual model of the three dimensions of child-rearing is intended to clarify the continuums of parenting styles. The parenting cube can also help counselors, teachers, and human service professionals teach and encourage positive behaviors among children and, as much as possible, within the whole family. As the case studies suggest, ineffective and poor parenting and family interactions have to be identified before steps can be taken to promote effective and positive interactions.

CHAPTER 4

SCHOOL ISSUES THAT RELATE TO AT-RISK CHILDREN AND YOUTH

▲ *If families do not . . .*
Then schools must
Provide roots for children . . .
So they stand firm and grow,
Provide wings for children . . .
So they can fly.
Broken roots and crippled wings
Destroy hope.
And hope sees the invisible,
feels the intangible,
and achieves the impossible.

J. J. McWHIRTER

CHAPTER OUTLINE

▲ In education, the term *at risk* refers primarily to students who are at risk of school failure. As we discussed earlier, *at risk* actually means much more than flunking reading or math, or even dropping out of school. And yet, from an educator's perspective, educational concerns define at-risk issues. School problems and dropout are linked to many other problems expressed by young people (Beauvais, Chavez, Oetting, Deffenbacher, & Cornell, 1996; Jessor, 1991, 1993; Mahoney, 1998). The strong relationships between school difficulties and other problems, as well as evidence that educational involvement is a protective factor influencing resilience (Miller & MacIntosh, 1999), highlight the pivotal position of schools. In schools prevention can reach the greatest number of young people, thus, examining the educational environment is critical.

THE VALUE OF EDUCATION

News reports compare the scores of students in the United States and in other countries on tests in geography and spelling, math and science. These reports consistently favor students in other countries. They imply that learning in U.S. schools is somehow not quite up to par. Does a student's ability to spell reflect his or her ability to think? Does recall of dates, locations, or facts indicate a student's problem-solving skills? The answer to these questions is no. Learning is the act of acquiring knowledge or a skill through instruction or study, yet these comparisons suggest a view of learning that reduces this cognitive act to an isolated and mechanical process (Comer, 1996).

How learning is valued is also reflected in the following statistics. According to the U.S. Census Bureau (2001) in 2000, the average household income was a bit over $55,000. Yet, according to the National Center for Educational Statistics, average teachers' salaries have hovered around $40,000 from 1987–88 through 1998–99 (National Center for Education Statistics [NCES], 2001). Schoolteachers and counselors, most with master's degrees, are actually paid less than the national average, and are poorly remunerated relative to other professionals. Low teacher salaries reflect the value society places on education, and are one contributor to the current teacher shortage. Former Senator Dennis DeConcini's words still hold true today:

> We will not attract the brightest and best people into the teaching field until we treat this profession as the priority we believe it to be. We will not attract and keep our teachers until we pay them truly professional salaries so that they can have the standard of living they should be able to earn with their skills and their abilities. (p. 115, 1988)

In response to the current shortage of 2.2 million teachers, many states are responding by lowering teacher standards, with one-fourth of new teachers not meeting states licensing requirements (CDF, 2000). During 1999–2000, over 70% of the students in ESL/bilingual education classes had teachers without certification. In addition, 17% of high school physics, 36% of high school geology, and between 29% and 40% of students in biology/life science and in physical science, were being taught by teachers without certification (Seastrom, Gruber, Henke, McGrath, & Cohen, 2002). Students learn more from better teachers. Interestingly, more affluent schools attract teachers with greater academic skills (Wayne, 2002), with a much greater percentage of teachers at poorer schools having poor academic skills. And the disparity between rich and poor schools is increasing (Berliner, 2001; Kozol, 1991). The richest school districts in the United States spend 56% more per student than the poorest schools. Those schools serving large numbers of poor children are likely to have fewer books and supplies and more teachers with less training and experience (CDF, 2000). If U.S. schools are expected to combat the societal problems of at-risk students, we must commit to the education of our children and youth as our highest priority, which includes attracting and training enough qualified teachers and counselors, encouraging them to work in poor districts, and providing them with adequate compensation.

Federal funding and policies provides further evidence regarding society's support of education. During Carter's presidency, Congress elevated the subcabinet agency of education to the Department of Education (DOE). In the 1980s, the Reagan and Bush administrations insisted that the DOE bring about educational reforms by "leadership and persuasion"—not by new programs or funds. In fact, during every year of Reagan's administration, educational funding was level or reduced for programs that provided aid for disadvantaged children, bilingual education, and work-incentive child-care initiatives; educational funding fell from 2.3% to 1.7% of the total federal budget (Carville, 1996; Shearer, 1990). The expenditure per pupil (dollar level adjusted) in public schools only rose from $6,343 in 1989–90 to $6,662 in 1997–98 (NCES, 2001). The 1990s saw a disturbing trend vis-á-vis prisons vs. education. For the first time, in 1995 states spent more on prisons than on colleges; university construction funds decreased by almost a billion (to $2.5 billion), and corrections funding increased by almost a billion (to $2.6 billion) (Ambrosio & Schiraldi, 1997). New York and California further illustrate this relationship. The New York State prison budget increased by $761 million and the higher education budget dropped by $615 million in the 1990s (Gangi, Schiraldi, & Ziedenberg, 1998), and between 1984 and 1994, there was a 209% funding increase in California's prison system but there was only a 15% increase in state university funding (Taqi-Eddin, Macallair,

▲ Box 4.1

Separate and Unequal 15-Year-Olds

A new look at the literacy of teens living in the industrialized world shows that American students are about average. "Average is not good enough for American kids," warns Education Secretary Rod Paige. True enough—but Paige and the Bush Administration miss the point. Hidden in those results is yet one more piece of evidence that American youngsters attend schools that are separate and markedly unequal.

The Program on International Student Assessment (PISA) seeks to understand what 15-year-olds in 27 industrialized nations learned in reading, mathematics, and science from school and nonschool sources. PISA's goal is to assess how well we teach them to think and solve common, everyday problems in those three disciplines. With 85% of a student's waking hours up to graduation from high school spent outside school, this is really a study of how well our society educates our young.

The answer depends on whether they are white, African American, or Hispanic. Overall, American 15-year-olds were close to the international averages in all three areas of literacy; about 10% scored in the top 10% worldwide on all three scales. The three tests correlated so highly that national scores on any one measure of literacy were almost a perfect proxy for scores on any other measure.

In reading, our strongest area, teens in only three nations—Finland, Canada and New Zealand—scored significantly higher than ours; in fact, 81% of U.S. teens scored at levels two and above on a five-level reading literacy scale (with Level Five being the top).

This is noteworthy because of what PISA says a "Level Two" teen can do: make a comparison or several connections between the text and outside knowledge, draw on personal experience and attitudes to explain the text, recognize the main idea when the information is not prominent, understand relationships or construe meaning within a selected part of the text, and locate one or more pieces of information, which may require inferences to meet several conditions. Only 12% of our teens, those classified in Level One, cannot reach this remarkably high standard. Even among the least-literate teens classified as at Level One, almost half were able to successfully respond to the more difficult items in Level Two.

On all three tests, our youth didn't do badly overall—but we didn't shine either. Why? The answer becomes clear when the scores of different 15-year-olds are viewed separately.

PISA clearly shows we have some ill-educated 15-year-olds, and most of those are poor and minority children. On the reading literacy scale white students in the United States are second in the world, but African American and Hispanic students rank 25th; in mathematics white students are seventh, African American students are 26th; in science white students are fourth, African American and Hispanic students are 26th.

The unpleasant reality is that the United States runs separate and unequal schools and neighborhoods. The conditions of the schools and neighborhoods for our poor, African American, and Hispanic youth are not designed for high levels of literacy in reading, mathematics, and science. We accept poverty, violence, drugs, unequal school funding, uncertified teachers, and institutionalized racism in the schools that serve these children and in the neighborhoods in which they live. These unequal conditions appear to be the major reason we fall short in international comparisons. We combine the scores of these ill-educated children with those of children who enjoy better resources. As long as these differences are allowed to exist, we will rank about average in international comparisons.

As PISA makes clear, accepting deficient schools and troubled neighborhoods for our poor and minority students diminishes our international competitiveness. In ignoring these data about who does well and who does not, we diminish our moral authority in the world as well.

PISA exposes what we have known for too long: that we have social problems to which we pay scant attention. In every international comparison of industrialized nations the United States is the leader in rate of childhood poverty. African American and Hispanic students attend public schools as segregated as they have ever been. Our poor and minority children are not getting the opportunities they need for the nation to thrive.

Politicians who spend their energy condemning the public schools for their supposed failure to educate American youth are ignoring what PISA tells the world: that we fail selectively, having organized our society to provide poor and minority 15-year-olds less opportunity to achieve. Shame on us.

David Berliner, Regents' Professor
Arizona State University
Tempe, Arizona

& Schiraldi, 1998). Apparently, the capital expenditure for a prison cell is $180,000; it costs $35,000 per year per inmate (Hora, Schma, & Rosenthal, 1999). This is a huge drain on public funds directly impacting schools.

A society loses by producing nonproductive citizens. If schools do not provide a safety net for children, health and well-being are reduced. Investing in prisons instead of education and prevention is an expensive, inefficient, and failing long-term strategy. America spends 50% more incarcerating 1.2 million nonviolent offenders than the federal government spends on welfare programs and 6 times more than on child care (Camp & Camp, 1999). Although the United States has only 5% of the world's population, it has 25% of the world's prisoners (Ziedenberg & Schiraldi, 1999). Yet 1 in 2 of America's children will never complete a single year of college; 1 in 8 will never graduate from high school; and 1 in 3 is behind a year or more in school (CDF, 2000).

The publication of *A Nation at Risk* (National Commission on Excellence in Education, 1983) led to two decades of public school education bashing and launched the high-stakes testing phenomena, in which consequences for not passing standardized tests include grade retention for the individual and decreased funding for schools that fail to achieve required pass rates (Amrein & Berliner, 2002). In *The Manufactured Crisis*, Berliner and Biddle (1995) provide convincing evidence of a political agenda underlying *A Nation at Risk* and present thorough and sound data indicating that public schools in the United States have done a marvelous job of educating American children. In fact, they demonstrate that children actually know more than earlier generations, compare very favorably to students educated in other countries, and perform better than ever before (see Box 4.1).

The No Child Left Behind (NCLB) Act of 2001 was signed into law by President George W. Bush in January 2002. This act has been described as the most sweeping reform of the Elementary and Secondary Education Act since its inception in 1965. It redefines the federal role in K–12 education and promises to help close the achievement gap between disadvantaged and minority students and their peers. NCLB contains four basic principles: stronger accountability for results (e.g., decreased funding for schools that do not meet pass rates for standardized tests), increased flexibility and local control, expanded school choice options for parents (e.g., parents can remove their children from failing schools), and an emphasis on scientifically supported teaching methods. While infusing resources to schools, there are significant concerns about the effects of the NCLB Act. For example, even more funding is likely to flow away from those public schools in most desperate need (Pierce, 2002). Others (Reville, 2002; Goldhaber, 2002) raise serious concerns about accountability and the ways that the NCLB Act may diminish attention to both above and below average students. Schools that want to show improvement will likely assist those children who test just below the minimum pass rates. Those children who have very poor test scores are unlikely to raise scores high enough to increase the school's pass rate, and those students with good scores are already part of the pass rates. Both are less likely to receive support or services.

Most teachers work hard, are concerned about children, and try to do a good job of teaching. Teachers *know* that all children need support, care, and nurturing. They also know that with the decline of economic stability, the pressures facing parents, and the fragmentation of neighborhoods and communities, the support and care children receive at school is even more critical. Teachers are expected to do more than ever before, in classrooms that some find increasingly unsafe. During the mid-1990s, 12% of all teachers were threatened with injury, and 4% were physically attacked by a student (NCES, 2001). Much gang activity occurs around schools (Esbenson, 2000). School shootings leave teachers questioning whether such shocking violence could happen "at *my* school?" (see Chapter 10). Amidst these concerns teachers are constantly bombarded about how "teachers are not doing their jobs," how "schools are inadequate and failing," and how teachers must "do more with less."

For education to succeed, increased financial support is needed for struggling schools and not simply for new schools. Such expenditures will not be forthcoming unless our society as a whole understands the value of learning (Comer, 1996). School reform is critical to the development of more effective schools. However, in

. . .our rush to reform education, we have forgotten a simple truth: Reform will never be achieved by reviewing appropriations, restructuring schools, rewriting curricula, and revising tests if we continue to demean and dishearten the human resource called the teacher on whom so much depends. Teachers must be better compensated, freed from bureaucratic harassment, given a role in academic governance, and provided with the best possible methods and materials (P. Palmer, cited in Obiakor, 2001, p. 4).

RESEARCH ON EFFECTIVE SCHOOLS

Variables in Research on School Effects

Researchers have identified a number of elements common to effective schools (Good & Brophy, 1994; Taylor, Pressley, & Pearson, 2000; Wohlstetter & Smyer, 1994). These can be classified into the general categories of leadership behaviors, academic emphasis, teacher and staff factors, student involvement, community support, and social capital.

Leadership behaviors.   Effective schools have autonomous staff management at the school site. Administrators, teachers, and counselors make many decisions about programs and program implementation without the need to seek approval of the school board or the district. Effective schools have a clear mission and place an emphasis on strong instructional leadership.

Academic emphasis.   Effective schools provide a curriculum that emphasizes academics. Students are expected to perform and they are frequently monitored. They recognize academic achievement on a school-wide basis, instructional time is maximized, and the curriculum is consistently improved.

Teacher and staff factors.   Effective schools are characterized by collegial relationships among the staff, encouragement of collaborative planning, and low turnover among the faculty. Further, staff development is provided on a school-wide basis.

Student involvement.   Students at effective schools tend to have a sense of community, a feeling of belongingness, and to feel safe at school. They also are likely to have clear goals. Teachers and counselors work to help students feel connected. Student discipline is fair, clear, and consistent but not oppressive or punitive.

Community support.   The communities in which effective schools are located have high expectations of the schools and their students. Further, district support and supportive parental involvement are evident, and relationships between home and school are strong and positive.

Social capital.   Social capital, the network of relationships that surround an individual child, is important for development (Coleman & Hoffer, 1987; Maeroff, 1998). One of the major reasons some schools perform significantly better than others is that they are so rich in social capital (Coleman & Hoffer, 1987). The nuclear and extended family, the neighborhood and church community, the social service agencies, and community organizations form a supportive enclave of adults who are united with school personnel around a system of similar educational beliefs and values. This network of relationships is extremely important to the education of all children. Most school systems are severely constrained today because of the general reduction of social capital in society (Maeroff, 1998).

Definitional Issues in Research on School Effects

Most research on effective schools measures effectiveness as students' performance on standardized achievement tests, an extremely narrow view of learning. Other cognitive criteria, such as decision making and critical thinking, are largely ignored (Adams & Hamm, 1994; Good & Brophy, 1994). Glasser (1990) states that "nothing of high quality, including schoolwork, can be measured by standardized, machine-scored tests" (p. 428). To judge school effectiveness by the narrow criterion of scores on standardized tests pressures teachers and districts to carry out test-driven curriculum. In one study examining a decade of data from 18 states that implemented high stakes testing, Amrein and Berliner (2002) found that scores on standardized tests such as the ACT and the SAT did *not* increase after high stakes testing was implemented, even when the high stakes test scores increased. Scores on the ACT, SAT, and content measures stayed the same or actually decreased.

Results of research on school effectiveness must be viewed with caution. For example, schools with higher dropout rates potentially have higher test score averages than do schools that retain their lower achieving students longer. If effectiveness is judged by performance on high stakes tests alone, a school that fails miserably with at-risk students by pushing them out may be deemed highly effective! Alternative indices, such as students' involvement in the community, attendance rates, the incidence of school vandalism and violence, or dropout rates, are seldom used in school effectiveness research (Aubrey, 1988), but these indices may be more relevant to the community. Obiakor (2001) suggests that "good" schools be redefined as those that are "culturally, racially, linguistically, and socioeconomically heterogeneous" and in which students "will not be misidentified, misassessed, mislabeled, miscategorized, misplaced, and misinstructed" (p. 129). Another dimension of school effectiveness is school culture. School culture focuses on aspects of education more directly relevant to at-risk youth. Let us consider the Diaz family case study.

School culture.   Every social organization has its unique culture, and schools are no exception. School culture is determined by student involvement, teacher factors, community support, curricular focus, and educational leadership—factors that also define effective schools. A culture provides its members with two things. First, it establishes a set of rules, expectations, and norms for members. Carlos's teachers encourage an English-only norm. In Lidia's school, retaining students who do poorly is the rule. Essentially, school culture provides an informal understanding of the way things are done. Second, culture can enhance self-esteem through shared values, beliefs, rituals, and ceremonies. Students, faculty, and staff who take pride in their school culture are likely to do better than those who do not. Many of Carlos's teachers share negative views of bilingual education; Lidia's feelings of stupidity are due in part to her exclusion from her school's culture. Participation and attendance in school activities can greatly enhance school connectedness and pride. These activities are generally hard hit when resources

The Diaz Family

Enrique Diaz came to the United States from El Salvador 16 years ago when he was 23 years old. He was forced to flee El Salvador when his membership in a small labor union was revealed to the government authorities, and left behind his parents, brothers, sisters, and extended family. He brought his sister's 2-year-old daughter Ramona with him, because the baby's father had been killed for his labor union activity and his sister feared for her own life. A church group participating in the Sanctuary movement of the 1980s provided Enrique and Ramona with shelter in a local safehouse, as well as assisting Enrique to find employment. Enrique works as a day laborer for growers and lawn maintenance companies. He met Alicia, a Mexican American woman volunteer at the safe house, during his first week in the United States. Alicia began spending a great deal of time caring for Ramona, and she and Enrique married 10 months after his arrival. One of the things that attracted Alicia to Enrique was the fact that he was a very hard worker and did not drink alcohol. Currently Enrique continues to work as hard as ever during the day, but he now consumes 1–2 six packs of beer most evenings. Alicia is the second child in a family of nine children. Her parents came to the United States from central Mexico as young adults. Alicia works as a motel maid and has a second part-time job doing custodial work at her church. Alicia and Enrique have raised Ramona, now 18, as their own daughter, and also have a son, Carlos, who is 13, and another daughter Lidia, who is 5 years old. They live in a small rented home and maintain a very modest standard of living. Enrique became a naturalized citizen just before the birth of Lidia.

Enrique understands but does not speak English. Alicia was raised in a monolingual Spanish household but learned to speak English in school. Although her English skills are solid, she is very reluctant to use English unless she has to, because she believes that she makes many mistakes and feels self-conscious about her accent. Both of the parents express concern about their children because family life is curtailed by the long hours the parents spend at work. They are especially concerned about their children's educational problems. Neither parent completed high school, and they desperately want their children to have a better life. They view education as a necessary step toward that goal. Their communication with the school system has been complicated by language barriers; in addition, Enrique and Alicia are convinced that the teachers think they are bad and uncaring parents because they have not learned enough English.

CASE STUDY

The Diaz Family *(continued)*

Upon entering kindergarten, Ramona Diaz was placed in an ESL (English as a second language) program. She was transitioned into an English-only classroom when she entered middle school because that was district policy; however, she did not seem prepared to enter this environment. Ramona associated only with other girls who were Spanish-language dominant and fell behind in all of her content areas. She resisted going to school, even skipping classes on occasion. In parent-teacher conferences, her teachers would consistently say that she was not turning in her homework, or would turn in work that was incomplete and inaccurate. Ramona would insist that she was turning it in but that her teachers were misplacing it and grading her unfairly because they thought she was "stupid" and didn't like her. Enrique was enraged by Ramona's attitude toward school, and they had explosive arguments two or three times per week, which were most likely to occur in the evening, after Enrique had been drinking for several hours. Finally, at age 16, Ramona dropped out of school and began working five nights per week at ABC Burgers. Although Enrique and Alicia did not approve, they had felt somewhat out of control of Ramona and were unsure of how to help her in school. With Ramona out of the house at night, and because homework was no longer a constant source of tension, the fighting between Enrique and Ramona decreased. Enrique's drinking did not decrease.

Ramona tells her parents that she will eventually earn her GED. Alicia is concerned that Ramona will become pregnant and be stuck in low-paying jobs for the rest of her life. She rarely sees Ramona. Ramona arrives home from work after her parents are in bed, and is still sleeping when Enrique and Alicia leave for work in the morning. Alicia suspects that Ramona has a boyfriend at work, but Ramona denies this and is very closed about her social activities. She has been contributing to the family income and is affectionate with her brother and sister when she sees them. Just last week, however, Ramona told her parents that she had lost her paycheck and would not be able to help out the family until the next one arrived.

Carlos Diaz is in the seventh grade. He has had a solid relationship with his parents, particularly his mother. Carlos has been in a regular classroom for the past two years. He has generally done well in his schoolwork, but he is not a model student. He has often had trouble with his peers and at times gotten into fights on the playground. Since he has moved into junior high school, his social problems have decreased somewhat. He has several teachers now, and the

The Diaz Family *(continued)*

classes are larger than those in the primary school. He has begun to make friends, although his lack of free time outside of school has made this difficult.

Because of Ramona's job at ABC Burgers, Carlos has the responsibility of watching his little sister after school, and he has had difficulty completing school assignments. His after-school activities now include cleaning the house and helping to prepare dinner in addition to baby-sitting, so he has only a limited amount of time to complete the homework assigned by his five teachers. When his assignments require use of a computer, Carlos has to stay in from recess to use one at school, because his family does not own one. Some nights he works on every subject for at least a short time, but on other nights he is able to complete an assignment for only one of his classes. At the time they entered counseling, Carlos was behind in every class and was falling asleep in school. Some of his teachers seem to think he is lazy, contrary, and unresponsive. Many of them seem frustrated that Carlos is not completely fluent in English by now.

Carlos's social studies teacher, Ms. Bassett, has taken a particular interest in him. At first, she found him inattentive in class and unresponsive to her questions, and she assumed this behavior was a combination of language and lack of ability. She noticed, however, that when he did complete his homework it was usually well done and accurate. After consulting with the school counselor, she gave Carlos a more active role in his own education. She found ways to give him more responsibility for learning, provided a means for him to monitor his own progress, and generally encouraged him to be more active in learning. The counselor also suggested that cooperative learning groups might be especially beneficial to Carlos, not only academically but as a means to help Carlos develop better peer relationships. Ms. Bassett is currently struggling with ways to modify her teaching style in a school that bases evaluations of her teaching on direct instruction, a method that typically works well for social studies recitation classes but fails to allow students to take an active role in learning. Enrique and Alicia view Carlos as a very responsible young man and hope that he will continue on in school. They are aware that he is under a lot of pressure at home and in school, but do not seem to know what to do about it. In spite of their concerns, they have not responded to Ms. Bassett's invitation to meet with them or talk on the phone. They seem to fear that she will be upset about Carlos's caretaking role and that she will not understand their family situation.

The Diaz Family (continued)

Lidia Diaz is in kindergarten this year. Last year she participated in Head Start, which greatly aided her language skills and helped prepare her for kindergarten. In spite of this advantage, she is progressing quite slowly. She is one of 30 kindergartners in the classroom. Some of her classmates attended private preschools and can already read. To deal with the large number of students in her class, Lidia's teacher groups the children according to their ability in reading and arithmetic. Lidia knows that she is in the lowest group in both subjects. Like her older sister, Lidia often feels stupid. Lidia's teacher believes that Lidia has the potential for school success and wishes she could spend more time with her. Lidia's elementary school has a retention policy for kindergarten students who do not make certain gains in achievement. In spite of her teacher's belief in her abilities, Lidia fits the criteria for the district retention policy, and if things do not improve, she will probably be kept back next year.

are scarce, and even when available, students such as Carlos are not able to take advantage of them. The culture of a school can be described in terms of student and teacher climate.

Student climate.   Several aspects of student climate relate directly to children and youth at risk. Children's experiences with their peers provide them with an opportunity to learn how to interact with others, develop age-relevant skills and interests, control their social behavior, and share their problems and feelings. As children get older, their peer group relationships increase in importance. The child's recognition of belonging to a group is an important step in development, and students with more friends at school feel more connected to their schools (McNeely, Nonnemaker, & Blum, 2002). But belonging to a group has both benefits and costs in the child's subsequent social development and behavior. Many students who are at risk for school failure know early that somehow they are different from—less acceptable and less accepted than—other students. Lidia Diaz is one such student. Consistent grouping of students by ability heightens such self-perceptions. Who of us did not know by the second grade which groups constituted the "good readers" and the "poor readers"? More important, the expectations of students depend on the group they are in. Students who succeed in school have both high expectations of themselves and a strong, positive sense of belonging to the school community. Students who are at risk for school failure are often placed in the lowest ability groups and excluded from the academic success community. Exclusion from the school community limits the potentially positive effects of school culture on students at risk for failure (Korinek, Walther-Thomas, McLaughlin, & Williams, 1999; Meggert, 2000; Sinclair, Hurley, Evelo, Christenson, & Thurlow, 2002).

In addition to academically based groupings, student climate is influenced by the peer groups that students form. Peers not only influence each other by offering support, advice, and opportunities to discuss conflicting points of view, but also negatively by coercion and manipulation. Thus, peer group pressure can be either a very powerful ally or a formidable antagonist, dissuading or encouraging problem behaviors (Dishion, Andrews, & Crosby, 1995; Kupersmidt, Burchinaal, & Patterson, 1995; Moffit, Caspi, Dickson, Silva, & Stanton, 1996). Behaviors such as misbehaving in class, fighting or arguing, and neglecting to turn in homework all interfere with learning and are related to school failure (Knitzer, Steinberg, & Fleisch, 1990; Walker, Colvin, & Ramsey, 1995). Carlos's earlier playground fights demonstrate how poor decision making among students can hinder positive student climate. Efforts to improve students' problem-solving and decision-making skills have a positive effect on the at-risk population (Beyth-Marom, Fischhoff, Jacobs, & Furby, 1989; Shure, 1999; and see Chapter 13). Some schools have reported a marked reduction in disruptive behaviors after students have been taught to mediate disputes on their own. Significant benefits accrue when students teach and model social skills (Blake, Wang, Cartledge, & Gardner, 2000). The ability of students to solve their own problems and peacefully settle disputes directly and positively affects student climate. School mediation programs (discussed in Chapter 14) have been especially helpful in this regard (Jones, 1998; Lane & McWhirter, 1992, 1996; Smith & Daunic, 2002).

Student climate is affected by students' ability to monitor their own behavior and progress, take responsibility for their own learning, and contribute to the school community (Korinek et al., 1999; McNeely, Nonnemaker, & Blum, 2002; Shapiro & Cole, 1994). Most learning research focuses on methods and procedures that increase desired student behaviors and center on strategies teachers and counselors can use. Research, however, often ignores the ways teachers and counselors can help young people help themselves. At-risk youth are capable, thinking people who are able to see and monitor their own progress. They need to be taught how to do so. They need to be encouraged to develop a shared responsibility for learning.

Teacher climate.   The working environment for teachers and other school employees is also part of school culture. Levels of collegiality and collaboration among staff members, community support, autonomy, adequacy of funding, and the effectiveness of leadership all contribute to teacher climate within the school.

Consistent and focused meetings with teachers and support staff (psychologists, counselors, social workers) encourage stability, development, collaboration, and collegiality. Unfortunately, school personnel usually meet for curative rather than preventive reasons—ultimately a costly and inefficient procedure (Comer, 1996)—largely because classroom teachers and support staff have a limited understanding of each other's efforts and strategies. Moreover, they generally have no training in a collaborative, collegial model of working together to prevent problems. If Carlos's teachers were able to work as a team, as middle school teachers often do, they might gain a better understanding of his previous bilingual problems and devise potential solutions. Models of shared decision making and leadership organized around shared values, commitments, and beliefs can make a dramatic difference in teacher climate (e.g., Sergiovanni, 1994, 2001). Box 4.2 illustrates one dimension of how teacher climates can vary.

When teachers are identified as professionals, the effect on teacher climate is positive. Unfortunately, it is frequently the case that teachers are not treated as experts on learning,

▲ Box 4.2
Teacher Climate
One of the authors of this text had the experience of spending 15 minutes in two different middle school teachers lounges in the same week, during a research project. The atmosphere within the two lounges could not have been more different and provided insight into the teacher climate at each school. In the first lounge, five teachers were filling coffee cups, organizing papers, and chatting energetically about the events of the week. One teacher approached the author/researcher, asking her name and making introductions to the others. Entering teachers were greeted by name. There was some joking about the "mountains of grading" that faced several of them. In the second lounge, two teachers were silently grading papers when a third entered and immediately began talking about a student using crude and insulting language. The other two teachers offered comparable stories about difficult students, also using language such as "asshole" and "bastard." Then the third teacher stated, "God I can't wait to retire" and left the room; the other two teachers returned to their grading. All three teachers completely ignored the author/researcher and did not make eye contact at any time.

pedagogy, and curriculum. Teachers have a base of professional knowledge, a professional language, and bring specific skills to their job. Yet teachers often are reduced to the status of clerks. Educational practices that stifle teachers from utilizing their knowledge produce a poor teacher climate and ultimately a poor student climate. This is true for school counselors as well.

Educational writers (S. M. Johnson & Boles, 1994; Smylie & Tuermer, 1992) describe the need for teacher empowerment in the workplace, particularly with regard to curriculum, and Shannon (1989) advocates that teachers' knowledge about lesson preparation should prevail over the prepared lesson plans found in teachers' manuals. Some educators view teachers as capable decision makers and encourage involvement in school-based management (Cambone, Weiss, & Wyeth, 1992; Johnson & Boles, 1994; Sergiovanni, 1994, 2001). Team-teaching is a way in which teachers contribute to high-performance schools (Wohlstetter & Smyer, 1994). Teachers in the teams receive immediate feedback from one another. The team provides teachers with a support group to help resolve judgment decisions. Consequently, teachers perform better in specific situations (Phillips, McCullough, Nelson, & Walker, 1992).

How do schools typically respond to increasing incidences of disruption? Often, schools respond with "zero tolerance" policies, the addition of security guards and video cameras, and the suspension or expulsion of disruptive students. Although removing disruptive students from the classroom or the school provides some immediate relief to the affected teachers and students, these short-term policies have a series of negative consequences. They shift responsibility away from the school, reinforce antisocial behavior and an environment of control, devalue the adult-child relationship, and weaken the ties between academic and social behavioral learning (Horner & Sugai, 2000). Positive Behavioral Support (PBS) is an alternative that involves a significant investment of resources and time, but that provides significant long-term benefits. PBS is a system-wide approach to school behavior management that combines a *system* that supports teacher behavior with *data* that supports effective decisions and *practices* that support student behavior. The purpose of PBS is to increase the effectiveness, relevancy, and efficiency of academic and social learning for all students, and especially those with emotional and behavioral problems by (1) increasing time devoted to teaching (instead of managing behavior problems) and (2) increasing students' academic engagement time and achievement. That is, PBS changes individual behavior by changing the context in which behavior occurs. PBS establishes a school-wide system for discipline with clear procedures and behaviors expected of students and teachers, and provides a clear continuum of reinforcement for positive behaviors and a continuum of discouragement for negative behaviors. Requiring collaboration throughout the school, the school staff are encouraged to work "smarter instead of harder and longer."

Initiating PBS requires a commitment of several years, with maintenance of the system a top priority. Other requirements include a team-based approach, active administrator support, proactive instructional approach, local behavioral expertise, and the use of data-based decision making. Implementation of PBS requires an enormous amount of time, resources, and energy. So why would a school select this intervention? Answer: Results. In one school, the average daily referrals in December dropped from 21 down to 6 per day the following December. Four years later the changes were maintained, with an average of 5 referrals per day in December with similar effects every month. The savings of time and energy that go into dealing with office referrals, as well as the increased satisfaction and security experienced by school personnel, are enough to convince many schools to adopt this program.

EDUCATIONAL STRUCTURE: SCHOOLS AND CLASSROOMS

The structure of education can be manipulated at two levels: the school structure itself (grade configuration, type of building) and the classroom (the teacher's philosophy and teaching style, the instructional method). Reform may be needed at both levels in order to optimize the academic success of students at risk.

School Structure

Grade configuration has been the primary organizing principle of our system. The rapid growth of high schools in the United States after the Civil War led some sections of the country to operate under an 8–5 schedule: eight years of elementary school, five years of high school. Other areas used a 6–6 plan: six years of elementary school, six years of high school. Toward the end of the century, the 8–4 pattern became popular. In 1909 the first junior high school was introduced. Since then, grades have been configured in a variety of patterns (6–3–3, 6–2–4, 7–2–3, 5–3–4, 4–4–4) in attempts to group students by developmental needs and to increase the cost-effectiveness of education. Bickel and colleagues (2001) present evidence that contradicts the widely held notion that large schools serving a small range of grades are uniformly more cost-effective than single-unit

(K–12 or K–8) schools. With respect to human costs, a larger size school is more damaging to disadvantaged students' achievement scores. After an in-depth analysis of a variety of indicators, Bickel and others (2001) conclude, "If we were also interested in balancing expenditure per pupil with achievement-based equity, the best configuration seems to be a small single-unit school. . . This makes the achievement advantage of small schools (where they are most needed, that is, in impoverished communities) more affordable than previously expected." It is important to engage in deeper-level examination of issues such as cost-effectiveness, and to raise questions such as, "beneficial to *whom?*" and "cost-effective with respect to *what dimensions?*" and "what dimensions have *not* been considered?"

The school-within-a-school concept is one way of structuring the school so that smaller groups of students are clustered together (Cuban, 1989; Seidman & French, 1997). For example, the school population of a specific secondary school is divided into four "houses." These houses become the major vehicles for social interaction, intramural athletics, school activities, discipline, and so forth (think of the organization of Hogwart's Academy of Witchcraft and Wizardry, featured in the popular Harry Potter books by J. K. Rowling). The main reference group can be reduced in this way from, for example, 2000 students in the comprehensive school to 500 students in the house, increasing the sense of community.

Some schools build before- and after-school supervised programs into their structure (Dryfoos, 1994). There is ample documentation that youth without supervision after school and who are with peers are more likely to engage in risky behaviors and to have poorer school achievement than unsupervised youth who are home alone, or youth who are with caretakers after school (Goyette-Ewing, 2000; Flannery, Williams, & Vazsonyi, 1999; Mulhall, Stone, & Stone, 1996). In addition, there are significant benefits to participation in quality after-school programs. The demand for school-based after-school programs exceeds the supply, and even existing programs are constantly threatened by decreasing funds. After-school care programs could be of significant benefit to at-risk students such as Carlos and Lidia Diaz. (See Chapter 6.)

School Choice

School choice has been offered as a solution to poor-quality schools. The proponents of school choice include political conservatives who view public education as overly controlled by the government, religious conservatives who view public schools as damaging to children because of exposure to immoral values and practices, private schools seeking increased enrollment, and activist, urban parents of color seeking better-quality education for their children (Miller-Kahn & Smith, 2001). Based on the belief that choice inspires competition and therefore higher quality, the school choice movement was supported by a 2002 U.S. Supreme Court decision upholding the constitutionality of the Cleveland school voucher program, enabling students to attend private religious schools. The National Education Association, the National Association of School Principals, and the American Federation of Teachers immediately indicated strong opposition to the voucher system believing that the effects will damage American public education. Miller-Kahn and Smith (2001) demonstrate how school choice policies reinforce and replicate inequities for lower SES, ethnic minority, and poor achieving students.

Charter Schools

The charter school movement has emerged from school choice (Wohlstetter & Smyer, 1994). Although charter schools are public schools that offer a free education, they differ from district-controlled schools in that they have a seperate board of directors. Charter schools embody many different visions of school improvement. Charter schools have the freedom to be innovative, and to become a source of good ideas. Supporters view charter schools as a promising way to raise academic standards, empower educators, involve parents and communities, and expand choice and accountability. Despite these promising possibilities, however, the variation in characteristics has made it extremely difficult to evaluate and compare their effects with one another and with traditional schools (SRI, 1997). Charter schools clearly have the potential to be an important educational innovation. However, the accessibility of charter schools must be addressed with respect to transportation, enrollment procedures and requirements, and a thorough understanding of who actually enrolls. This is particularly important given the No Child Left Behind Act.

Classroom Structure

Classroom structure affects the academic experience of at-risk students. The structure of the class can give at-risk students a feeling of control over their situation. An environment in which students are treated as unique individuals who have unique contributions to make to the group yields positive results (Elmore, Peterson, & McCarthy, 1996). Such an environment produces an acceptance and appreciation of differences, an increase in creativity, an enhancement of personal autonomy, an improvement in mental health, and the ultimate overall quality of learning (McNeely, Nonnemaker, & Blum, 2002). A caring relationship between teacher and student helps meet the needs of at-risk students (Birch & Ladd, 1997; Obiakor, 2001).

Class size also affects at-risk students. Certainly Lidia Diaz's teacher would be able to meet Lidia's needs more effectively if she were responsible for fewer children. Indeed, academic achievement and connection to school have been found to be related to class size (Ferguson, 1991; McNeely, Nonnemaker, & Blum, 2002). Because Lidia's class is large, students have been assigned to smaller groups based on ability levels. Although little advantage accrues to students assigned to the high groups, students assigned to the low groups suffer great disadvantage (Slavin, 1993). Educational researchers now advocate smaller heterogeneous groups that work cooperatively in lieu of homogeneous ability groups (D. W. Johnson & Johnson, 1988, 1989; Sharan, 1994; Slavin, Karweit, & Wasik, 1994; Slavin & Madden, 1989). When teachers and students are encouraged to work collaboratively, there is a positive effect on the overall school environment (Reminger, Hidi, & Krapp, 1992). Students who are at risk for school failure are usually several grades behind their age mates; school structures that emphasize cooperation over competition meet the needs of these students better (see Chapter 14).

Curricular and instructional practices also affect students who are at risk for school failure. Students have little enthusiasm for a curriculum that focuses simply on learning facts and isolated skills, and over time become passive players in the schooling process. Further, controversial and sometimes very interesting content areas are being omitted from the curriculum (Glasser, 1990). Educators agree that it is their responsibility, as well as the parents', to pass down the common values of society (Adams & Hamm, 1994; Wilson, 1993). Yet anything associated with "values clarification," "values education," or "morals" sets off alarm bells in some segments of the community. Many districts tightly regulate classroom discussion of topics such as sexual behavior and pregnancy prevention in an effort to avoid controversy.

Curriculum Issues

A curriculum that ignores moral education, development of social skills, student dialogue, and critical thinking does little to help at-risk students. For example, making contraceptives available to teens and providing information about effectiveness has been criticized as contributing to sexual activity among teenagers. However, even though sexual activity among teenagers is approximately equal in the United States and Europe, the teen birth rate is much lower in Europe, where contraception is available. In the year 2000, a narrowly defeated bill in Oregon would have prohibited school discussion of safe sex activities that prevent AIDS, because such information "promotes homosexuality." (We return to this important issue in Chapter 8.) The argument that children and adolescents should get their information at home is a hollow one in light of the vast numbers of families that do not provide this information.

Measures to assess the curriculum need to be broadened as well. Assessment of student learning should go beyond scores on standardized achievement tests to include critical thinking, decision making, and other factors (Cohen, McLaughlin, & Talbert, 1993). As a result of reforms in several states, students are required to pass benchmarks throughout K–12 that include social skills, problem solving, and other important career and life skills. Passing benchmarks in mathematics requires, for example, not simply providing the correct answer but being able to describe the reasoning process used to arrive at the answer, and to identify alternative strategies for finding the answer. (See Box 4.3.)

Vocational education is a critical element of all school curriculum (Blustein, Juntunen, & Worthington, 2000). Bizot (1999) described the seven elements of a strong vocational foundation: (1) provides a sense of competence based on genuine achievement via opportunities to attempt challenging tasks (2) exposes students to many areas of potential interest with the opportunity to explore some areas in greater depth and develop greater mastery; (3) fosters an ability to set goals, generate alternatives, evaluate options and results, and cope with obstacles; (4) provides a framework for understanding and organizing occupational information; (5) conveys respect for individual differences and an understanding of how individual values, interests, and skills lead to different choices, opportunities, and barriers; (6) provides for participation and opportunities to collaborate and contribute; and (7) imparts an understanding that education and career are life long, ongoing processes. Bizot (1999) noted that these key elements should be integrated into curricula. The Oregon educational reform represents a valuable model of how to integrate career and life skills throughout a curriculum. Perhaps if Ramona had been exposed to ongoing career education, and had a curriculum that made consistent connections between learning and life skills, she might have seen more benefits to staying in school. At a minimum, she may have had better-developed skills when she did drop out.

ESL and bilingual education programs are also an important part of school curriculum for students at risk. School dropouts are frequently poor, members of minority groups, lack skills in English, and have less access to English instruction (Watt & Roess-

▲ Box 4.3

Oregon's Educational Reform

The Oregon Educational Act for the 21st Century has effected changes throughout the Oregon education system. In 1997 Oregon became the only U.S. state with a "seamless connection between K–12 and college admissions" (Tell & Conley, 1998). This educational reform has detailed what students are expected to know as they pass through public education, with challenging content standards established in social science, the arts, second languages, English, mathematics, and science. Higher-order skills such as public speaking, analysis and synthesis, problem-solving, and teamwork are also expected and assessed. Both criterion-referenced and performance-based assessments are conducted every two or three years. Successful completion of all benchmarks at grade 10 results in the awarding of a "Certificate of Initial Mastery" (CIM). In grades 11 and 12, students identify interest areas: arts and communications, business and management, health services, human resources, industrial and engineering systems, and natural resource systems. Subsequent coursework utilizes these interest areas for real-world applications and students participate in work-based settings consistent with their interests. The final two years of the high school curriculum prepare students for school-to-work or school-to-school transition while continuing to require rigorous academic training. Successful performance consistent with eleventh and twelfth grade standards results in the awarding of the "Certificate of Advanced Mastery" (CAM). The standards and assessments are aligned with Oregon college admission requirements.

ingh, 1994). This group includes a great many ESL/bilingual students. Given the shortage of ESL teachers with appropriate credentials, and the fact that they live in a district characterized by many poor families, it is likely that the Diaz children did not have qualified teachers when they were in ESL classes.

Crawford (2002) points out that under No Child Left Behind, federal funds will continue to support the education of English language learners (ELLs) with the rapid teaching of English taking precedence at every turn. Annual English assessments will be mandated, and failure to show academic progress in English will be punished. Even though the additional resources provided by NCLB are good news for schools with substantial numbers of language-minority students, the money will be spread more thinly than before—between more states, more programs, and more students. Although districts will automatically receive funding based on their enrollments of ELLs and immigrant students, the impact of federal dollars will be reduced. Last year, for example, about $360 was spent per student in bilingual instructional programs. This year, despite the overall increase in appropriations, funding will provide less than $135 per student.

A final curricular issue we consider in this section is access to World Wide Web— the Internet. The information available to schools via the Internet is virtually limitless, and support services to assist teachers to incorporate this resource into their teaching are evolving rapidly. By the fall of 2000, 98% of public schools had Internet access (NCES, 2001), and this access is true for schools across poverty levels and locations (e.g., urban, rural). This compared to only 35% of schools connected in 1994. Similarly, the percentage of instructional classrooms (including libraries and computer labs) with Internet access increased from 3% to 77%. Yet, again, classroom access to the Internet varies with poverty. In schools serving 75% or more students eligible for free or reduced price lunch, only 60% of the instructional rooms have Internet access, whereas in schools with less poverty 82% of classrooms have access. When teachers are provided with the time and technological support to capitalize on the Internet, students benefit. And it is clear that access to and ability to navigate the Internet are critical skills for today's young people. Given the rapidity of change in this arena, we also offer some cautions about Internet use.

One of the primary functions of the Internet is for communication, and many proponents have convincingly described how the Internet expands the number of people with whom someone can be in easy communication. The social benefits of seem obvious. However, results of one longitudinal study of Internet use raise serious questions. Kraut and his colleagues (1998) followed people age 10 and older using the Internet for communication during their first two years of going on-line. Increased use of the Internet was associated with decreases in family communication and the size of their social circle, along with increases in loneliness and depression. The more time adults spend using the Internet, the less time they engage in family social activities (Nie & Erbring, 2000). As children and youth experience increased access, it will be critically important to monitor the effects of Internet use on their social interaction with family and peers.

CONCLUSION

Educators have control over some educational practices and policies, and elements of school climate that may improve the learning potential of at-risk students. They can promote curricular and teaching practices that emphasize the entirety of students' learning and development. Second, educators can increase collaborative efforts that encourage collegial support and collaborative decision making to improve school climate. Third, student empowerment can be promoted. Students need to approach their work and their interactions with tolerance and democracy. Teachers and counselors can be excellent models of such practices. Finally, educators can assist in raising public awareness about the value of extended support for children and youth who are at risk. Collaboration with researchers to provide evidence of successful prevention and intervention programs (or evidence that programs are *not* working) is one way to help draw attention to what does and does not work. Researchers in turn must consult with teachers to draw educators' first-hand classroom experience and wisdom into the development and implementation of prevention and intervention programs. Teacher expertise is a critical component of school-based programs that provide at-risk students with the skills and resources they need to be successful in school and in life. (Aksamit, 1990; Dryfoos, 1994)

CHAPTER 5

Individual Characteristics of High-Risk and Low-Risk Children and Youth

▲ *What makes some young people resolute and sturdy enough to chip away at the ore, locate the diamond, and polish it . . . while others weakly and feebly patter in the soil, haphazardly searching for a gem, finding only dirt?*

J. J. McWhirter

CHAPTER OUTLINE

▲   Within their unique family and community ecology, young people develop individual characteristics—likes and dislikes, talents and disabilities, strengths and weaknesses. These individual characteristics emerge from the societal environment and from the roots of family and school conditions. Most young people develop adequate knowledge, positive behaviors, pro-social attitudes, and other healthy characteristics with lower risk of future problems. Others are less fortunate.

At-risk children and adolescents do not acquire the knowledge, behaviors, attitudes, and skills they need to become successful adults. They frequently exhibit interlocking dysfunctional patterns of behaviors, cognitions, and emotions early in life and especially in their early school years (Schultz, Izard, Ackerman, & Youngstrom, 2001; Bellanti & Bierman, 2000). If this pattern is not reversed, it may develop into a self-fulfilling prophecy, a downward spiral of multiple problems that could include school failure, drug use, teen pregnancy, delinquency, and suicide (Jessor, 1991, 1993).

Individual characteristics exhibited by children and adolescents form the trunk of the at-risk tree, which links the soil of environment and the roots of family and school to the branches of behaviors. These characteristics can nourish positive and healthful development or risky behavior. When studies of at-risk youth are reviewed, a "multiple-problem syndrome" appears. School dropout, drug abuse, delinquency, teen pregnancy, and youth suicide are all associated with similar sets of psychosocial variables and skill deficits (Beauvais et al., 1996; Younge, Oetting, & Deffenbacher, 1996).

Teachers, counselors, and psychologists realize that many young people are lacking in fundamental skills. The term *skills* refers here not merely to mechanically performed actions but rather to proficiency in the behaviors, feelings, and thought patterns that are appropriate in recurrent circumstances or situations. All youth, including those defined as at risk, are capable of learning more adaptive strategies for addressing their life challenges, and the incorporation of skills acquisition into educational and counseling interventions is critical (Algozzine & Kaye, 2002; World Health Organization, 1999).

Some young people manage to survive extremely difficult life circumstances. Somehow they rise above poverty, chaotic families, poor school conditions—in short, those environmental conditions that we described in the first four chapters. These young people are considered to be at risk because their circumstances clearly suggest future problems. The greater the number of these risk factors, the greater their level of risk (Capaldi & Patterson, 1991; Deater-Deckard, Dodge, Bates, & Pettit, 1998). But resilient youth avoid falling into drug use, delinquency, and other at-risk behaviors. By examining their lives and circumstances, we may learn something that will inform our efforts with young people who are not so fortunate.

RESILIENCY AND INVULNERABILITY

Despite extremely debilitating environmental, familial, and personal experiences, many young people develop normally. They exhibit competence, autonomy, and effective strategies to cope with the world around them (Haggerty, Sherrod, Garmezy, & Rutter, 1994; Werner & Smith, 1992). These children and youth have been called *invulnerable, stress-resistant, superkids,* and *invincible.* These terms have been subject to criticism because they imply that the well-being of these young people is due to internal or constitutional factors only, that they are successful across all domains, and that they are consistently successful across time (McGloin & Widom, 2001). The terms *resilience* and *resiliency* will be used in this text and refer to those who demonstrate "a good outcome in spite of high risk, sustained competence under stress, and recovery from trauma" (p. 1022, McGloin & Widom, 2001). Resilience and resiliency are not static traits but are influenced by both internal and environmental factors.

Garbarino (1994) contends that every child has a "tipping point" between doing well (having hope, positive attitudes about self, functional behaviors) and doing poorly (feeling despair, having low self-esteem, dysfunctional behaviors). Thus, no child is immune to every possible amount of exposure to negative social, familial, and educational environments, and the idea of a tipping point may be even more useful than the concept of resilience. Another criticism of the term is that the justice system has used *resilience* to help punish offenders—contending that a violent and abrasive upbringing provides no explanation for violent behavior because some youth who grow up in the same environment do not engage in violence. We acknowledge these criticisms. However, we find the concept of resilience to be useful to distinguish between young people who do well and those who do not.

FACTORS THAT CONTRIBUTE TO RESILIENCE

The development of resiliency is a function of three related but distinct areas that provide protection to the child. First, the social environment can provide children with opportunities for development and support despite adverse conditions. External support systems can enhance the young person's competencies and provide a sense of meaning or a belief system by which to live. Second, the family milieu has both direct and indirect influences on a youth's resiliency. Ties within the family provide emotional support at times of stress. Third, individual characteristics and attributes (e.g., cognitive skills, styles of communication, interpersonal skills) have positive influences on at-risk children and are related to resiliency. Also important are dispositional attributes of an individual, such as activity level, sociability, and intelligence (Werner, 1995).

Social Environment

Resilient children derive support from the social environment—their school, their community, and their kinship network. The school environment is potentially a mediating milieu for children who experience numerous risk factors (Korinek, Walther-Thomas, McLaughlin, & Williams, 1999). When social support is low in one setting, other settings can compensate for that lack or provide assistance in rebuilding the support in the weakened area (Coleman, 1991). Caring relationships increase resiliency. Supportive and encouraging teachers are particularly important. Counselors and psychologists can make a crucial difference as well. Resilient children often succeed in academic areas and may also achieve in art, music, drama, or sports (Werner, 1995). Positive contact with peers and adults in these extracurricular areas provide support.

The social support networks of the larger community also help to ameliorate the effects of stress on children. Resilient youth frequently use community networks—ministers, older friends, youth recreation workers, and others. Resilient children often have at least one adult mentor outside the family throughout their development. These adults provide emotional support, encouragement, and advice. Resilient children also have one or more close friends and confidants among their peers. These networks provide at-risk children and adolescents with resources that enable them to develop the skills necessary for survival and success.

Children of color are often subjected to the stress of overt and covert racism and marginalization by the majority culture. Even though minority status is correlated with high risk, the way children learn to survive that stress makes a difference in their ability to maintain self-esteem and a positive identity (Stevenson, 1994). Many young people of color develop specific survival skills that work in their setting. These skills provide them with mechanisms for coping with an unsupportive, negative, or destructive environment (Arnold, 1995; Randolph, 1995). Unfortunately, some of these survival skills are functional and effective only within the subculture of the neighborhood; using the same skills in other contexts is often dysfunctional.

Carlos Diaz, whom we met in Chapter 4, is a potentially resilient youngster. His relationship with his mother has given him a secure foundation. His family responsibilities, although they interfere with schoolwork, have allowed him to develop important life skills such as cooking and caring for a younger child that improve his self-concept and self-esteem. Even though these responsibilities are stressful, knowing that he is contributing to his family gives him an important role in the family's well-being. His academic difficulties are associated with not having time and resources (e.g., a computer), but the work he completes reflects that he is learning and academically competent. Also important is the special interest his social studies teacher has shown in him. Ms. Bassett's interest and support, coupled with reasonable expectations, provides a solid relationship with a caring adult. Further, her willingness to modify her classroom and teaching style encourages responsibility for learning and contributes to his resiliency.

Family Milieu

As we have seen, family environment is probably one of the most important influences on the psychosocial development of young people. The characteristics of a positive family environment include a lack of physical crowding, consistently enforced rules with strict but fair supervision, and well-balanced discipline (Rak & Patterson, 1996). The child who has a good relationship with even one caregiver demonstrates greater resiliency (Bushweller, 1995; Contreras & Kerns, 2000; Werner, 1995). Adult support and involvement are useful for autonomy and self-direction that contribute to resiliency.

Healthy communication patterns often prevail in the homes of resilient youth (McCubbin & McCubbin, 1988). The parents model such skills as attending, focusing, and sustaining tasks. Focused, flexible, well-structured, and task-appropriate communication leads to academic and social competence (Wolin & Wolin, 1993). Parenting characterized by warmth, affective expression, anticipatory guidance, active teaching of social skills, and involvement reduces risk (Myers & Taylor, 1998; Pettit, Bates, & Dodge, 1997) and increases children's social competence (Mize & Pettit, 1997). Children in families that engage in "enabling" interactions—those that encourage and support the expression of independent thought and allow for give-and-take communication—are more likely to exhibit psychosocial competence (Baumrind, 1995). Parental monitoring and control is associated with better childhood outcomes in urban neighborhoods characterized by violence and poverty (Luthar, 1999; Tolan & Gorman-Smith, 1997). Good-quality parenting, parent support, and the quality of the mother-child relationship fosters resilience (Dubow, Edwards, & Ippolito, 1997; Klein, Forehand, & Family Health Project Research Group, 2000).

The family also contributes to resiliency indirectly, through its influence on the children's support networks. Some parents, for example, selectively expose their children to religious and church-related organizations or to such community organizations as the Girl Scouts and Boy Scouts or 4-H clubs. Adults in these organizations provide a useful support network that builds resiliency.

Christie Carter, whom we met in Chapter 3, may be resilient. She emerges in the family as a prim, priggish, and slightly unpleasant little girl. Her role as the family's angel relegates Jason to the role of devil, but perhaps her adoption of this role is what will save her. She does receive a great deal of attention, support, and reinforcement from both her father and her mother. The security that this support provides may be enough to inoculate her against the family dysfunction and prevent her from developing risky characteristics.

Individual Characteristics

Resilient children appear to have certain individual characteristics or skills: better verbal communication and social skills, an internal locus of control, impulse control and reflectiveness, and positive self-regard (Beardslee & Schwoeri, 1994; Berry, Shillington, Peak, & Hohman, 2000; Canino & Spurlock, 1994). Resilient children also demonstrate a well-developed sense of humor, an ability to delay gratification, and a focus on future orientation. Presumably these skills reinforce further resiliency; they elicit positive reactions from family members and from strangers (Sayger, 1996; Werner, 1995).

Daniella Baker, whom we met in Chapter 2, has a special relationship with her mother. She has developed good communication skills and has the ability to make her needs known. Her sweet, calm temperament elicits positive reactions from her mother and from others. At the same time, she has assumed the care of her younger brother. Although this responsibility sometimes frustrates her, it enhances her self-esteem. These personality factors contribute to her resiliency and may mitigate the effects of her environment.

COMMON CHARACTERISTICS OF RESILIENT YOUTH

Research (Haggerty, Sherrod, Garmezy, & Rutter, 1994; Rak & Patterson, 1996; Werner, 1995) points to several characteristics that resilient children exhibit:

- an active approach to life's problems, including a proactive problem-solving perspective, that enables the child to negotiate emotionally hazardous experiences;
- an optimistic tendency to perceive pain, frustration, and other distressing experiences constructively;
- the ability to gain positive attention from others, both in the family and elsewhere;
- a strong faith that maintains a vision of a positive and meaningful life;
- an ability to be alert and autonomous with a tendency to seek novel experience;
- competence in social, school, and cognitive areas.

These characteristics act as protective shields that allow the young person to avoid, regulate, or cope with aversive environmental or developmental conditions, modifying the impact of stressors and leading to less damaging results.

Resilient children and youth cope constructively with challenges by balancing short- and long-term needs of both themselves and others. This allows them to reap mostly favorable outcomes that bolster their self-definition and increase their future propensity for positive coping. These attitudes endear them to untroubled peers while alienating them from deviant peers.

Carlos Diaz, Christie Carter, and Daniella Baker are potentially resilient young people. All of them have personal characteristics that reflect influences from their social environment and their family milieu that may inoculate them against the stress of their current situations and help them to avoid future difficulty. Interestingly, these characteristics of resiliency correspond to specific skills that distinguish low-risk from high-risk children.

SKILLS THAT CHARACTERIZE HIGH-RISK VERSUS LOW-RISK YOUTH

As a result of our work in teaching and counseling at-risk children and adolescents, our discussions with other professionals, and an extensive review of research on at-risk children and youth, we have identified five characteristics that differentiate low-risk and high-risk youth (J. J. McWhirter, B. T. McWhirter, A. M. McWhirter, & E. H. McWhirter, 1994). We call these characteristics the "five Cs of competency":

- Critical school competencies
- Concept of self and self-esteem
- Connectedness

- Coping ability
- Control

These characteristics discriminate between young people who move through life with a high potential for success and those who are not doing well. Low-risk individuals exhibit proficiency, strength, or potential in the five Cs; high-risk individuals are deficient in one or more of these skills. The lack of these skills is closely related to the chronic dependency, aggressive behavior, or inability to cope with life that propels youngsters into the at-risk categories—school dropout, substance abuse, teen pregnancy, youth delinquency, and suicide.

Of course, these skills overlap. Critical school competencies, for example, may lead to connectedness and relate to skill in coping and control. Self-concept interacts in very important and powerful ways with the other characteristics. All the same, we can grasp their importance more firmly if we consider each in turn.

Critical School Competencies

Critical school competencies comprise those skills that are essential to success in school: basic academic skills, academic survival skills, and self-efficacy expectations (Arbona, 2000).

Basic academic skills. In a high-tech industrial society, young people must learn the basic skills of reading, writing, and arithmetic to survive. If they are to thrive, they also need a fund of information about themselves and the world around them. The lack of such skills reduces the prospects for a useful, productive life.

One of the most obvious characteristics of at-risk students is academic underachievement (Daly, Duhon, & Witt, 2002). Underachievement often results from a lack of basic numeracy and literacy skills. These academic deficits are an overwhelming cause of early school leaving and are often a contributing factor in many other problems. Mastery of academic skills encourages persistence in school. A lack of basic reading, writing, and arithmetic skills is often attributable to developmental delays, specific learning disabilities, a limited grasp of English, or emotional disturbance. These problems are compounded by contextual factors such as an inadequate educational structure, an uncaring and unresponsive school culture, limited instructional programs, or poor teaching. Elementary and secondary school students at risk for academic underachievement may be withdrawn and apathetic or, conversely, disruptive and overly aggressive (Coie, et al., 1993; Freeman, 1995). Early detection and intervention is critical to the prevention of ongoing academic difficulty (Daly, Duhon, & Witt, 2002).

Academic survival skills. In addition to numeracy and literacy skills, a core of social-behavioral skills is necessary for student success (Kamps & Kay, 2001). The lack of these essential competencies or "survival skills" predisposes students to failure because skills such as attending to tasks, following directions, and raising hands facilitate the acquisition of knowledge. Some research indicates that these skills are actually more important than academic achievement. Fad (1990), for example, provides evidence that some social-behavioral variables are more important for students' success than academic achievement and demographic characteristics. Work habits, coping skills, and peer relationships are three important areas. She identifies ten behaviors in each that are highly correlated with overall functioning. Strategies for mastering these behaviors may maximize students' chances for success.

Self-efficacy expectations. Finally, self-efficacy expectations are important for academic success (Arbona, 2000; Bandura, 1986). Self-efficacy expectations are beliefs about one's ability to successfully perform a specific task or behavior. These expectations are not necessarily accurate; individuals sometimes have low self-efficacy for tasks they are quite capable of doing, or high self-efficacy for tasks they do not do well. Self-efficacy expectations influence decisions about whether to attempt particular behaviors and how long to persist in those behaviors. If I believe that I am good at math, I am more willing to try a difficult new math problem; further, if my initial efforts yield poor results, I might continue working until I solve it. In contrast, if I perceive myself to be poor in math, I am unlikely to try the new problem, and if I do, I will probably read initial difficulty as evidence of my lack of skills and quit early. Academic self-efficacy expectations are an important influence on children's school performance (Arbona, 2000). When children believe they are capable of doing something, they are far more likely to successfully do it.

Ramona Diaz is at risk. She has not learned the basic academic skills she needs to function in society. Her lack of proficiency in English and her unconnectedness with successful peers probably reduced her academic self-efficacy expectations, and her decision to drop out of high school limits her potential for acquiring academic skills and developing more positive academic self-efficacy.

Concept of Self and Self-Esteem

Self-esteem refers to the extent to which we value ourselves and believe we are important and have something to contribute. Self-concept refers to our overall beliefs about who we are (values, traits, skills, characteristics). Both are global concepts; self-efficacy is specific to tasks (e.g., self-efficacy may be very high for driving, very low for speaking Spanish, and moderate for playing chess). Consider a teenage girl who has low self-efficacy for playing on an athletic team at school, based on her performance in gym class and earlier attempts to participate in school and neighborhood sports. Her self-concept may include the belief that she is not "the athletic type." If she and her family highly value sports participation and her closest friends are all varsity athletes, then her self-concept might be "lousy athlete" and her self-esteem may be lower. If her friends and family are not interested in sports and she herself does not enjoy them either, her self-esteem is unlikely to be negatively affected by her lack of confidence and success in athletics. A young man who is not succeeding in school, lacks a sense of belonging, and does not feel good about himself might begin to experiment with disruptive or deviant behaviors. If these result in attention and admiration from deviant peers, he may shift his self-concept from "failing student" to "daring student," develop increased self-efficacy for disrupting class, begin to devalue school performance even more, and may actually experience greater self-esteem. As children mature, their self-evaluations become more differentiated and less global. A strong relationship exists between young peoples' self-evaluations and their performance (Arbona, 2000; Harter, 1990; Kliewer & Sandler, 1992).

The environment around young people influences the value they place on something (academic success, popularity, etc.) and to whom they compare themselves. The below average student from a family of scholars is likely to have lower self-esteem than the below average student from a family in which no one has graduated from high school.

The path to deviance involves a negative learning process that results in a conditioned way of viewing oneself and one's relation to social institutions, such as the school. This negative learning process leads to a spiral of negative attitudes (Jessor, 1991, 1993). A self-perpetuating cycle or self-fulfilling prophecy is started when young people encounter situations that reinforce their more insecure, negative perceptions. They perceive things negatively and lower their own expectations. Building on these attributions, they exhibit learning, discipline, and acting-out problems, or, alternatively, passivity and withdrawal. When adults and peers react in an overly critical, judgmental, or punitive way, or exhibit limited caring and interest, the child is convinced that his or her subjective perceptions are valid. For example, the young person may determine that her test failure was due to "stupidity" instead of attributing it to factors such as not having studied, not attending class, or a learning disability. This confirmation of negative attitudes increases the cyclical nature of the self-confirming process and leads to increased alienation.

Thus, one of the common denominators among high-risk youth consists of biased attributions (e.g., beliefs that they cannot learn, that they are not acceptable) that result in alienation. These young people interpret new experiences in light of these beliefs. These learned expectations are reinforced by earlier experiences. The biases result from their interpretation of the meaning of an event rather than from the event itself.

These attributional biases operate powerfully to influence the individual's perceptions. Perceiving the world in a distorted way leads to miscommunication in interpersonal relationships. Young people who are aggressive and socially rejected, for example, negatively interpret their peers' intentions in ambiguous situations. They assume aggression in their peers when none is intended. Researchers have suggested that this attributional bias in children leads to risky behaviors (Coie, Dodge, Terry, & Wright, 1991; Schwartz, Kaslow, Seeley, & Lewinsohn, 2000). Negative attributions, combined with negative life events, combine to increase hopelessness and thereby increase depression (Joiner, 2000).

Obviously, attributional biases are important. Even when a peer's behavior is benign, a child who perceives the behavior as hostile is likely to respond aggressively. For example, nonaggressive boys view themselves as more aggressive than they are; aggressive boys underestimate their own aggressiveness with their peers (Lochman, 1987). Such cognitive distortions exacerbate problems. When aggressive boys perceive a threat, their attributional biases increase (Dodge & Somberg, 1987). Cognitive distortions of this nature lead to aggressive behavior and contribute to antisocial, deviant responses. Unfortunately, young people mistakenly conclude that the meanings they give events are unbiased and are accurate. They believe that a perfectly innocent bump is a personal attack.

Delinquents have lower self-esteem than nondelinquents (Oyserman & Markus, 1990), yet self-esteem does not predict delinquency when other factors are considered. As we have mentioned, some young people may shift their self-concept to incorporate their delinquent behavior and in that way increase their self-esteem. However, we (Herrmann, McWhirter, & Sipsas-Herrmann, 1997) found that young adolescents with lower self-concepts were significantly more involved in street gang activity than peers who possessed higher self-concepts. Beliefs of their own competence were particularly important. Middle school students who were involved with gangs had less confidence in their ability to solve problems, obtain their goals, bring about desired outcomes, and function effectively within the environment.

Seligman (1995) demonstrates that it is not low self-esteem that causes low achievement at school, but the opposite: Low achievement causes low self-esteem. Low self-esteem may reflect a realistic appraisal of negative life experiences. Undoubtedly, however, low self-esteem will continue to exacerbate the young person's problems. Attitudinal and self-concept deficiencies, especially when they are pessimistic, are critical determinants of school dropout. One study of African American high school students found that self-esteem, as well as perceptions of the benefits of staying in school and perceived ability to overcome barriers to school completion, were significant predictors of intentions to stay in school (Davis, Johnson, Miller-Cribbs, & Saunders, 2002). Interventions should aim directly at these variables.

Allie Andrews, whom we first met in Chapter 1, feels badly about herself and her behavior in part because of her negative relationship with her father. Her low self-esteem causes her to shift her concept of herself to include more and more deviant, antisocial behavior. She develops more biased, distorted attributions in regard to herself, to adults, and to nondeviant classmates. As she rejects her parents' (and other adults') beliefs and values, she becomes more closely aligned with and influenced by a negative peer cluster. As the value she places on parental approval decreases and the value of deviant peer approval increases, her self-esteem may actually increase. Unfortunately, her deviant behavior leads her down a path to potential disaster.

Connectedness

In the first two editions of this book, we identified "communication with others" as one of the five Cs of competency. Recent research (Lee, Draper, & Lee, 2001; Lee & Robbins, 1995, 1998, 2000; see Townsend & B. T. McWhirter, 2003 for a review) has convinced us that communication is actually subsumed under the broader and more encompassing construct of connectedness. Communication with others, of course, continues to be a very important construct and is, in fact, one of the main conduits that children and adolescents use to foster connectedness.

Connectedness is a ubiquitous and enduring experience of the self in relation to the world that includes a sense of close belonging in relationships with others (Lee & Robbins, 2000). In addition to communication, connectedness includes the idea of "mattering" (i.e., one knows that one matters to others), family, school, and community belongingness, peer clusters (see Chapter 14), and youth/adult linkage. Children and adolescents who lack connectedness experience social isolation or rejection and tend to suffer psychological distress and greater mental health problems as adults (Kupersmidt, Coie, & Dodge, 1990; Resnick, et al., 1998).

Communication with others.   Connectedness requires adequate social and interpersonal skills and they play an important role in psychological adjustment and psychosocial development (Kamps & Kays, 2001). Basic interpersonal skills are necessary for competent, responsive, and mutually beneficial relationships and are perhaps the most important skills that an individual must learn. Unfortunately, many at-risk individuals do not sufficiently master these skills.

The level of a young person's interpersonal skills has been related to several areas of adjustment in later life. A high incidence of mental health problems, juvenile delinquency, dropping out of school, and other at-risk behaviors has been related to social deficiencies in children and adolescents. Good social functioning in childhood and adolescence, in contrast, has been related to superior academic achievement and adequate interpersonal adjustment later in life (Dodge & Price, 1994). Further, an individual's ability to achieve and maintain positive interpersonal relationships is a prerequisite to success in work and in love.

Positive social interaction enhances social integration. Friendship is important not only for social reasons but also because of the interactive process involved in acceptable classroom and peer relationships (Richardson, Hammock, Smith, Gardner, & Signo, 1994). Children and adolescents who have positive peer relationships engage in more social interaction, and they provide positive social rewards for each other. They also use their abilities to achieve academically and to behave appropriately in the classroom. Positive relationships with peers and teachers are associated with better adaptation to school (Ladd, Kochenderfer, & Coleman, 1996; Birch & Ladd, 1997; Ladd & Burgess, 2001).

Perspective taking. Perspective taking has been broadly defined as the ability to understand the perceptual view, cognitive reasoning, emotional feelings, and actions of others. Individuals must be able to distinguish the perceptions and reasoning of other people from their own. A young person's perspective-taking ability is related to his or her cognitive development, and has implications for moral reasoning and empathy as well (Eisenberg, Fabes, Nyman, Bernzweig, & Piñuelas, 1994). Children with greater emotional knowledge are more empathic and popular with peers and less likely to withdraw and experience peer social problems (Schultz, Izard, Ackerman, & Youngstrom, 2001).

At-risk children not only have distorted perceptions but also lack the core abilities that make for satisfying social relationships. For example, Bellanti and Bierman (2000) found that kindergarten children with low cognitive ability and inattention had prosocial skills deficits in first grade with aggressive behavior and peer rejection. These children were at higher risk for poor peer relationships in elementary school. Kamps and Kay (2001) overview curricula and core skills areas for elementary students: (a) classroom survival skills (e.g., asking for help, ignoring distractions, bringing materials to class), (b) friendship-making skills (e.g., beginning a conversation, joining in, apologizing), (c) skills for dealing with feelings (e.g., knowing and expressing one's own feelings, showing understanding of another's feelings, dealing with anger), (d) skill alternatives to aggression (e.g., asking permission, responding to teasing, problem solving), and (e) skills for dealing with stress (e.g., deciding what caused a problem, being a good sport, reacting to failure, dealing with group pressure). In Chapters 13 and 14 we overview Kamps and Kay's (2001) recommendations for teaching social skills.

Solving relationship problems. The ability to solve interpersonal problems is an important skill. Shure (1999) describes problem solving as the integration of two skills: thinking of alternative solutions and understanding the consequences of behavior. Interpersonal problem-solving ability is related to interpersonal functioning in adults, adolescents, middle childhood, and children as young as 4 years old. Children usually develop this skill in the early grades (Shure, 1992a, 1992b, 1992c, 1999; Youngstrom, Wolpaw, Kogos, Schoff, Ackerman, & Izard, 2000). Even though Shure (1992a, 1992b, 1992c) has emphasized that the number of alternative solutions generated is most important, the work of

Youngstrom and colleagues (2000) demonstrated that the quality of children's interpersonal problem-solving solutions was at least equally as important as the quantity of solutions. That is, the ability to generate two prosocial solutions would be better than the ability to generate eight aggressive or withdrawing solutions.

Jason Carter, whom we introduced in Chapter 3, is not connected; he has not developed adequate communication skills. He is at risk precisely because he cannot communicate his wants and needs without resorting to explosive, impulsive, and ultimately self-defeating behavior. His poor peer relationships, his lack of respect for adults, and his aggressive outbursts suggest serious deficiencies in communication skills. He has not learned those fundamental social skills that might help him deal more effectively with his dysfunctional parents, his competitive sister, his rejecting classmates, and his upset teacher.

Coping Ability

The ability to cope effectively with anxiety and stress is another skill that differentiates low-risk from high-risk young people. All individuals confront situations that cause conflict and stress. All young people sometimes feel disappointment, rejection, fear, and anger in their interactions with others. How they cope with these emotions determines their adjustment.

Coping skills influence an individual's response to stress, which in turn affects the way that person deals with conflicts with other people. Some young people cope with humor and altruism, others by focusing their attention elsewhere. These methods result in a more relaxed and positive view of the situation. When young people are in a positive, relaxed state of mind, they are able to process information more objectively, exercise better judgment, and use common sense. They also demonstrate more effectiveness and competence in solving personal problems.

Some young people, unfortunately, are exposed to more stress and have greater difficulty coping with it, placing them at greater risk. They use evasive strategies such as compulsive acting out, withdrawal, and denial. Or they succumb to one of the twins of mental health problems: anxiety or depression. Anxiety interferes with the learning process, social judgment, and interpersonal relationships, and often leads to aggressive and destructive reactions. Depression can lead to suicide, suicide ideation, and other self-defeating behaviors (B. T. McWhirter, J. J. McWhirter, Hart, & Gat, 2000). Both anxiety and depression in children and adolescents are associated with cognitive distortions, negative self-talk, and anticipation of more negative future outcomes (Epkins, 2000; Lodge, Harte, & Tripp, 1998). Anxiety and depression in children place them at risk for learning problems, academic underachievement, conduct problems, and poor social problem solving (Kovacs & Devlin, 1998). Fortunately, there are a number of programs that have demonstrated effectiveness in enhancing children's skills for coping with stress, anxiety, and depression. For example, the FRIENDS program trains clinically anxious children and their parents to manage stress and anxiety while simultaneously fostering increased peer social support for children (Shortt, Barrett, & Fox, 2001).

Paul Andrews, Allie's brother, exhibits problems with stress. His bravado, aggressiveness, and destructiveness appear to mask considerable anxiety. His inability to modify his aggressive outbursts and his destructive hostility are a problem to him both at home and at school. His lack of skills in coping with the stress he feels foreshadows serious problems as he moves into adolescence.

Control

Lack of control—over decisions, over the future, over life—is a common characteristic of high-risk young people. Their inability to generate and follow through on competent decisions relates to failure to consider consequences, unwillingness to delay gratification, and an external locus of control. These problems influence the setting and achievement of goals. Many young people have an even more fundamental problem: Their sense of a purpose in life is limited, distorted, or lacking. Low-risk young people, by contrast, exert control in developmentally appropriate ways over their environment and their behavior.

Decision-making skills.   Decision making is a goal-directed sequence of affective and cognitive operations that leads to behavioral responses. Deficits in decision-making skills are clearly linked to at-risk behavior.

Low-risk children and adolescents have access to relevant information on which to base decisions. They accurately perceive, comprehend, and store this information. They personalize the information by relating it to their own beliefs, values, and attitudes. They evaluate their solutions by considering the consequences. They demonstrate behavioral skills in their efforts to implement these decisions in social situations. They have feelings of mastery and a belief in their personal competency (Harris, 1995). Young people who have high-perceived control and view their goals as important exhibit more mastery-oriented behavior, and have higher levels of achievement and satisfaction (Bandura, Pastorelli, Barbaranelli, & Caprara, 1999).

High-risk youth are deficient in the ability to make competent decisions (Cicchetti, Rogosch, Lynch, & Holt, 1993). Information on or knowledge of viable solutions is only part of the problem. Another problem lies in the ability to set constructive and attainable goals. Difficulty in this respect is significantly related to alcohol and drug use, delinquency, and low academic achievement. Further, high-risk youth are less likely to consider consequences fully (Bell & Bell, 1993) and they manifest an external rather than an internal locus of control. That is, they feel that forces outside of themselves control the events in their lives and even their own behavior and that they have no power to shape their own lives. Adolescents transitioning to middle school who did not believe they had control over their success in school, and were not invested in success, experienced significantly more school stress and depression (Rudolph, Lambert, Clark, & Kurlakowsky, 2001). Finally, many problems with decision making are related to an inability or an unwillingness to delay gratification.

Delay of gratification.   Individuals vary in their capacity to delay gratification even as early as preschool. In later years, lack of self-control expresses itself in an inability to delay gratification. Low-risk individuals voluntarily postpone immediate gratification, maintain self-control, and persist in behavior directed toward a larger goal to be reached when the appropriate foundation has been laid. At-risk young people value immediate gratification and behave in ways calculated to attain it. This behavior often becomes self-defeating. Inability to delay gratification is related to depression, low social responsibility, conduct disorders, antisocial behavior, and a variety of addictive disorders (Weisz, Sweeney, Proffitt, & Carr, 1993).

Tyrone Baker, whom we introduced in Chapter 2, is a young man who is unable to delay gratification. He is impulsive and lacks self-control. Because of the chaos in his home life, the lack of connectedness with his mother and siblings, and the absence of an adequate male role model, he simply has not developed skill in delaying gratification for the sake of a more important and more distant goal. His insistence on immediate gratification influences his decision-making ability and contributes to his high-risk potential.

Purpose in life.   A purpose gives life meaning. It is the positive end of a continuum whose negative end is meaninglessness or loneliness (B. T. McWhirter, 1990). Levels of future optimism and self-acceptance can discriminate between nonsuicidal adolescents and those who have attempted suicide (Gutierrez, Osman, Kopper, & Barrios, 2000). Lack of a purpose in life, with its accompanying sense of boredom, futility, and pessimism, is an essential mediating factor in the relationship between self-derogation, depression, and thoughts of suicide (Harlow, Newcomb, & Bentler, 1986; Seligman, 1995). Further, lack of purpose in life is related to the subsequent use of alcohol and other drugs. When life has no purpose, why worry about school or friends or goals or even life itself? Why say *no*?

Low-risk youth have a purpose in life that is potentially attainable and that propels them forward. Their purpose in life orients them toward the future and often suggests short-term, realistic goals. Researchers have consistently found that goals are important predictors of student achievement (Arbona, 2000; Drazen, 1994). Students who had realistic and hopeful visions for themselves as successful in the future achieved; those with weaker visions did not. This echoes the view of Clausen (1993) who identified "planful competence" as a strong influence on adjustment and overall success in adulthood.

Few high-risk youth give evidence of having a viable life purpose (see Box 5.1). If young people do not perceive themselves as having a viable future, "just say no" has no meaning. They need to discover what to say *yes* to. When young people feel that they have a limited future, they have little to lose by expecting little of themselves or by engaging in at-risk behaviors, including unsafe sexual behavior, delinquency, substance abuse, and suicide.

THINGS TO DO TO INCREASE THE FIVE CS

We have included specific behavioral strategies throughout the book that describe concrete and specific intervention skills to use with clients and students. Although these skills and activities are embedded in specific chapters, they usually have broader application beyond the particular problem area discussed. Most increase resiliency and they also are related directly to one or more of the five Cs just discussed. On the inside page of the back cover is a "Things to Do" chart that indicates the location of various activities and approaches that helpers can use with at-risk children, adolescents, and their families. We have suggested the most appropriate age groups for the use of these skills and activities and indicated which of the five competency areas we believe to be most affected by the intervention. We hope the "Things to Do" chart will help you locate intervention and prevention activities that work.

▲ Box 5.1

One Week at a Time

Young men and women who have just left high school or are close to graduation frequently struggle with the reality of poverty. Manolo, who lives in Huascar, Peru, is one such young man. His face is alive with enthusiasm and excitement. His wide grin often gets him out of trouble, and it also covers up some of his problems.

When we spoke during his last year of high school, he said to me, "You know, Peru is a great country, but I don't think about the future too much; not more than a few days ahead, anyway."

"Why is that?"

"Because I have no idea what will happen to me after next week. There are no jobs, a university costs too much, and when I'm at home, dry bread is sometimes the only thing we have to eat."

Then I asked him: "Are your high school studies going to help you later?"

"No," he replied with resignation. "School is taking up my time now, but what's the use? I'll never study in a university. I'll probably work in a factory somewhere, if there's a job to be found."

Educational opportunities in the Peruvian barrios and in American inner cities are extremely limited. For many young people, a career is out of the question; even a job is unlikely. What happens then to purpose in life and control of environment and self?

Conclusion

This chapter has highlighted an important issue that we emphasize throughout this book: The problems faced by children and youth are mediated not only by their social, family, and school environments, but also by the skills the children possess—skills they can develop to overcome their difficulties. One way we can assist young people is by recognizing how some of them have developed resiliency and by teaching these skills to those who are at risk. Professionals who can recognize the characteristics of high-risk versus low-risk youth are in a position to identify the youngsters who are at greatest risk and to make well-focused interventions. They can reduce the risk to young people by helping them develop the competencies we have presented in this chapter. The five Cs of competency are attended to in greater detail in Part II, where we describe problems in the at-risk categories and treatments for them, and in Part III, where we suggest strategies for preventing them.

AT-RISK CATEGORIES

▲ In Part II we consider six specific categories that reflect some of the principal problem areas for at-risk youth: school dropout, substance use, risky sexual behavior, juvenile delinquency and gangs, school shooters, and youth suicide. Although these topics represent a substantial portion of child and adolescent problem areas, they do not reflect all areas of concern. Nevertheless, we believe these core topics are highly representative of other problems as well. In each chapter we provide (a) a conceptualization of the problem, (b) a discussion of the scope of the problem, (c) characteristics of the problem and strategies to identify and assess it, and (d) consequences of the problem. Additionally, for each category we examine major prevention and intervention strategies that address the specific areas described in each chapter. Of course, the intervention ideas provided in each of these chapters can be generalized to other areas as well.

SCHOOL DROPOUTS

▲ *I'm stupid.*
At least, that's what they say when they tell me my ideas aren't good, or my hair is
too long, or I dress funny.
They tell me in so many ways that I can't.
I can't because I won't.
Why couldn't they just encourage me?

Or help me?
Or understand that can't doesn't always mean won't, but can't.
Why couldn't they tell me that I had something to offer?

Maybe if they had told me that, I would have finished school.

M. J. McWhirter

CHAPTER OUTLINE

▲   In this chapter we concentrate on those young people who leave school before they grad-uate. In the following pages we (a) discuss changing literacy standards that define the term *dropout*, (b) discuss the scope of the dropout problem, (c) outline some of the roots of the problem, (d) highlight the economic and social consequences of dropping out, (e) present information to identify potential dropouts, and (f) describe pragmatic individual interven-tions designed to reduce dropouts.

DEFINITIONAL ISSUES OF THE DROPOUT PROBLEM

Literacy Standards

To understand the apparent decline in academic proficiency of students, we must note the changes that have taken place in educational standards. In 1890 only 6.7% of the nation's 14- to 17-year-olds attended high school. By the late 1990s, more than 95% attended high school. In 1890, 3.5% of America's 17-year-olds graduated from high school. By 1970, 75.6% did so, and by the late 1990s, 89% were graduated. In addition, the criterion for functional literacy has risen steadily from three years of schooling in the 1930's, to six years in the 1950's, to the completion of high school in the 1970s. These climbing standards have placed increasing demands on students (Berliner & Biddle, 1995).

Additionally, many more children with widely diverse backgrounds are being educated than ever before in our history. High schools of one hundred years ago were mainly open to the most privileged children and only a handful of them were expected to graduate. Schools today are called upon to serve vastly larger numbers of children and children from very different social, cultural, and language backgrounds. They are also expected to deliver many more services and reach children with a much greater ability range. Today's high school dropouts are a major concern for educators and for society and there are strenuous efforts to reduce the high school dropout rate to zero. But, in general, the American educational system has been enormously successful (Berliner & Biddle, 1995).

Definition of Dropout

A *dropout* is a pupil who leaves school before graduation and before his or her program of study is complete. A student who dies is not considered a dropout and is not reflected in dropout statistics. Unfortunately, some districts count anyone who leaves school as a dropout, including those who enter college early, for example. The U.S. Department of Education has two classifications of dropout: event dropout and status dropout. Event dropouts are students who withdraw from school within a given time frame—during a given school year, for example. Status dropouts are students of a certain age group who are out of school without a high school credential. These definitions provide a consistent criterion for counting dropouts. However, educators, state governments, policymakers, and school district personnel sometimes use additional and inconsistent criteria, leaving us with statistics that are less than precise.

Quality of dropout data vary as a function of adequacy of school staffing, consistency of definitions of illnesses, leaves, and transfers, family transience, and specific state criteria for calculating dropout. For example, some states count students with equivalent high school degrees (GED) as graduates, while others do not. Finally, schools have a vested interest in keeping dropout rates low because their funds are often tied to student counts.

Even statistics based on common criterion rarely include students who dropped out before entering high school. For example, figures cited for Latino high school sophomores who drop out by their senior year may actually understate the dropout rate among Latinos. In one large secondary school district in Arizona, eighth-grade students who do not register for high school are never counted in the high school census, and therefore they are not counted in the dropout rate. Latino students fit this profile in greater numbers than do African American or European American students (Kaufman, Alt, & Chapman, 2001).

SCOPE AND CHARACTERISTICS OF THE PROBLEM

Despite ongoing inconsistency in tallying dropouts, educators and researchers have made headway in their attempts to profile the student who drops out of school. Indeed, teachers know from their own experience that students who drop out are likely to be those who are unmotivated by their classwork; who have had problems with either the school authorities, the police, or both; who skip classes or are often absent; who are pregnant or married; who are poor and must work; who have family problems; who have drug or alcohol problems; who are students of color; or who have fallen two or more years behind grade level (McMillen, Kaufman, & Whitener, 1995). The latter group includes many students who are learning English as a second language (ESL, also called second language learners or SLL). In fact, students from non-English-speaking homes drop out in much higher numbers than do students from homes where English is the only language spoken (Fashola & Slavin, 1998). Recall that Ramona Diaz (Chapter 4) gets poor grades and dislikes school. She does not think that school is meeting her needs, and she feels as though she does not belong there. Her family's economic situation is difficult, and Ramona feels strongly that she should work to help support her family. She also feels bad about herself and does not believe she has the ability to compete at school. Ramona has little social involvement with the school, partly because of the family's economic situation and partly because of her struggle with the English language. These factors make Ramona a prime candidate for dropping out.

In 2000, 11% of 16- to 24-year-olds were out of school without a high school credential. Although the status dropout rate remained fairly consistent from 1992 to 2000, it declined for young people as a group between the early 1970s and 2000. The rate of this decline, however, varied for European Americans, African Americans, Latino Americans, and American Indians (Kaufman, Alt, & Chapman, 2001). Between the early 1970s and 2000, the status dropout rate for European Americans was lower each year than the rate for African Americans or Latinos. During these years, the percentage of Latino young people who were out of school without a high school diploma was also higher than that of European Americans and African Americans in every year. In addition, status dropout rates for European Americans and African Americans declined by nearly 40%, whereas the rate for Latino young adults remained fairly constant.

Latino students are disproportionately represented among the status dropout rates in 2000 with a 27.8% dropout rate (Kaufman, Alt, & Chapman, 2001). This high dropout rate is partly attributable to the relatively greater dropout rate among Latino immigrants (44.2%) relative to first (21%) and second generation (15.9%) Latino youth.

Immigrant Students

Although all countries have experienced immigration, no country in the world has constantly experienced such a high immigration rate as the United States. Over 10% (or 28.4 million) of the U.S. population is foreign born (U.S. Census Bureau, 2001). The public school systems reflect these demographics, with children of immigrants accounting for nearly one in five of all U.S. school children. Most of the parents of these children arrived in the United States from Latin America and Asia.

Latino Students

The extensive literature on Latino dropouts indicates that there is not a single cause associated with the decision to leave school. For immigrants, the stress, confusion, and anxiety when first entering a U.S. school, combined with language problems, are issues. Others are poverty, pregnancy, poor academic achievement, parent's educational attainment, lack of motivation, low aspirations, disengagement from learning, and single-parent families (Velez & Saenz, 2001). A growing body of literature also points to school-related or institutional factors as playing an important role in the dropout process. For example, Hess (2000) suggested that a self-fulfilling prophecy phenomenon might be occurring in schools, such that teachers hold and unknowingly convey lower expectations of Latino students. One case study by Conchas (2001) examined immigrant and U.S.-born Latino students' perspectives on how the school structure mediates academic success and school engagement. Latino students in this case study expressed how the stereotypes held by teachers and other students about Latinos in general (e.g., "Latinos are lazy, don't try hard enough, etc.") affected their level of school engagement. For some students, such negative stereotypes foster pessimism about the usefulness of school in general.

Exceptional Students

In addition to students of color, immigrant, and English as second language students, dropout statistics include many students with disabilities. The dropout rate in special education is double that of general education despite the school's legal obligation to provide students with disabilities a free, appropriate education until they reach age 21 or receive a high school diploma, as mandated by the Individuals with Disabilities Education Act (IDEA) and the Americans with Disabilities Act (ADA). Students with specific learning disabilities who drop out of school are more socially alienated toward classmates and teachers than are students with learning disabilities who completed school. These young people also have far to go to reach the goals of adult adjustment. In one study, only 56% of learning disabled high school dropouts were employed full-time, and most were working in service work or labor occupations (Sitlington & Frank, 1993). Results are similar for adolescents with attention deficit hyperactivity disorder (ADHD). Gifted students, who often demonstrate high ability and intelligence, high creativity, and a strong drive to initiate and complete a task, drop out of school more often than one would think. In fact, they drop out more often than their non-gifted peers. All of these exceptional students must be kept in mind when we discuss the scope of the dropout problem.

Gay, Lesbian, Bisexual, and Transgendered Students

Another group of students who are particularly at risk of dropping out of school are students who are gay, lesbian, bisexual, and transgendered (GLBT) students. Many of the school problems of these adolescents are related to the physical and verbal abuse they receive from peers. Peer harassment contributes to poor school performance, truancy, and withdrawal from school. School is a dangerous and punishing place for many GLBT students who often experience threats, physical and psychological abuse from peers, and bias from teachers and other school personnel (Rivers & D'Augelli, 2001).

Unfortunately, too many educators do little to support GLBT teenagers in a world that reviles them and in a school environment that permits them to be called "dykes," "faggots," and an assortment of other names (Anderson, 1994). Ironically, although educators will challenge and correct other derogatory terms, the words *dyke* and *faggot* often go unnoticed or at least unchallenged. Making school safe for GLBT youth is the responsibility of all educators. In Chapter 11, we discuss how GLBT youth are susceptible to depression and are at high risk for suicide because of internal turmoil and environmental harassment. They also consistently report significant stress associated with school and related activities, no doubt contributing to their high dropout rate (Ryan, 2001).

THE CONSEQUENCES OF DROPPING OUT

Dropping out of school has a significant impact on the life of the individual, but the costs go far beyond individual consequences. School dropout has serious economic and social repercussions for society as well.

Economic Consequences

Students who drop out of school are at an economic disadvantage and will be throughout their lives: Unemployment and underemployment rates are high among high school dropouts; they earn significantly less over their lifetimes than high school graduates and less still than those graduates who attend some college (Grubb, 1999), and their unemployment rate is considerably higher.

Another aspect of the relationship between school, society, and dropping out is important. A high school diploma no longer ensures gainful employment as it did in the past; our economy needs large numbers of people to work at jobs that are not intellectually challenging. Unfortunately, most of these jobs do not pay well (Berliner & Biddle, 1995). Many adolescents do not see employment opportunities as contingent on a high school diploma, so many working high school students see no need to finish their education. The perception of a lack of employment opportunities—sometimes a realistic perception—accounts for the widespread belief among adolescents that school is irrelevant.

The economic consequences of the dropout problem include loss of earnings and taxes, loss of Social Security, and lack of qualified workers. A high school diploma is the minimum qualification for participation in the U.S. economy. A worker without one can find work in only the most menial occupations. The factory jobs that once allowed workers to make good incomes without a high school degree are diminishing or are being transferred out of the country; the educational requirements for jobs in general are increasing. The high school dropout is not easily absorbed into the workforce due to this ever-increasing demand for highly trained workers. Students who drop out of high school will lack the necessary skills to participate in the high-tech job market and are likely to be destined to marginal employment or outright dependence on society. The cost to society of one youth dropping out of high school followed by a life of drug abuse and crime is 1.7 to 2.3 million dollars (Cohen, 1998).

Not long ago, the Social Security checks of retirees were paid for by as many as 17 employed workers; people who retire in the next 20 years, however, will draw their Social Security from the wages of only three workers (Sklar, 1995), one of whom will be a person of color. As discussed in Chapter 2, projections indicate that the percentages of people of color entering the labor force will continue to increase over the next 15 years. Schools, communities, and legislators must ensure that adolescents of color graduate in increasing numbers both to meet the needs of the national labor market and to provide equal representation of people of color in society's labor force.

Social Consequences

Students who leave school before completing their program of study are at a disadvantage in other ways as well. Dropping out of school often has an impact on an individual's psychological well-being. Most dropouts later regret their decision to leave school (Kortering

& Braziel, 1999). Dissatisfaction with self, with the environment, and with lack of opportunity is also associated with lower occupational aspirations among young people. When high school dropouts are unemployed or earn less money than their graduated peers, their children also experience negative consequences because they live in lower socioeconomic conditions. Proportionately few of these homes provide the study aids that children of graduates can expect to have. Parents who are poor are less likely to provide non-school-related activities for their children than parents of higher socioeconomic status. Further, low wages require parents who are dropouts to work such long hours that it is difficult for them to monitor their children's activities. Because high school dropouts have lower occupational aspirations than their graduated peers, they also have lower educational expectations for their own children. The Andrews, Baker, and Diaz families (of Chapters 1, 2, and 4) are prime examples of this situation. In each of these families, at least one of the parents did not complete high school, and the children must face the consequences.

Dropping out of school truncates educational and vocational development in a manner that dramatically increases the probability of a downward spiral into greater physical, emotional, and economic problems. Less-educated adolescents are more likely to become pregnant outside of marriage and rely on public assistance. Dropping out of school is also highly correlated with such conditions as alcohol and drug abuse, delinquent and criminal activity, and other social problems to which communities of color are sometimes even more vulnerable (Cohen, 1998; Orthner & Randolph, 1999).

The idea that dropouts beget dropouts conveys an unnecessary hopelessness. Not all dropouts have children who want to drop out, and not all students at risk for school failure today are children of dropouts. Nevertheless, a continuing cycle of leaving school early seems likely if schools do not take action. Schools can break the cycle in a variety of ways.

PREDICTIVE INDICATORS AND TYPE OF DROPOUTS

Effective implementation of dropout prevention programs requires identification of students at risk. To facilitate this, we turn to research that teachers, counselors and psychologists, and other human service professionals may find useful in their daily work with students.

Differences Between Stayers and Leavers

Nearly 20 years ago, Ekstrom and her colleagues (1986) focused on a sample of high school sophomores over a two-year period. They found that those who stayed in school (*stayers*) differed significantly from those who left (*dropouts*) across a variety of dimensions: socioeconomic status, race/ethnicity, parent support for education, family structure, school behaviors, and attitudes/abilities toward schoolwork. Students who left school were more likely to be poorer, older, male, and ethnic minorities. They tended to come from homes with fewer study aids and fewer opportunities for non-school-related learning than students who stayed in school. Dropouts were less likely to have both birth parents living in the home, more likely to have employed mothers (who had less education and lower educational expectations for their children), and had less parental monitoring of their activities.

The students who dropped out of school also differed from the stayers in a variety of behaviors. They were less likely to be involved in extracurricular activities and had lower grades and lower test scores than the stayers. Interestingly, the gap between stayers' and dropouts' grades was greater than the gap between their scores on achievement tests. Dropouts did less homework: an average of 2.2 hours a week as opposed to the 3.4 hours reported by the stayers. The dropouts also had more discipline problems in school, were absent and late more often, cut more classes, got suspended from school more often, and had more trouble with the police.

Differences between dropouts and stayers also emerged in the affective domain. Many of the dropouts reported feelings of alienation from school. Most were not involved in clubs, sports, or student government. Not surprisingly, few dropouts reported feelings of satisfaction with their academic work. Dropouts did not feel popular with other students, and their friends were also alienated from school and had low educational expectations. Finally, the dropouts worked more hours than the stayers, and their jobs were more enjoyable and more important to them than school.

Ekstrom and her colleagues (1986) also investigated what had happened to the students who had dropped out of school between their sophomore and senior years. They found that 47% of them were working either full- or part-time (more whites and males reported working for pay than did minorities and females), 29% were looking for work, 16% were homemakers, 10% were enrolled in job-training programs, and 3% were in military service. Of these dropouts, 58% hoped to finish high school eventually, and 17% reported that they had already enrolled in an educational institution. Fourteen percent had already obtained a General Educational Development (GED) high school equivalency certificate. Very little has changed since Ekstrom's (1986) original report.

Predictive Variables and Dropout Types

Although the profile developed by Ekstrom and her colleagues (1986) tells us some of the characteristics of young people who drop out of school before graduation, it does not tell us enough about the complex interaction of variables nor about why younger students leave. Indeed, dropping out of school is a culmination of a developmental process that involves a complex ecology. Dropping out is a process that begins early in development, typically before a child even enters school, and continues through the time a student formally withdraws. In one study, the quality of early care giving, the early home environment, peer competence, and problem behaviors predicted high school status 15 years later (Jimerson, Egeland, Sroufe, & Carlson, 2000). Early experiences may affect a student's sense of agency and self-concept. These may directly influence school performance and later decisions to stay in school. Early experiences also lay foundations for relationships with teachers and differential interactions with peers that further propel the individual along the pathway toward dropping out. Success in school requires numerous capacities for behavioral control and self-regulation that are formed in earlier years.

In a study designed to test five theories of early dropout behavior, Battin-Pearson and her colleagues (2000) identified poor academic achievement as assessed by standardized achievement tests and grade point averages as consistently one of the strongest predictors of dropping out of high school early. Engaging in deviant behavior such as substance abuse or delinquency, having close connections to antisocial peers, and coming from a poor family increased risks for leaving school by age 14, even when the student had not experienced academic failure or difficulty. Clearly, dropout prevention efforts should be focused directly on improving academic achievement at early ages, but prevention programs should also focus on poor families, youth who associate with deviant peers, and those who participate in aggressive behavior and drug use.

Good dropout prevention programs have the ability to closely match their methods and content to the specific strengths, vulnerabilities, and needs of the participants. One helpful typology of dropouts comes from the work of Janosz and his colleagues (2000). Combining three axes of school-related behavior—academic achievement, school commitment, and behavioral maladjustment—Janosz and colleagues identified four basic, reliable, and valid dropout types—disengaged dropouts, low-achiever dropouts, quiet dropouts, and maladjusted dropouts. Each type has unique characteristics to consider in designing interventions.

Disengaged dropouts.   Although they believe that they are less competent than other students, disengaged dropouts obtain surprisingly high achievement scores considering their lack of school involvement. These young people care little about school grades and have few educational aspirations, generally do not like school, do not recognize the importance of education, and accord little value to both school and education in their lives.

Low-achiever dropouts.   Although they have relatively few behavior problems, low-achiever dropouts have a very weak commitment to education, experience poor grades, and learn little. Of all the dropout types, low achievers are distinct in their lack of ability to fulfill minimal course requirements.

Quiet dropouts.   Young people who fit this dropout category have few external problems although they exhibit poor school performance. They hold positive views about school attendance, appear to be involved in school activities, and do not create disciplinary trouble. They do not get very good grades, but also do not misbehave much and do not react openly to school difficulties. They generally go unnoticed until they drop out.

Maladjusted dropouts.   Dropouts in this category have high levels of misbehavior. They demonstrate a weak commitment to education, have poor school performance, invest little in school life, and frequently are in disciplinary trouble. Due to the variety and severity of difficulties, these dropouts have the most negative school profile of the four types.

Knowing these dropout types will assist counselors and educators to identify potential dropouts. Clustering variables that predict dropout types will improve interventions to reduce dropouts because prevention efforts can target specific behaviors and attitudes. Additionally, we must also consider another contributing factor: the student's instructional environment. Lunenburg (2000) argues that the instructional environment can seriously magnify a student's dislike for school, lack of motivation, and low self-concept. For example, at-risk, low-achieving students are treated differently than high-achieving students, and this kind of differential treatment can literally "push" them out of school. Differential treatment toward at-risk students includes that they are: called on less, given less wait time to answer questions, given less praise, and given less eye contact and other nonverbal communication of responsiveness (Janosz, LeBlanc, Boulerice, & Tremblay, 2000). At-risk students sense the teacher's lower regard for their personal worth as learners, come to believe it, and live up to those expectations.

GENERAL PREVENTION AND INTERVENTION STRATEGIES

Family and Community

Diversity. To understand family issues related to the dropout problem, one must acknowledge that schools are by and large designed to meet the needs of children from European American middle-class families. Programs for subsidized meals (breakfasts and lunches) and requirements that teachers take courses in multicultural education are evidence of concern for students with different backgrounds, but a great deal remains to be done. Children are still expected to be clean, alert, well-rested, and neatly dressed for school every morning. Despite the drastic changes that family life has undergone in the past several decades, schools still best serve those children from homes in which mom is always present with cookies and a smile; dad makes plenty of money; and everybody upholds the cultural and social values of the dominant-culture middle class.

Latchkey children. Carlos Diaz spends his afternoons taking care of his sister. He is like countless other children who wear their keys around their necks and stay home after school without supervision (Baker, 1990). The average latchkey child is left alone for approximately 2.5 hours a day (Sadker & Sadker, 1987), and evidence suggests that a direct relationship exists between the number of hours spent in after-school self-care and problem behaviors (Ross, Saavedra, Shur, Winters, & Felner, 1992). Many latchkey children are bored, lonely, and frightened. These experiences can be even more intense when children, unlike Carlos Diaz, do not have a structure to follow or responsibilities to carry out. Although physical well-being is of utmost concern to their parents, nearly one-third of latchkey children are unable to reach either parent by phone. As many as one in four latchkey children may be extremely fearful—fearful enough to arm themselves with baseball bats as they watch television. For the latchkey child, television becomes the baby-sitter, anesthetist, and constant companion.

Given that parents must work and that the number of latchkey children will rise, widespread pre- and after-school programs that extend the number of hours children receive supervision are necessary. Many after-school programs function as "afternoon schools." Such programs may seem too academic after a full day in the classroom, especially for young children. By the time students reach the age of 18, however, they will have watched 15,000 hours of television and attended school for only 11,000 hours (Sadker & Sadker, 1987). Indeed, the benefits of extra schooling and afternoon supervision may outweigh the possible excess of academia. This is particularly the case when after-school activities include games, sports, assistance with homework, counseling groups, tutoring, and opportunities to explore music and art.

Twenty-first century learning centers. The community already owns the school buildings by virtue of having invested one to two *trillion* dollars in these properties (Zigler cited in Dryfoos, 1994). Zigler advocates for opening the doors of schools all day, every day, from 7 A.M. to 6 P.M. In each school, he would establish whole-day childcare for 3- to 5-year-olds, ensuring developmentally appropriate and high-quality services. He would also provide before- and after-school care to 6- to 12-year-olds that would include enjoyable activities, recreation, and enrichment activities. These schools would also offer home visitors to all parents of newborns and organize and coordinate family day care for infants from birth to three years. Early childhood educators trained to bridge the gap between home and school would administer the center. Federal legislation pushed by Vice President Gore during the Clinton administration, and supported by the Bush administration, resulted in federal grants to allow schools to stay open before and after school hours including Saturdays and summers.

If schools are unable to obtain the funds to offer pre- and after-school programs, they can still meet some of the needs of latchkey students. For example, the school counselor or psychologist can conduct workshops for parents or children to help children deal with the fears they encounter during their unsupervised hours. Children can be taught what to do in case of emergency or danger, and how to maximize their safety. Latchkey children can be helped to devise productive ways to fill the time until a parent returns home, such as completing specific chores, doing homework, preparing nutritious snacks, and working on creative projects.

School

Schools can also organize programs that directly address the personal and success issues of dropouts. Efforts to prevent pupils from leaving school should include methods to reduce antisocial behaviors, increase academic achievement, and encourage positive school commitment.

Dropouts rarely mention a lack of desire to learn as a reason for their decision to leave school before graduation. The teenager, a possible quiet or disengaged dropout, who speaks to us in Box 6.1, expresses concerns that are common to many high school dropouts: a lack of relevance between the school's curriculum and the circumstances of students' lives, and a lack of belongingness. This teenager, though, at least has a goal: She is going to help her mother manage a restaurant. Clearly she is interested in learning, but the school she attends is not the place where most of her learning takes place.

Curriculum.   One way to prevent this teenager from leaving school is to take a serious look at her school's curriculum. Because she seems to be so eager to learn science, to read, and to use math skills, it is indeed a shame that she does not see the school curriculum in these areas as relevant to her life. Curricula that highlight the connection between learning and the "real world" should be selected whenever possible, with support for teachers to promote those connections.

Most potential dropouts benefit greatly from a curriculum that encompasses goal-setting techniques. Identifying and writing down long-term goals, developing a plan to implement those goals, and periodically reviewing the actions taken to achieve the goals are useful skills. Tyrone Baker, for example, would benefit from such a curriculum. (We discuss goal-setting techniques in Chapter 13.)

Schools can also organize programs to bring truant students back to the classroom. For example, requiring a daily after school study group could enable truant students to catch up, work at their own pace, and receive credit. These last-resort study sessions could prove to be a key element in a dropout prevention program.

Activities.   Social interaction, especially with antisocial peers, influences the decision to leave school. An opportunity to get involved with a social group and to work with the other members in a positive manner is beneficial to the potential dropout (Davalos, Chavez, &

▲ Box 6.1

Reflections of a Future Dropout

I wish I could leave school. It's so boring that I just daydream all day anyway. Why can't they just let me leave now, instead of waitin' till I'm 16?

When I leave I'm gonna help Mama in her restaurant. It's her own business and she runs it, but she also has to take care of my little sisters. We have it all worked out. I already help her every night when I get home from school. This week she let me work in the kitchen. I figured out a new way to make salad dressing, and it's really good. Mama says it's gonna be a house specialty. The first time we served it, I had to figure out how to make a batch for 100 people without messing it up.

Mama also lets me do the books. She don't have time for everything. If I didn't have to go to school, I could help her a lot more. Three weeks ago, we had a taxman in here checking through the books. He said he was impressed with the figures. We couldn't let him know I did them cuz I'm too young to work. Mama brings 'em home for me, and I do 'em at night. I'm usually right. I wish I could be like that in school. But man, those questions in my homework just get me all confused. I mean, once I was s'pose to figure out when two trains would meet if they was goin' toward each other and leavin' at different times and stuff like that. I mean, who cares? Someone's already got the train schedule all figured out so they don't run into each other, and I ain't never gonna be a train engineer, so why ask me? Usually, though, it don't make much difference cuz I'm so busy addin' up customers' bills that I don't have time to set down and figure out what some smart guy has already done. Mr. Larson is sorta gettin'

Guardiola, 1999). Perhaps if 9-year-old Tyrone Baker could get involved in healthy social activities run by the school, he would not be so susceptible to gang activities. School arts, music, and athletic programs provide valuable support and opportunities for disadvantaged students to participate in sports, clubs, and activities. Most school arts programs provide valuable outlets for young people and give them a sense of accomplishment, as does participation in the school band or choir. Too often, when funding is tight, the prevention value (in human and economic terms) of school arts programs are unacknowledged.

Some schools have addressed the social issues of potential dropouts by lengthening the school day by 20 minutes for an activity and club period during school hours. These programs help students gain a sense of working together; they make friends in a supervised setting and they relate to others with common interests. Because club meetings are held during the school day, all students can participate.

Peer and cross-age tutoring programs, too, can help young people at risk for dropping out of school. Such programs are popular because they blend learning with the development of social skills and a positive self-image. In Chapter 14 we provide an extensive discussion of the use of peer and cross-age tutoring programs to prevent school dropouts.

used to me not turning in my homework. So is Mr. Poland. He says I better start thinkin' about what I'm gonna do for the science fair or I'm gonna flunk his class. Well, excuse me, but I just don't have time to figure out how to make an atom bomb. I wish he'd just get off my case and stick to buggin' the smart kids.

If I didn't have to go to school, I could help Mama by takin' the kids to the library. They have story time, and my little sisters like to hear it sometimes. I just set and read the encyclopedias. The other day I was readin' that a kangaroo can have as many as three babies suckin' on her tits at once. There can be an embryo that attaches itself to the nipple, a newborn inside the pouch, and an older baby (they're called "joeys," in case you weren't aware) that hops in for some chow. I really enjoy the library. Especially in summer cuz the air conditioner works real good. Some of those librarians are real nice to me. Mrs. Bishop is my favorite. She always asks me about the books I check out, if I liked 'em, and then she says what's another good one to read. One librarian there is kinda mean, but she's nothing like the one at the school library. Man, that lady won't even let you read the inside cover flaps cuz it'll mess up her nice clean shelf. She looks at me like I'm lookin' to take something all the time. Mama says she must have a board up her butt. I just hate goin' in there. Anyway, it doesn't matter much cuz we're only allowed to go to the library with our English class, and I never finish my work in that class. I just can't get into prepositions and garbage like that. I mean, who cares anyway? In Mama's restaurant, nobody says I'm not talkin' right, and I know I never heard anybody discussin' conjugatin' verbs while they was eatin' a French dip roast beef sandwich. I sure wish I could leave school so I could start learnin' something.

In addition, classroom techniques that provide students with the opportunity to communicate with each other in a positive manner help to improve their social relationships. Jason Carter and Ramona Diaz would benefit greatly from working together with other students in supportive groups. Some specific classroom practices are discussed in Chapter 13, including peer support networks and cooperative learning groups.

Retention.   One issue of importance to a potential dropout is the practice of retaining students at a grade level, or retention. Although retention provides slower learners with the extra time they need to develop and mature physically, emotionally, or academically, retention in grade does not help them achieve success in school. In fact, retention at any time between kindergarten and eighth grade is associated with later poor academic, social, and personal outcomes regardless of the child's gender, socioeconomic status, or ethnicity (Jimerson, 1999). Children who were retained after kindergarten did not differ much academically from children who were considered to be at risk but were not retained. Their math scores were the same, and the retained group scored only one month ahead of the comparison group on reading measures at the end of the first grade. The biggest difference between the groups was found in their attitudes. The children who had been retained after kindergarten had more negative attitudes toward school than the children who had not been retained (Jimerson, 1999). Thus, retaining Lidia Diaz after her first year of schooling could be quite detrimental to her. Retention should be replaced by better teaching, counseling, and support strategies that help children experience success.

Early reading. Virtually all children, regardless of family background, social class, or other factors, enter first grade full of enthusiasm and motivation. They fully expect to succeed in school. By the end of first grade many of these students have already begun to discover that school can be negative and punishing. Children who have experienced early failure in school are likely to have poor self-concepts as learners, to be anxious about learning, to be unmotivated, and to hate reading and other school activities. Dropout prevention must begin in the earliest school years. Reform is needed at all levels of education, but no goal of reform is as important as seeing that all children start off their school careers with competence and success. Reading is the single most important foundational skill for learning.

All children must learn to read. Slavin (1994) argues forcefully that virtually every child can be successful in the early grades, and his Success for All program provides evidence that they can (Slavin, Karweit, & Wasik, 1994). He also argues that the most effective strategies by far for preventing early reading failure are those approaches that incorporate one-on-one tutoring of at-risk first-graders to help enhance their phonological awareness. One of the best established of these programs is Reading Recovery.

Reading Recovery, developed by New Zealand educator Marie Clay (1985), is an early intervention program designed to reduce reading failure. It is a one-on-one tutoring pullout program for first-grade students who are experiencing difficulty learning to read. It is based on the idea that high-quality intensive intervention in the very early grades is an efficient and cost-effective strategy for preventing reading failure, a pattern of frustration and other long-term academic difficulties, and school dropout. This approach helps prevent children from developing ineffective reading strategies.

In this program, the Reading Recovery teacher first discovers what the children know. This serves as a basis for developing instructional approaches. After this initial period, each daily 30-minute session has a similar format. Problem words are worked on. Then, the child rereads two familiar books with an emphasis on fluency, and the teacher explores strategies when the child experiences difficulty. A third book is used to create a running record of the child's accuracy in reading. After the reading session, the teacher goes back over the record with the student and asks questions: "How did you know that?" "What did you do here?" The teacher emphasizes the child's use of appropriate strategies in dealing with difficult sections. Next, the child dictates a sentence story to the teacher. This sentence is the basis for a writing activity and becomes part of the homework assignment. Then a fourth new book is introduced to the child. Upon conclusion of the session, the child is given a packet to bring home that includes a story to be read at home and a copy of the student-generated writing. When children begin to perform at the average reading level of their classroom, they are released from the program.

Reading Recovery has had substantial success in New Zealand (Glynn, Crooks, Bethune, Ballard, & Smith, 1992), Australia (Center, Wheldall, Freeman, Outhred, & McNaught, 1995), and the United States (Pinnell, Lyons, DeFord, Bryk, & Seltzer, 1994). Unfortunately, the size and mobility of the U.S. population, along with the intensive training and staff development required, make this tutoring program difficult for some schools to adopt. In Chapter 14 we discuss alternative one-on-one programs of peer and cross-age tutoring that can be implemented more easily.

Second-chance programs: Alternative education.   Besides prevention and early intervention, accommodations have been made for students who are at imminent risk of early school withdrawal or who have already dropped out. Alternative education programs provide ways for these young people to experience academic and personal success in technical vocational schools, alternative middle or high schools, schools for pregnant teens, homebound programs, and evening high schools.

A recent article by Dynarski and Gleason (2002) summarizes findings from a large evaluation of federally funded dropout prevention programs. Alternative middle schools with an intensive intervention approach were more effective at preventing early dropout than schools that only provided supplemental services. An intensive intervention approach involved: teaching students in smaller classes; implementing competency-based curricula that allowed students to work independently and progress at their own rate; developing challenging curricula that required students to use knowledge from several subject areas to address real-world issues; and pushing students to learn more and faster, so that those who were behind grade level could accelerate their progress.

In contrast, the supplemental program provided only tutoring or occasional classes to promote self-esteem or leadership, and had almost no impact on student outcomes (Dynarski & Gleason, 2002). An evaluation of alternative programs suggests that although supplemental services were relatively straightforward to implement, they did not appear to keep students in school, or improve their attendance or academic performance. Alternative programs that provide more attention to students, that create an environment geared to their specific needs, and that provide a more personal atmosphere with smaller classes seem to work best for students at risk for dropping out.

Most important, the choice of teachers was a more influential factor than the choice of the curriculum. The evaluators observed inspired and creative teachers engaging students intellectually with traditional material. More often, however, they observed classes with interesting subject material, but with traditional teaching format. Students were not engaged (Dynarski & Gleason, 2002).

Specific Intervention: Comprehensive, Competency-Based Guidance

Placements in alternative school settings are less critical when schools are systematically organized to intervene consistently. Research shows that most students who leave school before graduation did not receive school interventions to help them stay in school (Coley, 1995; Mattison, 2000). Over 60% indicated that no one on the school staff had tried to talk them into staying. Less than one-fourth saw a counselor or social worker to discuss their troubles or dropout plans. For many of these students, it was clear that they were struggling with academic and other problems in their final two years and no one caught the problem early enough to prevent dropout.

The 1990s have seen a major push by the American School Counseling Association and other concerned groups to encourage schools to adhere to the national standards for school counseling programs (Campbell & Dahir, 1997). The national standards are closely aligned to the Comprehensive Competency-Based Guidance (CCBG) model. Comprehensive competency-based guidance and counseling programs are rapidly becoming the program of choice for managing guidance and counseling in schools (Gysbers & Henderson, 2001). It is currently estimated that more than half of the states promote the use of CCBG programs.

Comprehensive competency-based guidance programs are developmentally focused and are designed to provide all students with experiences to help them grow and develop. These programs change the traditional responsibilities, roles, and contributions of school counselors, so that while they continue to meet the immediate counseling and crisis management needs of students, their major task is to identify competencies among all students and then to provide planned activities on a regular basis to assist students to achieve competencies and to learn new skills. Within the CCBG model, counselors provide a full range of services and activities—assessment, information sharing with teachers and parents, consultation, prevention, counseling, referral, placement, and follow-up work with children and youth and their families. CCBG programs incorporate unique components that typically include the following:

- A *guidance curriculum* that infuses career exploration into the academic curricula.
- *Individual planning* that consists of advising, assessing, and supporting students individually with their academic and career goals.
- *Responsive services* that include individual counseling, small-group counseling, large-group or classroom-level interventions, prevention work (also often through classroom delivery), consultation, and referral.

The student development aspect of CCBG encompasses a variety of desired student learning competencies. These competencies are comprised of specific knowledge, attitudes, and skills. They form the foundation of the developmental school counseling program. All students gain the specific competencies they need to be successful students and successful adults. The three areas or domains of student development in the CCBG model are:

- *Academic development*—that is, young people acquire the knowledge and skills that contribute to effective learning in school and across the life span.
- *Career development*—specifically, students employ strategies to achieve future career success and satisfaction.
- *Personal/social development*—students acquire the attitudes, knowledge, and interpersonal skills to help them understand and respect themselves and others.

Developmentally appropriate competencies in each of the three domains are identified at all levels, pre-K through 12. Typically, counselors are assigned to and become an expert in a particular domain. All students are systematically provided opportunities to develop competencies through classroom and small group presentations according to the master calendar developed by the counseling staff.

In the CCBG model, school counselors are more fully engaged in implementing prevention and intervention activities for all students. They move out of marginalized positions into roles that more effectively promote essential education and career objectives for students. Substantial research (Gysbers & Henderson, 2000, 2001; Lapan, Gysbers, & Petroski, 2001) indicates that the implementation of CCBG programs is associated with improving student success and safety.

In the traditional school counseling model, not every student receives the same quality or quantity of information from the counseling staff regarding post-secondary educational opportunities, career opportunities, or life-coping skills. Students with the most obvious personal difficulties and students with top academic skills receive the most attention from counselors. In this traditional counseling model, counselors are passive and wait for students to contact them, which is particularly disadvantageous to the potential school dropout. In the CCBG model, the potential dropout at least knows that somebody is attending to multiple dimensions of his or her development. Of course, because of the increase in the school counselor's job responsibilities, opportunities for long-term counseling of individual children are few, and outside referrals to appropriate counselors, social workers, or psychologists in the community may increase. The CCBG model provides more support and guidance to more students, and adoption of such a model can be a significant step toward dropout prevention.

SPECIFIC INTERVENTION: SOLUTION-FOCUSED COUNSELING

How can a school be transformed from a problem-focused environment into a solution-focused environment—one that fosters and highlights positive change? Solution-focused counseling is a positive and competency-based response to the problems experienced by children, adolescents, adults, and even organizational systems (Gingerich & Wabeke, 2001). Rather than focusing on what is wrong and how to fix it, this approach looks for what is already working and how to use and augment it. Its usefulness within the school system and its effectiveness with school problems have been well reported (Bruce, 1995; Durrant, 1995; Metcalf, 1995; Murphy, 1997; Murphy & Duncan, 1997; Sklare, 1997). The limited time frame of the solution-focused approach and its positive, competency-based, goal-oriented emphasis make it very well suited for counselors operating in a comprehensive competency-based guidance model.

Our focus here is on the use of a solution-focused approach within the context of counseling. However, the techniques are also useful to administrators working with teachers, parents, and students; in administrative meetings; and in case conferences. Teachers have found many of the strategies, skills, and concepts to be helpful in working with parents and students.

There are several key assumptions of solution-focused counseling.

- Change can occur rapidly and often a small change is all that is needed to prompt other changes.
- Problems are usually not pervasive; there will be times when the problem is less intense or not present at all.
- Students are more likely to change when they have a clearly defined goal and are able to generate solutions that fit.
- People have strengths and resources and are already doing some things to solve their problem.
- The problem is the problem, not the student, teachers, or parents.

Consistent with these assumptions, encouraging a student to make small changes in behavior has the potential to lead to bigger changes in behavior. Encouraging a student to complete a small portion of her English paper rather than complete the entire assignment is based on the idea that she needs success and encouragement to get some momentum started in her life. In addition, small shifts in role by one person in a relationship have the potential to cause the role shift of others in that relationship. Initially, the counselor's job is to push for small changes.

Using solution-focused questions helps the client identify exceptions and potential solutions to the problem. The counselor helps the client identify those times when the problem is not present or is less intense ("Can you describe a time in the past week when your teacher was *not* angry with you? What were you doing?), and these exceptions can be transformed into solutions. Next, the counselor builds on asking the client how the exception happened and how the client could make it happen more often.

The following pragmatic points appeal to clients' common sense.

1. If it works a little, try to do more of what is working;
2. Build on and add behaviors that are to what works;
3. If it is broke, stop what's not working and do something different to fix it;
4. And finally, "If it ain't broke, don't fix it."

In solution-focused counseling, goals are stated in positive and observable terms: Clients do better in obtaining goals that are specific and quantifiable. For example, the goal of "study harder" is inferior to the goal of "complete one homework assignment per day in study hall." Time in the counseling session is devoted entirely to increasing exceptions (doing more of what works) and identifying and pursuing specific goals. No time is spent trying to determine the cause of a problem, describing the history of a problem, or rehashing old, past experiences.

One simple strategy that counselors can use to implement solution-focused counseling is the "miracle question" (de Shazer, 1990). The miracle question is a future-oriented question that is very useful in goal setting and in shifting from focusing on the problem to focusing on the solution. In essence, the client is asked to visualize what their life would be like if suddenly the problems were solved. For example, "Suppose a miracle occurs tonight while you are sleeping. When you wake up, you suddenly realize that your problems are solved. What would things be like? What would you be doing that would tell you that the miracle had actually taken place?" A form of the miracle question useful for children is: "If I were to wave a magic wand and all of your problems went away, what would you do? If we could videotape you for one day, what would we see?" Older children and adolescents might respond better to a visualization of what their life would look like six months or a year from now if the problem were solved. "If we were to meet in a year and the problem we are talking about didn't exist anymore, what would you be doing differently and how would you know that things were okay?"

The miracle picture is elaborated through the use of solution-focused questions, such as "What else?" "What will others see?" "How would that make you feel?" and "How would that happen?" By engaging in this process students are essentially able to explore the positive change they would like to see occur and come up with possible solutions that they would like to implement.

Solution-focused counseling is non-blaming and emphasizes normalizing young people's experiences and problems. Solution-focused counseling may be especially effective with youth at risk for early school dropout because:

• Students are less likely to feel as if the counselor is attacking or blaming them for the problems they are experiencing;

- Students feel empowered knowing that the counselor believes they are capable of becoming their own agents of change;
- Students are able to recognize that they have many options besides dropping out of school;
- Counselors hone in on realistic solutions that can be readily implemented, thereby maximizing the effects of their brief encounters with each at-risk student.

Counselors should keep in mind the following five principles when working with at-risk youth from a solution-focused perspective (Davis & Osborn, 2000):

- Make the most of each brief encounter with a student, as it may be the only one that you have;
- Honor and respect students, especially the resources and strengths they already have, because these are the ingredients for positive change;
- Help students to transfer what they've heard and learned in their counseling interactions with you to the hallway, lunch room, gym, the bus or subway, and so on;
- As much as possible, engage in a collaborative, nonconfrontive exchange with students and their families;
- Instill in students a reason to be hopeful, because hope fuels change and change is always possible.

Solution-focused/brief counseling is uniquely suited to the school setting. It emphasizes resources and strengths; emphasizes natural forces within the environment; and uses effective, simple, and positive strategies to help students change behavior.

Overall research on the efficacy of solution-focused/brief counseling is limited; many are simply the anecdotal reports of solution-focused/brief counseling. However, the research that is available demonstrates that brief counseling has been effective when applied to students with behavioral disorders, anxiety, and depression (Dielman & Franklin, 1998; Triantafillou, 1997; Durrant, 1995; Littrell, Malia, & Vanderwood, 1995). This approach allows a busy school counselor to impact a larger number of students and is of great potential value in preventing dropout.

CONCLUSION

As literacy standards rise along with the demands of our increasingly technological society, we expect more from our young people than ever before. Unfortunately, these demands come at a time when economic resources are unequally distributed and many communities and families are unable to meet young people's educational and motivational needs. When we recognize the family, school, social, and personality issues involved, as well as the effects of the experience of failure, we are in a better position to understand why young people drop out of school. We must attempt to effect changes in all of these areas if we are to make any headway against the dropout problem and its wide-ranging consequences.

If at-risk children and adolescents do not stay in school, they move beyond the reach of effective prevention and intervention strategies that can be administered by and through the schools. And if young people do not develop the fundamental skills that schools can provide, they will continue to be dependent, unproductive, and discouraged members of society.

CHAPTER 7

SUBSTANCE USE AND ADDICTION

▲ *There is an assumption here that perhaps should be argued out rather than taken for granted. It is that the self is worth being.*

There is a philosophical dialogue that turns on the question of whether people are born good and become corrupted or are born evil and become civilized.

My own opinion is that each is equally true.

Thus, I cannot claim that if you strip yourself of the encrustation of attitudes and defenses, you are going to expose an angelic, euphoric, and expansive person.

But, certainly, neither are you going to find the cretinous and willful monster that most of us fear is lurking underneath.

There will be a human being, with the assets and limitations inherent in the definition of human being but, for the first time and most importantly, with the choice not to be ugly and cruel and stunted. . . .

. . . To give the self permission to be the self, a leap must be taken across the chasm of dread that the self may be little and mean and nasty toward a certain faith that the self is a good thing to be and that spontaneous behavior can be trusted.

J. J. McWhirter

Seek Wisdom

Chapter Outline

▲   In this chapter we describe the severity of substance use by children and adolescents, the problems associated with it, and potential solutions to this widespread problem. This discussion is especially pertinent to the United States, which has the highest rate of alcohol and drug use by adolescents among industrialized nations (Johnston, O'Malley, & Bachman, 2003). Throughout this chapter, we use the terms *substances* and *drugs* interchangeably, and include tobacco and alcohol as examples of drugs. In the following sections, we: (a) describe some of the definitional and assessment problems associated with substance use, (b) illustrate the scope of substance use among adolescents, (c) outline personal and social determinants leading to drug use and addiction, (d) discuss some of the consequences of alcohol and drug consumption, and (e) highlight child and adolescent substance use treatment and prevention approaches found to be effective.

Definitional Difficulties and Assessment

To determine the abusive nature of drug use, one must consider the context, the frequency, and the purpose for which a drug is used. There is often a fine line between drug use and drug abuse. The causes of *substance use* are often linked to social influences (e.g., peer drug use), whereas *substance abuse* may be more tied to internal processes, for example, using drugs as self-medication against persistent emotional distress. Yet for adolescents and pre-adolescents most of the correlates of substance use are identical to those of abuse. The term *substance abuse* is also an ideological term, suggesting that the results of drug use are always negative or harmful, which can be misleading. We use the term *substance use* throughout this text because it does not negate the harmful consequences of drug use nor does it exaggerate them.

Additionally, although tobacco products and alcohol are accepted and legal for adults, they can have severe negative consequences even when they are used in relative moderation. Alcohol and tobacco use are responsible for significant physical and personal problems and have greater social costs than all other drugs combined. Miller and Blincoe (1994) estimated that the total dollars spent or lost for alcohol misuse in one year in the United States to be 116.5 billion dollars. Cigarette smoking is estimated to account for over 430,000 premature deaths each year (National Center for Chronic Disease Prevention and Health Promotion [NCCDPHP], 2002). Nevertheless, we do not define the occasional smoker or drinker as an abuser of substances.

Criteria have been established for identifying substance abuse and substance-induced disorders, including substance intoxication, in adult populations. The Diagnostic and Statistical Manual of Mental Disorders (DSM-IV-TR)(American Psychiatric Association, 2000), distinguishes between substance dependence and substance abuse without making separate provisions for children and adolescents. Substance dependence is addiction. It involves the physiological responses of *tolerance* (increasingly larger doses of a particular drug are needed to maintain its physiological effects) and *withdrawal* (painful physical and psychological consequences result when the drug is withheld from the body). Substance use is maladaptive in DSM terminology if use of a particular substance causes impaired social, school, or occupational functioning. Drug use is identified as being "with or without physiological dependence," and the specific courses of drug use are identified as "early full remission," "early partial remission," "sustained full remission," or "sustained partial remission." Although not specifically listed as DSM criteria, substance abuse can be determined by examining: (a) the frequency of use, (b) the quantity typically used, (c) the variety of substances used at the same time (polydrug use), (d) the social context in which drugs are used (Is the user being dared to try drugs? Does the user usually use drugs with friends, alone, or with strangers?), and (e) the emotional state of the abuser (Is the user typically depressed or feeling positive before engaging in drug use?). Examining these criteria help to clarify the nature and extent of substance use and abuse among children and teenagers.

THE SCOPE OF THE PROBLEM

Although the overall use of drugs in the United States has fallen by 50% in the past 20 years, the past 10 years have shown some increase in drug use by adolescents (Johnston, O'Malley, & Bachman, 2003; U.S. Department of Health and Human Services, 2002). The National Institute on Drug Abuse (NIDA), through its Monitoring the Future Study (MFS), for example, found that 50% of high school seniors regularly use alcohol, with 26% having engaged in binge drinking and with over 20% of tenth-graders having engaged in binge drinking within two weeks of the survey (Johnston, O'Malley, & Bachman, 2003).

Additionally, experimentation with tobacco during adolescence is quite prevalent, and many children experiment with tobacco as early as age 9. Though daily use rates are declining, tenth and twelfth graders still have substantial use rates of 10% and 17% respectively. In addition, about 5% of eigth grade boys and 12% of twelfth grade boys had used smokeless tobacco (chewing tobacco, snuff, or dip) in the past 30 days (Johnston et al., 2003). The use of tobacco and alcohol are critical because both are considered "threshold" or "gateway" substances, which often precede use of illicit drugs such as marijuana and coca-based substances.

Close to 30% of high school students had been offered, sold, or given an illegal drug, often marijuana, on school property at some point during the 12 months preceding one survey (Grunbaum et al., 2002). These data are serious, especially because marijuana smoking may actually precede heavy tobacco smoking or abusing of alcohol among girls (which suggests it is also a gateway drug for girls). Further, marijuana use is often a forerunner to smoking heroin and cocaine (Golub & Johnson, 2001). Over 10% of students nationwide had tried marijuana before age 13, with male students more likely to use than female students across all ethnic groups (Grunbaum et al., 2002). Additionally, nearly 10% of adolescents have at least once used a form of cocaine (e.g., powder, "crack," or "freebase"), with Latino and European American students (15% and 10%, respectively) significantly more likely to do so than African American students (2%). It is also estimated that nearly 15% of adolescents have used inhalants (sniffed glue, aerosol spray, or paint) to get high. An increasing problem among youth—methamphetamine use—indicates that nationwide, nearly 10% of adolescents have used methamphetamines with European American and Latino young people (11.4% and 9%, respectively) using significantly more than African Americans (2%). Among twelfth graders, use of tranquilizers and barbituates has been steadily rising since the 1990's (Johnston et al., 2003).

Within these data there are points of hope. There is no evidence of increases in *early onset* of drug use. Use of most illicit drugs decreased or was stable between 2000 and 2002 (Johnston et al., 2003). Perceptions of risks associated with smoking and using most illicit substances increased (Johnston et al., 2003). Although these data are positive, drug and alcohol use among U.S. children and adolescents continues to be a serious behavioral, social, and health problem. The continuous introduction of new drugs, as well as the tendency for youth to "forget" the dangers associated with older drugs such as heroin, require ongoing efforts to educate the public (Johnston et al., 2003).

The often-held stereotype that adolescents of color abuse substances more than European American youth is not supported by research. African American youth are significantly less likely to use cigarettes, alcohol, and illicit drugs than European American youth (Johnston et al., 2003). In eighth grade, Latino youth have the highest use rates for all substances except amphetamines. It is European American youth that tend to have the highest use rates for all substances in tenth and twelfth grade (Johnston et al., 2003). Native American Indian adolescents use alcohol, tobacco, and other drugs significantly more than other groups, resulting in problems that include a high incidence of fetal alcohol syndrome (Plunkett & Mitchell, 2000).

Adolescents who are gay, lesbian, bisexual, or transgendered (GLBT) are at highest risk of substance abuse (Jordan, 2000). These young people are at risk because of an increase in suicidal ideation, levels of depression and hopelessness, and experiences of victimization (Russel & Joyner, 2001). Estimates suggest that over a third of GLBT youth are frequent and problematic users and are more likely to engage in poly-substance use, with marijuana and alcohol used most (Radkowsky & Siegel, 1997). Of course, gay and lesbian teenagers abuse drugs for the same reasons as straight youth, but the additional challenges and oppression they experience as members of a sexual minority group may drive many GLBT youth to use drugs as a way of buffering the social exclusion, ridicule, and torment that they experience (Radkowsky & Siegel, 1997). Clearly, a better understanding of substance abuse among GLBT young people can help the development of targeted prevention and treatment programs and a greater awareness and sensitivity to this underserved community can improve our prevention and intervention efforts right now.

SOME DETERMINANTS OF SUBSTANCE USE AND COMMON CHARACTERISTICS OF USERS

Family and peer influences, individual behavior, and personality characteristics consistently relate to child and adolescent substance use (Johnston, O'Malley, & Bachman, 2000; Scheier, 2001). Counselors and human service professionals can use knowledge of these factors to assess the likelihood of drug use and to provide appropriate interventions. Correlates and predictors of child and adolescent drug use influence each other in a variety of ways (e.g., Dishion, Kavanagh, Nelson, Schneiger, & Kaufman, 2002). Understanding the complex ecology of children's lives and how each aspect of their environment—social policy, media advertising, parenting practices, family and peer drug use, and individual characteristics—all interrelate in predicting substance use and its outcomes is important. Although correlates to adolescent drug use are presented here in discrete categories, these variables are highly interrelated and mutually influential.

Environmental and Social Correlates of Substance Use

There are a variety of environmental factors that contribute to drug use. In economically depressed communities young people often use drugs in response to the bleakness of economic and social conditions (Hawkins, Catalano, & Miller, 1992). The lack of educational, employment, and economic opportunities often leads to despair and escape in drugs, as we see in the Andrews and Baker children (Chapters 1 and 2). Traumatic events, poor neighborhoods, adverse school conditions, and negative peer influences also contribute to increased use of substances (Johnston et al., 2000) and to aggression. Consistent with this, drug use is typically heavier among lower socioeconomic groups.

Drug use is also reinforced through the media, which inundate the market with images of drug use as a helpful solution to all physical complaints and psychological problems. Alcohol is portrayed as necessary to lead the "good life." This message of drug acceptability further communicates to young people the usefulness of drugs as part of mainstream U.S. culture. The profit motive also leads advertising to glamorize products to appeal to and entice young people, such as use of cartoon characters to advertise cigarettes. Finally, modeling by older siblings, parents, and peers is highly correlated with drug use among children and adolescents (Kosterman et al., 2000). Two of the most important and direct predictors of adolescent drug use are peer drug use and low parental monitoring, or parents who are detached and disconnected from the everyday activities of their child's life (Dishion et al., 2002).

Peer Influence on Substance Use

Peer groups strongly influence a young person's decision to use drugs and they predict age of initial drug use, especially alcohol, marijuana, and tobacco (Dishion et al., 2002; Kosterman et al., 2000). Thus, interventions that focus on the peer group may be the most effective for preventing and treating substance use and associated problems. Unfortunately, *peer group* and *peer pressure* have been used so loosely that their meanings are ambiguous. As we clarified in Chapter 4, peer-cluster theory (Oetting & Beauvais, 1986; Beauvais, Chavez, Oetting, Deffenbacher, & Cornell, 1996) provides a specific framework for understanding and explaining the influence of peers on a young person's decisions and decision making. Peer-cluster theory emphasizes that drug use is linked to peer relationships. Peers provide information about drugs, shape attitudes toward them, create a social context for their use, give rationales for using them, and make them available.

This theory has been tested and supported by a series of research studies that highlight the importance of attending to peer clusters in both prevention and treatment (Oetting & Beauvais, 1987; Swaim, Oetting, Edwards, & Beauvais, 1989; Beauvais et al., 1996). This theory has also enjoyed some support in describing problem behavior among adolescents in other cultures as well (P. T. McWhirter, 1998), suggesting that the theory may be culturally sensitive and broadly applicable.

Adolescent drug use is also a function of positive reinforcement. When children and adolescents use certain substances, they frequently experience not only physiological reinforcement (e.g., euphoria, stimulation), but also social reinforcement by peers, who bestow attention and status on the using adolescent. Such reinforcement is a powerful force for maintaining substance use and for experimenting with more potent drugs.

Family Correlates of Substance Use

Research consistently identifies family factors, such as parenting style, as central to the etiology of multiple problem behavior outcomes, including early-onset substance use (Webster-Stratton, 1997). Lower socioeconomic status and parental substance use are significant contextual predictors of onset of alcohol and tobacco use (Dishion et al., 2002). Low parent monitoring in particular predicts early alcohol, tobacco, and marijuana use. Therefore, increasing parental monitoring may serve as a key protective factor for reducing substance use among children exposed to it by their siblings or peers (DiClemente et al., 2001). Poor parent-child relationships, deficient parental limit setting, and weak problem-solving and communication skills within families all predict higher use as well (Dishion & McMahon, 1998; Kosterman et al., 2000). At the same time, authoritarian and punitive approaches in schools and in families also tend to contribute to higher drug use among children and adolescents. And teens are more likely to use drugs if their family environments are disruptive or disorganized, include an adult who uses drugs, or have no family religious affiliation (Webster-Stratton, Reid, & Hammond, 2001). Thus the children in the Andrews, Baker, and Carter families are at serious risk. Jason Carter's dysfunctional family, his poor school adjustment, and his underlying emotional distress provide particularly fertile ground for the development of drug-use problems. Because family factors are central to the risk of adolescent drug use, it is not surprising that family-based approaches are quite promising for reducing early-onset substance use and would be quite helpful to each of our described families (Dishion et al., 2002; Hawkins, Catalano, Kosterman, Abbott, & Hill, 1999; Kumpfer, Molgaard, & Spoth, 1996).

Personal Correlates of Substance Use

Although some adolescents never experiment with drugs, others experiment briefly and never use them again, and others develop long-term patterns of use. Drug dependence may be associated with two additional and critical factors: psychic pain and inability to cope (Clark & Sayette, 1993; Simons, Whitbeck, Conger, & Melby, 1991). Psychic pain can emerge from pervasive self-criticism and a chronic sense of failure that often leads to lower self-esteem and to young people believing that they are primarily responsible for the problems they experience. Many adolescents internalize these attributions for problems and experience subsequent depression and anxiety (B. T. McWhirter & Burrow-Sanchez, 2004; B. T. McWhirter, J. J. McWhirter, Hart, & Gat, 2000). Adolescents with poor coping skills are vulnerable to intense emotional pain, and drug use can become a relief-seeking behavior aimed at alleviating both internal problems (frustration, stress, depression, feelings of low self-worth) and external problems (poor school performance, family discord, violence). These kinds of pain can be overwhelming and draw many young people into substance use as a form of self-medication. But because relief through drugs is only temporary, drug use itself becomes part of a downward spiral and is ultimately self-defeating. Jason Carter of Chapter 3, for example, is experiencing considerable psychological pain and his coping methods are ineffective and exacerbate his distress. He is a prime candidate for potential chronic drug abuse and dependency.

Pervasive substance use, rather than experimentation, is also associated with a variety of other personality characteristics. Among these are pleasure-seeking and sensation-seeking behaviors (Comeau, Stewart, & Loba, 2001), such as rebelliousness; nontraditionalism, tolerance for deviance, adventuresomeness, and need for excitement (P. T. McWhirter, 1998); an acute desire for independence and autonomy, along with low interpersonal trust and low impulse control with poor ability to delay gratification (Comeau et al., 2001). Drug interventions should focus on the problematic aspects of these personal risk factors. Some of these characteristics (e.g., high risk-taking behavior and adventuresomeness) are not necessarily a problem and, in fact, can be used in treatment. Some prevention and treatment programs use adventurous activities to help adolescents channel their energies in a positive direction along with building self-efficacy and appropriate trust in self and in peers.

Finally, two specific personality correlates or psychological phenomena that make abstention from drugs difficult for adolescents who wish to quit using are *cognitive dissonance* and *personal attribution*. These thought processes make it difficult for an individual to stay off drugs after a period of abstention. *Cognitive dissonance* is a result of conflicting internal messages. For example, the statements "I don't smoke anymore" and "After three months without a cigarette, I just smoked most of a pack" are inconsistent. They create dissonance, which brings on feelings of guilt, depression, and failure. These feelings are relieved when the internal messages are made harmonious: "I just smoked most of a pack" and "I'm a smoker." *Personal attribution* is the act of placing responsibility for a break from abstention on personal weaknesses and inadequacies. Despite situational factors that may greatly influence their behavior, such as unusually strong peer pressure or the actual addictive properties of the drug, people blame themselves for using substances again after they have decided to quit. The feelings of loss of control, failure, and guilt that result from both of these cognitive processes can lead abstainers to turn again to substances in an effort to cope, to alleviate their negative feelings, and to engage in behaviors consistent and congruent with their self-concept.

▲ Box 7.1

Joe

One of us worked with a 13-year-old boy named Joe for two months after Joe's mother requested that he receive counseling. She and her husband, Joe's stepfather, were concerned about his poor school performance, his acting out, his group of "delinquent" friends, and his alternately hostile and completely withdrawn behavior at home.

Joe's stepfather was a machine operator who provided severe yet inconsistent discipline. Joe disliked his stepfather, and he reported that the dislike was mutual. He described his mother as "nicer," but complained that she did not permit him to do what he wanted. His mother was primarily a homemaker, but occasionally she did temporary office work. She frequently placated her husband so that he would not get angry with Joe. She felt Joe needed to change, however, and believed that counseling might "fix" him. Joe's parents refused to come in for counseling as a family because Joe was the problem.

Joe spent a great deal of time with his friends both during and after school. He reported smoking marijuana and cigarettes fairly regularly. Shortly after our first counseling session, he was arrested for possession of drug paraphernalia. His parents refused to let him see any of his friends after the arrest.

Joe's school performance and effort were poor. Joe probably had a mild learning disability, but a recent psycho-educational evaluation had been inconclusive. Joe's primary problem at school was his acting out. Unfortunately, when Joe got into trouble with a teacher, he was inadvertently rewarded for his disruption. He could effectively avoid the schoolwork that he found so difficult and distasteful by sitting in the assistant principal's office "listening to stupid stories." Joe was doing so poorly at school and misbehaving with such frequency that his stepfather threatened to send him to a strict boarding school unless his behavior improved. Joe said that would be fine with him because he had heard that the work was easier there. His stepfather's threat to cut his hair short was the only consequence he seemed concerned about.

Joe primarily used marijuana, which did not change during the two months he was in counseling. We don't know whether Joe experimented with more powerful substances because he showed a great deal of resistance to coming to counseling and seemed very disinterested in changing himself, although he did want his stepfather to move out. Joe was a frustrated and angry adolescent who resented his parents and received little direction or consistent structure from them. He was unsure of their expectations, hated school, felt isolated from his friends, and could see no solution to his problems. He directed his anxiety and poor

(continued)

Box 7.1 *(continued)*

self-esteem inward and acted out by skipping school, talking back to his teachers, or roaming the streets with his friends.

Like many other young people, Joe faced difficult challenges in life and had few resources for coping with them. He had never learned to delay gratification, he did not know how to relate to others in a healthy and positive way, he received no consistent discipline and failed to develop a sense of responsibility for his actions, and he felt mistreated and betrayed by the school and by his parents. Drug use was simply a means for Joe to escape from the problems that troubled him so much.

Joe's parents did not accept that his difficulties might be symptomatic of larger family problems. They refused to enter family therapy and eventually withdrew Joe from counseling.

Some Consequences of Substance Use

The long-term consequences of substance use require additional research, but some of the physiological, psychosocial, and legal consequences are clear. Examples of each are briefly presented here.

Physiological Consequences

The physiological consequences of drug use vary with the drug. Most substances (alcohol, nicotine, marijuana, narcotics, hallucinogens) have relatively immediate physical effects with alterations in one's sense of reality, judgment, and sensory perceptions. These effects are caused by interference with the normal functioning of the central nervous system. The effects may be felt for hours (as with alcohol) or for days (as with marijuana). But part of the difficulty with communicating the physiological risks of substance use to young people is that not all substances have severe or immediate consequences. Although marijuana impairs perception and judgment, for example, it is not physiologically addictive when it is used in moderation (although its ability to become psychosocially addictive is quite high). So to focus exclusively on the short-term negative effects of marijuana in counseling on drug education classes actually reduces the perceived truthfulness and therefore the effectiveness of the prevention strategy.

Although short-term feelings associated with use of a substance are obvious, the long-term consequences of drugs are more severe. In the United States, alcohol is a factor in approximately half of all adolescent deaths from motor vehicle crashes and long-term alcohol misuse is associated with liver disease, cancer, cardiovascular disease, and neurological damage (NCCDPHP, 2000). One of the most troublesome effects of marijuana smoking is an impairment to processing newly learned material and storing it for future use (Ameri, 1999). Like tobacco, marijuana use also has adverse respiratory effects: chronic cough, recurrent bronchitis, and irritation of the respiratory tract (Lynskey & Hall, 2000).

Physiologically addictive substances (cocaine, crack, heroin, other narcotics) used over a long time can cause severe impairment of the nervous system and internal organs. *Addiction* is typically defined as a physiological state in which the body needs increased amounts of a substance to maintain *homeostasis* (physiological balance). Users become *tolerant* of a drug and need increasing amounts of it to achieve the desired effect. *Withdrawal* is a painful physical experience that occurs when the drug is withheld from the system and the body reacts to the resulting lack of homeostasis. When the use of substances results in tolerance and withdrawal processes, treatment often includes in-patient detoxification because physical dependence on the drug needs to be eliminated for behavioral and psychological interventions to be effective.

Psychosocial Consequences

Typically, drug use during childhood and adolescence leads to more serious problems in early adulthood. Early and risky sexual involvement, failure to pursue educational opportunities, early entrance into the workforce, and early unemployment or underemployment are associated with high levels of drug use by teenagers (Dishion et al., 2000). Essentially, adolescents enter into adult roles before they are ready, without critical life skills, leading to even poorer outcomes for themselves and their offspring (Gragg & E. H. McWhirter, 2003). Alcohol use has been linked to physical fights, academic failure, occupational problems, and juvenile criminal behavior (NCCDPHP, 2000). Drug use contributes to HIV/AIDS, and to infant morbidity and mortality (NCCDPHP, 2000). Adolescent cigarette smoking is associated with poorer achievement on standardized tests (Jeynes, 2002). Interestingly, moderate use of alcohol in the later teen years tends to increase a young person's sense of being integrated with others, positive self-feelings, and positive affect, while reducing loneliness and feelings of self-derogation in early adulthood (Shedler & Block, 1990). But heavy use of more serious drugs (e.g., intravenous drugs, cocaine-based derivatives such as crack, methamphetamines) during adolescence increases loneliness, depression, and suicide ideation, and decreases social support in early adulthood (Newcomb & Bentler, 1989).

GENERAL PREVENTION AND INTERVENTION STRATEGIES

The soil that nurtures drug use (see Chapter 2) includes poverty, racism, community and interpersonal violence, lack of educational and job opportunities, the dissolution of communities, and interpersonal and family problems. The U.S. "war on drugs" has been unsuccessful in large part because it has been a military/geopolitical response to what is fundamentally a social and public health issue. The "war" also underscores that the United States focuses much effort on dealing with drugs and their related problems through the criminal justice system, contributing to the U.S. status as the most incarceration-oriented country in history. But this response does not address the reasons adolescents turn to drugs in the first place. Effective child and adolescent drug prevention and intervention must address these fundamental contributing factors to be successful (August, Realmuto, Winters, & Hektner, 2001; Huang, Unger, & Rohrbach, 2000; Kosterman et al., 2000). The most effective interventions do attend to underlying problems, skills deficiencies, and systemic problem deficiencies (such as poor family life, lack of school programs) that are core to successful prevention programs.

Prevention

Prevention programs are a common form of drug use intervention because many young people have not yet experimented with drugs or alcohol. Additionally, treatment to deal with the use of tobacco and alcohol, as gateway drugs, is also considered prevention for use of other drugs. Because some children experiment with drugs early, universal and indicated prevention programs should begin in the early school grades, commensurate with the prevention/intervention framework we present in Chapter 12. The goals of drug use prevention are generally twofold: to delay age of first use of drugs and to reduce the incidence of use of gateway substances. We know that delaying the age of initial drug use is associated with better outcomes in nearly all indices: social, academic, and economical (Kosterman et al., 2000), and evidence shows that exposure to school-based prevention programs is significantly related to reduced susceptibility to use of gateway substances, such as tobacco (Huang, Unger, & Rohrbach, 2000).

School interventions.   Information-based intervention is probably the most common school strategy. This approach attempts to increase students' knowledge about the effects of drugs and foster healthy attitudes about them. To be most effective, educators and counselors must provide accurate information about the effects and consequences of substance use. Young people's ability to make healthy decisions about drugs is undermined if they perceive that information is inaccurate, irrelevant, or phony. In fact, providing inaccurate information may actually encourage youth to connect with drug-using peers to satisfy curiosity about drugs.

The role of schools in prevention programs is extensive and varied (August, Realmuto, Winters, & Hektner, 2001; Botvin, Schinke, & Orlandi, 1995; Dishion et al., 2002; Durlak, 1995; Huang, Unger, & Rohrbach, 2000). Yet efforts to prevent drug use must go beyond factual information to provide skills that young people need to resist drugs and their social reinforcement (see Chapters 12–14). Some school intervention programs provide alternative activities, such as adventurous recreational activities and service-related community projects. Other schools encourage awareness and better learning opportunities for drug education, increase teachers' awareness of drug use, provide more drug counseling, and support law enforcement efforts to limit drugs on the school campus. Some schools are enlisting the help of community organizations. The most successful school-based programs for drug use prevention are ecological in nature; they include work with families, school personnel and policy, and peer clusters; they include efforts to strengthen the relationships between families, schools, and communities (e.g., August, Realmuto, Winters, & Hektner, 2001; Dishion et al., 2002).

In the Safe and Drug-Free Schools and Communities (SDFSC) programs, the U.S. Department of Education has identified both "exemplary" and "promising" programs that have been implemented for preventing drug and alcohol use (U.S. Department of Education, 2001). Effective treatment components that are common across some of the best programs include: resistance and refusal skill training, accurate education about the consequences of alcohol and drug use, social and problem-solving skills training, parent training to help parents understand and reinforce program goals, examining the social pressure of peers, training in citizenship and leadership skills, and helping children to see how drug use interferes with their personal goals. Programs that include many of these components have been found to be most effective and successful in preventing drug and alcohol use. One of our prevention programs has been included as a promising program by the SDFSC

(Herrmann & McWhirter, 1999). We encourage you to review SDFSC programs for more information on effective prevention.

Family interventions.   Because parental use of drugs and the family environment are key predictors of whether a young person will use substances, prevention and treatment efforts should focus on the family. Family environments that expose children to physical and sexual abuse, alcoholism, and other drug-abuse problems put adolescents at risk for drug use. Inconsistent parents who do not monitor their children's activities also contribute to high risk for drug use (Dishion et al., 2002). Single-parent and blended families are particularly challenged in contemporary society and are at greater risk for adolescent drug use. Additionally, teens who use drugs report greater parental conflict (Lowe, Foxcroft, & Sibley, 1993). Counselors and human service professionals can work with families through parent education or family therapy. Prevention efforts targeting parents' management practices and family norms regarding adolescent substance use are promising for preventing early initiation of substance use (Kosterman et al., 2000). Family counseling is more successful when it addresses the family's cognitive, behavioral, moral, ethical, spiritual, and interpersonal problems (Wallace & Estroff, 2001). Jason Carter's family could use some help of this nature (see Chapter 3).

Community Treatment Programs

Only recently have drug and alcohol treatment programs been designed specifically for children and adolescents. Most juvenile programs are patterned on the traditional drug-free treatment models developed for adults in the 1960s. Few programs are designed to take into account the family situations or the developmental problems faced by young users. But in 2002, the Substance Abuse and Mental Health Services Administration (SAMHSA) joined the Center for Disease Control in an educational "Youth Media Campaign" to influence the attitudes of youth about alcohol abuse. Further, programs in the later part of the 1990s began to respond more to the developmental needs of youth. Although continued research is needed, programs tailored to youth have demonstrated promise (Drug Strategies, 2003; Hser, Grella, Hubbard, Hsieh, Fletcher, Brown, & Anglin, 2001).

A few examples of federally supported and other community treatment programs include the following. *Drug-free programs* offer counseling usually in outpatient settings and use no medication. Some offer drop-in services; others are organized around activities, such as camping trips or challenge experiences; and some offer highly intensive group counseling or biweekly individual brief or long-term counseling. *Therapeutic communities* are community-based residential programs that utilize a structured, isolated, mutual-help environment relying on peer influence and confrontation and group action to change self-destructive values and behavior and to "resocialize" the adolescent into more productive behavior. *Residential adolescent treatment programs* are private residential treatment programs for adolescents operated by profit-making corporations that usually have psychiatrically trained staff and operate on a mental health residential rehabilitation model. Generally, these programs attempt to help adolescents gain understanding of their problems, develop recovery goals, and prepare for long-term recovery by helping them learn skills for relapse-prevention and abstention. Many insurance plans include such treatment, but because treatment does not include other ecological factors that contribute to substance use their effectiveness is limited to nonexistent. *Day-care programs* are treatment programs that also provide alternative schooling, are less structured than residential communities, and provide more comprehensive services than drug-free outpatient programs. Most provide academic instruction, counseling, and recreational and social activities for several hours daily and include greater attention to ecology. Finally, *aftercare programs* work on the philosophy that recovery is a lifelong process and they incorporate therapeutic elements carried out after the young person has been discharged from treatment, including ongoing professional contact and participation in self-help groups such as Alcoholics Anonymous or Narcotics Anonymous. Unfortunately, a serious shortage of treatment programs for adolescents is a major problem in most communities.

School Treatment Programs

Students involved in the early stages of drug use may benefit from school-wide or specific preventive and intervention programming. Such programs often include (a) accurate education, (b) assertiveness training, (c) decision-making strategies, and (d) peer-cluster involvement.

Accurate education.   Effective drug education should (a) provide accurate information about drugs, (b) teach skills for evaluating the social and personal costs of drug use so that young people can realistically assess the consequences and begin to develop a clear sense of the role of drugs in their lives, and (c) address the factors that have led to their substances use, such as their peers' use, family problems, limited interpersonal skills, and poor self-esteem. Educational approaches are not salient unless they address these fundamental issues. Accurate education will help young people make more clearly thought-out decisions about drugs and will help adolescents develop reasoning skills and decision-making strategies.

Assertiveness training: resistance and refusal skills.   Students who are trained in assertiveness develop skills to avoid use of tobacco, alcohol, and marijuana (Herrmann & McWhirter, 1997; 2000). They are less willing to use drugs after intervention and assertiveness training, called resistance training in this context. This training provides youth with the skills needed to recognize and resist the external pressures to use drugs. But developing refusal skills alone, such as the "just say 'No' " campaign, is not effective. Young people need to enhance interpersonal skills, develop better self-awareness, remain free of drug-using peers and be assisted in developing social networks and friendships with low-risk peers, for intervention to be successful in the long term.

Allie Andrews might well profit from confrontation, accurate education, and assertiveness training. Her interaction with her stepfather suggests that she has few ways to respond to stress, mostly acting-out and self-defeating responses. Her peer interaction hints that she may be turning to her friends for the acceptance she does not receive at home. Thus her resistance to drug use is probably quite low. Assertiveness and resistance training might help her develop the skills she needs to change her self-defeating patterns and prevent substance use.

Decision-making strategies.   Good decision making requires that the benefits and consequences of drug use be spelled out clearly and accurately. Unfortunately, neither all the benefits nor all the consequences of drug use (and drug abstinence) are known. Nevertheless, decision-making strategies help users to (a) define the nature of their choice, (b) enlarge the number of alternatives under consideration, (c) identify all benefits and consequences of each alternative, and (d) implement their desired alternative. Because these steps are effective with many of the root problems of substance use, they represent a valuable resource for at-risk youth. (We present the DECIDE model in Chapter 13 as one example of decision making.)

Peer involvement.   Because peers play such an important role in drug use, prevention and treatment efforts should focus not only on individual youth but also on their peer clusters. Peer-based programs represent a direct approach to the problems of substance use, and can be used in conjunction with the information-based approaches discussed earlier. Peer programs that emphasize training in assertiveness and other social skills have the best success rate (Herrmann & McWhirter, 1997). If these skills are not taught to the whole peer cluster, or if adolescents return to the same peer cluster after receiving treatment away from their peers, they often regress to past patterns of use.

In-school approaches that make use of the peer cluster may be helpful. First, schools can organize professionally led, weekly group counseling sessions for young people and their peers who use substances. Also, schools can assign young people to a form of in-school suspension that requires them to spend one or more days each week together as a group, learning why they have been using drugs, learning the short- and long-term consequences of prolonged drug use, and developing the skills necessary to stop using drugs. Both strategies are designed to engage the peer cluster and modify norms and attitudes that support drug use. But, as we have advocated for the past 12 years, be cautious. The peer group may reinforce norms that adults are helpless to modify, especially if groups are provided with unstructured time. Dishion, McCord, and Poulin (1999) discuss the *Iaotragenic effect*, whereby group interventions intended to help actually cause harm, because peers within groups negatively influence each other and encourage drug use. This is particularly problematic in informal and unstructured groups. To reduce the potential harmful effects of a group intervention, it is wise to keep the group highly structured and to include, as we discuss in Chapter 14, trained peer or cross-age facilitators in the group.

Student assistant programs.   Student assistant programs (SAP) within schools are useful because they deal directly with two major problems. First, students involved with alcohol and other substances are hesitant to seek counseling services. Second, the illegal nature of substance use contributes to the reluctance of adolescents to seek assistance and accentuates the denial of problems associated with abuse. The typical SAP has a team that includes representatives from key units in the school and a substance abuse specialist (Moore & Forster, 1993). The composition of this team includes administrators involved in student discipline, school counselors, and faculty representatives. SAPs have a structure and process for identifying substance-abusing students, a network to community resources that provide treatment and recovery interventions, and a reentry program that includes case management and follow-up for students returning to school after treatment.

One particularly important component of follow-up is the school recovery support group. The type of support received when a young person leaves a treatment center and reenters the "real world" is extremely important in preventing relapse. On average, teens who take a leave of absence from school for drug treatment are faced with pressure to use drugs again within the first 20 minutes of returning to school (Hanson & Peterson, 1993). The recovery support group provides an opportunity for students to discuss emotional difficulties of being clean and sober. Because they include students who are "working a program," they accentuate a pro-social peer cluster. In fact, it is detrimental to a school recovery support group to include students who are not actively engaged in their own recovery. Other types of group counseling should be available to drug-using adolescents who choose not to be committed to a drug-free lifestyle.

Guidelines for Best Practices in Drug/Alcohol Intervention

The best practices in interventions for adolescent drug and alcohol use across all settings include some basic core components. Treatment should be (a) multimodal, (b) foster a sense of individual choice in participation, (c) consider risk and protective factors of the individual, and (d) be multiculturally sensitive by considering and integrating cultural and individual differences in prevention and treatment.

Multimodal.   Typically, the most successful interventions for adolescent drug and alcohol use involve individual counseling, family counseling, group therapy, and recreational, vocational, and educational activities (Crits-Christoph & Siqueland, 1996; Liddle & Dakof, 1995).

Individual counseling, which is particularly effective, involves helping adolescents develop better coping, life skills, and decision-making strategies as a form of relapse prevention, versus more psychoanalytic or confrontational therapies (Friedman, Glickman, & Morrissey, 1987; Friedman, Utada, & Glickman, 1987). *Family therapy* and parent training for prevention has been associated with eliminating or reducing drug use, especially with younger children. Family therapy alone is not ideal because it does not attend to all contextual and internal factors of drug use. Family therapy, however, seems to be more effective than unstructured peer group therapy for adolescents and should be used when possible (Crits-Christoph & Siqueland, 1996). *Cross-age peer group therapies* show promise, as do guided group activities. The most effective treatment programs include involving adolescents in peer group activities (such as the recreational and other activities) during treatment incorporating cross-age role-modeling. Finally, *recreational, vocational, and educational activities* should also be included in multimodal treatment. In particular, programs that allow adolescents to develop pro-social skills and healthy behavior and to learn information applicable to their lives are highly related to post-treatment success and should be incorporated as part of a comprehensive treatment approach (Catalano, Hawkins, Wells, Miller, & Brewer, 1990–1991).

Individual choice in participation.   Perceived choice at all levels of treatment consistently predicts both treatment retention and post-treatment outcomes. According to the research, perceived choice at entry and during treatment predicts a positive attitude toward treatment, positive treatment progress, and reduced post-treatment drug use (Miller & Rollnick, 2002). So, strategies such as motivational interviewing and others based on encouraging self-selected change and self-decisions are apt to have greater long-term effectiveness for reducing or ameliorating drug and alcohol use (Miller & Rollnick, 2002).

Individual risk and protective factors. To understand the differential patterns of adolescent drug involvement, previous research points to the influence of biological, social, and psychological "risk factors" and "protective factors." Reducing risk factors and enhancing protective factors is central to treatment. Risk factors for adolescent drug use include exposure to peer, sibling, or parental substance use, availability of drugs, family pathology, poor parental monitoring, peer drug use, and other factors (Dishion, 2001; P. T. McWhirter, 1998). Interestingly, Newcomb and Felix-Ortiz (1992) have found that risk factors for substance use tend to be social and environmental in nature, whereas protective factors tend to be psychological and interpersonal. Thus, an effective treatment program should counter salient environmental risk factors while enhancing personal and interpersonal protective factors, and build on intrapersonal skills and interpersonal strategies that young people already have.

Multiculturally sensitive. Intervention must consider ethnic, cultural, and individual differences. For example, many young people of color are struggling with acculturation issues along with common developmental concerns. Different ethnic groups have social norms about acculturation that must be integrated into treatment (Gloria & Robinson-Kurprius, 2000). So, substance use treatment must include attention to human diversity, the cultural and ethnic differences of young people and what this means in terms of developing relationships and influencing behavior, and additional pressures, such as "minority stress," that children and adolescents of color usually face each day of their lives.

SPECIFIC INTERVENTION: MOTIVATIONAL INTERVIEWING

Motivational interviewing (MI) is a counseling approach that has been applied to drug and alcohol use problems, is well supported by research, and includes the core components of best practices (Millers & Rollnick, 2002). Using the "Stages of Change" meta-theory proposed initially by Prochaska and DiClemente (1983, 1986), MI is based on the idea that people proceed through a process of preparing to make a change before actually doing so. Motivational interviewing helps to "motivate" people to both desire and prepare for making a life change. The assumptions of MI are that someone abusing alcohol or drugs will not change their behavior (that is, quit) unless they are ready. Thus, intervention focuses on helping the person realize that the negative consequences outweigh the positive effects of drug use and understand for themselves how the costs are greater than the benefits. Thus, instead of a confrontational approach, traditional in drug and alcohol intervention, MI provides people with personalized feedback and focuses on pointing out discrepancies and inconsistencies in people's self-view with their actual behavior. The counselor is always supportive throughout the process. Current studies (e.g., Stephens, 2001) indicate that MI is effective in reducing adolescent smoking by increasing adolescents' motivation to change and by increasing their interest in participating in smoking cessation programs. For instance, students receiving a motivational enhancement intervention had more favorable outcomes regarding tobacco use (such as trying to quit more frequently and showing greater self-efficacy in their perceived ability to quit) than students who received a school-based tobacco education group intervention (Stephens, 2001).

Relying on the Prochaska and DiClemente (1983) stages of change model, MI is designed to motivate people to progress along the change process, regardless of where they are in the process. The stages of change suggests that people change when they are ready and that the change process is dynamic: People move through established stages from one to the other, but also can move in and out of stages depending on a variety of circumstances and the specific nature of the problem. Therefore, intervention helps people progress through the stages and develop their readiness to change, and provides the skills needed to effect and maintain change.

Prochaska and DiClemente (1983) describe the stages as follows:

- *Pre-contemplation.* Example: Not considering quitting drug or alcohol use.
- *Contemplation.* Example: Considering quitting within a specific time frame, such as within the next month.
- *Preparation.* Example: Characterized by making active plans and attempts to quit drug or alcohol use, sometimes characterized by following through with at least one quit attempt.
- *Action.* Example: Being engaged in and actively involved in treatment.
- *Maintenance.* Example: Typically defined as maintaining abstinence for a specific time period after treatment.

These stages of change describe the discrete steps in the process of an individual's intentional behavior change during treatment. Assessment of where people are along this sequence may also help to monitor and guide substance use treatment and prevention planning in adults and in adolescents (Annis, Schober, & Kelly, 1996; Prochaska & DiClemente, 1983, 1986; Prochaska & DiClemente, 1993; Prochaska, Velicer, DiClemente, & Fava, 1988; Werch & DiClemente, 1994). The appropriateness and potential impact of any given intervention is contingent upon the young person's readiness to change. For example, the clinically appropriate response to a relapse is qualitatively different when an adolescent is in an initial stage of the change process (that is, internally more at the preparation stage) versus the final stage (maintenance). Fundamentally, interventions designed to enhance readiness to change may be necessary before people engage in and benefit from other active treatment strategies (Freeman & Dolan, 2001).

Motivational interviewing includes core intervention components, referred to as FRAMES. Each letter stands for the following important, but not sequential, aspects of counseling:

- *Feedback* of personal status allows the counselor to simply reflect back behavior to an individual without judgment or pressure to change. Sometimes showing a mirror to a client can be very powerful.
- *Responsibility* for change is an emphasis that keeps counseling focused on the choices, consequences, and personal responsibility of the adolescent for changing and reduces focus on external excuses that adolescents may make for engaging in behaviors that they have chosen.
- *Advice* to change allows the counselor to simply suggest to the adolescent that they may be much better off if they consider and follow through with a behavior change. Advice always comes after developing a trusting relationship with the client.
- *Menu* of change options allows counselors to suggest to teens and to parents treatment alternatives. As opposed to narrowing options, this method lets adolescents and

families choose what they believe will work for them at any given time. Providing a menu of treatment options is central to the idea of allowing adolescents and families to make choices about the treatment they receive.

- *Empathetic* counselor style is something that occurs from the very outset of counseling and highlights the importance of accepting people where they are, being nonjudgmental about their behavior, and accepting them as people who are struggling. Acceptance facilitates change and skillful reflective listening is a powerful intervention for understanding clients and for helping them to feel heard.
- *Self-efficacy* for change means that adolescents develop the skills needed to quit or reduce use, find and enter into more positive social and support environments, and develop confidence that they can quit.

Some of the fundamental principles of MI are well integrated into the FRAMES list and include the following. *Expressing empathy*, as described above, is paramount. Helping clients *develop discrepancies* is also critical. This involves helping clients see for themselves the consequences of their actions, and that the consequences of their actions are often in conflict with stated goals. By pointing out discrepancies, clients present their own arguments for change rather than the counselor doing it for them as is more common in traditional interventions. *Avoiding argumentation* is important because arguments are counterproductive. Defending a position (e.g., "Abstinence is the only way to improve your life!") nearly always breeds defensiveness in the client and enhances a client's resistance to change. *Rolling with resistance* means that instead of "boxing with" the client (that is, trying to get clients to see the counselor's point of view and entering into a power struggle with clients), it is best to "dance with" clients (that is, see their resistance as a coping strategy, which suggests that clients have some important strengths that you can build on) (Miller & Rollnick, 2002). Finally, *supporting self-efficacy* means communicating belief in the clients' ability to change. This can be a powerful motivator. It means providing clients with hope and with a range of available behavioral alternatives that they might use to act differently. Supporting self-efficacy means to communicate clearly to clients that responsibility for personal change rests solely within them and that they have the capacity to make the change.

Motivational interviewing meets the core components of best intervention practices. It is multimodal. It is well adapted to include individual counseling, can be applied to family counseling (e.g., Dishion & Kavanagh, 2000), can involve peers in the treatment process, and is sensitive to cultural and individual differences. Motivational interviewing also highlights the notion of perceived choice. Adolescents make their own decisions about change, and interventions are based on where an adolescent is along the change path. Using the stage model framework, therapeutic interventions at each stage incorporate stage-appropriate strategies to motivate and prepare the adolescent for the next stage. These interventions increase the adolescent's intrinsic sense of choice throughout treatment. Motivational interviewing is also sensitive to individual, cultural, and ethnic group differences. This is essential because studies show that the reasons adolescents use drugs vary according to their ethnicity. Additionally, youth of color may have a higher risk of post-treatment relapse due to the greater number of environmental and contextual risk factors they face (e.g., possibly greater overall presence and availability of drugs within some communities). Motivational interviewing accounts for potential cultural and environmental differences and is flexible enough to integrate specific risk and protective factors in its approach. Fundamentally, MI is very respectful of clients' world-view, helps clients to identify their own strengths, and supports their own decisions of what changes to make and when. Similar to the solution-focused brief therapy model we presented in Chapter 6, we encourage you to read more about MI as an effective approach to working with adolescents who have a drug or alcohol problem.

CONCLUSION

Drugs and alcohol are widely used and their abuse imposes great social, economic, and personal costs on individuals, communities, and society as a whole. The most effective prevention strategies involve schools and families, and treatment is most effective when families, schools, and the community collaborate. Understanding and attending to the influence and attitudes of the peer cluster are critical for both deterring and treating the problems caused by drug use. Only by helping young people to understand themselves, their motives and coping strategies, and their responsibility for their actions and for creating change in their own lives will the negative influences of alcohol and drug use among adolescents be diminished.

CHAPTER 8

TEENAGE PREGNANCY AND RISKY SEXUAL BEHAVIOR

▲ *A young girl-woman, without education,*
without resources, stressed and depressed,
rears her baby alone and
bends like the poplar.
Gentle summer rains nourish the soil . . . but
where do the poplars and the waters meet?

J. J. McWhirter

Chapter Outline

▲   Problems related to adolescent sexual activity are broad-ranging and complex, including pregnancy, abortion, sexual identity difficulties, human immunodeficiency virus (HIV), acquired immunodeficiency syndrome (AIDS), other sexually transmitted diseases (STDs), childhood molestation and incest, and sex-related violence. No one chapter can fully attend to the interpersonal, psychological, and social implications of these issues. We focus on two critical problems related to a young person's sexuality, sexual development, and sexual activity: the problem of "babies having babies," and HIV/AIDS and other STDs.

More specifically, in this chapter we discuss (a) the incidence and frequency of teenage sexual behavior and teenage pregnancy, (b) factors associated with teen pregnancy, (c) the consequences of teen pregnancy, (d) incidence of AIDS and HIV among teens, and finally, (e) we discuss prevention and treatment strategies.

The Scope of the Problem

After steady increases in births to adolescent mothers in the 1980s, teen pregnancy, abortion, and birth rates have been steadily declining every year since the early 1990s (National Campaign to Prevent Teen Pregnancy, 2001). The decline has been attributed to the leveling off of sexual activity and increased use of contraceptives (Ventura, Martin, Curtin, Mathews, & Park, 2000). Not only have these rates maintained their downward trend among all racial and ethnic groups, but according to one source, teen birth rates are now at their lowest recorded level ever (National Campaign to Prevent Teen Pregnancy, 2001). Analysis of data from an ongoing national survey of high school students concluded that although overall sexual experience decreased 11% among American high school students between 1991 and 1997, sexual activity among female and Latino students showed no significant decrease (Centers for Disease Control & Prevention [CDCP], 1998). Even with the reported decreases, more than four in ten teenage girls get pregnant before age 20, which translates into nearly 900,000 teen pregnancies/year (National Campaign to Prevent Teen Pregnancy, 2001). There are nearly 500,000 live births annually among 15- to 19-year-olds in the United States (National Center for Health Statistics, 1999).

Even with recent declines the United States still has the highest teen pregnancy and birth rates among comparable industrialized nations, twice as high as Great Britain, ten times higher than the Netherlands (National Campaign to Prevent Teen Pregnancy, 2001), and higher than pregnancy rates in over 50 developing nations (McDevitt, 1996). In countries with lower teen pregnancy rates, contraceptive services are confidential, widely available, and very inexpensive or free (Brown & Eisenberg, 1995). Approximately 78% of teen pregnancies are unplanned (Alan Guttmacher Institute [AGI], 1999), with childbirths among unmarried girls higher among African Americans than European Americans (Dixon, Schoonmaker, & Philliber, 2000).

Eight in ten girls and seven in ten boys are sexually inexperienced at age 15 — so most very young teens have not had intercourse (AGI, 1999). By the time they graduate from high school, however, about two-thirds of all students have had intercourse. The younger women are when they first have intercourse, the more likely they are to have had involuntary or unwanted first sex (National Campaign to Prevent Teen Pregnancy, 2001). Regular use of alcohol, cigarettes, and marijuana by 14- and 15-year-olds is also related to their engagement in sexual intercourse (AGI, 1994). According to the Youth Surveillance Survey by the CDCP (2002), among the 33.4% of currently sexually active students nationwide, 25.6% had used alcohol or drugs at last sexual intercourse. Male students (31%) were significantly more likely than female students (21%) to have used alcohol or drugs at last sexual intercourse. Overall, European American and Latino students (28% and 24%, respectively) were significantly more likely than African American students (18%) to have used alcohol or drugs at last sexual intercourse (CDCP, 2002).

Although contraceptives can prevent pregnancy, they can be complicated to use and difficult and expensive to obtain. They may also seem unnecessary to teenagers, even though a sexually active teenage girl who does not use contraceptives has a 90% chance of becoming pregnant within one year (AGI, 1999). Teen girls use contraceptives much more sporadically than older women (AGI, 1999). Teenage women's contraceptive use at first intercourse rose from 48% to 65% during the 1980s, mostly due to the doubling in condom use. By 1995, contraceptive use at first intercourse reached 78%, with two-thirds of it being condom use (AGI, 1999). However, 41% of African American, 60% of Latina, and 51% of European American female students failed to use condoms at last sexual intercourse, leaving them at risk for pregnancy and sexually transmitted diseases (Kann, Kinchen, Williams, et al., 1998). Meanwhile, consistent contraceptive use has been significantly related to factors such as high academic expectations, good relationships with both parents, lower rates of involvement in delinquency and substance use, lower association with deviant peers, and for males, more frequent attendance of religious services (Costa, Jessor, Fortenberry, & Donovan, 1996).

Additional data shows that about 33% of students in grades 9 through 12 nationwide report that they are currently sexually active (CDCP, 2002) and among those, nearly 60% reported that they had used a condom during last sexual intercourse. Male students were significantly more likely than female students to report condom use, and African American students were more likely to report condom use than European American or Latino students. Nearly 20% reported that either they had used birth control pills before last sexual intercourse, with female and European American students more likely to report birth control pill use than male, Latino, and African American students. It has been estimated that teenage women would experience an estimated 385,800 additional unintended pregnancies annually if publicly subsidized contraceptive services were not available; therefore, publicly funded contraceptive services annually avert about 154,700 teen births, 183,300 abortions, and 47,800 miscarriages or spontaneous abortions every year (Forrest & Samara, 1996).

The response of adolescents to pregnancy is changing as well. The teen abortion rate in the United States declined by 21% between 1991 and 1995 and more teens chose to give birth rather than to terminate their pregnancies (Henshaw, 1998a). Nonetheless, teenagers receive more than 25% of all the abortions performed in the United States, giving the United States the highest rate of teen abortion among developed, industrialized countries (Brown & Eisenberg, 1995). Additionally formal adoption among teens has declined sharply over recent decades, with less than 1% placing their children for adoption (Child Trends, 1996). Children of teens in Latino, African American, and Native American families are often parented or informally adopted by a member of the extended family. Current trends also suggest that adolescent girls would rather have an abortion than carry an unwanted pregnancy to term and relinquish the baby for adoption.

The rise in adolescent sexual activity and subsequent pregnancies, abortions, and births that occurred up until the 1990s has been attributed to a variety of factors. We review these next.

PRECURSORS OF TEEN PREGNANCY: COMMON BACKGROUND CHARACTERISTICS

Family and social issues as well as psychological and interpersonal characteristics contribute to teen pregnancy. In this section we discuss (a) issues related to adolescent development; (b) antecedent characteristics that set the stage for teen pregnancy; (c) interpersonal influences, such as peer relationships and family dynamics; and (d) the media.

Adolescent Development

In view of the normal challenges of adolescence, it is not surprising that many teens are involved in sexual activity or that pregnancy so frequently results. One of the primary ways in which adolescents attempt to negotiate the transition from childhood to adulthood is through sexual activity. Even though more than 80% of teenage parents never expected or wanted to conceive a child, many teens see sexual activity as a way to develop adult identity (Melchert & Burnett, 1990; Musick, 1993). Teens look to the opposite sex for valida-tion and approval. Sexual behavior also provides a means of challenging parents on the way toward independence (Musick, 1993).

Adolescence is an important time in the formation of identity, including sexual iden-tity. Experimentation with opposite and same-sex partners is often a part of the learning ex-periences that assist young people in understanding their sexual selves. Young people engaging in same-sex activity often do not identify as gay or lesbian. One study of male ado-lescents who reported same-sex intercourse found that 54% identified themselves as gay, 23% as bisexual, and 23% as heterosexual (Ryan & Futterman, 1998). Models of gay/lesbian identity development characterize the process of developing a positive gay, lesbian, or bi-sexual (GLB) identity as a series of nonlinear and potentially reoccurring stages (Fassinger, 2000; E. H. McWhirter, 1994; O'Connor, 1992). For GLB teens of color, the process of de-veloping a positive ethnic identity may conflict with the development of a positive sexual identity. GLB adolescents confront the task of forming a stigmatized identity just at a time when sameness and affiliation with peers are very important, and they may withdraw from their peers, stifle expression of their feelings and experiences, or develop a false identity. All of these strategies create anxiety. Not surprisingly, drug use, running away, family rejection, and risky sexual behavior are significant problems among GLB adolescents

Preparation for career, marriage or partnership, and family life is part of this devel-opmental period for all adolescents, and sexual activity serves as a way for young people to test these future roles. When an unwanted pregnancy occurs, the developmental process is accelerated. Adolescents must cope immediately with adult roles: parenthood, finding a job, and dealing with social isolation and loneliness. In many cases they become depen-dent on public aid for survival. For many girls, pregnancy limits life options. However, if they already believe themselves to be restricted in their educational, occupational, and economic opportunities, having a child may not alter their perceptions of life options.

Antecedent Characteristics

A variety of personal and demographic characteristics place teens at risk for premature pregnancy. Higher self-esteem decreases the risk of pregnancy for Latino and African American teens (Berry, Shillington, Peak, & Hohman, 2000), but delinquent activity and alcohol use have been found to precede teen pregnancy (Hockaday, Crase, Shelley, & Stockdale, 2000). Among urban African American girls, living in a more disorganized neighborhood, having low school expectations, holding deviant values, being a gang mem-ber, and engaging in status offenses in early adolescence were found to be the greatest risk factors for adolescent sexual activity. For these girls pregnancy may represent a source of gratification and independence (Lanctot & Smith, 2001). African American pregnant girls are proportionally more likely to participate in status offenses than their sexually active but nonpregnant peers (Berry, Shillington, Peak, & Hohman, 2000). Teens at risk for preg-nancy are also likely to reject social norms, to have limited knowledge of their own physi-ology, to have difficulty using information about birth control, to be biologically mature, and to have little structured religious orientation (Brown & Eisenberg, 1995; Haveman & Wolfe, 1994). Finally, a young woman's socioeconomic status (Berry, Shillington, Peak, & Hohman, 2000), perception of opportunity, and her educational expectations are crucial determinants of pregnancy (Hockaday, Crase, Shelley, & Stockdale, 2000; National Cam-paign to Prevent Teen Pregnancy, 2001).

Teens born to poor and less-educated teenage parents are more likely to bear children during adolescence (Berry, Shillington, Peak, & Hohman, 2000; Haveman & Wolfe, 1994; National Campaign to Prevent Pregnancy, 2001). Lower educational and career opportunities and coming from a single-parent family or from a family marked by marital strife and instability also increase risk. School dropouts are more likely to start sexual activity earlier, fail to use contraception, become pregnant, and give birth (Brewster, Cooksey, Guilkey, & Rindfuss, 1998; Manlove, 1998; Darroch, Landry, & Oslak, 1999). Teens who give birth are much more likely to come from poor or low-income families (83%) than teenagers who have abortions (61%) or teenagers in general (38%) (AGI, 1999). Finally, early childbearing is associated with conduct disorder, as well as lower IQ, educational attainment, and SES (Jaffee, 2002).

Interpersonal Influences

One of the primary interpersonal variables associated with adolescent pregnancy is the teen's relationship with his or her parents. Perceptions of high levels of warmth, love, caring, and connection with parents, as well as parental disapproval of teen sex, have been associated with delay of sexual activity among teenagers (Resnick et al., 1997). A close mother-daughter relationship, in particular, encourages girls to turn to their mothers for nurturance. Communication between mother and daughter about sexual issues and feelings and behaviors can significantly help daughters learn and practice responsible sexual behavior. Such communication desensitizes the topic of sex, helps teens overcome negative feelings about the changes in their bodies, and provides information about birth control. In addition, girls who are close to their mothers are more likely to abstain from sex or to practice birth control (Dittus & Jaccard, 2000; Levin, Whitaker, Miller, & May, 1999). A good mother-daughter relationship also provides a girl with a model for responsible sexual behavior and for maintaining a good relationship with a future partner (Apter, 1990).

On the other hand, families characterized by poor interpersonal relationships, ineffective communication, and limited problem-solving skills typically foster in teens the need to turn to peers for nurturing relationships. In turn, pressure from peers can lead to norms of risky behavior and irresponsibility. In one study, Cowley and Tillman (2001) found that boyfriends' attitudes toward having children was the only significant predictor of teenage girls' attitudes about pregnancy. Peers can provide support, fairly clear norms, and the structure that most adolescents want and, along with the media, are a primary source of information about sex. Unfortunately, adolescents who confidently share information may lack knowledge about their own bodies and about contraception, and may often encourage premature and irresponsible sexual decisions in others.

Finally, once a girl becomes pregnant, her mother usually has the most influence on the outcome, but not always (see Box 8.1). Often the mother pressures her pregnant daughter to keep the child. In this case, the relationships between mother, daughter, and baby tend to become confused, with the new grandmother taking on primary responsibility for the infant. Although these teen mothers may indeed have family support, the pressure to keep the baby in the family usually restricts their educational and occupational attainment (Haveman & Wolfe, 1994). Often this choice places the babies in a similar situation of restricted future options, and the cycle of "babies having babies" is perpetuated.

▲ Box 8.1

Daddy's Girl

When 16-year-old Susan and her father came for counseling to work on their relationship, she appeared sullen, depressed, and angry. When I met with her alone, she explained that her father had tricked her into coming by telling her he was taking her shopping. She confided that she was pregnant, that her father did not know, and that she hadn't been able to hold down food for three straight days. Susan's mother had "run off years ago." Susan reported that she had had one abortion already and was very reluctant to have another one. When I saw her father alone, he told me that he knew she was pregnant—"Well, that's why I brought her to you." He emphasized several times, "I'm a hundred percent behind her. I support Susan all the way." He told her the same thing when the two were brought together and she acknowledged her pregnancy. In the same breath he told her, "The decision is totally up to you. But of course, if you decide not to get an abortion, you'll have to live somewhere else."

Susan did not show up for her next appointment. She sounded tearful when she answered the phone.

"Couldn't you make it in today?" I asked.

"No, I'm sick. Well . . . I had an abortion this morning."

Despite repeated calls and letters to her father, he would not bring her in for additional counseling. So far as her "supportive" father was concerned, Susan no longer had a problem.

Media Influences

Young people are bombarded with sexual messages and images in entertainment and advertising that reflect premature, risky, and irresponsible sexual behavior. More than one-half of the programming on television has sexual content (Cope & Kunkel, in press). Further, the CDCP (2001) found that 38.3% of students watch television for more than 3 hours per day during an average school day, with male, African American, and Latino students having the highest rates of television viewing. Rock music videos, rap music, cable channels and movies are even more sexually explicit than television. Virtually every R-rated movie contains at least one nude scene, and some favorites contain as many as 15 instances of sexual intercourse in less than 2 hours (DuRant et al., 1997). Finally, children have easy access to pornography on the Internet. Children's chat rooms have linked sexual perpetrators to their victims. Among young people 10 to 17 years of age who regularly use the Internet, one-fourth had encountered unwanted pornography and one-fifth had been exposed to unwanted sexual solicitations or approaches (Finkelhor et al., 2000). Parental monitoring of children's Internet use is critical; however, sexually explicit Web sites may be entered even when there are no indicators of sexual content at that link.

Running parallel to media inundated with sexual content is a reluctance to depict contraception use. For instance, in 2001, only Fox, CBS, and NBC permitted condom advertising, which was largely restricted to late night television (Wilke, 2001). These policies are far more conservative than the average American. In a national random survey of adults, 60% believed that cigarettes and 47% believed that hard liquor should not be advertised on television, while only 25% believed that condoms should not be advertised on television (Princeton Survey Research Associates, 2001). Nearly 40% of the sample believed that condom advertising *should* be permitted throughout daytime and nighttime television.

Interestingly, 95% of U. S. adults and 85% of U.S. teenagers think that children and teenagers should receive a strong societal message that they should abstain from sex until after high school, and nearly 60% of U.S. adults think that sexually active teenagers should have access to contraception (Princeton Survey Research Associates, 1997). Just as the mass media can encourage risky sexual behavior, it has an undeniable potential for presenting helpful and healthy information. For example, more than one-half of the high school students in a national survey reported that they had learned about birth control, contraception, or preventing pregnancy from television; almost two-thirds of the girls and 40% of the boys said they had learned about these topics from magazines (Sutton, Brown, Wilson, & Klein, 2002).

CONSEQUENCES OF EARLY CHILDBEARING

When a teenage girl becomes pregnant, her physical, social, educational, and career development is significantly altered. An unwanted child has consequences for the mother's socioeconomic status, educational attainment, health, and family development.

Socioeconomic Consequences

A teenage girl who decides to keep her baby is likely to suffer consequences in the form of substandard housing, poor nutrition and health, unemployment or underemployment, an end to her schooling, inadequate career training, and financial dependency (Robinson, Watkins-Ferrell, Davis-Scott, & Ruch-Ross, 1993; Way & Leadbeater, 1999). She is three times more likely to live in poverty than women who delay childbirth until age 20 or older, earns half the lifetime income of her counterparts who mother after age 20, and is far more likely to require public assistance (National Organization on Adolescent Pregnancy, Parenting, and Prevention, 1995; Robin Hood Foundation, 1996). The cost of adolescent pregnancy has been estimated at nearly 9 billion dollars annually, in the form of health care, foster care, and the incarceration rates associated with adolescent childbearing (Robin Hood Foundation, 1996).

Educational Consequences

Teen pregnancy is associated with low achievement scores and limited vocational and educational expectations. Clearly, youth at risk for becoming parents are also at risk for dropping out of school and are more likely to be unemployed or underemployed throughout much of their lives. In recent years, the proportion of teenage mothers with high school diplomas has increased, in large part because many school districts now provide alternative high schools or school programs for student mothers. The High School Equivalency Program (HEP) is a federally funded program that can be helpful to teenage mothers and fathers, although it is not specifically designed for them. This program brings adult Latino farm workers or their family members to a university campus for 8 weeks of study, career planning, and preparation for the GED (see *http://www.uoregon.edu/~hep/home.html*). However, although 70% of teenage mothers eventually complete high school, they are much less likely to go on to college (AGI, 1999).

The educational problems faced by adolescent parents are frequently carried over into the next generation. A disproportionate number of the children born to teenagers show more emotional and behavioral problems while growing up (Thomson, Hanson, & McLanahan, 1994; Zill, Morrison, & Coiro, 1993). These children also have more erratic attendance records, poorer school performance, and lower college expectations (Astone & McLanahan, 1991; Moore, Morrison, & Greene, 1997). As might be expected, teen parents' children have been found to have less supportive and stimulating home environments, poorer health, and lower cognitive development, and are more likely to become teen parents themselves (National Campaign to Prevent Teen Pregnancy, 2001).

Health-Related Consequences

Pregnant adolescents commonly experience poor nutrition, poor health, and limited access to and use of health services. One-third of pregnant teens receive inadequate prenatal care. Prenatal, perinatal, and postnatal problems are more common among younger than among older mothers, and more of their babies die, likely because younger mothers infrequently seek prenatal care in their first trimester. The younger the mother, the higher the incidence of pregnancy-related problems such as anemia, toxemia, infections of the urinary tract, cervical trauma, and premature birth (Advocates for Youth, 1994). Of course, these problems are compounded for teenagers who live in poor socioeconomic conditions. In comparison with older women, younger girls also have problems with premature delivery and are at greater risk of very long labor (American College of Obstetricians and Gynecologists, 1993). Additionally, the maternal mortality rate for mothers under age 15 is 60% greater than for mothers in their 20s (Advocates for Youth, 1994).

Children of teenage mothers also have serious health problems. Babies born to teen mothers are more likely to be low birth weight, to have childhood health problems, and to be hospitalized than those who are born to mothers in their 20s or older (AGI, 1994; National Campaign to Prevent Teen Pregnancy, 2001; Robin Hood Foundation, 1996). Infant mortality is highest among younger teen mothers and African American teen mothers (Ventura, Matthews, & Hamilton, 2002). Low birth weight, congenital problems, and sudden infant death syndrome account for nearly half of infant deaths in the United States (Ventura, Matthews, & Hamilton, 2002).

Family Development

Few teen pregnancies actually involve marriage. Of the girls who do marry, nearly a third are divorced within 5 years, compared to 15% among couples who marry later. Most children born to teen mothers will spend at least part of their lives in single-parent homes (AGI, 1994). Indeed, many teenage fathers never acknowledge parenthood. Some of these boys never know that they are fathers, but many do know and are simply unwilling to deal with the responsibilities of parenthood (Arendell, 1995; Kiselica, 1995).

Teenage mothers are at a great disadvantage when they attempt to create a healthy and stimulating environment for their children. They are often forced to work long hours and may have little time to spend with their babies. These problems may be compounded by neglect, because teen mothers often know little about what babies need to thrive. Teen mothers experience a great deal of stress, and the potential for child abuse is significant (Becker-Lansen & Rickel, 1995). Boyer and Fine (1992) and Walker (1996) suggest that the high rate of maltreatment inflicted by adolescent mothers on their own children is more likely to be associated with the stress of their histories as abuse victims rather than the immaturity associated with their young age. In one study, 65% of pregnant and parenting teen mothers reported nonvoluntary sexual activity and 44% reported having been raped, with the average age of first rape at 13.3 years (U.S. Department of Health and Human Services, 1998). Children of adolescent mothers are 83% more likely to become mothers before age 18, two to three times more likely to run away from home, and more than twice as likely to become victims of abuse and neglect as children of mothers in their 20s or older; and sons of teen mothers are 2.7 times more likely to end up in prison (Robin Hood Foundation, 1996). The multiple environmental and developmental challenges that adolescent mothers must deal with often result in a lack of attention to and knowledge about promoting the optimal development of the baby, which lays a foundation for a continued cycle of teen pregnancy.

Even in the best of circumstances, the developmental tasks of adolescence and parenthood stand in sharp contrast. Sadler and Catrone (1983) identified points of conflict between adolescence and the demands of parenthood, including narcissism vs. empathy, egoism vs. mother and child mutuality, identity formation vs. maternal identity, role experimentation vs. maternal role definition, emancipation from the family vs. family role assignment, sexual identity development vs. body image changes, and cognitive development from concrete to formal operations vs. requirements for high-level problem solving. There is evidence that psychosocial adjustment is an important predictor of a variety of outcomes for teen mothers. For example, one longitudinal study found that prenatal socioemotional adjustment (as measured by measurements of social competence, self-esteem, depression, anxiety, and attachment to mother) predicted later parenting stress, child abuse potential, and maternal socioemotional functioning, and was also the best predictor of their children's later socioemotional adjustment (Whiteman, Borkowski, Keogh, & Weed, 2001). Finally, Hunt-Morse (2002) found that teenage mothers with higher levels of psychosocial development experienced less parenting stress, reported using fewer dysfunctional parenting practices, and were more confident in their maternal role and their ability to overcome parenting barriers.

AIDS AND OTHER SEXUALLY TRANSMITTED DISEASES

Sexually transmitted diseases (STDs) have extremely serious health consequences that may be irreversible and in the case of herpes and AIDS are incurable. Chlamydia, an infection of the vagina or urinary tract, is the most frequently diagnosed STD among adolescents. Gonorrhea, genital warts, herpes, and syphilis are also common. Approximately one in four teens contract STDs every year (Kirby, 2001). In a single act of unprotected sex with an infected partner, a teen girl has a 1% risk of acquiring HIV, a 30% risk of getting genital herpes, and a 50% chance of contracting gonorrhea (AGI, 1999). African American teenage girls are 24 times more likely to contract gonorrhea than their European American counterparts (CDCP, 1997b). In one study of urban adolescent women, 15.6% were infected with human papilloma virus (HPV), 11% were infected with chlamydia, 7% with gonorrhea, and over 5% with trichomoniasis (Jamison, et al., 1995).

Each day in the United States, as many as 54 young people under the age of 20 are infected with HIV. The total number of reported AIDS cases among 13- to 24-year-olds in the United States was over 31,000 in the year 2000 and most of those in the 20- to 24-year-old age group were infected during their teens. African Americans and Latinos are vastly overrepresented in AIDS cases and the proportion of females among adolescent AIDS cases has grown to 50% (CDCP, 1997a, 1997b). Young men and young women are most likely to have contracted AIDS via sexual contact with men, with only about 10% of reported cases through intravenous drug injection (CDCP, 1997b, 2000). Finally, although rates of contracting AIDS are declining overall, there has not been a comparable decline in the number of newly diagnosed HIV cases among youth (CDCP, 2002).

Knowledge regarding STDs is low in the United States, among teenagers and among adults. For example, one survey found that only 12% of American teens and 4% of adults were aware that STDs infect as many as one-fifth of people in the United States, and 26% of adults and 42% of teens could not name a single STD other than HIV/AIDS (American Social Health Association, 1995). Even more alarming, in a study of sexually active female adolescents, 81% of students indicated that they had "never done anything that could give them a chance of getting AIDS" and most believed that their chance of contracting HIV was "very low" (36%) or "nonexistent" (37%). Asked to indicate reasons for assessing their personal risk as they did, the main reasons included that they were currently monogamous, that they believed their partner was safe and faithful, they believed that they were good at choosing partners carefully, they used condoms, and they did not use injection drugs (Overby & Kegeles, 1994). Note that only one of these reasons, using condoms, is a reliable (though not guaranteed) means of reducing risk of HIV transmission.

Perhaps more than adults, teens tend to feel invulnerable to something as catastrophic as AIDS—"It can't happen to me!" or else "Even if I get it, there will be a cure before it affects me." That attitude coupled with sexual activity, multiple sex partners, and ineffective, sporadic, or no condom use make teenagers very vulnerable for contracting HIV/AIDS. The urgency of dealing with teenage sexual issues as early and as informatively as possible cannot be overestimated. In a nationwide survey of youth in grades 9 through 12, 89% of students reported being taught in school about acquired immunodeficiency syndrome (AIDS) or HIV infection. Overall, European American students (91.1%) were significantly more likely than African American and Hispanic students (86.1% and 80.5%, respectively) to have been taught about AIDS or HIV infection in school. There were no racial/ethnic differences for male students; however, European American female students (90.4%) were significantly more likely than Hispanic female students (81.4%) to have been taught about AIDS or HIV infection in school (CDCP, 2002).

Sexually active adolescent gay males, who are less likely to identify with adult gay communities, are particularly vulnerable to HIV infection (Besner & Spungin, 1995; Cranston, 1991). When adolescents experiment sexually with both male and female partners, teenage boys who experiment with unprotected sex with other males may not see themselves at risk if they do not self-identify as gay, which many do not (Ryan & Futterman,

1998). Research on young men who have sex with men indicates high rates of risky activity; one Los Angeles study found that 55.3% of young men who have sex with men reporting unprotected anal intercourse or bare-backing in the last 6 months (HIV Epidemiology Program, 1996), whereas in a 1996 study of 1,781 young men who have sex with men, 38% reported having unprotected anal sex and 27% reported having unprotected receptive anal sex (Valleroy, MacKellar, & Jacobs, 1996).

GENERAL PREVENTION AND INTERVENTION STRATEGIES

For every dollar spent on adolescent pregnancy programs, 1 cent is spent on primary prevention (Feijoo, 1999). Given the potentially lifelong and life-threatening consequences of risky sexual activity for teens, primary prevention requires far greater resources. The U.S. Surgeon General recently issued a Call to Action in which he described the deplorable state of sexual health in the United States and requested nationwide collaboration in providing, among other things, high-quality sex education in schools and communities (Office of the Surgeon General, 2001). Abstinence cannot be counted on as the major means to reduce unintended pregnancy or HIV/AIDS among teenagers. However, abstinence is a critical element for inclusion among available prevention methods. One survey found that eight in ten girls and six in ten boys who were sexually active reported that they wished they had waited until they were older to have sex (National Campaign to Prevent Pregnancy, 2002). Well-being is optimized when sexual intercourse occurs only in the context of a major personal commitment based on caring and mutual consent and on the exercise of personal responsibility, including steps to avoid both STDs and unintended pregnancy. The prevention and treatment interventions presented in this section all reflect this position.

All children and adolescents need appropriate family-life education from the early school years through high school that addresses health, development, family life stages, and so on. Unfortunately, many young people receive little systematic information about sexuality from their parents. Access to information about human sexuality, reproduction, and birth control is a prerequisite for responsible sexual behavior. Because the reasons for teen pregnancy are varied, programs designed to prevent pregnancy should vary as well. In his review of the empirical literature on pregnancy prevention, Kirby (2001) divided prevention programs into three categories: those that focus on the "sexual antecedents" of pregnancy (i.e., sexual attitudes, beliefs, and skills), those that focus on "other antecedents" (i.e., poverty, parental relationships, school failure, depression), and those that address a combination of the two. Programs focused on sexual antecedents are typically referred to as sex education or HIV prevention programs. Unfortunately, most existing programs need to be better evaluated.

Sexual Antecedent Programs

Among those providing outcome data and that focus on sexual antecedents, Kirby (2001) identifies characteristics common to the most effective sexual antecedent programs. These programs deliver and consistently reinforce a clear message about abstaining from sexual activity and/or using condoms or other forms of contraception. They focus on reducing one or more risky sexual behaviors, provide basic and accurate information about the risks of teen sexual activity and ways to avoid intercourse or use protection against pregnancy and STDs, and include activities that address social pressures that influence sexual behavior. Successful programs provide examples of and practice with communication, negotiation, and refusal skills, and they tailor program goals, methods, and materials to the age, sexual experience, and culture of the students. Such programs are based on theoretical approaches that have been demonstrated to influence other health-related behavior and identify specific important sexual antecedents to be targeted. They employ teaching methods designed to involve the participants and have them personalize the information, last a sufficient length of time (i.e., more than a few hours), and select teachers or peer leaders who believe in the program and then provide them with adequate training (Kirby, 2001, p. 10).

Nonsexual Antecedent Programs

Programs focusing on the nonsexual antecedents of teen pregnancy addressed such issues as poverty, school detachment, lack of parental connections, and vocational aspirations. Kirby (2001) categorized these programs into several subgroups: early childhood programs, service learning programs, vocational education programs, and other youth development programs. Participants in one early childhood program that provided developmental enrichment and parent involvement components had, by age 21, delayed childbearing by more than a year longer than control group members. The four empirically evaluated vocational education programs, which provided an intensive focus on academic development, vocational development, and support services, were *NOT* effective in decreasing sexual activity or pregnancy rates, or in increasing use of contraceptives. Clearly, vocational education is not in and of itself a tool for preventing pregnancy. Two programs designed to increase parental connection by teaching parenting skills showed evidence of reducing pregnancy rates.

The most effective nonsexual antecedent programs were service learning programs. These programs combined voluntary community service with structured time for preparation and reflection before, during, and after the service activity. The programs were successful in reducing rates of pregnancy. Kirby (2001) speculates that the success of these programs may have been due to one or more of the following elements: participants form relationships with caring adults, participants increase their sense of autonomy and social competence, participants are supervised after school while carrying out their service activities, or participants see themselves as able to make a contribution to others.

Although sex education is still controversial in some communities, less than 5% of parents excuse their children from sex education classes (Haffner, 1994). Despite sentiments to the contrary, HIV and sex education programs do not increase the frequency of sexual activity or hasten the onset of intercourse (Kirby et al., 1994; Kirby, 2000, 2001). The National Campaign to Prevent Teen Pregnancy (2001) reports that in addition to *not increasing* rates of sexual activity, many sex and HIV education programs have actually been found to delay the onset of sex, reduce the frequency of sex, reduce the number of partners, and increase contraceptive use and thereby substantially decrease unprotected sex. An overwhelming majority of Americans support providing sex education in junior and senior high schools. Most Americans want students to have information to protect themselves against unplanned pregnancy and STDs and oppose the portion of the federal law that funds abstinence-only-until-marriage education (Advocates for Youth, 1999;

Smith, 2000). Of course, teaching young people about contraception while denying their access to it is unlikely to be effective.

School-based interventions for pregnant and parenting adolescents also significantly decrease the occurrence of repeat births among adolescents (Key, Barbosa, & Owens, 2001). Useful components of such programs include peer and/or group counseling, education and career planning, facilitated access to contraceptives, and a project coordinator who is a close cultural match to participants. Preventive strategies aimed at more distant social contextual factors such as urban and family disadvantage are also important. The impact of these preventive strategies is likely to be mediated through day-to-day student experiences such as school bonding. By intervening with more proximal day-to-day factors, premature transition toward adulthood may be postponed. Therefore, directing preventive efforts toward both distant and proximal risk factors is recommended (Lanctot & Smith, 2001).

Kirby's (2001) review of effective pregnancy prevention programs suggests that skills acquisition is an important part of pregnancy prevention. Young people need skills to avoid pregnancy—skills in decision making, assertiveness, and building self-esteem. (We discuss strategies to teach such skills in Chapter 13.) Young people must learn such skills if they are to know how to regulate intimacy, how to behave in accordance with their personal values and boundaries, and how to avoid the unwanted consequences of sexual activity.

Any skill-building program designed to alter sexual behavior needs to personalize the information so that young people apply it directly and concretely to themselves. Self-understanding aids in personalizing information and increasing motivation. Awareness of the purpose and goals of one's behavior is an extremely important component of self-understanding. Young people at risk for pregnancy need to be encouraged to explore and understand why they are engaging in sexual activity and especially why they are unwilling to use methods that prevent pregnancy and disease. Such understanding helps the young person make better decisions. Adults who work with young people at risk for pregnancy need to understand these underlying goals and purposes as well because they are in a position to help young people make better decisions.

SPECIFIC INTERVENTION: AN ADLERIAN MODEL

One of the best models for understanding child and adolescent behavior is found in Alfred Adler's (1930, 1964; Ferguson, 2001; Hoffman, 1994) concepts of social interest, mistaken goals, and purposive behavior. Rudolf Dreikurs (1964, 1967), the foremost interpreter of Adler's ideas as they apply to the American scene, added another concept: the goals of misbehavior. These concepts are useful for understanding and dealing with a wide range of adolescent problems and issues, and we apply it here specifically as a tool for responding to teenagers in the sexual realm (Clark, 1994; Pryor & Tollerud, 1999; Sweeney, 1998). The concepts are also helpful for younger children. Indeed, Adler, and later Dreikurs, developed child guidance clinics that provided education and counseling to families and parents, not infrequently with very young children. Many school counselors use these ideas to assist young children as well.

In the following paragraphs, we first present the general framework of the model, and then we detail its specific application to issues of sexuality. These recommendations are not a substitute for sexual health education, but are adjunctive to it.

According to Adler, much individual behavior is directed toward finding a place or position in the group. All young people need a sense of belonging and an arena in which to contribute. Low-risk children find belonging first in their families and later in the school environment with peers and adults. In their interaction with their social environment, they find ways to contribute to the common welfare. These contributions increase their social interest, build their feelings of self-worth, and solidify their sense of belonging. Unfortunately, other young people struggle to belong and are frustrated in their attempts to contribute to the social group. But the need to belong continues, and these youth often behave in ways that are less acceptable in the mistaken belief that a particular action will fulfill a certain social need. These mistaken beliefs contribute to what Dreikurs calls the goals of misbehavior. Negative, antisocial, and self-defeating behavior has an underlying purpose—to allow the individual to fit in the group. One way to help at-risk children is to attend to the underlying purposiveness of their behavior: first, to understand their mistaken goals and to respond more appropriately to them, and second, to reveal to the young people their own underlying goals and the purposiveness of their actions.

Purposiveness of Behavior

Purpose is not the same as cause. Cause is past-oriented; purpose is future-oriented. Cause implies a need to search through past history to identify what event, person, or situation brought about the child's present behavior. It also implies that the individual has no agency or influence over his or her own behavior. Purposiveness reflects the goals the youth wants to achieve and the consequences he or she anticipates. In this sense, the young person's behavior is a means to an end and is based on his or her perceptions of reality. Young people behave in ways that they believe will lead to desirable consequences and help them avoid unpleasant ones. Purpose operates in the present and looks toward the future, toward the outcome of behavior, and therefore is more directly open to intervention. The purpose of adolescent sexual activity has been associated with an underlying tendency to nonconformity; Lanctot and Smith (2001) suggest that girls are more likely to respond to this tendency by being self-destructive rather than destructive to others. Adolescent pregnancy may be considered self-destructive behavior, especially when prenatal care is neglected (Lanctot & Smith, 2001).

Goals of Misbehavior

In the Adler/Dreikurs model, a young person's misbehavior may be designed to achieve one or more of four goals: (a) attention (the child wants service and attention), (b) power (the child wants to be boss), (c) revenge (the child desires to hurt others), and (d) inadequacy or assumed disability (the child wants to be left alone). Although young people usually do not think about their behavior in these terms, they do see their actions as logical. Whether they seek attention, attempt to assert power, take revenge, or capitalize on their inadequacy, the corresponding misbehavior is designed to get special recognition. Their behavior, regardless of their goal, results from the belief that this is the most effective way to function in the group, which includes the family and the peer cluster.

Attention.   When children do not achieve acceptance and belonging through useful contributions to the family, they may seek inclusion through attention. At first they may seek attention through socially acceptable means. If these efforts are unsuccessful, they may try any of a vast array of negative behaviors calculated to get attention. The *purpose* of such attention-getting mechanisms (AGMs) is to engage the adult. The young person's underlying goal is to get adults to pay attention. The adult's intervention reinforces the young person's desire for attention, because it's better to be punished than to be ignored.

Attention-getting behaviors are usually negative, but overly cooperative behavior may also be a bid for special attention. It is sometimes difficult to distinguish between behavior that stems from a genuine willingness to be helpful and behavior that is aimed primarily at getting attention. If the youth's behavior seems directed to becoming the best or better than the other children (the teacher's pet), he or she is probably motivated by a desire for attention. Children and adolescents need to be able to derive satisfaction from performing positive, cooperative behaviors rather than simply from the reinforcement that follows. Consider an adolescent girl who gains satisfaction from her pro-social acts only when adults notice them. If her siblings (at home) and classmates (at school) are more successful at gaining adults' attention, she may try to gain attention by being the worst among her peers. Many youth behave negatively because the positive roles they really want are already "taken."

Recognizing when attention is the goal of misbehavior is not simple, but may be inferred when the adult's initial reaction to the behavior is annoyance, irritation, or surface anger, and the child responds to correction by temporarily stopping the disturbing action. Essentially, the scolding, coaxing, helping, reminding, and so forth provide the desired attention, so the behavior stops—temporarily. Understanding the purpose of irresponsible sexual behavior is a more complex task because the behavior may be aimed not only at adults but at peers as well. In some cases, AGMs evoke attention and concern from permissive or indifferent parents. In other cases, AGMs derive from a desire for attention and affection from peers or a specific peer. Sometimes the AGM is directed toward the idealized infant in the hope that the baby may fill an emotional gap left by rejecting parents or the romantic partner. In each instance, the need to belong, to feel needed, to be loved, or to feel increased self-esteem underlies the AGMs.

As part of a research project, one of the authors was debriefing eighth-grade students after they filled out questionnaires about stress. One student, a 12-year-old eighth grader, offered shyly, "well, I don't have a boyfriend, but I met a boy at the mall and I let him put it in me. I know that's how you get a baby, but he said he took it out in time. I hope he's gonna meet me there again." In the course of a subsequent conversation, it was quickly apparent that she was not interested in physical pleasure, nor did she seem to have romantic notions about babies; she simply wanted to feel special.

Boys exhibit purposiveness and mistaken goals in their sexual behavior in experiencing sexual interaction as a means of gaining affection and attention from girls. Sometimes boys establish desired reputations as their sexual exploits gain the attention of their male peers. In some subgroups, fathering a child increases the boy's status and brings him into what he perceives to be a more mature and powerful stage of development.

Power.   When the goal of misbehavior is power, young people attempt to establish their position in the group by dominating, controlling, and manipulating adults and peers. They demonstrate their control and power by refusing to be commanded and by breaking rules. Many use manipulation to demonstrate to themselves and to the world that they do have power over others. If the adult responds to the power struggle by exerting more control or power to force compliance, the young person becomes even more convinced of the value of power. The goal is less to win the struggle than to get the adult involved in it. Once the adult engages in the battle, the teenager has won, regardless of the outcome.

If the adult's anger goes beyond mere annoyance and if the anger is coupled with feelings of being challenged and provoked, then the young person's goal is probably to gain power. The sentences that run through the adult's mind at this point also provide clues to the nature of this power struggle ("I'll show you whose boss around here." "I'll make you do it." "You can't get away with that."). When the adult behaves in accordance with these thoughts, the adolescent may escalate his or her actions or comply outwardly while subtly sabotaging the adult's efforts. Either way, the teenager wins the power struggle.

The underlying goal of power in sexual acting out may be directed against parents who are inconsistent, too permissive, or too strict. On the surface the young person appears to be expressing independence, but in reality the behavior is designed to establish a position vis-à-vis the parents. Willingness or unwillingness to engage in sex may provide girls and boys with perceived power over others or over a specific partner. Willingness to coerce a girl into unprotected intercourse may be based on the mistaken belief that a subsequent pregnancy would secure the relationship. Boys may use sexual activity to demonstrate independence and power over their parents. With their partner or even someone unknown to them, boys may use sex as a physical expression of domination or control through rape and other forms of sexual assault. Sometimes the boy's domineering attitude and his unwillingness to use a condom are attempts to demonstrate power. Assuming that girls are responsible for contraception and denying fatherhood when pregnancy occurs are other ways in which the young male may express domination and power over others through sexual behavior.

Revenge. The child who seeks revenge is extremely discouraged and poses the greatest problem. If children have not been able to attain and maintain a desired position by gaining attention or power, they may consider that the only other way to gain attention is to hurt someone. It is as if they conclude, "I can't be liked and I don't have power—but I *can* be hated." This often violent antagonism provides them with a specific role to play in the group.

Revenge is sought only after a long series of failures has convinced the young person of his or her utter lack of belonging. Revenge is frequently the result of an unrecognized problem (depression, severe learning difficulties, conduct disorder) and of unrealistic expectations and pressures by significant adults. The unrecognized problem may prevent the young person from accomplishing a particular task. Assuming negative motives, adults punish the youth for "not trying." Young people are hurt by such encounters and want to hurt back. In taking this position, they are likely to evoke responses that justify the continuation of revenge, and the cycle escalates.

Feelings of intense anger with underlying hurt and shock in response to a young person's behavior indicate to the adult that the goal of misbehavior is probably revenge. The adult may think: "How could he possibly do that to me?" "This kid is just nasty and unlovable." "How could she be so vicious and cruel?" If the adult's response is full of anger, the adolescent will continue trying to get even. If the adult responds with hurt, sadness, and tears, the youth may actually smile (see Box 8.2).

Premature and irresponsible sexual activity is sometimes a way to get back at parents. One of the authors of this book worked with an angry father whose son had dressed in women's makeup and clothing, and had sexually explicit pictures taken of himself on the

▲ Box 8.2

Lying for Revenge

Some years ago I was co-conducting a consultation with several teenagers and their families. The model we were using called for a large-group meeting that included both parents and teenagers, in which participants discussed family and school concerns. We then broke into smaller groups, the adults in one group and the young people in another.

After several weekly sessions, a girl who had a particularly stormy relationship with her mother used the large-group session as an opportunity to tell her parents that she thought she was pregnant. Her mother's horror and embarrassment were vividly evident. Later, during the session with peers and siblings, the girl reported that she was *not* pregnant and currently wasn't even sexually active. Her earlier false self-disclosure, she concluded, was intended to hurt her mother: a clear instance of revenge. In a later family session this incident became a springboard that enabled us to help her look at the self-defeating aspects of her behavior and to help her family confront their own dysfunction.

family's front porch in daylight. The son left these photos for his father to find, which achieved the desired effect. Sexual behavior can also be used to obtain revenge on the partner if one feels rejected. The person who acts out sexually may intend to get back at the former partner. So, ultimately, the dynamics of revenge are played out not only within the family but also between partners.

Assumed inadequacy. Children and teenagers who expect failure rely on their assumed inadequacy to escape participation in the group and family system. They want to be left alone. As long as nothing is expected of them, they can still appear to be members of the group. Some children and adolescents believe that by hiding behind a display of real or imagined inferiority, they can avoid even more embarrassing and humiliating experiences. Those who feel inadequate and incapable of functioning will not try, whether their deficiency is real or merely assumed.

This goal poses serious problems for parents, teachers, and counselors because these young people realize that underachievement and lack of effort are the most effective ways to keep adults involved with them. Thus, it is convenient for them to continue their lack of effort even when it is no longer necessary. Adults often fail to distinguish between a real lack of ability and a lack of ability that the child or adolescent merely assumes.

Feelings of despair, frustration, and hopelessness in the adult are good signs that the young person is operating on the assumption of inadequacy. Adults should reflect carefully upon the feelings aroused by a young person's misbehavior, because whatever they feel is often exactly what the young person intends them to feel. Despair and hopelessness may be what the child wants, but when the adult responds with despair, inadequacy is reinforced. Such responses encourage continued inadequacy.

Assumed inadequacy in the sexual realm may be expressed by lack of assertiveness regarding sexual activity. The term *assumed* suggests that these adolescents have the skills to resist sexual pressure—from a partner or from peers—or to insist on protection if they do engage in sex but that they do not use these skills. Of course, we know that some young people's inadequacy is not assumed; the lack of skill is real. In such situations the concerned adult can use specific cognitive and behavioral strategies to provide success experiences and reduce the young person's sense of inadequacy. In Chapter 12 we provide a model for building skills, and in Chapter 13 we discuss specific cognitive and behavioral strategies from which young people may benefit.

Summary.   Having reviewed the four goals, we must emphasize that young people are often in pursuit of more than one goal at the same time and that their goals can shift depending on the people with whom they interact. Some young people actually pursue all four goals at one time, a situation that causes parents, counselors, teachers, and other adults a great deal of distress. Some children or teenagers may have one goal at school, another goal with their peers, and still another at home. If the misbehavior is to be understood, the child's actions have to be seen as a whole, as part of the total social environment, not as emanating solely from one situation.

Additionally, sexual behavior does not have an underlying negative purpose for all teens. Needs gratification, reinforcement, pleasure, and desire for warmth, closeness, and validation are all components of sexuality. When teens become pregnant, mixed goals are probably the rule rather than the exception. Allie Andrews, for example, appears to use sex to gain attention from boys. Further, lacking a positive position at home, she has progressed from sex-as-attention to sex-as-power to show her stepfather that she counts. Unfortunately, his criticisms and accusations have led her now to use sex to shock and hurt him. She has adopted the goal of revenge (on her stepfather), and uses her sexual behavior at least partly as a way of getting back at him.

Among the methods that have proved helpful in efforts to intervene with young people who are struggling with these four mistaken goals are corrective procedures, logical and natural consequences, and encouragement. We describe these techniques in the context of risky sexual behavior; however, they can be used with any kind of misbehavior.

Corrective Procedures

Corrective procedures involve (a) altering adults' responses to adolescent's risky sexual behavior and (b) helping the young people to interpret the goals of their sexual activities. Altering the adult's responses (e.g., the parent, teacher, or counselor) begins with identifying the feelings aroused by the youth's behavior (anger, disgust, resentment, despair, whatever) and then *not acting* on those feelings. Helping young people interpret their goals is a bit more complex. If you ask them why they didn't use a condom, the response may be an honest "I don't know," or a hindsight rationalization rather than a factual account of motives ("I just finished a period and didn't think I would get pregnant" rather than, "At that moment, I didn't care what happened to me, even if I got some disease, I was so lonely"). The sensitive counselor or teacher can help young people by proposing some possible goals of their behavior. Such a confrontation can be the first step toward change. To confront the behavior, however, is not to label it ("You're being stupid"). Labeling has no meaning for the young person, does not explain the behavior, and does nothing to change it. Confrontation helps adolescents understand their own motivation and gives them the option of continuing or discontinuing their behavior. Sometimes the behavior loses its appeal once the underlying intention has been brought into the open; other times, the young person is able to identify more effective and less harmful ways of getting their needs met.

The most useful approaches are tentative, beginning with "Could it be that . . ." or "I was thinking that maybe . . ." All questions must be asked in a nonjudgmental way, and not during an argument. It is not enough to help young people identify their goals; it is important to provide them with alternative and less self-defeating goals. All corrective procedures should be geared toward helping young people choose more constructive goals and behaviors.

Corrective procedures for AGMs.   When the goal of risky sexual behavior is attention, the following questions may be helpful: "Could it be that you want him to see you as more special than other girls, by sleeping with him?" "Do other guys respond differently, say with more respect or admiration, when they know you've had sex?" Recognize that punishing, giving service, coaxing, and scolding are forms of attention and may only serve to reinforce the negative behavior. Although ignoring the behavior while it occurs is normally a corrective procedure for AGMs, this strategy isn't useful in the case of risky sexual behavior because adults are not typically present. However, if the young person is bragging about their sexual escapades, ignoring the behavior in the moment may be the most appropriate response.

Corrective procedures for power.   Interpretive questions for power-seekers might include, "Could it be that you want to show your mother that she isn't in control of you?" "It seems to me as though you want her to see you as stronger and in charge, as if that will make her think you are more masculine." It is important to recognize and acknowledge that the young person does indeed have power and choices regarding sexual behavior, even though that behavior has consequences. Refrain from engaging in arguments over sexual behavior, and rather than insisting that rules be followed, put energy into being consistent about imposing consequences when rules are broken. Be willing to negotiate on issues where it is possible for you to do so. And, outside of the context of arguments, help the young person identify other means to establish their sense of power in ways that do not pose health risks to themselves or others. This may include broadening their circle of activities and engaging their leadership and responsibility skills.

In addition to interpreting goals, provide alternative goals that are less self-defeating. One of the authors worked with an adolescent male client who had been having unprotected sex with an older young woman in his father's garage. He quite readily admitted that part of him wanted to be caught, to show his father he was "practically a man" now. After several counseling sessions he decided to, at least temporarily, abandon this tactic and get his ear pierced instead. This action provoked a confrontation with his father that allowed him to express some of his resentment quite directly. When last seen, he and his father had begun a tense but hopeful process of negotiating a new set of freedoms and responsibilities.

Corrective procedures for revenge.   It is of critical importance that the adult refrains from punishment and retaliation, and does not take the young person's revenge behavior personally or show feelings of hurt. When the adult is also the parent, this can be especially difficult and the parent will need support and time to learn better responses. Questions to help the young person identify their goals might include "Could it be that you want to punish your mother for her boyfriend's behavior?" "I'm wondering if you are consciously trying to hurt me, and if you are, I want to understand that."

Corrective procedures for assumed inadequacy.   When the child sees himself or herself as a failure, it may be helpful to ask, "Do you think you're going to flunk out, so you might as well have a child to take care of ?" "I wonder if you think you don't deserve to be protected against diseases." It is important that the adult helper shows encouragement and optimism in the face of the young person's despair. Arranging situations in which he or she can experience success may be critical, and this may require engaging the assistance of teachers, tutors, parents, and siblings.

Some general suggestions for corrective procedures in response to risky sexual activity also include participation in skill-building groups and activities to increase self-esteem, assertiveness, and self-efficacy (see Chapter 13); individual, group, or family counseling; social competency skills building; sex education for the young person and parents; and finally, all interventions and corrections should be geared toward empowering adolescents to identify healthier ways to meet their goals of belonging, inclusion, and recognition.

Natural and Logical Consequences

Natural and logical consequences are also effective ways of dealing with misbehavior. Traditional discipline involves reward and punishment: Adults punish kids for unacceptable behavior and reward them for complying with their wishes and commands. Natural and logical consequences differ from reward and punishment in a number of ways and have certain advantages. The goal of consequences is to teach young people responsibility, cooperation, respect for order and the rights of others, good judgment, and careful decision making, and to give them a sense of control and choice. The goal is not to force submission and compliance, nor is it to obtain retribution and revenge (often the real goal of punishment). To some degree, reliance on consequences removes from the adult the function of meting out rewards and punishment, which de-emphasizes the traditional authority position of the adult. When authority is de-emphasized, young people feel more independent, and that feeling itself decreases undesirable behavior.

Natural consequences are those consequences directly resulting from the behavior. Examples are getting an STD or becoming pregnant. Because natural consequences in this case threaten health and safety, logical consequences should be used, and hopefully, the natural consequences will never be experienced. Clear and unequivocal communication about the natural consequences of risky sexual behavior should be accompanied by encouragement to engage in healthier behavior. Logical consequences are determined in advance, are logically connected to the behavior, and are applied when the misbehavior occurs, for example, "If you have your boyfriend over while I'm at work one more time, you will not be permitted to have any friends over for one month." It is important that logical consequences are not arbitrary or invoked during the heat of an argument. Consequences are administered and experienced in an impersonal, matter-of-fact fashion, without moralizing, judgment, or excessive emotional involvement.

Sometimes another young person can share natural consequences in a way that communicates more effectively than adults can do so. A student of one of the authors gave a speech on how becoming pregnant earlier in high school had drastically changed her life.

She did not "preach" to her classmates, nor was she dramatic in her descriptions. She simply told her story. Her straightforward, unromantic portrayal of daily life had a profound effect on her classmates and generated a lively discussion on the belief that "it could never happen to me." Although the actual effects of her speech cannot be measured, her matter-of-fact and nonjudgmental approach certainly provoked a good deal of nondefensive discussion. Exposing students to the natural and logical consequences of risky sexual behavior through other people's lives may promote some behavior change so they do not have to experience the consequences themselves.

Reliance on consequences is intended to help children develop responsibility for their own behavior. It is not meant to be a vehicle to express the adult's displeasure or anger. Care should be taken that the nonverbal aspects of the interaction do not turn it into covert punishment and thereby defeat the purpose of the entire procedure.

Encouragement

Encouragement greatly enhances the relationship between child and adult and reduces the child's need to resort to undesirable behavior to feel significant. Encouragement is the process of increasing young peoples' sense of worth and self-esteem by focusing on their *actual* strengths and assets, not on *expected* or potential strengths. Encouragement conveys to young people that the adult has faith in them, trusts and respects them, and values them as people despite any mistakes or flaws.

All too often children and teens are exposed to ongoing discouraging experiences. Some adults focus only on the mistakes children make, attributing them to basic defects of character or ability ("He's just lazy." "She's always been clumsy."). Some adults set standards that are difficult or impossible to reach; they compare young people to each other in such a way that there is always a loser. The discouragement and self-doubt that arise from these practices may be manifested in misbehavior and in useless, inappropriate attempts to gain recognition.

Encouragement should be a regular aspect of interactions with all adolescents and children. When a young person is deeply discouraged, the teacher or counselor has the difficult task of counteracting a host of negative experiences. Adults can offer encouragement by recognizing effort and improvement as well as accomplishment, expressing appreciation, separating the deed from the doer when the deed is unacceptable, focusing on the child's or teenager's unique talents and contributions, and treating youth with respect and courtesy. Nonverbal messages are also important. Listening without interruption, using a friendly, nonjudgmental tone of voice, treating mistakes as opportunities for learning rather than as failures, and choosing the right moment for a remark are as important as the choice of words.

Keep in mind that some words that purport to be encouraging have the opposite effect. Some ill-advised attempts at encouragement include: competitive encouragement ("See what you can do when you try?"), coupling encouragement with expectations ("You got an A; that's great. Now let's keep up that average."), expressing surprise at success ("You *did?* I never thought you could do it!"), using someone else as an example ("If Kristin can do it, you can too, I'm sure."), and blaming someone else for a young person's failure ("If it hadn't been for that referee, I'm sure you'd have won.").

In general, anything that perpetuates low self-esteem, that lowers confidence in a child's ability to master problem situations, or that fosters feelings of inadequacy and insignificance is discouraging. Anything that gives a sense of being an important member of the group and a feeling that the child's participation, contribution, and cooperation are valued is encouraging. Above all, it is important for young people to learn that they are good enough as they are.

CONCLUSION

Premature and irresponsible sexual activity, teen pregnancy, and HIV/AIDS are significant social problems. Understanding some of the environmental, family, and peer dynamics that young people encounter and helping adolescents change the goals of their misbehavior may help prevent some of these problems. Because of the long-term consequences of teenage sexual activity, it is critical to provide young people with accurate, comprehensive sex education, including the skills they need to carry out their own informed decisions about sexuality. The growing literature on successful prevention programs indicates that there are specific characteristics associated with reducing pregnancy and unprotected sex, increasing abstinence, and delaying first intercourse.

Additionally, young people's optimistic and positive beliefs about themselves and their capacity to set the direction of their future is an important part of a comprehensive effort to prevent pregnancy and risky sexual behavior. According to Edelman, "The best contraceptive is a real future" (1987, p. 58), and a future requires opportunities to build academic and work-related skills, job opportunities, and life-planning skills. As such, we believe that greater funding to support prevention and promote awareness of program effectiveness is one of the only methods to reduce problems related to teen sexual activity.

ANTISOCIAL BEHAVIOR, DELINQUENCY, AND YOUTH GANGS

▲ *When I feel bad and can't do anything about it,*
Don't even know it, maybe,
I can still pound somebody, smash a windshield, maybe.
At least I have a good reason for feeling bad.
And so what if they do too?

When I feel bad, I can do something about it.
Ripping off lunch money, or something from the store shelf, or the Jacksons' yard,
or even living room, maybe, helps.
The rush covers up bad feelings.
And so what if the feeling becomes me?

When I feel bad, the kids on the street help
I like colors and coats and bright-green shoelaces.
Out here, bad is good.
And being feared is better.

J. J. McWhirter

CHAPTER OUTLINE

▲   In this chapter we present an ecological and developmental model to discuss (a) the nature and scope of antisocial behavior, delinquency, and gang activity; (b) the roots of antisocial behaviors that lead to conduct disorder and delinquency; (c) the development and consequences of youth gangs; (d) several general intervention strategies for youth violence; and (e) a specific intervention based on Glasser's choice theory and reality therapy.

THE SCOPE AND NATURE OF ANTISOCIAL BEHAVIOR, DELINQUENCY, AND GANGS

We use the term *antisocial behavior* to refer to any activity that conflicts with social norms. Sometimes it includes criminal activity, but not always. *Delinquency* implies breaking the law. Not infrequently, antisocial behavior and delinquency include violence. Violence takes many forms, among them organized gang violence, school and community shootings, and self-inflicted violence. Antisocial behavior, delinquency, and violence have common roots and similar consequences. Although not exhaustive, the following list represents the most frequently encountered antisocial behaviors expressed by children and teenagers: (a) expressions of aggression and coercive misbehaviors within the family; (b) aggression in school often leading to the designation of conduct disorder; (c) community and school problems such as fighting and the destruction of property; (d) minor infractions of the law, or *non-index* crimes such as vandalism, substance use, and running away; (e) major infractions of the law, or *index* crimes like theft, robbery, and larceny; and (f) violence and gang membership. An additional category of antisocial behavior, school shootings, warrants more detailed review and is discussed in Chapter 10. Although these areas are related, we discuss them separately to make clear their unique characteristics.

Family Aggression and Violence

Family aggression and violence occur with alarming frequency and can lead to the development of severe antisocial behavior. It is estimated that children witness 10% to 20% of the nation's homicides (Pynoos & Eth as cited in van Dalen & Glasserman, 1997). Violence is the leading cause of injury to women in the home. Between two and four million women are battered by their partners each year (Hughes & Hasbrouck, 1996). An estimated 3.3 million children witness violence in their homes (Krajewski, Rybarik, Dosch, & Gilmore, 1996).

Chronic exposure to violence can have a detrimental developmental effect on children including identification with the aggressor, truncated moral development, and pathological adaptation to violence. Children who observe parents using violence observe not only the violent behavior but also the circumstances of violence, the emotional triggers for violence, and the consequences of violence. These observations significantly influence behaviors.

A related problem in families is poor parental response to challenging children, such as children who are irritable, inattentive, and impulsive. Children with these characteristics tend to be violent later in life (Osofsky, 1997). Often these difficult children are responded to with anger and hostility, followed by attempts to appease the child, leading to inconsistent discipline. Children who view the world as hostile and inconsistent will attempt to get their way regardless of social rules, which creates problems in other contexts as well.

School Problems

Problem behavior at school is often a precursor to more severe antisocial behavior. In fact, well-developed antisocial patterns coupled with high levels of aggression early in a child's life are among the best predictors of delinquency in later years. The general principle is that less serious problem behaviors precede more serious delinquency. Thus, the development of disruptive and delinquent behaviors generally progresses in an orderly fashion following three distinct developmental pathways: authority conflict (e.g., defiance and disobedience); covert actions (e.g., lying and stealing); and overt actions (e.g., delinquency and violent behavior). The first two of these pathways are frequently seen in the school setting. Individuals may proceed along single or multiple developmental pathways toward serious antisocial behavior.

There is also increasing evidence that overall aggression in the classroom increases individual aggression. Aber and his associates (1998) found that children in classrooms with higher overall levels of aggression were at increased risk of developing lower levels of competent strategies, and higher levels of aggressive strategies, aggressive fantasies, and hostile attributional perceptions. Apparently, this higher level of classroom aggression can affect future behavior. In another study (Kellam, Ling, Merisca, Brown, & Ialongo, 1998), overall classroom level of aggression in the first grade increased boys' risk of being aggressive in middle school. Further, the more aggressive first-grade boys who were in more highly aggressive first-grade classrooms were at a markedly increased risk for aggressive behavior 6 or 7 years later. Early aggression patterns characterized by high frequency, intense severity, and occurrence across multiple settings predict a number of ominous outcomes later on, including victimization of others, delinquency, and violent behavior (Loeber & Farrington, 1998).

Conduct disorder (CD) is another problem that impacts schools. CD and its less severe diagnostic cousin, oppositional defiant disorder (ODD), encompass most of the antecedent, precursor behaviors that predict and lead to delinquent and violent behavior in juveniles. CD in particular refers generally to clinically severe antisocial behavior including physical aggression, stealing, fire setting, truancy, and running away. Various estimates of this disorder suggest that it is of serious magnitude with a 2% to 16% prevalence rate (Sommers-Flanagan & Sommers-Flanagan, 1998). The effects of CD and associated delinquent behavior patterns constitute a major social problem; evidence suggests, for example, that disruptions in the classroom that interfere with their teaching and threats to public school personnel have increased (U.S. Department of Education, 1998).

Vandalism

Vandalism is a serious and growing problem in the United States accounting for millions of dollars in damage to school property (Goldstein, 1996). In addition to schools, vandals target parks and playgrounds, city streets, museums, libraries, mass transit vehicles, and numerous other venues.

In the 1980s and 1990s, school and community personnel became increasingly preoccupied with student fights, assaults of teachers, weapon violations, youth gangs, and similar "high-level" aggression. Since then the importance of vandalism has diminished as a social concern. This relative indifference to lower levels of a given negative behavior is unfortunate because it comes at a substantial cost. Aggression toward both property and people is learned behavior. Just as the oppositional child may develop into the conduct-disordered preadolescent and ultimately to the delinquent adolescent, so too may successful young vandals evolve into youth who are assaultive.

Juvenile Delinquency

According to data released by the FBI, youth crime has actually declined over the last 30 years. Arrest figures from 1999 indicate that juveniles account for 17% of all arrests, compared to the all-time high of 26% in the mid-1970s (Snyder, 2000). Also in 1999, 16% of all violent crime arrests were juveniles. The substantial growth in juvenile violent crime arrests that began in the 1980s peaked in 1994. In 1999, for the fifth consecutive year, the rate of juvenile arrests or Violent Crime Index offenses—robbery, forcible rape, aggravated assault, and murder—declined. In 1999, the juvenile violent crime arrest rate was the lowest in the decade.

Ironically, most people continue to believe that juvenile crime is increasing. This may be for a few reasons. First, many young people who engage in antisocial behavior never come to the attention of the justice system and are thus not counted in arrest statistics. Second, the public's misconstrual about juvenile crime may be related to the media sensationalizing of crime, particularly when it is violent and involves young victims and perpetrators. Following the national trend of "get tough on youth crime," a number of states enacted laws to prosecute young juvenile offenders as adults. A fourteen-year-old alleged murderer being tried as an adult makes headline news, and continuing reports of the trial often go on for weeks. Third, the public may believe that youth crime is increasing because although juvenile arrests have actually decreased over the last decade, the average *age* of first offense has become increasingly *younger* over the same time period, making the problem seem worse (Snyder, 2000). Fourth, child and adolescent use of certain drugs, particularly methamphetamines, has risen since 1995, and substance use is highly correlated with law violation by young people. The use or possession of alcohol and other substances has also led to the arrest of many boys and girls. Thus, crime and drug use are highly correlated and their relationship influences social perception. As such, it should also influence our prevention and intervention efforts (see Chapter 7).

Although the decrease in youth crime and juvenile arrests is encouraging news that suggests we have been doing some things well, it is no time for complacency. The Surgeon General reports that surveys consistently find that between 30% to 40% of male youth and 15% to 30% of female youth report having committed a serious violent offense by age 17 (Office of the Surgeon General, 2001). About 2.5 million of the 25 million U.S. children aged 10 to 17 years, 10% of our youth, were arrested in the year 1999 (Snyder, 2000) and about the same in the year 2000 (Lykken, 2001).

Additionally, even though crime statistics in general have gone down across the United States in the last few years, the opposite is true for adolescent girls. The number of girls in the juvenile justice system has been increasing both in percentage and numbers (Acoca, 1999). For example, loitering and curfew violations for girls have increased 150% and drug use violations have increased almost 200% in the last decade.

Gang Membership and Youth Violence

A youth gang is a group consisting primarily of adolescents and young adults who interact frequently with one another, share a common identity expressed through a gang name and common symbols, claim control over a certain geographical area, and are deliberately involved in illegal activities. Estimates indicate that nearly 25,000 gangs with over 770,000 gang members were active across the United States in 2000 (Egley & Arjunan, 2002). Youth in these gangs were responsible for a wide variety of offenses including street crime, drug trafficking, and witness intimidation, and they are highly likely to use firearms in an assault crime (Esbensen, 2000). A high percentage (95%) of gang activity occurred within one or more high schools with as nearly as high of a percentage (91%) of gang activity occurring within one or more intermediate schools. Involvement with gangs remains one of the most powerful predictors of violence (Office of the Surgeon General, 2001).

When one gang gains power and control in an area, rival gangs sometimes relocate to other areas of the city or even to other cities. These divisions of power and region are frequently related to ethnicity, although there is some evidence to suggest that a new type of gang, *hybrid gangs*, is emerging. Hybrid gang culture is characterized by mixed racial and ethnic participation within a single gang (Starbuck, Howell, & Lindquist, 2001). Economic opportunities, such as the availability of new markets for drug profits, may also play a part in a gang's decision to relocate. Many communities and neighborhoods once untouched by organized violence now find themselves threatened by gang activity. The proliferation of youth gangs in recent decades is of concern, and of particular concern is the spread of homegrown youth gangs to rural communities (Esbensen, 2000). These findings highlight the importance of continuing systematic response in combating youth gang problems.

THE ORIGINS OF THE PROBLEM

The origins of antisocial behavior, including conduct disorder, delinquent activity, and gang involvement among children and adolescence, are developmental and ecological. The model of antisocial behavior we present here (see Figure 9.1 for a graphic representation) provides one way to conceptualize this multifaceted and complex problem.

A Developmental and Ecological Model

In an ecological model the social contexts of society, community, and neighborhood are viewed as remote predictors of antisocial and delinquent behavior (as we reviewed in Chapter 2). As depicted in Figure 9.1, family, school, and peer influences as well as individual characteristics of the youth all contribute to the ecology of the problem as well.

Society, Communities, and Neighborhoods

The ecological model (Bronfenbrenner, 1989) highlights the importance of the microsystems of community and neighborhood as well as other environmental influences in predicting and understanding antisocial behavior. Economic conditions—prosperity, employment rates, family income—are important and help to predict the degree and severity of antisocial behavior and delinquency. In fact, significant correlations between rates of unemployment and juvenile delinquency have been found in over 100 American cities, and youth crime is most common in urban areas that are economically depressed (Esbenson, 2000). The impact of media and the access to guns are important components as well (and we discuss these in the next chapter).

Indeed, social influences also include historical and social changes. The civil rights movement of the 1960s, for example, created hopes and expectations among many communities of color that have been largely unfulfilled. Racism continues to be a major social factor in the United States, and its effects continue to be insidious and far reaching, with large portions of our ethnically diverse communities experiencing serious violence, crime, and continued economic, social, and educational marginalization. Such marginalization is associated with poorer parenting, lower levels of parental monitoring, and less-integrated family structures, which have all been associated with an increase in criminal behavior among children and teenagers of color (Dishion & Kavanagh, 2002; Patterson, Reid, & Dishion, 1992).

Because parents who are struggling with social, economic, and community problems are often less able to provide the structure that young teenagers need, many young people are drawn to gangs that often provide structure (such as rules and norms) and a sense of

A Progressive, Developmental Model of Aggression and Violence

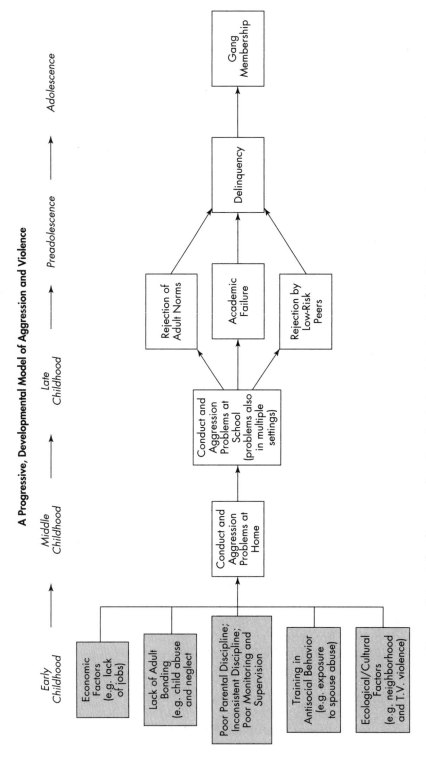

FIGURE 9.1   A developmental and ecological model of antisocial, delinquent, and gang behavior

Source: Adapted from Patterson, DeBaryshe, & Ramsey, 1989.

belonging and group and individual identity. Adolescents of color living in inner cities have much higher levels of personal victimization than national norms (Sheley, McGee, & Wright, 1992), and so gangs also provide a sense of safety for many youth.

Regarding gay, lesbian, bisexual, and transgendered (GLBT) youth, most studies suggest higher incidence of negative encounters with police, including jail, compared to heterosexual youth (Rotheram-Borus & Langabeer, 2001). But probably more important than crime done by GLBT adolescents is the violence done to them. GLBT youth are uniquely subject to violence resulting from societal homophobia. Forms of violence in school and in the community range from name calling to "gay bashing" to physical attacks, and there is a high and increasing number of hate crimes toward GLBT persons in the United States (Herek, Gillis, Cogan, & Glunt, 1997). This amplified vulnerability to victimization of GLBT youth is especially problematic because of the distinctive developmental struggles reported by GLBT youth during their adolescent years (Savin-Williams, 1995).

Antisocial behavior is a developmental process that begins early in life and continues through childhood and adolescence into adulthood (Patterson, 1993). Chronic delinquency emerges in a series of predictable steps that place young people at increasingly greater risk for long-term criminal behavior. Unfortunately, by the time offenders come to the attention of the juvenile justice system, they may have spent several years committing minor offenses and developing serious behavior problems that eventually led to crime. Next, we review risk factors that contribute to this developmental process.

Risk Factors in Society, Communities, and Neighborhoods

Although the primary social environments for most children are family and school, children also interact with others in their neighborhood, with peers who attend other schools, and with other adults. Children develop a set of expectations about themselves and others in these social contexts and are faced with many challenges. Among other things, the following risk factors provide an environment that makes antisocial behavior, delinquency, and gang activity more likely.

- Poor economic prosperity of the nation as a whole and unequal distribution of wealth.
- High rates of unemployment, underemployment, and limited work opportunities.
- Failure of communities to meet their economic and educational expectations and poor community response to economic marginalization.
- High frequency of social marginalization and racism in the community, including presence of hate groups and hate crimes.
- Public policy that fails to meet community, economic, family (e.g., accessible quality day care), and/or educational needs.
- High frequency of neighborhood vandalism, crime, gang activity, and violence.
- Limited transportation, health, and social services.
- Ready access to guns and drugs.
- Low family income and high likelihood of economic hopelessness.

Family and Home Environment Risk Factors

The family can mitigate against delinquency or encourage it. Parents whose discipline is harsh and inconsistent, for example, who have little positive involvement with their children, and who do not monitor their children's activities foster early aggressive behavior, which is strongly related to later delinquency (Baumrind, 1993; DeBaryshe, Patterson, & Capaldi, 1993). When parents and grandparents are negative and inconsistent in their parenting styles, are explosive, and when parents are antisocial themselves, aversive and aggressive behavior is reinforced (Fry, 1993). Family stressors, such as family violence, marital discord, divorce, or stresses related to acculturation or bicultural adjustment all contribute to the development of a youth's antisocial behavior.

Certain family demographic features are also highly correlated with delinquency. SES is not directly related to the incidence of delinquency, but ethnicity, the type of neighborhood, and parents' education, occupation, and income can influence the type of delinquency children exhibit (Tolan & Guerra, 1994). Children of families of color who live in poor communities, whose parents have unskilled jobs or are unemployed, and whose schools and community economic opportunity are poor are at greatest risk for violent forms of delinquent behavior (Tolan & Guerra, 1994). This risk is partly attributable to the difficulty of raising children in a poor environment and to parents' lack of education, resources, and problem-solving skills. Parents with this profile often monitor their children less, show little involvement with them, and provide less educational stimulation and positive reinforcement for pro-social behaviors (Dishion & Kavanagh, 2002; Dishion, Kavanagh, Schneiger, Nelson, & Kaufman, 2002).

Early parenting patterns can lead to antisocial behavior in two ways. First, a negative and hostile interaction style and inconsistent discipline lead to poor bonding between parent and child. This lack of bonding contributes to the child's failure to accept society's values and to develop internal control mechanisms. This problem is exacerbated when the family is isolated. Second, coercive and violent behaviors may be modeled and reinforced by grandparents, parents, and siblings. Children learn to use aversive and aggressive behaviors to counteract the hostile and negative behaviors of other family members, and aggressiveness is rewarded. Learned aggressiveness in such an environment is functional for survival, and hitting, screaming, and other aggressive behaviors are sometimes accepted as normal early in life.

Families that reinforce aggressive and antisocial behavior fail to provide the appropriate skills that children need for survival in the school and social environment. The significance of positive parental involvement, healthy parent-child interaction, and consistent discipline is supported by the fact that when parents change their discipline and monitoring styles to become more consistent, more positive, less physical, and more aware and observant, their children's antisocial behavior almost invariably declines significantly (Aktan, Kumpfer, & Turner, 1996; Cunningham, Bremner, & Boyle, 1995; Kumpfer & Tait, 2000). Conversely, if children receive training in antisocial behavior in the home, they will most certainly experience significant difficulties in and out of school (see Box 9.1).

School Environment and Risk Factors

Coercive behavior learned at home usually leads to aggression at school and often an assessment of ODD or CD. School aggression also leads to academic failure. Uncontrolled behavior adversely affects a child's ability to concentrate, to stick to a task, and to complete homework. The correlation between antisocial behavior and poor academic performance is strong (Catalano & Hawkins, 1996; Stormshak, Bierman & the Problems Prevention Research Group, 1998).

▲ Box 9.1

Training for Violence

At one time I was a school counselor for two brothers, Tom, a freshman, and John, a sophomore. Almost every week one or the other or both got into a fistfight at school—sometimes with each other, more often with another student. The vice principal provided appropriate discipline, which progressed from talking to detention to more detention to in-school suspension to suspension. Because the parents refused to attend parent-teacher or parent-administrator conferences, and because I worked with the boys in a counseling relationship, the vice principal asked me to make a home visit to discuss the problem with the parents.

The boys' father was home when I arrived. It quickly became clear that the boys' problem was their dad. The overriding family value he expressed was: "Don't take nothing off of nobody. If someone bothers you, hit him." In this family, aggression and violence were not only being modeled and reinforced, they were being actively encouraged through verbal instruction.

Once I understood the situation, I was able to work with the boys to help them understand their aggression, to develop different standards of behavior at school, and to learn more appropriate problem-solving skills.

The link between aggression and poor academic performance is due to several factors, most of which have developmental roots. Children who are aggressive are disruptive, and disruption itself means less on-task behavior, leading to less concentration and study. Disruptive young people are more often placed in time-out, sent to the principal's office, spend more time in a responsibility room, and are suspended more often. All of these consequences contribute to less learning time, leading to poor performance. Limited academic achievement contributes to the student's negative self-perception that encourages more negative behavior, that in turn leads to even more limited academic achievement.

Many of the risk factors that emerge in the school environment are symptomatic of other problems, such as learning disabilities, emotional problems, or a temporary difficulty in the family. Nevertheless, some of the following risk factors in the school environment lead to or are symptomatic of more severe antisocial or delinquent behavior expressed outside of school. In school, children and teens may:

- Behave aggressively or violently toward other students and toward teachers in the classroom or on the playground.
- Use money as a means of winning other students' approval and acceptance.
- Disrupt the classroom by failing to attend to the tasks of the class, stay in their seats, respond appropriately to the teacher, or participate in appropriate classroom behavior (such as raising a hand before speaking).

- Vandalize school property and classroom materials.
- Make sexual gestures toward other students and teachers.
- Perform poorly in academic work, regularly scoring low on tests and consistently failing to complete classroom and homework assignments.
- Spend free time with older students who behave aggressively in and out of the classroom.
- Describe themselves as "bad" or "dumb," or in other ways deride their ability to do the required schoolwork and behave appropriately around other students and teachers.

Peer Group Environment

Rejection by low-risk peers. As young children become socialized to the behavioral standards and norms of society, they gradually reduce their level of aggressive and acting-out behavior. However, older children with antisocial behavioral patterns display rates of aggression that are more typical of younger children. They are usually not cooperative or helpful in their social interactions. Indeed, antisocial students seem to have a particular disinclination to cooperate with others in peer-related activities. Their aggressive and antisocial behaviors lead to nonacceptance and eventual rejection by low-risk peers (Fraser, 1996). They continue to experience difficulty entering positive peer groups; they misperceive peer group norms, and they inappropriately interpret the reactions of their peers. Considerable evidence suggests that even benign actions by other students—an innocent, accidental bump in a crowded hallway, for instance—are interpreted as hostile, deliberate, aggressive attacks (Dodge & Price, 1994).

Membership in a deviant peer group. Uncontrolled and aggressive behavior ultimately leads young people to join deviant peer groups as a means of achieving support and acceptance. Aggressiveness and antisocial behavior, then, is learned at home and is exacerbated by academic failure and rejection by normal peers. It becomes a precursor to membership in a deviant peer group. But the relationship between inappropriate and aggressive behavior and academic failure and peer rejection may be circular. That is, school failure and social rejection may in fact stimulate behavior problems, enhance aggressiveness, and contribute to delinquent and hostile reactions by the struggling student. This relationship needs to be assessed more carefully, however. Some studies suggest that training in academic and social skills can be effective but must be introduced early in the child's life to prevent or reduce antisocial behavior (Goldstein, Harootunian, & Conoley, 1994; Kazdin, 1994; Lipsey, Wilson, & Cothern, 2000).

As we discussed in Chapters 4 and 7, the peer cluster is a major training ground for the development of a young adolescent's attitudes, beliefs, and behaviors. Peers supply the attitudes, motivations, rationalizations, and opportunities for engaging in antisocial and delinquent behaviors. Further, delinquent peers reinforce deviant behavior and punish behavior that is socially conforming (Dishion, McCord, & Poulin, 1999; Patterson, Crosby, & Vuchinich, 1992). Pressure from the peer cluster makes it difficult for children and adolescents to modify antisocial behavior once they have started to engage in it. Many delinquent youth actively resist efforts to change their behavior. If they adopt more positive social behavior, they may alienate themselves from their major source of companionship and acceptance.

Onset of Delinquent Behavior

The age of onset of aggressive and delinquent behavior is an important factor in determining severity. Youth who begin delinquent activities early are at greatest risk for becoming chronic offenders (Patterson, Reid, & Dishion 1992; Walker, Colvin, & Ramsey, 1995). Boys who are first arrested between the ages of 6 and 10, for example, have more criminal charges and convictions than "late starters," or, those who commit their first offense in middle adolescence. About one-half of conduct-disordered children become adolescent delinquents, and about one-half to three-fourths of adolescent delinquents become chronic adult offenders (Blumstein, Cohen, & Farrington, 1988). These data argue for the importance of early assessment and intervention.

Focusing on the developmental perspective (Patterson, DeBaryshe, & Ramsey, 1989; Patterson, Crosby, & Vuchinich 1992) and ecological model (Bronfenbrenner, 1979), as it relates to delinquency development, Figure 9.1 shows how ecological, cultural, and economic factors place external pressure on families, schools, and children. As young people pass through their developmental milestones, their interactions with families, schools, and peer groups change. For children who are at risk for antisocial behavior, identification with and commitment to a deviant peer cluster encourages delinquent behavior and, for some, eventual membership in a gang.

Gang Involvement

Gangs have significant negative consequences not only for society but also for their young members. However, a gang may be the only means many young people have to satisfy their need for affiliation and affirmation (Decker & Van Winkle, 1996). Gangs also provide an opportunity for economic gain and an image of success for young people who have no other means to establish it. Gangs provide security, protection, companionship, and opportunities for excitement. Thus, gang membership gives young people ways to enhance their perception of their worth and acceptance (Howell, 1998).

In one of our studies (Herrmann, McWhirter, & Sipsas-Herrmann, 1997), we found that high gang involvement was associated with low competence self-concept. That is, those middle-school-aged students who were most involved (members) and/or wanted to be involved (wannabes) believed themselves to have very little impact or influence on their environment, with adults, or with their peers. Apparently, if young people believe themselves impotent, gang membership is viewed as a way to increase their competency and power. These consequences of gang involvement make intervention a complicated and challenging task and further highlight the importance of early prevention.

Gang Risk Factors

Research has identified risk factors for juvenile gang membership at a variety of levels: individual, peer group, school, family, and community (Howell, 1998). These risk factors range from lack of parental role models to academic failure to neighborhood drug availability. Many duplicate the risk factors in community, families, and schools noted earlier. Some of the most important risk factors that lead to gang membership are:

- A community characterized by poverty, residential mobility, and other examples of social disorganization often avowing cultural norms that support gang behavior.

- Families experiencing extreme economic deprivation.
- Parents with management problems and violent attitudes and households with siblings with antisocial behavior.
- Low commitment to school with low achievement test scores and low school attachment; high levels of antisocial behavior in school; and identification as being learning disabled and/or conduct disordered.
- Interaction with and high commitment to delinquent peers coupled with a low commitment to positive peers; friends who use drugs or are drug distributors, or who are gang members.
- Problem attitudes and behaviors including hyperactivity, drinking, lack of refusal skills, externalizing behaviors, and early sexual activity.

All of these risk factors and contexts in which we find the roots of the problem of youth violence and delinquency need to be considered in prevention and intervention. Youth gangs represent a particularly acute concern because gang members account for a disproportionate number of delinquent acts and for a greater number of more serious crimes. Additionally, substance use and abuse, drug trafficking, and gang membership are related (Bilchik, 1999). The following section provides ideas and strategies for prevention and intervention.

GENERAL PREVENTION AND INTERVENTION STRATEGIES

General approaches for dealing with delinquency focus on family, school, and community issues. Specific intervention models, such as Glasser's reality therapy, help young people establish the healthy relationships they need to be able to reduce antisocial behavior and to avoid delinquency. We first examine some general prevention and intervention approaches.

Family Prevention and Intervention

The family's cooperation in minimizing the risk of delinquency, violence, and gang involvement is critical. Parent training in child management is a promising family intervention strategy (Kosterman et al., 2000; Kumpfer & Tait, 2000). It is most effective, however, if parents learn to recognize and deal with the signs of risk before their child reaches adolescence. Training in behavior modification, in management of rewards and consequences, and in communication skills is most effective with younger children whose behavioral problems have not yet developed into violence or delinquency. If children are already violent and delinquent, parent training is relatively less effective in reducing the children's offenses, perhaps because the delinquent behaviors have already become part of the young persons' repertoire, because they have already identified with deviant peers, and/or because they have achieved a high level of autonomy (Dishion, Capaldi, & Yoerger, 1999).

Current research supports the use of multiple interventions aimed not only at the family but also at the school and social environments. Behavior modification procedures used in halfway houses, for instance, have had immediate results but produce little long-lasting changes after teenagers return to their natural environments. However, more recent work with multidimensional treatment foster care (MTFC) homes with well-trained foster parents demonstrated markedly improved behaviors of chronic juvenile delinquents (Chamberlain & Reid, 1998). In other areas, a combination of efforts designed to improve the young person's academic performance and social skills, to modify the adolescent's peer cluster, and to train the parents for better family management offers the greatest promise for averting or reducing the problems of youthful violence and delinquency (Patterson, DeBaryshe, & Ramsey, 1989; Patterson, Crosby, & Vuchinich, 1992).

Multisystemic therapy (MST) has emerged as a leading intervention for adolescent delinquent behavior (Henggeler, 1999). Working from a social-ecological model of human development, MST counselors focus on providing parents with skills to effectively monitor and discipline their children and on increasing family cohesion. MST also discourages continued contact with peers that provide reinforcement for delinquent behavior and promotes contact with pro-social peers (Henggeler, 1999; Huey, Henggeler, Brondino, & Pickrel, 2000). When treating conduct problems in young people, helpers must involve multiple systems in treatment and should attend to negative or positive roles that peers play in undermining or facilitating intevention.

School Prevention and Intervention

School programs that let kids know the rules and how they are expected to behave are very effective. Children can learn to behave more responsibly if they are taught to do so. These programs range from schoolwide anti-bullying campaigns to programs that reward children who behave well. Life skills training (discussed in Chapter 12), and similar programs that teach young people to develop self-control, manage stress, solve problems, and make responsible decisions also help prevent crime, delinquency, and other problems. Educational interventions such as cooperative learning, conflict resolution, and mediation programs (discussed in Chapter 14) are extremely helpful. Programs such as unified discipline, a proactive, schoolwide approach for managing problem behavior, are very important in maintaining discipline (White, Algozzine, Audette, Marr, & Ellis, 2001). Schools that have a consistent, clear, and graduated consequence for misbehavior and that provide recognition for positive behavior reduce antisocial behavior and conduct disorders (Sugai & Horner, 1999, 2001). Finally, bringing together only aggressive and delinquent youth to engage in school and community activities is likely to be counterproductive. Programs that integrate delinquent youth into pro-social groups can prevent the development and perpetuation of delinquent peer groups when certain criteria are met, such as maintaining a high level of structure (Dishion, McCord, & Poulin, 1999; Poulin, Dishion, & Burraston, 2001).

The school can also play an effective role in limiting and mitigating the influence of gangs. The effectiveness of such efforts depends on the level of communication among school personnel and the speed of their response. School personnel need to be in close communication with one another, with each employee having a clearly designated response role when the threat of gang activity is present (Lal, Lal, & Achilles, 1993). A number of strategies can limit gang activity in schools:

- Acknowledge the problem immediately and get help from local police and community groups; work closely with the local police; establish procedures to share information with them.

- Control points of access to the school; institute a strict visitor/trespasser policy; educate security personnel; use cameras to take pictures of suspicious visitors or trespassers.
- Maintain a high profile: consider posting uniformed security personnel in strategic places to ensure maximum visibility.
- Form or access a community network; engage community members and parent groups to help monitor the school and the neighborhood.
- Establish informal communication networks with students.
- Remove graffiti as quickly as possible; be aware of gang dress, colors, and signs; discourage the use of gang names at school.

These procedures help restrict many gang-related activities and may discourage some students from being influenced by gangs. However, because delinquency generally precedes gang membership, efforts should not be limited to only gang intervention or suppression (Esbenson, 2000).

Community Prevention and Intervention

Schools can play a crucial role in developing communication with the community and in building coalitions with community organizations and government agencies. Community groups that are recruited and educated by schools can help to minimize violence and gang activity. Community organizations that meet an adolescent's need for inclusion, affirmation, and acceptance also discourage gang involvement. Youth service centers, recreational centers, and religious organizations can all fill this role and help to prevent gang activity and delinquency, and it is critical to encourage community organizations to provide young people with educational and social opportunities to offset the attraction of gangs.

A variety of proactive local citizen groups have been developed to deal specifically with the youth gang problem, sometimes with the aid and supervision of local police. These community groups patrol streets, supervise social events, and monitor students in school buildings and in the neighborhood. Some of the groups have taken on a vigilante character interrupting drug deals, holding offenders until the police are called, and even shooting at gang members (Esbensen, 2000). Some cities have similar groups somewhat analogous to Mothers Against Drunk Driving. Their members provide mutual support for parents whose children are victims of gang violence. They lecture in schools, pressure police and other agencies to focus greater attention on gang problems, and advocate stricter gun control. Local community groups can make a positive difference but they require close coordination with schools, churches, youth agencies, and the police (Spergel et al., 1996).

All of these approaches are designed to confront a general situation. To deal with a specific troubled youth, a specific intervention, such as reality therapy, is called for.

SPECIFIC INTERVENTION: REALITY THERAPY

Dr. William Glasser and Dr. G. L. Harrington developed reality therapy, one of the more promising approaches to the deterrence of delinquency. When Glasser was a resident in psychiatry at the Veterans Administration Neuropsychiatric Hospital in West Los Angeles, California, in the 1950s, both he and his supervisor, Dr. Harrington, were frustrated by the inability of traditional psychotherapy to solve the problems of many of their patients. Harrington was in charge of a "back" ward that had a very low success rate. The 210 patients averaged 17 years of confinement; the last discharge had occurred two years earlier, and the patient had returned within a short time. Although the staff was compassionate and well intentioned, the patients were not getting better. Harrington began to confront the patients, chiding them for their unacceptable behavior and supporting them when their behavior improved. Nurses and aides began to follow suit; they became more involved with the patients and less tolerant of their "crazy" symptoms.

At this time Glasser was taking a similar approach to delinquent girls at the Ventura School for Girls, an institutional facility of the California Youth Authority. In view of the populations they were serving, both men were achieving a remarkable degree of success. Forty-five patients on Harrington's ward went home the first year. They were followed by 85 the second year and 90 the third. Many returned, of course, as they were encouraged to do, but only a very few remained more than a month after their return. The others reentered mainstream society immediately. Glasser obtained similar results at the Ventura School. Roughly 400 girls, with offenses ranging from "incorrigibility" to murder, were confined there for 6 to 8 months for rehabilitation. After applying the new therapy, Glasser reported that 80% of the girls were released and did not return.

Reality therapy grew out of the experiences and discussions of Glasser and Harrington. Glasser first described this treatment in *Reality Therapy* (1965) and has continued to elaborate and expand his approach through numerous publications (Glasser, 1972, 1976, 1984). In his most recent work (Glasser, 1998, 2001, 2002), he has developed the concept of choice theory that embeds reality therapy within it.

Assumptions of Reality Therapy

Reality therapy and choice theory are based on the assumption that human beings must have human communication and contact to thrive, much like the notion of connectedness that we present as one of the 5 Cs of competency in Chapter 5. Within the context of this communication and contact, people must balance their five basic drives: (1) belonging, (2) power, (3) fun or enjoyment, (4) freedom, and (5) survival (Wubbolding, 2000). Humans have a basic desire to be with other people, to care for others, and to be cared for in return. Individuals who seek help or who are sent for help suffer from one basic inadequacy—they are unable to achieve such contact successfully.

Striving for human contact reflects two fundamental needs: (a) to love and be loved and (b) to be worthwhile as a person. Low-risk young people are able to satisfy these needs in an appropriate way. They develop a success identity that allows them to be involved with respected people who care for them and for whom they care. They have the capacity to give and receive love. They have at least one other person who cares about them and one person whom they care about. They also develop a feeling of personal self-worth. They believe they have a right to be in the world, and they behave in socially responsible ways.

High-risk young people are unable to satisfy these two basic needs. Instead, they either ignore or deny reality. In the process, they develop a failure identity. Young people who ignore reality cope with life by acting as if the rules did not include them (see Box 9.2). They are described as antisocial, sociopathic, delinquent, or criminal. Those who deny reality cope in one of two ways, through substance abuse or mental illness. The young person who says "The world is no good, so I must change it" and proceeds to change

▲ Box 9.2

Mikey the Menace

When Mikey arrived at the classroom door each morning, the atmosphere changed. A subtle wave of tension would pass among the children as he entered the room shouting, "Hi everybody!" Within minutes, someone would be crying, complaining, or retreating from his awkward overtures and fast-moving fists, and he would be temporarily relocated to the timeout chair. He would beam at me from the chair. "Teacher, I'll be good." And he tried.

Mikey was the youngest of seven children. His father was in prison for selling drugs, and his mother had described her current boyfriend as a "damn scary alcoholic." Child Protective Services closely monitored the family and was close to taking the younger children away from the mother. During one home visit, I observed her grab Mikey roughly, pull his hair, and hit him on the head, all in response to appropriate attention-seeking behavior. Each time he was punished, Mikey scowled and then quickly turned his sunniest smile back on; each time, his mother failed to notice.

One evening I was still working in my classroom as darkness fell, and I was suddenly startled to hear him shout, "Hi, every . . . Where's the kids?" There was Mikey in the doorway, cheerful as ever, having just walked seven long blocks through projects so crime-ridden that the classroom mothers had warned me to "never go in there." Mikey was very disappointed to learn that "the kids" had gone home. His desperate efforts to gain affection and attention were all that a 4-year-old could do. Mikey should be 19 years old now. What new methods has he learned?

the world by getting "high" or "wasted" is essentially denying reality and escaping it. Withdrawing from the world through delusions and other symptoms of mental illness is another way of denying reality.

The reality therapist assumes that all problems result from an inability to fulfill essential needs. Psychological problems are caused by lack of responsibility, the choice of behaviors, and toxic relationships (Glasser, 2001). Thus, individuals must fulfill their needs without preventing others from fulfilling theirs. The person who cannot do so is irresponsible, not mentally ill or bad. Perhaps more than any other approach, reality therapy holds that it is impossible to maintain self-regard while living irresponsibly. The practice of reality therapy is based on teaching at-risk individuals satisfactory standards of behavior, praising them when they act appropriately, and correcting them when they are wrong. Self-respect comes through self-discipline and closeness to others. In learning to face reality, young people fulfill their needs. In doing so they become socially responsible people who can achieve honest human relationships.

Theoretical Components of Reality Therapy

Reality therapy has three basic components: involvement, rejection of unrealistic behavior, and relearning. We consider each of these components in detail as they might apply to Ty Baker of Chapter 2.

Involvement.   Involvement is the initial and most difficult phase of counseling and requires the most therapeutic skill. Involvement, and the process of developing it, is a prerequisite to the other steps and forms a consistent theme running through the entire helping relationship. In creating involvement with young people it is important to not give up, nor to push too hard. In the language of choice theory (Glasser, 2001) if Tyrone is internally controlled, the adults cannot work "on" him (external control); they can only be effective by working "with" him, and to do that a good relationship is necessary.

In Tyrone's case, the helper must be able to become emotionally involved with him and must be able to accept him uncritically at first. The adult cannot be frightened by or angry about Ty's behavior, thoughts, or attitudes. By demonstrating interest, warmth, and sensitivity while discussing Ty's values, interests, hopes, and fears, the adult helps Tyrone grow beyond his problems. The counselor must know and understand Tyrone and express interest in him as an individual with great potential.

Further, the helper must be open and present himself or herself as a model of transparency and integrity. Glasser says that helpers must be willing to have their own values tested. The helper must be tough and able to withstand Tyrone's intense criticism and anger. In addition, the helper must be willing to admit imperfection and yet demonstrate to Tyrone that he has the ability to act responsibly. The helper, in effect, supports and strengthens Ty's conscience by demonstrating honesty, concern, and personal authenticity.

The counselor develops an "I/you" pattern of interaction. The personal "I," Glasser says, must be used instead of the more impersonal "we," "the school," and "they." The adult says: "I'd like you to do your homework for me." "It's important to me that you're here every day." "I'm concerned about you and interested in you." "I want to explain how your life can go better." Such statements emphasize the personal; they lead the adult to involvement not only as helper to client but as person to person. They communicate that the adult cares enough to risk an emotional, personal involvement. This allows Tyrone to look at his unacceptable behavior and to learn better ways to lead his life. By being responsible, tough, and sensitive, the helper shows confidence that Tyrone can change his irresponsible behavior.

Rejection of irresponsible behavior.   In the second phase of treatment, the client's irresponsible behaviors are rejected first by the counselor and later by the client. The counselor ignores the past and works in the here and now with a view to the future. The focus is on Ty's behavior rather than on his feelings and attitudes. In fact, the feelings and emotions that accompany deviant behavior are de-emphasized.

The counselor working with Tyrone insists that he recognize and assume responsibility for his own behavior. Tyrone is helped to evaluate and to judge his behavior against an established standard of social responsibility. The counselor does not accept excuses or help him justify irresponsibility. Ty is helped to "own" his behavior and to view that behavior in light of his values and needs and of society's system of values and needs (Glasser, 2001). "The skill of therapy is to put the responsibility upon the client and, after involvement is established, to ask him why he remains in therapy—if he is not dissatisfied with his behavior" (Glasser, 1965, p. 29).

Of course, emphasizing responsibility is fruitless if the client is not ready. Irresponsibility is discussed with stubborn clients only when they are ready to change. Even then, the counselor should discuss only the fact that the client's behavior is irresponsible and that only the client can do something about it. Tyrone's recognition that his current behavior is irresponsible or wrong and therefore not effective in getting his needs met provides powerful motivation for positive change. Consequently, the counselor is free to pose such questions as: "Are you taking the responsible course of action?" "Are you doing right or wrong?" Questions of this sort underline the unrealistic aspects of negative behavior and set the stage for the next level of interaction.

Relearning.   The third procedure employed by the reality therapist is to help clients learn more realistic ways to fulfill their needs. By modeling consistently responsible behavior, the counselor can guide Tyrone toward an understanding that happiness results from responsibility.

Counselors instruct clients to examine their "constructive" thinking about the present and future, in other words, to evaluate their plan for getting what they want out of their current situation so that they can be where they would rather be (Glasser, 1965). By working out this plan of action with Tyrone, the counselor helps identify alternatives to his negative, self-defeating behavior. Developing a realistic plan of action that accords with Tyrone's previously articulated values serves as a means for the counselor to teach responsibility.

After the counselor and the client jointly agree upon a plan, they make a mutual commitment to resolve the problem. Tyrone's plan, for instance, must lead to behaviors that will allow him to satisfy his needs for acceptance and connection with others. The mutual planning and mutual commitment demonstrate that the counselor does not accept Tyrone's negative behavior but cares about him and is willing to help him do something definite that will lead to the fulfillment of his needs. The plan and the commitment always involve much positive reinforcement for Tyrone's responsible behavior and the rejection of excuses for irresponsible, self-defeating behavior.

When Tyrone behaves irresponsibly, the counselor refrains from punishing him. The helper does, however, freely express praise when Tyrone behaves responsibly and shows disapproval when he does not. In varying degrees, then, the counselor teaches Tyrone more realistic ways to meet his needs.

The Seven Principles of Reality Therapy

Glasser has elaborated his three-stage framework by providing seven principles of reality therapy. These principles constitute the essential mechanics of reality therapy, and we list and briefly describe them here with sample statements that reflect the interactions of client and counselor.

It should not be assumed that every session will incorporate all seven principles. Involvement is essential in every session, but the other principles emphasized will depend on the particular client, the circumstances, and the progress of counseling. Early sessions tend to focus on identification and evaluation of current behavior. Later sessions tend to deal with planning and commitment issues.

Involvement.   Involvement means development and maintenance of a close, emotional relationship between client and helper. It implies a positive, caring attitude and gives the relationship a warm, personal quality. The thread of involvement is woven throughout the therapeutic process and intertwines with all other principles. (Client: "I'm going out of my head. I've got to get some help quick." Helper: "I'd really like to help you.")

Dozens of studies have provided evidence of the importance of an empathic therapeutic relationship in achieving positive outcomes (Garfield, 1994; Orlinsky, Grawe, & Parks, 1994; Sexton & Whiston, 1994). It is critically important for difficult and defiant adolescents as well (Bernstein, 1996; Hanna, Hanna, & Keys, 1999). Further, strong relationships based on mutual respect and trust are one of the seven attributes of effective prevention programs (Schorr, 1997).

Current behavior.   The focus is on behavior here and now. The counselor helps the client become aware of his or her current behavior and its ramifications. The client is also helped to see that this behavior is self-selected and therefore the consequences of the behavior are self-inflicted. (Client: "My mother is always angry at me. She's always been angry at me. I never do anything right." Helper: "What are you doing now about that situation?")

Evaluating behavior.   The client is made to look critically at his or her behavior and judge whether or not the behavior is in his or her best interest. The counselor helps the client make value judgments about what is contributing to a lack of success. At this stage, the client realistically determines what is good for himself or herself and what is good for people the client cares about or would like to care about. (Client: "To keep her off my back, I don't stay home much." Helper: "Is that productive for you?")

Planning responsible behavior.   The counselor helps the client develop a realistic plan to implement the identified value judgment. At this stage the counselor is strongly involved in teaching responsibility to the client. Working with the client to develop a realistic plan for changing behavior is an important step in teaching responsibility. (Client: "It's not productive because when I do come home she complains even more." Helper: "Is there a plan that we could make together that would keep your mother from complaining so much?")

Commitment.   When the plan of action has been agreed upon, the client and counselor make a commitment to follow it. The commitment may be a written agreement, but usually it consists of an oral exchange. Equivocations—"I'll try," "Maybe," "I think I can do it"—are not acceptable. (Client: "Yes, I guess I could stay home a couple of nights a week." Helper: "Are you willing to make a commitment to stay home two nights next week?")

The principles of reality therapy are designed to help clients learn to become involved with others in a responsible way and to learn to say yes and no at appropriate times. Clients are also encouraged to try new patterns of behavior to fulfill their needs, regardless of fears that these behaviors may not work. Essentially, clients learn not only to face reality but also to fulfill their needs. They commit themselves to a plan that has no loopholes. In the process they evaluate their current behavior and develop a plan for the future.

Reality may be painful, but when at-risk young people can admit to the irresponsibility of their actions, the last phase of counseling—the relearning process—can begin.

Then there is potential for growth, fulfillment, and self-worth. When at-risk young people take responsibility for their actions, they gradually find better ways to meet their needs and change inappropriate patterns of behavior. At-risk young people can learn to control themselves (Glasser, 2001).

Accept no excuses.   The helper must help the client gain the experience that will enable the client to keep the commitment he or she made. In addition, the new behavior needs time to become satisfying and thus self-reinforcing. Consequently, the helper cannot accept excuses for failure to keep a commitment. Glasser makes it clear that counselors, teachers, parents, and other adults who care about young people must not make excuses for them. Nor should adults tolerate the excuses that young people offer. (Client: "Yes, I'll stay home unless something more important comes up." Helper: "If you make the commitment, no excuses are acceptable. You have to decide now whether to commit yourself or not.")

No punishment.   A counselor will not implement sanctions that have not been agreed upon in the commitment. Punishment changes the relationship that is necessary for success and reinforces the client's loneliness and isolation. (Client: "What will happen if I don't stay home two nights?" Helper: "Well, then we'd have to restudy the plan and the commitment. I would be disappointed; you wouldn't have helped your situation. It would be better to come up with a plan you can live with than not to follow through on your commitment.")

Engaging adolescents in a process that reflects the assumptions and principles of reality therapy can be very helpful to counselors, teachers, and parents. Adults who use this approach can effectively confront a potential or current delinquency problem. Although the principles of reality therapy were developed in a structured, controlled setting, they can be applied successfully in many less-controlled environments.

CONCLUSION

Young people have to cope with many interpersonal, personal, and environmental pressures. Some children react to these pressures by aggressive acting out. Unless they are helped to control such behavior, and unless our interventions help modify and change school and family environments as well, aggressive and acting out children may be very likely to develop antisocial behavior, criminal activities, and gang involvement as teenagers. The problems of delinquency are multifaceted, so understanding the problem, prevention, and intervention must focus not only on the individual youth but on the family, school, peer group, and community. The principles of reality therapy can be usefully applied to help adolescents understand the consequences of their actions and form a plan for changing their self-defeating behaviors.

CHAPTER 10

SCHOOL SHOOTERS

▲ *Long day coming*
where any corner I turn
any door opening
any hallway minute
can end up with everyone watching
all those eyes seeing
and no one is there

Later you'll say 'just ignore them'
like it would be so easy,
like breathing
You'll tell me stories
listen to my plans
nod and then smile
and look at your watch
like I'm not even talking
like I'm not really there

We'll sit in your office
with posters of baby animals
on the endangered list
(they aren't the ones who belong on that list)
but you'll pretend, and then we'll both pretend
that our little talks make it better
that I will bravely endure
that this story has a nice quiet ending
and that I will be OK

E. H. McWhirter

CHAPTER OUTLINE

▲   In the previous chapter, we discussed serious deviant and maladjusted behaviors that contribute to family, community, and school violence. Aggression, conduct disorders, antisocial behavior, delinquency, and youth gangs are all forms of violence that manifest in schools and communities. In this chapter we focus specifically on the school shooter. In the last decade, since the first edition of this book appeared, society repeatedly has witnessed an increasingly lethal dimension of youth violence—school shootings. The developmental and ecological model of antisocial behavior presented in the last chapter (see Figure 9.1) has some relevance here. However, school shooting violence emerges from some differing experiences and ecological pressures. In this chapter, we discuss (a) prevalence of the problem, (b) contributing factors, (c) problem identification, (d) general prevention and treatments suggestions, and (e) a specific intervention for school shooters that focuses on anti-bullying programs in schools.

SCOPE OF THE PROBLEM

An unprecedented number of school shootings that resulted in the deaths of students and teachers in Arkansas, Mississippi, Kentucky, California, Oregon, Colorado, and California have created widespread concern about school safety. These seemingly random and irrational acts in relatively affluent rural and suburban areas have demonstrated that school violence extends far beyond our poor, inner-city schools and that no school is safe.

Ironically, the last few years have shown a marked decrease in violent youth crime overall. The Urban Institute chronicles a steady increase in violent youth crime between 1980 and 1994, followed by a rapid decline through 2000 (Butts, 2002). Although youth under 18 comprise a much lower percentage of overall arrest rate, they make up one-third of the overall violent crime drop of the past decade. Violent juvenile crime between 1994 and 2000 dropped 34%.

Although attention to and concern about *school* violence has increased in recent years, school violence has also shown a decline. For example, the overall school crime rate between 1993 and 1997 declined from about 155 school-related crimes for every thousand students in 1993 to just over 100 such crimes in 1997 (Riley & McDaniel, 2000). Furthermore, most injuries that occur at school are not the result of violence. Fewer students are carrying weapons and engaging in physical fights on school grounds (U.S. Department of Education & Justice, 1999). Students age 12 to 18 are more likely to be victims of serious crimes away from school than at school (National Center for Education Statistics, 2000). Researchers found that young people are more than twice as likely to be victims of violence (Butts, 2002).

Tragic events like the shooting at Columbine High School in Colorado captured public attention and concern but are not typical of youth violence. Most adolescent homicides are committed in inner cities and outside of school. They most frequently involve a single victim and an interpersonal dispute with a clear territorial, retaliation, or economic motive. With the recent acts of school shooting, a new type of violent teenager seems to have emerged, and this teenager lives in suburbs, small towns, and rural areas. Most of the perpetrators of school shootings have been from affluent and middle-class communities, and many from intact families; the majority of the shooters were honor, advanced placement, or academically able students, and they were European American.

Even though school crimes and violence have decreased, young people do not feel safe at school. One in five Latino and African American teens indicate that the threat of crime and violence have kept them from attending school—cutting classes or staying home (Butts, 2002). In one large national survey of young people students from grades six to twelve reported that they had changed feelings or behavior because of school victimization or violence. Half of the students knew someone who moved to another school to feel safer; 37% did not feel safe in their school; 45% avoided school grounds; 43% avoided school rest rooms; 20% avoided school hallways (Ansley, 1997, p. 5). The ripple effect of concern and fear is manifested in settings far from those in which the shootings took place.

It is really not very surprising that so many members of the American public, including young people, think that school is not safe: We are all exposed to repeated televised pictures of students who have used handguns to kill their fellow students; media broadcasts and newspaper stories describing a teacher disarming a student in the classroom; telephoned weapon threats that necessitate closing down schools for a thorough search, while students stand and shiver in parking lots and on sidewalks, watching. These are powerful images that encourage the belief that schools are no longer safe regardless of the facts. Two ingredients of the ecology are present here that contribute to the school shooter problem: guns—especially handguns—and the media.

ECOLOGICAL CONTRIBUTIONS TO THE PROBLEM

Guns

The ownership of firearms in the United States has persisted throughout American history and is unique among western industrialized nations. In fact, the United States has more firearms than any other industrialized nation in the world. A police officer is killed by a gun every five days whereas a child dies of a gunshot wound every two hours in the United

States. Two times as many children under the age of ten have died as a result of firearms than U.S. soldiers killed in Somalia and the Persian Gulf War combined.

Firearm-related death rates for both boys and girls reveal that the most vulnerable age group among young people is 15 to 19. During this age range, their death rates from guns jump precipitously from younger teens and children. However, a child under the age of 15 in the United States is 15 times more likely to be killed by gunfire than a child growing up in Northern Ireland. Finally, the overall firearm-related death rate among U.S. children under 15 years of age is nearly 12 times higher than that of children in 25 industrialized countries (Prothrow-Stith, 2001).

The easy and excessive availability of firearms is a major contributor to the problem. The availability of guns makes youth violence more lethal and provides school shooters with access to the means to create their mayhem. A recent report suggests that a disproportionately high number of children fall victim to homicide (and suicide and accidental shooting as well) in those areas where purchase and possession of guns is especially prevalent (Miller, Azrael, & Henenway, 2002). A comparison of five states with the lowest gun availability compared to the five states with the highest gun availability shows the number of non-gun murders is similar. Those states with high gun availability, however, have 250% more shooting murders of children. When compared to other upper-income nations, the homicide rate for U.S. children is 17 times higher (Miller, Azrael, & Henenway, 2002). Among urban youth, 40% from both working and welfare families reported that at one time they had had a gun in their homes. Eighty-eight percent thought it was acceptable for children and teens to have guns. Nearly half (47%) stated that a gun had injured either a relative or themselves (Kahn, Kazimi, & Mulvihill, 2001).

In discussing ways to prevent school shootings, it is important to acknowledge the legal and economic decisions that adults have made that have increased gun accessibility to young people during the last two decades. Canada (1995) points out that young people have come to believe they need handguns for their own protection. Handgun manufacturers have been quick to take advantage of this situation, making their guns more attractive to teens and marketing their product to them. In spite of efforts to raise awareness of the problem of gun accessibility, stricter gun legislation has not been passed, typically in the name of misinterpreted Second Amendment rights.

Media

Over five decades of research on film and television viewing have documented the consistent exposure of American children to high levels of media violence. The relationship between television viewing and violence has been empirically established: There is absolutely no doubt that increased acceptance of aggressive attitudes and increased aggressive behavior are correlated with higher levels of viewing violence on television (e.g., Huesmann, Moise-Titus, Podolski, & Eron, 2001). Further, younger children's exposure to media violence can have harmful lifelong consequences. A study by Bushman and Anderson (2001) reaffirms modern society's exposure to massive doses of violent media. By the time the average American child graduates from elementary school, he or she will have seen more than 100,000 assorted acts of violence (e.g., rapes, assaults) and more than 8,000 murders on network television (Bushman & Anderson, 2001). If the child has access, as most do, to a VCR, DVD player, or to cable television, the numbers are higher. In movies as well as television, violence dominates. Even G-rated films now contain more violence than they ever have before (Yokota & Thompson, 2000).

Media games also contain violence, with 85% of the most popular video games using violence. Even young children play violent video games. Fourth-grade boys and girls reported that the majority of their favorite games were violent ones (Buchman & Funk, 1996). Playing violent video games can increase aggressive thoughts, feelings, and behavior in real life (Anderson & Dill, 2000). Violent video games teach children to practice aggressive solutions to conflict. In the short run, the violent games teach children to think violent thoughts. Over a longer period of time, the child practices new aggressive strategies during the game and becomes more likely to use those strategies when real-life conflicts arise. Some of the most worrisome games are: Doom, Doom2, Duke Nukem (video games played extensively by Harrison and Klebold, the Columbine shooters), Destrega, and Carmageddon. The latter two are advertised by "Let the slaughter begin!" and "More fun than shooting your neighbor's cat."

Music is another media influence that is often imbued with violence. The FBI surmised in their study that all the shooters had listened to music lyrics that promoted violence (Band & Harpold, 1999). Youth today have access to gangsta rap, Marilyn Manson, Eminem, and other performers who saturate their lyrics with murder, violence, aggression, and vicious disturbing images. Eminem, for example, raps about slitting parents' throats and sticking needles through eyelids. Some evidence suggests that many school shooters listen to acid rock and rap more than 40 hours per week (Buchman & Funk, 1996). This overwhelming saturation by the combined media highlights aggressive and antisocial behavior and promotes an appetite for more violence. The teenage worldview is influenced by the media that increases the fear of becoming a victim and sets the stage for "justified" violent behavior. At the same time, the media has led to increased desensitization to violence and depersonalization toward the victims of violence.

IDENTIFYING POTENTIAL SHOOTERS

In the aftermath of the highly publicized tragic injuries and loss of life at the hands of school shooters, school personnel, law enforcement personnel, mental health professionals, and policymakers have taken increased steps to prevent future violence from happening in their schools. Often, their efforts have focused on providing resources, funding, and hiring of school security officers. They have increased physical security with metal detectors and cameras. They have developed tactical plans for responding when a shooting occurs. Although some of these approaches might be moderately helpful, they do not get to the root of the problem (Hyman & Perone, 1998). Two other approaches consist of profiling and problem checklists. These approaches have been recommended by a number of authorities and are designed to allow school and laws enforcement personnel to identify future shooters.

Profiling and Checklists

Historically, profiling has consisted of carefully studying a crime scene and based on the physical evidence, generating a set of hypotheses about the demographic, physical, personality, and other characteristics of the person most likely to have committed the crime. Profiling has been very helpful in identifying suspects and solving crimes. More recently, profiling has been used in an attempt to identify perpetrators of violence *before* an incident occurs. The profile is developed based on demographic, personal, and behavior characteristics of past school shooters. A number of professionals and agencies have developed prospective profiles of school shooters including the "classroom avenger" profile (McGee & DeBernardo, 1999) and the FBI profile (Band & Harpold, 1999) in an attempt to improve the prediction of an individual student's potential for violence.

Unfortunately, profiling potential shooters is not an exact science. Even though there are similarities across shooters, accurate prediction depends upon a very high degree of concordance. The demographic, social, and personality characteristics of the shooters have varied considerably. In addition, many students who fit shooter profiles will not become shooters even without intervention. For example, shooters are described as moody, confrontational, angry, and having low self-esteem. This description can be used to describe almost any young person at some point in their adolescence. Undoubtedly, the use of profiles will fail to identify some dangerous students who share only a few characteristics with prior attackers, and will identify as dangerous many students who do not actually pose a risk to others.

Checklists of warning signs are a less scientific alternative to profiles, designed to help identify potentially violent youth without assuming that all young people fitting the description are potential shooters. Several agencies and groups, including the U. S. Department of Education, the FBI (Band & Harpold, 1999), and the National School Safety Center, have provided checklists of warning signs and risk factors. The best use of these checklists is usually to motivate schools to develop prevention and early intervention procedures, as well as safe school plans, because warning list items are so commonly found among adolescents at a given school. Most developers of checklists emphasize that the list is not intended to predict future violent behavior by otherwise nonviolent students. The Department of Education warning sign checklist explicitly cautions that their list does not constitute a profile and was never intended to serve as a predictor of violent behavior. Yet there is some evidence that even explicit cautions are disregarded (Sewell & Mendelsohn, 2000). In spite of the variability among warning list items and the cautions about their use, in many school settings warning sign checklists are applied as profiles. This can result in the unfair labeling of students who do not pose a threat to the school, particularly students who differ from the majority with respect to sexual orientation, race, and appearance. Lonely, isolated, "weird," young people who dress "funny," have quirky personality characteristics, and otherwise don't fit the norms of their peer group are likely to receive even more harassment, rejection, and ostracism than they already do. Warning lists may actually promote the profiling concept, creating an environment of both suspicion and false security (Lord, 1999; Bender, Shubert, & McLaughlin, 2001).

Predicting Versus Preventing

The process of predicting future incidences of school violence is fraught with methodological and practical problems. Predicting any low base rate or infrequent behavior, even if reasonably accurate, results in many false positives for every true positive (Mulvey & Cauffman, 2001). Further, although social scientists are able to predict with some accuracy the approximate numbers of individuals in a given cohort group likely to behave in a certain way, their ability to predict which *specific* individual is likely to engage in the behavior, and *when*, is far more limited (Borum, 1996, 2000; Mossman, 1994; Otto, 1992).

There is an important distinction between *predicting* violence and *preventing* it (Reddy et al., 2001). Violence prediction involves maximizing the accuracy of predicting who will be violent and under what circumstances the probability of violence is greatest (Sewell & Mendelsohn, 2000). Violence prevention emphasizes not who and when, but understanding common underpinnings of violence, and intervening so as to maximize protective factors and minimize risk factors.

GENERAL PREVENTION AND INTERVENTION STRATEGIES

A recent report based on a collaboration between the U.S. Secret Service and the U.S. Department of Education (Reddy et al., 2001) focused on 37 school shootings from 1974 to 2000 involving 41 attackers. Shootings that were drug related, gang related, or stemming from disputes that just happened to occur on school property were not analyzed. Rather than building a profile of attackers from a set of personality traits and demographic characteristics, the Secret Service focused on behavior and motives, tracing the shooters' thoughts and actions from the day of the attack back to when the perpetrator first developed a notion to make the attack. Based on a systematic analysis of investigative, educational, judicial, mental health, and other files, along with interviews of some of the shooters, the report provides useful information about the patterns of relationships, emotions, and attitudes of others in the shooter's environment.

Bender, Shubert, and their colleagues (Bender, Shubert, & McLaughlin, 2001; Shubert, Bressette, Deeken, & Bender, 1999) came to remarkably similar conclusions as those of the Secret Service, even though they proceeded with different data sources. Using national press reports, the researchers constructed a list of factors consistently associated with the shooter's psychological and social environment. They used the term *invisible kids* to describe the school shooters, underscoring the finding that these students were not known for overt behavior problems or aggression; indeed, they were simply unknown.

Targets of Intervention

Drawing together the results of the reports by Reddy et al. (2001) and Bender et al. (1999), five clusters of emotions and behaviors emerge as critical indicators of potential violence. Each of these is an important target of intervention. The five areas are: access to guns, emotional pain and confusion, aggressive hatred toward self and others, planning and leakage, and vigilante motivation. We describe each of the five areas in the following sections; these should be seen as the basis for general prevention and intervention.

We followed the sentencing hearing in Lane County Circuit Court for Kip Kinkel, a 15-year-old high school student from Springfield, Oregon. On May 20, 1998 Kinkel was suspended from school for stashing a stolen pistol in his school locker. That evening he killed his mother and father at home, and the next morning took several guns and hundreds of rounds of ammunition to school and proceeded to shoot 26 of his high school classmates. Two were killed. At the time of his hearing, Kinkel had accepted a 25-year prison term after pleading guilty to killing his parents and two classmates. The hearing was held to help the court decide whether to add more prison time for the 26 counts of attempted murder and for trying to stab a police detective after his arrest. His final sentence was for 112 years without possibility of parole. In Box 10.1 and in Box 10.2 we present excerpts from Kip's journals, which were documents presented at the hearing. They graphically illustrate the five target areas we now describe. Notice that these target areas do not

▲ Box 10.1

The Words of a Shooter: Kip's Journal

These excerpts are from a journal hidden in the loft of Kip Kinkel's home. Investigators discovered the black, hard-cover book tucked away in a chest. Passages read in court are filled with violent images, with Kinkel's wishing for his own death, with visions of his classmates' death. The journal offers a window into Kinkel's state of mind leading up to the tragic shooting at Thurston High School in Springfield, Oregon. It also illustrates concepts we have discussed in this chapter.

Aggressive Hate

I sit here all alone. I am always alone. I don't know who I am. I want to be something I can never be. I try so hard every day. But in the end, I hate myself for what I've become.

Every single person I know means nothing to me. I hate every person on this earth. I wish they could all go away. You all make me sick. I wish I was dead.

The only reason I stay alive is because of hope. Even though I am repulsive and few people know who I am, I still feel that things might, maybe, just a little bit, get better.

I don't understand any (expletive) person on this earth. Some of you are so weak, mainly, that a 4-year-old could push you down. I am strong, but my head just doesn't work right. I know I should be happy with what I have, but I hate living.

Motivational Vigilantism

Every time I talk to her, I have a small amount of hope. But then she will tear it right down. It feels like my heart is breaking. But is that possible? I am so consumed with hate all of the time. Could I ever love anyone? I have feelings, but do I have a heart that's not black and full of animosity?

Plan and Leakage

I know everyone thinks this way sometimes, but I am so full of rage that I feel I could snap at any moment. I think about it every day. Blowing the school up or just taking the easy way out, and walk into a pep assembly with guns. In either case, people that are breathing will stop breathing. That is how I will repay all you (expletive) for all you put me through.

Motivational Vigilantism

I need help. There is one person that could help, but she won't. I need to find someone else. I think I love her, but she could never love me. I don't know why I try.

End. New day. Today of all days, I ask her to help me. I was shot down. I feel like my heart has been ripped open and ripped apart. Right now, I'm drunk, and I don't know what the hell is happening to me.

I gave her all I have, and she just threw it away. Why? Why did God just want me to be in complete misery?

Aggressive Hate

Oh, (expletive). I sound so pitiful. People would laugh at this if they read it. I hate being laughed at. But they won't laugh after they're scraping parts of their parents, sisters, brothers, and friends from the wall of my hate.

Please, someone, help me. All I want is something small. Nothing big. I just want to be happy.

It is clear that no one will help me. Oh, God, I'm so close to killing people. So close.

Every time I see your face, my heart is shot with an arrow. I think that she will say yes, but she doesn't, does she? She says "I don't know." The three most (expletive) words in the English language.

Guns

I need to find more weapons. My parents are trying to take away my guns. My guns are the only things that haven't stopped me—that haven't stabbed me in the back.

Emotional Pain/Confusion

I want you to feel this, be this, taste this, kill this. Kill me. Oh God, I don't want to live. Will I see it to the end? What kind of dad would I make? All humans are evil. I just want to end the world of evil.

I don't want to see, hear, speak or feel evil, but I can't help it. I am evil. I want to kill and give pain without a cost. And there is no such thing. We kill him—we killed him a long time ago.

Anyone that believes in God is a (expletive) sheep.

If there was a God, he wouldn't let me feel the way I do. Love isn't real, only hate remains. Only hate.

refer to personality traits, family background, or demographic characteristics as profiles do. Rather, they address features of the ecology common among past school shooters.

Access to guns. Most of the shooters had a history of gun use with some demonstrating a fascination with weapons and explosives. Most of the attackers had easy access to weapons and were able to take guns from their own home or from a relative or friend. Harris and Klebold, the Columbine shooters, easily purchased them. Some received them as gifts from parents. The Glock used by Kip Kinkel was a gift from his father, an attempt to demonstrate confidence in the young man who was such a concern to his parents.

Access to weapons among students is common, and not in and of itself a cause for concern. Interventions that address gun access include parent education about the role of guns in the deaths of young people, the frequency with which "secured" guns are accessed by children, and the importance of requesting assistance when a child seems obsessed with guns and other weapons. Parents and teachers should know that students' new or extraordinary efforts to acquire, prepare, or use weapons may signify the progression from idea to action. Appropriate investigation and inquiry about weapon access and use is important.

Relying on metal detectors in schools to prevent weapons from entering the building provides false security. Most of the shooters made no effort to conceal their weapons. In addition, metal detectors are very expensive, require at least two operators, and are subject to relatively frequent breakdowns with high maintenance costs. In discussing this issue with young people in an alternative high school, the adolescents we talked to scoffed at the idea of metal detectors. They told us: "School starts at 8:15. Security people get here at 7:30; so we just get here at 7:15." When we asked them what happened if the school locked the doors until 7:30, the response was: "We just give it (the weapon) to the girls. They (the security officers) don't like to check purses." We asked further: "Well, what if they did check the girls' purses?" "All of us get there at 8:10, they don't want us to be late to class, so we all rush by the machine." We persisted: "But what if they don't let you get by the machine and just mark you tardy?" Their response: "Oh, in that case, a friend goes in, we go to the outside fence and toss the gun over to him."

Emotional pain and confusion.   Very few of the shooters had been diagnosed with any mental illness. Relatively few of them had histories of alcohol or drug abuse, but most demonstrated an incredible range of conflicting emotions. (See Box 10.1.) Each of the students responsible for the shootings demonstrated some type of emotional trouble. More than half had a history of feeling extremely depressed, almost desperate. Most threatened to kill themselves, made suicidal gestures, or tried to kill themselves before the attack. A number did kill themselves during the attack.

The shooters were young people bursting with anger and rage. But under the anger and rage was an enormous range of feelings including pain, fear, shame, and sadness. These conflicting emotions interfered with reasonable problem solving. Many of the shooters saw the attack as the way to solve a personal problem: a parent planning to move the family, a lost or unreturned love, a school suspension. Unfortunately, to the emotionally confused shooters, the problems appeared devastating and without solution. For those who did not commit suicide, most experienced intense regret, remorse, and guilt afterwards. Developmentally appropriate life skills curriculum would assist them in dealing with negative feelings, disappointment, and loss, as well as in learning skills in developing and maintaining intimate friendships.

Aggressive hatred toward self and others.   The shooters had very favorable and narcissistic views about themselves, concurrent with very poor self-esteem. They believed that they were different from other people, and at the same time, disliked those who were different. Along with the narcissism, they were filled with self-loathing. Apparently these narcissistic young people with fragile, unstable self-esteem erupted into violence when their egos were threatened (Baumeister, Bushman, & Campbell, 2000).

Almost all of the attackers had come to the attention of someone, often fellow students, for their disturbing behavior. Behind this disturbing behavior were feelings that exemplified a callous disregard for the life of others and for their own lives. Some wrote poems about homicide and suicide. One student talked often of putting rat poison in the cheese shakers at a local pizza restaurant. One shooter claimed that he did not dislike his English teacher, who he killed. His goal was to kill two people because killing *any* two people made him eligible for the death penalty. She happened to be an opportune target. Because other teens may have knowledge of potential problems, peer assistance programs and supportive, compassionate adults are an important component of an environment that increases protective factors of support and belonging.

Planning and leakage.   In almost all of the incidences of school shooting, the attacker developed the idea to harm the target well before the attack, most at least two weeks earlier. The attacks were neither spontaneous nor impulsive. The attackers developed the idea in advance; they acquired weapons; and most developed a plan at least two days prior to the attack. So, these young people took a long, planned public path toward violence.

Additionally, prior to most incidences, the shooter told someone about his plan. The FBI describes this communication as *leakage*. In over half of the incidents, the shooter told more than one person about his plans. In virtually all of the cases the person told was a peer—a sibling, a school mate, or a friend. Sometimes the attackers told their friends directly, providing detailed information about the plan and the target. In other cases the information was oblique with the peers knowing that something spectacular was going to happen at school on a particular date. In almost half the cases the shooters were encouraged or influenced by other students.

Even though the shooter told a sibling, schoolmate, or friend about their ideas about a possible attack before it occurred, in almost no case was that information relayed to adults. Thus, a few young people at school usually knew what would happen because the shooters had told them, but these bystanders didn't warn anyone. Ironically, this disturbing pattern gives hope: If shooters plan, there is time to intervene. If shooters tell peers, adults might be able to learn what is planned.

Vigilante motivation.   School shooters had more than one motive, with the most frequent motive being revenge. Most of the shooters were known to hold a real or imagined grievance against the targets. Coupled with the grievance was the shooter's difficulty in coping with a major change of a significant relationship or with a personal failure prior to their school attack. These young people had built up such a huge reservoir of pain, resentment, hostility, anger, and rage that, in the end, it took relatively little to tip the scale.

It must be emphasized that a precipitating event alone did not cause the shooters to act. Rather, most had been persecuted, threatened, attacked, injured, or bullied by others prior to the incident. Shooters described experiences of being bullied in terms that approached torment. They described behaviors that, if they occurred in the workplace, would meet the legal definitions of harassment.

The experience of bullying appeared to play a major role in motivating the school attacks. More important, perhaps, was the common belief held by most of the shooters that they had not been safe at school. They had come to believe that adults would not or could not protect them. They concluded that adults did not care.

▲ Box 10.2

The Words of a Shooter: Kip's Letter

This second document is the text of a letter written after Kip Kinkel killed his parents. He left it on the living room coffee table. We have divided it into segments to provide examples of key points in the text.

Emotional Pain/Confusion

I have just killed my parents. I don't know what is happening. I love my mom and dad so much. I just got two felonies on my record. My parents can't take that. It would destroy them. The embarrassment would be too much for them. They couldn't live with themselves. I am so sorry.

Aggressive Hatred

I am a horrible son. I wish I had been aborted. I destroy anything I touch. I can't eat. I can't sleep. I didn't deserve them. They were wonderful people. It's not their fault or the fault of any person or organization or television show. My head just doesn't work right. God damn these voices inside my head!

Emotional Pain/Confusion

I want to die. I want to be gone. But I have to kill people. I don't know why. I am so sorry.

Why did God do this to me? I have never been happy. I wish I was happy. I wish I made my mother proud, but I am nothing. I try so hard to find happiness, but you know me: I hate everything. I have no other choice. What have I become? I am so sorry.

SPECIFIC INTERVENTION: PREVENTING SCHOOL SHOOTINGS

An effective plan for prevention of school shootings should target the above areas. More specifically, quiet, withdrawn, or "bizarre" youth who are frequently rejected, disrespected, teased, and bullied by classmates, and who have a tenuous relationship with parents need attention from compassionate adults. Young people who talk with hate and hostility and plan on "getting revenge on" or "getting even with" need to be heard. This is even more so for teens who have lost status or a relationship or a loved one recently. It may be that the single most effective school safety measure is the presence of caring adults in the school who spend time listening to young people. Teachers, para-educators, as well as administrative, cafeteria, and maintenance staff can all be provided with skills for listening and identifying troubled students.

The skill-building programs described in Chapter 13 provide an avenue to help develop competencies in young people who are struggling. These programs help the potential shooter directly by providing a range of useful skills. The peer interventions discussed in Chapter 14 engage invisible kids with their peers in a positive way. In addition to connecting the troubled teen with positive peers—itself a great help—the responsible adult has access to these adolescents in a meaningful way.

In almost every school shooter case, adults were not especially concerned or even knowledgeable about the behavior and feelings of the perpetrators prior to the shootings. Other students knew something was wrong. Schools need to use the peer group as a vehicle to identify and assist these young people. Peer support networks, cross-age and peer tutoring, mediation, and leadership programs provide links to connect understanding adults to the youth peer culture. Once connected to the youth peer culture, caring and sensitive adults can connect with young people in trouble. Students must believe that (a) telling an adult is an appropriate and positive behavior, and (b) that telling an adult will lead to positive outcomes. If they do not believe both of these, students are unlikely to confide in adults.

Two other potential interventions emerged from the above analysis. Because bullying played such a major role in most school shootings, school personnel must strongly support ongoing efforts to combat bullying in schools. Second, uncontrolled feelings of anger, hostility, and rage were also a major factor in the shootings. Often the anger was connected to experiences of rejection, isolation, and persecution with hurt and fear underlying the anger. We turn now to a discussion of the prevention strategies of anger management and anti-bullying programs.

Anger Management

Learning to deal with anger and other emotions must be one component of an anti-bullying program. Unfortunately, most anger reduction programs have not been empirically validated. Without validation, practitioners do not know whether their interventions are effective. More important is the possibility that the intervention is doing more harm than good. Most interventions are designed to put young people together in a group to help them reduce their anger and aggression, but this can be risky if youth are given unstructured time in which they may reinforce each others' aggression. Few anger programs have dealt with this issue, and few have been directed at the roots of aggressive and violent behavior in younger, middle-school-aged populations.

One exception is the SCARE (Student Created Aggression Replacement Education) program by Herrmann and McWhirter (2001). The SCARE program was specifically developed to prevent violence and aggression through appropriate management of anger for early adolescents. A growing body of literature has consistently indicated that these years are critical to a young person's social development, and this time period is potentially one of the best times for prevention programs for at-risk youth. Additionally, because a review of the literature revealed a lack of aggression replacement and anger management packages available to teachers, counselors, and youth workers for this age group (McWhirter, Herrmann, Jefferys, & Quinn, 1997), the curriculum was designed for broad scale implementation by such individuals.

One premise of the SCARE program is that negative actions perceived as intentional will elicit anger, and anger in turn motivates hostile behavior. Therefore, the SCARE program focuses on the reattribution of perceived offenses, and the control and management of resulting anger. In recent years empirical evidence has linked high levels of anger to a number of negative social consequences, including an increased propensity to cause physical damage to oneself and others, increased psychological problems, and school-related problems (Deffenbacher, Lynch, Oetting, & Kemper, 1996). Because the literature has also indicated that anger *can* be effectively reduced through therapeutic intervention (Achmon, Granek, Golomb, & Hart, 1998; Deffenbacher, McNamara, Stark, & Sabadell, 1990; Moon & Eisler, 1983; Novaco, 1975), the SCARE program was constructed as a meta-theoretical treatment package focusing on anger management and coping skills for adolescents and young adults. Primary objectives embraced by the SCARE program include (a) teaching young people about emotions, including aggression and anger, (b) helping young people recognize alternatives to violent behavior and aggressive responses, and (c) encouraging young people to make good decisions in response to provocative situations. The program involves a total of 15 different sessions that are clustered into three distinct yet related sections: (a) *recognizing anger and violence in the community*, (b) *managing and reducing self-expressions of anger*, and (c) *defusing anger and violence in others.*

In *recognizing anger and violence in the community*, primary objectives include (a) providing a clear definition of anger and violence, and (b) introducing the topic of anger and violence in such a way that promotes intrigue and interest for acquiring anger management and coping skills. We know that learning is facilitated among youth who have cultivated an interest for a particular subject, and who feel that the material presented to them is relevant to their lives. By combining national statistics with descriptive images obtained from popular media resources, this section aims to stimulate motivation for learning anger reduction skills, and cultivates an awareness that such skills are vitally important to *all* adolescents.

The second section, *managing and reducing anger in the self*, was developed to inform youth about effective pro-social strategies for managing their own aggressive impulses and feelings of anger. This section is based on Novaco's (1975, 1979) adaptation of Michenbaum's (1972) stress inoculation model, and consists of three separate phases: (a) education and cognitive preparation, (b) skill acquisition, and (c) application training. Education and cognitive preparation provides youth with information about the cognitive, physiological, and behavioral interactions of anger arousal. They learn about internal triggers that can provoke anger, and about steps they can take to effectively manage their expression of anger. Skill acquisition consists of training adolescents in cognitive-behavioral coping skills to effectively manage situations involving anger and aggression. Application training consists of practicing newly acquired skills within the context of experiential group sessions or role-plays until such skills are mastered. In studies assessing the efficacy of this model, Novaco (1975, 1979) reports evidence in support of stress inoculation training for reducing anger, whereas others have reported the effectiveness of this model with adolescent populations (Hains & Ellmann, 1994; Wilcox & Dowrick, 1992).

Finally, the third section, *defusing anger and violence in others*, draws upon an eclectic model involving skills and techniques for (a) preventing situations involving anger and violence from developing, and (b) promoting peaceful resolutions to hostile situations that have developed. To promote these objectives in as many different ways as possible, this section is not grounded in any one theoretical orientation, and combines techniques from different schools of thought. In a review of the treatment literature, Greenwood (1994) notes that multimodal approaches that combine several treatment modalities (e.g., cognitive skills, relaxation skills, social skills training) are usually more efficacious than unimodal approaches. In addition, multimodal approaches are of special value when treating behaviorally disordered and "acting-out" youth. As such, several sessions have been developed in the *defusing anger and violence in others* section, which draw upon diverse yet complementary theoretical tenants, including sessions on verbal and paraverbal techniques, body language training (proxemics and kinesics), identifying creative alternatives to aggression, diversity appreciation training, and no-violence contracting.

Based on a series of experimental research studies, this anger control program for children and adolescents has been designated a Promising Program by the U.S. Department of Education's (USDE) Expert Panel on Safe, Disciplined, and Drug-free Schools. The process through which the USDE evaluates program effectiveness is described in detail in Chapter 12. In addition to reducing state and trait anger and the inclination to use guns and violence to solve disputes, *SCARE* participants also significantly increased their cognitive perspective taking, the inclination to see the other person's point of view. We are hopeful that this intervention disrupts the process by which intense and deep-rooted anger evolves into calculated, destructive behavior, thus making children and schools safer.

Another way to make children and schools safer is to eliminate or reduce some of the immediate, school-based sources of anger and rage. Reducing school bullying will help accomplish this.

Anti-Bullying Interventions

The bullying that students, parents, and educators face today differs from that of earlier years in part because of young people's access to more lethal forms of aggression. So, even when the bully is not actually accessing weapons, the perception of threat and the psychological effects of bullying is intensified.

Bullying is a specific subset of hostile aggression in which (1) there is an imbalance of power with a more powerful person or group attacking a less powerful one, (2) a behavior is intended to disturb or harm, and (3) the behavior occurs repeatedly over time. The aggressive behavior may be verbal (e.g., threats, name calling), psychological (e.g., exclusion, rumors), or physical (e.g., hitting, kicking). Bullying can be done directly in the classroom, hallway, or playground; it can be accomplished indirectly and anonymously through e-mail messages. The power differential may be psychological or physical. Thus, bullying can take many forms but retains the same essential spirit. Bullies are characterized by the need to dominate others through hostile means and they show little or no empathy for their victims (Ballard, Argus, & Remley, 1999). Of particular concern is frequent bullying, typically defined as bullying that occurs once a week or more. In a large World Health Organization study (Nansel et al., 2001), 30% of the sample reported frequent or moderate involvement in bullying either as a victim (over 10%), as a bully (13%), or both (over 6%). Frequency of bullying was higher in middle-school grades than in secondary schools. Males were more likely than females to be both the victims and the perpetrators of bullying. Simmons (2002) argues that much of girls' aggression is not captured in many studies of bullying. She notes that girls normatively use relational aggression to bully their victims, and that relational aggression is characterized by high frequency and invisibility to teachers, and that girls are often reluctant to acknowledge that it occurs.

Research examining personal characteristics of young people involved in bullying has consistently found that both the victims and the bullies demonstrate poorer psychological functioning than their less involved peers. Bullies generally demonstrate more dislike of school, higher levels of conduct problems, with increased risk of having a criminal record as adults (Olweus, 1993). Ninety percent of young adolescents who were bullied believe that the victimization caused them significant problems including the loss of friendships, feelings of isolation, and hopelessness (Hazler, Hoover, & Oliver, 1992). Young people who are bullied generally show higher levels of anxiety, depression, and unhappiness, and they display significant behavioral difficulties even two years after the bullying (Rigby, 1999; Schwartz, McFadyen-Ketchum, Dodge, Pettit, & Bates, 1998; Swearer, Song, Cary, Eagle, & Mickelson, 2001). Fortunately, actions taken by school personnel and others can significantly reduce the occurrence of bullying (Crawford, 2002; Espelage & Swearer, in press; Teacher Education Institute, 2002).

Schoolwide plan.   Although individual efforts can be helpful, developing a systemwide plan is necessary to significantly reduce bullying. Begin with a clear, agreed upon definition of bullying and make a plan for action. This plan for action should include answers to these questions. Does the plan develop an effective way to eliminate or reduce student-to-student put-downs? Are there as many opportunities for students to be recognized for pro-social, positive behaviors as opportunities to be recognized for antisocial, negative behaviors? How would the students answer this question? Does the plan include recognizing and promoting students' pro-social behavior and their random acts of kindness? Does the plan establish ways to recognize and support positive and kind acts done by staff and faculty? Faculty and staff must be backed up in their efforts to identify and halt bullying. Inconsistent application of the plan, or administrative failure to support the efforts of those implementing it, will reduce student confidence and decrease effectiveness.

The purpose of the schoolwide plan is to change the context in which bullying occurs (Espelage & Swearer, in press). Norms of looking the other way, intermittent punishment, and classroom Darwinism must be changed to norms of attending to bullying incidents, consistent application of consequences, and the fostering of a strong sense of community within every classroom. In addition to responding systemwide, the plan needs to consider interventions with the specific people involved in the bullying. This includes victims, bullies, parents, and bystanders.

The victim.   Concerned adults need to consider the bullying victim's realistic options, given the particular situation and persons involved. The coping skills and support network of bullied students may need to be strengthened before the student can act more assertively on their own behalf. Victims of bullying often feel a great deal of shame and mistrust, which may make it harder for them to attempt using the skills that they do have. Sometimes students can be helped to identify behaviors and strategies that will reduce their risk of further bullying. The assertiveness training program described in Chapter 13 attends to one dimension that may be important for students who are bullied. Bullies can benefit from assertiveness training as well, learning appropriate ways to meet their needs for importance, validation, and esteem.

The bully.   Incidences of bullying should not be ignored, but they do vary widely in seriousness and severity. Thoughtless teasing might merit an informal discussion; group harassment with threats might need formal procedures including interviews with perpetrators and parents and possible disciplinary action. Pikas (cited in Rigby, 2000) has developed an approach known as the Method of Shared Concern, which involves a two-stage process. In the first stage, perpetrators are identified and spoken to individually. The adult shares his or her concern with the bully for the person being victimized and invites the bully to act in a constructive and responsible way to remedy the situation. No threats are used. This is followed by a careful monitoring of subsequent behaviors. In the minority of cases where this approach is not successful and the bullying continues, the second step includes sanctions and application of consequences.

The bystander.   Observers of victimization and bullying often receive little attention. This is unfortunate because they contribute to the problem. Many want to help, but are insecure and afraid that they themselves will be targeted next. Remaining silent leads to guilt and anxiety. Encouraging bystanders to discuss their feelings, along with the provision of assertiveness skills and exploration of various options for responding, can encourage them to become more active in reducing bullying. Bystanders can provide personal support to victims, showing their concern, encouraging the victim's efforts and accomplishments, and can also refuse to reinforce the bully with verbal encouragement or laughter. More direct intervention might take the form of protecting the victim and confronting the bully during the incident.

"The toadies."   There is another type of bystander who is more interested in encouraging bullying and the bully. Indeed, bullies are sometimes bolstered by the presence of "passive bullies." These passive participants in bullying behavior support the primary aggressor by expressing approval and encouragement. This elevates the status of the perpetrator and reinforces him (Ballard, Argus, & Remley, 1999). These passive bullies should be dealt with in the same way as the overtly aggressive bully.

Parents.   Parents are essential allies in implementing a schoolwide anti-bullying program. Understanding the problem of bullying, the prevention program, and the definitions of bullying used by the school are all important in parental acceptance and support of the program. In the process of learning about the program, parents may realize the importance of exploring bullying with their children in a more focused way, which may lead to surprises for the parents of both victims and bullies. Many children suffer, and dole out suffering, in silence.

The parents of bullied children need information and support to help their child. The parents of students who bully may respond in numerous ways to their child's behavior: denial, blame of the victims, the school, or society, or with requests for assistance with an out-of-control child. Blaming the bully—or his or her parents—is not helpful.

A developmental and comprehensive approach to reducing bullying is important. Prevention programs that are supported throughout the school building, that include consistent responses to individual behavior, and that incorporate aspects of the social context of bullying are most likely to reduce the number of young people victimized by bullying.

CONCLUSION

Even though there has been a decrease in youth crime and school violence in the last decade, sensational incidences of school shootings have created concern and fear. The characteristics of shooters are different than the characteristics of other perpetrators of youth violence. Their access to guns, their emotional pain and confusion, their aggressive hatred, and their vigilante motives mark them as distinct offenders in contrast with the stereotypical juvenile offender. The detailed planning and subsequent leakage of information about their eventual shootings highlight the need to listen more closely to our young people. It suggests the need to engage the shooter's peer group in a more pro-social way. Finally, reducing the incidence of bullying within schools and providing consistent opportunities to develop anger management skills will decrease the likelihood that an angry and discouraged young person will ultimately become a school shooter.

Youth Suicide

▲ *Wet the top of the glass*
and run your finger around the rim.
That's me in the shimmering squeal; the sound of
glass.
Drop the vase to the floor
and listen to it shatter.
That's me in the piercing shatter; the sound of
glass.
Crush the mirror and watch the image
crack and splinter.
That's me in the crack, the splinter; the sound of
glass.
There is not much left of me.
Why not just silence the sound of glass, too?
If only I could find
Some meaning for myself that
Death won't take away.

J. J. McWhirter

CHAPTER OUTLINE

▲   In the last two decades the number of people 15 to 24 years old who committed suicide rose 200% (Marris, Canetto, McIntosh, & Silverman, 2000). To prevent suicide we must understand the influences that contribute to suicidal behavior. They may range from a child's chaotic family life to not knowing how to manage relationships, from a child's perception that the future is doomed, to a teenager's feeling that the present is hopeless. To prevent suicide we also should know the warning signs and available intervention strategies.

Among the aspects of suicide that we discuss in this chapter are (a) the incidence of childhood and adolescent suicide, (b) precursors to suicide and the characteristics of suicidal children and teens, (c) warning signs and behaviors, (d) common misconceptions of suicide, (e) identification and assessment of suicide ideation, and (f) prevention and intervention strategies, including early intervention, crisis management, and follow-up treatment. Particular attention is given to childhood and adolescent depression and early onset of bipolar disorder. Finally, for each intervention, we focus on the potential role of the teacher, counselor, psychologist, and other human service professionals and the role of the school, family, and inpatient settings in effecting change.

THE SCOPE OF THE PROBLEM

Suicide is the third leading cause of death among adolescents in the United States after unintentional injury and homicide (McIntosh, 2000; National Center for Health Statistics, 2000; Centers for Disease Control and Prevention, 2001). In recent years, it is estimated that approximately 5,000 individuals whose death certificate indicated suicide were between the ages of 15 and 24. In 1996, 4,358 suicides were by those between 15 and 24 years of age (McIntosh, 2000). Some research suggests that 11% of young people attempt suicide (Andrews & Lewinsohn, 1992; Lewinsohn, Rohde, & Seeley, 1993). This rate climbs to about 33% among troubled adolescents (Tomlinson-Keasey & Keasey, 1988) and to 61% in some groups of juvenile offenders (Alessi, McManus, Brickman, & Grapentine, 1984). Over the past two decades, the suicide rate among adolescents has increased by 200% and the number of youth who attempt suicide is predicted to increase (Robertson & Mathews, 1989; McIntosh, 2000). Suicide rates among children and adolescents are highest in the western regions of the United States and lowest in the Northeast (National Center for Health Statistics, 2000).

These estimates are probably low. Many suicides are not reported as such because of the family's embarrassment or religious beliefs or the discomfort of the school and community in acknowledging that a suicide has occurred (see Box 11.1). Consider also that accidents, the leading cause of death among adolescents, are often associated with recklessness and use of alcohol, both of which are related to suicide ideation. Many accidental deaths may be a result of a wish to be dead. Similarly, drug overdoses, recorded as accidental deaths, may be unrecognized or unreported suicides. These deaths are considered *passive suicides*. Of course, researchers are unable to determine the number of passive suicides that occur each year.

Sex differences have been found in the rates and the lethality of suicide attempts. Three times as many females as males attempt suicide, but about three times as many males as females are successful (Canetto & Lester, 1995; McIntosh, 2000). Differences can be partially attributed to the lethality of the method. Males tend to choose more violent means to kill themselves, such as firearms, while females more often use pills and poisons. Six out of ten suicides among all adolescents are through the use of firearms (McIntosh, 2000).

Latino children and adolescents have a higher rate of suicide than European American youth (Smith, Mercer, & Rosenberg, 1989; Queralt, 1993). The suicide rate of African American teens has increased, and although the rate is still lower than for European Americans, the gap is closing. African American females have a low rate of suicide compared to other ethnic groups (Range et al., 1999), however, recent increases in suicide attempts by male and female African Americans are quite dramatic (Centers for Disease Control, 1998).

Although there is considerable variability from tribe to tribe, Native Americans have the highest adolescent suicide rate of any ethnic group in the United States (Gould & Kramer, 2001). The high suicide rate has been associated with factors such as substance abuse and alcoholism, child abuse and neglect, unemployment, the availability of firearms, and lack of economic options that lead to hopelessness (Berman & Jobes, 1991; Middlebrook, Lemaster, Beals, Novins, & Manson, 2001). Although little data exists for Asian American adolescents, some researchers hypothesize that cultural values may contribute to lower rates of suicide among this group (Range et al., 1999).

▲ Box 11.1

Accidental Death

Jarrod was a senior in high school who loved to play the guitar and compose songs. He had dreamed of being a musician for as long as he could remember. It was a dream his parents did not share. Jarrod was the oldest child in the family and he had hoped to study music in college, but his parents insisted that he attend a business school because they didn't want to "send good money after bad." Jarrod expected a lot of himself and he knew that his parents also expected a great deal of him. He had few friends, but the friendships he had were quite intense. His friends looked up to him and had high expectations for his career in music. They were disappointed about his parents' plan to send him to business school and told him to "fight for his rights." Feeling unable to live up to his friends' expectations, he retreated from them. That spring Jarrod was sleeping only 3 to 4 hours a night. He alienated himself from his friends and his parents and grew increasingly distraught over his seeming inability to please the people he loved. Four days after his high school graduation, local newspapers reported that Jarrod, aged 18, had died in a car accident. Investigators could not explain why, in the absence of traffic or bad weather, he had suddenly veered off the road and crashed, at high speed, into a very prominent cement wall.

Suicide among gay, lesbian, bisexual, and transgendered (GLBT) youth has received considerable attention during the last several years. Rates of attempted suicide range from 20% to 42% with suicide the leading cause of death among gay, lesbian, and bisexual youth, primarily because of the dehabilitating effects of growing up in a homophobic society (Ryan, 2001). The rate of suicide among gay and lesbian youth is considerably higher than that for heterosexual youth: They are two to three times more likely to commit suicide and constitute 30% of all adolescent suicides. Several researchers (Remafedi, French, Story, Resnick, & Blum, 1998; Noell & Ochs, 2001) suggest that suicide attempts by this population are frequently linked with sexual milestones, such as self-identification as homosexual, coming out to others, or resulting loss of friendship. GLBT youth often report higher rates of intravenous drug use, lifetime history of suicide attempts, and recent depression and suicidal ideation (Noell & Ochs, 2001). Such risk factors increase when homosexual youth are faced with additional difficulties, such as homelessness. According to French, Story, Remafedi, Resnick, and Blum (1996), homosexual males are also more likely to report poor body image, binge-eating, or purging behaviors. Gay male suicide attempters tend to adopt a homosexual identity at a younger age, express more feminine gender roles, and often come from dysfunctional families (Savin-Williams, 1994).

Attempts are most likely to occur after same-sex sexual activity or when individuals question their heterosexual identity. During this period, they are faced with additional stressors and experience feelings of social isolation, self-revulsion, disenfranchisement, and rejection from family and peers (Remafedi et al., 1996; Savin-Williams, 1994). This particularly high-risk group requires special attention in order to reduce suicide attempts.

Disability status may also be a factor in youth suicide. Children and adolescents with disabilities often feel isolated (Bauer, 2001), and are frequently the only member of their family with a disability. Although the presence of disabilities can affect both male and female children, some researchers have noted the multiple minority status for females with disabilities (Bauer, 2001). Feelings of isolation and "differentness" can cause additional stress leading to loneliness, depression, and thoughts of suicide.

RISK FACTORS AND CHARACTERISTICS OF YOUTH SUICIDE

To understand the causes of suicide among children and adolescents, it is helpful to recognize behaviors that are considered "normal" during development. Many adolescents of all cultures enjoy life, are happy most of the time, and are able to develop nurturing friendships (Diener & Diener, 1996). They feel positive about their development and their futures. They experience physical changes and new social roles without undue trauma, even though they may regularly experience situation-specific anxiety. For the most part, they are able to cope with the changes that are taking place in their lives.

For other adolescents, however, this period of change and growth is filled with stressful events and adjustments. Depression, aggression, and divergent thinking are common during this transitional period. These characteristics can be exacerbated by low socioeconomic status, absence of parental support, and lack of educational and economic opportunity. Girls tend to express more negative feelings toward themselves than boys, and report more loneliness, sadness, and vulnerability (Tang & Cook, 2001). These experiences may provide fertile ground for suicide ideation and attempts.

It is often difficult for parents, teachers, and mental health professionals to differentiate between the normal turmoil that occurs during childhood and adolescence from turmoil that is life-threatening (King, Price, Telljohann, & Wahl, 2000). Many children and adolescents at risk for suicide have been mistakenly viewed as simply "going through a stage." Certain psychological and relationship characteristics help to identify those who are at risk for self-destructive behavior.

Interpersonal, Family, and Psychosocial Characteristics

A variety of interpersonal, family, and psychosocial characteristics are associated with suicidal ideation and suicide attempts. Several of these are described in the following paragraphs, however, this is not an exhaustive list.

Substance abuse.   Alcohol and drug abuse is often related to adolescent risk for suicide (Gould & Kramer, 2001). Although adolescents who are chemically dependent are generally at higher risk for suicide, interrelated factors, such as homelessness or social isolation, can add to the likelihood of a suicide attempt (Noell & Ochs, 2001). Substance abuse can exacerbate suicide risk in a myriad of ways. For example, alcoholics or drug users are often inaccessible for suicide prevention and may not seek the adequate support that is needed (Roy, 2001). In Chapter 7 we provide detailed information about the risks associated with substance use.

Under- and overachievement.   Academic under achievement has been linked to suicide, although impaired academic functioning may follow and be a consequence of suicide attempts (Lewinsohn, Rohde, & Seeley, 1993; Mazza & Eggert, 2001). Perfectionism, overachievement, and living up to high expectations are characteristic of many academically talented suicidal children and adolescents. Some researchers suggest that suicide among children is related to high intellectual ability (Tomlinson-Keasey & Keasey, 1988). Deterioration in the academic performance of young people, whether they are high or low achieving, can be a warning sign of suicidal potential.

Catastrophic worldview.   In addition to negative thoughts and feelings about the self, a negative or catastrophic view of the world and the future is associated with suicide risk. Some children and adolescents view the world as an unpredictable, dangerous, and hostile place. These intimations of catastrophe are exacerbated by threats of nuclear weapons, the AIDS crisis, racism, poverty, regional wars, and civil violence. Consequently, some young people feel desperate and helpless and are potential victims of a suicide crisis. Unfortunately, films and television influence catastrophic feelings by modeling and glorifying violence and death (Levine, 1996; Gould & Kramer, 2001).

Cluster suicides.   Cluster suicides are suicides that follow or imitate another suicide. They may also follow a television program or movie that depicts teenage suicide (Capuzzi & Golden, 1988; Gould & Shaffer, 1986; Gould & Kramer, 2001). When one child or adolescent commits suicide, the act somehow becomes normalized for others. After one suicide, those who have already been experiencing despair may begin to see suicide as a viable response to their stress and feelings of hopelessness. Adolescents who are at risk for self-destructive behavior are even more vulnerable after someone they know or know of commits suicide (Lewinsohn, Rohde, & Seeley, 1993). Suicide in the media primarily affects teenagers and young adults, rather than young children (Gould & Kramer, 2001). Suicide clusters, often trivialized as "copycat" suicides, are a particular problem on American Indian reservations (Tomlinson-Keasey & Keasey, 1988). For this reason, appropriate postvention or follow-up treatment after a suicide crisis is essential.

Disruptive family experiences.   Suicidal youth often come from dysfunctional or disintegrated families (Fergusson & Lynskey, 1995). The rise in single-parent households as well as lack of skill and experience in parenting, communication, and discipline (see Chapter 3) exacerbate the risk of suicide. Family interactions that are characterized by anger, emotional ambivalence, and rejection are also associated with self-destructive behavior in youth. When single parents are overloaded with work and financial obligations and have limited support from others, they have less energy to devote to the parent-child relationship. "Blended" families or stepfamilies may also be at high risk for suffering from uncertain, inconsistent, and confusing family interactions. Parental support and consistency are important protective factors against children at risk for suicide, and youth who lack family stability are at increasingly higher risk for suicide (Mazza & Eggert, 2001; Randell, Eggert, & Pike, 2001).

Violent families.   Violence is common in the families of many suicidal children. In one study, attempters were three to six times more likely to have experienced sexual or physical abuse at home (Blumenthal, 1990). Suicide is also more prevalent among young people whose families have a history of suicide (Pfeffer, Normandin, & Kakuma, 1994; Gould

& Kramer, 2001). One study found that nearly 38% of adolescent suicide attempters had a close relative who committed suicide (Metha & Dunham, 1988). The age of a child is also significant: As many as 75% of children who were under 11 years old when a family member committed suicide attempted suicide themselves when they became adolescents (Roy, 1983), a greater percentage than older children who experience this tragic event.

Poor communication. Children who grow up in a dysfunctional family system frequently develop inadequate communication skills. Young people who grow up in an environment where communication of their thoughts and feelings is unsafe do not learn to express their distress to others. As feelings and thoughts fester and become increasingly negative, these children may withdraw into themselves, making it difficult for others to recognize and respond to their increasing pain, depression, and possible suicidal feelings. The progressive isolation that results from poor communication skills can be a warning sign of self-destructive behavior (Marttunen, Aro, & Lonnquist, 1993). Other children may develop problems in acting out, also associated with higher levels of suicide risk (Evans, Marte, Betts, & Silliman, 2001).

Loss and separation. Suicidal youth are more likely than other youth to have experienced the loss of a parent through separation, divorce, or death (Marttunen, Aro, & Lonnquist, 1993). Even when one has not lost a parent or other close relative, suicidal thoughts may arise in response to the loss of a friendship or dating partner (Tang & Cook, 2001). Separation and differentiation from parents is an important developmental task of adolescence, but death and divorce are life-changing events over which a child has no control. The natural feelings of grief, abandonment, and anger call for coping skills that not all children have developed. The surviving parent may be experiencing tremendous emotional adjustment as well, and may be unable to provide the direction and support the child needs. In contrast with steady nurturing of autonomy, the loss of a parent may push children rapidly into adult roles before they are ready.

Intrapersonal and Psychological Characteristics

Certain intrapersonal and psychological characteristics are associated with suicide ideation, attempts, and completions. These deserve specific attention.

Self-image. Low self-esteem, poor self-concept, and feelings of worthlessness are typical of suicidal children and may predispose a child or adolescent to suicide ideation. Poor self-esteem and self-concept often lead to feelings of hopelessness and depression (Bagley, 1992; Stivers, 1990; Tang & Cook, 2001). A distorted view of the self can also lead to irrational and unrealistic expectations of others, the world, and the future. Children and adolescents who dislike themselves and who are unable to see themselves in positive ways require special attention from counselors, teachers, and parents. Girls are at an increased risk of problems with self-esteem, especially during middle school (Tang & Cook, 2001). Female adolescents who physically mature earlier than others and date at an early age may have particularly negative outlooks on their body and appearance (see Box 11.2).

Anger. Anger, aggression, and anger control difficulties are also predictors of risky suicidal behavior (Randell, Eggert, & Pike, 2001). As we discussed in the last chapter, inappropriately expressed anger is a major problem, and suicidal adolescents often display

▲ Box 11.2

She Didn't Want to Die

Jennifer was a 12-year-old girl, just finishing her sixth-grade year in elementary school. Unlike other girls her age, she began developing physically and emotionally into a young adult over the past year in school. Although Jennifer had a close circle of friends, she often worried about other girls teasing her and gossiping about her behind her back. She felt different than everyone else. She was ashamed to shower after gym class and uncomfortable about her rapid physical development. Jennifer often found herself hanging around boys several years older than herself and enjoying their company. She no longer felt comfortable giggling and gossiping with her friends. She was too ashamed to tell her parents how she felt and believed her friends would not understand. Slowly Jennifer started speaking with her friends less and spending more time with her older male buddies.

One day after school, Jennifer headed home and flipped on the television as she normally did. There on the news, she saw a young girl in high school who had committed suicide the previous week. The news coverage was quite extensive, showing her memorial service, her saddened classmates, and all of the flowers around the school laid out for her. It was at that moment that Jennifer grabbed a bottle of pills and swallowed over 30 of them in hopes of recovering some sense of importance and belonging. Later, in the emergency room, she told her mother that she really didn't want to die; all she wanted was to stop feeling so unbearably alone.

increased levels of hostility. In a recent study conducted in the Rocky Mountain region, the area with the highest rate of adolescent suicide, researchers found a relationship between reported suicide risk and initiation of fights, threatening of other children, and use of weapons to assault (Evans, Marte, Betts, & Silliman, 2001). Those who act aggressively toward their peers, are victims of violence, or witness such hostility are at increased risk for suicidal behavior.

Loneliness.   Loneliness, isolation, and lack of connectedness are clearly implicated in suicide (B. T. McWhirter, 1990; Mazza & Eggert, 2001). Most suicidal children and adolescents generally have problems with their peers and are sensitive to rejection. Usually loneliness begins in childhood and continues into adolescence. Teenagers who feel lonely and isolated in a period marked by developing social relationships do not experience the support of friends. Without these nurturing and bonding relationships, children feel expendable and unnoticed—feelings that often lead to suicide ideation.

Impulsivity.   Impulsivity is often related to a suicidal response in young people. Teenagers and pre-teenagers who are part of a peer cluster, for example, may attempt suicide out of an impulsive reaction to someone else's self-destructive actions. Impulsive children are also influenced by others' responses to suicide and by the impact that a suicide has on others (Lipschitz, 1995; Gould & Kramer, 2001).

Impulsivity is also related to a risk-taking style. Although young people may be ambivalent about ending their lives, an impulsive or daredevil reaction to stressors often leads to suicide. In other words, adolescents may not be intent on killing themselves, but attempt to gain attention or approval from others through risky behavior. High-risk behaviors and impulsivity, fairly common during adolescence, allow young people to test their fears of death against their feelings of immortality (Bell & Bell, 1993). Impulse control may be a key predictor of the outcome of a suicidal crisis: Impulsive children who contemplate suicide may attempt it before they have time to think of an alternative.

Depression and hopelessness.   Depression is clearly a strong contributing factor to suicidal behavior in adults, with 35% to 80% of adult suicide attempters reporting depression before the attempt. Before the 1970s, many researchers and clinicians believed that depression did not occur in children (Fergusson & Woodward, 2002). Recent studies have suggested that approximately 2% to 8% of children experience a first episode of major depression before reaching age 16 (Fergusson & Woodward, 2002). Current research indicates that depression is linked to suicidal thoughts and behaviors among children and adolescents in both clinical and nonclinical settings (Gould & Kramer, 2001; Mazza & Eggert, 2001). As we have argued elsewhere (B. T. McWhirter, J. J. McWhirter, Hart, & Gat, 2000), depression, although not present in all cases of youth suicide, remains an important common denominator among suicides.

Hopelessness, one component of depression, is a solid predictor of the feeling or state that leads some young people to self-destructive behavior (Levy, Jurkovic, & Spirito, 1995; Metalsky & Joiner, 1992; Whisman & Kwon, 1993; Gould & Kramer, 2001). Other psychological disorders, such as anxiety disorders, obsessive-compulsive behavior, hostility, and psychosis, also play important roles in some teenage and child suicides. Recognition of the signs of depression and other psychopathology in children may help to avert a suicidal crisis.

Adolescents who develop depression are at increased risk for a variety of adverse outcomes later in life (Fergusson & Woodward, 2002), including subsequent depression, anxiety, suicidal behavior, nicotine dependence, difficulties in academia and employment, as well as unplanned pregnancy. As many as two-thirds of those between the ages of 14 and 16 showing depression will experience another episode before the age of 21 (Fergusson & Woodward, 2002).

Thinking patterns.   Faulty thinking and irrational beliefs, consistently found in conjunction with depression and low self-esteem, are prevalent among suicidal youth (Metalsky, Joiner, Hardin, & Abramson, 1993). Children at risk for suicide possess fewer positive coping strategies and often do not seek assistance for their problems (Randell, Eggert, & Pike, 2001). If faulty thinking can be modified at an early age, many suicide crises may be avoided. Here are some thinking patterns common to suicidal children and adolescents:

- *Cognitive constriction:* inability to see options for solving problems, which leads to dichotomous thinking, common in the critical stages of suicide ideation. The child is able to see only two solutions to the problem: continue to exist in a living hell or find relief through death. (For example, "I will feel this way forever unless I kill myself.")

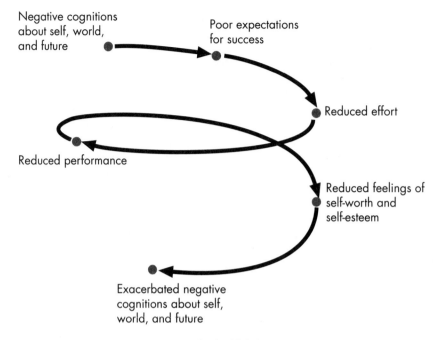

FIGURE 11.1 Spiral of self-defeating cognitions

- *Cognitive rigidity:* a rigid style of perceiving and reacting to the environment, which restricts a person's ability to cope with stress and to formulate realistic alternative approaches to problems. Cognitively rigid individuals see the problem, their inability to solve it, and the future as catastrophic. (For example, "I have no place to live and no one to help me; there's absolutely nothing I can ever do about it.")
- *Cognitive distortion:* overestimation of the magnitude and insolubility of problems. The difficulty of a problem is also generalized to all situations. Distorters assume that they are the cause of their problems. The past is forgotten and the future is unimaginable. (For example, "I didn't get an A on that test so I must be stupid and everything in my life is a complete mess.")

These consuming negative beliefs about the self, the insolubility of problems, and the future are pervasive. They can lead to withdrawal, to an inability to create change, and ultimately to suicide. Faulty thinking patterns have a self-defeating spiral effect in which youngsters' problems grow increasingly worse and their ability to conceive solutions becomes increasingly limited (Figure 11.1).

WARNING SIGNS OF SUICIDE

Suicide Motivations

The reasons that young people attempt suicide are, themselves, initial warning signs, if they can be detected. Suicide can be a method of *self-punishment* to deal with guilt or shame. Self-punishment is not uncommon for a young girl who discovers she is pregnant,

▲ Box 11.3

The Girl Who Had Everything

Shelley was an intelligent, beautiful, and popular high school senior. She was dating the homecoming king, was earning straight A's, was the star of the girls' softball team, and was liked by everybody. She seemed to have everything her girlfriends wanted without even trying. When her parents went through a sudden and angry divorce, Shelley continued to be the same smiling, fun-loving friend; her girlfriends believed that this "courage" was just another strength that their talented friend possessed.

One weekend she got into a fight with her mother just before her mother and brothers were to leave for an overnight visit with friends. In what was probably an attempt at revenge, Shelley called a large number of her friends and had a party at her mother's house. After several hours of drinking, Shelley got into another argument, this time with her boyfriend, and he broke off the relationship. Her girlfriends reported that Shelley seemed to be her "normal, laughing self" for the rest of the evening; at the time, they assumed she thought the breakup was only temporary. But when her family arrived home the next morning, the car was running in a closed garage and Shelley had been dead for hours.

She left no note. Shelley had not done or said anything to her friends to suggest that she wouldn't be around the next day. It appeared to be an impulsive decision, carried out in haste. Clearly her outgoing high spirits and bravado were masking despair and anger. Perhaps they also masked the fact that this girl who "had everything" had never really learned how to cope with disappointment and pain.

for a teenager who begins to have memories of sexual molestation, or for an adolescent in conflict about sexual orientation. Suicide may also seem to provide *absolution* for past behaviors; this motivation is not uncommon among alcoholics who end their lives to absolve themselves of past behaviors. Suicide may be motivated by *perverted revenge*, a perceived means to get back at those who caused the individual pain, such as parents who got divorced. *Retaliatory abandonment* is another motivation for suicide. A boy who has been dumped by his girlfriend can "retaliate" by showing her how awful she was to cause him to end it all. He would rather leave than to be left by someone. Both perverted revenge and retaliatory abandonment may have been operating in the case of the girl described in Box 11.3. *Fantasy of omnipotent mastery* is a desire to have absolute control over the self and others, to control life and death itself, and to be completely autonomous. Finally, children or adolescents may attempt suicide, not intending to end their lives but rather as a cry for help; of course, these attempts can be just as lethal. Decreasing suicidal ideation is essential in reducing actual attempts, and being aware of suicide motivations can assist in detection and prevention.

Verbal Messages

Most children who feel self-destructive give verbal hints that life is too difficult to handle and not worth living. Children and adolescents may say any of the following statements or similar statements:

- "I don't see how I can go on."
- "I wish I were dead."
- "There's only one way out of my problems."
- "I won't be around much longer."
- "I'm tired of living."
- "You'll be sorry you treated me this way."
- "Pretty soon my troubles will be over."

They are hinting or saying directly that they are considering suicide. Suicidal children also talk about death, wonder aloud what it will be like to be dead, and may be preoccupied by thoughts of others who have died. They may also joke about killing themselves. Many messages that are communicated as jokes are actually indications that a suicidal crisis is imminent; these jokes should not be taken lightly. In an effort to get help or to find out how others will respond, some children make direct threats of suicide. Verbal warnings should be taken seriously and not seen as just a "stage" that children go through. Failure to respond to a verbal warning or to a direct threat of suicide may be interpreted as confirmation that the child is worthless, expendable, and unloved. These feelings only increase the risk of a suicide attempt.

Behavioral Changes

Parents, teachers, and counselors can help prevent suicide attempts in children and adolescents by familiarizing themselves with behavioral changes that may suggest the risk of a suicide attempt (Mazza & Eggert, 2001). These include:

- Mood swings or fluctuations.
- A change from happy and positive interactions with others to withdrawal and negativity.
- Apathy or a lack of activity, such as neglect of hobbies that once were important to the person.
- Changes in sleeping or eating patterns—insomnia or lethargy, lack of appetite or ravenous hunger.
- Giving away prized possessions.

School personnel in particular may recognize (Mazza & Eggert, 2001):

- A decline in the child's productivity and performance.
- An increase in truancy.
- More acting out in class.
- Possible drug or alcohol use and hanging out with the "wrong crowd" at school and after school hours.
- Higher levels of social activity than the average student if they are at risk for school dropout as well.

General Risk Factors

As we observed earlier, suicidal children typically have a rigid and unrealistic style of thinking (Randell, Eggert, & Pike, 2001). The content of their preoccupations may also be a warning sign. When children seek to escape from a situation, to join a dead friend or family member, to be punished for their actions, to get revenge or to hurt someone else, to control their death, or to solve a problem that they see as intolerable or unresolvable, they are at risk for self-destructive behavior (Capuzzi, 1994; Capuzzi & Gross, 1996). A negative outlook and poor self-image are also warning signs. Most children will express their thoughts in some way. Knowing the state of mind and the style with which a child resolves or fails to resolve problems is the first step in preventing suicide. (Strategies for cognitive change are discussed in Chapter 12.)

As we saw in Chapter 1, Paul Andrews exhibits many of the warning signs of suicide. The conflict with his parents, although less focused than that of his sister, Allie, could be a precursor to a suicide attempt. Parent-child conflict is a common prelude to a suicidal attempt (Randell, Eggert, & Pike, 2001). Paul's stepfather, Jack, either is overtly aggressive toward him or ignores him completely. His mother passively encourages Paul not to upset Jack. Paul acts out in school, is aggressive with other children, and yet at times is very withdrawn. He also receives attention (and subsequent rejection) from other children by repeating gory news stories related to death and human pain. Paul's interactions with his peers therefore reinforce both his aggressiveness and his feelings of guilt, worthlessness, and anger at himself and at the world. Paul demonstrated warning signs in those areas that serve as red flags—verbal messages, behavioral changes, and cognitive preoccupations. Unfortunately, his strategies for getting attention and support were not effective.

COMMON MISCONCEPTIONS OF SUICIDE

There are a number of common misconceptions or myths about suicide (Capuzzi, 1994; King, Price, Telljohann, & Wahl, 2000). Here are some of the most common ones:

• *A person who has considered or attempted suicide will always be suicidal.* In fact, most children and adolescents think about suicide at some point. Most suicide attempts are a desperate means of crying out for help. If the crisis is resolved effectively, many will not become suicidal again, with those who did not actually attempt suicide at lower risk of reoccurance.

• *After a suicide crisis has passed, the child is no longer at risk for suicide.* Although children may not continue to feel suicidal after an attempt, they are not out of danger. Because suicide attempters have already overcome a social taboo by trying to kill themselves once, subsequent attempts are easier for them. If parents, counselors, psychologists, and school personnel do not attend to the child and the reasons for the attempt, a subsequent attempt is possible. Suicide takes a great deal of emotional energy. A child or adolescent who displays a calm reaction after an initial suicide attempt may be gaining strength for another. Later suicide attempts frequently involve more lethal methods. In one study, adolescents with a history of suicide attempts were almost 18 times more likely than those with no attempt history to try to commit suicide during a one year time period (Lewinsohn, Rohde, & Seeley, 1994).

- *Talking about suicide can make people more inclined to make an attempt.* Talking to children and adolescents about suicide can allow them to express their feelings and concerns, and can lead to increased supports and coping skills. Adults should not avoid the topic of suicide, there is *no* evidence that this increases risk.
- *People who commit suicide always leave a note.* Actually, only a small proportion of children and teenagers who commit suicide leave a note, even though they may leave numerous clues or hints. This misconception can perpetuate a family's bewilderment after a suicide, because not only are they helpless to change what happened but they are also uncertain about the reason for the suicide. Many suicides are classified as accidents because no note has been found and the deaths are not recognized as suicides.
- *Suicide happens without warning.* Though few people who are thinking about committing suicide actually spell out their intention directly, most do give numerous clues and hints of despair and suicidal ideation. After a young person has committed suicide, it is not uncommon for friends and family members to retrospectively identify many of the warning signs that we have reviewed.
- *The person who talks about committing suicide never actually does it.* Nearly every suicide has been preceded by some kind of warning. Even if such threats seem to be bids for attention, it is better to respond to a child's potential risk than to regret a completed suicide. Always take threats seriously.
- *Suicide occurs more frequently among the lower socioeconomic groups than among the more affluent.* Although age and gender differences persist (suicide is on the rise among children and adolescents) and some ethnic differences persist (Native Americans have the highest suicide rate), suicide is a problem in all socioeconomic and ethnic groups.
- *Suicidal people are mentally ill or severely depressed.* Suicide is an ineffective, maladaptive solution to a problem that appears unsolvable. Suicidal youth usually are not mentally ill, nor can any genetic markers for the incidence of suicide be distinguished from ineffective coping mechanisms learned from others in the environment. And even though many suicidal children and adolescents are depressed, not all are. Some children and adolescents who are not depressed consider suicide in the absence of adequate problem-solving skills.

Awareness of these misconceptions about suicide helps parents, teachers and counselors to identify suicidal behaviors and risk among children and adolescents. Next, we consider specific identification and risk assessment strategies.

IDENTIFICATION AND ASSESSMENT STRATEGIES

Several useful strategies have been devised to determine if children will act on suicidal thoughts. Recognizing signs of depression and familiarity with its various forms and manifestations can be very helpful. Two other methods are clinical interviews, which can disclose the severity and lethality of suicide ideation, and self-report measures.

Forms of Depression

Building on earlier works on adult suicide, two studies (Garrison, Addy, Jackson, et al., 1992; Lewinsohn, Rohde, Seeley, & Fischer, 1993) focused on increase of depression among children and adolescents. Depression affects approximately 30% of the adolescent population with similar trends present in young children. The assumption is that the precursors of depression begin quite early in a child's life. Referring to "epidemic proportions" of depression, Seligman (1995) suggests that we are in an "Age of Melancholy." Early onset bipolar disorder is also being more effectively identified and is more pervasive than ever thought (Papolos & Papolos, 1999). One tool for more clearly understanding depression and bipolar disorder in young people is the fourth edition of the Diagnostic and Statistical Manual of Mental Disorders (DSM-IV), which has been published with a revised text (TR), or DSM-IV TR.

The DSM-IV TR clarifies differences in the expression of depression in childhood, adolescence, and adulthood. For example, children commonly display irritable moods rather than depressed moods, somatic complaints, and social withdrawal. Depressed adolescents typically display psychomotor retardation and hypersomnia. Also, children typically display major depressive episodes along with disruptive behavioral disorders, anxiety disorders, and ADHD. Adolescent depression is more commonly associated with ADHD, disruptive behavior disorders, anxiety disorders, substance-related disorders, and eating disorders.

Mood disorders in the DSM-IV TR are divided into three major categories: Depressive Disorders, Bipolar Disorders, and Mood Disorders due to a General Medical Condition. The Depressive Disorders include Major Depressive Disorder, characterized by one or more depressive episodes without a history of mania, and Dysthymic Disorder, characterized by conditions indicating mood disturbance that has been chronic or intermittent for at least two years, but without the degree of severity to warrant diagnosis of Major Depressive Disorder.

Bipolar Disorders include Bipolar I Disorder, Bipolar II Disorder, and Cyclothymic Disorder. Bipolar Disorders are distinguished by the presence of a Manic Episode. Cyclothymia, a milder form of Bipolar Disorder, is indicated by the presence of numerous episodes with hypomanic symptoms and numerous periods with depressive symptoms that do not meet the criteria for a Major Depressive episode. The final category includes mood disturbances judged to be of medical origin. This condition is found with increasing frequency among younger populations. The DSM-IV TR also describes conditions such as Seasonal Affective Disorder, in which people become more depressed during certain times of the year, and Adjustment Disorders in which the adjustment to a major external stressor is accompanied by depressed mood. In sum, the DSM-IV TR is a useful tool for clarifying certain types of depression in childhood and adolescence.

In view of the relationship between depression and suicide, the use of depression inventories is warranted in efforts to determine the risk of suicide. Two that are useful for children and adolescents are the Beck Depression Inventory (BDI), which has an adolescent version (Beck, Ward, Mendelson, Mock, & Erbaugh, 1961), the Child Depression Inventory (CDI) (Kovacs & Beck, 1977; Kovacs, 1981). The BDI contains 21 items that yield a single score reflecting a client's symptomatology for depression. It indicates whether an adolescent may be severely depressed and at risk for suicide. The CDI was modified from the BDI for use with children between the ages 8 and 17.

Later, we present strategies for early intervention, crisis intervention, and postvention for child and adolescent suicide. Interventions to prevent depression itself are extremely important in preventing suicide. Two such programs, optimism training (Seligman, 1995) and the SOAR program (Gilboy, McWhirter, J. J., & Wallace, 2002), are described in Chapter 13.

Interviews for Suicide Lethality

Interviews are probably the most effective and informative way to assess suicide risk (J. J. McWhirter, 2002). Interviews are conducted with parents, teachers, and the child or adolescent who appears to be at risk of suicide. Because suicidal children are typically angry at themselves, upset at the world, and are caught up in emotional turmoil, it is critical to establish a professional relationship that expresses confidence, helpfulness, and trust.

The interviewer should attempt to assess (a) the history of the presenting problem (e.g., depression, anxiety, loneliness), (b) the family constellation and family relationships, (c) a developmental, medical, and academic history, (d) the status of interpersonal relationships, (e) verbal and behavioral warning cues, and (f) any current stressors that may trigger a suicide attempt. Changes in behavior, in sleep and eating patterns, and in emotional status as well as any previous suicide attempts should be noted. Discrepancies between the parents' and the child's reports may indicate a problem. The following high-risk factors should receive particular attention:

- Symptoms of *clinical depression* and *hopelessness*.
- *Recent loss* of an important relationship or life goal.
- Serious *family problems*, such as divorce, alcoholism, physical abuse, or incest.
- *Personal history* of physical disability, alcohol or drug abuse, or psychiatric treatment.
- *Interpersonal impoverishment*, or the absence of friends, family, church members, or others who can provide direct emotional support in a crisis.

When suicide ideation is present, the lethality of the risk must be assessed. The severity of the threat depends on the specificity and the lethality of the method of choice. Ideation alone is not a great risk. Progressively worse are (a) ideation with a plan, including a time, place, and method; (b) a lethal method (such as a gun or a leap from a tall building); (c) accessibility of a means to commit suicide (such as a loaded gun in the house); and (d) a history of previous suicide attempts (Pfeffer, Hurt, Kakuma, Peskin, Siefker, & Nagabhairava, 1994).

Holinger, Offer, Barter, and Bell (1994) have devised useful guides for determining many of these risk factors. Readers are encouraged to consult their work and other sources, such as J. J. McWhirter (2002), for sample interview procedures.

Self-Report Inventories

Researchers have developed a variety of inventories to identify suicidal children and adolescents. (See Thompson and Eggert, 1999, for a review of these.) In particular, the Suicide Risk Screen is a pragmatic and effective method for identifying suicide-risk students among potential dropouts in school settings (Thompson & Eggert, 1999). In addition to his depression measures, other scales by Beck and his associates are the Beck Hopelessness Scale (BHS) (Beck, Weissman, Lester, & Trexler, 1974) and Scale of Suicide Ideation (Beck, Kovacs, & Weissman, 1979). The Scale of Suicide Ideation includes questions related to attitudes about living or dying, the characteristics and specificity of suicidal ideation, and background factors such as previous suicide attempts. These measures can help identify the risk of suicide among children and adolescents.

Schoolwide screening strategies have demonstrated encouraging results in preventing suicidal behavior (Gould & Kramer, 2001). Through use of interviews and self-report inventories as described above, preventive screening methods in schools can generate information about suicidal ideation, substance abuse, depression, and previous suicide attempts. This is critical for identifying those at-risk.

GENERAL PREVENTION AND INTERVENTION STRATEGIES

General Prevention

In general, efforts to prevent suicide focus on the factors that lead to a suicide crisis while treatment occurs after an unsuccessful attempt or in a response to acute suicide ideation. Postvention, or follow-up treatment, consists of interventions for the surviving family members, friends, and community after a completed suicide. One of the goals of postvention is to prevent cluster suicides. Prevention strategies, treatment (that is, crisis intervention), and postvention could all have been helpful to Paul, and may still be helpful to him. (Figure 12.2 in Chapter 12 shows a useful framework of prevention, early intervention, and treatment.)

Primary prevention involves the removal or modification of environmental and interpersonal characteristics that are commonly associated with suicide. It usually takes the form of a generic program carried out in all grades of an elementary or secondary school. Many primary prevention programs focus on the development of affective skills, such as building self-esteem, social skills, and problem-solving skills (Seligman, 1995; Shure, 1992a, 1992b, 1992c; Hyson, 1994; Gould & Kramer, 2001; King, Price, Telljohann, & Wahl, 2000). Workshops, staff and teacher outreach programs, and direct classroom instruction can focus on stress, family communication, problem-solving, cognitive distortions, and other factors associated with suicide. With younger children, puppets can be a useful medium for teaching problem-solving and the communication of feelings, and have been successfully used for a variety of educational purposes (J. J. McWhirter & A. M. McWhirter, 1987).

Another preventive strategy includes the restriction of firearms (Gould & Kramer, 2001). In the United States, the most common method for attempting suicide is through the use of firearms. Having a gun in the home is a significant suicidal risk factor for children and adolescents.

Women who attempt suicide often choose the method of overdosing on medication. Although this method is less lethal than the use of firearms, it is still harmful and can result death. Another prevention strategy involves educating medical personnel about risks and safety precautions when prescribing medication to suicidal individuals (Gould & Kramer, 2001). Gould and Kramer (2001) also recommend educating news reporters, television producers, and others in the entertainment and media industries to reduce the risk of cluster suicides.

Brief Therapy and Skills Training

Brief therapy and skills training exposes children and adolescents to protective factors against suicidal ideation and behavior. These include exposure to positive coping strategies, emotional support from others, instrumental support, and positive affirmations. Brief therapy attempts to achieve maximum benefit in a short period of time. In one particular study (Randell, Eggert, & Pike, 2001), researchers implemented two brief therapy suicide prevention interventions—Counselors CARE (C-CARE) and Coping and Support

Training (CAST). The C-CARE intervention exposed the child to alternative perspectives, acknowledgement of distress, positive affirmations, and support in school and at home. It consisted of a brief assessment interview and brief counseling. Following administration of C-CARE, children went through the 12-session training program of CAST. This skills training program focused on decreasing drug use, increasing school performance, group support, setting goals, building self-esteem, anger management, decision-making skills, and recognizing progress. Participation in C-CARE and CAST was effective in enhancing self-esteem, reducing depressed mood, improving self-efficacy, and reducing suicide risk behaviors.

SPECIFIC EARLY INTERVENTION, CRISIS MANAGEMENT, AND POSTVENTION

Early intervention programs target early detection and treatment of depressive disorders, anxiety, loneliness, stress, and family problems. Parents and teachers, the adults most accessible to the child and adolescent, play crucial roles in early intervention, but other school personnel and community professionals are also important (King, Price, Telljohann, & Wahl, 2000). Early intervention programs in the school minimize the frequency and severity of the suicide ideation experienced by high-risk youth. Early detection can be managed conveniently and inexpensively through group screening devices. Suicide threat can also be detected through gatekeeper training programs (Grossman & Kruesi, 2000; Gould & Kramer, 2001). In these programs, adults who come into contact with youth in school on a daily basis are trained to identify suicidal youth. The principle behind these programs is that suicidal children and adolescents are often under-identified. Had such an early intervention program been in place in Paul's school, he might have been identified earlier and appropriate interventions could have been implemented before the suicide crisis emerged.

School crisis response teams are an important part of deterring suicide and providing support when a suicide occurs (Vidal, 1989; McKee, 1993; Kalafat, 1994). Of course, a crisis response team also deals with other tragedies, such as school shootings described in the last chapter. Response teams are made up of trained teachers and administrators, school counselors, school nurses, and social workers, as well as parents and community members. Although response teams are designed for crisis intervention, part of their purpose is to provide education and intervention before an actual crisis emerges.

Four early intervention activities are central to the response-ready crisis team (Vidal, 1989; McKee, 1993). The school must develop a prevention and early intervention plan. Referral resources should be prepared and procedures established so that team members can take direct, immediate action when it is needed. Schools should involve families and parents in this program. In addition, schools must incorporate the unique experiences of diverse populations into their early intervention plan.

- Teams coordinate their activities with those of mental health agencies and other organizations that serve families and children in the community. They may also engage law enforcement agencies, private therapists, medical professionals, and church and hospital personnel. Developing a network is critical for preventing suicide and for dealing with attempts.

- Response teams can participate in education and training. Continuing education on suicide risk and response should be provided to teachers, other school personnel, and parents (King, Price, Telljohann, & Wahl, 2000). Response teams can also maintain appropriate audiovisual materials and a library of information on suicide and intervention resources. In one study, researchers found that after viewing videos on suicide, parents' knowledge increased regarding suicidal signs, responses toward suicidal youth, and appropriate help-seeking and strategies (Maine, Shute, & Martin, 2001).
- Response teams should review and maintain the program to ensure that referral resources are updated, procedures are efficient, and the prevention and early intervention activities are appropriate for the students.

Finally, response teams should consider recommendations by Vidal (1989; see also Capuzzi, 1994) when instituting suicide prevention and early intervention procedures:

1. Don't wait for a crisis before planning a response. Response plans need to be instituted before a crisis.
2. Don't avoid talk about suicide. Suicide issues should be dealt with openly and honestly.
3. Don't prepare students to deal with suicide before significant adults are prepared, especially teachers and other school personnel. Capuzzi (1994; Capuzzi & Gross, 1996) argues that it is unethical not to prepare school faculty and staff in advance of the presentation of suicide information to students.
4. Don't show an educational film or video on suicide without first discussing the content with students. After the film or video, allow time for students to discuss their thoughts and feelings about it. The same is true for parents.

Crisis Management and Response

Suicide treatment is a response to a threat of suicide with severe and acute ideation or to a failed attempt at suicide. A suicide crisis is managed with the same concern and immediacy as any other emergency. Counselors, teachers, and administrators who are members of the response-ready crisis team should free themselves from normal duties to respond to such an emergency. Mental health professionals, such as school counselors, play primary roles in a crisis response.

First, counselors need to assess the lethality of the suicide threat (J. J. McWhirter, 2002; Holinger, Offer, Barter, & Bell, 1994). If a suicide plan is specific and lethal or if an attempt has been made, counselors must assess whether or not the child or adolescent is stable, using referral procedures as needed. Hospitalization may be called for.

Second, a written contract is developed between the student and the counselor. This contract establishes an agreement that the student will not attempt suicide before talking to or seeing a counselor again. Most children who sign a contract comply with it. Providing the child with an emergency crisis number is also important. Crisis hotlines have been used for decades to prevent suicidal behavior (Gould & Kramer, 2001). Suicidal behavior is often related to a crisis, and "cries for help" can be handled by trained workers at crisis centers. Although hotline resources may be especially important for at-risk teens, few studies have examined their efficacy.

Third, observation is critical. The child or adolescent must be monitored during the crisis for a period of at least 24 to 72 hours. This may involve arranging for hospitalization or a "suicide watch," in which family members and friends keep constant track of the youth's affect and behavior (Capuzzi, 1994; Capuzzi & Gross, 1996). Counseling should be action-oriented, directive, and aimed at dealing first with the danger of suicide. Once a child is stabilized, the underlying causes of the suicide crisis can become the focus of intervention.

Finally, counselors must notify parents of the danger of suicide when they are aware of suicide ideation. Parent-counselor contact is often the first step of a crisis response. *Although this contact may break confidentiality, it is an ethically and legally appropriate response to a child's suicide threat.* The counselor must make clear to all minor clients and to relevant adults the limits of confidentiality at the onset of the relationship. The counselor who informs others of the danger of suicide shows concern for the youth's welfare.

Crisis intervention steps.   Six steps must be taken to defuse a suicide crisis:

1. Listen and show respect for the feelings a suicidal youth expresses. Suicidal children feel that their problems are severe, and their feelings should not be brushed aside. Schools should incorporate peer assistance programs to aid in crisis intervention and decreasing suicidal behavior (King, Price, Telljohann, & Wahl, 2000).
2. Reinforce the child for seeking help. Admitting suicide ideation or attempting suicide brings shame and embarrassment. These feelings should be acknowledged. The counselor can also help the child recognize and voice the part of him or her that wants to survive. This can help deter a later attempt.
3. Be specific about assessing lethality. Ask direct questions: "Are you thinking about killing yourself?" Be particularly specific about assessing the concreteness of the plan. Ask: "How do you plan to kill yourself?" "Do you already have the pills?" "Have you attempted suicide before?" Don't be afraid that asking such questions will increase the risk for a suicide attempt.
4. Make decisions. Children or adolescents who give indications that they will attempt suicide within the next few hours should be hospitalized for consistent care and monitoring.
5. Have the youth sign a written contract. An oral contract may be adequate, but a written contract is more powerful. Sometimes the suggestion of hospitalization is enough to persuade a child to sign a written contract. Be very careful about this tactic, though. *The child who feels coerced into signing a contract may feel under no obligation to abide by its terms.*
6. Use the resources that are available. Community mental health agencies and private therapists are often the primary resources for helping children and their families after a suicide attempt or acute suicidal ideation.

Immediately after a crisis.   After a nonfatal attempt, school personnel or the crisis team should attend to a number of other issues. Because most suicide attempts are not made at school, a member of the crisis team should call the parents to verify the suicide attempt. The call also provides an opportunity to offer assistance to family members. After this call, a team member should notify teachers and administrators, emphasizing confidentiality. It is also important to monitor the attempter's friends, to follow up on others who are perceived to be at risk for suicide, and to respond to friends who may be traumatized by the attempt. While the student is recovering, a team member should keep the student informed about what is going on at the school and encourage the parents to report on the child's progress.

This collaborative relationship is continued when the student returns to school. Members of the crisis team should help to make the student's return to school as comfortable as possible. Teachers should also remain aware of the appropriate steps necessary when a student returns to school after a suicide attempt (King, Price, Telljohann, & Wahl, 2000). Both individual and group counseling have been effective in helping a child deal with the aftermath of a suicide attempt, although group counseling should be postponed a few months so that the attempter is not the primary focus of the group (Robertson & Mathews, 1989). Medications for depression and anxiety may also be effective after a suicide attempt and may be used in conjunction with therapy. It is important that the prescribing physician is aware of the young person's suicide attempt (Grossman & Kruesi, 2000).

Family interventions.   After a suicide attempt, family treatment is often recommended in place of or in addition to individual interventions. An attempt at suicide by any member of the family is very stressful for all the other members, particularly when the family is already struggling. Even when the family is relatively healthy and functioning well, normal nurturance and family care may not be adequate to deal with a child's stress, anxiety, depression, and suicide ideation.

When working with families, counselors must emphasize certain key issues (McLean & Taylor, 1994). First, counselors must establish the significance of the problem. Although parents may see their child's concerns as minimal, they may be overwhelming to the child. Parents must understand that a suicidal child's problem is a family problem. The involvement of Paul's parents, for example, is critical because much of his despair is rooted in family problems.

Second, counselors must deal with the shame, guilt, and anger that parents often experience when their child is suicidal—and with the denial that may be operating within the family. Oftentimes, individual meetings are helpful after a suicide attempt in a family (Grossman & Kruesi, 2000). Third, the family must begin to recognize that the problems that led up to the suicide crisis have developed over a long time and the extent to which they reflect family dynamics. Families should be encouraged to recognize, understand, and modify these dynamics as a means of managing a suicide crisis and of effecting long-term change. Finally, counselors should assess for suicide ideation among each member of the family.

Family counseling is probably the most effective method for dealing with the primary causes of self-destructive behavior. For example, modifying the communication styles and helping each family member to clarify and modify his or her role in keeping the dysfunctional family in balance would be useful for Paul and his family. Unfortunately, many suicidal children and adolescents do not have a family and are in the child protection system. In these situations, interventions should involve alternative caretakers (Grossman & Kruesi, 2000). (Family counseling interventions are discussed in Chapter 14.)

Postvention and Follow-Up Treatment

A great deal of suffering goes on in the aftermath of a teen's or child's suicide. Surviving family members, friends, and schoolmates of the suicide victim often need follow-up treatment or postvention. Individual, group, or family counseling may be needed to help them deal with the event. Sharing information about the suicide and discussing it with community members and with fellow students helps to prevent cluster suicides. Indeed, mental health professionals and school personnel have important responsibilities after a successful suicide (King, Price, Telljohann, & Wahl, 2000). Most postvention efforts involve the school and the family.

Schools.   The school is the major setting not only for prevention and early intervention but also for attention to the aftermath of a student's suicide. School personnel can provide information about suicide, help survivors cope with their loss, and offer counseling to students who may need special attention. Suicide should be discussed because a fear of discussing self-destructive behavior actually increases the risk to other students. In discussions of the suicide, the deceased child should not be glorified or romanticized, but students should be allowed to grieve. For example, the school should not hold a memorial for the student or plant a tree in honor of the student. However, students should be allowed to miss school if necessary to attend the funeral service of the deceased student. Neglect of these factors may increase the possibility of cluster suicides and complicate the grieving process for students.

Postvention, like crisis intervention, is the responsibility of the crisis team. The response team should take the following steps after a student has committed suicide (Vidal, 1989; Grossman, Hirsch, Goldenberg, & Libby, 1995; King, Price, Telljohann, & Wahl, 2000):

- Administrators should call an emergency faculty meeting to relay the facts and to give teachers "talking points" for class discussions.
- Designated team members call parents and offer assistance, contact the district counseling department, and prepare written information for parents about the event, the school response, and how to support their children and secure outside support as needed.
- The school should *not* hold an assembly to announce the suicide or issue a public statement about it. Some students may perceive these actions as positive consequences of suicide. In addition, the school must prepare for possible media coverage of the suicide.
- The school should *not* hold a memorial service, nor should it prepare a memorial statement for publication in the student newspaper. These activities can increase the perception that suicide is an acceptable form of death.
- Opportunities should be provided for friends and schoolmates to meet to share their grief, and emergency or crisis hotline numbers should be made available to students. The school may need to enlist community resources to manage these groups and to provide emergency and information services.
- Depending on the nature of the event, the school should hold a *critical incident stress debriefing* (CISD) of staff members (Juhnke, 1997; E. H. McWhirter, 1994). This process includes a structured review of the event and allows personnel to ventilate their feelings, fears, and frustrations. Although the usefulness of CISD has been questioned (Rose, Bisson, & Wessely, 2001; Mayou, Ehlers, & Hobbs, 2000), its use very soon after the incident and its continuing use (Campfield & Hills, 2001) suggest it has value in preventing future problems.
- The school should identify and monitor the well-being of close friends of the student who committed suicide.

Families.   Some of the strategies used in working with families after a suicide attempt are also useful for postvention. Besides experiencing feelings of guilt, shame, and embarrassment, however, family members also feel grief, loss, and helplessness after a suicide. We discuss specific interventions in Chapter 14; here, we simply encourage those who must deal with a youth suicide to pay particularly close attention to the needs of the surviving family after the death of a family member.

CONCLUSION

Suicide attempts and completions can have a catastrophic effect on children and adolescents and on those around them. The prevention of suicide and the provision of early intervention in the presence of suicide ideation is essential. Because teachers, school counselors, and other school personnel play primary roles in the lives of children and adolescents, their knowledge of the symptoms, causes, misconceptions, warning signs, and related problems of adolescent and child suicide is of particular importance. Understanding child and adolescent risk factors can help to prevent suicidal behavior, and prevention and early intervention strategies will help minimize the likelihood and long-lasting effects of self-destructive behavior.

Prevention, Intervention, and Treatment Approaches

▲ In this section we provide a systematic framework and model of prevention, early intervention, and treatment of children and teenagers at risk. In Chapter 12 we describe the conceptual framework. In Chapter 13 we suggest ways to address the roots of the problem in the social environment and address intervention components that draw on social skills, cognitive-behavioral strategies, and other approaches aimed at decreasing negative behaviors and attitudes and increasing positive ones. In Chapter 14 we describe several intervention programs that can be used to help young people by harnessing pro-social peer group influences. Chapter 15 focuses on family-based interventions. We conclude Part III with Chapter 16, which presents a discussion of legal and ethical issues that must be considered by helping professionals who work with children and adolescents.

CHAPTER 12

A Prevention/Early Intervention/Treatment Framework and Other Environmental Considerations

▲ *The teacher says, "If it weren't for*
those parents . . . counselors . . ."
The counselor says, "If it weren't for
those teachers . . . parents . . ."
The parent says, "If it weren't for
those schools . . . agencies . . . society . . ."
Society says, "If it weren't for
those kids . . . "
The kids say—
But who listens to kids anyway?

The spiral of blame and guilt,
incrimination and rationalization,
circles like buzzards over a
gritty desert.

Can we ever find a way to straighten
the spiraling circle—to roll up our
sleeves and get to work?

J. J. McWhirter

CHAPTER OUTLINE

▲   In this chapter we introduce a multifaceted prevention and treatment framework that helps integrate concepts addressed throughout the book and that provides an overall context for the interventions described in later chapters. We precede our description of the framework with clarification of the relationship of prevention, treatment, and risk and a brief history of prevention strategies. We define prevention. After a thorough description of the framework, we address relationships, empowerment, and social activism as factors that can reduce child and adolescent risk.

A COMPREHENSIVE PREVENTION/
EARLY INTERVENTION/TREATMENT FRAMEWORK

What serves as a *treatment* intervention for one problem frequently serves as a *preventive strategy* for a more advanced problem. In a sense, problem behaviors form a continuum. If we involve Tyrone Baker (of Chapter 2) in a smoking-reduction group, for example, we are providing a treatment for his cigarette smoking; but because cigarette smoking puts Ty at risk for the use and possible abuse of alcohol, marijuana, and other drugs, our treatment also serves as a prevention strategy. If we engage the Carter family (of Chapter 3) in treatment for their troubled family system, we are providing treatment for their ongoing negative interactions. We are helping Jason Carter deal more effectively with both his maladaptive and self-defeating behaviors, and we are also potentially preventing Jason's further progression toward one or more of the at-risk categories.

Risk also forms a continuum, from remote risk to imminent risk. Factors that contribute to risk include demographic characteristics such as social class and economic conditions; family, community, and school stressors; and personal characteristics. As we discussed in Chapter 5, some young people are resilient enough to flourish even though their environments and contexts place them at risk. Unfortunately, other young people develop specific personal behaviors that interact with poor family and social contexts to increase their potential for problems and place them at further risk for even more severe problems. As risk factors increase, children and adolescents become increasingly likely to be at imminent risk. Our framework incorporates the relationship between prevention and treatment as well as the continuum from remote to imminent risk.

In understanding risk, it is also important to consider protective factors, that is, factors that serve to buffer or protect young people who might otherwise be at greater risk. Just as risk factors can be thought of with respect to individual characteristics, family, community, and other contextual characteristics, so too are protective factors potentially present at each level. Individual protective factors include but are not limited to social skills and intelligence; familial factors include authoritative parenting and strong attachments between parents and children; community factors include accessible resources such as social and medical services and parks, as well as strong linkages between family and community. Prevention efforts that support and maximize protective factors while reducing risk factors are most likely to be successful.

Any model that incorporates prevention, early intervention, and treatment raises complex issues. The role of the school, the linkage between the problems of young people and prevention, and the interplay between treatment and prevention are all important considerations in formulating such a model (Conyne & Cook, in press; Lowenthal, 1996; O'Shaughnessy, Lane, Gresham, & Beebe-Frankenberger, 2002). It is also critical to understand previously successful and unsuccessful efforts at prevention in order to improve interventions now.

HISTORY OF PREVENTION PROGRAMS

During the 1960s, drug prevention programs emerged with a focus on providing information. Early efforts were based on scare tactics, moralizing, and often inaccurate information, and many programs contained fear-arousal messages regarding the social and health consequences of drug use. The emphasis was on the drugs themselves rather than on the reasons people used them. Perhaps even more significant, youth reported that the information lacked credibility. Drug use also actually increased among adolescents during this time. A consensus emerged that relying on knowledge alone to change problem behavior is misguided (Dielman, 1994; Montagne & Scott, 1993).

By the 1970s, drug prevention programs began to address personal and social factors that correlated with drug abuse and to provide more accurate information. Affective education became the major preventive approach. Rather than focusing on drug abuse, educational efforts focused on factors associated with the use of drugs and attempted to eliminate the presumed reasons for using drugs. Affective education programs targeted self-esteem on the assumption that if young people understood their motivations for drug use and had greater self-esteem, they would not want to use drugs. This approach also failed to lower substance-abuse rates. Indeed, trying to eliminate most problem behaviors by focusing on self-esteem alone is not effective. Seligman (1995) provides an interesting discussion of "feel-good" self-esteem versus "do-good" self-esteem and their relative contributions to childhood depression and other problems. "Do-good" self-esteem is helpful; "feel-good" self-esteem is not.

During the 1980s, prevention efforts began to emphasize behavioral strategies. These programs focused on developing social competency and pro-social coping, subsumed under the rubric of "life skills." Following the behavioral tradition that includes a strong empirical foundation, research was conducted across some at-risk areas to test the efficacy of prevention and early intervention programs. The results of this research are promising, and life skills education has been adopted around the world as an important prevention tool (World Health Organization, 1999).

The 1990s built on these previous efforts. Models developed in the 1990s began to systematically incorporate affective, cognitive, and behavioral areas and emphasized development of both skills and pro-social attitudes. Programs became more comprehensive and broad-based. Some efforts were made to develop programs to increase protective factors but the main focus continued to be on eliminating risk.

Concern with program effectiveness also emerged in the 1990s. Unfortunately relatively little is known about the effectiveness of the hundreds of youth prevention programs currently used in communities and schools throughout the United States. It has become evident, as serious attempts have been mounted to evaluate their impact, that many well-intentioned prevention programs were found to be ineffective and to even have negative effects on their young participants.

To deal with this concern some university institutes (e.g., Blueprints Program at the University of Colorado) and a number of federal agencies (e.g., National Institute of Mental Health, Substance Abuse and Mental Health Services Administration, Office of Juvenile Justice and Delinquency Prevention) have developed procedures for identifying empirically supported prevention programs. These procedures, and greater use of empirically supported programs, are now, in this decade, considered standard practice. The procedures include establishing a set of evaluation standards for selection, most often including an experimental design, evidence of a statistically significant effect, replication of the original study with an experimental design and demonstrated effects, and—sometimes—evidence that the effect was sustained for at least one year post-treatment. Based on adherence to criteria, programs are designated by evaluative category. For example, the Safe and Drug Free Schools and Communities (SDFSC) Program of the U.S. Department of Education has a rigorous process for identifying prevention and intervention programs that have evidence of being successful (U.S. Department of Education, 2000). Using expert field reviewers, programs are submitted, reviewed, and evaluated according to the criteria. Evidence of program efficacy is a critical dimension of their evaluation; other criteria include program quality, educational significance, and usefulness to others. After a series of field reviews, the full expert panel then meets to consider all of the reviews and to make recommendations to the Secretary of Education of those programs successfully meeting the criteria. Programs are designated as Best Practices or Promising Programs. In this text, we offer descriptions of many of the programs that have been deemed valid and effective through this process.

PREVENTION DEFINED

Commensurate with this brief history of prevention programs, definitions of prevention have varied over time and across disciplines (e.g., Caplan, 1964; Gordon, 1987; Mrazek & Haggerty, 1994; Romano & Hage, 2000). Literally, prevention means to stop something before it happens (Romano & Hage, 2000). In 1964, Caplan added the categories of primary, secondary, and tertiary prevention. These terms refer to the reduction of new incidence rates of a disorder (primary), prevalence rates for those at risk of developing a disorder (secondary), or the harmful effects of an existing disorder (tertiary). In 1987, Gordon created a different classification system making distinctions among universal, selected, and indicated prevention. This classification system identified targeted populations, including everyone in a population (universal), an individual or subgroup of a population (selected), or only individuals and groups at high risk (indicated). More recently, the Institute of Mental Health defined prevention efforts in a very limited way as only those that occur before the onset of a disorder (Mrazek & Haggerty, 1994).

There are several criticisms regarding the applicability of these more recognized definitions and classification systems to the prevention of mental disorders (Lorion, Price, & Eaton, 1989; Romano & Hage, 2000). Caplan's (1964) and Gordon's (1987) prevention definitions, for example, were originally created to classify prevention efforts for physical disorders. Unlike most physical disorders, however, it is more difficult to identify the cause or origin of a psychological disorder and to classify complex mental disorder prevention efforts into a single category such as primary or universal prevention. Similarly, the Institute of Health's prevention definition (Mrazek & Haggerty, 1994) has been criticized for using a disease-based prevention model and excluding social and political change, as well as health-promoting interventions, as part of prevention. Romano and Hage (2000) addressed these criticisms and created a new definition for the prevention of mental disorders.

Romano and Hage (2000) define prevention efforts as those having one or more of the following five dimensions: (1) stops (prevents) a problem behavior from ever occurring, (2) delays the onset of a problem behavior, (3) reduces the impact of an existing problem behavior, (4) strengthens knowledge, attitudes, and behaviors that promote emotional and physical well-being, and (5) supports institutional, community, and government policies that promote physical and emotional well-being. This definition of prevention encompasses the goals of primary, secondary, and tertiary prevention practices and also includes risk-reduction and health promotion strategies. Moreover, this definition includes prevention efforts within larger social systems and acknowledges counselors' and other human service professionals' role as agents of social change. To engage in prevention efforts along any of these dimensions, however, counselors are challenged to determine what prevention practices and implementation strategies will be most effective with what individuals and communities at what time. This requires consideration of individual and context-specific factors, as well as the interaction among these factors, in the creation and implementation of interventions (Bronfenbrenner, 1979, 1989). The framework we describe next is designed to assist toward this end.

DESCRIPTION OF THE FRAMEWORK

This comprehensive framework we describe is conceptualized as operating along several continuums and provides intervention components that encompass society/community, family, and schools. Universal primary prevention, secondary prevention/treatment programs (that is, early intervention and selected programs), and second-chance treatment intervention strategies are included. Figure 12.1 shows the several continuums that comprise the framework.

The Risk Continuum

The risk continuum introduced in Chapter 1 is at the top of the figure. Problems faced by young people are conceptualized as following a continuum from minimal risk to actual participation in an activity in one of the at-risk categories. Beginning at the left of Figure 12.1, a remote degree of risk is associated with certain demographic characteristics. As young people develop and mature, personal characteristics that lead to increasingly higher risk may become evident. If these personal characteristics are not modified, young people may soon be beyond remote risk and high risk and considered at imminent risk for many problems. The end of this continuum describes children or adolescents who are already engaged in one or more of the risk behavior categories discussed in earlier chapters.

The Approach Continuum

The second strand in the arch in Figure 12.1 identifies various intervention approaches to the problems that may appear at each level of risk: universal approaches, selected approaches, indicated treatment approaches, booster sessions, and second-chance ap-

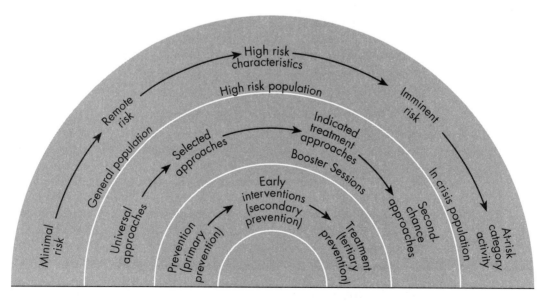

FIGURE 12.1   **Risk, approaches, and prevention continuums**

proaches. Although the labels of "universal, selected, and indicated" are used in different ways in the prevention literature (for example, Mrazek and Haggerty [1994] use these terms to define levels or types of primary prevention only), we use these terms more broadly here as a way to help conceptualize the continuum of possible interventions for at-risk youth. The relative placement of each approach between the anchors of the risk continuum above reflects the relation of the approach to the level of risk. Thus, a universal approach is the most appropriate type of intervention when a child exhibits minimal or remote risk. As a child moves from remote risk to high risk, a selected approach is more appropriate. As a young person moves from high risk to imminent risk and then to at-risk category activities, an indicated treatment approach and then a second-chance program are more useful. Each of the approaches in the second strand of the arch can operate in the domain of the community, family, or school, but we will focus here on the school setting for our examples.

Universal approaches.   Universal strategies are considered to be appropriate for all children, not just those who are presumed to be at risk. All children within a given catchment area (a community, a neighborhood, a school) may receive a common or universal intervention. All children in a low-income neighborhood, for example, are given access to a program even though some are at only minimal risk and some of their families are more affluent. All children in a classroom are engaged in interactive and cooperative learning groups rather than just those who are educationally deficient; all children are involved in a schoolwide program of positive behavioral support (Lewis & Sugai, 1999; Horner, Crone, & Stiller, 2001; see Chapter 4).

In universal school approaches, the intent is to maintain or increase the educational achievement, pro-social coping skills, and mental health of large numbers of children. Ideally, universal content is integrated throughout a comprehensive health-oriented school curriculum. Basic life-skills competencies (discussed in the following two chapters) — such as problem-solving and decision-making skills, communication and other social skills, and impulse control — help young people respond to a variety of social situations. Developmentally appropriate personal, social, and cognitive skills are important components of a universal life-skills program. These programs can be beneficial at any time in the life of a young person, but they have the greatest influence early in life. Ideally, universal programs should be an integral part of preschool, elementary, and middle school curricula.

Selected approaches.   Selected approaches are aimed at groups of young people who share some circumstance or experience that increases the probability that they will develop problems in the future. Demographic parameters, specific environmental stressors, and skill deficits indicate the need for target prevention programs. Perhaps the best example of a selected group defined by demographic factors are the children from low-income families who qualify for a Head Start program. Because of their economic situation (which presumes other stressful circumstances), they are provided with an enriching preschool experience that increases their chances for later academic success.

Specific environmental stressors also provide a useful way to target young people either when they appear to be in a vulnerable situation or during specific developmental stages. Children from families in which there has been an acrimonious divorce, mental health problems, or drug abuse or alcoholism, for example, are quite vulnerable. Individual or group counseling or school support programs are very useful interventions for these students. The transitions from elementary school to middle school and from middle school to secondary school are stressful developmental periods that are often followed by a significant increase in absenteeism, increased susceptibility to substance use and delinquency, and a sharp decline in psychological well-being (Felner et al., 1993; Lord, Eccles, & McCarthy, 1994; Reyes & Hedeker, 1993; Rudolph, Lambert, Clark, & Kurlakowsky, 2001).

A third group of children appropriate for selected programs are those whose behaviors indicate deficits in skills. Sometimes these children are identified in psychological terms, such as lonely, depressed, anxious, aggressive; sometimes by educational categories, such as learning disabled or behavior disordered; and sometimes in terms of their limitations in the five Cs (critical school competencies, concept of self, connectedness, coping, and control skills, discussed in Chapter 5). Most often, these children are identified and referred because of behavior disruptions. Unfortunately, many classroom interventions designed for these children focus on reducing behaviors that disrupt the class, but do not attend to behaviors such as increasing literacy skills that are also vital to the child's ability to succeed in school in the long run (O'Shaughnessy, Lane, Gresham, & Beebe-Frankenberger, 2002).

The risks, problems, and needs of the selected group must be identified before an appropriate intervention can be designed and implemented. The appropriate content for a selected approach often consists of the same social and cognitive skills that are addressed in universal approaches. Some children need increased attention, more intensive emphasis, and more applied practice to acquire these life skills. This is the case in any classroom, but school personnel need to give particular attention to students with special education classifications. Lane, Gresham, and O'Shaughnessy (2002) recommend that social skills competency interventions for children with emotional and behavioral disorders address each of the following components: skill acquisition, skill performance, removal or reduction of competing problem behaviors, and generalization and maintenance of skills. Because of their emotional, behavioral, and learning problems, children identified for special education are especially suited for selected approaches.

Booster sessions.   Prevention efforts should be intensive, sequential, and comprehensive, with continued involvement over a long time period. One-shot prevention efforts are not very effective because program effects dissipate in a relatively short time (Elmquist, 1991; O'Shaughnessy, Lane, Gresham, & Beebe-Frankenberger, 2002). Recall that Kirby (2001) included "sufficient length" as one of ten elements of successful pregnancy prevention programs. Short-term interventions achieve, at best, short-term results. Consequently, periodic and sequential "booster" follow-up sessions should be added to help maintain the effects of the initial intervention (Elmquist, 1991). Few programs without booster sessions have achieved positive long-term results (Durlak, 1995).

Indicated approaches.   On the right-hand side of the middle continuum in Figure 12.1 are indicated treatment approaches for individuals who are at imminent risk for problem behavior or who have actually begun to engage in the behavior. Indicated treatment approaches must be developed for young people whose underlying characteristics, problems, and behaviors are associated directly with at-risk activity. A smoke-reduction treatment group, for example, is an indicated treatment for smokers, and it is also a prevention strategy for the use of other substances. Attitudes and skills that are particularly relevant for each at-risk category are also addressed in indicated treatment approaches. Alternative behaviors and coping skills specific to the problem are also taught in indicated treatment.

Second-chance approaches.   Finally, "second-chance" interventions are needed for those children and adolescents who are already engaging in substance use, have dropped out, have become pregnant, or are engaging in violent and aggressive behaviors. Young people who have made poor choices need an opportunity to change those choices to more constructive ones; they need a second chance. In the six chapters of Part II we provided concrete examples of both specific treatment interventions and second-chance approaches for the specific at-risk categories.

The universal, selected, indicated, and second-chance approaches address, in sequential order, those risk factors that are the most salient contributors to young people's problems. These intervention efforts are most successful when they are comprehensive and cover a broad range of risk and protective factors. The problems of children and youth at risk have multiple antecedents, and interventions must focus on many causal factors if they are to be effective. The intent of such approaches is to set individuals on new paths as early as possible, to open opportunities, to modify life circumstances, and to aim for long-term change.

The Prevention/Treatment Continuum

Prevention, early intervention, and treatment programs also form a continuum, which is represented by the bottom strand of the arch in Figure 12.1. Conceptually, these three terms are closely aligned with the four-decade-old formulation of primary, secondary, and tertiary prevention that Caplan (1964) used to define prevention in the psychiatric field. As we mentioned earlier, Caplan used these terms to describe efforts for "reducing (1) the incidence of mental disorders of all types in a community (primary prevention), (2) the duration of a significant number of those disorders which do occur (secondary prevention), and (3) the impairment which may result from disorders (tertiary prevention)" (pp. 16–17). Caplan's terms are included on the continuum for some grounding; however, we use the prevention, early intervention, and treatment designations to more appropriately anchor our framework.

Environmental Settings

In the comprehensive framework we attend to the environment by including society/community, family, and school settings, and we acknowledge the relationship between these components. Intervention in each of these settings is also conceived as following a continuum from (a) early broad-based prevention to (b) early intervention efforts to coordinate support and training activities, and ultimately to (c) treatment approaches. The three rectangles in Figure 12.2 represent the three settings, and each is divided by a diagonal line to indicate that some strategies and programs are best implemented earlier in the risk continuum and some are more appropriate later. The diagonal line also suggests that some aspects of prevention need to be maintained and supported throughout the model. In some circumstances treatment begins early and may accompany prevention. Early intervention falls in the middle of Figure 12.2 and has elements of both prevention and treatment.

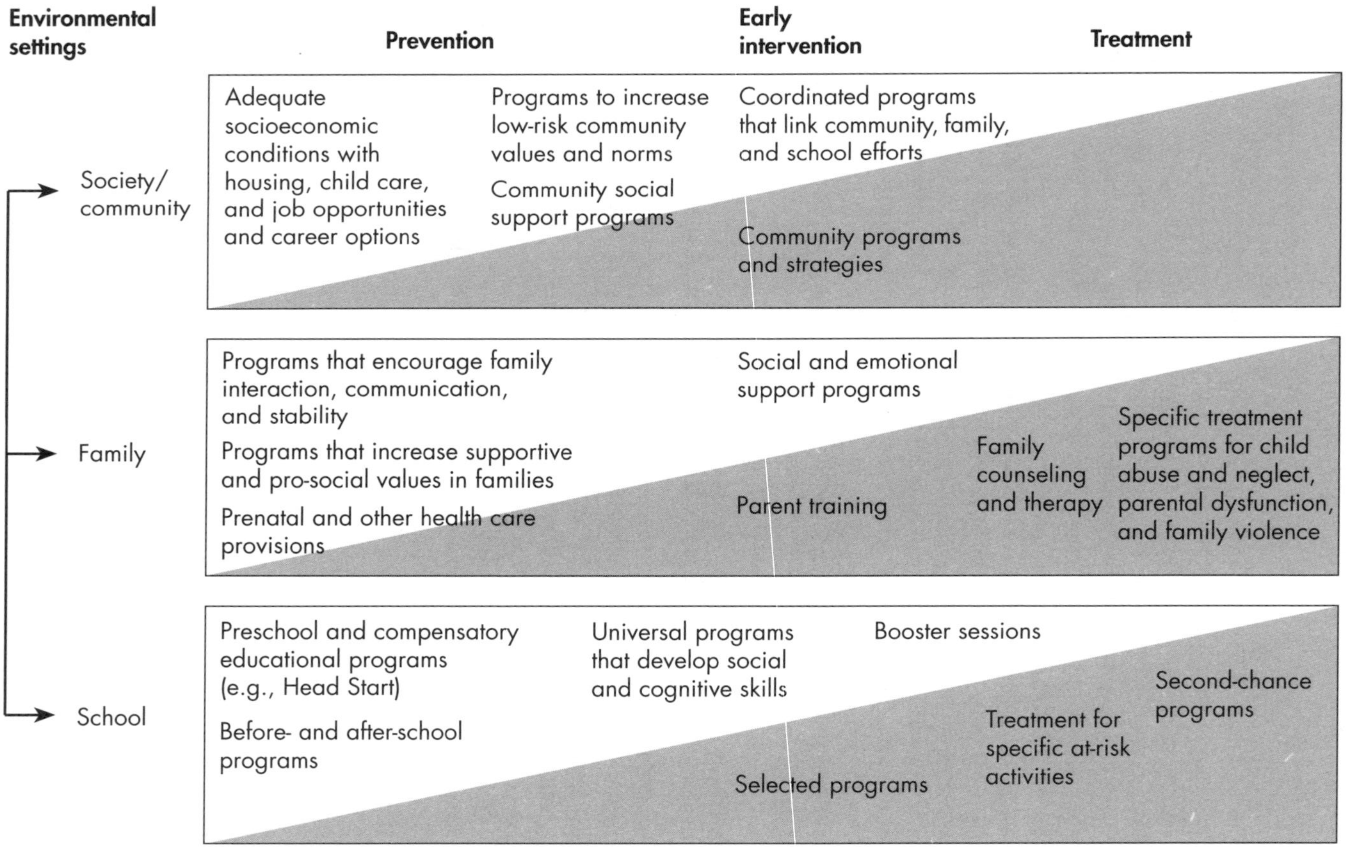

FIGURE 12.2 Environmental settings for prevention/early intervention/treatment framework for at-risk children and youth

Society/Community

The society/community continuum interacts with both family and school continuums but encompasses the community and larger society. Prevention efforts in this setting consist of improving socioeconomic conditions; increasing the supply of low-cost housing, child care, job opportunities, and career options; providing community social support programs; and developing healthy community norms and values.

Along the early intervention portion of the continuum are community programs that involve family members and school personnel. That is, there is a need to provide social support and coordinated programs that enable community members to assist young people. There is a need to strengthen existing support for families in the schools and in community organizations. There is a need for schools to work with the community. Below the diagonal line are treatment strategies that include system-level interventions, such as empowerment and social activism. Empowering young people and helping them to develop plans for social action are a preventive approach on the individual level, but they serve as treatment on the society/community level. The target here is not individuals or even groups of individuals but rather the norms, structures, and practices of organizations, communities, society, and the nation.

Family

Prevention, early intervention, and treatment for families forms a continuum that begins with strategies designed to strengthen families—strategies that encourage interaction, consistency, communication, stability, support, and pro-social values. Prenatal and health-care programs are included as well. As family problems increase, social and emotional support programs and training in parenting skills are implemented. Counseling is critical for dysfunctional families. At the extreme end of the continuum, programs designed to address child abuse and neglect, parental dysfunction, and family violence are especially important. (See also Chapter 15.)

School

Prevention in schools begins with adequate comprehensive preschools, compensatory programs (such as Head Start), and before- and after-school programs. All school-based efforts are enhanced and the effects prolonged if there is a strong level of collaboration between school and home. Such collaboration is difficult to achieve, due to parents' anticipation of being treated with cultural insensitivity, being patronized by school personnel or blamed for their children's difficulties, as well as teachers' anticipation that parents will not respect their expertise, will not participate, or will blame their children's problems on the teachers (Kay, Fitzgerald, & McConaughy, 2002). Indeed, these fears are all too often realistic and the presumed common goal of serving the child is often not enough to overcome these barriers. Rather, multicultural competence, communication skills, time, resources, empathy, and patience are also required. Kay and her colleagues (Kay, Fitzgerald, & McConaughy, 2002) describe the successful development and implementation of parent-teacher partnership to prevent problem development among children at risk for behavioral and emotional disorders. One important element of their program is the inclusion of parent liasons; paraprofessionals from the local community who support parent-teacher interactions and facilitate and direct the meetings. In addition, a parent-teacher action research team is formed to develop plans for learning about, intervening with, and supporting the optimal development of the identified children, utilization of ground rules such as "Parents talk first, then teachers," and ongoing evaluation of all dimensions of the process.

Universal school programs for teaching social and life skills to all children begin early in this model, although the diagonal line indicates that they can be implemented at any point (see Figure 12.2). In Chapter 13 we provide detailed information about teaching these skills. The need for selected programs increases chronologically; specific early intervention is necessary for targeted children in specific problem situations or for those who exhibit problem behavior.

Figure 12.3 presents early intervention and treatment concepts for each of six at-risk categories (discussed in Chapters 6 through 11.) The universal programs specified at the left in each box of figure 12.3 represent the preventive efforts that are directed toward all young people. As children develop, efforts shift from universal approaches to programs aimed at selected groups or individual children experiencing the specific problem areas listed.

Selected interventions should begin by grade 3 or earlier for children who engage in risky behavior (e.g., aggressiveness, withdrawal), or who exhibit such negative emotions as depression, anxiety, or hostility. In a given third-grade classroom, quite accurate predictions can be made as to who will drop out of school before graduation (Slavin, 1994). Evidence also suggests that delinquency in adolescence can be predicted on the basis of early behavior patterns. Researchers have shown that a pattern of antisocial behavior established by fifth grade (Walker, Colvin, & Ramsey, 1995) or even earlier (Patterson, Reid, & Dishion, 1992) is the single best predictor of criminal behavior in adolescence. This is especially the case if the antisocial behavior occurs in a wide variety of settings and involves more than one type of act.

As young people progress through school, indicated treatment programs are required to assist those with more specific and serious concerns. Figure 12.3 also highlights second-chance programs for adolescents who have already engaged in risk category behavior.

A universal life-skills curriculum, modified and adapted for developmental skill level, cultural appropriateness, and social class variables, should be provided to all students as they move through school. Curriculum should include information on study skills and time management, how to study for tests, how to make friends, how to manage emergencies when home alone, how to avoid or report abuse, and, as the young adolescent matures, how to prepare for intimate relationships, how to prevent pregnancy and STDs, how to avoid drug use and resist peer and media pressure to engage in behavior that has negative consequences, and other life events. In order to be effective these programs should be ongoing components of the curriculum rather than one-session classes. Training in problem-solving, decision-making, empathy, communication, assertiveness, and coping skills should also be ongoing. Teachers, with support from and in consultation with school counselors, psychologists, and social workers, should be prepared to teach cognitive and life skills, avoidance of substance use and delinquency, and sex education. Implementing such a model will have far-reaching effects for young people and for society as a whole.

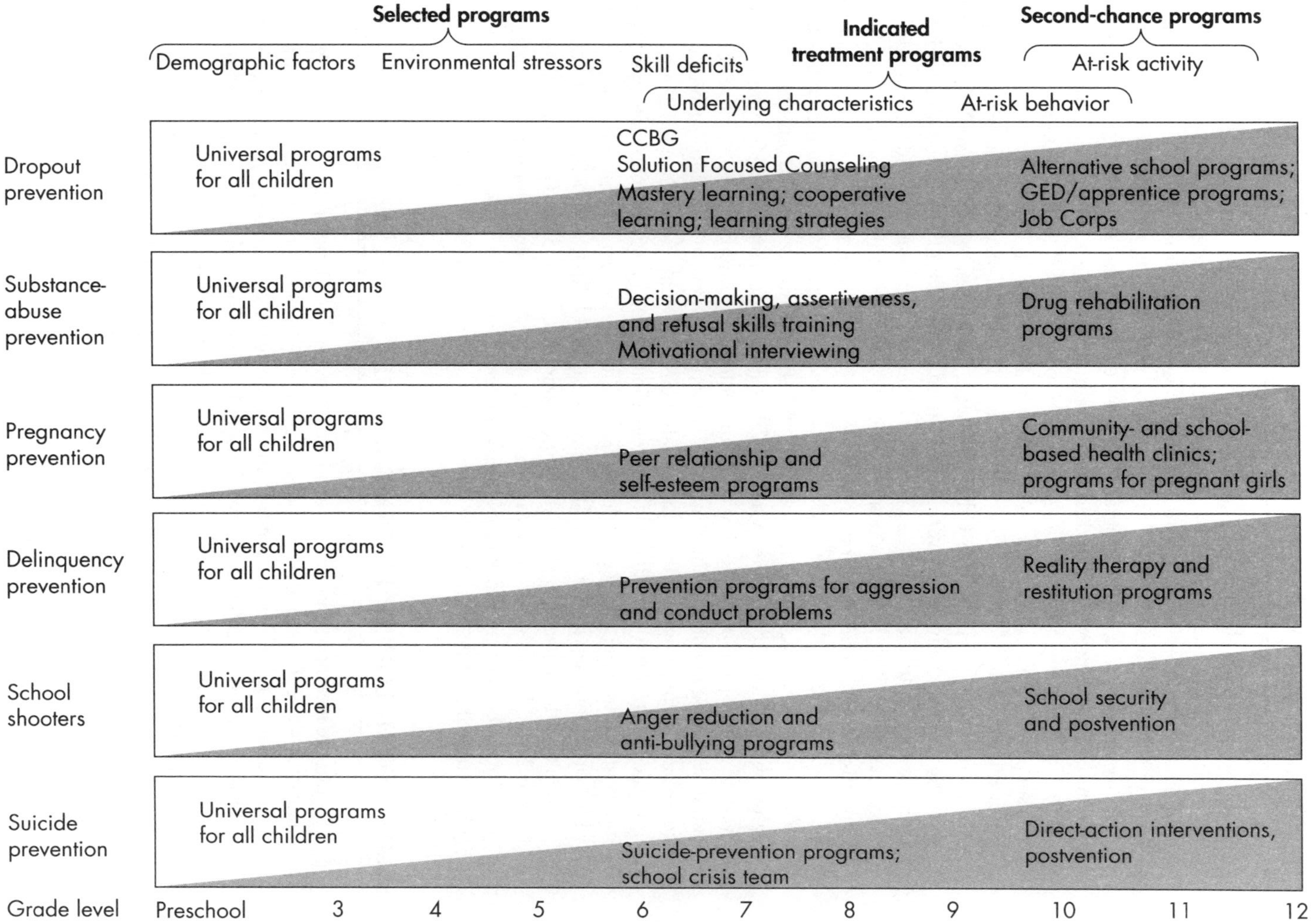

Selected programs

	Selected programs			Indicated treatment programs		Second-chance programs
	Demographic factors	Environmental stressors	Skill deficits	Underlying characteristics	At-risk behavior	At-risk activity

Dropout prevention
- Universal programs for all children
- CCBG Solution Focused Counseling; Mastery learning; cooperative learning, learning strategies
- Alternative school programs; GED/apprentice programs; Job Corps

Substance-abuse prevention
- Universal programs for all children
- Decision-making, assertiveness, and refusal skills training; Motivational interviewing
- Drug rehabilitation programs

Pregnancy prevention
- Universal programs for all children
- Peer relationship and self-esteem programs
- Community- and school-based health clinics; programs for pregnant girls

Delinquency prevention
- Universal programs for all children
- Prevention programs for aggression and conduct problems
- Reality therapy and restitution programs

School shooters
- Universal programs for all children
- Anger reduction and anti-bullying programs
- School security and postvention

Suicide prevention
- Universal programs for all children
- Suicide-prevention programs; school crisis team
- Direct-action interventions, postvention

Grade level: Preschool 3 4 5 6 7 8 9 10 11 12

FIGURE 12.3 Early intervention and treatment for six at-risk categories

Practical Considerations

Would such a comprehensive program be expensive? Certainly. But it is useful to consider the social costs if certain behaviors are not prevented. The costs of comprehensive prevention and intervention programs must be weighed against the sometimes overlooked costs of future residential treatment programs, medical bills, long-term incarceration, property damage, and welfare programs. When we calculate all of these costs, the expense of comprehensive prevention and early intervention become a bargain. To illustrate, it is estimated that in 1996 the federal government spent over $38 *billion* to provide services and support to families that began with a birth to a teenager. In that same year, the federal government invested $138.1 *million* — less than one-seventh of one billion dollars — to prevent teen pregnancy (Bess, Leos-Urbel, & Green, 2001). That is more than 275 times *less* than the amount the federal government spent to support families begun with a birth to a teen. Of course, the long-term costs of teen mothering calculated here did not include lost wages associated with limited education, or costs associated with the increased likelihood that sons born to adolescent mothers will spend at least some time in prison. In Chapter 4 we described the parallel increases, and decreases, in funding for prisons and educational institutions, respectively. And in a study by the Urban Institute on the costs of protecting vulnerable and abused children, Green, Waters Boots, and Tumlin (1999) found that for every $1 states spend on "other services" (including prevention, child protective services, and case management activities), over $3 is spent to cover interventions such as out-of-home placement, adoption, and administrative costs. Several years later, a follow-up report from the Urban Institute indicated that prevention funding is still dramatically lower than intervention funding; whereas at least $1.5 billion was expended on other services, of which prevention services only constitute one part, $9.4 billion was spent on maintenance payments and services for children in out-of-home placements (Bess, Leos-Urbel, & Green, 2001). Of course, simply withdrawing money from intervention and investing in prevention does not solve our problems. We need to continue to assist those who are already struggling while dramatically increasing our investment in prevention.

Counselor/Psychologist/Teacher Interface

Many of the techniques we discuss can be used by a school-based interventionist with elementary, middle, or secondary school students. Mental health counselors, social workers, and psychologists employed in public and private agencies and hospitals can incorporate aspects of these strategies and interventions in their practice. Many of the suggestions can be used by a teacher with an individual child, a group of children, or an entire classroom. These interventions, with appropriate modifications, lend themselves to both individual and group work. They are most effective when concerned adults work together, and as we have indicated, parents are essential collaborators in work with children. When teachers, human service professionals, and parents collaborate in their efforts, putting the needs of an individual child or one classroom full of children uppermost on their agenda, they increase the effectiveness of their work.

Teachers, especially those in special education, can incorporate aspects of the suggested programs in their classrooms. There is an increasing need for adults to serve as mentors, to become positive role models for young people, and to provide practical information about communication and human relationships. Comprehensive life-skills training programs (discussed in Chapter 13) effectively meet this need. Teachers, perhaps with help from counselors and well trained parents, are in an excellent position to implement these programs. They need training, time, encouragement, and support in their efforts to do so.

The school or agency counselor or psychologist, and other human service professionals, are in a good position to consult with teachers about implementing life-skills programs. Counselors have the training to apply cognitive-behavioral approaches, small-group processes, and other developmental, psychoeducational strategies to improve young peoples' social skills. The developmental and educational role of the counselor is crystallized in the concept of the counselor as a psychoeducator. Psychoeducational group interventions are applicable in a wide variety of problem areas and are especially useful for at-risk children and youth and their parents.

ADDITIONAL ENVIRONMENTAL ISSUES

The prevention/early intervention/treatment framework considers need for environmental changes. Other environmental issues are of particular importance. These include *relationships* between caring adults and at-risk youth and *empowerment* as a central component of any intervention effort. Direct participation in the process of social change, or *social activism*, is one fundamental part of empowerment and is also central to being effective advocates for young people.

Relationships

Relationships between at-risk youth and stable, nurturing adults provide a means by which young people learn academic skills and knowledge as well as social skills. Adults can increase a sense of self-worth in children and adolescents.

The importance of relationships is particularly critical in prevention efforts. Recall from Chapter 5 that resilient, invulnerable children are consistently found to have established a significant, positive relationship with at least one adult, particularly (but not necessarily) a parent. Connectedness is one of the five Cs of competency. So, relationships make a difference, and caring relationships with at-risk children and adolescents can prevent or disrupt the negative spiral and raise self-expectations. Healthy adults provide a model of appropriate behavior and mentoring to help guide young people to more healthy and happy life experiences.

Relationships also increase the social interest of the child or teen (Pryor & Tallerud, 1999; Sweeney, 1998). Given the learning and adjustment problems facing at-risk children, teachers and counselors must be sensitive to issues related to social interest (Obiakor, 2001). Feelings of belonging, along with the ability and desire to cooperate, participate, and contribute, are critical to the common welfare. Social interest is also necessary for good mental health, and the degree to which it is present is a measure of the individual's adjustment. Experiences that increase a child's feelings of belongingness and that convey social status and significance foster social interest. Conversely, whatever makes a child feel inadequate, inferior, or humiliated decreases his or her social interest.

Children learn effective or ineffective social behavior in their relationships with family members, school personnel, and other significant adults. Through this socialization process, children learn to adapt their interests to those of society. Children who do not learn to accomplish tasks, overcome obstacles, and relate with peers in a pro-social way are at significant risk, as we have documented throughout this text. Settings and environments that increase children's social interest are characterized by order, consistency, opportunities to contribute to the group, and recognition, encouragement, and belonging. Mutual respect and tolerance for mistakes and failures, along with experiencing natural and logical consequences, but not punishment, are also essential elements (Adler, 1964; Dreikurs, 1964, 1967; Pryor & Tollerud, 1999; Sweeney, 1998).

Empowerment

Empowerment is another way in which adults can help at-risk children and adolescents address limiting environmental conditions. Empowerment helps people actively confront their environment rather than passively accept their conditions as unalterable (E. H. McWhirter, 1994, 1998).

The term *empowerment* is frequently used in education, social work, and counseling literature. We have elsewhere defined empowerment as "the process by which people, organizations, or groups who are powerless or marginalized (a) become aware of the power dynamics at work in their life context, (b) develop the skills and capacity for gaining some reasonable control over their lives, (c) which they exercise, (d) without infringing on the rights of others, and (e) which coincides with actively supporting the empowerment of others in their community" (E. H. McWhirter, 1994, p. 12). For young people this means learning how their lives are influenced by family, school, and the larger society; developing the skills to combat negative influences and make positive choices for their lives; and supporting the healthy choices of other young people in their families, schools, and communities. The benefits of contributing to the welfare of others is consistent with Adlerian principles and supported by findings such as those associated with service learning programs that reduce pregnancy (Kirby, 2001). Here we will discuss four aspects of empowerment in more detail: critical consciousness, skill development, exercising new choices and behaviors, and social activism.

Critical consciousness.   Part of facilitating empowerment means raising critical consciousness, that is, awareness of power dynamics that affect a person's life ecology, and critical self-reflection, or understanding the person's own contribution to that ecology (E. H. McWhirter, 1994; Gragg & E. H. McWhirter, 2003). Analysis of power dynamics can focus on family systems, school and community factors, and local and national government policies; it can also be applied to racism, sexism, ageism, ecology, nuclear weapons, pollution, and a multitude of other topics. The key is to help students understand how these issues affect them as individuals and as members of a community. The more immediate dynamics of popularity, peer pressure, and media influences such as advertising are especially salient to adolescents, and a basic knowledge of reality television shows and MTV can help facilitate discussions when discussing classroom social politics is not warranted. For example, "Who has ideas about why (character name) on *Real World* got so drunk in last week's episode? What kind of decision-making strategy did she use?" "Has anything happened in the past two weeks at school that is similar to the way (the characters) are treating (other character)?" Even young children can be taught in simple ways to examine how their behavior is influenced by context. For example, "I laughed at Sarah when all the other kids did, even though I didn't really think it was funny" is a statement of awareness many children could achieve. Adolescents are often quite willing to explore how their behavior is shaped by peers, by the school, and by their community, but need assistance with developing a norm and a language for doing so. Critical self-reflection, or understanding what they contribute to peer dynamics, social pressure, family tension, or class projects, requires a safe and nonjudgmental atmosphere that is free of blame. When they understand how they are influenced and can explore the choices they have made and are making without being criticized for those choices (that is, allowing natural and logical consequences to serve their powerful roles), adolescents have a basis for choosing different attitudes and behaviors. Power analysis and critical self-reflection, the two components of critical consciousness, can be integrated into a variety of standard subjects, such as history, language arts, government, creative writing, and literature. Fostering critical consciousness helps young people identify social influences, identify what they are and are not able to change or control among those influences, and consider possibilities for change.

Skill development.   Empowerment also involves development of the concrete skills necessary for responsible choices. Teaching children more effective social skills increases their power over their personal environment. Learning cognitive-behavioral skills helps them control and cope better with their internal processes. Providing them with learning strategies facilitates their intellectual growth. Decision-making and assertiveness training, imagery and relaxation techniques, and other psychological tools enhance people's ability to negotiate the barriers and take advantage of the opportunities in their environment. Training in other skills, such as research, writing letters, organizing meetings, public speaking, and leadership, enable at-risk youth to take more active roles in confronting or joining various power structures influential in their lives. Much of the discussion in the following chapters is designed to help teachers and counselors empower their students and clients through the development of important skills. Kamps and Kay (2001) note that social skills programs that *do not* work are often characterized by poor teaching and modeling of the skill, inadequate reinforcement of the skills over time, and negative modeling. Negative modeling could be group reinforcement of aggressive behavior in a group for boys with conduct disorder (e.g., Dishion, McCord, & Poulin, 1999), and could also refer to poor modeling on the part of the social skills trainer. For example, the classroom teacher instructs students on social skills and at the same time is disrespectful to them, violating the basic principles of the skills that are being taught.

Exercising new choices and behaviors.   Through enhancing critical consciousness, the teacher or counselor helps at-risk youth realistically appraise the impact of socialization, economic stratification, and discrimination on their lives, as well as more immediate influences of peers and family members. To ignore the political, economic, and social context within which the young person operates and survives is to risk identifying the source of the problems as the individual. It is the responsibility of the teacher or counselor to help individuals identify contributing factors, for most young people are all too willing to shoulder all the blame themselves.

If young people are led to believe that "the system" caused all of their problems, however, their apathy and withdrawal may simply increase. Growing critical consciousness must be accompanied by the development of concrete skills and, equally important, the motivation and encouragement to utilize the skills, to identify new alternatives, and to change the individual's behavior. When the norms for behavior change within a classroom or a school, the child's environment is significantly affected. Empowerment suggests that although problems are often rooted in systems, individuals can and must share the responsibility for addressing and alleviating the problems. Identifying new choices and behaviors is essential, as is providing students with opportunities to practice those behaviors and actively pursue those choices. Otherwise, teachers and counselors will leave their students and clients feeling even less in control of their lives. The natural outgrowth of the empowerment process is social activism.

Social activism.   One hindrance to the development of adequate services for youth is the fact that so many of the solutions require fundamental sociopolitical changes (E. H. McWhirter, 1998; Albee, 1995; Prilleltensky, 1997). Poverty, inadequate nutrition and housing, and discrimination cannot be prevented with crisis-oriented programs. One means of prevention is to change the environment that fosters such problems. Thus, some aspects of prevention must involve critical analysis of the structure of society and reflect the results of such analysis in planning, programming, and action.

The issue of action is critically important. Empowerment by its very nature requires not just reflection and change on the part of those served by human service professionals, but by service providers themselves. We cannot facilitate critical consciousness in others without becoming aware of how we ourselves participate in maintaining systems that perpetuate inequity, injustice, and ongoing community and individual problems. We need to develop awareness of existing community organizations, support groups, neighborhood action committees, and other channels of collective effort. We need to inform our students, their families, our communities, and our colleagues of opportunities to participate in social and community affairs. We have suggested elsewhere (Gragg, B. T. McWhirter, & Kerewsky, 2004; J. J. McWhirter & E. H. McWhirter, 1989; E. H. McWhirter, 1994, 1998, 2001) that it is time to add a new dimension to the traditional roles of counselor and teacher. Traditionally, both teachers and counselors have been advocates of individual development and growth. With the growing acknowledgment of the role the environment plays in human development, however, social activism is the natural arena into which counselors and teachers must move if they are to remain faithful to that advocacy. Counselors especially can urge adoption of mental health programs that address specific environmental circumstances, limitations, and inadequacies. Teachers and counselors can make their views known to local and national leaders through votes and letters, publications, and seminars. Both can be more aware of how local politics is affecting mental health policy in their communities. Teachers and counselors can enhance awareness of the influence of the environment, encourage recognition that change is possible, and facilitate development of resources and skills for creating change.

The social and economic risk factors in the larger society can be directly modified by mental health and school personnel only modestly at the grassroots level. However, educational and mental health policy and practice at every level of government, pre-service training, school district and building, and agency service can be modified to improve the health and learning of students at risk. Further, teachers and counselors need to be involved in the process of seeking change at the level of those who have the power to fund, to legislate, and to affect the structure of the environment. Teachers and counselors have both the resources and the knowledge to address the needs of the poor and to break the cycle of poverty. Counselors for Social Justice (*www.counselorsforsocialjustice.org*) is just one example of an organization designed to provide mutual support, information, and ideas for social action that promote community well-being.

CONCLUSION

The comprehensive prevention/early intervention/treatment framework presented in this chapter highlights how intervention is related to and modified by the developmental sequence through which children progress as they become increasingly at risk. Prevention efforts include universal approaches for all children, as well as selected programs that attend to issues of concern that are identified early on. As children come to be increasingly at risk, they may require indicated intervention or specific treatments focused on specific problem areas. For youth already engaged in an at-risk category activity, treatment that includes second-chance programs may be necessary. Each of these interventions, provided for children and teenagers at a specified level of risk, can be offered in the society/community, family, and school settings. Meanwhile, helping youth examine other environmental issues, such as the relationships at work in their lives, and helping to foster positive, healthy relationships between youth and nurturing adult role models are also central to intervention. From an empowerment perspective, it is important that we work to increase critical consciousness and help children and teens to learn and practice skills not only for self-improvement but for the advancement of other similar young people. Finally, for full effectiveness, counselors, teachers, and other human service professionals must be socially active. Their activism should be focused on improving resources and the accessibility of resources for all children and youth. Indeed, modeling social activism alone can serve as a powerful tool to help young people recognize their own potential to change and improve the course of their lives.

CORE COMPONENTS OF PROGRAMS FOR PREVENTION AND EARLY INTERVENTION

▲ *To change your way of thinking is to move great,*
huge trunks around in the attic.
To change your way of acting is to push toothpaste
back into the tube.
To change your way of feeling is to take a great,
irretrievable leap of hope into the dark void.

To change means to develop and grow.
And to develop and grow
You have to
move the trunk,
push the paste,
and leap.
If you don't change, develop, grow
You lie in the muck down in the dark hole.

The truth and reality of your existence
will continue to bury you.
If you do not work to execute your past,
how shall you construct your future?

J. J. McWHIRTER

CHAPTER OUTLINE

▲   Specific affective, cognitive, and behavioral skills play a large part in a young person's personal and social success. Resilient youth develop social competencies that help them to negotiate life's vicissitudes and to emerge as healthy, strong, and contributing individuals. High-risk youth do not develop such competencies and frequently find themselves on a downward spiral of lowered expectations, deviant behavior, rejection by society, and a dead-end future. They have not mastered those fundamental life skills that allow them to survive and thrive in the world.

In Chapter 5 we discussed resiliency and how some young people have the ability to thrive despite exposure to severe risks. To be considered resilient, children must both experience significant negative life events that ensure their status as high risk, and they must also demonstrate successful and positive adaptation to that risk. In Chapter 5 we highlighted five major areas—the five Cs of competency—that appear to be important in the lives of young people who are resilient. The five Cs distinguish between high-risk and low-risk young people.

In this chapter we lay out a series of prevention and early intervention strategies that are core components in improving resiliency among young people. In presenting these various programs we use the general framework of the five Cs. This serves as a useful framework to guide our thinking. However, an intervention to improve one specific competency is likely to improve others as well.

Most of these prevention and early intervention programs are designed to be implemented with young people early in their school careers, in some instances even preschool. The reason for this, of course, is that most problem behavior often develops according to an orderly progression from less to more serious problems. Nothing precludes implementing these programs later in a young person's life if the person has not developed the competency.

Although some competency skills seem to tie in directly with specific problem behaviors that we presented in Chapters 5 to 11, specific problems do not exist in isolation from others. For example, delinquent youth are likely to have reading problems, use drugs, engage in risky sex, and join gangs. Additionally, specific problem behavior tends to weaken protective factors (such as, commitment to school, attachment to parents). Improving the five Cs, using some of the programs identified here, will help to strengthen and increase protective factors.

CRITICAL SCHOOL COMPETENCIES

Critical school competencies consist of both basic academic skills and academic survival skills. Again, we acknowledge the very important role that good academic skills—reading, writing, arithmetic, and so forth—play in the success and happiness of citizens. Exposing young people to high quality schools is critical for developing basic academic skills. Academic survival skills include social competency, critical for school survival initially and survival in life as the young person matures.

Social competence can be described as the ability to make use of personal resources to influence the environment and to achieve a positive outcome. Social competence is made up of a variety of skills that provide effective ways of being with others. Such skills include behaving appropriately in the classroom, the formation of relationships and friendships, nonviolent resolution of conflicts, assertiveness and resistance to peer pressure, and negotiation of relationships with adults. Without these essential skills, children and adolescents are susceptible to high-risk problem behaviors (Allsopp, Santos, & Linn, 2000; Botvin, Schinke, & Orlandi, 1995; Wagner, 1996), and deficits in personal, cognitive, and social skills are an underlying cause of social incompetence. So, young people, especially those at risk, need specific help to acquire the social competence to cope with academic work, to make good decisions about life's options, to adopt health-promoting behaviors, to form stable human relationships, and to maintain hope about their future (see Box 13.1).

Training in Life Skills

Life-skills training programs emphasize the acquisition of generic social and cognitive skills. The theoretical foundation of these approaches consists primarily of Bandura's (1977) social learning theory and Jessor and Jessor's (1977) problem-behavior theory. From these perspectives, deviant behaviors are seen as socially learned, functional behaviors that

▲ Box 13.1

The Birthday Party

As we walked up the sidewalk to the front porch, the front door opened and Mary exclaimed, "Grama, Papa . . . Thank you for coming to my birthday party!" Said in a clear, precise, and thoroughly taught voice that only a 3-year-old can muster.

At 3 years old, Mary's social and interpersonal skills were in stark contrast to the group of inner-city children I had worked with all that afternoon. Too bad all children don't have a mother who teaches them what to say and when to say it. But if parents don't, teachers can.

result from the interplay of personal and environmental factors. Skill-building training programs typically employ some combination of interpersonal communication and social skills, strategies for cognitive change, and coping mechanisms.

The life-skills model.   With its emphasis on education and training rather than counseling and therapy, the life-skills model is ideal for use in elementary, middle, and secondary schools. Programs that include a few core elements are useful, but comprehensive programs are more effective (Dryfoos, 1994; Durlack, 1995; Lowenthal, 1996). The life-skills model can enlist the efforts of mental health counselors, psychologists, social workers, school nurses, nurse practitioners, and teachers in such varied fields as physical education, home economics, and health educators (Allsopp, Santos, & Linn, 2000). School counselors, psychologists, and special education teachers are key participants in this plan. Life-skills modules can be incorporated into the curriculum at all developmental levels, from kindergarten through high school and in a variety of course content areas. Life-skills training can also be included in adult and continuing education programs and in parent education programs offered by the school system as well as by community colleges and community service agencies.

Training model.   Procedures for teaching life skills resemble those used in teaching any other skill. The overall task is broken down into small stages or component parts, which are taught systematically, step by step, from the simple to the more complex. Training in each session follows a five-step model: (1) instruction (teach), (2) modeling (show), (3) role-play (practice), (4) feedback (reinforce), and (5) homework (apply). Specific tasks are presented in sequence, and frequent rewards are given for desired behavior. In this model, directed practice and an emphasis on influential models play equal parts. Although the order may vary somewhat, all five training steps are important in teaching specific skills.

1. *Teach.* Explanations and instructions are provided. A rationale for the skill is provided, and students are given oral instructions on how to perform it.
2. *Show.* The specific skill is modeled for the student. The skill can be "shown" by videotape, or the trainer or another child can demonstrate it.

3. *Practice.* The child is encouraged to imitate and use the skill by role-playing in the training session. The performance is evaluated with emphasis on the correct aspects of the student's imitative behavior.

4. *Reinforce.* As the child role-plays additional problem situations, feedback and encouragement are given. Further coaching is provided as needed to shape and refine the performance.

5. *Apply.* Students are requested to perform the newly acquired skill in various real-life situations. They record their experiences and report back at the next session. The characteristics of successful and unsuccessful performances are reviewed and refinements introduced as needed.

Components of the life-skills program can be included in regular and special education classes and in a program designed for use throughout a school or a district. To be most effective, these skills programs should start early in a child's life, such as in preschool, and continue to be reinforced throughout the young person's school career (Forness et al., 2000). Ideally, the program would be universally applied so as to not stigmatize students with limited or deficient skills. Of course, provisions need to be made to teach or reteach the skills to those children who miss or otherwise do not get them.

Prevention Strategy for Children: Interpersonal Cognitive Problem Solving (ICPS)

Several useful models for academic survival, life, and social problem-solving skills were discussed in Chapter 12. Others include "think aloud" (Camp & Bash, 1985a, 1985b, 1985c), the "skill streaming" programs (Goldstein, Sprafkin, Gershaw, & Klein, 1980; McGinnis & Goldstein, 1992, 1984), and "I can problem solve" (Shure, 1992a, 1992b, 1992c). This last program includes the interpersonal cognitive problem-solving or "I can problem solve" (ICPS) manuals for preschool, kindergarten and primary grades, and intermediate elementary grades. This cognitive problem-solving program is the result of more than 30 years of research by Spivack and Shure and their colleagues at Hahnemann University (Shure, 1999). It is designed to enhance interpersonal thinking skills that reduce or prevent high-risk behaviors. The underlying goal of the program is to help children learn *how* to think, not *what* to think.

Rebelliousness, aggressive and antisocial behavior, poor peer relationships, and poor academic achievement are important early predictors of later delinquency, alcohol and substance abuse, psychopathology, and school dropout (Shure & Spivack, 1988). Often by the third grade, schoolchildren with poor academic survival and life skills exhibit behavior that indicates a high-risk pattern for subsequent behavioral maladjustment, special school placement, academic problems, and grade retention. Considerable evidence exists to suggest that some children do not have adequate problem-solving skills. Available evidence suggests that problem solvers draw on (or are limited by) their repertoire of social behavioral and social cognitive competencies (for example, role-taking and assertiveness skills), as well as by their store of social knowledge (for example, familiarity with social roles and conventions) in generating, evaluating, and applying potential solutions to social and interpersonal dilemmas that confront them.

Spivack and Shure (1974) investigated how these cognitive interpersonal skills might be taught and how early they could be successfully absorbed. They assumed that the earlier these skills could be learned the greater the cumulative benefit and the broader their usefulness for confronting life challenges. Focusing on African American inner-city nursery schoolchildren, these researchers found that children as young as 4 years old could benefit from the program. The interpersonal cognitive problem-solving program (ICPS), later nicknamed by the children "I can problem solve," was the result.

The researchers also investigated whether the level of effective problem solving was correlated with level of intelligence, asking, in essence: Do smarter people make better problem solvers? Results suggest that general verbal skills and IQ scores are not related to effective problem solving (Spivack, Platt, & Shure, 1976). Another investigation focused on how overly impulsive (i.e., impatient and quick to act) or overly inhibited (i.e., passive and very shy) children would respond to problem-solving training. Both of these extremes are examples of children deficient in the ability to foresee the consequences of their actions and limited in solutions to interpersonal problems. Both impulsive and shy children responded well to training in interpersonal problem solving. The ICPS program has even been successfully implemented with parents being trained to work with their children on problem solving (Shure, 1996a, 1996b). The program is applicable to different age groups, social classes, and to children of diverse ethnic and racial backgrounds.

Program description. The format of the preschool program is a script (Shure, 1992a), which is upgraded in sophistication for use in kindergarten and early elementary school (Shure, 1992b) and even further upgraded for intermediate grades (Shure, 1992c). The program has a particularly strong advantage as an intervention strategy in that teachers in a typical classroom, mixing quiet and talkative youngsters in smaller groups, easily implement it. Ideally, teachers work with small groups of six to ten students for about 20 minutes per day.

As a school-based program, the ICPS intervention includes all the children in a class because even good problem solvers can get better. The classroom-based approach has several advantages: No student is left out, because children initially competent in problem solving help avoid group silence; it helps those children incorrectly identified as being at low risk (the unidentified false negatives); and more youth can be reached in a shorter period of time.

It is recommended that the formal classroom curricula be implemented on a daily basis for 4 months. However, informal use of the approach should continue throughout the time the children are in school. The ICPS manuals (Shure, 1992a, 1992b, 1992c) include formal lessons as well as specific suggestions for incorporating problem-solving approaches into ongoing classroom curricula and interactions. Each lesson includes a stated purpose, suggested materials, and a teacher's script. The teacher's script is intended to be a flexible guideline for implementing the basic steps of the lesson. Lessons are grouped into two major categories: pre-problem-solving skills and problem-solving skills.

Pre-problem-solving skills. Pre-problem-solving concepts set the stage for the acquisition of problem-solving skills by teaching the ICPS vocabulary, teaching cause-and-effect relationships, encouraging listening and paying-attention skills, and helping children identify feelings.

The first and second weeks of the program focus on basic word concepts that lay a foundation for problem solving. For example, the words *different* and *same* help children develop a habit of thinking about a variety of different alternatives. Kicking and hitting are the same in that they both hurt; asking is different from hurting. The words *all* and *some* help children learn to recognize that certain solutions may not be successful with all people but with some. The word *or* helps children think about more than one way to solve a problem: "I can do this" or "I can do that."

Cause-and-effect relationships are also taught. For example, "Lidia hit Denise because Denise hit Lidia first." Children learn to understand cause and effect but also to think in such a way that they will see the cause-and-effect connection between an act and its consequence. The words *because* and *why*, *might* and *maybe*, *now* and *later*, and *before* and *after* are all included and set the stage for problem-solving consequences that come later in the program.

Approximately 20 lessons are included that teach children the concept of emotions and about how people feel. Children are encouraged to identify another's feelings in a problem situation; they learn to be sensitive to feelings. Obviously, they must learn a language for emotions. They are encouraged to learn "if . . . then" logic. For example, a child learns to identify and label emotions: "If he is crying, then he is sad." Teaching feelings is important; if people's feelings are to be considered in decision making, it is necessary to identify, understand, and verbalize them.

Problem-solving skills.   Problem-solving skills are taught through lessons on alternative solutions, consequences, and solution–consequence pairs. The intermediate grade school program also includes a section on means–ends thinking, which is believed to be too advanced for younger students.

Alternative solutions lessons are designed to help children recognize problems and generate possible solutions. The goal is to stimulate children to think of as many different solutions as possible to everyday interpersonal problem situations that are presented to them. All solutions are accepted equally. Solutions are never evaluated for being "good" but are praised for being "different." Later, the children evaluate for themselves whether an idea is good or not, and why.

The objective of the consequences sessions is to help children learn to think sequentially and to engage in consequential thinking. Children are guided to think about what might happen next if a particular solution is carried out. Children are encouraged to identify consequences for their own solutions and then to decide whether the idea is good or not.

The lessons for solution–consequence pairs are designed to give children practice in linking solutions with consequences. Children are encouraged to suggest a solution to a problem and then follow it up with a consequence. They then return to the same problem for a second solution and look at the consequence of that solution, and so on. These exercises provide experience in linking a variety of pairs of solutions and consequences. For example, in trying to get a friend to leave the room, a child might say "Push him if he won't go" (solution), "but he might hit me back" (consequence) or "If I ask him" (solution), "he might go" (goal).

The curriculum for older children includes means–ends thinking. Means–ends thinking is a higher order skill that does not emerge until sometime in middle childhood. In these sessions, children are taught to elaborate or plan a series of specific actions to attain a given goal. They are encouraged to recognize and devise ways around potential obstacles. They are helped to develop a realistic time frame in constructing a means to the goal.

In addition to the formal curriculum, the teacher is encouraged to extend the approach from helping children think about hypothetical situations and their problems to helping them think about actual problems that arise during the day, including those that occur in the classroom. This informal problem-solving dialogue technique, which focuses on the real-life world of the child, contributes to another advantage of the program—generalization—that is built in as an integral part of ICPS.

In addition to the preschool and elementary school programs, ICPS curricula have been developed for adolescents through high school and young adulthood (Spivack, Platt, & Shure, 1976). Taken as a whole, available findings suggest that ICPS training has beneficial effects going beyond improved cognitive test performance (Shure, 1993, 1999; Shure & Spivack, 1988). Changes in social behavior have been noted, including decreases in aggressive and impulsive behavior and increases in cooperative and pro-social behavior. Behavioral gains have been achieved with numerous groups, ranging from preschoolers showing early signs of behavioral maladjustment to disturbed schoolchildren in residential treatment to juvenile delinquents (Shure, 1999). Long-term follow-up data are sparse, but initial findings suggest substantial holding power for behavioral treatment effects, at least in the early years. So, ICPS helps instill academic survival skills and has the potential to prevent serious behavioral problems later on.

CONCEPT OF SELF

In Chapter 5 we identified self-concept and self-esteem as the second "C" of competency. We pointed out that generally, high-risk young people tend to struggle with negative self-concepts and with low self-esteem. We do know that high-risk young people have biased attributions and that these biased attributions influence their perceptions including self-perceptions. Providing interventions to modify biased attributions is a reasonable prevention approach, and one of the best early primary prevention programs was developed by Seligman and colleagues (Peterson, Maier, & Seligman, 1993; Seligman, 1990, 1993, 1994, 1995) at the University of Pennsylvania.

Training to Prevent Depression

For over 30 years, Seligman has been a major researcher in the general area of depression, with his first contributions identifying, clarifying, and establishing the concept of learned helplessness. He also devoted major effort and energy to the opposite side of the coin, *learned optimism,* establishing a robust link between pessimism and eventual depression (Seligman, Schulman, DeRubeis, & Hollon, 1999). The Penn Prevention Program (PPP) sought to inoculate children against the effects of pessimism—with spectacular results. The children in the Penn Prevention Program spent a total of 24 hours learning and practicing cognitive-behavioral skills. They were also asked to practice the skills in homework assignments. Because the PPP worked so well in preventing depression when it was taught to children in schools, Seligman (1995) developed an approach to teach it to parents. This program is primarily a depression prevention program, but it helps youth improve their concept of self, which is strongly related to depression.

In this intervention, children who reported parental conflict, depressive symptoms, or both were targeted because these factors increase children's risk for future depression

(Jaycox & Repetti, 1993; Nolen-Hoeksema, Girgus, & Seligman, 1992). Children who participated in the prevention program reported fewer depressive symptoms than did children in the control group immediately after the program and at a 6-month follow-up. A later study explored the program's effects after a 2-year delay (Gillham, Reivich, Jaycox, & Seligman, 1995). The effects of the prevention program actually grew *stronger* after the program was over, suggesting that psychological immunization against depression can occur by teaching social and cognitive optimism skills to children.

The PPP contains two major components: a social problem-solving component and a cognitive component. The social problem-solving component focuses on interpersonal and conduct problems that are often associated with depressed children. Children are taught to think about their goals before acting. They generate lists of possible solutions for various problems, and are encouraged to make decisions by weighing the pros and cons of all the options. The cognitive component is based on the theories developed by Ellis (1962, 1985, 1996), Beck (1976), and Seligman (1990). Briefly, children are taught to identify negative beliefs and to evaluate these beliefs by examining evidence for and against them. Children are taught explanatory style and how to identify pessimistic explanations. They learn to generate alternative explanations that are more realistic and more optimistic. Finally, children are also taught behavioral techniques to enhance assertiveness, negotiation, and relaxation, as well as techniques for coping with parental conflict.

Optimism

The PPP also focuses on the concept of optimism. Optimism is a style of engaging in or adapting to a situation that follows from the belief that what one has an effect of achieving one's desired goal or making the possibility of achieving that goal more likely. It is a set of skills on how to talk to oneself when suffering a setback. When people do badly, they ask themselves, "Why?" There are three components to the answer to this question: Who is to blame? How much of life will be undermined? How long will it last? The distinctions among these three aspects are critical. The first issue attaches blame to the self or to the world. The second and third questions—how pervasive is the cause and how permanent is the cause—govern what people do to respond to failure. Feeling bad about oneself does not directly cause failure. However, the belief that problems undermine everything in life and that problems will last forever cause people to stop trying. Giving up leads to more failure, and more failure leads to an even more pessimistic explanatory style. Thus, in the face of a bad event, a pessimist characteristically thinks that it is pervasive and permanent and that he or she is personally at fault. For example, a child may attribute a poor school performance to a personal failure or inability and begin to believe that all school efforts will result in failure. This explanatory style leads to destructive actions and becomes a kind of self-fulfilling negative prophecy. Positive events are believed by pessimists to be temporary, limited, and caused by something other than their own actions.

By contrast, optimists characteristically employ an explanatory style in which they think the bad event is temporary, limited to the specific event, and with many possible causes other than themselves. This cognitive mind-set saves the person from stress and mobilizes energy toward constructive goals. When a positive event occurs, an optimist characteristically thinks that he or she had a personal hand in causing the outcome and that it is pervasive and permanent. Thus, the three critical dimensions used to explain why any particular good or bad event happens are personal, permanent, and pervasive.

Internal versus external: Personal.   When events happen, children either blame themselves (internal) or they blame circumstances or other people (external). Pessimistic children have a habit of blaming themselves when bad things happen and frequently explain good events by attributing them to other people or to the situation. To change the explanatory style from pessimism to optimism, and thus inoculate against future depression, children need to learn to take appropriate responsibility for events that occur in their lives, but also to not blame themselves when things go wrong—because most problems are caused by a complex set of contributing factors. Some children shoulder the entire blame and think of things in black-and-white terms. This leads to overwhelming feelings of worthlessness and guilt, causing them to withdraw and further increasing their risk for depression.

Sometimes versus always: Permanent.   Pessimistic and depressed children believe the cause of bad events and the reasons for their failure are permanent. Because the cause will persist forever, bad events are always going to occur. Optimistic children believe that the causes for bad events are temporary; this serves to inoculate them against depression. For the pessimistic child, mistakes, rejections, failures, and so forth are thought of in terms of *forever* and *always*. The optimistic child explains bad events with words such as *sometimes* or *lately* or another time-limiting term.

Pessimistic and optimistic children react differently to positive events in their lives as well. Children who believe that good events have temporary causes tend to be more pessimistic than children who believe that good events have permanent causes. This is just the opposite of the explanation for bad events.

Specific versus global: Pervasive.   If the cause of the event is pervasive, its effect is distributed across many different situations in life and becomes global. Children who focus on global explanations for bad events give up on everything when they fail in one area. Pessimistic and depressed children tend to let a bad situation expand into all parts of their lives. This limits the number of positive outlets available to them, and catastrophizes everything.

Children who attribute global causes to bad events need to learn to be more specific in their explanations. Instead of a test failure meaning, "I am stupid," children can learn to say "I didn't prepare very well this time." Children who think about good events as having more global causes do better in more areas of their lives. When it comes to good events, the optimist believes that the causes enhance everything they do. Pessimists believe that good events are caused by specific factors: "That just happened because she felt sorry for me." Global negative causes are pervasive and lead to despair and passivity. Seligman (1995) argues that the dimension of pervasiveness is not easily taught to children, although it is routinely taught to adults, and may be used for middle and secondary school students.

Basic Skills of Optimism

The PPP has incorporated the main techniques of cognitive therapy for depression into a prevention program for people who are not depressed. The PPP helps individuals develop new skills of optimistic thinking. There are four basic skills of optimism:

Thought catching.   People must first learn to catch the negative things they say to themselves, about themselves, and about events that occur. These almost imperceptible thoughts affect behavior and mood. By learning to recognize thoughts, they can then be changed.

Evaluation.   The second skill is to evaluate the automatic and habitual thoughts or beliefs that have been identified. These can be acknowledged as being hypotheses that need to be tested rather than "Truths," and evidence can be gathered and considered to determine the accuracy of the beliefs.

Accurate explanations.   When bad events happen, more accurate explanations can be developed to challenge the automatic thoughts. By interrupting the chain of negative explanations, attitudes and mood can improve.

Decatastrophizing.   Catastrophizing, or thinking about the worst possible case, is counterproductive. Most often, the worst case is very unlikely. Ruminating on potential terrible implications and the worst possible consequences creates frustration, drains energy, and interferes with correcting problems.

Identifying automatic thoughts, searching for evidence, generating alternatives, and decatastrophizing are extremely important in developing optimism and lowering pessimism and depression in children.

Application for At-Risk Problem Prevention

Early primary prevention programs can be very helpful to children. Skills for optimism can serve as a means of problem prevention. Children who drop out, and even children who attend school but have given up on themselves academically and personally, lack hope that school will benefit their future or that they can succeed in school. They may internalize their lack of success as their own fault, due to pervasive personal characteristics ("I'll never be able to read. I'm stupid."), as well as blaming it on pervasive global factors ("Teachers don't care." "School is useless."). Teachers or school counselors could initiate classroom discussions to identify thoughts students face in response to negative school experiences (thought catching). The class can assist in evaluating sample thoughts, helping to generate accurate explanations to substitute for sample negative thoughts. Decatastrophizing can be illustrated. When working individually with students, the same series of steps can be followed, reinforcing and further personalizing optimism skills. With practice, students will begin to utilize these skills to encourage each other.

Teaching these skills to children is important, but it is equally important for the helping adults to learn and practice these skills themselves. Using these skills may improve the mental health of the helper—not an unimportant consideration given the nature of the work, the consistent drain of personal resources and energy, and the constant stress of budget cuts and limited resources. Increased optimism gives the helper more energy and greater impact as well.

Optimism can also be taught to parents. Parental (and other adult) criticism often reflects the bad habits and biases of the adult and contributes to increased pessimism in children. If they are aware of their children's attributions, parents can provide more helpful feedback and criticism to their children. Children view ability as permanent, so blaming failure on lack of ability fosters pessimism. In contrast, blaming lack of success on conduct, effort, or attention is less malignant because these are temporary and changeable. Children can be challenged and supported in their efforts to improve conduct, increase effort, or focus attention. If they believe they lack ability, they will be at greater risk of dropout and other problems.

We have developed a middle-school classroom application of the optimism program that we call SOAR (Gilboy, McWhirter, & Wallace, 2002) and are currently researching it using the SCARE program (described in Chapter 10) as a contrast treatment. The SOAR (Students Optimistic Attitudes and Resiliency) program is a proactive program, multi-theoretical in foundation and multimodal in intervention techniques. The purpose of SOAR is to increase students' control over their thoughts, attitudes, and attributions with a view of developing realistic optimism (Schneider, 2001). It is designed to build resiliency and to promote well-being. The theoretical foundations for SOAR lie in the previously described learned optimism (Seligman, 1990) and with the additional component of Hope Theory.

Snyder (1994) has developed a cognitive model of hope. Hope is a goal-directed form of thinking that includes both *agency* or goal to be achieved and *pathways*, optional paths to reach the goal. Individuals with high hope have multiple benefits. Hope is positively associated with success in academic performance (Snyder, Wiklund, & Cheavens, 1998). Hope is also related to positive mental health including positive emotion and subjective well-being, optimism, coping, and planning (Snyder et al., 1996). Conversely, low hope is related to symptoms of psychopathology, including anxiety and depression. In addition to helping students learn optimistic attributions, the SOAR program is designed to help them set goals in a manner that makes success likely, increase goal-directed determination, develop additional pathways to reach goals, and avoid and cope with obstacles to goals. In the Osborn Prevention Project, students who participated in the SOAR treatment group decreased depressive thoughts but maintained angry emotions and aggressive attitudes compared to students in the SCARE intervention (Gilboy, 2003).

CONNECTEDNESS

Connectedness with others is critical in peoples' lives and is a major component of more effective and comprehensive life-skills training programs. Connectedness involves both intrapersonal awareness and interpersonal skills. Both have to do with understanding self and others. The interpersonal communication skills that are core to connectedness are sometimes termed *social skills, social competence,* or *human relations skills.* Such skills in interpersonal communication are necessary for people to have effective and healthy interpersonal relationships. As we mentioned in Chapter 5, interpersonal communication skills are necessary for responsive, confident, and mutually beneficial relationships. A lack of good communication skills often leads to social isolation and rejection, which in turn results in poor psychological adjustment and a lack of connectedness. Positive adult reactions and peer acceptance are related to friendly, positive interpersonal communications, and each of these form a sense of connectedness that is critical in people's lives for sustained happiness (Lee, Draper, & Lee, 2001).

Training in Interpersonal Communication

Acquisition of basic communication skills begins in early childhood; by adolescence most individuals have acquired a complex repertoire of social skills. Most programs designed to promote communication skills offer training in verbal and nonverbal communication, creation of healthy friendships, avoidance of misunderstandings, and development of long-term love relationships.

Programs to promote interpersonal communication should be developmentally appropriate. The variables that seem to play a role in the development and maintenance of interactions from age 1 to 3 years are: attention to the listener, to the speaker, or to the object of interest; proximity and turn-taking with others; relevance of content; and provision of feedback from the listener. From age 3 to 5 years, behaviors that may be incorporated in training programs include the use of attention-getting cues, listener responses, reinforcement of turn-taking and mutual attention, and the use of routines to maintain attention. Mutual attention and feedback are still important skills for 6- to 8-year-olds, and appropriate role taking is developed during this age period. From ages 9 to 12, the use of positive, cooperative, and helpful communication, as opposed to negative, is important. Gazda and colleagues (1999) provide a comprehensive list of interpersonal communication and human relation skills and indicate the approximate age at which each skill is usually acquired.

Interpersonal communication skills represent the major component of many prevention programs. A particularly useful package is an integrated program of training in communication skills for adolescents (Goldstein, Sprafkin, Gershaw, & Klein, 1980) and younger children (McGinnis & Goldstein, 1984, 1990). Other useful programs have been developed for elementary school students (Cartledge & Milburn, 1986; Jackson, Jackson, & Monroe, 1983; Wiig, 1983) and for secondary school pupils (Kelly, 1982; Wilkinson & Canter, 1982). Stephens's (1992) social skills program is appropriate for both children and adolescents. Communication skills training used in prevention include the work of Cummings and Haggerty (1997), Dupaul and Eckert (1994), and Jones, Sheridan, and Binns (1993).

Jason Carter (of Chapter 3) could profit from training in communication skills. As described, he is disconnected from most other children and from most adults. His difficulty in dealing with his dysfunctional family has extended to his classroom interactions. Although parent training and family counseling approaches are probably necessary to help modify the family dysfunction, Jason's ineffective interpersonal communication is contributing to the aversive nature of his school experience. Better interpersonal communication skills would allow him to interact more positively with classmates and adults at school. This improvement could bring greater acceptance by Jason's peers and increase his self-esteem.

Assertiveness Skills

Some at-risk young people get into trouble because they are timid and withdrawn and appear to be incapable of dealing with other students, teachers, and family members in effective ways. Others express themselves in hostile, angry, aggressive ways that cause problems for people around them and ultimately for themselves. Still others find themselves going along with the crowd because they are overly susceptible to influence by their peers. They do not recognize pressure or have the skills to resist it. Many at-risk children and youth need training in general assertiveness and in specific ways to resist peer pressure.

General assertiveness training. Assertiveness training is a psychoeducational procedure designed to reduce deficits in specific social skills and to help the individual interact more effectively with others. Assertiveness training also reduces the maladaptive anxiety that prevents young people from expressing themselves directly, honestly, and spontaneously.

Assertiveness training usually includes modules on the expression of positive feelings, the expression of negative feelings, and the ability to initiate, continue, and terminate conversations. Besides these basic interpersonal communication skills, assertiveness training focuses on limit setting and self-initiation. The person who knows how to set limits can say no to unreasonable requests. Self-initiators have the capacity to ask for what they want and to actively seek opportunities for enjoyment, advancement, and intimacy.

Nonverbal communication is also an important aspect of assertiveness training. The way a message is delivered is given as much attention as the message itself. Loudness of voice, fluency of spoken words, facial expression, body expression, interpersonal distance, and method and degree of eye contact all deliver their own messages. Students are taught to look others squarely in the eye during both positive and negative social confrontations. Looking people in the eye is a sign that one is sure of one's position, knowledge, or attractiveness in mainstream United States culture. Students are taught that passive behavior can be replaced by assertive techniques and that assertive responses are more adaptive than aggressive ones in handling conflict and anger. All assertiveness training programs should attend to students from cultural backgrounds in which direct eye contact is considered disrespectful or aggressive. Rather than exclude "eye contact," this component of the program as well as others should acknowledge cultural differences and provide guidance in exploring when using assertive behavior may be more or less effective.

One school-based assertiveness training program has been reported to yield extremely positive results (M. J. Smith, 1986). The children trained in assertiveness had better school attendance records than their untrained counterparts, were ill less often, scored higher in reading and math, had better self-images, and showed positive changes in those negative attitudes that predict future drug abuse. Three years after completing the program, the trained students were more resistant to peer pressure to use tobacco, alcohol, and illicit drugs. The assertiveness-trained youth also achieved higher grades than the students who were not trained in assertiveness. This social thinking and reasoning program, called STAR (Benn, 1981), provides techniques and methods to train children from grades 3 through 5 in how to respond more effectively in social conflict situations. Another program for promoting learning and understanding of self, called PLUS (Benn, 1982), is an adaptation of STAR for high school students and has demonstrated similar success.

Resistance and refusal training.   Specific resistance and refusal skills help at-risk students resist negative social influences (Herrmann & J. J. McWhirter, 1997). Resistance training focuses on helping young people (a) identify and label social influences and pressure situations and (b) develop behavioral skills to resist such influences. Skills are needed to resist various types of pressures, from those exerted by the entertainment media and advertising to those of peers. Students are taught to identify and label various forms of pressure. Peer pressure, for instance, can take the form of teasing, friendly pressure, tricks, dares, lies, physical threats, social threats, or silence. Typical examples of each kind of pressure are demonstrated.

Students are then taught strategies for resisting pressure and for refusing to succumb to it. Particular techniques are described, demonstrated, and modeled. Students practice and observe others practicing each resistance or refusal strategy. They engage in role-playing to develop competence in each technique. All of them are given opportunities to rehearse and refine their performances so that in real-life situations they can respond with confidence.

COPING ABILITY

The fourth "C" identified in Chapter 5 is coping ability. Many at-risk young people are affected by stress and anxiety. Anxiety is associated with a number of undesirable intrapersonal and interpersonal characteristics: lack of responsiveness, inability to perform independently, overdependence on conformity, excessive concern about evaluations, and self-critical and self-defeating attitudes. Anxiety from such sources leads to chronic stress. Because many aspects of the educational process are greatly affected by anxiety and stress, providing coping methods to deal with them is particularly beneficial. Mounting evidence suggests that school-based prevention and early intervention programs have the potential of reducing future instances of serious anxiety disorders (Dadds, Spence, Holland, Barrett, & Laurens, 1997).

Relaxation and imagery are helpful tools to offset some of the negative aspects of anxiety and stress. These two techniques are combined in relaxation and imagery training (RIT), a program that promises to help at-risk children realize more of their potential (J. J. McWhirter, 1988; J. J. McWhirter & M. C. McWhirter, 1983). Similar programs improved students' test anxiety, study skills, and academic self-esteem (Wachelka & Katz, 1999).

Beneficial Relaxation

Relaxation techniques alone can reduce stress and many of its negative psychological and physical effects. Relaxation has been reported to help clients overcome fatigue, avoid negative reactions to stress, reduce anxiety, improve social skills and interpersonal relationships, and improve self-assurance (Burns, 1981). Relaxation can also help to reduce depression and improve self-esteem (Kahn, Kehle, Jenson, & Clarke, 1990). Relaxation is both effective and efficient in helping students to behave more appropriately in school, to think more positively about themselves, and to interact more positively with their peers. Relaxation also reduces anxiety—an especially important effect because anxiety is associated with dependence, hostility, low peer status, poor relationships with teachers, and aggression (McReynolds, Morris, & Kratochwill, 1989).

Relaxation techniques are useful in learning school material as well as in the social arena. A variety of studies have demonstrated the positive effects of relaxation techniques on reading, spelling, mathematics, music, and athletics (Carter & Russell, 1980; Frey, 1980; Glantz, 1983; Oldridge, 1982; Olrich, 1983; Proeger & Myrick, 1980; J. J. McWhirter & M. C. McWhirter, 1983; Zenker, 1984; Zenker & Frey, 1985). In addition to improving social and academic performance, relaxation has been used successfully as an intervention strategy for hyperactivity. Relaxation is a viable tool for increasing attention to task and decreasing impulsiveness. And relaxation training teaches young people to use the relaxation response when anxiety and fear arise.

Relaxation training promotes anxiety reduction by teaching the individual to reduce muscle tension. Essentially, relaxation training accomplishes two objectives. First, it is a means to counter-condition the anxiety associated with a stressful environment. Second, it is a self-management tool. Through the self-regulation training of relaxation, children can increase their control over their lives, be responsible for their behavior, and improve their academic performance. This tool has a spin-off effect. As children gain confidence in the ability to become calm in learning and social situations, they gain approval from adults and peers, improve their attention span, are less distractible, and learn more. This procedure shows considerable promise for improving the self-management skills of children (Brennan, 1984; Rivera & Omizo, 1980).

Progressive Relaxation

Several techniques are useful in relaxation training, including biofeedback, autogenic training, meditation, the quieting reflex, and progressive relaxation. Most training in relaxation uses a procedure originally outlined by Jacobson (1938), which he referred to as progressive (deep-muscle) relaxation. Merely telling an individual to relax is not enough. Jacobson developed a more structured and concrete procedure by which the individual achieves a state of deep muscular relaxation. To achieve relaxation in a specific muscle or muscle group, the client lies down comfortably and alternately tenses and relaxes the major muscle groups. The contraction phase is then gradually decreased until it is eliminated as the individual develops awareness of and releases muscle tension.

In the relaxation technique used in RIT, the youth tenses and then relaxes various muscle groups. This procedure continues until the person is aware of the contrast between a tense and a relaxed state. Early in relaxation training it is necessary to repeat the tension and relaxation phases several times during several sessions. Eventually the need for tensing is eliminated and the individual achieves relaxation quickly. Once students develop this technique, they can relax on their own without instructions from the adult, thereby exercising a greater degree of self-control. After practice, most individuals can learn to achieve a relaxed physical and mental state within a few minutes. Lazarus (1971) and Carkhuff (1969) have published guides for conducting relaxation sessions, and elsewhere (J. J. McWhirter, 1988) we have developed relaxation strategies for younger people.

At least some of the problems faced by Paul Andrews (of Chapter 1) can be attributed to his stressful environment. The tension in his dysfunctional family and his intense dislike of school have led to angry, hostile, aggressive acting out. Adults' reactions to his behavior increase his stress. His aggressiveness and anger appear to be methods for coping with underlying anxiety. Relaxation training would enable him to cope better with his own emotional reactions to his situation. Relaxation would provide Paul with the skill needed to redirect his aggression and attend to his underlying apprehension and anxiety.

Visual Imagery

Visual imagery is an important adjunct to relaxation training. It is used to lessen tension and to enhance comfort, to engage various muscle groups, and to cue a relaxation response. The counselor or teacher might ask the child to imagine a peaceful scene, such as waves lapping on a shore at night, rocking on a porch swing, or sitting in front of a warm fireplace. Many excellent scripts and audiotapes are available to set imaginary scenes for students (Davis, Robbins-Eshelman, & McKay, 2000). Commercial tapes have music, narrative, and distinctive environmental sounds (bird songs, flowing water, rustling leaves). Of course, the subject matter of the tape or script must be appropriate to the age and environment of the targeted youth. For example, an ocean scene may be outside the experience of many students. Students must be given ample time and practice to develop skill in imagery.

Visual images in the form of guided fantasies allow the child or youth to confront areas of difficulty, to learn tasks, and to develop self-control. Through imagery, the child is guided through an event as if the activity were actually happening. The child enters a rich world of internal experiences where imagination is recruited to promote specific psychological and physiological changes to aid performance or behavior. In addition, imagery should include positive suggestions, especially when the youth is anticipating a negative outcome or condition. Positive imagery is obviously important for an at-risk child or adolescent such as Paul Andrews, who has come to expect failure and negative reactions.

Several key elements go into guided fantasy scripts for young people. The scripts should be as realistic and focused as possible and incorporate words, phrases, and situations that apply to the individual. Paul Andrews's counselor might enlist other adults as collaborators. Paul's mother could become a technical consultant and suggest words, language, and fantasies as well as key events and details that would make the fantasy a rich and realistic experience. If we were to construct a fantasy for Paul, we would follow these guidelines:

1. Help Paul use all his senses—touch and hearing as well as vision. Internal emotional and muscular cues that are experienced before and during a scene should not be neglected.
2. Set the scene as vividly as possible by describing it clearly. If specific details are available, provide them. If not, ask Paul to supply them.
3. Work from the outside environment (the classroom, the home) to the inside environment or the emotional state.
4. Guide the fantasy from Paul's viewpoint, as if he were actually in the situation. Paul is not simply observing himself as a spectator but is actually participating in the event— feeling the emotion it arouses, thinking about it, observing others in the situation, and so forth.
5. Use positive statements and autosuggestions to help Paul develop self-reinforcing statements. Be sure to close the fantasy with a positive image.

Imagery improves learning and retention of materials in most academic subjects (J. J. McWhirter, 1988). It seems to be useful in all areas of the curriculum, as it can create an appropriate readiness and mental set for learning. In the sciences and mathematics, imagery aids creative problem solving and memory. It promotes learning in the language arts by lending vitality to poetry and prose. In educational contexts imagery (a) creates a readiness to learn, (b) aids comprehension, (c) enhances memory and recall, and (d) facilitates problem solving and creative thinking.

Helping students prepare their minds, emotions, and bodies for learning may be as important as the instruction itself. Anticipation of a mental event and openness of mind create a state of readiness for whatever is to be learned. We have had success using imagery, along with other techniques, to enhance group experiences of high school students (Wenz & J. J. McWhirter, 1990).

Affirmations

In view of the generally negative cognitions of at-risk young people, use of positive affirmation to acknowledge and increase personal strengths is critical. RIT provides an opportunity for the teacher or counselor to encourage the child by making positive affirmations. These affirmations should be used consistently and frequently throughout both the relax-

▲ Box 13.2
The Little Train

It's three A.M. again and she wakens full of dread
Another day coming
another endurance test to mark
how many taunts, snubs, stares
a girl can bear in silence.
The clock ticks on relentlessly
then in its rhythm she begins to hear

"I think I can I think I can"

She smiles, remembering stories and laps, comfort
Smiles at herself for this lapse into silly optimism
Smiles at the thought of her teacher—
trying so hard to push this "positive thinking"
That no one will ever use . . .

Sleep finds her
Still smiling.

ation and imagery segments of the program. Most children know the story *The Little Engine That Could* with its refrain of "I think I can, I think I can, I think I can." This saying can be the basis of a class discussion of other positive sayings (see Box 13.2). Children repeat these sayings to themselves to reduce stress and to build confidence. Several phrases seem particularly useful: "I can do it"; "I've studied for this test, and I'll do my best"; "I am special because. . ."; "I can relax and remember the right answer"; "I have lots of strengths." Specific phrases and sentences need to be developed from the repertoire of the at-risk children and adolescents.

Affirmations represent one technique in a wide range of useful cognitive strategies. In the following section, we attend to a number of cognitive restructuring approaches known to be helpful to children and adolescents. With the RIT program, children will begin to understand that they have the power and self-control to overcome the effects of stress and anxiety and get on with living and learning. Counselors and other adults can facilitate development of that power and that self-control.

CONTROL: STRATEGIES FOR COGNITIVE CHANGE

The final and fifth "C" denoted in Chapter 5 is control—control of decisions, control of self, and control of the future. A variety of cognitive-behavioral techniques have been devised to help children and young people develop control over their internal reactions and overt behavior. Three points in cognitive-behavioral theory are particularly important in this respect: First, cognitive events mediate behavior; therefore, a focus on cognition can be an effective approach to changing behavior. Second, young people are active partici-pants in their own learning and can exercise control over it. And third, cognition, behav-ior, and the environment are related: Each affects and is affected by the others. Among the cognitive-behavioral strategies with demonstrated utility in dealing with control are inter-ventions to improve decision making.

Control of Decisions

At-risk young people are more likely to engage in rigid thinking and perceive fewer alter-natives to problems when they emerge. Thus, their ability to generate and select from al-ternative choices of action or cognition needs to be improved.

Early models of problem solving and decision making were based on the assumption that adequate and accurate information would lead to better choices. There was an im-plicit assumption that prudent choices would flow from a rational review of options. We now know that accurate information is necessary but not sufficient for effective decision making. Even for adults with substantial life experience and mature cognitive skills and abilities, the processes of problem solving and decision making are far less rational than they were once thought to be. Children and adolescents are at least as irrational as adults in their problem solving and decision making.

At the same time, young people have the potential to make competent decisions. Dodge and Price (1994) suggest that children who accurately perceive and effectively solve interpersonal problems use a five-stage sequential problem-solving, decision-making process. In stage one, they attend to relevant environmental cues. In stage two, they accu-rately encode and interpret these cues. In stage three, they generate many and varied so-lutions to the problems. In stage four, they accurately evaluate each of the solutions and determine the best possible solution. Finally, in stage five, they plan the steps necessary to carry out and actually perform the favored solution. For high-risk youth several things stand in the way of effective problem solving and decision-making. These include: the emotional component of most problems, the tendency to appraise situations from an ego-centric perspective, the perception of limited alternatives, and failure to use systematic decision-making procedures. For example, social-cognitive deficits in aggressive children have been reported in the area of social attention and recall (stage 1), generating multiple solutions to interpersonal problems (stage 3), and performance of favored responses (stage 5). Social-cognitive distortions in antisocial children occur when errors are made in the inter-pretation of social stimuli (stage 2) and misjudgments are made concerning the conse-quences of hostile acts (stage 4) (Dodge & Price, 1994).

Explicit instruction in problem-solving and decision-making processes helps to avert problems and over come areas of limitation. The steps involved in problem solving require specific skills, which need to be learned and practiced. We have adopted a model for gen-eral problem-solving training that we call DECIDE, which is similar to that of the DE-CIDES model of career counseling developed by Kinnier and Krumboltz (1984) but contains some variations for problem solving.

We developed the DECIDE model specifically for improving the skills in general problem solving for at-risk children and adolescents. DECIDE stands for the steps to be taken: (1) Define the problem, (2) Examine variables, (3) Consider alternatives, (4) Isolate a plan, (5) Do action steps, and (6) Evaluate effects. Teaching at-risk children and adolescents these six problem-solving steps will contribute to a more internal locus of control—that is, students will feel that their behavior is under their own control—and will help modify impulsive, self-defeating behavior. An internal locus of control, in turn, can improve self-esteem, increase a sense of self-efficacy, and strengthen resistance to problem behaviors. The steps are:

1. *Define the problem.* The problem is defined as clearly as possible and is stated as a goal to be achieved. This goal is assessed: Will it address the problem? If it is attained, does it help the individual achieve satisfaction?
2. *Examine variables.* The specifics of the total situation are examined. Background issues and environmental factors are considered, so it may be necessary to gather and appraise additional information. It is particularly important to identify the feelings and thoughts of the young person at this step. Both here and in step 1, questions and suggestions from other students in the classroom or the group are useful.
3. *Consider alternatives.* Various means of solving the problem are considered. The strengths and weaknesses of each possibility are evaluated. Again, the teacher or the counselor may call for brainstorming to generate ideas from other students about alternatives and strategies.
4. *Isolate a plan.* The alternatives are gradually narrowed down until what seems like the best response or solution remains. A plan for carrying out this alternative is prepared, and the potential consequences are considered in more detail.
5. *Do action steps.* After a plan is decided upon, action must be taken to implement it. Youngsters are systematically encouraged to follow through on the necessary steps to carry out their plan. They perform the behaviors that make up the solution plan.
6. *Evaluate effects.* Finally, children and adolescents need to evaluate the effectiveness of the solution. Teaching them to look for effects in their thoughts and feelings is important. They analyze and evaluate the outcome, review the decision, and if necessary develop another plan to achieve their goal.

Self-Management and Self-Control

Self-management and self-control are related. Self-management is the ability to maintain or alter goal-directed behavior without depending on discernable external forces. Young people with good self-management skills are able to respond to situations based on their internal standards. Self-control is an important component of self-management and refers to control over one's affective, cognitive, and behavioral reactions. It is particularly important for high-risk children and adolescents because it helps them prevent problem situations, limit negative emotional reactions, resist problematic behaviors, and delay gratification.

Training in self-management and self-control includes the following skills: (a) self-assessment (being able to compare present functioning with internal standards and evaluate significant differences between the performance and the standard), (b) self-monitoring (being attuned to and aware of one's present functioning), and (c) self-reinforcement (providing positive consequences when performance meets standards and negative consequences for failure to perform adequately).

Self-assessment.   Self-assessment is the systematic evaluation of one's own behavior to determine whether or not it has been adequate. Young people need to be able to evaluate and assess their behavior to improve it. Most young people evaluate themselves on the basis of standards acquired from significant others in their environment. Both parents and teachers provide young people with standards against which to evaluate their behavior in various situations. For a variety of reasons, many at-risk young people fail to acquire clear standards for self-evaluation.

Self-ratings can be used to teach youth to assess their behavior. First, the student and adult decide together which specific behavior needs to be changed. After a target behavior is identified, the next step is to devise a rating system—a scale of 0 to 10, say, or 0 to 100—by which the specific behavior can be assessed and evaluated. Paul Andrews of Chapter 1, for example, might be asked to rate his classroom outbursts by rating his underlying mood and behavior: 0 (no desire to hit or to explode) to 10 (several outbursts). Number 5 on this rating scale might be "resisted desire to hit or explode." Such a rating scale would provide Paul with a subjective measure of mood and behavior, and the self-assessment would help him to develop self-control. Although Paul has several behaviors that need to change, he needs to deal with only one behavior at a time. An attempt to change too many behaviors simultaneously would lower the probability of success and serve to confuse him. If he started out by attempting to change a single behavior, Paul's chance for success would be increased. (Workman [1982] is an excellent source of self-assessment techniques.)

Self-monitoring.   Self-monitoring is focusing attention and awareness on one's characteristics, emotions, thoughts, or behavior and is closely related to self-assessment. Self-monitoring requires students to observe their own behavior and to record it. Essentially students are taught to collect data on their own behavior. Self-monitoring helps students become more aware of their own negative and positive behaviors, putting their behavior more firmly under their own control (DiGangi, Maag, & Rutherford, 1991). Several authors (Kaplan, 1991; Shapiro & Cole, 1992; Workman, 1982) provide useful information on observation and recordkeeping forms for the self-monitoring process.

Self-reinforcement.   Self-reinforcement is the act of supplying one's own consequences for performance. Such consequences may be intangible and intrinsic (such as silent self-praise for meeting a personal goal) or tangible and external (such as buying oneself a present after meeting a personal goal). Consequences may also be negative. A negative consequence might be self-criticism or forgoing a particular pleasure.

Self-reinforcement energizes the self-management process. People anticipate and work for possible positive consequences. Self-reinforcement keeps the person on the track of establishing and pursuing goals. The effects of self-reinforcement on school performance are found to be as beneficial as those of external reinforcement (Kaplan, 1991). The self-reinforcement of behaviors conducive to learning works powerfully to improve school achievement and personal performance.

In summary, when young people are taught to assess their own behavior, to monitor their academic and personal performance, and to reinforce their improved behavior with positive consequences, their school performance is likely to improve, and their personal problems are minimized.

Control for Learning

Self-management and self-control help in the educational process too. Self-management training produces both short- and long-term gains in achievement. Students who have received this training have been found to raise their levels of academic aspirations, increase their efforts on future tasks, improve their nonacademic skills, and decrease their disruptive behaviors (D. J. Smith, Young, Nelson, & West, 1992). Self-control skills help students make adaptive attributions: Students are encouraged to take responsibility for their successes and failures by learning when failure is attributable to their own lack of effort and when success results from their own ability, efforts, and skills. These modified attributions result in enhanced efforts in similar tasks in the future.

One consistent difference between academically successful and unsuccessful students is their awareness of their own learning strategies. Many at-risk students are unaware that their learning strategies are limited or ineffective. Another way for adults to intervene in the learning process is to teach successful learning strategies to at-risk students. A learning strategy is a plan for merging cognitive skills and metacognitive ability in the process of acquiring information (Cohen & de Bettencourt, 1991; Zigmond, 1990). In this educational approach, students are taught to observe, monitor, and think about their learning strategy or plan.

Children's awareness of their cognitive strategies is correlated with enhanced performance on reading measures. That is, children who can describe the thinking processes they use as they read are able to comprehend more than students who cannot. Duffy and his colleagues recommend that teachers model their own mental processes to stimulate metacognitive skill in their students (Duffy, Roehler, & Hermann, 1988). The purpose of instruction in metacognitive strategies is to increase students' awareness of themselves as learners, place students in control of their own learning activity, and provide them with a method to use to improve their own learning.

Reciprocal teaching is a similar learning strategy that is successful with poor learners. To implement this strategy, the teacher and a small group of students talk about the texts they read. The students take turns being "teacher" and practicing the four components of reciprocal teaching: They (a) generate questions about the content of the reading material, (b) summarize the content, (c) clarify points, and (d) predict future content on the basis of prior knowledge or clues within the text. Reciprocal teaching has improved achievement of low achievers (Lysynchuk, Pressley, & Vye, 1990; Rosenshine & Meister, 1991), providing success for students with learning problems.

Cognitive Restructuring

The term *cognitive restructuring*, as we use it here, simply means modifying, changing, or restructuring one's beliefs. A belief is a rule that a person applies to all situations regardless of his or her current experiences. When the belief is maladaptive, it can be unlearned to produce a new and better belief. As more adaptive beliefs replace incomplete or faulty ones, behavior changes too.

The best-known approaches to changing maladaptive beliefs or cognitive patterns are rational-emotive behavioral therapy (REBT) (Ellis, 1962, 1996) and cognitive therapy (CT) (Beck, 1976, 1991). Both approaches are based on the assumption that faulty cognitions cause detrimental self-evaluations and emotional distress and that these experiences lead to behavioral problems. The goal is to help people develop their cognitive ability to recognize faulty self-statements and to substitute more positive ones. There is growing evidence that children and adolescents can understand the principles of REBT (Vernon [1983] reviews the evidence) and CT (Garber, Deale, & Parke, 1986).

Rational-emotive behavior therapy (REBT).   Ellis's rational-emotive therapy, the oldest and probably best known of the cognitive therapies, is based on the belief that people need to change their faulty thinking and correct irrational beliefs to lead healthier, happier lives. Ellis (1996) suggests that emotional disturbances are the result of illogical and irrational thinking in the form of internalized beliefs. Thus, emotional disturbances arise from cognitive or thinking processes around an activating event. Ellis recognized, however, that emotion is complex and is tied to a variety of sensing and response processes and states.

The major assumption of REBT is that thoughts create feelings. In other words, it is not events or other people that make one feel upset or inadequate but one's belief about them. A young boy who does not succeed at football and feels depressed, for example, may assume that his poor performance has caused the depressed feeling. Ellis argues, however, that it is the assumptions about the event or the failure—the thoughts about it, not the event itself—that cause the depressed feeling.

Ellis (1985) proposes an A-B-C-D-E model as a cognitive intervention strategy. The child or adolescent learns to recognize the activating event (A), the corresponding belief (B) about the event, and the emotional and behavioral consequences (C). The counselor then helps the young person to dispute (D) the old belief system and attend to the new emotional and behavioral effects (E) of more rational thinking.

At-risk children and adolescents develop many irrational ways of thinking. These irrational thoughts lead to maladaptive behavior. Cognitive restructuring efforts are designed to help young people recognize and change these irrational beliefs into more rational ones. Attainment of this goal requires a confrontive and supportive counselor who is able to actively engage the client (Ellis, 1996).

Cognitive therapy.   Beck (1976, 1991) suggests that cognition and affect are interactive. Like Ellis, he believes that an individual's cognition about an event determines the affective response to the event. If cognitions are distorted or inaccurate, the individual's emotional response will be inappropriate.

Three elements are central to Beck's CT model: the cognitive triad, cognitive schemas, and cognitive errors. The cognitive triad is composed of thoughts that focus on three major aspects of life: view of the world, the self, and the future. When the cognitive triad is negative, the individual views the world, self, and future as negative, and depression and despair result.

A schema is like a personality trait; it is a stable cognitive pattern that an individual creates from the cognitive triad. Schemas are underlying cognitive structures that help the individual organize and evaluate information, events, and experiences. At-risk children and adolescents develop schemas that distort environmental stimuli in a negative way. Often their schemas include a derogatory self-image. Because these schemas are a person's "core beliefs," they influence both behavioral and affective responses to an event.

Dysfunctional or negative schemas are often maintained and exacerbated by faulty information processing or consistent errors in logic. These are called cognitive errors. At-risk young people make these automatic cognitive errors when they evaluate events. These errors—negativistic, categorical, absolute, judgmental—cause the person to consistently misread or misinterpret even benign experiences.

Treatment and training strategies flow directly from Beck's cognitive model. His cognitive therapy has both behavioral and cognitive components that are designed to reduce automatic negative cognitions. The client learns to challenge the assumptions that maintain the faulty cognitions. Behavioral strategies are used first in the therapeutic or training process. Positive activities are established and augmented through role-playing, graduated task assignments, activity schedules, assertiveness training, and behavioral rehearsal. After these strategies are successfully used, cognitive interventions are introduced to identify, test, and modify the cognitive distortion. Clients are taught (a) to recognize the connections between cognitions, affect, and behavior; (b) to monitor negative automatic thoughts; (c) to examine evidence related to distorted automatic cognitions; (d) to substitute more realistic interpretations for distorted cognition; and (e) to learn to identify and modify dysfunctional beliefs.

Cognitive therapy is dedicated to the goal of helping clients discover maladaptive thoughts, recognize their negative impact, and replace them with more appropriate and positive thought patterns. Cognitive restructuring techniques have been successfully applied in clinical settings and are used increasingly in training modules to help at-risk young people make cognitive changes so that they can lead more productive lives.

Tyrone Baker (of Chapter 2) could benefit from cognitive change strategies. Interpersonal problem solving could help him make better decisions. Self-assessment, self-monitoring, and self-reinforcement could provide him with tools to help him delay gratification. Through cognitive restructuring, he could modify his irrational thoughts, the nature of his cognitive triad, and his negative schemas. Cognitive errors could be corrected to modify and improve his negative behavior.

CONCLUSION

Communication and life skills, cognitive change strategies, and coping techniques are critical elements in programs for prevention and early intervention. Young people who have acquired these tools have the ability to avoid problem behavior. Comprehensive training programs to teach these skills need to be instituted early and *universally* for all youth in order to prevent problems. For at-risk youth, *indicated* programs to teach these skills are needed as early as possible—ideally before third grade. For long-term benefits, young people need the skills reinforced over time and from a variety of people. Finally, for older children and adolescents who are at higher risk, these skills need to be included in special education classes, school counseling programs, and in community treatment programs.

School-based psychoeducational groups, peer (and cross-age) tutoring, and school mediation programs are strong environments in which to teach and reinforce these skills. By learning these skills, young people will improve their interactions with others, perform better in school, and realize their potential for a more positive future.

PEER INTERVENTIONS

▲ *Dear Jenny,*
I am really, really sorry that I did something to make you mad at me. If you would tell me what it is I would change it but you won't talk to me. Please be my friend again, I will try to be the best friend that I can be.
Kayla

▲ *Dear Jenny,*
It has been 2 weeks that you won't talk to me and I still don't know what I did. Did you tell Angie and Kara something about me, because now they won't talk to me either. I can't eat or sleep, this is making me very upset, I am going to go talk to the peer helper even though we think she is weird, that's how upset I am about all of this, so you should think about what you are doing to me. Your friend (still, even though you won't talk to me).
Kayla

▲ *Dear Jenny,*
Jackie is actually nice and she isn't weird at all. She asked me what a friend is and I said that you are a friend. Hah! I would tell you more but I am going to go study with a FRIEND.
Kayla

▲ *Dear Jenny,*
Well I guess this is my last note to you because after all this time of wanting to be your friend and wanting to know what I did wrong, now it doesn't matter to me any more. I liked being your friend and you are pretty and fun, but there are girls who don't act like you and they are my friends now. If that means I'm not cool that's ok with me. A friend is someone who talks to you and listens to you so we aren't really friends any more. Maybe you should talk to Jackie too and tell her how mean you are, she could probably help you be a better friend, and then you wouldn't have to hang around girls that say mean things.
Kayla
PS I know you are going to show this to Kim and Angie so don't think it will shock me.

CHAPTER OUTLINE

▲   In the previous chapter, we provided a series of core interventions designed to build personal resiliency and to increase the individual competencies of young people at risk. We presented prevention strategies to be implemented in curriculum-based developmental programs in schools. In this chapter, we present major prevention strategies that utilize the power of the peer group in helping young people decrease negative and increase positive behaviors. These interventions help prevent and reduce the negative behaviors discussed earlier in this book.

IMPORTANCE OF PEERS

The history of prevention of problem behaviors over the last four decades has included educational and "scare" approaches during the 1960s, self-esteem and ego-enhancing approaches during the 1970s, and social skills training approaches during the 1980s. Each of these approaches is necessary, but not sufficient in preventing or decreasing problem behaviors. The core competency approaches described in the last chapter, which include components of education (cognitive), self-esteem and optimism building (affective), and social skills training (behavioral) show great promise and characterize preventive interventions prevalent during the 1990s. Many of these interventions have proven efficacious in modifying the abuse of substances, in reducing teen pregnancy, and in preventing other problems. In making interventions specific, focused, and personalized, high-risk children and adolescents are aided in improving their resiliency and competency skills.

Unfortunately, for many high-risk young people, learning to be competent is not enough. For example, virtually all young people can learn resistance and refusal skills. They can learn to "just say no." However, knowing how to say "no" is a very different thing from actually saying "no," which takes us to the focus of this chapter. As we move into a discussion of preventing behavior so troublesome to at-risk children and adolescents, we discuss the influences of peer pressure in encouraging and maintaining deviant behavior. We also consider the potential of peer cluster theory to explain peer influence on problem behavior and how to use it as a potential model for helping young people to overcome problems. Later in the chapter we highlight several prevention and intervention strategies that are designed to modify negative peer clusters or engage youth in identifying more closely with positive peer clusters. For example, we examine cooperative learning groups with a particular emphasis on peer support networks. We also describe strategies that utilize peers to help other peers by enhancing academic and social success in school settings. Thus we provide models for peer and cross-age tutoring, peer mediation programs, and other peer-assisted or peer-mediated interventions.

Peer Influence—For Good or Bad

As children grow older, the importance of parents decreases as a reference group and as a model for conformity (McGoldrick & Carter, 1999). Interestingly, the degree of emotional closeness and values consensus between parents and youth has been directly related to problem behavior (Jessor, 1993). Although parental influence is more important for some young people than for others, peer influence becomes the dominant factor for many teenagers. Peer influence clearly can be part of the problem, but it also can be part of the solution.

Young people are very responsive to peer group comments as measures of self-worth and self-esteem. The peer group represents the transfer vehicle for transition from childhood to adulthood. It is within the peer group that the young person learns to relate to different roles and to experiment with interpersonal interaction skills that will eventually transfer to the world of adults.

The peer group exemplifies the world outside the home. Compliance, aggression, leadership, and need satisfaction are developed within peer group interaction. A teenager who is attracted to a peer group that values antisocial activity inevitably finds that resisting the encouragement of group members to engage in negative behaviors is an insurmountable task. In this situation the adolescent is faced with a decision—either abandon the relationships that provide social support or capitulate to the dictates of peer group pressure. The most consistent risk factor for urban middle school students is having friends who exhibit problem behavior (Jessor, Van Den Bos, Vanderryn, Costa, & Turbin, 1995). Interestingly, the most powerful protective factor was having an attitude that was intolerant of deviant behavior.

Peer Cluster Theory

Peer cluster theory (Beauvais, Chavez, Oetting, Deffenbacher, & Cornell, 1996; Oetting & Beauvais, 1986) provides a way of operationalizing peer pressure, especially as it relates to problem behaviors. This theory suggests that antisocial behavior and school problems are major factors in creating deviant peer clusters. Young people who engage in troublesome behavior have a tendency to find each other. These individuals form peer cluster groups. These deviant peer cluster groups normalize, support, and encourage a wide range of deviant behaviors.

Peer cluster theory suggests that the dominant influences on an adolescent's drug use and other problem behaviors are the attitudes, beliefs, and behaviors of the young person's immediate peers (Beauvais et al., 1996; Oetting & Beauvais, 1987). According to this theory, social and environmental factors such as poverty, prejudice, family, community, and the presence of emotional stressors, as well as personality traits, values, and beliefs, provide a framework that can increase or decrease adolescents' susceptibility to problem behaviors. Against this background, the peer cluster is a dominant influence on young people's behavior. Alternative models examining the influences of peers and family patterns on adolescent delinquency and violence have suggested that the direct influence of family functioning is stronger than that suggested by peer cluster theory (Dishion, Patterson, et al., 1994; Henry, Tolan, & Gorman-Smith, 2001).

A peer group can be a large or small reference group; a peer cluster is a small subset of a peer group that influences the values, attitudes, and beliefs of each member. Peers within a particular cluster are likely, in the case of a substance-using adolescent, to use the same drugs, use them for the same reasons, and use them together. These characteristics are much more specific than those implied by the term *drug lifestyle*, which can refer to heavy and occasional drug users alike. Similarly, peer clusters influence sexual behavior, delinquency, gang membership, and school dropout. Adolescents at risk of dropping out have more friends who are dropouts, more working friends, and fewer school friends than adolescents at low risk of dropping out (Ellenbogen & Chamberland, 1997). *Peer pressure* implies the heavy influence of a group on an individual who usually has limited ability to resist it. Peer clusters are much more dynamic; every member of the peer cluster is an active participant in developing the norms and behaviors of the cluster. The cluster is an interactive whole. Although some members will wield more influence than others (as in any group), the group as a whole determines the behavior, attitudes, and beliefs of the entire cluster (Oetting & Beauvais, 1987).

The dynamics of peer clusters may explain why many prevention and intervention treatments fail. Most adolescents return to their original environment and peer cluster after treatment. The norming influence of the peer cluster can diminish or eliminate the treatment effects. Treatment strategies must consider peer clusters and provide alternatives for adolescents who may be drawn back into a peer cluster that engages in unproductive, unhealthy, or antisocial behavior. In fact, removing young people from their peer cluster alone sometimes ameliorates their problem (Oetting & Beauvais, 1987). Another alternative is providing treatment for the whole cluster. However, as Dishion, McCord, and Poulin (1999) have documented, interventions that provide group treatments to high-risk youth can inadvertently exacerbate problem behaviors. In addition, interventions that fail to incorporate caretakers and focus exclusively on children tend to be less successful. A young person who returns from treatment into the same family dynamics, as well as the same peer cluster, is unlikely to be consistently reinforced for treatment gains that were made.

COOPERATIVE LEARNING AND PEER SUPPORT NETWORKS

Cooperative learning groups are one of the most basic ways to influence peer clusters. Any teacher can develop this approach from the primary grades through high school, and beyond. Children learn the skills of collaboration, manage conflicts and disputes, and develop a cooperative spirit with their classmates. Peer clusters lose some of their negative influence when this strategy is adopted.

The practice of grouping students by their ability to learn, as determined by some objective measure, has a negative impact on the children in low-ability groups, and it tends to reinforce initial inequalities (Barr, 1992; Berliner & Biddle, 1995). Teachers treat high-ability groups differently from low-ability groups. Students with lower ability have been found to receive fewer opportunities to answer analytical questions, to be given less time to respond, and to receive less praise than the students in high-ability groups. These students begin to think little of their own ability. Overall, ability grouping as a practice has decidedly negative effects for children with lower ability.

Cooperative Learning

Still, the wide range of skills and abilities they find in heterogeneous classrooms frustrates teachers. Various grouping procedures (Vaughn, Hughes, Moody, & Elbaum, 2001) including cooperative learning groups are one solution to this problem (Slavin, Karweit, & Wasik, 1994). Cooperative learning is implemented in various ways. First, it can vary in task structure. In some programs, students work independently on a task that has been divided up. In others, students work on the task as a group. The latter format encourages peer helping and a truly cooperative learning environment. Second, cooperative learning can vary according to incentives. For example, the group's grade or reward may be the sum or average of the individual members' performances, or it may be contingent on the product that the group as a whole has created. In most cooperative learning implementations, students work in small, heterogeneous groups (usually numbering between four and six) and are rewarded according to the group's performance.

Cooperative learning groups also have the potential to provide at-risk students with a peer support group. In this section, we present cooperative learning groups as a major intervention approach, and we discuss the deliberate adaptation of them to augment a peer support network. These networks are a counterpoint to peer clusters.

Positive Effects of Cooperative Learning Groups

Cooperative learning has several aims. First, a cooperative model is a healthy alternative to an individual competitive model. Individual competition can have devastating effects on the motivation of at-risk students. Membership in a successful group permits students to experience success with all its attendant advantages—perceptions of themselves as able to perform well, satisfaction in their performance, and the esteem of their peers— regardless of each student's personal individual performance. This experience is of particular benefit to at-risk students who have known few academic successes (see Box 14.1).

In cooperative learning groups, students are encouraged to help and support one another rather than to compete. As in most athletic activities, individual excellence is encouraged because it benefits the whole team. Both high- and low-ability children profit

▲ Box 14.1

Getting Smart

One teacher recently experimented with cooperative learning groups. She joined two children of middle ability with one child of high ability and one of low ability for a social studies project. They worked together cooperatively on the reading material. When they were finished with their project, she quizzed each child on the material.

The next day, when the low-ability child received his score on the test, he looked perplexed and said, "I'm not this smart." The teacher smiled and replied, "I guess you must be." She decided to continue to organize cooperative learning groups in her classroom.

from the experience. The low-ability children benefit from the assistance of their peers, and the high-ability children achieve a higher level of understanding after providing that assistance. Incidentally, high-ability students in cooperative learning situations, compared to those in individualistic competitive ones, demonstrated higher achievement on factual recall and high-level reasoning measures and had higher academic self-esteem and greater cohesion (Johnson, Johnson, & Taylor, 1993).

Cooperative learning increases academic performance (Stevens & Slavin, 1995). Whether students are questioning factual information, discovering new concepts, or solving problems, a cooperative learning approach has been shown to develop academic skills. Students, especially those from diverse linguistic and cultural backgrounds, make significant academic gains compared to student gains in traditional settings. Classroom interaction with peers offers students many chances to use language and improve speaking skills, especially important for ESL students.

Cooperative learning encourages active learning. Extensive research and practice have indicated that students learn more when they are actively engaged in discovery and in problem solving. As students talk and reason together to solve a problem or complete a task, they become more involved in communicating and in thinking. These activities automatically engage a child in an active way that is quite different from the passive listening and learning required by most approaches (Carpenter, Bloom, & Boat, 1999).

Cooperative learning prepares students for work in today's world. Team approaches to problem solving, individual efforts to accomplish group goals, interpersonal harmony, and the work setting are all valued skills in today's society of interdependent workplaces. Cooperative learning teaches students how to work together and builds students' social nature, social understanding, and personal efficacy.

Finally, cooperative learning groups provide an opportunity to improve race relations in the school (Davidson & Worsham, 1992). Students who work together in cooperative learning groups are more likely to value mixed racial and ethnic acquaintances and friendships and develop a respect for diversity, including greater acceptance of students with physical and learning disabilities. When students cooperate to reach a common goal, they learn to respect and appreciate each other. Ms. Basset, Carlos Diaz's social studies teacher, is working toward this goal by placing her students in cooperative learning groups.

As her students of different ethnic backgrounds work with each other, prejudice diminishes. Consequently, Carlos is now establishing friendships with other students. Dividing a class into interracial learning teams reduces prejudice by undercutting stereotypes and encouraging group members to pull together (Costa, 1991).

Cooperative learning takes numerous forms. Programs are known by names such as Learning Together, Group Investigation, Team Assisted Individualization, Student Teams-Achievement Divisions, Teams-Games-Tournaments, and Jigsaw (Slavin, 1983, provides a complete review of these cooperative learning methods). These strategies are a group of instructional methods that utilize interdependence among students in the learning of content (Carpenter, Bloom, & Boat, 1999).

Cooperative learning programs have demonstrated positive affective outcomes that directly address the needs of at-risk youth: motivation, peer support, self-attributions, and self-esteem (Slavin, Karweit, & Wasik, 1994; Stevens & Slavin, 1995). After 30 years of research, the evidence is impressive supporting the claim that cooperative learning groups enhance academic achievement; increase positive self-esteem, internal locus of control, altruism, and perspective taking; improve intergroup relationships between students without and with disabilities, as well as the relationship between students of different cultural backgrounds; and provide positive peer support. Because they entail positive peer support, cooperative learning groups seem to be a natural way to promote feelings of connectedness among students at risk of dropping out or those who have other social and emotional problems. The potential to increase social capital and pro-social peer influence are especially important in cooperative peer learning groups.

Peer Support Networks

Grouping students together because they share a problem may increase interaction, mutual support, and camaraderie, but it can also have other unwanted effects: Positive peer models and influences on academic performance and behavior may be drastically reduced; negative peer modeling may escalate; the entire group may perform according to anti-adult and antisocial norms. Nevertheless, to be successful, classroom interactions must foster caring communities in which students feel they belong and where they believe teachers and peers support them (Carpenter, Bloom, & Boat, 1999).

To increase their positive impact and to minimize their potential negative influence, we propose that cooperative learning groups be formed deliberately to increase the socioemotional supports for students (Meyer & Henry, 1993; Meyer, Williams, Harootunian, & Steinberg, 1995). We have found that by purposefully and deliberately designing peer support networks, high-risk students are provided with positive peer support, which promotes their feelings of connectedness with other students and with the school. High-risk students are not identified in any formal or obvious way, but they are put in situations where they can maintain relationships with peers who provide positive models of academic performance and behavior. In this way, peer support networks are accessible to students regarded as being at risk. They also form a natural structure for psychoeducational support groups recommended by Morganett (1990, 1995) and O'Rourke and Worzbyt (1996).

In developing peer support networks, first identify students at risk. Then identify students who are more grounded, resilient, and pro-social. The five Cs of competency (see Chapter 5) can be used to help identify both groups of students.

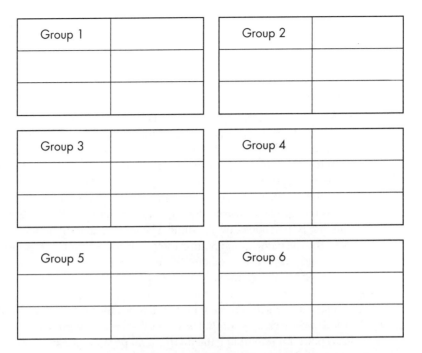

FIGURE 14.1   Peer support network form: Classroom grouping

After students have been identified, the teacher or counselor deliberately structures a cooperative learning group that also functions as a peer support network. Figure 14.1 shows a classroom grouping form that can be used to structure peer support networks. Students with the greatest support needs are targeted, and their names are put in one of the five slots in each cluster. If at all possible, only one high-risk student is included in any single group. Attempts should be made to avoid putting together individuals who form friendship bonds that are a negative influence on academic motivation, school achievement, and behavior. The other four students in each peer support network cluster should be chosen with the intent of making the group as heterogeneous as possible with regard to gender, race, ability, and achievement (for example, European American, Latino, and African American; female and male; one low, one high, and three average achievers).

For each cooperative learning peer support group, include at least one student who is generally on-task in group activities and, if possible, one student who is a peacekeeper diplomat. Also, include at least one group member who might be a potential friend to the student at risk. Ideally, students in the peer support cooperative groups would be very much like the student at risk with an important exception—the potential friends are positive influences. Try to avoid individual personalities that may create negative group combinations. For example, two physically aggressive, volatile students may create a potentially explosive group; or timid or quiet students may be manipulated or intimidated by "macho" boys.

These peer support cooperative learning groups should stay together for their class cooperative learning activities for at least a 9- or 12-week grading period. Although modifications may need to be made when group combinations are not working, the intent is to put together high-risk students with less risky students to provide a peer support network.

Elements of Cooperative Learning

After formation of the groups, it is important that the students engage in cooperative learning activities to help the interaction and mutual interdependent collaboration. In a recent study (Bassett, McWhirter, & Kitzmiller, 1997), we found that teachers who reported a commitment to cooperative learning groups were not really using the method. Many teachers believed that they were implementing cooperative learning when in fact they were missing its essence. Structured cooperative learning among students is more than just putting students into groups to learn. Students sitting together at the same table and talking with each other is not cooperative learning. Having one student do all the work on a group report and others in the group putting their name on it is not cooperative learning. A student who finishes a task early and helps slower students complete it is not cooperative learning.

The five basic elements (Johnson, Johnson, & Holubec, 1990) that are essential to cooperative learning groups are *positive interdependence, individual accountability, face-to-face interaction, social skills,* and *group process.* Slavin (1991) identifies similar elements and adds a sixth: *group rewards.* He argues that awards accruing to the whole group are useful and powerful in building the prestige and power of the cooperative learning group.

Positive interdependence.   Students are linked with others in such a way that one cannot succeed unless the other members of the group succeed and vice versa. Goal interdependence, role interdependence, shared rewards, dependence on each other's resources, and a distributed division of labor helps ensure positive interdependence.

Individual accountability.   The performance of each individual student in the group is assessed and the results are reported back to the student and to the group. Randomly selecting one student's work to represent the entire group or randomly asking one group member to explain a problem, solution, or concept are ways to accomplish this element. Students need to know that they can't "ride" on the backs of others.

Face-to-face interaction.   This element exists when students assist, help, support, and encourage one another's efforts to learn. Discussion of strategies and concepts, explanations of how to solve problems, teaching knowledge, and making connections between past and present information fulfill this requirement.

Social skills.   Working cooperatively requires specific social and interactional skills. Leadership, communication, trust-building, decision-making, and conflict management skills are necessary components of effective cooperative learning groups. As we have made clear elsewhere in this book, these skills have to be taught just as purposefully and precisely as academic skills. Many students have never had an opportunity to work cooperatively in a group before, and they need the social skills to do so.

Group process.   Monitoring and discussing the interactional process of the groups is necessary. Students need to become aware and be encouraged to maintain effective working relationships in their groups and to consider whether they are achieving their goals. Group maintenance, feedback about participation, and other process issues need to be developed.

To develop and increase group cohesion, productivity, and interaction, ask the cooperative learning group members to respond to these two questions after each session: What was something that each member did that helped the group today? What can each person do at the next meeting to make the group better? The ten minutes that this processing takes provides feedback for members on their collaborative skills, allows the group to focus on group maintenance, and reminds students to use their collaborative skills consistently.

Cooperative learning groups that are deliberately structured to provide a social support network can change the way young people experience school. The social support network provides high-risk students with systematic opportunities to develop positive interaction patterns and to form friendships with peers who have been carefully selected as potential supports and friends based on personal, cultural, and social characteristics. Teaching social skills, critical thinking, and academic content is integrated in the context of group support.

PEER AND CROSS-AGE TUTORING PROGRAMS

Peer and cross-age tutors are students who teach other students in formal and informal learning situations that are delegated, planned, and directed by an educator. Peer tutoring is a one-to-one teaching process in which the tutor is of the same academic age as the partner. Cross-age tutoring involves matching an older student tutor with a younger student learner. Peer tutoring alters the environmental and social climate in a school and can enhance and increase learning. It provides a cost-effective way to meet the individual needs of students and to improve the performance of students who need help with their studies. Tutoring programs are designed to aid at-risk children by improving their academic performance and their emotional well-being (Arreaga-Mayer, 1998; Keller, 2002; Tansey, Santos de Barona, McWhirter, & Herrmann, 1996). Peer tutoring improves social interactions, self-concept (Fantuzzo, Davis, & Ginsburg, 1995), motivation, attitudes toward the school (Roswal et al., 1995), peer status, and overall school experience (Cushing & Kennedy, 1997; Tansy, Santos de Barona, McWhirter, & Herrmann, 1996). The concept of peer tutoring has deep roots in our educational system.

Systematic planning is a critical component of successful peer or cross-age tutoring programs. Administrators, teachers, students, and families more readily accept programs that attend to readiness, preparation, selection, implementation, supervision, and evaluation components.

Well-planned programs can be integrated into schools more effectively than programs that are not well articulated from the outset (Greenwood, Carta, & Maheady, 1991). Elements essential to implementing a successful peer or cross-age tutoring program include considerations of cost, school readiness, and teacher, student, and parent preparation.

Cost-Effectiveness

Cost-effectiveness is an important consideration for administrators in the implementation of academic interventions. Levin, Glass, and Meister (1984) studied the cost-effectiveness of four educational intervention strategies designed to raise student achievement in reading and mathematics: (a) computer-aided instruction; (b) cross-age/peer tutoring; (c) reduced class size; and (d) a longer school day. When student gains and program costs were compared, peer tutoring produced math and reading gain scores more than twice those resulting from computer-aided instruction, three times those achieved through reducing class size from 35 to 30 students, and almost four times more than lengthening the school day by one hour. Information regarding the relative utility of peer or cross-age tutoring interventions is vital to administrators in a time of reduced resources, increased demands, and increased accountability.

Readiness

Much of the success of peer tutoring depends on the readiness of the school to accept the program. Readiness is a function of both attitudinal factors and availability of resources to support the program. As administrator of the school, the principal is instrumental in allowing for program adjustments such as release time, schedule modifications, allocation of space, and active encouragement of peer tutoring. Teachers support the peer tutoring program by participating in peer selection, curriculum development, ongoing evaluation, and program development activities. Teacher readiness requires thorough training in peer tutoring methods through in-service training and ongoing consultation and supervision (Hawryluk & Smallwood, 1986). Specialized training and instruction in peer and cross-age tutoring methods for teachers are often available from school psychologists and counselors. Counselors may encourage teachers to acquaint themselves with tutoring methods and materials through published resources, including the *Cross-Age Tutoring Handbook* (S. Johnson, 1977), *Tutoring for At-Risk Students* (Gaustad, 1992), *Increasing Student Productivity Through Peer Tutoring Programs* (Pierce, Stahlbrand, & Armstrong, 1984), and *Peer Tutoring: A Guide for School Psychologists* (Ehly, 1986).

Preparation

Sufficient preparation of participating individuals increases the likelihood that the peer/cross-age tutoring program will be successfully established and accepted in both the school and the community. Students may be readied for peer tutoring through written and oral information about the program. Because peer/cross-age tutoring is a nontraditional means of instruction, presenting the program and its participants in a positive light is important.

Teachers play a central role in determining the content to be tutored, explaining how learning is approached by tutors, monitoring student progress, and facilitating student interaction. To increase teachers' acceptance of and commitment to the program, training and preparation of teachers should encompass several components, including: (a) understanding the purpose, advantage, and features of the peer tutoring program; (b) planning lessons and material preparation for student use; and (c) developing competence in teaching interactional and problem-solving skills to students. This training is accomplished through consultation, exposure to written material on peer tutoring, and in-service training. Teacher training includes instruction of tutoring methods, simulation exercises to familiarize teachers with student and teacher roles, modeling strategies for social and conflict resolution skills, and discussion of anticipated problems that may interfere with implementation. Our experience suggests that training programs developed for this pur-pose can accomplish these objectives in a minimum of three to five 40-minute training ses-sions if ongoing in-service, consultation, and coordination for maintenance purposes is provided.

The degree to which students are prepared to tutor is another critical element of an effective peer tutoring program. Children who have a fuller understanding of a task and its rationale are better prepared to perform the task themselves and better equipped to teach it to others (Barron & Foot, 1991). Students planning to tutor are better prepared when trained in various aspects of tutoring, including: (a) developing and presenting in-structional material, (b) recognizing and reinforcing correct learner responses appropri-ately, (c) providing corrective feedback effectively, (d) redirecting off-task behavior, (e) communicating with learners, and (f) working closely with teachers. Tutor prepara-tion includes a mix of didactic instruction, practice in specific skills, and group discussion of possible problems. Tutors also benefit from ongoing training to strengthen their skills and reinforce the purpose of the program. Ongoing training can be accomplished through brief refresher training sessions offered periodically during the peer/cross-age tu-toring program.

Advance preparation of parents is essential to the program's acceptance. If not prop-erly informed, parents may perceive their child's participation in the peer/cross-age tutor-ing program negatively. Advance preparation of participating parents in the form of written information, group discussions, and personal contact may convert potentially doubting parents to agents of support. Because peer tutoring activities involve individual students se-lected from the entire class, parental consent is needed. Parents should be provided with a clear explanation of the program, reasons for their child's involvement, and safeguards against possible negative effects. Parent preparation may be accomplished through letters to the parents, meetings between parents and school personnel, and presentations at meet-ings such as the PTA and the PTSO.

Sample Method: Pause, Prompt, and Praise

To illustrate the nature of peer tutoring, we selected one method for fuller description. The "pause, prompt, and praise" method is very helpful for tutoring oral reading. The first part of the tutoring procedure, "pause," requires the tutor to delay attention to the student's reading error for more than five seconds or until the end of the sentence. The second part of the procedure, "prompt," requires the tutor to supply a prompt if no self-correction oc-curs. The prompts are the self-correction strategies that the student learner has already learned as part of program preparation. They are often graphic or contextual clues that pro-vide meaning. If no correct response is elicited following two prompts, the tutor supplies the correct word and moves on. The final part of the procedure, "praise," requires the tu-tor to verbally reinforce positive behaviors and to encourage development of independent self-correcting skills. Therefore, in addition to the general praise for behaviors such as fin-ishing a whole page, the tutor praises self-corrections and prompts corrections made by the learner.

This method supplies the tutor with a procedure for dealing with both correct and error behavior by the reader. It encourages him or her to reinforce the desired behaviors. Perhaps more important, it allows the reader to develop independence and independent self-correction strategies. It is also a simple method for peer tutors to learn.

Program Implementations

Educational interventions such as peer or cross-age tutoring often emerge from a need to remediate students who are failing or at risk of failure. The impetus to develop new programs often reflects a sense of urgency. Initially, however, a modest peer/cross-age tutoring program is most viable. Avoid overtaxing available resources during the initial implementation stage of a program, and expand later when the program is well established.

In spite of how thoroughly a program has been planned, unforeseen problems will arise. After initial start-up, slight adjustments will be necessary. Administrative support is essential to the program. As well, teachers will need some release time and other forms of support to develop materials, assess and supervise program participants, and provide ongoing training (in-service and discussion groups) related to the program. Now let's take a closer look at the elements of a successful peer tutoring program.

Tutor selection. In cross-age tutoring programs, older tutors are matched with younger partners. In peer tutoring programs, tutors and student learners (or partners) are the same age, class, or grade. When selecting tutors, consideration may be given to students with a variety of characteristics, including those who are academically accomplished and able to instruct, those who are positive role models and influential with their peers, and others who are at greater risk of school failure and may benefit academically and emotionally from their role as tutors. Each type of tutor offers a degree of assurance that the program will be accepted. The academically accomplished tutor will bring mastery of the subject matter to the tutoring session, the influential peer will popularize the program within the peer culture, and the "at-risk" tutor will provide evidence that the program is of benefit to those who tutor.

When choosing whom to include as student learners, educators might consider the degree of learning difficulties, motivation, and behavioral adjustment the learner presents. Learners with severe problems may not be good candidates for initial implementation of the program. These students may be introduced to the peer tutoring program in subsequent years, once introductory concerns are resolved and the program is established.

Once matched, it is advisable that tutor-learner interactions be observed and pairs assessed for compatibility. Supervising teachers or coordinating counselors should intervene in difficult relationships and reassign unworkable matches. This kind of support will prevent tutors and learners from feeling frustrated or discouraged with the program and will increase their enjoyment of the process.

Tutoring sessions. The program coordinator, scheduling several 20- to 30-minute sessions each week, should develop a tutoring schedule. Tutoring schedules must be followed consistently. Failure to hold tutoring sessions at their scheduled times conveys the message that the program is unimportant relative to other activities.

Tutoring sessions typically are held in a designated area within the classroom, isolated somewhat from other student activities. This seating arrangement allows for privacy and reduces distractions but enables the teacher to directly monitor the tutoring session.

Materials. Tutoring materials are generated by the teacher or adapted from published sources. With supervision, experienced tutors can learn to develop materials for the learner, resulting in increased understanding of the materials by the tutor and decreasing the teacher's required time commitment somewhat.

Student incentives.   Students' motivation to participate in a peer or cross-age tutoring program will not be sustained without some form of incentive. Incentives for participating in the program can be provided for both tutors and their partners on a regular basis. Although most students are motivated through immediate praise and verbal approval, school personnel can recognize student involvement by making schoolwide announcements and providing activities such as social events and learning games. Time set aside for personal reflection and discussion of students' experiences in the program is especially useful. In some schools, tutors receive elective credit for their participation in the program. Some programs recognize tutors and their partners by awarding certificates of completion and recognition. School newsletters and plaques hung in the central hallways are other ways to recognize students for their involvement. Schools can be very creative in developing incentives to enhance student involvement.

Teacher supervision.   Teachers need to meet with tutors before each session to review instructional materials. Prior to the session, the teacher ascertains that the tutor has a clear grasp of the content of the instructional material and the objectives for the learner. These meetings become shorter as the tutor demonstrates competence in the tutorial role.

Initially, after each session, the tutor meets with the teacher to discuss how the session went, the partner's progress, and any difficulties encountered. The teacher reinforces and instructs the tutor at this time. Post-session supervision is reduced as the tutor establishes competence. The motivational aspects of these meetings, however, must be kept in mind; reinforcement of tutors is an ongoing activity and is extremely important. As part of their supervisory role, teachers should directly observe the tutoring session in about one of every three or four sessions to monitor the tutoring process.

Evaluation.   Program evaluation is important to a tutor program for several reasons. Ongoing evaluation of student progress can be used to motivate both the student receiving tutoring and the tutor. Also, feedback from student performance can be used to determine aspects of the program that are effective and those that could benefit from modification. Evaluation results can be used to demonstrate the value of the program to interested parties, such as administrators faced with decisions about funding special programs or parents who express doubts about the quality of alternative educational approaches.

Evaluation activities should be linked to the goals and objectives of the program. Tutoring programs are often designed to improve the academic achievement of both the tutor and the student learner in the specific area tutored. Another common goal of tutoring programs is enhancing both students' academic self-concept. The effectiveness of a tutoring program may be gauged by whether the tutor and the learner have achieved gains in academic performance in the subject being tutored and in academic self-concept.

The use of global measures of academic achievement or self-concept for evaluating the effectiveness of the program may result in ambiguous feedback on student progress. Overall academic achievement is a composite of several academic areas (mathematics, reading, spelling, and so forth). It is unrealistic to expect change in overall academic achievement through tutoring in only one academic area. It is equally unrealistic to anticipate change in global self-concept as a result of improved performance in a specific academic area (Craven, Marsh, & Debus, 1991). Efforts to evaluate program effectiveness using global indices will underestimate the actual benefits of the program. The best way to measure the effect of the tutoring program is to evaluate academic and self-concept change specifically related to the subject tutored.

Students participating in the tutoring program should be assessed before, during, and after participating in the program. Academic achievement can be assessed through teacher-developed curriculum-based measures that are inexpensive, directly related to the academic subject matter, and sensitive to improvement in academic performance.

Several tests designed to measure children's self-concept have academic self-concept factors (Harter, 1985; Piers, 1984). Each of these tests mixes academic self-concept items among the other self-concept items, which does not readily allow measurement of academic self-concept alone. The Multidimensional Self-Concept Scale (MSCS) is well suited to isolating academic self-concept because its 25 academic self-concept items are not woven into the body of the instrument; rather, they are presented on a separate page and may be administered, scored, and compared to national norms without giving or scoring the entire test (Bracken, 1992). The academic scale of the MSCS, about a five-minute test, can be used throughout the course of program participation as a measure of academic self-concept.

PEER MEDIATION PROGRAMS

School peer mediation (Lane & McWhirter, 1992, 1996) is a mode of conflict management employed by students for the purpose of resolving conflicts. Trained peer mediators work as a team of two to facilitate problem solving between disputants. Students' involvement in the mediation process ensures practice with critical thinking, problem solving, and self-discipline. Students' participation in efforts to change their own and their peers' behavior is directly related to the developmental construct of self-regulation. Awareness of socially approved behaviors is a critical feature.

The setting for this mediation process is often the playground. Used in conjunction with traditional means of discipline, such as suspension for serious violent acts, peer mediation provides a structured forum for the resolution of in-school disputes. Student involvement in the mediation process provides practice in critical thinking, problem solving, and self-discipline. "The process of peer mediation is a self-empowering one—it enables students to make decisions about issues and conflicts that affect their own lives" (Maxwell, 1989, p. 150). This element of student participation in self- and peer behavior change is directly related to the developmental construct of self-regulation. Awareness of socially approved behaviors is a critical feature of self-regulation, which involves the ability to postpone acting on a desired object or goal. Self-regulation requires being able to generate socially approved behavior in the absence of external monitors. The ability to self-regulate is a developmental skill that must be practiced regularly. School peer mediation programs provide daily opportunities for reinforcement.

Background

School peer mediation programs have sprung up across the nation in the last two decades, and many of them are based on community mediation models such as the San Francisco Community Board Program (1982). Developers of the San Francisco Community Board Program had five years of experience settling disputes between neighbors and businesses before introducing this school-based Conflict Manager program. In this program, students receive 16 hours of training and role-play practice. They eventually become team mediators on the playground and in the lunchroom. Similar programs now exist in almost all major cities in the United States. The assistance of a community mediation school initiative trainer, although not essential, may be valuable in training school personnel and students.

Models for both adults in the community and children in schools promote conflict mediation through the application of communication skills, listening to evoke varying perspectives, eliciting mutual contributions to the problem's eventual solution, and attending to feelings—all in an atmosphere of respect for the parties involved.

Theoretical Assumptions

Advocates of peer mediation in the schools assume that "children helping children" is a valid perspective from which to view program implementation and outcomes. A wealth of research literature supports this perspective. Peer leaders have been found to have greater credibility regarding student social interactions. They serve as potent role models and can demonstrate pro-social behaviors. Peers can create and reinforce norms supporting the notion that certain behaviors are deviant rather than acceptable, and they can promote alternatives to deviant behaviors. The student mediators who are the direct recipients of program training receive the most impact; students without direct training also benefit (Jones, 1998).

Another strength of such programs is that they emphasize student involvement and student management. Thus, participants tend to feel more committed to program goals and more interested in producing change among their peers. A more specific description of benefits follows.

Benefits to Students and to the School

Both student behavior and school discipline problems improve as a result of peer mediation. McCormick (1988) reported that at-risk disputants (students who had been referred frequently for discipline problems) were observed by teachers to exhibit shifts to cooperation after experiencing peer mediation, a change supported by a 47% decrease in self-reported aggressive conflicts. Also, "at-risk students who directly participated in the program developed more 'prosocial' attitudes towards conflict, but those who had only indirect exposure to the collaborative process maintained their 'antisocial' attitudes towards conflict" (McCormick, 1988, p. 73). For example, when one at-risk student was trained as a peer mediator, his previous preference for resolving conflict in an aggressive style was replaced (over one semester as a mediator) with a reported preference for a collaborative style of dispute resolution. Such metamorphoses are also described by McCormick: " 'Troublemakers' were just as enthusiastic about the problem-solving process and just as competent to guide others through it as those peer mediators who were thought to be ideal students" (p. 63).

Araki, Takeshita, and Kadomoto (1989) found that peer mediation increased empowerment and volunteerism, with both mediators and disputants developing increasing capacities for self-control. Disputants who were nonlisteners became listeners through participation in the mediation process. All students—both disputants and mediators—found a place for talking about problems, learning more about the views of others, and practicing better communication in a nonviolent, nonjudgmental atmosphere. The words of one student summarize peer mediation's impact:

> All I ever wanted to do was to fight. If someone said something to me I didn't like, I didn't think about talking, I just thought about fighting. I came into a mediation session as a disputant with four girls on the other side. I thought, "Who needs this? What am I doing here?" I just wanted to punch these girls out. I figured that the mediator would tell me what I was going to have to do. But she didn't. Instead she drew me out, listened to me. It felt so good to let it all out; then I wasn't angry anymore. I thought, "Hey, if this can work for me, I want to learn how to do it." (McCormick, 1988, p. 54).

Peer mediation also provides benefits for schools by reducing the number of discipline events. In one Hawaii school, the number of on-campus fights dropped from 83 to 19 over a 2-year period (Araki, Takeshita, & Kadomoto, 1989). At a New York school, these events declined by 50% (Koch, 1988), and an Arizona school reported a 47% decrease in the average number of aggressive incidents per month (McCormick, 1988). Finally, out of 69 mediated cases at a Milwaukee high school, 60 agreements were reached, and researchers recorded an 80% success rate for disputes mediated during the 1986–87 school year (Burrell & Vogel, 1990). As more instruments for program evaluation become available, the benefits to students and to school climate will become increasingly apparent.

Training Staff Members

The training sequence begins with presentation of the mediation program to the entire school staff. The school counselor and principal often conduct this introductory session. Given the time and resources required to implement a peer mediation program, it is very important that the initial presentation include evidence of the benefits to students and to the school. After the presentation, each staff member completes a level-of-interest questionnaire to determine his or her degree of commitment to the process. If staff support for mediation is adequate (usually 80%), training for teachers and support personnel is initiated. Elementary and middle school staff training usually requires about 8 hours. The content of this training includes communication skills that encompass active listening, reflection of feeling, message clarification, body language, giving "I" messages, brainstorming, types of questioning, and effective problem solving. The mediation sequence is identified, and adult responsibilities are delineated. Role-play is used extensively with the adult staff members, as it is later with the students.

Training Student Peer Mediators

Once the adults have been trained, they plan and implement an orientation assembly to motivate students and alert them to the qualities of a good mediator. Role-plays and skits are used to outline aspects of the program and the process.

As the time for implementation nears, students who wish to become peer mediators nominate themselves or are nominated by others. Nominations may also come from counselors, teachers, and administrators. Final selection of mediators is completed by student vote. Adult staff members then train selected students, sometimes with the assistance of a community mediation training consultant. Training for elementary and middle school students consists of five half days. The adult staff members teach the communication skills that they reviewed in their own training. They guide the students through role-plays not unlike those they engaged in during the adult training.

The mediation sequence is introduced and practiced until it becomes a comfortable process for the children. This sequence involves four basic stages: introduction, listening, wants, and solutions.

In the first stage of the peer mediation sequence, the student mediators introduce themselves, offer their services ("Do you need a mediator?"), and walk to a different area to cause physical and psychological separation from the initial point of conflict. When the disputants and mediators are ready, the rules are reviewed and commitment to them is elicited. An assurance of confidentiality is given to disputants by the mediators.

In stage 2 of the mediation sequence, the peer mediators listen to each disputant in turn. They reflect and restate content and feelings as they address each disputant. Because no interruptions are allowed, disputants have the opportunity to hear the others' perspective of the conflict and their resultant feelings.

With guidance from the peer mediators, disputants express their wants in stage 3 of the sequence. As the requests are heard and restated by mediators, clarity reduces anxiety about possible hidden agendas.

In stage 4, disputants are asked what they can contribute to the resolution of the problem. The peer mediators restate and check solutions for balance. Then each disputant is asked if the proposed solution is acceptable. An important step in this phase is asking if the problem is solved. Disputants may wish to express a need to receive or to give an apology to smooth hurt feelings. The mediators then ask disputants how such a conflict could be handled differently in the future. Peer mediators close the sequence by asking former disputants to tell their friends that the conflict has been solved, thus reducing the potential for rumors. After congratulating the students on solving their problem, the peer mediators complete a mediation report form. In this last step of the sequence, the peer mediators have an opportunity to review the quality of their guidance because they do their record-keeping together.

When training is complete, student mediators receive recognition and uniform T-shirts, banners, or hats at an assembly. They are then assigned to recess duty in pairs. They meet twice a week with a staff program coordinator to discuss their successes and problems, to maintain and build new skills, and to handle scheduling problems. School counselors often introduce classroom guidance curriculum activities to promote general student awareness of the peer mediators and the services they offer.

Implications

The simplicity of the peer mediation process contributes to its success. The student mediators can easily implement the steps. They also provide support for each other. In the San Francisco Community Board Program (1982) demonstration video, a young man who was formerly a "conflict maker" became a "conflict manager." Sonny had this to say about his peer mediation experience:

> "I used to be a bully. I think because I wanted to get the authority—the power. Now, as a conflict manager, I get the authority and status I used to take. I've changed. Now I can feel what the kids feel, and I can help them solve their problems."

Cahoon (1988), an elementary principal, noted that her "mediators learn valuable problem-solving skills: to think logically about processing the information presented to them, to see issues impartially, and to advise without censoring. They also gain recognition for their efforts" (p. 94). Roderick (1988) emphasized a valuable aspect of school mediation programs: "Young people have many choices besides passivity or aggression for dealing with conflict . . . [through mediation] we give them the skills to make those choices real in their own lives" (p. 90).

The Ripple Effect

Program implementation results in fewer playground problems and fewer referrals to the nurse or the principal's office. Families may also experience the program's impact with parents and students in peer mediation schools reporting that conflict in the home is modified (Daunic, Smith, Robinson, Miller, & Landry, 2000).

Another ripple effect of peer mediation programs is a perceived improvement in school climate. For example, Jones (1998) reports that peer mediation programs had a sustained and significant impact on both staff and teacher perception of school climate at all educational levels—elementary, middle, and secondary. The program also increased students' perceptions of school as a healthy and safe environment.

Counseling Ramifications

Peer mediation helps youth develop self-regulation and other skills. When students are given an opportunity to participate in decisions relating to their own lives, more self-regulation and positive self-esteem are likely to be a result. School counselors can promote peer mediation programs (and are in a strong position to open up mediation training to parents as part of a school–community outreach program). Conflict resolution through peer mediation is a preventive program as well—in the form of leadership training. It is also an integral component of a school's discipline plan. Finally, it is a way to meet the communication objectives of a guidance curriculum. Regardless of its placement in the overall picture of school pupil development, its importance for children and its implications for society are clear.

The conflict resolution model of peer mediation addresses the skills of listening, problem solving, oral language expression, and critical thinking. These essential skills are directly taught in the process of mediation training. They are modeled and reinforced by the peer mediators.

Carlos Diaz would benefit in several ways from being trained as a peer mediator. The experience of being nominated by a peer, teacher, or counselor would bolster his confidence. The skills he learns as a mediator would help him to reduce the number of fights he has with peers. Providing a valuable service to his school would help him view himself as more a part of the school community. This participation might influence teacher perceptions, increasing the amount of support and positive feedback he receives from teachers. The verbal skills learned and utilized by peer mediators might enhance Carlos's language acquisition efforts. Finally, Carlos could be an effective mediator for monolingual Spanish-speaking children at the school. Given Carlos's responsibilities at home, however, staff would have to ascertain whether the time demand of the program would hinder Carlos more than the benefits would be an enhancement. Nevertheless, a young man reinforced for his contributions to the school community who is being supported in the development of useful life skills is a young man with a lowered risk of dropout.

PEER FACILITATION

Peer facilitation (sometimes referred to as peer leadership, helping, or counseling) is very helpful in increasing the impact and efficiency of professional counseling. Peer facilitation is a process in which trained and supervised students perform interpersonal helping tasks—listening, offering support, suggesting alternatives, and engaging in other verbal and nonverbal interactions—that qualify as counseling functions with similar-aged clients who either have referred themselves or have been referred by others. Like peer tutoring and peer mediation, peer facilitation appears to be a useful way to counter negative peer cluster influence (Coker & Borders, 2001). It also reinforces and supports the use of life skills.

Peer facilitation programs generally have two major components: training and service. In the training phase, adult leaders provide designated peer helpers with intensive training. In the service or implementation phase, peer leaders offer direct service to other youth.

Training Phase

The training phase usually has certain common content. Communication skills in particular are emphasized. Active listening, empathic understanding, and paraphrasing are included. Equally important are the nonverbal cues that the peer helper is projecting through his or her behavior.

In addition to basic communication skills, peer leaders almost always acquire skills in problem solving and decision making. These are useful skills that they can transfer to those whom they help although peer facilitators are almost always prohibited from giving advice. Their role is to listen, to question, to reflect, and to be a friend.

The young people in training usually spend a fair amount of time learning about important community resources. For example, information on alcohol and drug use, crisis intervention programs, and treatment facilities are emphasized. Peer leaders are an important source of referrals to community agencies.

Service Phase

Peer leaders can be helpful in many areas. In addition to tutoring and mediation discussed earlier, peer facilitators can help introduce new students to school, befriend lonely and alone children who seem to have no friends, and work with special education students. They can also provide classroom information on tobacco, alcohol, and drug abuse problems; on healthy life styles; and on many other topics. With training they can facilitate small discussion and support groups. Most important, they can provide supportive and caring listening to troubled youth. Often, peers are the first to know when someone is considering suicide. As we discussed in Chapter 10, in every incident of school shootings, the event "leakage" was usually to another peer. Peer facilitators can make school safer by providing a link between troubled young people and caring adults.

The role of the adult supervisors is just as important in the service phase as it is in the training phase. In addition to being models of empathy, understanding, and caring, adults are necessary to coordinate and organize the program. They must be available to help the young leaders with the particularly difficult problems. Of course, problems of extremely urgent or serious nature must be referred to responsible adults.

Successful facilitator programs attempt to involve a representative and diverse group of students as peer helpers. Using the natural helper method described earlier, students and school personnel are asked to identify those students who are perceived to be individuals other students talk to if they need help with a problem. If students perceive the peer helper group as only an elite collection of class leaders or high achievers, many of the students who are in most need of support will stay away.

Facilitation assignments can vary from helping other students with specific problems to being available to provide encouragement and support in a common office area, to assisting on a survey of student needs. Whatever the assignment, peer facilitation programs create a pool of helpers who are trained to be sensitive to student needs and concerns.

CONCLUSION

In this chapter we have described several school-based peer programs designed to directly or indirectly prevent student problems. Such programs are an effective means of reducing some of the correlates of at-risk categories: depression, interpersonal conflict, communication deficiencies, loneliness, and lack of purpose. They can be also implemented at all levels of education—elementary, middle, and secondary settings—and can be organized within a single classroom, a whole school, or an entire district. Schools can also help mobilize peer groups as a force for good. When children are allowed to work cooperatively in small groups, they are provided with a classroom community that encourages them to discuss their work with others, accept one another's viewpoints, weigh their options, and make decisions on the basis of reasoning.

Peer tutoring, mediation, and facilitation programs provide the direct help to at-risk young people in improving academic abilities, in mastering new skills, and in connecting them to the school environment. The peer leaders also benefit by gaining confidence and increased self-esteem. Although requiring the resources of teachers, counselors, and administrators in a time of increasing demands and fewer resources, peer-based programs have positive effects—both current and future—that outweigh their costs.

FAMILY INTERVENTIONS

▲ *In some families words are like*
barbed wire, they cut and puncture.

In some families messages are like
exploding shrapnel, they rip and tear.

In some families secrets are like
land mines, step on one and they
erupt in explosion.

In some families even love and affection
are tools in the battle.

All war, especially the war in families, is
at once horrible and dehumanizing
and obscenely senseless.

J. J. MCWHIRTER

CHAPTER OUTLINE

▲ As discussed earlier, the nature of the family structure is shifting in response to changes in social, political, and economic conditions. More and more families are called upon to deal with the stresses of divorce, remarriage, and stepchildren, and the loss of the extended family network. Even negotiating the inevitable developmental changes that are part of the family life cycle can be highly stressful and can generate family conflict. Sometimes the symptoms of family distress emerge when a reasonably healthy family goes through a difficult transition, such as the marriage of the first child. In other cases, family symptomatology reflects ongoing dysfunction and emerges in response to everyday stresses.

To illustrate, a father might abuse alcohol for several weeks following a layoff, then engage in productive coping strategies, adjust to the new situation, and then return to his pre-layoff, nonproblematic level of drinking alcohol. Or, a father may consistently go on alcoholic binges, whenever the extended family gathers, when the mother confronts him, when the children fight, or when the traffic is heavy. The patterns of behavior that the various family members use to cope with the father's drinking may in themselves represent symptoms of family dysfunction. For example, sometimes roles are frequently assumed by members of families with an alcoholic parent (Devine & Braithwaite, 1993; Brook & Coll, 1994). The scapegoat role is played by a child who acts out (fighting in school, setting a fire, failing a class), thus drawing attention away from the alcohol problem. The parents temporarily unite while they deal with the "problem child." Sometimes, the youth whose behavior appears self-destructive and irrational is actually trying to help a family member. This also inadvertently serves to perpetuate dysfunction (see Box 15.1).

When teachers and counselors become frustrated by the destructive and aggressive behaviors of their students, it is helpful to keep in mind that these behaviors are often goal-directed and represent attempts to meet needs (see our discussion of goals of misbehavior in Chapter 8). Much behavior originates in response to the family dynamics to which the students return every night.

▲ BOX 15.1
The School Slut

He was always angry with her. Every aggressive retort, every call from the school, every violation of curfew drew his rage like flies to butter. But the failing grades, her reputation as the "school slut," and the constant battles were all worth it. Because as long as his attention was focused on his anger with her, it would not be directed at her sister, the "good" daughter. And he wouldn't come into her sister's bedroom. Her sister wouldn't be forced to endure those long nights, the hideous emptiness, the vomiting afterward. At least, this much she could control.

And that's one reason why the rage overwhelmed and consumed her ten years later; that's one reason why the tears in my office were so torrential that her whole body convulsed with agony. Because ten years later, her sister said, "It was happening to me too."

It is a mistake, however, to attribute all student problems to some growing malevolence in the American family. As we have indicated, the family is changing in response to societal trends over which the individual family has little control. Too often society appears too eager to blame families for individual problems, as evidenced by attempts to solve those problems by "fixing" families. Blaming families diverts attention from the fact that our society lacks a coherent national family policy and that the structural supports required for family life are grossly inadequate (Kagan & Weissbourd, 1994; Lott, 2002). In this chapter we describe to interventions for individual families as one point of entry for addressing the problems of youth at risk. These interventions are family counseling, parent support groups, parent education, and parent training.

FAMILY COUNSELING

Working with the entire family is often the optimal approach for dealing with young people at risk for dropout, substance use, pregnancy, delinquency, suicide, or other problems. When a child or adolescent is contemplating or engaged in life-threatening behavior, it is of utmost importance that the family be involved in efforts to avert the problem. In general, family counseling is appropriate when: (a) the presenting problems are affected by and affect the family system; (b) the child or adolescent is living in the family or is working through unfinished business with the family and is in contact with them even though not living at home; and (c) both the counselor and the client agree that family counseling is an appropriate intervention.

Family counseling is not always a viable option. The following questions are often considered in exploring the option of family counseling: Does the family have resources such as transportation? Are there any language or cultural factors that might prohibit or discourage the family members from availing themselves of counseling services? Is the family willing and able to commit to attending counseling sessions? Is there a family member who has access to counseling services through an employee assistance program or some other work benefit? Discussion of these questions and familiarity with community resources will set the stage for appropriate referrals.

Referring the Family for Counseling

For many family members, attending a counseling session is tantamount to acknowledging severe mental illness within the family. When a teacher or counselor believes that a particular family might benefit from family counseling, several steps can be taken to lay a foundation for success. First, the family needs to know why. On what basis has the referring professional made this decision? The identified problem—that is, the behavior of the child that attracted attention—should be explained in specific and concrete terms. For example, Lidia Diaz's teacher (Chapter 4) might say: "For three weeks now, Lidia has been withdrawn and quiet. She seems to be avoiding her school friends, she's refusing to participate in class, and she has cried at school three or four times this week. When I asked her how things were going at home, she simply stared at the floor and said, 'It's probably my fault anyway.' This is so different from Lidia's usual behavior that I thought it was important to contact you to talk about some possible ways to help her." Notice that Lidia's teacher does not assign blame or sound judgmental; nor does she draw conclusions from her observations.

A second step in family referral is to help the family understand that family counseling may help in the achievement of mutual goals. Counseling provides an opportunity for the family to work as a cohesive unit; the needs of all family members are considered in developing solutions to problems. Potential benefits include more appropriate behavior by the "problem child," increased responsibility among family members for voicing their opinions and feelings, better grades for the children, and more support and less stress for all family members. The teacher or counselor who knows the general nature of the problem can identify the benefits appropriate to the specific situation.

Family members are often more accepting of recommendations for counseling if they have a sense of what to expect. When Jason Carter (of Chapter 3) was first seen as a client, he asked the family counselor, "Where's your black couch? Aren't you going to write down everything I say?" Adults, too, may have misconceptions. The teacher or counselor can dispel some of the mystique surrounding counseling by discussing some of the common reasons families go to a counselor and what the process might be like. Common reasons include problems with discipline and communication, lack of trust among family members, school problems, and tension related to divorce, dating, or remarriage of a parent. There are many approaches to family counseling, and individual therapists vary in style even if they ascribe to the same approach.

Families should be encouraged to ask potential counselors, "What do you expect of your clients?" "How long have you been practicing and what are your credentials?" "What can we expect of you?" "How do you structure your counseling sessions?" "How can we make best use of our time and money here?" "Do you have experience working with families like mine?" A family that has a sense of its own role in the therapeutic process may be more willing to consider the option of counseling.

Some families resist counseling because they are unsure how to begin the process. Let them know that once they call for an appointment, it may be anywhere from a day to a month or more before they have their first session. This first session may be an intake session, during which a counselor gathers information about the family's background and history. The family may work with the intake counselor and in later sessions may be assigned to a different counselor. If families are unprepared for this sometimes drawn-out process, they may become frustrated and discontinue prematurely.

Some parents may want to meet with the counselor alone first without their children. Some counselors may request such an arrangement; others may refuse it. This decision depends on the theoretical orientation and judgment of the counselor. Encourage parents to let the counselor know their preference.

Teachers and counselors are more likely to be successful in referring families for counseling if they are knowledgeable about a variety of local counseling agencies and practitioners. It is especially important to make referrals that are consistent with the family's cultural and language needs. Not all counselors have multicultural training, though the importance of multicultural competence increasingly is reflected in professional ethics codes and accreditation standards. And certainly not all agencies have counselors fluent in languages other than English. When a counselor or teacher approaches an ethnic minority family, it is important to consider that counseling as we know it has historically been a Western, white, middle- and upper-class phenomenon. Recent immigrants in particular will need a thorough explanation of the nature of counseling and may need time to consider whether it is consistent with their cultural values and practices (see Box 15.2).

When referrals are made for family counseling, the family should be provided with accurate information about agencies and practitioners, including addresses, phone numbers, specializations, and whether the agency adjusts fees to the client's ability to pay. Follow up with the family and find out what might help them to take action if they haven't followed through with the referral. For those who follow through, ask for feedback regarding the counseling facility for the benefit of future families.

The Nature of Family Counseling

In family counseling, problems are examined within the context of the family interactions, or system. Problems are viewed not as the result of individual issues but as the consequence of the complex dynamics that characterize every family system. Often, the family comes to a counselor expecting that the "problem child" will be fixed. The family counselor's first task is to assist family members to recognize that a family system is composed of a number of both positive and negative interlocking relationships. Family members must be helped to understand their contribution to the maintenance of the identified client's symptom. Finally, the family must agree to work together to change their situation.

Working with the entire family is advantageous in many ways. It enables the counselor to establish a more accurate perspective on the problem. The counselor may discover, for example, that what has been portrayed by a 15-year-old son as cruel authoritarianism is a belated attempt by his parents to impose control over curfew limits and homework completion. A mother who describes herself as loving and affectionate may truly believe she is so, in comparison with her own unavailable mother. But the objections and disagreements of her family can be a way to clarify the words *loving* and *affectionate* and the expectations that surround them. Watching arguments in progress provides the counselor with a picture of the family's interaction that no series of descriptions could convey. In addition to enhancing problem identification, working with the whole family makes problem solving more cohesive, efficient, and timely. The outcome of family counseling depends on many variables, including the therapist's skill, the willingness of family members to exert effort and take risks, their willingness and ability to take responsibility for their behavior, and the range of coping skills they possess.

Strategies in Family Counseling

In the 1950s Gregory Bateson and others at the Mental Research Institute (MRI) developed a communication framework for working with families. Focusing on the family as a system (see Chapter 3), family counseling attends to the interactional styles of family members. Notable members of this group include Paul Watzlawick, John Weakland, and Don Jackson, as well as Virginia Satir and Jay Haley. Jackson, Satir, and Haley, and to some extent Murray Bowen and Salvador Minuchin and most other system family theorists, share four core concepts: (1) two major tasks are involved in the process of forming and maintaining a relationship; deciding *what* the rules of the relationship *are* and negotiating *who* actually makes the decisions regarding the rules; (2) the exchange of messages is accomplished through the task of setting rules and negotiating who has control over the rules; (3) the basic elements of the interactional process are the messages that form the substance of communications between people in the relationship; and finally, (4) messages have two major aspects: the communication (the content of the message) and the meta-communication (the message about the message).

Thus, family counselors attempt to understand the family by analyzing the communication and meta-communication aspects of the interactions. They identify problems through observation of the family's interactions, including such behaviors as seating arrangement, control of the children, and who speaks most and least frequently, and so forth. They also sometimes employ techniques that include "paradoxical messages" and "prescribing the symptom." *Paradoxical messages* direct the family to do something that seems opposite to the stated goal; they are particularly useful with resistant families. For example, a family might be directed to refuse to cooperate during a session. The family has the choice of either cooperating (to maintain control *vis-a-vis* the counselor) or to continue their lack of cooperation and thereby give the counselor therapeutic leverage, because they are following a directive.

The counselor who *prescribes the symptom* asks the family to continue their problem behavior, perhaps because "I don't yet understand it well enough." This technique is also beneficial with resistant families because in order to resist they must change their problem behavior. *Relabeling* or *reforming* consists of describing the problem behavior in such a way that makes it sound positive. A therapist might relabel an adolescent's use of foul language, for example, as a creative way of directing her parents' attention away from her school performance. After establishing that this teen is creative and purposeful, the therapist can draw upon her creativity to devise more effective means of getting what she wants.

Other family counselors focus on the structural context of the family interaction. They examine the organizational dynamics and boundaries both within the family system and between the family and the environment. *Boundaries* can be seen as a manifestation of the rules and regulations governing the system and separating the system from its environment. How the family regulates and modifies these boundaries is of interest to the family counselor. Two fundamental concepts are "differentiation of self" and "triangulation." A chronic high level of anxiety within a family causes tension to escalate. If unchecked, this tension eventually exceeds the capacity of the family's normal coping mechanisms, and a variety of family symptoms result. *Differentiation of self* is the individual's ability to discriminate between emotional and cognitive processes and to achieve independence from the emotional climate of the family. Highly differentiated family members can respond to conflict on a cognitive level, on the basis of conscious beliefs and values, whereas the undifferentiated individual responds in an emotional and unstable manner. The greater the differentiation of self, the more effectively the family member can cope with anxiety. The failure of family members to differentiate is termed "fusion." *Fusion*, that is, a low level of differentiation, is characterized by inability to separate emotional from intellectual interaction.

Poorly differentiated family members are more likely to be part of a family triangle. *Triangulation* occurs when the anxiety in a two-person system is more than the system can handle, and a third person is engaged in the system to diffuse the tension. Triangulation is a specific type of enmeshment (see Chapter 3). For example, to diffuse marital tension, the mother establishes a close "friendship" with her daughter, and together they exclude the father. Triangulation generally increases problematic communication within a family.

As a family moves through the stages of the family life cycle (see Chapter 3), it must change structurally to accommodate changing roles and tasks. Such adaptation occurs through the renegotiation and modification of boundaries. Clear boundaries fall between enmeshed and disengaged boundaries and allow for optimal functioning. Family subsystem boundaries that are pervasively enmeshed or consistently rigid, especially those between the parent and child subsystems, are the primary basis for dysfunction.

By identifying the boundaries and transactional patterns within the family system and subsystems, the family counselor affects the goal of therapy, which is to change the structure of the family so that it is more consistent with the developmental needs of its members. One technique to do this is to present the family with a scenario and assign roles to the individual members. The roles require them to act out new patterns of behavior. This changes the behavior patterns that support the symptom and alters the sequences between family members, thereby restructuring the family system.

There are several ways in which a family counselor might work with the Carter family of Chapter 3. For example, the counselor might help the Carter family identify the sequence of acts in which the family's problems are embedded. The counselor would note the relationships among Lois's constant negative affect, lack of eye contact with her husband, fatigue, and refusal to ask for what she wants and needs; Doug's telling Jason, "If you. . .I'll. . ." without ever following through, his black-and-white views of Jason, the "bad one," and Christie, the "good one," and his sarcastic tone when he talks to his wife; Jason's feeble attempts to cheer up his mother, his belligerence toward his father, and his rapt attention whenever his parents interact; Christie's subtle teasing of Jason, her aloof primness when asked a question, and her fingernail biting. The counselor might attempt to understand how these behaviors maintain or threaten the power balance in the family and might view each symptom as a tactic employed by one person to deal with the others. He or she would see Jason's acting out as his way of defining his relationship with his parents: Jason sets the pace and they respond. The counselor might direct Jason to continue to misbehave at school and at home, (assuming his misbehaviors are not dangerous or harmful) and ask him to keep a log of each misbehavior and to note why he chose each behavior when he did. This use of symptom prescription gives Jason the choice of cooperating with the others, setting the stage for change, or resisting the therapist by reducing his symptoms.

In another approach the counselor would focus on helping each of the Carters to separate emotionality from objective thinking. He or she would begin by looking for clear and well-defined boundaries between family members. The counselor might view Doug's anger at his wife and his feelings of inadequacy as overriding his cognitive knowledge of the importance of consistency and consequences in discipline. He or she might view Lois's guilty feelings as an indication of her inability to separate her own feelings and behavior from those of her son. The unexpressed anger between Lois and Doug is diffused and focused on Jason, with the result that Doug feels excluded by both his wife and his son. The counselor might help the couple to express and explain their feelings to each other objectively. As the process of triangulation diminished, the members of the family would achieve a greater degree of differentiation.

Another approach would acknowledge the sociocultural context in which the Carter family operates. The counselor might conceptualize the problem in terms of two stressors: a developmental transition (Jason is entering adolescence) and an idiosyncratic problem (Lois is chronically depressed). The family's dysfunction is a result of their failure to renegotiate boundaries in response to these stressors. In light of the enmeshed boundaries between Jason and his mother and the lack of a defined parental subset, the counselor might work to increase the strength of the parental subset by engaging Doug and Lois in tasks together. He or she might ask Jason and Christie to reverse roles as a means of unbalancing the homeostasis and creating an opportunity for change.

Each of these strategies or techniques share an emphasis on the family as a system. A systems framework is often a major foundation for family counseling. But in what other ways might we be helpful to families with youth at risk? We now consider alternatives to family counseling.

ALTERNATIVES AND ADJUNCTS TO FAMILY COUNSELING

There are a number of other channels through which families can gain the support, knowledge, and skills they need to address their problems. Family counseling is not always the best way to pursue change. In addition, some families referred for counseling do not choose to follow through. Counseling may cost more than they are able or willing to pay.

Family members may have had negative experiences with counselors in the past, or they may perceive the time commitment as too demanding. Underlying these reasons are often a variety of others. Parents may be insecure about their child-rearing practices and fear exposure. Family members may be concerned that issues such as alcoholism, domestic violence, incest, and neglect will come to the surface. Often these fears are expressed as "We can deal with these problems alone" or "My family doesn't need some stranger getting into our business." In this section we describe four alternatives to family counseling, beginning with the Family Check-Up.

The Family Check-Up

The Family Check-Up (FCU) is a brief family intervention developed by our friends and colleagues Tom Dishion and Elizabeth Stormshak at the University of Oregon (Stormshak & Dishion, 2002; Dishion et al., 2002). The FCU is based on principles of motivational interviewing (Miller & Rollnick, 2002; see also Chapter 7) and is designed for families experiencing mild to severe problems. The FCU consists of three sessions conducted with the parent(s) or caregiver(s) and the child or children. The first session is an interview that takes place in the home when possible, so that the family is observed in their usual and familiar setting. The second session consists of an assessment of multiple dimensions of the family, including communication, discipline and other aspects of parenting, characteristics of each family member, functioning in home and school settings, and peer relationships. In the third session, the family is presented with feedback that is designed to facilitate several goals: supporting and enhancing positive parenting by identifying strengths and weaknesses; reducing harm by identification of impending, serious events such as a suicide attempt or school expulsion, and preventing such problems through provision of concrete recommendations; tailoring of feedback to maximize motivation for change; and supporting motivation for change through identification of family strengths and resources. During the feedback session, parents provide a self-assessment of their family and the clinician clarifies and contributes to this assessment using the information gained through the prior assessment stage. This session culminates in the collaborative development of a menu of options that emerge logically from the assessment and feedback.

The menu of options targets changes that the family perceives as important, and includes specific behaviors that the parents want to engage in on their own (e.g., meeting the parents of the children's friends; initiating Family Game Night once a week). The menu may also include parent education, parent training, support groups, or individual, couples, or family therapy. Because this 3-step model places a strong emphasis on forming a trusting relationship with the family and collaborative identification of concerns, families that may have initially resisted a recommendation for family therapy are often willing to pursue this option after a Family Check-Up. There are multiple positive outcomes associated with the Family Check-Up (Dishion et al., 2002; Stormshak & Dishion, 2002).

Parent Education and Training

Parent education and training refers to programs, support services, and resources offered to parents and caregivers that are designed to provide support and increase skills and efficacy for raising a family in a healthy and constructive manner (Carter, 1996). Teachers, counselors, and other human services professionals can often provide effective prevention and intervention in the form of parent education and training. The parents of a student who is acting out sexually may shy away from discussing sex, birth control, and sexually transmitted diseases. The parents of a student who doesn't turn in homework may lack a consistent system for monitoring school progress. The parents of a student who is belligerent and aggressive may have lost control of their child. These issues and others may be effectively addressed by educating parents on dealing with specific aspects of their children's behavior. Family-oriented programs designed to prevent chemical dependency and to strengthen families by teaching parents behavioral management, effective discipline, sex education, nutrition, and family budgeting can be very effective (Ashery, Robertson, & Kumpfer, 1998; Kumpfer, 1998; Kumpfer & Alvarado, 1995), although cultural appropriateness is critical to the success of parent training programs (Kumpfer & Alvarado, 1995; Norwood, Atkinson, Tellez, & Saldana, 1997).

Before we describe specific parent education and training programs, a few basic principles of parenting can go a long way to help parents be more effective. Two of our "favorite" parenting principles are: the Premack Principle and logical consequences.

The Premack Principle.   The Premack Principle, or Grandma's Rule, is a relatively simple and highly effective guide that parents can quickly put to good use (J. J. McWhirter, 1988). The Premack Principle tells us that "for any pair of responses, the more probable one will reinforce the less probable one" (Premack, 1965, p. 132). In other words, behaviors that youngsters are quite likely to perform (playing videogames, riding a bike, watching television, talking on the telephone) can serve as reinforcements for those behaviors that they are less likely to perform (completing homework, drying dishes, caring for younger siblings, cleaning their rooms). As Grandma might put it: First you work, then you play. The parent's task is to identify what their child wants to do and then require that a less-favored activity occur first: "Clean your desk and then we can play a game"; "Pick up the room before you go out to play"; "Do the dishes before you watch television."

Application of the Premack Principle is most effective when parents break down tasks into subtasks (e.g., clean desk = put away all loose books and papers + put away all crayons, pens, pencils + dust desktop + water plant on desk), and sometimes it is also helpful to reward the performance of each subtask. Frequent small rewards provide more effective reinforcement than infrequent, large rewards. Parents should provide rewards immediately after the behavior is accomplished, and they should reward the behavior *only* after it occurs. This last point is very important. Parents will hear rationalizations ("But my show will be over by the time I finish the dishes!"), and they are guaranteed to hear many more if they give in to them.

Logical consequences.   Carrying out a system of logical consequences not only encourages children to take responsibility for their behavior but can greatly reduce the amount of arguing. Consider the Carter family of Chapter 3. Doug Carter is unhappy with the fact that Jason stays up very late on weekends watching television. Because he stays up so late, Jason sleeps late the following morning, leaving his chores undone until the afternoon or forgetting them altogether. Jason's behavior is only one of the problems here; the other problem is that his behavior has no logical consequences. A logical consequence of staying up very late is to be quite tired when one is roused from sleep to do one's chores. By allowing Jason to sleep late, his parents condone his late-night TV habits. By requiring Jason to get up and do his chores no matter what time he went to bed, his parents would give

TABLE 15.1   **Sample Logical Consequences**

Action	Consequence
Leaving toys out	The toys are taken away for one day; only one toy allowed out at a time
Talking on the phone too long	All calls are limited to 3 minutes for two days
Fighting over a bike	The bike is taken away for a day and the children must play peacefully together for 30 minutes
Violating family curfew	Staying home the next evening or weekend
Stealing from a store	Apologizing to the store manager; returning the item; working to earn the cost of the item and giving the money to the store, a church, or a charity organization

him responsibility for deciding how late to stay up (reducing the likelihood of a "But I'm thirteen years old!" argument) and still have the satisfaction of knowing his work is done (reducing the likelihood of a "You live in this house too" argument).

Parents once brought to us a 4-year-old who stubbornly clenched her teeth and refused to eat when she didn't like the dinner she was served. She often threw her food on the floor. Her parents responded in a number of ways, arguing with the little girl, with each other, threatening her, and rewarding each bite, and typically concluded by cleaning up the mess and providing an alternative meal. Mealtime had become "a living hell." At first, the parents were horrified when we informed them that the logical consequence of such behavior was to go without eating until the next meal was served. But finally they conceded that she really would not be harmed by her hunger pains and agreed to try this approach. Upon their daughter's next refusal to eat, they explained to her that if she threw her dinner on the floor, she would get nothing to eat until breakfast. When she promptly and predictably flipped her dinner to the floor, her parents were prepared. They didn't yell or argue or rush to clean it up. Instead, they calmly reminded her that it would be a long time until breakfast, and finished their own dinner before attending to the mess she had made. She kept them awake most of the night with her tearful cries, but they didn't back down. The next day, she ate breakfast and lunch without incident (lunch, eaten at day care, had never been a problem), and dinner the next evening was relatively peaceful. She complained about the food, but she ate most of it. The next evening she once again overturned her plate, and endured the same logical consequence. She cried for only two hours that night. Two months later her parents reported that she had never again overturned her plate and was eating at least a small portion of everything they served her.

If logical consequences are to work, parents must be prepared to apply them without fail. Table 15.1 provides some sample behaviors and their logical consequences. Each consequence is modified according to the severity of the misbehavior and the number of times the behavior recurs after consequences have been applied. If a child continues to leave toys about the house, for example, the parents may remove the toys for two or more days at a time. Children should always know the logical consequences of their misbehaviors and be informed when the consequences are changing. With older children, parents may draw up a contract that specifies, for example, rules for using the family car and consequences of failure to follow those rules. By signing the contract, families formalize the agreement and establish a clear standard of conduct.

Parent Education and Training for Families of Color

An important focus for the teacher, counselor, or parent-trainer in getting acquainted with the family is to understand family culture, values, identity, and practices. Expectations regarding child behavior and accepted modes of child discipline are often associated with culture, though level of acculturation influences traditional values and practices. There is often more variability within an ethnic/cultural group than there is between ethnic groups. Sensitivity to family differences associated with religion and SES is also important. The following parent education and training programs are examples of programs that have been developed for parents who are members of specific ethnic/cultural groups (Pines, 1991; Bickel & Ertle, 1991).

The Effective Black Parenting Program. The Effective Black Parenting Program, developed by the Center for Improvement of Child Caring, is most appropriate with African American parents with children ages 2 to 12. The program contains 15 two-hour sessions; each session includes a review, demonstration, role-playing of skills, and homework assignments.

In this program parents are taught a variety of management strategies, including African American self-discipline, family rules guidelines, effective phrase and verbal confrontation, as well as time-out and the point system. The importance of African heritage and pride and the courage and strength of African American families are continually reinforced. The program is intended to foster effective family communications, healthy African American identity, extended family values, child growth and development, and healthy self-esteem.

Los Niños Bien Educados. This program was also developed by the Center for Improvement of Child Caring specifically for Latino parents. This cognitive-behavioral program fosters positive family communication, healthy Latino American identity, child growth and development, and healthy self-esteem. The program focuses on one of the dominant goals Latino parents often have in carrying out their parental functions: raising children to be academically, socially, and personally well-educated. It emphasizes child management skills, family meetings, effective praise, problem assessment, time-out, increasing respectful behaviors, and other approaches. Los Niños Bien Educados consists of 12 three-hour training sessions with a suggested group size of about 15 to 20 parents. Results and benefits associate with both Los Niños and Effective Black Parenting have been summarized by the Center for Improvement of Child Caring on their Web site: *http://www.ciccparenting.org.*

Positive Indian Parenting. The Positive Indian Parenting curriculum is a practical, brief, culturally specific training program with the goal to help American Indian parents explore and apply the values and attitudes expressed in traditional Indian child-rearing practices. The curriculum is published by the National Indian Child Welfare Association. Parents are helped to develop positive and satisfying values, attitudes, and skills that have roots in Native American Indian cultural heritage.

Because there is no one child-rearing tradition among Native American people, the curriculum draws examples from numerous tribes. The program is designed to be adapted to fit various tribal cultures. It does, however, build on universal values, attributes, and customs that include the oral tradition, storytelling, and the role of the extended family. The curriculum consists of eight sessions, each with specific learning objectives, and each session is designed to take two or three hours (see http://www.hec.ohio-state.edu/famlife/nnfr/ctf/curricul/97.html).

Family effectiveness training.   José Szapocznik and his associates (1986a, 1989, 2000) present a prevention model for Hispanic families of preadolescents who are at risk for drug abuse. This program is based on the premise that intergenerational family conflict related to the acculturation process may exacerbate existing maladaptive patterns of interaction in families and contribute to drug use. It is one of only a few empirically tested programs that directly address cultural differences. The three components of family effectiveness training (FET) are designed to change maladaptive interactional patterns and to enhance the family's ability to resolve intergenerational and intercultural conflict.

The first component, family development, helps the family to negotiate their children's transition to adolescence. Family members learn constructive communication skills and take increased responsibility for their own behaviors. Parents develop the skills to direct their children in a democratic rather than authoritarian style. This component also includes drug education for the parents, so that they can effectively teach their children about drugs.

The second component, bicultural effectiveness training (BET) (Szapocznik et al., 1984, 1986b), is designed to bring about family change by temporarily placing the blame for the family's problems on the cultural conflict within the family. Alliances are established between family members through the development of bicultural skills and mutual appreciation of the values of their two cultures. BET helps the family handle cultural conflicts more effectively and reduces the likelihood that conflicts will occur. BET is itself an excellent parent training program, of obvious value to families of nonmajority cultures.

The third component of FET is brief strategic family counseling (Szapocznik & Williams, 2000), the most experiential aspect of this model. The FET counselor meets with the family for 13 two-hour sessions and assists the family in addressing conflicts and improving relationships. The FET model may be modified to deal with issues other than drug use. One final parent education and training program is now described. This one is based on European American norms, but it has potential benefit with other cultural groups as well.

Parent Effectiveness Training

Parent effectiveness training (PET) (Gordon, 1970, 1977) is a method of parent training based on two principles stressed by the psychologist Carl Rogers: unconditional positive regard and empathy. A fundamental premise of the method is that everyone in the family can "win," with power negotiated and shared by parents and children. Although the program was originally designed for parents of problem children, its contents are also valuable for parents of well-functioning children. The PET program teaches parents skills in confrontation, conflict resolution, active listening, and giving "I" messages. Training provides parents with an opportunity to practice and refine those skills throughout the sessions. These skills enable parents to communicate more effectively with their children and to resolve problems constructively (J. J. McWhirter & Kahn, 1974; Wood & Davidson, 1993).

A PET training course is typically 24 hours in duration, ordinarily presented in eight weekly three-hour sessions. Brief presentations, group discussions, audiotapes, dyads for skill practice, role-playing, workbook assignments, and textbook reading are among the training methods used. Gordon continues to develop new applications for his ideas (1989), and in 1997 published a home study version of his program. Core components of the program include problem ownership, active listening, I-messages, and mutual problem solving. These are briefly described below.

Problem ownership.   In accord with the PET model, parents are trained to identify whether the parent, the child, or the relationship (both parent and child) have ownership of the problem. Determining who owns the problem sets the stage for problem resolution. The child owns the problem when he or she is blocked in satisfying a need, but his or her behavior does not interfere with the satisfaction of the parents' needs. The parent owns the problem when the child's attempts to satisfy a need interferes with the parent's needs. The relationship owns the problem when neither the child nor the parent is able to satisfy their needs. Problem solving is achieved via three different pathways, depending upon problem ownership. Active listening is used when the child owns the problem, sending I-messages is used when the parent owns the problem, and mutual problem solving is used when both own the problem.

Active listening.   The purpose of active listening is to communicate a deep sense of acceptance and understanding to the child. The parent tries to understand what the child is feeling and to communicate empathy to the child. The affective and emotional dimensions of the communication process is reflected in eye contact, tone of voice, and body movement. If parents reflect their children's feelings accurately, the children will feel understood, freed from the emotion of the problem, and better able to deal with the problem. When children amplify and fully express their thoughts and feelings at the heart of the problem, they are moving toward the desired goal and often are able to suggest their own solutions. Sometimes active listening helps children accept an unchangeable situation (e.g. the family must move to a new apartment) and simply gives them a chance to get their feelings out and experience genuine acceptance.

Active listening requires getting inside the child, viewing the world through his or her eyes, and communicating that understanding. Essentially, then, the parent must respond to both the words that the child uses and the feelings that lie behind the words. The following examples demonstrate the skill.

CHILD 1 (CRYING): Tommy took my truck away from me.

PARENT 1: You sure feel bad about that. You don't like it when he does that.

CHILD 1: Yeah, it makes me mad.

CHILD 2: Boy, do I have a lousy teacher this year. I don't like her. She's an old grouch.

PARENT 2: Sounds like you are really disappointed with your teacher.

CHILD 2: I sure am; I miss being in Mrs. Chang's class. She *liked* me.

In each illustration, the parent has accurately understood the child, and the child has responded by verifying the parent's accuracy and elaborating on the feeling. Each interchange sets the stage for a continued and meaningful conversation.

Parents should never use active listening to draw out and then put down the child ("Oh, so you want to flunk and go back with Mrs. Chang, do you?"). Parents sometimes begin active listening but subsequently slam the door shut because their own attitudes get in the way or because of lack of time. At other times, parents simply echo back a message to the child without empathy. Over time, this will result in demoralization and mistrust.

Sending I-messages.   When the parent determines that he or she owns the problem, that is, his or her needs are directly and tangibly affected, there are several possible responses. For example, the parent can modify the environment, him or herself, or the child directly. Often with younger children, changing the environment will promote a change of the child's behavior and thus solve the parent's problem. Such changes may include enriching the environment (bringing out crayons and paper; scheduling times for friends to come over and play), simplifying the environment (turning down or turning off the television; requiring that one activity be cleaned up before another is initiated), or substituting one activity for another (tag on the front lawn instead of wrestling in the living room).

Parents who own the problem may also decide to change themselves. For example, a father might decide that he will work on becoming more tolerant of noise in the house, and will follow through and supervise his children more after asking them to do a task; a mother might reduce the amount of pressure she puts on her children to behave in a particular manner.

Finally, the parent can seek to modify the child directly. Sometimes parents use spanking or some other form of punishment, which may produce short-term compliance but is detrimental in the long term (Gershoff, 2002). Verbal punishment is also ineffective; it typically consists of derogatory labeling or put-down statements: "You are so lazy." "You are a real pest." "You are no good; you just *want* to be a mean person don't you!" This kind of communication is called "You-messages."

Rather than punishment or ineffective you-messages, a simple I-message is a powerful tool in modifying a child's behavior. In an I-message the adult clearly expresses to the child the problem and the feelings about the problem while letting the child know that the adult owns the problem. Often the child is willing to modify behavior based on the adult's feelings. An I-message is less apt to provoke rebellion and resistance and it places the responsibility on the child for changing behavior. The following examples demonstrate the contrast between you-messages and I-messages.

You-message: You didn't do your chores this morning. You are so lazy and irresponsible!
I-message: I'm angry because you didn't do your chores
Comment: The focus is on the problem of the chores. and not on the character or
    personality of the child. The parent's feelings of annoyance and anger are not directly
    expressed in the you-message; the anger is clear and direct in the I-message.
You-message: Stop being such a pest. You're *always* interrupting your mother and me
    when we are talking.
I-message: I am frustrated with you because I want to finish my conversation with your
    mother and you keep interrupting us; this has been happening a lot lately.
Comment: The I-message communicates the parents' feelings, puts responsibility on the
    child for the behavior, and does not lower the child's self-esteem.

By sending an I-message, the adult anticipates that the child will understand the adult's problem, respect the adult's needs, and therefore discontinue acting in a negative way. Frequently, an I-message is adequate for modifying the child's behavior. Occasionally it is necessary to follow the I-message with a change in the environment. For example, after communicating frustration at being interrupted, the father could require the child to go play in another room until he has finished the conversation with the child's mother.

Mutual problem solving.   Mutual problem solving is the PET strategy used when the problem is owned by both child and parent, that is, when the needs of both the child and the adult are being blocked by a problem. Too often solutions to problems and conflicts result in a win-lose situation. The loser (adult or child) feels defeated and regardless of who loses, the child is denied opportunities to develop behavior that is self-disciplined, sensitive to others, and inner directed.

Gordon (1970) recommends following a six step, no-lose method whenever an adult and a child encounter a conflict-of-needs situation, so that the parent and child can construct a solution that is acceptable to both of them. These steps are common to many problem-solving models.

1. *Identify and define the conflict.* It is important to determine if the disagreement is actually over the issue at hand. Sometimes the conflict is really over a different matter, and the current problem reflects another concern. Both parent and child need to be clear on the nature of the conflict.
2. *Generate possible solutions.* Both parent and child need to indicate as many alternative solutions as possible. The child should be encouraged and praised for identifying solutions even when they don't seem feasible.
3. *Evaluate the alternative solutions.* The feasibility and potential effectiveness of each solution is critically evaluated. Both the adult and child should consider the consequences of the various solutions and decide which solutions they can live with. The parent does *not* stop being the parent at this step. For example, the parent should not enter into false "equal" arrangements in which the child also picks out the *mother's* clothes, or the child gets to use profanity every time the parent does.
4. *Decide on and get commitments for the most acceptable solution.* Both must agree to commit themselves to the solution, including modifying their own behavior as needed.
5. *Work out ways of implementing the solution.* The adult and child must agree upon who is going to do what and when it is to be done.
6. *Follow up and evaluate how the solution worked.* After an agreed upon time limit, parent and child review the solution to determine satisfaction with it. If the parent is consistent about following up when the problem and solution are "easy," the child will be more trusting and willing to try out solutions when those solutions demand more risk or effort on the child's part.

By engaging the child in the process of mutually solving the problem, over time, both parent and child will be more satisfied, and the child will learn to anticipate problems and generate solutions independently. Thus, conflicts can be resolved in a healthy manner that builds a relationship that is mutually satisfying, constructive, and loving.

Effective parenting derives from a philosophy in which respect for the child is uppermost. This means respecting individuality, uniqueness, complexity, idiosyncratic potential, and capacity for making choices. This philosophy is expressed in effective communication. Of course, these skills are just as important to the effective teacher or counselor as they are to parents (Gordon, 1989). The PET program, like all parent training programs, reflects a particular set of values and assumptions. Exploration of parent values is an important prerequisite to carrying out any parent training program.

In addition to these multiple parent education and training programs just reviewed, it is important to consider programs specifically for other caretakers—such as guardians and foster parents—who are often underrepresented in the family intervention treatment literature. Foster parents and foster families play key roles in many young people's lives and may play critical roles in the lives of high-risk youth. In Box 15.3 we describe one example program for foster parents of high-risk young people who might otherwise be placed in institutional settings with little intervention or monitoring. The program illustrates how multidimensional and ecologically oriented interventions can be very effective for some of our most at-risk adolescents.

Parent Support Groups

The final alternative or adjunct to family counseling is participation in a parent support group. These groups are also very useful to foster parents and others serving in primary caretaking roles. Many parents would benefit from experiencing a sense of accompaniment with other parents who have "been there" or are currently "in the same boat." Each new generation of parents deals with issues that their own parents never imagined. Your grandparents, for example, are unlikely to have had a son who came home with a pierced nipple. Many of the underlying issues are the same, however, and are related to the movement through the family life cycle: dealing with stress, change, loss, and anger; problems of communication, discipline, and authority; and the passing down of values and traditions. Especially in light of the decline of the extended family network, a parent support group is an ideal way for parents to express their concerns and learn what other parents have experienced and attempted (Allen, Brown, & Finlay, 1992). It also allows parents to share the pain and frustration as well as the joys and successes of raising children. Parent support groups are available through local churches, YMCAs, schools, counseling agencies, day-care centers, and workplaces. Many areas of the country also have local parent crisis lines or Parents Anonymous groups, which can provide information about parent support groups.

One parent support group that is active throughout the United States is ToughLove. ToughLove is a self-help group for parents and guardians of teenagers who are uncontrollable, addicted, abusive, or otherwise in trouble with the school or the law. With over 1500 groups, this organization provides ongoing support, assistance in crises, and referrals to professionals, as well as many practical ideas for helping teenagers stop their self-destructive behavior. Parents are encouraged to make their own plans for addressing their teenager's behavior. The group functions as a sounding board, a source of suggestions, and a backup support team. One ToughLove mother we know enlisted the help of other ToughLove parents in planning a constructive confrontation with her drug-abusing daughter. One of the other couples provided an alternate place for the daughter to stay for a week in case she decided she could not stay with her mother after the confrontation. The same mother had just posted fliers for a ToughLove parent in another part of the country whose runaway son had been seen locally.

Alateen and Al-Anon Family Groups are broad-based teen and family support groups that operate throughout the country. Teens or families of alcoholics meet together much

▲ BOX 15.3
Multidimensional Treatment Foster Care

Association with pro-social peers and inclusion in a functional, well-adjusted family are both key factors in the socialization process of youth. Association with deviant peers, even while in a treatment program, often is predictive of problematic behavior (Dishion, McCord, & Poulin, 1999). Youth outside of a functional family system are also less likely to thrive. The Multidimensional Treatment Foster Care Program (MTFC), from the Oregon Social Learning Center in Eugene, Oregon, combats these two risk factors by recruiting community foster families to be members of a treatment team that monitors daily family and child activities, monitors peer associations, and tracks school behavior of the high-risk, pre-delinquent youth who are enrolled in the program (Chamberlin, Fisher, & Moore, 2002).

The program is multidimensional and comprehensive because it responds to the whole ecology of children's lives. The *foster parents* receive increased financial compensation in comparison to general foster parents, are considered to be primary members of the treatment team, receive over 20 hours of pre-service training, attend weekly training and technical assistance meetings, and have 24-hour, 7-days-a-week on-call access to psychological support staff. The *children* in the program, who would otherwise be placed in a nonfamilial institutional setting, receive services within a structured, supportive, teaching-oriented family environment; are closely supervised in regards to their whereabouts, activities, and peer associations; receive daily monitoring of their participation and progress in school; receive

like the members of Alcoholics Anonymous. Participating teens and families learn about alcoholism and are helped to achieve a loving detachment from the alcoholic, to increase their self-esteem and independence, and to rely on the group for encouragement and support. Through the sharing of common problems, members of alcoholics' families discover that they are not alone and that they have the ability to cope with their situation.

Parent support groups can provide invaluable information and support for parents and guardians who feel hopeless, angry, and alone in dealing with the problems of their troubled children. ToughLove, Alateen, and Al-Anon provide support for family members who may feel trapped in an impossible situation. These are only three such groups; there are literally thousands of others. There are support groups for parents of children with problems ranging from spina bifida and cerebral palsy to bipolar disorder and schizophrenia. Teachers and counselors can assist families by keeping informed about these resources and by encouraging families to contact local chapters of these support groups. Refer to Appendix A for more information and addresses for many of the organizations discussed earlier in the chapter.

social skills building from a skills trainer; and receive individual therapy. The young person's *family of origin* receives intensive training and support, has 24-hour, 7-days-a-week access to program staff, receives family therapy, and is provided with aftercare services (e.g., ongoing support and consultation). The young person's *school* is involved in a collaborative support meeting to set up a system before the youth is enrolled, and receives support monitoring the child or young adolescent's behavior at school through use of a school "card" on which attitude, homework completion, and attendance are all evaluated. The performance ratings on the school card are checked nightly by MTFC foster parents and are linked with a three-level point system to reinforce positive behavior and decrease problematic behavior.

A number of well-designed studies have shown MTFC to be more effective than normal foster care and than group treatment facilities for youth. For instance, in follow-up studies comparing youth in MTFC with control group youth have shown the MTFC youth, in general, spent 60% fewer days incarcerated in follow-up treatment, had 50% less subsequent arrests, ran away from the program three times less often, returned to live with parents or relatives more often, and had significantly less hard drug use (Chamberlin, Fisher, & Moore, 2002). Although the program costs nearly $130 per day to keep a child in MTFC, it is substantially more cost-effective than placing a youth in treatment or standard youth detention. For instance, during a 2-year follow-up study comparing incarceration rates of youth placed in a group facility to those placed in MTFC, the reduced incarceration costs alone accounted for substantial savings (Chamberlin, Fisher, & Moore, 2002).

CONCLUSION

A family systems framework is a realistic and viable way to view the problems of troubled children and adolescents. Too often work with an individual provides only partial solutions. All young people live in a montage of overlapping systems: families, schools, neighborhoods, larger communities, the nation. Family counselors address the family as a system in order to change dysfunctional patterns of behavior and communication. Parent training and parent support groups provide alternatives and adjuncts to family counseling. Counselors, teachers, and other helping professionals can be of invaluable assistance by providing these services or by helping families gain access to such programs.

LEGAL AND ETHICAL ISSUES

▲ *Federal law, state statutes, court*
rulings, civil codes,
administrative procedures, ethical
codes. . . . When two or more
stretch out like railroad rails or
telephone lines reaching perfectly
parallel to an infinity point in
the distance, the choice and the
decision are easy. But sometimes
two or more are like a pair of
scissors—so joined they seem not
to be separated, yet seemingly
moving in opposite directions—
punishing anyone who comes between.

J. J. McWhirter

CHAPTER OUTLINE

▲   To work with at-risk youth is to be at the cutting edge of society's problems, which is also the cutting edge of the law. There is often great difference in the way practitioners (psychologists, counselors, and other human service professionals) and lawyers approach a situation. Indeed, Rowley and MacDonald (2001) suggest that the differences among approaches to handling legal and ethical issues might be seen as a "cross-cultural" phenomenon. In this chapter we provide some insights for mental health and teaching professionals into the "culture" of the legal world and suggest important ethical considerations in working with at-risk youth.

As practitioners we have our own ethics codes that are specific to our disciplines in human services. This chapter treats ethical issues only within the context of their legal ramifications. At the same time, this chapter is no substitute for reviewing the law of one's own state, so we encourage all practitioners to become very familiar with laws relevant to working with youth and families. Additionally, the American Psychological Association has produced a good series of state-specific books on state legal and ethical issues in its *Law & Mental Health Professionals* series. After reading this chapter, these books form a good start for seeking answers to specific legal and ethical questions and problems.

In this chapter we first provide a general explanation of the legal system and issues of criminal and civil liability. Next, we focus on specific legal considerations related to the at-risk categories of substance use, sexuality, delinquency, suicide, and the legal aspects of work with families. We have added a new section to this edition on what to do if you are called to testify in court. Finally, we conclude the chapter by listing some "dos and don'ts" for working with at-risk youth that will also help improve ethical decision making and avoid legal liability.

THE LEGAL SYSTEM

Although a complete discussion of the American legal system is obviously beyond the scope of this chapter, the rudiments of how American law works should clarify some issues. Generally, the law is divided into two broad categories: criminal and civil.

Criminal Law

Criminal cases are the ones most often seen on television and movies. Though the issues can be interesting, their relevance to most of us is often exaggerated. One can see a trend, however, toward holding practitioners and teachers criminally liable for failure to report suspected child abuse to authorities, which we discuss in detail at the end of this section.

General criminal law.   Criminal cases are tried by a prosecutor—a representative of the state or federal government who will often refer to him or herself as representing "the people," "the commonwealth," or "the government." He or she has the burden of proving "beyond a reasonable doubt" that the defendant committed the crime for which he or she stands accused. The accused is usually defended by a lawyer—retained private counsel or a public defender. Each side presents its case to a "tier of fact," usually a jury, but sometimes a judge, who decides innocence or guilt based on the evidence presented. Over several centuries our society has found this adversarial system to be the best way, despite its flaws, to find "truth."

Criminal law is rarely a major concern to practitioners, because their work seldom confronts them with criminal liability. Because it is illegal to contribute to the delinquency of a minor, however, it is possible for a practitioner with good intentions to run afoul of someone's idea of what constitutes a contribution to a minor's delinquency (Hopkins & Anderson, 1985; Hopkins, 1989). Obviously, providing drugs to a child or adolescent counts as contributing to delinquency. Suppose an adolescent such as Jason Carter, of Chapter 3, was using a drug as a form of self-medication and the practitioner, hoping to build a better relationship, facilitated his access to the drug. In the past, pharmacists and osteopaths who prescribed dangerous drugs for minors have been convicted of contributing to their delinquency (*People v. Brac*, 1946; *State v. Tritt*, 1970). The best legal advice is obvious: do not provide illegal drugs to anyone.

Perhaps the most obvious situation in which a practitioner could be accused of contributing to the delinquency of a minor is in the sexual realm. Of course, it comes as no earth-shattering news that practitioners should never engage in sexual liaisons with underage persons, whether or not they are clients. Moral and ethical considerations aside, states across the country are increasing the legal penalties for such activity, and these penalties are increasingly applied equally to men and women, so that women who violate this ethical and legal code receive punishments similar to those given to men.

The child-abuse quagmire.   Every state has mandatory child-abuse reporting laws (Walker, 1990) and the U.S. Congress has its version for practitioners working on federal land or in a federally operated or contracted facility (Crime Control Act of 1990). These laws require health-care and educational professionals to report suspected child abuse and the federal law even requires commercial film and photo processors to report evidence of child abuse. In addition, all states other than Maryland and Wyoming impose criminal liability for failure to report child abuse (Small, Lyons, & Guy, 2002). This section of this chapter will highlight the most important points, but see Kalichman (1999) for greater depth on the issue.

Practitioners are generally immune from criminal and civil liability for reporting suspected child abuse that turns out to be unfounded. States have provided this immunity to obtain federal grant money (Small, Lyons, & Guy, 2002). The reporting, however, must still be "in good faith" with "reasonable cause" to believe abuse occurred. Small, Lyons, and Guy (2002) state that "to date, there are no reported cases in which psychologists have been denied immunity for failing to act in good faith." Generally, courts treat all practitioners the same as psychologists. Conversely, there is no immunity for false reporting and several states have laws that make this a crime as well (Small, Lyons, & Guy, 2002).

The extent of a practitioner's duty to report suspected child abuse varies, with some states requiring that past abuse be reported no matter how old. Others have time limitations. The Andrews family, of Chapter 1, conceivably might represent a reporting issue of this kind. If Allie Andrews confided that her natural father, John Meadows, had sexually abused her, in some states this admission would create a duty to report the abuse, even though it occurred many years earlier. Practitioners must consult the laws of their own state to find the precise definition and their legal responsibilities. State and local professional associations may well have this information prepared and Small, Lyons, and Guy (2002) provide a useful survey and helpful charts of state statutes that we encourage you to consult.

Most state laws require reporting of child abuse when a teacher, mental health, or other human service professional has a "reasonable suspicion" that abuse has occurred. What constitutes reasonable suspicion is often left to the individual state court, legislature, or practitioner to decide (Walker, 1990). The best advice in an unclear legal situation is to trust one's own professional training and ethical standards. Consultation with a supervisor and/or team of colleagues, and documentation of that consultation, is always important. Write it down or tape it so you can corroborate what you did and why (Renninger, Veach, & Bagdade, 2002).

It is not unusual for licensed psychologists, who consider themselves relatively well informed, to demonstrate knowledge deficits regarding the details of actual reporting laws. At the same time, just knowing the definition of "child abuse" and what constitutes "reasonable suspicion" is not sufficient information to assist practitioners in responding ethically. In a survey of psychologists, nearly one-third of the respondents stated that they had seen children who they suspected were abused but did not report their suspicions to child protection agencies; and only 15% believed that a subjective suspicion alone was sufficient to require reporting (Kalichmant & Brosig, 1993). Conversely, confusion exists among mental health practitioners as to whether to report when someone tells them of abuse but they do not believe the abuse actually happened. After reviewing the literature, Foreman and Bernet (2000) concluded that mandatory reporters generally are not required to report abuse allegations if they themselves do not believe the allegation. They encourage mandatory reporters to report abuse as required by law but not to make unnecessary reports out of confusion or misinformation (Foreman & Bernet, 2000).

One motivation for not reporting is that practitioners are concerned about destroying the counseling relationship with the young person if they report. Weinstein and colleagues (2000) studied the some of the issues surrounding reporting and client-practitioner relationships. In their study, the majority of practitioners who informed their clients that they had a duty to report child abuse and their limits to confidentiality before therapy began found that this information did not deter clients from speaking during therapy. They also found that over 35% of the clients were not informed of the practitioner's duty to report child abuse until after the practitioner suspected or knew that abuse had occurred. Furthermore, the study reported that after the practitioner reported the abuse, about 20% of the therapy relationships ended, 7% deteriorated, 32%

▲ Box 16.1

When the Abused Is the Abuser

Janey, age 8, was sexually abused by the son of her mother's best friend when she was 4 years old. Her mother, Tanya, at first attributed the change in Janey's behavior to the fact that she herself was absent for long hours. In addition to working full-time, Tanya was taking care of her dying father and her newborn daughter, Kelsey. When Janey finally described the abuse to her mother, Tanya informed the authorities and sought counseling for herself and Janey. She responded quickly and appropriately, and did everything she could to help Janey recover from the trauma she had experienced. Two years later, however, she discovered that Janey was sexually abusing Kelsey. Janey was deeply ashamed and begged her mother not to tell anyone. Somehow Tanya found the courage to seek appropriate help once again, and entered both girls in individual and group therapy for child survivors of sexual abuse. This is not an isolated case; the fact is that many child survivors of sexual abuse replay the abuse on other children. In this case, the mother's painful decision to report her older daughter's actions resulted in the provision of effective and appropriate support services for both children.

did not change, and 41% improved. The authors of this study suggest that statewide consultation networks and training beyond "identification" of abuse be available to all practitioners because the nuances of this issue requires that practitioners receive better training (Weinstein et al., 2000).

Ambiguity in the statutes and practitioners' lack of understanding of legal responsibility often lead practitioners to hesitate to report suspicions that may, in the end, be unfounded. Perhaps the biggest factor in the failure to report, however, is the practitioner's concern regarding the negative consequences to the child and family. To appreciate this problem, suppose a practitioner suspects that a mother abused her child. Perhaps the practitioner knows that the mother was recently laid off and lost her own mother to cancer, and that the abuse, if it occurred, appears to have been an isolated incident. The law views this matter in black-and-white terms, but to the practitioner this situation may look to be many different shades of gray. Indeed, most practitioners are trained for work in the gray areas, and so continued education around ethical decision making will help practitioners make better law-related decisions.

Another example might be when a practitioner suspects that a child is abusing a younger sibling (see Box 16.1). In this case, most child-abuse statutes mandate reporting. But if the practitioner believes the abusing child is very near a major breakthrough in therapy work, reporting may actually be the more harmful alternative or choice of action. This is another example of a gray area.

Fortunately, despite the universality of reporting laws, prosecution of practitioners under them is rare. In the one case of such a prosecution, *Barber v. State* (1992), the counselor had not reported the alleged abuse because he found it to be unsubstantiated. But, the alleged abuser later murdered the victim and the counselor was subsequently convicted for failure to report the original child abuse (Small et al., 2002). Given the lack of other reported cases, the *Barber* case represents an extreme, and relatively rare, situation.

Civil Law

Civil law is more likely than criminal law to affect counselors, human service professionals, teachers, and other practitioners. Before discussing the legal issues related to the at-risk categories, we attend here to general concepts of civil law, the duty to warn, and confidentiality.

General civil law.   Under civil law, unlike criminal law, nobody is in danger of going to jail. Instead, a person who believes he or she has been wronged, the plaintiff, sues another, the defendant. Both usually have lawyers. There can be several defendants and even several plaintiffs. The plaintiff has the burden of proving the case but the standard of proof is lower than in a criminal case: "a preponderance of the evidence" and not "beyond a reasonable doubt." This means that in order to win, the plaintiffs have to convince the jury that their version of what happened is more probable than the other side's version. If the defendant loses a civil case, he or she must compensate the plaintiff. When the defendant is a practitioner, more often than not the defendant's insurance company has to pay.

One point to clarify here is that being sued is different from being liable. Anyone can sue for a moderate court fee; but winning the lawsuit is another matter. Without solid legal reasons, a judge or jury will not hold a practitioner liable. Some people file lawsuits without much consideration of this fact.

To establish the practitioner/defendant's civil liability, or malpractice, the client/plaintiff must prove four things:

1. The practitioner/defendant owed the client/plaintiff a duty of care. In this context this usually means that a professional relationship had been formed;
2. The practitioner/defendant was negligent in performing the duty owed. Again, the duty must be demonstrable and the client/plaintiff must show the defendant practiced below the standard of care;
3. The client/plaintiff suffered a tangible harm or injury; and
4. The practitioner/defendant's not meeting or "breaching" the standard of care was the "proximate cause" of the client/plaintiff's injury. In other words, the client/plaintiff's harm or injury was a reasonably foreseeable consequence of the practitioner/defendant's breach of care (Bennett, Bryant, VandenBos, & Greenwood, 1990).

For example, mental health practitioners assume several duties when they accept a client. One of these duties is to conform to the ethical standards of the profession, including those of maintaining the client's confidentiality. If the practitioner violates this duty by divulging a confidence, he or she could be liable for damages. A plaintiff, however, must still show that the practitioner's conduct actually caused the plaintiff harm.

Suppose a psychiatrist fails to provide necessary medication to a young person—say, to Jason Carter of Chapter 3. If Jason commits suicide, his parents, Doug and Lois, could certainly sue the practitioner for negligently failing to prevent Jason's death and might win a jury award of money. Again, this is because the practitioner assumed a *duty*, performed it *negligently*, and *caused* the *harm* to Jason's family.

This system of civil law, in which a jury decides that the defendant must pay if the plaintiff can prove duty, negligence, causation, and harm, helps to prevent or redress the more serious forms of negligence in society. This legal system encourages professional associations to establish a standard of ethical conduct to guide the behavior of professionals. Following these standards, or not following them, can make the difference in whether one is found liable in court. Because of this, the practitioner who works with at-risk youth should always conform to the ethical standards of their particular human service profession.

Confidentiality and privilege in general.   The terms confidentiality and privilege are not synonymous, but they are related. Although both concepts exist for the benefit and protection of the client and not the practitioner (cf., McGuire, Parnell, Blau, & Abbott, 1994), important distinctions exist.

Confidentiality usually refers to the ethical obligation of the practitioner not to disclose confidential information obtained during the counselor-client relationship. Under rules of confidentiality, the practitioner must protect the confidence of the client. The rules of confidentiality are a professional standard of conduct. These standards are often defined and governed in many states by statute (laws passed by legislatures), case law (decisions of appellate courts interpreting statues or other norms), or professional associations. Confidential relationships are based on the idea that the practitioner and the patient have some type of understanding to protect the communication except in specific situations.

Privilege refers to the patient's legal right to prevent certain professionals (lawyers, doctors, psychologists, and possibly counselors) from providing information to a party in a lawsuit or to testify regarding information the client gave them. Unless the law specifically mandates or allows the health-care practitioner to reveal the information from the patient, the communication between patient and practitioner remains protected. Thus, we often say that the client "holds" the privilege.

The genesis of both concepts is that the law has long protected certain communications. This protection came from the relationship between priest-penitent, with all its sacramental overtones. A natural outgrowth of this relationship is the attorney-client privilege. Doctors and patients enjoy a similar privilege, and in most states so do psychologists, counselors, and other mental health practitioners. Glosoff, Herlihy, and Spence (2000) report that out of 45 states with a system of licensed professional counselors, 44 states had statutes or evidentiary rules granting privileged communication status to the counselor-client relationship. The problem is that the extent of the privilege varies from state to state.

In the federal context, the United States Supreme Court in *Jaffe v. Redmond* (1996) confirmed that a psychotherapist-patient privilege exists with such communications being "protected from compelled disclosure. . . ." The extent of this privilege, however, is not absolute, as with the "duty to warn" notion that we discuss in the next subsection.

Further complicating this problem is that in a given state the degree of privilege accorded a psychologist may differ from that accorded to another practitioner, such as a school counselor. Again, the best advice is to consult specific state law. This information is generally not too difficult to obtain; most states have an office that publishes a brochure or pamphlet on the issues, and state and local professional associations often compile this information as well.

Under the notion of privilege, practitioners can discuss clients' statements with colleagues, but those colleagues have the same duty to guard that communication as the practitioner themselves. This is a critical point because practitioners must consult regularly with colleagues and discuss their client cases to effectively treat at-risk youth. Consultation is also important for avoiding civil liability, especially when dealing with ambiguous matters.

Confidentiality and privilege issues arise in the school setting. Some state courts hold that parents of public school children are entitled to inspect their children's records because they are public records. The reasoning behind this position is that because the youth is a minor, the parents have the privilege and are therefore entitled to know their children's statements (Hopkins, 1989). Other states, however, hold that a young person's confidential communications should have the same protection as any other communication (Hopkins, 1989). One study found that among 354 licensed school psychologists in Minnesota there was great variability in the frequency with which practitioners told parents of communication from minors that they worked with in the school setting (Manheim et al., 2002). There was also great variation in the professionals' willingness to share information with parents, even when this may have been in the best interests of the child, in part due to the concern that divulging information would irreparably damage the client-counselor relationship.

In certain situations, however, the law requires practitioners to reveal a confidence. We have already discussed child-abuse cases as one example (McGowan, 1991). Different states have carved out other exceptions for revealing confidential information as well (see Glosoff, Herlihy, & Spence, 2000). These include:

- When the client's condition poses a danger to self;
- When there is imminent threat of harm to a specific third person (discussion follows);
- When the counselor has knowledge that the client will commit a crime;
- When a dispute exists between the client and the practitioner;
- When the client raises the issue of mental condition in court, including court-ordered psychological examinations;
- For purposes of involuntary hospitalization;
- When the practitioner has knowledge that a client has been a victim of a crime, and in cases of harm to vulnerable adults.

Again, on these issues practitioners should check the law in their jurisdiction to see if any of these exceptions apply. Glosoff, Herlihy, and Spence (2000) provide a good table outlining the exceptions to confidentiality in each state.

In some situations, such as in group counseling, a client can waive confidentiality. Practitioners should discuss the limits of confidentiality in the relationship at the outset, especially when the therapy group includes the youth's family (Ford, Thomsen, & Compton, 2001).

Aside from these possible exceptions, a practitioner should not divulge any communication given in confidence, regardless of the client's age. Unless a clear therapeutic benefit is possible or a court has ordered disclosure, it simply is not appropriate to divulge confidential communications. Glosoff, Herlihy, and Spence (2000) recommend the following:

- Use disclosure/informed consent statements;
- Inform clients of the situation and involve them in the process;
- Take reasonable steps to protect client confidentiality;
- Provide minimal disclosure;
- With permission, contact the client's attorney;

- Document all actions and factors involved; and
- Consult with colleagues regarding clinical judgments and with lawyers regarding legal obligations.

With the above in mind, practitioners may still find themselves in court, ordered to reveal confidential information, despite being ethically and even morally bound not to do so. Refusal would truly put the practitioner at the cutting edge of the law, and could lead to a jail sentence for contempt of court. One consolation is that given our current legal environment, a practitioner is not likely to suffer the fate of those priests who went to their deaths rather than break the seal of the confessional.

Duty to warn.   A practitioner may have a special duty to warn third persons of danger. In *Tarasoff v. Regents of the University of California* (1976), the California Supreme Court held that psychologists, and potentially all practitioners, have a duty to take reasonable steps to warn a specific third person or persons to whom the patient poses a danger. The important point here is that in most states the patient or client must pose a serious risk to a specific third person before the practitioner has the duty to warn.

The *Tarasoff* case concerned a patient at a university psychiatric center who had stated during therapy that he intended to kill an unnamed but readily identifiable girl (Tatiana Tarasoff). The therapist did not warn the Tarasoff family of the threat, and when the patient did in fact kill Ms. Tarasoff, her family sued the university. The Supreme Court of California held that the family had the right to sue. Again though, what the Tarasoff family won was just the right to sue; the California Supreme Court's ruling did not mean that a jury found the therapist or university liable.

Not all states have a *Tarasoff* rule that includes a duty to warn, so practitioners must consult the laws of their own state. In states that do have a *Tarasoff* rule, practitioners who work with at-risk youth must consider whether any of their clients poses a possible danger to a specific third person. If the youth is dangerous, then the practitioner may have a duty to warn the third party or to take other measures to prevent imminent harm (Costa & Alteruse, 1994). Of course, as the American Psychological Association argued in *Tarasoff*, warning may well destroy the therapeutic relationship leading to more harm in the long run.

This raises the question of how the privilege of confidentiality affects the legal duty to warn. As discussed previously with the duty to report child abuse, a given state or federal court rule or statute may prevent divulging such information as privileged (*Jaffee v. Redmond*, 1996). Some states may provide the answer to this question in statutes, which the practitioner should check.

In a case following the United States Supreme Court's decision in *Jaffe*, the Ninth Circuit Court of Appeals ruled that a defendant could not have a case dismissed for making threats to FBI agents because his psychotherapist had betrayed his confidence (*United States v. Chase*, 2002). In *Chase*, the defendant, who had a history of bipolar disorder and was under the care of a psychologist, expressed anger at various officials and others, including FBI agents. The psychologist decided that the threats to "kill them" became concrete enough to warn the agents. The defendant was convicted at trial. On appeal, Chase argued that there was no "dangerousness" exception to the psychotherapist-patient privilege. The Ninth Circuit held otherwise and upheld his conviction. The court explained that though Chase never acted on his threats, they were tangible enough so that in the therapist's professional opinion there was an imminent danger that only disclosure of the communication could prevent.

Although *Chase* provides interesting guidance on the duty to warn in the context of a privileged or confidential relationship, the case does not end the question. The Ninth Circuit Court, in holding that an exception existed, sided with the prior Tenth Circuit case of *United States v. Glass* (1998) but against the Sixth Circuit case of *United States v. Hayes* (2000), which held that there is not a "duty to warn" exception to a privilege relationship.

On questions of what to do, the best advice remains to consult with colleagues when one is in doubt as to the law or the gravity of the threat to the third person. Also, it is both wise and expected practice to inform clients about the limits of confidentiality in the first session. Such a procedure clarifies the practitioner's responsibility and helps avoid the client feeling betrayed. We will return to the duty to warn when we address sexuality issues.

SPECIFIC LEGAL CONCERNS

The behaviors that put young people at serious risk—the use of illegal substances, irresponsible sexual activity, delinquency, and suicide—all present unique legal complications.

Legal Issues in Problems of Substance Use

In state-funded drug programs, state laws and regulations control the practitioner's activities. Programs that receive federal funds, however, follow guidelines found in the Code of Federal Regulations (CFR). Technical reports from the U.S. Department of Health and Human Services periodically explain these guidelines.

The general requirement for federally funded substance use programs is that confidentiality must be maintained in nearly all aspects of treatment (42 CFR 2.12[e]). This regulation applies to any program that specializes in providing treatment, counseling, assessment, or referral services for youths with alcohol and other drug problems. These regulations generally do not apply to teachers or practitioners in a traditional school setting who may deal with substance problems of at-risk youth.

Practitioners can, of course, obtain a youth's consent to release information. Under this standard of confidentiality, it is hard to conceive of a situation in which a practitioner could be found negligent for failing to disclose substance use. Indeed, federal regulations require the exact opposite. That is, in most cases, confidentiality must be maintained unless a young person has a specific self-destructive or suicidal intent in using substances (Brody & Waldron, 2000).

Legal Issues in Youth Sexuality

Although confidentiality is central to dealing with youth sexuality, a practitioner may have a duty to warn third persons of a youth's sexually transmitted disease (STD). As the number of sexually active teenagers in the country continues to be substantial (Brown & Eisenberg, 1995), sexuality issues are common topics in therapeutic settings.

Warning parents.   The law is ambiguous as to whether the practitioner must tell parents of a child's sexual activity. On the one hand, it would be very difficult for parents to prevail in a lawsuit against a practitioner for failure to report sexual activity among teenage clients because this is communication that ordinarily must stay confidential to maintain the therapeutic relationship. Thus, when an irate parent calls a practitioner and demands to know if his or her child is sexually active, as Jack Andrews of Chapter 1 might well do in his rage about Allie's behavior, the law is almost certain to support the practitioner's professional judgment not to reveal the information. On the other hand, this is the age of fatal and incurable sexually transmitted diseases. If Jack sought information from the practitioner as to whether Allie was sexually active and the practitioner refused to divulge the confidence, conceivably, Jack could sue the counselor if Allie later contracted AIDS. In this situation, Jack could come into court and say that if he had known that Allie was sexually active, he would have discussed "safe sex" with her, but because the practitioner refused him the information he sought, he was denied the chance to protect her. Although the potential for this type of lawsuit exists, the practitioner certainly has defenses: Obviously Jack suspected that Allie was sexually active or he would not have asked. What was to prevent him from discussing safe sex with her even if his suspicions were not confirmed? A practitioner cannot be held liable for a parent's failure to communicate with his child. Consequently, though legal risks exist, practitioners cannot afford to exaggerate them or let them get in the way of their work.

Contraception and abortion.   The laws relating to a practitioner's duties in regard to contraception and abortion are very inconsistent. If the counseling facility is not a family planning program, some state laws may require that parents be notified of any contraception or abortion counseling provided to minors. This presents special problems if the adolescent is homeless or orphaned (Blustein, Levine, & Dubler, 1999). However, because of the U.S. Supreme Court's decision on abortion in *Roe v. Wade* (1973) and the extensions of that ruling to minors (*Bellotti v. Baird*, 1979; *Carey v. Population Services International*, 1977), parental notification laws may not bind a practitioner who works with minors in a family planning program. Minors share in the constitutionally protected right of privacy regarding contraception and abortion decisions. Thus, communications that practitioners in a family planning program receive from minors are confidential. Parents simply do not have the right to know of those communications, despite any state law to the contrary. The law here is not fixed. Every new appointment to the U.S. Supreme Court as well as to a federal circuit court of appeal has a bearing on this question.

Thus, the practitioner in a family planning program can provide access to birth-control pills or other contraceptives. In general the courts have held that the minor's right to privacy outweighs the parent's right to be informed. Consequently, even if Jack Andrews demands to know whether Allie is receiving contraceptives, the practitioner should not divulge the information to him if the practitioner works in a family planning program. If not, however, state law may require parental notification, although the age of the minor in question is an important factor to consider and varies from state to state. Of course, any prescribing of contraceptives to a minor requires the practitioner have the appropriate qualifications and medical training to do so, without which the practitioner could be successfully sued.

The inconsistency of rulings on the confidentiality of contraception counseling extends to abortion counseling. The practitioner who does not work in a family planning situation may have a duty under state law to inform the parents of a minor's decision to have an abortion. Conversely, the practitioner who works in a family planning situation is exempt from the requirements that state law may impose. In *H. L. v. Matheson* (1981), however, the U.S. Supreme Court held that a Utah law requiring a physician to notify a parent of an unemancipated minor's plans for an abortion was not unconstitutional. If a given state law requires notification to parents but allows for a mature or emancipated minor to go independently to a judge for permission to have an abortion, apparently the statute is constitutional. By extension, a mental health practitioner can provide a minor with abortion counseling and the opportunity to obtain judicial consent for an abortion without parental notification.

Most of the U.S. Supreme Court case law in this respect involves medical doctors. Mental health practitioners, however, need to stay abreast of the duties set forth for physicians and draw parallels with their own practice. In the right set of circumstances, the applications could as easily be extended to teachers and practitioners.

STDs/AIDS. The *Tarasoff* standard, imposing on a practitioner the duty to warn a third person of an explicit threat of danger from the client, could very well apply to the threat of sexually transmitted diseases. A patient with AIDS can pose an "explicit threat" to a specific foreseeable victim. If Allie Andrews became infected with HIV, for example, and was sleeping with a specific noninfected person, the law might require the practitioner to warn that person of his/her risk. As of 1993, no courts had addressed a practitioner's duty to warn sexual partners in a case involving HIV (Harding, Gray, & Neal, 1993). Since then, however, Chenneville (2000) has summarized recent cases relating to a physician's duty to warn partners of HIV-positive adults. Some courts have held that hospitals and physicians are not responsible for disclosing HIV status to patient's spouses (e.g., *Diaz Reyes v. United States*, 1991/1992; *N.O.L. v. District of Columbia*, 1996; *Santa Rosa Health Care Corp. v. Garcia*, 1998), whereas others (*Chizmar v. Mackie*, 1995) found that physicians are free to inform a patient's spouse upon the diagnosis of a fatal sexually transmitted disease (Chenneville, 2000). How this relates specifically to adolescents appears to be an open question.

Physicians have resolved this ethical problem by requiring all "reportable" or "communicable" diseases to be reported to the state or county department of health. These departments then take action to protect the public from the disease, which may include a warning to a third party who is at high risk. Further, these departments must protect confidentiality by not disclosing the source of the information.

Thus, it is good practice for the practitioner to notify the state public health agency of possible communicable or reportable diseases, including AIDS and other STDs. Before reporting, the practitioner should determine exactly what measures will be taken to protect confidentiality. This protects both the third person and the client's confidence. In addition, notifying a department of health of an at-risk youth's STD may protect the practitioner from civil liability. If a client transmits a disease to a third person, that person may sue the practitioner for being aware of the situation and taking no action. By confidentially reporting to a public health agency, the practitioner may be able to demonstrate that he or she took measures to prevent harm to the specific third person. Although not perfect, this action provides at least a partial solution.

Legal Issues in Delinquency

In general, the criminal law does not require the reporting of criminal activity, with the exception of child abuse. Thus, even if you see a crime committed, you are unlikely to be prosecuted if you fail to report it. If you benefit from the crime or in any way facilitate it, however, you may be charged as an accessory to the crime (La Fave & Scott, 2002).

▲ Box 16.2

When Suicide Was a Crime

The legal system has never known what to do with suicide. Suicide was long a crime under English law. Punishments included refusal of burial in consecrated ground, mutilation of the body, burial at a crossroad, and a stake driven through the victim's heart. Although these sanctions were not transported to the United States, suicide was once a crime in most parts of this country (Marzen O'Dowd, Crone, & Balch, 1985). This legal prohibition created obvious problems. How does one punish a suicide? The victim, of course, is immune to punishment, at least in this life. Sanctions, therefore, tended to be imposed on the surviving family. Partly in response to this inherent injustice and inconsistency, state legislatures abolished their suicide laws, so that today it is no longer a crime to commit suicide (Marzen O'Dowd, Crone, & Balch, 1985).

A practitioner who learns of a youth's crimes through confidential communications, then, is not likely to face criminal charges for failure to report them. Indeed, in federally funded programs for drug use treatment, a mental health practitioner cannot even request a court order to permit the reporting of any crime less serious than a felony, such as homicide, rape, or kidnapping (42 C.F.R. 2.65[d][1]). Even in these circumstances, the practitioner must refer to a particular client by a fictitious name.

Under civil law, however, the practitioner may have a duty to warn in certain circumstances. Under *Tarasoff*, a mental health worker who knows of a danger to specific third persons may have a civil duty to warn them. For example, if a practitioner hears in a therapy session with a gang member that the gang is planning a drive-by shooting of a specific person at a specific time and place, the practitioner may have a duty to warn that person. If the person is killed, the surviving relatives could conceivably sue the practitioner and the institution for failure to warn the victim.

Legal Issues in Youth Suicide

Suicide. Contrary to popular belief, suicide is no longer a crime in the United States, although aiding a suicide is still illegal, despite the movement in support of assisted suicide for the terminally ill (see Box 16.2). So, counselors, social workers, psychologists, and other human service professionals need not fear criminal penalty if a client commits suicide unless they have aided the client in the act.

Traditionally, civil law has viewed suicide as an intentional, willful act by one individual, with no blame attaching to any other party. This is not to say, however, that a practitioner may not be sued, and courts have allowed the victim's relatives and heirs compensation in exceptional circumstances (Jobes & Berman, 1993). After a youth's death, surviving family may seek an outlet for grief by casting blame elsewhere and the practitioner may become the target. Numerous suits for malpractice reported by practitioners involve suicide or attempted suicide (Bongar, 1992). These lawsuits not only relieve guilt-ridden family members, they also protect the image of the victim. Given the psychological makeup of Doug Carter of Chapter 3, no one would be surprised if he sued the practitioner if Jason committed suicide.

In the few suits filed against practitioners families do not claim that the hospital, psychiatrist, or practitioner "caused" the death of their loved one. Rather, they claim that the practitioner or institution had a duty to prevent the suicide and failed to meet that duty. Because it is difficult to prove that anyone has a duty to prevent suicide, practitioners are protected against most charges of malpractice in such instances.

The setting where the practitioner works may also offer protection against lawsuits (J. J. McWhirter & R. J. McWhirter, 1988). The courts have reasoned that the primary responsibility of schools and their personnel is to educate students, not to treat their emotional problems. In other words, schools do not have a duty to care for the psychological health of students, so they do not have a duty to prevent suicide (*Bogust v. Iverson*, 1960). Although a school is not now liable for the suicide of a student, it is possible that under a particular set of circumstances a jury could hold school personnel liable (Anderegg & Vergason, 1992).

A practitioner who works at a hospital has a greater chance of being sued if a patient commits suicide (J. J. McWhirter & R. J. McWhirter, 1988). Because the insurance industry recognizes that one need not be a psychiatrist to be a valid health-care provider (*Blue Shield of Virginia v. McCready*, 1982), the courts may begin to hold nonmedical practitioners liable for the suicidal deaths of their clients. This acknowledgment, in combination with the fact that many practitioners now have malpractice insurance, increases the likelihood of lawsuits.

When the practitioner has acted with reasonable professional judgment, the chance of being successfully sued is minimal. Reasonable professional judgment, however, is often not an objective standard (Berman & Cohen-Sandler, 1983). A practitioner may not believe, for example, that a patient's history of assaults and homicidal tendencies necessarily signifies suicidal tendencies. Another therapist may think otherwise. Generally the courts will hold a practitioner to the "generally accepted view of the profession" on a given point (*Fernandez v. Baruch*, 1968). Codes of professional ethics and discussions with colleagues are the best means to acquire information about the accepted professional standard of care (Jobes & Berman, 1993).

Attempted suicide.   Persons who have attempted suicide can conceivably sue their therapists for the injuries caused by the attempts. Other legal considerations, too, enter the picture when a youth makes suicidal gestures. In certain circumstances, the courts may intervene after an adolescent attempts suicide. That is, although the courts today generally do not punish people for attempting suicide, they may commit them to a psychiatric hospital (Wright, 1975). Most states have statutes that empower the courts to commit persons judged to pose a danger to themselves to the state psychiatric hospital. This power is especially likely to be exercised when the person who has attempted suicide is an adolescent ward of the court.

When an adolescent's suicide attempt is serious enough to require hospitalization, an agency or hospital staff member should evaluate the patient. The evaluators may recommend a hearing to determine whether the adolescent should be committed to the state hospital. Thus, practitioners must be aware of the possibility that their client may be committed.

State hospital systems are often too underfunded to handle all mental health problems, especially those of children and adolescents. In view of their financial stability, the Carter family could probably overcome this problem by finding a private mental health facility for Jason. When the family lacks the Carters' resources, however, the counseling professional must diligently try to locate the resources available in the state mental health system through state agencies and mental hospitals. In some situations the only way to help a suicidal young person is to petition a court to order the client's commitment.

Practitioners should inject themselves into the state or county evaluation process. If no one contacts the practitioner after the attempted suicide of an adolescent client, the practitioner should contact the appropriate evaluating team or agency. His or her comments and recommendations to them may be invaluable and the evaluation team may decide that it would be best for the practitioner to maintain a therapeutic alliance with the client.

Similarly, the practitioner should be familiar with legal resources in the community. If hospitalization is necessary, the therapist may be responsible for finding a suitable facility for a youth at risk for another suicide attempt. Contact with administrative agencies and the state court system can often yield helpful information on how to make appropriate resources available to the client.

Testifying in Court

At some point in your career as a practitioner you might be called to testify. Under most rules of evidence including the Federal Rules of Evidence "every person is competent to be a witness except as otherwise provided in these rules" (Federal Rule of Evidence, 601). Thus, unless you are somehow "incompetent," such as a very small child or a person with a mental or psychological defect, there is nothing to bar you from being a witness. The question, then, is whether you are going to testify as a "lay" or "expert" witness.

Generally, a lay witness only testifies about something that they perceived at the time, such as something that they actually heard. They could also testify as to what they touched, or smelled. In short, anything that a person perceives by their very own five senses at the time that it occurs can be testified to as long as it is relevant. In fact, the only time a lay witness can opine is when it is "rationally based on the perception of the witness, be helpful to a clear understanding of the witness's testimony or determination of a fact or issue, and not based on scientific, technical, or other specialized knowledge. . ." (Federal Rules of Evidence, 701).

Conversely, an "expert" witness can offer opinions based on their "specialized knowledge" (Federal Rule of Evidence, 703). Their testimony is supposed to help the jury to better understand the evidence, not to testify as to "ultimate issues" (see Federal Rule of Evidence, 702). For example, experts are not allowed to give an opinion as to whether the defendant is guilty. Thus, an expert could testify as to cause of death, but not who caused the death. The jury decides such "ultimate issues," not the expert.

As a practitioner you may be called to testify as a lay witness for what you actually perceived with your senses of a given situation. Also, you may be called because of your specialized knowledge or skill—indeed, the very thing that makes you a practitioner. Here, you are an expert witness. In a given case, you could be called as both. The attorney who calls you as a witness should explain it to you at the time.

CONCLUSION

Legal Dos and Don'ts in Work with At-Risk Youth

Practitioners can minimize the risk of lawsuits by understanding the legal system, ethical guidelines, and some of the legal quagmires entailed in working with at-risk youth (Jobes & Berman, 1993). The following suggestions can be both helpful to the practitioner and therapeutically beneficial to the young client:

1. In an emergency situation, avoid a display of anger or sarcasm toward the client. Paradoxical intentions are also highly risky. With a client who has recently attempted suicide, for example, a statement like "Next time cut vertically instead of horizontally and you'll get the main artery" would not impress a jury should the client later follow your advice.
2. Document your actions fully and professionally. Documentation should include your assessment of the risks involved in a particular treatment and your reasoning. The "reasonable professional judgment" standard will protect you against liability if you have clearly used reasonable professional judgment. A client's records can be offered at a trial and can show that you did the best that could be done in the situation.
3. Consult frequently with your colleagues on therapeutic, ethical, and legal questions and document this. Common sense tells a juror that "two heads are better than one." If your colleagues supported your decision at the time, negligence will be hard to prove.
4. Maintain good staff communication. Bad communication between the "professionals" will negatively impress a juror because poor communication may indicate negligence.
5. Deal with the family, particularly after a suicide. This approach has a dual purpose. First, it facilitates the family's resolution of grief and is a matter of humane and responsible treatment. Second, the family's contact with you helps deter a hasty, emotion-driven decision to file a malpractice suit.
6. Know the ethics code in your field such as those that the American Psychological Association, the American Counseling Association, or the National Education Association have developed. These codes define the standard practice on many points and are often produced to help professionals avoid legal as well as ethical problems.
7. Continue to update your professional training and keep a record of the seminars and classes you attend. This will indicate to a jury or judge that you are a conscientious practitioner who works to provide the best for your clients. These practices not only help practitioners defend themselves against lawsuits but enhances the professional practice of counseling and human services.

These suggestions can help all practitioners protect themselves and at the same time to work more effectively with the young people who seek their help.

REFERENCES

42 Code of Federal Regulations; United States Code § 13031 (1990).

Aber, J. L., Jones, S. M., Brown, J. L., Chandry, N., & Samples, F. (1998). Resolving conflict creatively: Evaluating the developmental effects of a school-based violence prevention program in neighborhood and classroom context. *Development and Psychopathology, 10,* 187–213.

Achmon, J., Granek, M., Golomb, M., & Hart, J. (1998). Behavioral treatment of essential hypertension: A comparison between cognitive therapy and biofeedback of heart rate. *Psychosomatic Medicine, 51,* 152–164.

Acoca, L. (1999). Investing in girls: A 21st century strategy. Washington DC: U.S. Department of Justice Office of Justice Programs, *Journal of the Office of Juvenile Justice and Delinquency Prevention,* (6)l.

Adams, D., & Hamm, M. (1994). *New designs for teaching and learning: Promoting active learning in tomorrow's schools.* San Francisco: Jossey-Bass.

Adlaf, E. M., Paglia, A., & Ivis, F. J. (2000). Nonmedical drug use among adolescent students: Highlights from the 1999 Ontario Student Drug Use Survey. *Canadian Medical Association Journal, 162*(12), 1677.

Adler, A. (1930). *The education of children.* South Bend, IN: Gateway.

Adler, A. (1964). *Social interest: A challenge to mankind.* New York: Capricorn.

Advocates for Youth. (1994). *Adolescent sexual behavior, pregnancy, and parenthood.* Washington, DC: Author. Retrieved from *http://www.health.state.ok.us/ program/ahd/FP2002.pdf* on July 8, 2002.

Advocates for Youth and Sexuality Information & Education Council of the United States. (1999). *Poll on America's Attitudes toward Sexuality Education.* Washington, DC: Hickman-Brown.

Aksamit, D. (1990). Mildly handicapped and at-risk students: The graying of the line. *Academic Therapy, 25,* 277–289.

Aktan, G., Kumpfer, K. L., & Turner, C. (1996). Effectiveness of a family skills training program for substance use prevention with inner city African-American families. *Substance Use and Misuse, 31*(2), 57–175.

Alan Guttmacher Institute. (1994). *Sex and America's teenagers.* New York: Author.

Alan Guttmacher Institute. (1999). *Teenage pregnancy: Overall trends and state-by-state information.* New York: AGI.

Alan Guttmacher Institute. (2002). *Teen Sex and Pregnancy — Revised 9/1999.* Retrieved from *http://www. agi-usa.org/pubs/fb_teen_sex.html* on May 5, 2002.

Albee, G. W. (1995, February). The answer is prevention. *Psychology Today,* 60–64.

Albee, G. W., & Gullota, T. P. (1997). *Primary prevention works.* New London: Sage Publications.

Alessi, N. E., McManus, M., Brickman, A., & Grapentine, L. (1984). Suicidal behavior among serious juvenile offenders. *American Journal of Psychiatry, 141,* 286–287.

Algozzine, B., & Kaye, P. (Eds.). (2002). *Preventing problem behaviors: A handbook of successful prevention strategies.* Thousand Oaks, CA: Corwin Press, Inc.

Allen, M. L., Brown, P., & Finlay, B. (1992). *Helping children by strengthening families: A look at family support programs.* Washington, DC: Children's Defense Fund.

Allsopp, D. H., Santos, K. E., & Linn, R. (2000). Collaborating to teach prosocial skills. *Intervention in School and Clinic, 35*(3), 141–146.

Alvarado, R., & Kumpfer, K. (2000). Strengthening America's families. *Juvenile Justice,* (7) 8–18.

Alvy, K. T. (1994). *Parent training today: A social necessity.* Studio City, CA: Center for the Improvement of Child Caring.

Ambrosio, T., & Schiraldi, V. (1997). *From classrooms to cellblocks: A national perspective.* Washington, DC: The Justice Policy Institute.

Ameri, A. (1999). In Schwartz, R. (2002), A decade and a half later, still a crude drug with underappreciated toxicity, *Pediatrics, 109,* 284–290.

American College of Obstetricians and Gynecologists. (1993). Special needs of pregnant teens. ACOG *patient education pamphlet no. AP103.* Washington, DC: Author.

American Medical Association. (1990). *Healthy youth 2000: National health promotion and disease prevention objectives for adolescents.* Chicago: Author.

American Psychiatric Association. (2000). *Diagnostic and statistical manual of mental disorders* (4th ed.). Washington, DC: Author.

American Psychological Association Presidential Task Force on Violence and the Family. (1996). *Violence and the family.* Washington, DC: Author.

American Social Health Association. (1995). *Gallup study: Teenagers know more than adults about STDs, but STD knowledge among both groups is low.* Research Triangle Park, NC: The Association.

Amrein, A. L., & Berliner, D. C. (2002, March 28). High-stakes testing, uncertainty, and student learning. *Education Policy Analysis Archives, 10*(18). Retrieved from *http://epaa.asu.edu/epaa/v10n18/* on July 1, 2002.

Amundson, K. (1991). *Building self-esteem: A guide for parents, schools, and communities.* Arlington, VA: American Association of School Administrators.

Anderson, C. A., & Dill, K. E. (2000). Violent video games can increase aggression. *Journal of Personality and Social Psychology, 78*(4), 772–790.

Anderson, G. L. (1987). *When chemicals come to school: The student assistance program model.* Milwaukee, WI: DePaul Training Institute.

Anderson, J. D. (1994, March–April). Breaking the silence: Creating safe schools for gay youth. *Student Assistance Journal*, 21–23.

Anderegg, M. L. & Vergason, G. A. (1992). Preparing teachers for their legal responsibilities in facing school-age suicide. *Teacher Education and Special Education, 15*, 295–299.

Anderson, S., Cavanagh, J., Hartman, C., & Leonard-Wright, B. (2001). *Executive excess 2001: Layoffs, tax rebates, the gender gap.* Boston, MA: Institute for Policy Studies and United for a Fair Economy.

Andrews, J. A., & Lewinsohn, P. M. (1992). Suicidal attempts among older adolescents: Prevalence and co-occurrence with psychiatric disorders. *Journal of the American Academy of Child and Adolescent Psychiatry, 31*(4), 644–661.

Annie E. Casey Foundation. (1994). *Kids count data book: State profiles of child well-being.* Washington, DC: Author.

Annie E. Casey Foundation. (1995). *Kids count data book: State profiles of child well-being.* Washington, DC: Author.

Annis, H. M., Schober, R., & Kelly, E. (1996). Matching addiction outpatient counseling to client readiness for change: The role of structured relapse prevention counseling. *Experimental and Clinical Psychopharmacology, 4* (1), 37–45.

Ansley, L. (1997, August 13–14). Just keeps getting worse. *USA Weekend,* 5.

APA Help Center. (1999). *Warning signs of teen violence: Recognizing violence warning signs in others.* Retrieved from *http://helping.apa.org/warningsigns/* on March 2001.

Apter, T. (1990). *Altered loves: Mothers and daughters during adolescence.* New York: St. Martin's Press.

Araki, C. T., Takeshita, C., & Kadomoto, L. (1989). *Research results and final report for the dispute management in the school project.* Honolulu, HI: University of Hawaii at Manoa, Program on Conflict Resolution. (ERIC Document No. ED312750)

Arbona, C. (2000). The development of academic achievement in school aged children: Precursors to career development. In R. Lent & S. Brown (Eds), *Handbook of counseling psychology* (3rd ed., pp. 270–309). New York: John Wiley & Sons.

Arendell, T. (1995). *Fathers and divorce.* Thousand Oaks, CA: Sage.

Arnold, D. S., O'Leary, S. G., Wolff, L. S., & Acker, M. M. (1993). The parenting scale: A measure of dysfunctional parenting in discipline situations. *Psychological Assessment, 5*(2), 137–144.

Arnold, M. S. (1995). Exploding the myths: African-American families at promise. In B. B. Swadener & S. Lubeck (Eds.), *Children and families "at promise"* (pp. 143–162). Albany, NY: State University of New York Press.

Arreaga-Mayer, C. (1998). Increasing active student responding and improving academic performance through classwide peer tutoring. *Intervention in School and Clinic, 34*(2), 89–94, 117.

Ashery, R., Robertson, E., & Kumpfer, K. (Eds.). (1998). *Drug abuse prevention through family interventions.* Rockville, MD: National Institutes of Health.

Astone, N., & McLanahan, S. (1991). Family structure, parental practices, and high school completion. *American Sociological Review, 56*, 309–320.

Aubrey, R. F. (1988). Excellence, school reform, and counselors. In J. Carlson & J. Lewis (Eds.), *Counseling the adolescent* (pp. 189–204). Denver: Love.

August, G. J., Realmuto, G. M., Winters, K. C., & Hektner, J. M. (2001). Prevention of adolescent drug abuse: Targeting high-risk children with a multifaceted intervention model—The early risers "skills for success" program. *Applied and Preventive Psychology, 10*, 135–154.

Bagley, C. (1992). Development of an adolescent stress scale for use by school counselors. *School Psychology International, 13*, 31–49.

Baker, L. (1990, August 16). After school: Some programs help latchkey kids find something to do. *Southeast Community: Arizona Republic*, pp. 1, 3.

Ballard, M., Argus, T., & Remley, T. P. (1999). Bullying and school violence: A proposed prevention program. *NASSP Bulletin*, 83, 38–46.

Band, S. R., & Harpold, J. A. (1999, September). School violence: Lessons learned. *FBI: Law Enforcement Bulletin*, 68, 9–16.

Bandura, A. (1977). *Social learning theory*. Englewood Cliffs, NJ: Prentice-Hall.

Bandura, A. (1986). *Social foundations of thought and action*. Englewood Cliffs, NJ: Prentice-Hall.

Bandura, A., Pastorelli, C., Barbaranelli, C., & Caprara, G. V. (1999). Self efficacy pathways to childhood depression. *Journal of Personality and Social Psychology*, 76, 258–269.

Barber v. State, 592 So.2d 330 (Fla. App. 2nd Dist. 1992).

Barnett, W. S. (1992). Benefits of compensatory preschool education. *Journal of Human Resources*, 27, 279–312.

Barr, R. (1992). Teachers, materials, and group composition in literacy instruction. In M. J. Dreher & W. H. Slater (Eds.), *Elementary school literacy: Critical issues*. Norwood, MA: Christopher-Gordon.

Barron, A. M., & Foot, H. (1991). Peer tutoring and tutor training. *Educational Research*, 33, 174–185.

Barry, D. (1990, April). *Music and the at-risk child*. Paper presented at the Music Educators National Conference, Washington, DC.

Bassett, C., McWhirter, J. J., & Kitzmiller, K. (1997). *Teacher implementation of cooperative learning groups*. Unpublished manuscript. Arizona State University, Tempe, AZ.

Bates, J. E., Bayles, K., Bennett, D. S., Ridge, B., & Brown, M. M. (1991). Origins of externalizing behavior problems at 8 years of age. In D. J. Pepler & K. H. Rubin (Eds.), *The development and treatment of childhood aggression* (pp. 93–120). Hillsdale, NJ: Erlbaum.

Battin, M. P. (1995). *Ethical issues in suicide*. Englewood Cliffs, NJ: Prentice-Hall.

Battin-Pearson, S., Newcomb, M. D., Abbott, R. D., Hill, K. G., Catalano, R. F., & Hawkins, J. D. (2000). Predictors of early high school dropout: A test of five theories. *Journal of Educational Psychology*, (92)3, 568–582.

Bauer, A. M. (2001). "Tell them we're girls": The invisibility of girls with disabilities. In P. O'Reilly, E. M. Penn, & K. deMarrais (Eds.), *Educating young adolescent girls* (pp. 29–45). Mahwah, NJ: Lawrence Erlbaum Associates.

Baumeister, R. F., Bushman, B. J., & Campbell, W. K. (2000). Self-esteem, narcissism, and aggression: Does violence result from low self-esteem or from threatened egotism? *Current Directions in Psychological Science*, 9(1), 26–29.

Baumrind, D. (1990). Rearing competent children. In W. Damon (Ed.), *New directions for child development: Child development today and tomorrow*. San Francisco: Jossey-Bass.

Baumrind, D. (1993). The average expectable environment is not good enough: A response to Scarr. *Child Development*, 64, 1299–1317.

Baumrind, D. (1995). *Child maltreatment and optimal caregiving in social contexts*. New York: Garland.

Beardslee, W., & Schwoeri, L. (1994). Preventive intervention with children of depressed parents. In G. P. Sholevar (Ed.), *The transmission of depression in families and children: Assessment and intervention*. Northvale, NJ: Aronson.

Beauvais, F., Chavez, E. L., Oetting, E. R., Deffenbacher, J. L., & Cornell, G. R. (1996). Drug use, violence, and victimization among White American, Mexican American, and American Indian dropouts, students with academic problems, and students in good academic standing. *Journal of Counseling Psychology*, 43(3) 292–299.

Beck, A. T. (1976). *Cognitive therapy and emotional disorders*. New York: International Universities Press.

Beck, A. T. (1991). Cognitive therapy: A 30 year retrospective. *American Psychologist*, 46(4), 368–375.

Beck, A. T., Kovacs, M., & Weissman, A. (1979). Assessment of suicidal intention: The scale for suicidal ideation. *Journal of Clinical and Consulting Psychology*, 47, 343–352.

Beck, A. T., Ward, S. H., Mendelson, M., Mock, J., & Erbaugh, J. (1961). An inventory for measuring depression. *Archives of General Psychiatry*, 4, 561–571.

Beck, A. T., Weissman, A., Lester, D., & Trexler, L. (1974). The measurement of pessimism: The hopelessness scale. *Journal of Consulting and Clinical Psychology*, 42, 861–865.

Becker, E. (1981). *The denial of death*. New York: Free Press.

Becker, W. C. (1964). Consequences of different kinds of parental discipline. In J. L. Hoffman & L. W. Hoffman (Eds.), *Review of child development research* (Vol. 1, pp. 169–208). New York: Russell Sage Foundation.

Becker-Lansen, E., & Rickel, A. U. (1995). Integration of teen pregnancy and child abuse research: Identifying mediator variables for pregnancy outcome. *Journal of Primary Prevention*, 16(8), 39–53.

Bell, N. J., & Bell, R. W. (Eds.). (1993). *Adolescent risk taking.* Newbury Park, CA: Sage Publications.

Bellanti, C. J., & Bierman, K. L. (2000). Disentangling the impact of low cognitive ability and inattention on social behavior and peer relationships. *Journal of Clinical Child Psychology, 29*(1), 66–75.

Belle, D. (1990). Poverty and women's mental health. *American Psychologist, 45,* 385–389.

Bellotti v. Baird, 428 U.S. 132 (1979).

Belsie, L. (2001). USA: America by the numbers: Surprise: More nuclear families. *The Christian Science Monitor, 93*(97), 1,5.

Benard, B. (1991). *Fostering resiliency in kids: Protective factors in the family, school, and community.* Portland, OR: Western Center for Drug-Free Schools and Communities.

Bender, W. N., Shubert, T. H., & McLaughlin, P. J. (2001). Invisible kids: Preventing school violence by identifying kids in trouble. *Intervention in School and Clinic, 37*(2), 105–111.

Benn, W. (Ed.). (1981). *STAR: Social thinking and reasoning.* Irvine, CA: Irvine Unified School District.

Benn, W. (Ed.). (1982). *PLUS: Promoting learning and understanding of self.* Irvine, CA: Irvine Unified School District.

Bennett, B. E., Bryant, B. K., VandenBos, G. R., & Greenwood, A. (1990). *Professional liability and risk management,* Washington, DC: American Psychological Association.

Benson, H. (1992). *The relaxation response* (2nd ed.). New York: Random House.

Berg, C. A., & Clough, M. (1990/91). Hunter lesson design: The wrong one for science teaching. *Educational Leadership, 48*(4), 73–78.

Berliner, D. (2001, January 28). *Our schools vs. theirs: Averages that hide the true extremes.* Education Policy Project CERAI-01-02, Center for Education Research, Analysis, and Innovation. Milwaukee: University of Wisconsin—Milwaukee.

Berliner, D. C., & Biddle, B. J. (1995). *The manufactured crisis: Myths, fraud, and the attack on America's public schools.* Reading, MA: Addison-Wesley Publishing Company.

Berman, A. L. & Cohen-Sandler, R. (1983). Suicide and malpractice: Expert testimony and the standard of care. *Professional Psychology: Research and Practice, 14,* 6–19.

Berman, A. L., & Jobes, D. A. (1991). *Adolescent suicide: Assessment and intervention.* Washington, DC: American Psychological Association.

Bernhardt, G. R., & Praeger, S. G. (1985). Preventing child suicide: The elementary school death education puppet show. *Journal of Counseling and Development, 63,* 311–312.

Bernstein, N. (1996). *Treating the unmanageable adolescent: A guide to oppositional defiant and conduct disorders.* Northvale, NJ: Jason Aronson.

Berry, E. H., Shillington, A. M., Peak, T., & Hohman, M. M. (2000). Multi-ethnic comparison of risk and protective factors for adolescent pregnancy. *Child and Adolescent Social Work, 17,* 79–96.

Besner, H. F., & Spungin, C. I. (1995). *Gay and lesbian students: Understanding their needs.* Washington, DC: Taylor & Francis.

Bess, R., Leos-Urbel, J., & Green, R. (2001). *The cost of protecting vulnerable children II: What has changed since 1996?* The Urban Institute. Retrieved from *www.urban.org* on July 10, 2002.

Bettencourt, H., & Blair, I. (1992). A cognition (attribution) emotion model of violence in conflict situations. *Personality and Social Psychology Bulletin, 18*(3), 342–350.

Beymer, L. (1995). *Meeting the guidance and counseling needs of boys.* Alexandria, VA: American Counseling Association.

Beyth-Marom, R., Fischhoff, B., Jacobs, M., & Furby, L. (1989). *Teaching decision making to adolescents: A critical review.* Washington, DC: Carnegie Council on Adolescent Development.

Bianchi, S., & Caspar, L. (2000). American families. *Population Bulletin, 55*(4), 3–42, Washington DC: Population Reference Bureau.

Bickel, A., & Ertle, V. (1991, February). *Parenting skills curricula: A descriptive guide.* Portland, OR: Western Regional Center for Drug-Free Schools and Communities.

Bickel, R., Howley, C., Williams, T., & Glascock, C. (2001). High school size, achievement equity, and cost: Robust interaction effects and tentative results. *Education Policy Analysis Archives, 9*(40). Retrieved from *http://epaa.asu.edu/epaa/v9n40.html* on October 8, 2001.

Bilchik, S. (1999, August). *OJJDP research: Making a difference for juveniles.* Report. Washington, DC: Office of Juvenile Justice and Delinquency Prevention, 1–22.

Birch, S., & Ladd, G. W. (1997). The teacher-child relationship and children's early school adjustment. *Journal of School Psychology, 35,* 61–79.

Bizot, E. (1999, May). Paper presented at Vocational Society Conference, Milwaukee, WI.

Bjerregaard, B., & Smith, C. (1993). Gender differences in gang participation, delinquency, and substance abuse. *Journal of Quantitative Criminology, 9*(4), 329–355.

Blake, C., Wang, W., Cartledge, G., & Gardner, R. (2000). Middle school students with serious emotional disturbances serve as social skills trainers and reinforcers for peers with SED. *Behavioral Disorders, 25,* 280–298.

Blechman, E. A., Prinz, R. J., & Dumas, J. E. (1995). Coping, competence, and aggression prevention: Part 1. Development model. *Applied and Preventive Psychology, 4,* 211–232.

Blue Shield of Virginia v. McCready, 457 U.S. 465 (1982).

Blumenthal, S. J. (1990). Youth suicide: Risk factors, assessment, and treatment of adolescent and young adult suicidal patients. *Psychiatric Clinics of North America, 13*(3), 511–556.

Blumstein, A., Cohen, J., & Farrington, D. P. (1988). Criminal career research: Its value for criminology. *Criminology, 26,* 1–35.

Blustein, D. L., Juntunen, C. L., & Worthington, R. L. (2000). The school-to-work transition: Adjustment challenges for the forgotten half. In S. Brown & R. W. Lent (Eds.) *Handbook of counseling psychology* (3rd ed., pp. 435–470). New York: John Wiley & Sons.

Blustein, J., Levine, C., Dubler, N. N. (Eds.). (1999). *The Adolescent Alone: Decision Making in Health Care in the United States.* New York, NY: Cambridge University Press.

Bogust v. Iverson, 10 Wis. 2d 129, 102 N.W. 2d 228 (1960).

Bongar, B. (1992). Effective risk management and the suicidal patient. *Register Report, 18*(6), 22–27.

Bortner, M. A. (Ed.). (1993). *Confronting violent crime in Arizona.* Phoenix, AZ: Arizona Town Hall.

Borum, R. (1996). Improving the clinical practice of violence risk assessment: Technology, guidelines, and training. *American Psychologist, 51,* 945–956.

Borum, R. (2000). Assessing violence risk among youth. *Journal of Clinical Psychology, 56,* 1263–1288.

Botvin, G. J., Schinke, S., & Orlandi, M. S. (Eds.). (1995). *Drug abuse prevention with multiethnic youth.* Thousand Oaks, CA: Sage Publications.

Botvin, G. J., Baker, E., Dusenbury, L., Botvin, E. M., & Diaz, T. (1995). Long-term follow-up results of a randomized drug abuse prevention trial in a white middle-class population. *Journal of the American Medical Association, 273,* 1106–1112.

Bowen, M. (1978). *Family therapy in clinical practice.* New York: Jason Aronson.

Boxer, A. M., Cook, J. A., & Herdt, G. (1991). Double jeopardy: Identity transitions and parent-child relations among gay and lesbian youth. In K. Pillemer & K. McCartney (Eds.), *Parent-child relations throughout life.* Hillsdale, NJ: Erlbaum.

Boyer, D., & Fine, D. (1992). Sexual abuse as a factor in adolescent pregnancy and child maltreatment. *Family Planning Perspectives, 24*(1), 4–11.

Bracken, B. A. (1992). *Multidimensional self-concept scale.* Austin, TX: Pro-Ed, Inc.

Bransford, J. D., & Stein, B. S. (1984). *The IDEAL problem solver.* New York: W. H. Freeman.

Brennan, T. R. (1984). The reduction of disruptive classroom behavior of emotionally disturbed adolescents through the use of a relaxation procedure. Ph.D. dissertation, Columbia University Teachers College, 1983. *Dissertation Abstracts International, 44,* 3347A.

Brewster, K. L., Cooksey, E. C., Guilkey, D. K., & Rindfuss, R. R. (1998). The changing impact of religion on the sexual and contraceptive behavior of adolescent women in the United States. *Journal of Marriage and the Family, 60*(2), 493–504.

Briesmeister, J. M. S., & Charles E., (Eds.). (1998). *Handbook of parent training.* New York, John Wiley & Sons, Inc.

Brindis, C. (1992). Adolescent pregnancy prevention for Hispanic youth: The role of schools, families, and communities. *Journal of School Health, 62,* 345–351.

Brindis, C. D. (1991). *Adolescent pregnancy prevention: A guidebook for communities.* Palo Alto, CA: Health Promotion Resource Center.

Brody, J. L. & Waldron, H. B. (2000). Ethical Issues in Research on the Treatment of Adolescent Substance Abuse Disorders. *Addictive Behaviors, 25,* 217–228.

Bronfenbrenner, U. (1979). *The ecology of human development: Experiments by nature and design.* Cambridge, MA: Harvard University Press.

Bronfenbrenner, U. (1989). Ecological systems theory. *Annals of Child Development, 6,* 187–249.

Brook, J. S., Cohen, P., Whiteman, M., & Gordon, A. S. (1992). Psychosocial risk factors in the transition from moderate to heavy use or abuse of drugs. In M. Glantz & R. Pickens (Eds.), *Vulnerability to drug abuse.* Washington, DC: American Psychological Association.

Brooks, V., & Coll, K. (1994). *Troubled youth: Identification and intervention strategies.* Paper presented at the National Convention of the American Alliance for Health, Physical Education, Recreation, and Dance, Denver, CO, April 12–16.

Brown, S. A., Myers, M. G., Mott, M. A., & Vik, P. W. (1994). Correlates of success following treatment for adolescent substance abuse. *Applied and Preventive Psychology, 3,* 61–73.

Brown, S. S., & Eisenberg, L. (Eds.). (1995). *The best intentions: Unintended pregnancy and the well-being of children and families*. Washington, DC: National Academy Press.

Brownsworth, V. A. (1992). America's worst-kept secret. AIDS is devastating the nation's teenagers, and gay kids are dying by the thousands. *The Advocate*, 38–46.

Bruce, M. (1995). Brief counseling: An effective model for change. *The School Counselor*, 42(5), 353–364.

Bruton, S. (Ed.). (1994). *On alert! Gang prevention*. Sacramento, CA: Department of Education.

Buchman, D. D., & Funk, J. B. (1996). Video and computer games in the '90s: Children's time commitment and game preference. *Children Today*, 24, 12–16.

Bumpass, L. L. (1984). Children in marital disruption: A replication and update. *Demography*, 21, 71–82.

Burns, L. E. (1981). Relaxation in the management of stress. In J. Marshall & C. L. Cooper (Eds.), *Coping with stress*. London: Gower.

Burrell, N., & Vogel, S. (1990). Turfside conflict mediation. *Mediation Quarterly*, 7(3), 237–251.

Burt, M., & Cohen, B. (1993). *America's homeless*. Washington, DC: Urban Institute Report, 89–109.

Bushman, B. J., & Anderson, C. A. (2001). Media violence and the American public: Scientific facts versus media misinformation. *American Psychologist*, 56(6/7), 477–489.

Bushweller, K. (1995). The resilient child. *The American School Board Journal*, May, 18–23.

Butts, J. (2002). *The rise and fall of the American youth violence: 1980–2000*. Washington, DC: Urban Institute.

Byrne, D., Kelley, K., & Fisher, W. A. (1993). Unwanted teenage pregnancies: Incidence, interpretation, and intervention. *Applied and Preventive Psychology*, 2, 101–113.

Cahoon, P. (1988). Mediator magic. *Education Leadership*, 45(4), 92–95.

Calfee, B. E. (1992). *Lawsuit prevention techniques: For mental health professional, chemical dependency specialists, and clergy*. Sarasota, FL: Professional Resource Press.

Cambone, J., Weiss, C. H., & Wyeth, A. (1992). *We're not programmed for this: An exploration of the variance between the ways teachers think and the concept of shared decision making in high schools*. Cambridge, MA: Harvard University, National Center for Educational Leadership.

Camp, B. W., & Bash, M. S. (1985a). *Think aloud: Increasing social and cognitive skills—A problem-solving program for children, Classroom program grades 1–2*. Champaign, IL: Research Press.

Camp, B. W., & Bash, M. S. (1985b). *Think aloud: Increasing social and cognitive skills—A problem-solving program for children, Classroom program grades 3–4*. Champaign, IL: Research Press.

Camp, B. W., & Bash, M. S. (1985c). *Think aloud: Increasing social and cognitive skills—A problem-solving program for children, Classroom program grades 5–6*. Champaign, IL: Research Press.

Camp, C. G., & Camp, G. M. (1999). *The Corrections Yearbook, 1998*. Middletown, CT: The Criminal Justice Institute.

Campbell, C. A., & Dahir, C. A. (1997). *National standards for school counseling programs*. Alexandria, VA: American School Counselors Association.

Campfield, K. M., & Hills, A. M. (2001). Effects of timing of Critical Incident Stress Debriefing (CISD) on posttraumatic symptoms. *Journal of Traumatic Stress*, 14, 327–340. *http://www.cdc.gov/maso/factbook/Fact%20Book.pdf*.

Canada, G. (1995). *Fist stick knife gun: A personal history of violence in America*. Boston: Beacon Hill.

Canetto, S. S., & Lester, D. (1995). Gender and the primary prevention of suicide mortality. *Suicide and Life-Threatening Behavior*, 25(1), 58–69.

Canino, I. A., & Spurlock, J. (1994). *Culturally diverse children and adolescents: Assessment, diagnosis, and treatment*. New York: Guilford.

Capaldi, D. M., & Patterson, G. R. (1991). Relation of parental transition to boys' adjustment problems: Mothers at risk for transitions and unskilled parenting. *Developmental Psychology*, 27, 489–504.

Caplan, G. (1964). *Principles of preventive psychiatry*. New York: Basic Books.

Capuzzi, D. (1994). *Suicide prevention in the schools: Guidelines for middle and high school settings*. Alexandria, VA: American Counseling Association.

Capuzzi, D., & Golden, L. (1988). *Preventing adolescent suicide*. Muncie, IN: Accelerated Development Inc.

Capuzzi, D., & Gross, D. R. (1996). "I don't want to live": The adolescent at risk for suicidal behavior. In D. Capuzzi & D. R. Gross (Eds.), *Youth at risk: A prevention resource for counselors, teachers, and parents* (2nd ed., pp. 253–282). Alexandria, VA: American Counseling Association.

Carey v. Population Services International, 431 U.S. 678 (1977).

Carkhuff, R. R. (1969). *Helping and human relations, Vol. 1*. New York: Holt, Rinehart & Winston.

Carlson, L., Grossbart, S., & Stuenkel, J. K. (1992). The role of parental socialization types on differential family communication patterns regarding consumption. *Journal of Consumer Psychology, 1*(1), 31–52.

Carnegie Council on Adolescent Development. (1995). *Great transitions: Preparing adolescents for a new century.* New York: Carnegie Corporation of New York.

Carnegie Task Force on Meeting the Needs of Young Children. (1994). *Starting points: Meeting the needs of our youngest children.* New York: Carnegie Corporation of New York.

Carnine, D., Silbert, J., & Kameenui, E. J. (1990). *Direct instruction reading* (2nd ed.). Columbus, OH: Merrill.

Carpenter, C. D., Bloom, L. A., & Boat, M. B. (1999). Guidelines for special educators: Achieving socially valid outcomes. *Intervention in School and Clinic, 34*(3), 143–149.

Carter, D. J., & Wilson, R. (1991). *Ninth annual status report: Minorities in higher education.* Washington, DC: American Council on Education.

Carter, E., & McGoldrick, M. (Eds.). (1999). *The changing family life cycle: A framework for family therapy* (2nd ed.). Needham Heights, MA: Allyn & Bacon.

Carter, J. L., & Russell, H. (1980). Biofeedback and academic attainment of LD children. *Academic Therapy, 15*, 483–486.

Carter, N. (1996). *See how we grow: A report on the status of parenting education in the U.S.* Philadelphia: Pew Charitable Trust.

Cartledge, G., & Milburn, J. F. (Eds.). (1986). *Teaching social skills to children: Innovative approaches* (2nd ed.). New York: Pergamon Press.

Carville, J. (1996). *We're right, they're wrong: A handbook for spirited progressives.* New York: Random House.

Catalano, R. F., & Hawkins, J. D. (1996). The social development model: A theory of antisocial behavior. In J. D. Hawkins (Ed.), *Delinquency and crime: Current theories.* New York: Cambridge University Press, pp. 149–197.

Catalano, R. F., Hawkins, J. D., Wells, E. A., Miller, J., & Brewer, D. (1990–1991). Evaluation of the effectiveness of adolescent drug abuse treatment, assessment of risks for relapse, and promising approaches for relapse prevention. *The International Journal of the Addictions, 25* (9A, 10A), 1085–1140.

Center for Disease Control and Prevention. (2001). *CDC Fact Book 2000/2001: Adolescent and young adult health.* Retrieved from *http://www.cdc.gov/nchs/releases* on May 2, 2002.

Centers for Disease Control. (2002). *Teen birth rates decline in all states during the 1990's.* Retrieved from *http://www.cdc.gov/nchs/releases/02facts/teenbirths.htm* on August 7, 2002.

Center for Disease Control. (2001). *Out-of-wedlock births.* Retrieved from *http://www.cdc.gov/nchs/faststats/unmarry.htm* on August 7, 2002.

Center for Substance Abuse Prevention. (1993). *Signs of effectiveness in preventing alcohol and other drug problems.* Washington, DC: U.S. Government Printing Office.

Center, Y., Wheldall, K., Freeman, L., Outhred, L., & McNaught, M. (1995). An experimental evaluation of Reading Recovery. *Reading Research Quarterly, 30*, 240–263.

Centers for Disease Control. (1992). *Selected behaviors that increase risk for HIV infection, other sexually transmitted diseases, and unintentional pregnancy among high school students—United States, 1991.* Atlanta, GA: Author.

Centers for Disease Control and Prevention. (1993). *Mortality trends, causes of death, and related risk behaviors among U.S. adolescents.* Atlanta: Author.

Centers for Disease Control and Prevention. (1994). HIV/AIDS. *Surveillance Report, 6*(2), 1–39.

Centers for Disease Control & Prevention. (1995). Youth risk behavior surveillance, U.S., 1995. *MMWR CDC Surveillance Summaries, 45* (SS-4), 1–56.

Centers for Disease Control & Prevention. (1997a). HIV/AIDS Surveillance Report 1997; 9(2):1–39.

Centers for Disease Control & Prevention. (1997b). HIV/AIDS Surveillance Report 1997; 9(1):1–39.

Centers for Disease Control & Prevention. (1997c). Division of STD prevention. Sexually transmitted disease surveillance, 1996. Atlanta, GA.

Centers for Disease Control & Prevention. (1998). Trends in sexual risk behaviors among high school students: United States, 1991–1997. *MMWR 47*, 749–752.

Centers for Disease Control (March 20, 1998). Suicide Among Black Youths—United States, 1980–1995. *MMWR Weekly, 47*(10), 193–106.

Centers for Disease Control & Prevention. (2000). *Youth risk behavior surveillance—United States, 1999.* Morbidity and mortality weekly report (MMWR); June 09, 2000 / 49(SS05); 1–96.

Centers for Disease Control & Prevention. (2001). *Youth tobacco surveillance—United States, 2000.* Morbidity and mortality weekly report (MMWR); November 2, 2001; 50 (SS04).

Centers for Disease Control & Prevention. (2002a). *Trends in sexual risk behaviors high school students—United States, 1991–2001.* (MMWR); September 26, 2002; 51(38); 856–859.

Centers for Disease Control and Prevention. (2002b). *Young people at risk: HIV/AIDS among America's youth.* Retrieved from *http://cdc.gov/hiv/pubs/facts/youth.htm* on May 5, 2002.

Centers for Disease Control & Prevention. (2002c). *Youth risk behavior surveillance—United States, 2001.* Morbidity and Mortality Weekly Report (MMWR); June 21, 2002; 51(SS04); 1–64.

Chamberlain, P., Fisher, P. A., & Moore, K. J. (2002). Multidimensional Treatment Foster Care: Applications of the OSLC intervention model to high-risk youth and their families. In J. B. Reid, G. R. Patterson, & J. Snyder (Eds.), *Antisocial behavior in children and adolescents: A developmental analysis and model for intervention* (pp. 203–218). Washington, DC: American Psychological Association.

Chamberlain, P., & Reid, J. B. (1998). Comparison of two community alternatives to incarceration for chronic juvenile offenders. *Journal of Consulting and Clinical Psychology, 66,* 624–633.

Charney, R. S., & Clayton, M. K. (1994). The first 6 weeks of school. *The Responsive Classroom, 6*(2), 1–3.

Chavers, D. (1991). Indian education: Dealing with a disaster. *Principal, 70,* 28–29.

Cheng, W. D. (1996). Pacific perspective. *Together, 24*(3).

Chenneville, T. (2000). HIV, Confidentiality, and Duty to Protect: A Decision-Making Model. *Professional Psychology: Research and Practice, 31,* 661–670.

Child Trends, Inc. (1996). *Facts at a glance.* Washington, DC: Child Trends, Inc.

Children's Defense Fund. (1991). *The state of America's children yearbook.* Washington, DC: Author.

Children's Defense Fund. (1994). *The state of America's children yearbook.* Washington, DC: Author.

Children's Defense Fund. (1995). *The state of America's children yearbook.* Washington, DC: Author.

Children's Defense Fund. (2000). *The state of America's children yearbook 2000.* CDF: Washington, DC.

Children's Defense Fund. (2001a). *Weakening economy and vanishing safety net also clouds news of last year's decline in child poverty.* Retrieved from *http://www.childrensdefense.org/release010925.htm* on April 17, 2002.

Children's Defense Fund. (2001b). *Fair Start-FAQs.* Retrieved from *http://www.childrensdefense.org/fairstart-faqs.htm* on April 7, 2002.

Children's Defense Fund. (2001c). *Facts on youth, violence and crime.* Retrieved from *http://www.childrensdefense.org/ss_ydfs_viocrime.php* on May 10, 2002.

Children's Defense Fund. (2001d). The state of America's children yearbook. Retrieved from *http://www.childrensdefense.org/keyfacts.htm* on July 29, 2002.

Chizmar v. Mackie, 896 P.2d 196 (Alaska, 1995).

Cicchetti, D., Rogosch, F. A., Lynch, M., & Holt, K. D. (1993). Resilience in maltreated children: Processes leading to adaptive outcome. *Development and Psychopathology, 5,* 629–647.

Clark, A. J. (1994). Conflict resolution and individual psychology in the schools. *Individual Psychology: Journal of Adlerian Theory, Research, and Practice, 50*(3), 329–340.

Clark, D. B., & Sayette, M. A. (1993). Anxiety and the development of alcoholism. *The American Journal on Addictions, 2*(1), 59–76.

Clarke-Stewart, A. (1989). Infant day care: Malignant or maligned? *American Psychologist, 44,* 266–273.

Clarke-Stewart, K. A., Gruber, C. P., & Fitzgerald, L. M. (1994). *Children at home and in day care.* Hillsdale, NJ: Erlbaum.

Clausen, J. A. (1993). *American lives: Looking back at the children of the great depression.* New York: Free Press.

Clay, M. M. (1985). *The early detection of reading difficulties.* Exeter, NH: Heinemann.

Cobb, P. (1994). Constructivism in mathematics and science education. *Educational Researcher, 23*(7), 4.

Cohen, D. K., McLaughlin, M., & Talbert, J. E. (1993). *Teaching for understanding: Challenges for policy and practice.* Hoboken, NJ: Jossey Bass.

Cohen, M. (1998). The monetary value of saving a high risk youth. *Journal of Quantitative Criminology, 14*(1), 5–33.

Cohen, S. B., & de Bettencourt, L. V. (1991). Dropout: Intervening with the reluctant learner. *Intervention in School and Clinic, 26,* 263–271.

Coie, J. D., Dodge, K. A., Terry, R., & Wright, V. (1991). The role of aggression in peer relations: An analysis of aggression episodes in boys' play groups. *Child Development, 62,* 812–826.

Coie, J. D., Watt, N. F., West, S. G., Hawkins, J. D., Asarnow, J. R., Markman, H. J., Ramey, S. L., Shure, M. B., & Long, B. (1993). The science of prevention: A conceptual framework and some directions for a national research program. *American Psychologist, 48*(10), 1013–1022.

Coker, J. K., & Borders, L. D. (2001). An analysis of environmental and social factors affecting adolescent problem drinking. *Journal of Counseling & Development, 79,* 200–208.

Cole, J. D. (1990). Toward a theory of peer rejection. In S. R. Asher & J. D. Coie (Eds.), *Peer rejection in childhood* (pp. 365–401). New York: Cambridge University.

Coleman, J. (1991). *Parental involvement in education.* Policy Perspectives, U.S. Department of Education.

Coleman, J. S., & Hoffer, T. (1987). *Public and private high schools: The impact of communities.* New York: Basic Books.

Coley, R. J. (1995). *Dreams deferred: High school dropouts in the United States.* Princeton, NJ: Educational Testing Service.

Comeau, N., Stewart, S. H., & Loba, P. (2001). The relations of trait anxiety, anxiety sensitivity and sensation seeking to adolescents' motivations for alcohol, cigarette, and marijuana use. *Addictive Behaviors, 26,* 803–825.

Comer, J. P. (Ed.). (1996). *Rallying the whole village: The Comer Process for reforming education.* New York: Teachers College Press.

Comiskey, P. E. (1993). Using reality therapy group training with at-risk high school freshman. *Journal of Reality Therapy, 12*(2), 59–64.

Compas, B. E., Banez, G. A., Malcarne, V., & Worsham, N. (1991). Perceived control and coping with stress: A developmental perspective. *Journal of Social Issues, 47,* 23–34.

Conchas, G. Q. (2001). Structuring failure and success: Understanding the variability in Latino school engagement. *Harvard Educational Review, 71*(3), 579–589.

Conger, J. J. (1988). Hostages to fortune: Youth, values, and the public interest. *American Psychologist, 43*(4), 291–300.

Conger, R. D., & Elder, G. H., Jr. (Eds.). (1994). *Families in troubled times: Adapting to change in rural America.* New York: Aldine de Gruyter.

Contreras, J., & Kerns, K. A. (2000). Emotion regulation processes: Explaining links between parent-child attachment and peer relationships. In K. A. Kerns, J. M. Contreras, & A. M. Neal-Barnett (Eds.), *Family and peers: Linking two social worlds* (pp. 1–25). Westport, CT: Praeger.

Conyne, R. K., & Cook, E. P. (in press). *Ecological counseling: An innovative approach to conceptualizing person-environment interaction.* Alexandria, VA: American Counseling Association.

Cooper, M. L. (1994). Motivations for alcohol use among adolescents: Development and validation of a four-factor model. *Psychological Assessment, 6*(2), 117–128.

Cope, K. M., & Kunkel, D. (in press). Sexual messages in teens' favorite prime-time TV programs. In J. D. Brown et al. (Eds.), *Sexual teens, sexual media.* Mahwah, NJ: Lawrence Erlbaum.

Corbin, S. K. T., Jones, R. T., & Schulman, R. S. (1993). Drug refusal behavior: The relative efficacy of skills-based and information-based treatment. *Journal of Pediatric Psychology, 18*(6), 769–784.

Costa, A. L. (Ed.). (1991). *Developing minds: A resource book for teaching thinking.* Alexandria, VA: Association of Supervision and Curriculum Development.

Costa, F. M., Jessor, R., Fortenberry, J. D., & Donovan, J. E. (1996). Psychosocial conventionality, health orientation, and contraceptive use in adolescence. *Journal of Adolescent Health, 18,* 404–416.

Costa, L., & Altekruse, M. (1994). Duty-to-warn guidelines for mental health counselors. *Journal of Counseling & Development, 72*(4), 346–350.

Cowley, C., & Tillman, F. (2001). Adolescent girls' attitudes toward pregnancy: The importance of asking what the boyfriend wants. *The Journal of Family Practice, 50* (7), 603–607.

Cranston, K. (1991). HIV education for gay, lesbian, and bisexual youth: Personal risk, personal power, and the community of conscience. *Journal of Homosexuality, 22*(3/4), 247–259.

Craven, R. G., Marsh, H. W., & Debus, R. L. (1991). Effects of internally focused feedback and attributional feedback on enhancement of academic self-concept. *Journal of Educational Psychology, 83,* 17–27.

Crawford, J. (2002). Obituary: The Bilingual Education Act, 1968–2002. Education Policy Studies Laboratory. Retrieved from *http://www.asu.edu/educ/epsl/LPRU/features/article2.htm* on Oct. 20, 2002.

Crawford, N. (October, 2002). New ways to stop bullying. *APA Monitor, 33* (9), 64.

Crits-Christoph, P., & Siqueland, L. (1996). Psychosocial treatment of drug abuse: Selected review and recommendations for national health care. *Archives of General Psychiatry, 53,* 749–756.

Cuban, L. (1989). At-risk students: What teachers and principals can do. *Educational Leadership, 45*(5), 29–33.

Culhane, D., Dejowski, E. F., Ibanez, J., et al. (1993). *Public shelter admission rates in Philadelphia and New York City: Working paper.* Washington, DC: Fannie Mae Office of Housing Research.

Cummings, C., & Haggerty, K. P. (1997). Raising healthy children. *Educational Leadership, 54*(8), 28–30.

Cunningham, C. E., Bremner, R., & Boyle, M. (1995). Large group community-based parenting programs for families of preschoolers at risk for disruptive behaviour disorders: Utilization, cost effectiveness, and outcome. *Journal of Child Psychology and Psychiatry, 36*(7), 1141–1159.

Cushing, L. S., & Kennedy, C. H. (1997). Academic effects of providing peer support in general education classrooms on students without disabilities. *Journal of Applied Behavior Analysis, 30,* 139–151.

D'Augelli, A. R. (1991). Gay men in college: Identity processes and adaptations. *Journal of College Student Development, 32,* 140–146.

D'Augelli, A. R., & Dark, L. J. (1994). Lesbian, gay and bisexual youths. In L. D. Eroh, J. H. Gentry, & P. Schlegel (Eds.), *Reason to hope: A psychosocial perspective on violence and youth.* Washington: APA, 177–196.

Dadds, M. R., Spence, S. H., Holland, D. E., Barrett, P. M., & Laurens, K. R. (1997). Prevention and early intervention for anxiety disorders: A controlled trial. *Journal of Consulting and Clinical Psychology, 65,* 627–635.

Daly III, E. J., Duhon, G. J., & Witt, J. C. (2002). Proactive approaches for identifying and treating children at risk for academic failure. In K. L. Lane, F. M. Gresham, & T. E. O'Shaughnessy (Eds.), *Interventions for children with or at risk for emotional and behavioral disorders* (pp. 18–32). Boston: Allyn & Bacon.

Darroch, J. E., Landry, D. J., & Oslak, S. (1999). Age differences between sexual partners in the United States. *Family Planning Perspectives, 31*(4),160–167.

Daunic, A. P., Smith, S. W., Robinson, T. R., Miller, M. D., & Landry, K. L. (2000). School-wide conflict resolution and peer mediation programs: Experiences in three middle schools. *Intervention in School and Clinic, 36*(2), 94–100.

Davalos, D. B., Chavez, E. L., & Guardiola, R. J. (1999). The effects of extracurricular activity, ethnic identification, and perception of school on student dropout rates. *Hispanic Journal of Behavioral Sciences, 21*(1), 61–77.

DaVanzo, J., & Rahman, M. O. (1993). *American families: Trends and policy issues.* Santa Monica, CA: RAND.

Davidson, N. (Ed.). (1990). *Cooperative learning in mathematics: A handbook for teachers.* Reading, MA: Addison-Wesley.

Davidson, N., & Worsham, P. (Eds.). (1992). *Enhancing thinking through cooperative learning.* New York: Teachers College Press.

Davis, L., Johnson, S., Miller-Cribbs, J., & Saunders, J. (2002). A brief report: Factors influencing African-American youth decisions to stay in school. *Journal of Adolescent Research, 17,* 3.

Davis, M., Robbins-Eshelman, E., & McKay, M. (1988). *The relaxation and stress reduction workbook* (3rd ed.). Oakland, CA: New Harbinger Publications, Inc.

Davis, S. (1989). Evening classes for at-risk kids cost only a little, but they help a lot. *American School Board Journal, 126,* 33.

Davis, T. E., & Osborn, C. J. (2000). *The solution-focused school counselor: Shaping professional practice.* Ann Arbor, MI: Edwards Brothers.

de Shazer, S. (1990). What is it about brief therapy that works? In J. K. Zeig & S. G. Gilligan (Eds.), *Brief therapy: Myths, methods, and metaphors* (pp. 90–99). New York: Brunner/Mazel.

Deater-Deckard, K., Dodge, K. A., Bates, J. E., & Pettit, G. S. (1998). Multiple risk factors in the development of externalizing behavior problems. *Development & Psychopathology, 10,* 469–493.

DeBaryshe, B. D., Patterson, G. R., & Capaldi, D. M. (1993). A performance model for academic achievement in early adolescent boys. *Developmental Psychology, 29,* 295–804.

Decker, S. H., & Van Winkle, B. (1996). *Life in the gang: Family, friends, and violence.* New York, NY: Cambridge University Press.

DeConcini, D. (1988). America's little red school house: How is it holding up? *American Psychologist, 43,* 115–117.

Deffenbacher, J. L., Lynch, R. S., Oetting, E. R., & Kemper, C. C. (1996). Anger reduction in early adolescents. *Journal of Counseling Psychology, 43*(2), 149–157.

Deffenbacher, J. L., McNamara, K., Stark, R. S., & Sabadell, P. M. (1990). A comparison of cognitive-behavioral and process oriented group counseling for general anger reduction. *Journal of Counseling Development, 69,* 167–172.

Devine, C., & Braithwaite, V. (1993). The survival role of children of alcoholics: Their measurement and validity. *Addiction, 88,* 69–78.

Devries, D., & Slavin, R. (1978). Teams-Games-Tournaments (TGT): Review of ten classroom experiments. *Journal of Research and Development in Education, 12,* 28–38.

Dewey, J. (1916/1944). *Democracy and education.* New York: Free Press.

Diaz Reyes v. United States, 770 F. Supp. 58 (D.P.R. 1991), *aff'd without op.,* 971 F.2d 744 (1st Cir.), *cert. denied,* 504 U.S. 957 (1992).

Dickerson, B. J. (1995). *African American single mothers: Understanding their lives and families.* Thousand Oaks, CA: Sage.

DiClemente, R., Wingood, G. M., Crosby, R., Sionean, C., Cobb, B. K., Harrington, K., Davies, S., Hook III, E., & Kim, M. (2001). Parental monitoring:

Association with adolescents' risk behaviors. *Pediatrics, 107,* 1363–1369.

Dielman, M. B., & Franklin, C. (1998). Brief solution-focused therapy with parents and adolescents with ADHD. *Social Work in Education, 20,* 261–268.

Dielman, T. E. (1994). School-based research on the prevention of adolescent alcohol use and misuse: Methodological issues and advances. *Journal of Research on Adolescence, 4,* 271–293.

Dielman, T. E., Butchart, A. T., Shope, J. T., & Miller, M. (1990–1991). *The International Journal of the Addictions, 25,* (7A & 8A), 855–880.

Diem, R., & Katims, D. S. (1991). Handicaps and at risk: Preparing teachers for a growing populace. *Intervention in School and Clinic, 26,* 272–275.

Diener, E., & Diener, C. (1996). Most people are happy. *Psychological Science, 7*(3), 181–189.

DiGangi, S. A., Maag, J. W., & Rutherford, R. B., Jr. (1991). Self-graphing of on-task behavior: Enhancing the reactive effects of self-monitoring on on-task behavior and academic performance. *Learning Disabilities Quarterly, 14,* 221–230.

Dishion, T., Capaldi, D., & Yoerger, K. (1999). Middle childhood antecedents to progression in male adolescent substance use: An ecological analysis of risk and protection. *Journal of Adolescent Research, 14,* 175–206.

Dishion, T. J., & Bullock, B. M. (2001). Parenting and adolescent problem behavior: An ecological analysis of the nurturance hypothesis. In J. G. Borkowski, S. L. Ramey, & M. Bristol-Power (Eds.), *Parenting in your child's world: Influences on academic, intellectual, and social–emotional development* (pp. 231–249). Hillsdale, NJ: Erlbaum.

Dishion, T. J., & Bullock, B. M. (2002). Parenting and adolescent problem behavior: An ecological analysis of the nurturance hypothesis. In J. G. Borkowski, & S. L. Ramey (Eds.), *Parenting and the child's world: Influences on academic, intellectual, and social-emotional development. Monographs in parenting* (pp. 231–249). Mahwah, NJ: Lawrence Erlbaum Associates.

Dishion, T. J., & Kavanagh, K. (2000). *Adolescent problem behavior: An intervention and assessment sourcebook for working with families in schools.* New York: Guilford.

Dishion, T. J., & Kavanagh, K. (2000). A multilevel approach to family-centered prevention in schools: Process and outcome. *Addictive Behaviors, 25,* 899–911.

Dishion, T. J., & Kavanagh, K. (2002). The Adolescent Transitions Program: A family-centered approach. In

J. B. Reid, J. J. Snyder, & G. R. Patterson (Eds.), *Antisocial behavior in children and adolescents: A developmental analysis and the Oregon Model for Intervention* (pp. 257–272). Washington, DC: American Psychological Association.

Dishion, T. J., & McMahon, R. J. (1998). Parental monitoring and the prevention of child and adolescent problem behavior: A conceptual and empirical formulation. *Clinical Child and Family Psychology Review, 1,* 61–75.

Dishion, T. J., Patterson, G. R., & Griesler, P. C. (1994). Peer adaptation in the development of antisocial behavior: A confluence model. In L. R. Huesmann (Ed.), *Aggressive behavior: Current perspectives* (pp. 61–95). New York: Plenum.

Dishion, T. J., & Stormshak, E. (2002). *An ecological approach to child clinical and counseling psychology.* Washington DC: American Psychological Association.

Dishion, T. J., Andrews, D. W., & Crosby, L. (1995). Antisocial boys and their friends in early adolescence: Relationship characteristics, quality, and interactional process. *Child Development, 66,* 139–151.

Dishion, T. J., Kavanagh, K., Schneiger, A., Nelson, S., & Kaufman, N. (2002). Preventing early adolescent substance use: A family-centered strategy for public middle school. In R. L. Spoth, K. Kavanagh, & T. J. Dishion (Eds.), *Universal family-centered prevention strategies: Current findings and critical issues for public health impact* [Special Issue]. *Prevention Science, 3,* 191–201.

Dishion, T. J., McCord, J., & Poulin, F. (1999). When interventions harm: Peer groups and problem behavior. *American Psychologist, 54,* 755–764.

Dittus, P. J., & Jaccard, J. (2000). Adolescents' perceptions of maternal disapproval of sex: Relationship to sexual outcomes. *Journal of Adolescent Health, 26*(4), 268–278.

Dixon, A. C., Schoonmaker, C. T., & Philliber, W. W. (2000). A journey toward womanhood: Effects of an afrocentric approach to pregnancy prevention among African-American adolescent females. *Adolescence, 35,* 425–429.

Dixon, W. A., Heppner, P. P., & Anderson, W. P. (1991). Problem solving appraisal, stress, hopelessness, and suicide ideation in a college population. *Journal of Counseling Psychology, 38,* 55–61.

Dodge, K. A. (1992). Youth violence: Who? what? where? when? how? WHY? *Tennessee Teacher,* Oct. 9–13.

Dodge, K. A., & Price, J. M. (1994). On the relation between social information processing and socially competent behavior in early school-aged children. *Child Development, 65,* 1385–1397.

Dodge, K. A., Price, J. M., Bachorowski, J., & Newman, J. P. (1990). Hostile attributional biases in severely aggressive adolescents. *Journal of Abnormal Psychology, 99,* 385–392.

Dodge, K. A., & Somberg, D. R. (1987). Hostile attributional biases among aggressive boys are exacerbated under conditions of threats to self. *Child Development, 58,* 213–224.

Dolbeare, C. N. (1991). *Out of reach: Why everyday people can't find affordable housing.* Washington, DC: Low Income Housing Information Service.

Doll, B., & Lyon, M. (1998). Risk and resilience: Implications for the delivery of education mental health services in the schools. *School Psychology Review, 27,* 348–363.

Donmoyer, R., & Kos, R. (1993). *At-risk students: Portraits, policies, programs, and practices.* Albany, NY: State University of New York Press.

Donovan, P. (1993). *Testing positive: Sexually transmitted disease and the public health response.* New York: The Alan Guttmacher Institute.

Drazen, S. M. (1994, August). *Factors influencing student achievement from early to mid-adolescence.* Paper presented at the meeting of the American Psychological Association, Los Angeles.

Dreikurs, R. (1964). *Children: The challenge.* New York: Hawthorne.

Dreikurs, R. (1967). *Psychology in the classroom.* New York: Harper & Row.

Driver, R., Asoko, H., Leach, J., Mortimer, E., & Scott, P. (1994). Constructing scientific knowledge in the classroom. *Education Researcher, 23*(7), 5–12.

Drug Strategies (2003). *Treating teens: A guide to adolescent drug programs.* Washington, DC: Author.

Dryfoos, J. G. (1990). *Adolescents at risk: Prevalence and prevention.* New York: Oxford University Press.

Dryfoos, J. G. (1994). *Full-service schools: A revolution in health and social services for children, youth, and families.* San Francisco: Jossey-Bass.

Duany, L., & Pitmann, K. (1990). *Latino youths at a crossroads: Adolescent pregnancy prevention clearinghouse report.* Washington, DC: Children's Defense Fund.

Dubow, E., Edwards, S., & Ippolito, M. (1997). Life stressors, neighborhood disadvantage, and resources: A focus on inner-city children's adjustment. *Journal of Clinical Child Psychology, 26,* 130–144.

Duffy, G., Roehler, L., & Herrmann, B. A. (1988). Modeling mental processes helps poor readers become strategic readers. *Reading Teacher, 41,* 762–767.

DuPaul, G. J., & Eckert, T. L. (1994). The effects of social skills curricula: Now you see them, now you don't. *School Psychology Quarterly, 9*(2), 113–132.

DuRant, R., et al. (1997). Tobacco and alcohol use behaviors portrayed in music videos: A content analysis. *American Journal of Public Health, 8,* 1131–1135.

Durlak, J. A. (1995). *School-based prevention programs for children and adolescents.* Thousand Oaks, CA: Sage.

Durlak, J. A., Fuhrman, T., & Lampman, C. (1991). Effectiveness of cognitive-behavior therapy for maladapting children: A meta-analysis. *Psychological Bulletin, 110,* 204–214.

Durrant, M. (1995). *Creative strategies for school problems: Solutions for psychologists and teachers.* New York: W. W. Norton.

Duvall, E. M., & Miller, B. C. (1985). *Marriage and family development* (6th ed.). New York: Harper & Row.

Dwyer, K., Osher, D., & Warger, C. (1998). *Early warning, timely response: A guide to safe schools.* Washington, DC: U.S. Department of Education.

Dyk, P. H. (1993). Anatomy, physiology, and gender issues in adolescence. In T. P. Gullotta, G. R. Adams, & R. Montemayor (Eds.), *Adolescent sexuality: Advances in adolescent development: Volume 5* (pp. 35–56). Newbury Park, CA: Sage.

Dynarski, M., & Gleason, P. (2002). How can we help? What we have learned from recent federal dropout prevention evaluations. *Journal of Education for Students Placed At Risk, 7*(1), 43–69.

D'Zurilla, J. (1986). *Problem-solving therapy: A social competence approach to clinical intervention.* New York: Springer.

Ebb, N. (1994). *Child care tradeoffs: States make painful choices.* Washington, DC: Children's Defense Fund.

Edelman, M. W. (1987). *Families in peril: An agenda for social change.* Cambridge, MA: Harvard University Press.

Edelsky, C. (1991). Authentic reading/writing versus reading/writing exercises. In K. S. Goodman, L. B. Bird, & Y. M. Goodman (Eds.), *The whole language catalog* (p. 72). Santa Rosa, CA: American School Publishers.

Edelsky, C., Altwerger, B., & Flores, B. (1991). *Whole language: What's the difference?* Portsmouth, NH: Heinemann.

Egley, A. Jr., & Arjunan, M. (2002). Highlights of the 2000 National Youth Gang Survey: Fact Sheet. U.S. Dept. of Justice, Office of Justice Programs, Office of Juvenile Justice and Delinquency Prevention. Washington, DC: U.S. Department of Justice.

Ehly, S. (1986). *Peer tutoring: A guide for school psychologists.* Washington, DC: National Association of School Psychologists.

Eighth Biennial California Student Survey, 1999–2000. *Preliminary Findings: Alcohol and Other Drug Use: Grades 7, 9, and 11.* Los Alamitos, CA: WestEd.

Eisenberg, N., Fabes, R. A., Nyman, M., Bernzweig, J., & Piñuelas, A. (1994). The relations of emotionality and regulation to children's anger-related reactions. *Child Development, 65,* 109–128.

Ekstrom, R. B., Goertz, M. E., Pollack, J. M., & Rock, D. A. (1986). Who drops out of high school and why? Findings from a national study. *Teacher's College Record, 87,* 356–373.

Elder, G. H., Jr., Conger, R. D., Foster, E. M., & Ardelt, M. K. (1992). Families under economic pressure. *Journal of Family Issues, 13,* 5–37.

Elder, J. P., Wildey, M., de Moor, C., Sallis, J., Eckhardt, L., Edwards, C., Erickson, A., Golbeck, A., Hovell, M., Johnston, D., Levitz, M., Molgaard, C., Young, R., Vito, D., & Woodruff, S. (1993). The long-term prevention of tobacco use among junior high school students: Classroom and telephone interviews. *American Journal of Public Health, 83*(9), 1230–1244.

Ellenbogen, S., & Chamberland, C. (1997). The peer relations of dropouts: A comparative study of at-risk and not at-risk youths. *Journal of Adolescence, 20,* 355–367.

Ellickson, P. L., Bell, R. M., & McGuigan, K. (1993). Preventing adolescent drug use: Long-term results of a junior high program. *American Journal of Public Health, 83,* 856–861.

Ellis, A. (1962). *Reason and emotion in psychotherapy.* New York: Stuart.

Ellis, A. (1985). *Overcoming resistance: Rational-emotive therapy with difficult clients.* New York: Springer.

Ellis, A. (1996). *Better, deeper, and more enduring brief therapy: The rational emotive behavior therapy approach.* New York: Brunner/Mazel.

Elmore, R., Peterson, P. L., & McCarthy, S. J. (1996). *Restructuring in the classroom: Teaching, learning, and school organization.* San Francisco: Jossey-Bass.

Elmquist, D. L. (1991). School-based alcohol and other drug prevention programs: Guidelines for the special educator. *Intervention in School and Clinic, 27*(1), 10–19.

Entwisle, D., & Alexander, K. (1992). Summer setback: Race, poverty, school composition, and mathmatics achievement in the first two years of school. *American Sociological Review, 57,* 72–84.

Epkins, C. C. (2000). Cognitive specificity in internalizing and externalizing problems in community and clinic-referred children. *Journal of Clinical Child Psychology, 29,* 199–208.

Esbensen, F. (2000). Preventing adolescent gang involvement. Youth Gang Series Bulletin. Washington DC: U.S. Department of Justice, *Bulletin of the Office of Justice Programs, Office of Juvenile Justice and Delinquency Prevention.*

Espelage, D., & Swearer, S. (Eds.). (in press). *A social ecological view of bullying and victimization.* Mahwah, NJ: Erlbaum.

Evans, W. P., Marte, R., Betts, S., & Silliman, B. (2001). Adolescent suicide risk and peer related violent behaviors and victimization. *Journal of Interpersonal Violence, 16*(12), 1330–1348.

Fad, K. S. (1990). The fast track to success: Social-behavioral skills. *Intervention in School and Clinic, 26*(1), 39–43.

Falco, K. (1991). *Psychotherapy with lesbian clients.* New York: Brunner/Mazel, Inc.

Falco, M. (1988, June). *Preventing abuse of drugs, alcohol, and tobacco by adolescents.* Working paper, Carnegie Council on Adolescent Development, New York.

Falco, M. (1992). *The making of a drug-free America: Programs that work.* New York: Times Books.

Fantuzzo, J. W., Davis, G. Y., & Ginsburg, M. D. (1995). Effects of parent involvement in isolation or in combination with peer tutoring on student self-concept and mathematics achievement. *Journal of Educational Psychology, 87,* 272–281.

Fashola, O. S., & Slavin, R. E. (1998). Effective dropout prevention and college attendance programs for students placed at risk. *Journal of Education for Students Placed at Risk, 3*(2), 159–183.

Fassinger, R. E. (2000). Gender and sexuality in human development: Implications for prevention and advocacy in counseling psychology. In S. D. Brown & R. W. Lent (Eds.), *Handbook of counseling psychology* (3rd ed., pp. 346–378). New York: John Wiley & Sons, Inc.

Federal Bureau of Investigation. (2000). Hate crime statistics. Retrieved from *http://www.fbi.gov/ucr/ucr. htm* on September 13, 2002.

Federal Rule of Evidence 601

Federal Rule of Evidence 701

Federal Rule of Evidence 702

Federal Rule of Evidence 703

Feijoo, A. N. (1999). *Teenage pregnancy, the case for prevention: An updated analysis of recent trends & federal expenditures associated with teenage pregnancy.* Washington, DC: Advocates for Youth.

Felner, R. D., Brand, S., Adan, A. M., Mullhall, P. F., Flowers, N., Sartain, B., & DuBois, D. L. (1993). Restructuring the ecology of the school as an approach to prevention during school transitions: Longitudinal follow-ups and extensions of the School Transitional Environment Project (STEP). *Prevention and Human Services, 10,* 103–136.

Fenstermacher, G. (1986). Philosophy of research on teaching: Three aspects. In M. Wittrock (Ed.), *Handbook of research on teaching* (3rd ed., pp. 37–49). New York: Macmillan.

Ferguson, E. D. (2001). Adler and Dreikurs: Cognitive-social dynamic innovators. *The Journal of Individual Psychology, 57*(4), 324–341.

Ferguson, R. F. (1991). Paying for public education: New evidence on how and why money matters. *Harvard Journal on Legislation, 28,* 465–498.

Fergusson, D. M., & Lynskey, M. T. (1995). Childhood circumstances, adolescent adjustment, and suicide attempts in a New Zealand birth cohort. *Journal of American Child and Adolescent Psychiatry, 34*(5), 612–621.

Fergusson, D. M., & Woodward, L. J. (2002). Mental health, educational, and social role outcomes of adolescents with depression. *Archives of General Psychiatry, 59*(3), 225–231.

Fernandez v. Baruch, 52 N.J. 127, 244 A2d 109 (1968).

Fincham, F. D. (1994). Understanding the association between marital conflict and child adjustment: Overview. *Journal of Family Psychology, 8*(2), 123–127.

Fincham, F. D., & Osborn, L. (1993). Marital conflict and children: Retrospect and prospect. *Clinical Psychology Review, 13,* 75–88.

Fincham, F. D., Grych, J. H., & Osborn, L. N. (1994). Does marital conflict cause child maladjustment? Directions and challenges for longitudinal research. *Journal of Family Psychology, 8,* 128–140.

Finkelhor, D., et al. (2000). *Online victimization: A report on the nation's youth.* Washington, DC: National Center for Missing and Exploited Children.

Flannery, D. J., Williams, L. L., & Vazsonyi, A. T. (1999). Who are they with and what are they doing? Delinquent behavior, substance use, and early adolescents' after school time. *American Journal of Orthopsychiatry, 69,* 247–253.

Fleming, M. (1990). *Conducting support groups for students affected by chemical dependence: A guide for educators and other professionals.* Minneapolis, MN: Johnson Institute.

Ford, C. A., Thomsen, S. L., & Compton, B. (2001). Adolescents' interpretations of conditional confidentiality assurances. *Journal of Adolescent Health, 29,* 156–159.

Foreman, T. & Bernet, W. (2000). A misunderstanding regarding the duty to report suspected abuse. *Child Maltreatment. Journal of the American Professional Society on the Abuse of Children, 5,* 190–196.

Forness, S. R., Serna, L. A., Neilsen, E., Lambros, K., Hale, M. J., & Kavale, K. A. (2000). A model for early detection and primary prevention of emotional or behavioral disorders. *Education and Treatment of Children, 23*(3), 325–345.

Forrest, J. D., & Samara, R. (1996). Impact of publicly funded contraceptive services on unintended pregnancies and implications for Medicaid expenditures. *Family Planning Perspectives, 28,* 188–195.

Fraser, B. J. (1994). Research on classroom and school climate. In D. Gabel (Ed.), *Handbook of research on science teaching and learning.* New York: Macmillan.

Fraser, M. W. (1996). Aggressive behavior in childhood and early adolescence: An ecological-developmental perspective on youth violence. *Social Work, 41*(4), 347–356.

Freeman, A., & Dolan, M. (2001). Revisiting Prochaska and DiClemente's stages of change theory: An expansion and specification to aid in treatment planning and outcome evaluation. *Cognitive and Behavioral Practice, 8,* 224–234.

Freeman, B. (1995). Power motivation and youth: An analysis of troubled students and student leaders. *Journal of Counseling and Development, 73,* 661–671.

French, S. A., Story, M., Remafedi, G., Resnick, M. D., & Blum, R. W. (1996). Sexual orientation and prevalence of body dissatisfaction and eating disordered behaviors: A population-based study of adolescents. *International Journal of Eating Disorders, 19*(2), 19–26.

Frey, H. (1980). Improving the performance of poor readers through autogenic relaxation training. *Reading Teacher, 33,* 928–932.

Friedman, A. S., Glickman, N. W., & Morrissey, M. R. (1987a). Prediction to successful treatment outcome by client characteristics and retention in treatment in adolescent drug treatment programs: A large-scale cross validation study. *Journal of Drug Education, 16,* 149–165.

Friedman, A. S., Utada, A., & Glickman, N. W. (1987b). Outcome for court-referred drug abusing male adolescents of an alternative activity treatment program in a vocational high school setting. *Journal of Nervous and Mental Disease, 174,* 680–688.

Fry, D. P. (1993). The intergenerational transmission of disciplinary practices and approaches to conflict. *Human Organization, 52,* 176–185.

Fuller, B., Kagen, S. L., Loeb, S., Carroll, J., McCarthy, J., Kreicher, G., Carrol, B., Cook, G., Chang, Y., & Sprachman, S. (2002). *New lives for poor families? Mothers and young children move through welfare reform. The growing up in poverty project-wave 2 findings California, Connecticut, and Florida: Technical Report.* Retrieved from *http://wwwgse.berkeley.edu/research/PACE/gup_tech_rpt.pdf* on August 10, 2002.

Gangi, R., Schiraldi, V., & Ziedenberg, J. (1998). *New York state of mind: Higher education vs. prison funding in the empire state, 1988–1998.* Washington, DC: The Justice Policy Institute.

Garbarino, J. (1994). *Raising children in a socially toxic environment.* San Francisco, CA: Jossey-Bass.

Garbarino, J. (1998). The stress of being a poor child in America. *Child and Adolescent Psychiatric Clinics of North America, 7*(1), 105–119.

Garber, J., Deale, S., & Parke, C. (1986, November). *The coping with depression pamphlet revised for adolescents: Comprehensibility and acceptability.* Paper presented at the annual meeting of the Association for the Advancement of Behavior Therapy, Chicago.

Gardner, S. E., Green, P. F., & Marcus, C. (Eds.). (1994). *Signs of effectiveness II: Preventing alcohol, tobacco, and other drug use: A risk factor/resiliency-based approach.* Washington, DC: U.S. Government Printing Office.

Gardner, W., & Herman, J. (1991). Adolescents: AIDS risk taking: A rational choice perspective. In W. Gardner, S. Mielstein, & B. Wilcox (Eds.), *Adolescents in the AIDS epidemic.* San Francisco: Jossey-Bass.

Garfield, S. L. (1994). Research on client variables in psychotherapy. In A. E. Bergin & S. L. Garfield (Eds.), *Handbook of psychotherapy and behavior change* (4th ed., pp. 190–228). New York: Wiley.

Garland, A. F., & Zigler, E. (1993). Adolescent suicide prevention: Current research and social policy implications. *American Psychologist, 43*(2), 169–182.

Garrison, C., Addy, C., Jackson, K., et al. (1992). Major depressive disorder and dysthymia in young adolescents. *American Journal of Epidemiology, 135,* 792–802.

Gaustad, J. (1992). *Tutoring for at-risk students.* Oregon School Study Council Bulletin, 36(3), 1–74. (ERIC Document Reproduction Service No. ED353642)

Gazda, G. M. (1989). *Group counseling.* Boston: Allyn and Bacon.

Gazda, G. M., Asbury, F. R., Balzer, F. J., Childers, W. C., Phelps, R. E., & Walters, R. P. (1999). *Human relations development: A manual for educators* (6th ed.). Boston: Allyn & Bacon.

Gershoff, E. T. (2002). Corporal punishment by parents and associated child behaviors and experiences: A meta-analytic and theoretical review. *Psychological Bulletin, 128,* 539–579.

Gersten, R., & Carnine, D. (1984). Direct instruction mathematics: A longitudinal evaluation of low-income elementary school students. *Elementary School Journal, 84,* 395–407.

Gersten, R., & Keating, T. (1987). Long-term benefits from direct instruction. *Educational Leadership, 44*(6), 28–31.

Gest, S., Neemann, J., Hubbard, J., Masten, A., & Tellegen, A. (1993). Parenting quality, adversity, and conduct problems in adolescence: Testing process-oriented models of resilience. *Development and Psychopathology, 5,* 663–682.

Gibbs, J. T., & Huang, L. N. (Eds.). (1991). *Children of color: Psychological interventions with minority youth.* San Francisco: Jossey-Bass.

Gibson, P. (1989). Gay male and lesbian youth suicide. *Report of the secretary's task force on youth suicide, Vol 3: Prevention and interventions in youth suicide.* Rockville, MD: U.S. Department of Health and Human Services.

Gilboy, S. F. (2003). *Prevention and amelioration of depression: A school based prevention model.* Unpublished doctoral dissertation, Arizona State University, Tempe, Arizona.

Gilboy, S. F., McWhirter, J. J., & Wallace, R. (2002). *SOAR: Students' optimistic attribution and resiliency program: A depression prevention and amelioration program.* Unpublished manuscript. Arizona State University.

Gillham, J. E., Reivich, K. J., Jaycox, L. H., & Seligman, M. E. P. (1995). Prevention of depressive symptoms in schoolchildren: Two-year follow-up. *Psychological Science, 6,* 343–351.

Gingerich, W. J. & Wabeke, T. (2001). A solution-focused approach to mental health intervention in school settings. *Children and Schools, 23,* 33–47.

Gingras, R. C., & Careaga, R. C. (1989). Limited English proficient students at risk: Issues and prevention strategies. *New Focus: National Clearinghouse for Bilingual Education, 10,* 1–11.

Giroux, H. A. (1989). Critical literacy and students' experience: Donald Graves' approach to literacy. *Language Arts, 64,* 175–181.

Glantz, K. (1983). The use of relaxation exercises in the treatment of reading disability. *Journal of Nervous and Mental Disease, 171*(12), 749–752.

Glasser, W. (1965). *Reality therapy: A new approach to psychiatry.* New York: Harper and Row.

Glasser, W. (1976). *Positive addiction.* New York: Harper and Row.

Glasser, W. (1984). Reality therapy. In R. J. Corsini (Ed.), *Current psychotherapies* (3rd ed., pp. 320–353). Itasca, IL: F. E. Peacock Publishers, Inc.

Glasser, W. (1990). The quality school. *Phi Delta Kappan, 72,* 425–435.

Glasser, W. (1998). *Choice theory: A new psychology of personal freedom.* New York: HarperCollins.

Glasser, W. (2001). *Counseling with choice theory: The new reality therapy.* New York: HarperCollins.

Glasser, W. (2002). *Unhappy teenagers: A way for parents and teachers to reach them.* New York: HarperCollins.

Gloria, A., & Robinson-Kurprius, S. (2000). I can't live without it: Adolescent substance abuse from a cultural and contextual framework. In D. Capuzzi & D. Gross, (Eds.), *Youth at risk: A prevention resource for counselors, teachers, and parents* (3rd ed., pp. 409–440). Alexandria, VA: ACA Press.

Glosoff, H. L., Herlihy, B., Spence, E. B. (2000). Privileged communication in the counselor-client relationship. *Journal of Counseling & Development, 78,* 454–462.

Glynn, T., Crooks, T., Bethune, N., Ballard, K., & Smith, J. (1992). Reading Recovery in context: Implementation and outcome. *Educational Psychology, 12*(3 & 4), 249–261.

Goetting, A. (1995). *Homicide in families and other special populations.* New York: Springer Publishing Co.

Goldfield, M. (1997). Race and labor organization in the United States. *Monthly Review, 49*(3), 80–97.

Goldhaber, D. (2002). *What might go wrong with the accountability measures of the "No Child Left Behind Act?"* The Urban Institute. Retrieved from *http://www.edexcellence.net/NCLBconference/* on May 29, 2002.

Goldstein, A., Sprafkin, R., Gershaw, N. J., & Klein, P. (1980). *Skill streaming the adolescent: A structured learning approach to teaching prosocial behavior.* Champaign, IL: Research Press.

Goldstein, A. P. (1996). *The psychology of vandalism.* New York: Plenum Press.

Goldstein, A. P., Harootunian, B., & Conoley, J. C. (1994). *Student aggression: Prevention, management, and replacement training.* New York: Guilford Press.

Golub, A., & Johnson, B. D. (2001). *The rise of marijuana as the drug of choice among youthful adult arrestees.* National Institute of Justice: Research in Brief. Washington, DC: US Department of Justice.

Good, T. L., & Brophy, J. E. (1994). *Looking into classrooms* (6th ed.). New York: HarperCollins Publishing.

Good, T. L., & Weinstein, R. S. (1986). Schools make a difference: Evidence, criticisms, and new directions. *American Psychologist, 41,* 1090–1097.

Goodlad, J. I. (1994). *Educational renewal: Better teachers, better schools.* San Francisco: Jossey-Bass.

Goodman, S. H., Adamson, L. B., Riniti, J., & Cole, S. (1994). Mothers' expressed attitudes: Associations with maternal depression and children's self-esteem and psychopathology. *Journal of the American Academy of Child and Adolescent Psychiatry, 33,* 1265–1274.

Gordon, T. (1970). *Parent effectiveness training.* New York: Wyden.

Gordon, T. (1974). *Teacher effectiveness training.* New York: Wyden.

Gordon, T. (1977). *Leader effectiveness training.* New York: Putnam.

Gordon, T. (1989). *Teaching children self-discipline. . .at home and at school: New ways for parents and teachers to build self-control, self-esteem, and self-reliance.* New York: Random House.

Gormley, W. T. (1995). *Everybody's children: Child care as a public problem.* Washington, DC: Brookings Institution.

Gould, M. S., & Kramer, R. A. (2001). Youth suicide prevention. *Suicide and Life Threatening Behavior, 31* (Suppl.), 6–31.

Gould, M. S., & Shaffer, D. (1986). The impact of suicide in television movies: Evidence of imitation. *New England Journal of Medicine, 315,* 690–694.

Goyette-Ewing, M. (2000). Children's after school arrangements: A study of self-care and developmental outcomes. *Journal of Prevention & Intervention in the Community, 20,* 55–67.

Gragg, K. M., McWhirter, B. T., & Kerewsky, S. D. (2004). Counseling Prevention from an ecological framework. In R. K. Conyne & E. P. Cook (Eds.). *Ecological counseling: An innovative approach to conceptualizing person-environment interaction:* Alexandria, VA: ACA Press.

Gragg, K. M., & McWhirter, E. H. (2003). Applying social cognitive career theory to the empowerment of battered women. *Journal of Counseling & Development.*

Grant, G. (1982). The elements of a strong positive ethos. *National Association of Secondary School Principals Bulletin, 66*(452), 84–90.

Green, R., Waters Boots, K., & Tumlin, C. (1999). *The cost of protecting vulnerable children.* The Urban Institute. Retrieved from *www.urban.org* on June 8, 2002.

Greenberg, B. S., Siemicki, M., Dorfman, S., et al. (1993). Sex content in R-rated films viewed by adolescents. In B. S. Greenberg, J. D. Brown, & N. L. Buerkel-Rothfuss (Eds.), *Media, sex and the adolescent.* Cresskill, NJ: Hampton Press.

Greenwood, C. R. (1999). *Costs and benefits of early childhood intervention.* Office of Juvenile Justice and Delinquency Prevention, No. 94. Washington, DC: U.S. Department of Justice.

Greenwood, C. R., Carta, J. J., & Maheady, L. (1991). Peer tutoring programs in the regular classroom. In G. Stoner, M. R. Shinn, & H. M. Walker (Eds.), *Interventions for achievement and behavior problems* (pp. 179–200). Washington, DC: National Association of School Psychologists.

Greenwood, P. W. (1994). What works with juvenile offenders: A synthesis of the literature and experience. *Federal Probation, 58*(4), 63–67.

Grossman, J. A., & Kruesi, M. (2000). Innovative approaches to youth suicide prevention: An update of issues and research findings. In R. Marris, S. Canetto, J. McIntosh, & M. Silverman (Eds.), *Review of suicidology, 2000* (pp. 170–201). New York: The Guilford Press.

Grossman, J., Hirsch, J., Goldenberg, D., & Libby, S. (1995). Strategies for school-based response to loss: Proactive training and postvention consultation. *Crisis, 16*(1), 18–26.

Grubb, W. N. (1999). *Learning and earning in the middle: The economic benefits of sub-baccalaureate education.* New York: Community College Research Center, Columbia University. Retrieved from *http://www.tc.columbia.edu/~iee/ccrc/papers/grubb1.pdf* on April 28, 2002.

Grunbaum, J. A., Kann, L., Kinchen, S. A., Williams, B., Ross, J. B., Lowry, R., & Kolbe, L. (2002). *Youth risk behavior surveillance survey, United States, 2001.* National Center for Chronic Disease Prevention and Health Promotion, Division of Adolescent and School Health. Retrieved from *http://www.cdc.gov/mmwr/preview/mmwrhtml/ss5104a1.htm* on June 28, 2002 / 51(SS04), 1–64.

Gueron, J. M., & Pauly, E. (1991). *From welfare to work.* New York: Russell Sage Foundation.

Guetzloe, E. C. (1991). *Depression and potential suicide: Special education students at risk.* Reston, VA: The Council for Exceptional Children.

Guiterrez, P., Osman, A., Kopper, B. A., & Barrios, F. X. (2000). Why young people do not kill themselves: The reasons for living inventory for adolescents. *Journal of Clinical Child Psychology, 29,* 177–187.

Guy, S. M., Smith, G. M., & Bentler, P. M. (1993). Adolescent socialization and use of licit and illicit substances: Impact on adult health. *Psychology and Health, 8*(6), 463–487.

Guy, S. M., Smith, G. M., & Bentler, P. M. (1994). The influence of adolescent substance use and socialization on deviant behavior in young adulthood. *Criminal Justice and Behavior, 21*(2), 236–255.

Gysbers, N. C., & Henderson, P. (2000). *Developing and managing your school guidance program* (3rd ed.). Alexandria, VA: American Counseling Association.

Gysbers, N. C., & Henderson, P. (2001). Comprehensive guidance and counseling programs: A rich history and a rich future. *Professional School Counseling, 4*(4), 246–256.

H.L. v. Matheson, 450 U.S. 398 (1981).

Haberman, M. (1993). In M. J. O'Hair & S. Odell (Eds.), *Diversity and teaching: Teacher Education Yearbook I.* Orlando, FL: Harcourt Brace Jovanovich.

Hacker, A. (1992). *Two nations: Black, white, separate and unequal.* New York: Scribner.

Haffner, D. (1994). *Sexuality education and contraceptive instruction in U.S. schools.* Paper prepared for the Committee on Unintended Pregnancy. Washington, DC: Institute of Medicine.

Haggerty, R. J., Sherrod, L. R., Garmezy, N., & Rutter, M. (Eds.). (1994). *Stress, risk, resilience in children and adolescents: Processes, mechanisms, and interventions.* New York: Cambridge University Press.

Hains, A. A., & Ellmann, S. W. (1994). Stress inoculation training as a preventative intervention for high school youths. *Journal of Cognitive Psychotherapy, 8*(3), 219–232.

Haley, J. (1976). *Problem-solving therapy.* San Francisco: Jossey-Bass.

Haley, J. (1984). *Ordeal therapy.* San Francisco: Jossey-Bass.

Haley, J. (1991). *Problem-solving therapy.* San Francisco: Jossey-Bass.

Hambright, J. E. (1988). *Effects of perceived life options on female adolescent sexual responsibility: A test of a conceptual model.* Ph.D. dissertation, Arizona State University, Tempe.

Hamburg, D. A. (1994). *Today's children: Creating a future for a generation in crisis.* New York: Time Books.

Hamburg, D. A. (1995). *A developmental strategy to prevent lifelong damage*. New York: Carnegie Corporation of New York.

Hammer, C. J. (1993) *Youth violence: Gangs on main street, USA*. Philadelphia: PEW Charitable Trust.

Hammond, W. R., & Yung, B. R. (1994). *African Americans*. In L. D. Eron, J. H. Gentry, & P. Schlegel (Eds.), *Reason to hope: A psychosocial perspective on violence & youth*. Washington: APA, 105–118.

Hanna, F. J., Hanna, C. A., & Keys, S. G. (1999). Fifty strategies for counseling defiant aggressive adolescents: Reaching, accepting, and relating. *Journal of Counseling & Development, 77*, 395–404.

Hanson, M., & Peterson, D. S. (1993). *How to conduct a school recovery support group*. Portland, ME: J. Weston Walch.

Hara, P. F., Schma, W. G., & Rosenthal, J. T. A. (1999). Therapeutic jurisprudence and the drug treatment court movement: Revolutionizing the criminal justice system's response to drug abuse and crime in America. *Notre Dame Law Review, 74*(2), 439–537.

Harding, A. K., Gray, L. A., & Neal, M. (1993). Confidentiality limits with clients who have HIV: A review of ethical and legal guidelines and professional policies. *Journal of Counseling and Development, 71*, 297–305.

Harlow, L. L., Newcomb, M. D., & Bentler, P. M. (1986). Depression, self-derogation, substance use, and suicide ideation: Lack of purpose in life as a mediational factor. *Journal of Clinical Psychology, 42*(1), 5–21.

Harris, S. M. (1995). Psychosocial development and black male masculinity: Implications for counseling economically disadvantaged African American male adolescents. *Journal of Counseling and Development, 73*, 279–287.

Harris, S., & Harris, L. B. (Eds.). (1986). *The teacher's almanac*. New York: Facts on File.

Harter, S. (1985). *Manual for the Self-Perception Profile for Children* (revision of the *Perceived Competence Scale for Children)*. Denver, CO: University of Denver.

Harter, S. (1990). Causes, correlates and the functional role of global self-worth: A life-span perspective. In R. Sternberg & J. Kolligian (Eds.), *Competence considered* (pp. 67–97). New Haven, CT: Yale University Press.

Haveman, R., & Wolfe, B. (1994). *Succeeding generations* New York: Russell Sage Foundation.

Hawkins, J. D., Catalano, R. F., Kosterman, R., Abbott, R., & Hill, R. (1999). Preventing adolescent health-risk behaviors by strengthening protection during childhood. *Archives of Pediatric Adolescent Medicine, 153*, 226–234.

Hawkins, J. D., Catalano, R. F., & Miller, J. Y. (1992). Risk and protective factors for alcohol and other drug problems in adolescence and early adulthood: Implications for substance abuse prevention. *Psychological Bulletin, 112*(1), 64–105.

Hawryluk, M. K., & Smallwood, D. L. (1986). Assessing and addressing consultee variables in school-based behavioral consultation. *School Psychology Review, 15*, 519–528.

Hazler, R., Hoover, J., & Oliver, R. (1992). What kids say about bullying. *The Executive Educator, 14*, 20–22.

Hechinger, F. (1992). *Fateful choices: Healthy youth for the 21st century*. New York: Carnegie Corporation of New York.

Henggeler, S. W. (1999). Multisystemic treatment of serious clinical problems in children and adolescents. *Clinician's Research Digest, 21*, 1–2.

Henry, D. B., Tolan, P. H., & Gorman-Smith, D. (2001). Longitudinal family and peer group effects on violent and non-violent delinquency. *Journal of Child Clinical Psychology, 16*, 203–220.

Henshaw, S. K. (1998a). Abortion incidence in the United States, 1995–1996. *Family Planning Perspectives, 30*, 263–270.

Henshaw, S. K. (1998b). Unintended pregnancy in the United States. *Family Planning Perspectives, 30*, 24–29 & 46, Table 1.

Henshaw, S. K. (1992). Abortion trends in 1987 and 1988: Age and race. *Family Planning Perspectives, 24*, 85–86.

Herek, G. M., Gillis, J. R., Cogan, J. C., & Glunt, E. K. (1997). Hate crime victimization among lesbian, gay, and bisexual adults. *Journal of Interpersonal Violence, 12*, 195–215.

Herring, R. D. (1994). Substance use among Native American Indian youth: A selected review of causality. *Journal of Counseling & Development, 72* (July/August 1994), 578–584.

Herrmann, D. S., & McWhirter, J. J. (1997). Refusal and resistance skills for children and adolescents: A selected review. *Journal of Counseling and Development*.

Herrmann, D. S., & McWhirter, J. J. (2000). *SCARE: Student created aggression replacement education* (2nd ed.). Trainer's manual and student workbook. Dubuque, IA: Kendall/Hunt.

Herrmann, D. S., & McWhirter, J. J. (2001). *SCARE: Student created aggression replacement education*. Dubuque, IA: Kendall/Hunt.

Herrmann, D. S., McWhirter, J. J., & Sipsas-Herrmann, A. (1997). The relationship between dimensional self-concept and juvenile gang involvement: A focused examination. Unpublished manuscript: Arizona State University.

Hess, R. S. (2000). Dropping out among Mexican-American youth: Reviewing the literature through an ecological perspective. *Journal of Education for Students Placed at Risk, 5*(3), 267–289.

Hewlett, S. A. (1991). *When the bough breaks: The cost of neglecting our children.* New York: HarperCollins.

Hilton, J., Desrochers, S., & Devall, E. L. (2001). Comparison of role demands, relationships, and child functioning in single-mother, single father, and intact families. *Journal of Divorce & Remarriage, 35*(1–2), 29–56.

HIV Epidemiology Program. (1996, February). Young Men's Survey: Los Angeles, August 1994–January 1996. Paper presented to Los Angeles County Adolescent HIV Consortium, Los Angeles, CA.

Hockaday, C., Crase, S. J., Shelley, M. C., & Stockdale, D. F. (2000). A prospective study of adolescent pregnancy. *Journal of Adolescence, 23,* 423–438.

Hofferth, S. L. (1987). Social and economic consequences of teenage childbearing. In S. L. Hofferth & C. D. Hayes (Eds.), *Risking the future: Adolescent sexuality, pregnancy, and childbearing, Vol. II.* Washington, DC: National Academy Press.

Hoffman, E. (1994). *The drive for self: Alfred Adler and the founding of individual psychology.* Reading, MA: Addison-Wesley.

Holinger, P. C., Offer, D., Barter, J. T., & Bell, C. C. (1994). *Suicide and homicide among adolescents.* New York: Guilford Press.

Holloman, F. W. (1993). Estimates of the population of the United States by age, sex, and race. U.S. Bureau of the Census, *Current population reports,* Series P-25, No. 1095.

Holmes, G. R. (1995). *Helping teenagers into adulthood: A guide for the next generation.* Westport, CT: Praeger/Greenwood.

Hopkins, B. R. (1989, February). Counselors and the law. *Guidepost,* p. 13.

Hopkins, B. R., & Anderson, B. S. (1985). *The counselor and the law* (2d ed.). Alexandria, VA: American Association for Counseling and Development.

Horner, R. H., & Sugai, G. (2000). School-wide behavior support: An emerging initiative (special issue). *Journal of Positive Behavioral Interventions, 2,* 231–233.

Horner, R. H., Crone, D. A., & Stiller, B. (2001). *The role of school psychologists in establishing positive behav-ior support: Collaborating in systems change at the school-wide level.* National Association of School Psychologists. Retrieved from *http://www.naspcenter.org/teachers/IDEA_pbs.html* on July 10, 2002.

Horner, R. H., Sugai, G., & Horner, H. F. (2000). A school-wide approach to student discipline. *The School Administrator, 57*(2), 20–24.

Howell, J. C. (1998). *Youth gangs: An overview.* Washington, DC: U.S. Department of Justice, Office of Justice Programs, Bulletin of the Office of Juvenile Justice and Delinquency Prevention.

Hser, Y., Grella, C. E., Hubbard, R. L., Hsieh, S., Fletcher, B. W., Brown, B. S., & Anglin, D. (2001). An evaluation of drug treatments for adolescents in 4 US cities. *Archives of General Psychiatry,* 689–695.

Huang, T. T., Unger, J. B., & Rohrbach, L. A. (2000). Exposure to, and perceived usefulness, of school-based tobacco prevention programs: Associations with susceptibility to smoking among adolescents. *Journal of Adolescent Health, 27*(4), 248–254.

Hudelson, S. (1989). *Write on: Children writing in ESL.* Englewood Cliffs, NJ: Prentice-Hall.

Hudson, R. A. (1980). *Sociolinguistics.* Cambridge: Cambridge University Press.

Huesmann, L. R., Moise-Titus, J., Podolski, C., & Eron, L. D. (2001). *Longitudinal relations between children's exposure to television violence and their aggressive and violent behavior in young adulthood: 1977–1992.* Washington DC: APA. Retrieved from *http://www.lionlamb.org/research_articles/ctvout.2001.ver12_pdf.pdf* on December 15, 2002.

Huey, S. J., Jr., Henggeler, S. W., Brondino, M. J., & Pickrel, S. G. (2000). Mechanisms of change in multisystemic therapy: Reducing delinquent behavior through therapist adherence and improved family and peer functioning. *Journal of Consulting and Clinical Psychology, 68,* 451–467.

Hughes, J. N., & Hasbrouck, J. E. (1996). Television violence: Implications for violence prevention. *School Psychology Review, 25,* 134–151.

Hunter, M. (1991). Hunter design helps achieve the goals of science instruction. *Educational Leadership, 48*(4), 79–81.

Hunt-Morse, M. C. (2002). *Adolescent mothers' psychosocial development: Implications for parenting.* Unpublished doctoral dissertation, University of Oregon.

Hyman, I. A., & Perone, D. C. (1998). The other side of school violence: Educator policies and practices that may contribute to student misbehavior. *Journal of School Psychology, 36* (1), 7–27.

Hyson, M. C. (1994). *The emotional development of young children: Building and emotion-centered curriculum.* New York: Teachers College Press.

In re Gault, 387 U.S. 1 (1967).

Information please almanac, atlas, and yearbook (44th ed.). (1991). Boston: Houghton Mifflin.

Jackson, N., Jackson, D., & Monroe, C. (1983). *Getting along with others: Teaching social effectiveness to children.* Champaign, IL: Research Press.

Jacobson, E. (1938). *Progressive relaxation* (2nd ed.). Chicago: University of Chicago Press.

Jaffe v. Redmond, 116 S.Ct. 1923 (1996).

Jaffee, S. R. (2002). Pathways to adversity in young adulthood among early childbearers. *Journal of Family Psychology, 16,* 38–49.

Jamison, J. H., Kaplan, D. W., Hamman, R., Eagar, R., Beach, R., & Douglas, J. M., Jr. (1995). Spectrum of genital human papillomavirus infection in a female adolescent population. *Sexually Transmitted Diseases, 22,* 236–243.

Janosz, M., LeBlanc, M., Boulerice, B., & Tremblay, R. E. (2000). Predicting different types of school dropouts: A typological approach with two longitudinal samples. *Journal of Educational Psychology,* (92)1, 171–190.

Jarjoura, R. G., Triplett, G. P., & Brinker, G. P. (2002). Growing up poor: Examining the link between persistent childhood poverty and delinquency. *Journal of Quantitative Criminology, 18*(2), 159–187.

Jaycox, L. H., & Repetti, R. L. (1993). Conflict in families and the psychological adjustment of preadolescent children. *Journal of Family Psychology, 7,* 344–355.

Jaycox, L. H., Reivich, K. J., Gillham, J. K., & Seligman, M. E. P. (1994). Preventing depressive symptoms in school children. *Behaviour Research and Therapy, 32,* 801–816.

Jemmott, J. B., Jemmott, L. S., & Fong, G. T. (1992). Reductions in HIV-risk-associated sexual behaviors among Black male adolescents: Effects of an AIDS prevention intervention. *American Journal of Public Health, 82,* 372–377.

Jessor, L. D., & Jessor, S. L. (1977). *Problem behavior and psychosocial development: A longitudinal study of youth.* New York: Academic Press.

Jessor, R. (1991). Risk behavior in adolescence: A psychosocial framework for understanding and action. *Journal of Adolescent Health, 12,* 597–605.

Jessor, R. (1993). Successful adolescent development among youth in high-risk settings. *American Psychologist, 48,* 117–126.

Jessor, R., Donovan, J. E., & Costa, F. M. (1991). *Beyond adolescence: Problem behavior and young adult development.* New York: Cambridge University Press.

Jessor, R., Van Den Bos, J., Vanderryn, J., Costa, R. M., & Turbin, M. S. (1995). Protective factors in adolescent problem behavior: Moderator effects and developmental change. *Developmental Psychology, 31,* 923–933.

Jeynes, W. (2002). The relationship between the consumption of various drugs by adolescents and their academic achievement. *American Journal of Drug Alcohol Abuse, 28,* 15–35.

Jimerson, S., Egeland, B., Sroufe, L. A., & Carlson B. (2000). A prospective longitudinal study of high school dropouts: Examining multiple predictors across development. *Journal of School Psychology,* (38)6, 525–549.

Jimerson, S. R. (1999). On the failure of failure: Examining the association between early grade retention and education and employment outcomes during late adolescence. *Journal of School Psychology,* (37)3, 243–272.

Jobes, D. A., & Berman, A. L. (1993). Suicide and malpractice liability. Assessing and revising policies, procedures and practice in outpatient settings. *Professional Psychology: Research and Practice, 24,* 91–99.

Johnson, D., & Johnson, R. (1993). What we know about cooperative learning at the college level. *Cooperative Learning, 13*(3), 17–19.

Johnson, D. W., & Johnson, R. T. (1988). Critical thinking through structured controversy. *Educational Leadership, 45,* 58–64.

Johnson, D. W., & Johnson, R. T. (1989). Toward a cooperative effort: A response to Slavin. *Educational Leadership, 46,* 80–81.

Johnson, D. W., & Johnson, R. T. (1989). *Cooperation and competition: Theory and research.* Edina, MN: Interaction Book Company.

Johnson, D. W., Johnson, R., & Holubec, E. (1990). *Circles of learning: Cooperation in the classroom.* Edina, MN: Interaction Book Company.

Johnson, D. W., Johnson, R. T., & Taylor, B. (1993). Impact of cooperative and individualistic learning on high-ability students' achievement, self-esteem, and social acceptance. *The Journal of Social Psychology, 133*(6), 839–844.

Johnson, S. (1977). *Cross-age tutoring handbook.* Corcoran Unified School District, AC. (ERIC Document Reproduction Service No. ED238826)

Johnson, S. M., & Boles, K. C. (1994). The role of teachers in school reform. In S. A. Mohrman &

P. Wohlstetter (Eds.), *School-based management: Organizing for high performance* (pp. 109–137). San Francisco: Jossey-Bass.

Johnston, L. D., Bachman, J. G., & O'Malley, P. M. (1992). *Smoking, drinking, and illicit drug use among American secondary school students, college students, and young adults, 1975–1991.* Rockville, MD: National Institute on Drug Abuse.

Johnston, L. D., O'Malley, P. M., & Bachman, J. G. (1995). *National survey results on drug use from the monitoring the future study, 1975–1994.* Rockville, MD: National Institute on Drug Abuse.

Johnston, L. D., O'Malley, P. M., & Bachman, J. G. (2000). *National survey results on drug use from the monitoring the future study, 1975–1999. Volume I: Secondary school students.* Ann Arbor, MI: University of Michigan.

Johnston, L. D., O'Malley, P. M., & Bachman, J. G. (2003). The Monitoring the Future national survey results on adolescent drug use: Overview of key findings, 2002 (NIH Publication No. 03-5374). Bethesda, MD: National Institute on Drug Abuse.

Joiner, T. E., Jr. (2000). A test of the hopelessness theory of depression in youth psychiatric inpatients. *Journal of Clinical Child Psychology, 29,* 167–176.

Joint statement on the impact of entertainment violence on children: Congressional Public Health Summit. (2000, July 26). Retrieved from *http//www.senate.gov/Brownback/violence1.pdf* on December 4, 2000.

Jones, C. A. (1998, November). *Preventing school violence: A review of the literature.* Paper presented at the annual meeting of the Mid-South Educational Research Association, New Orleans, LA.

Jones, L. K. (1996). A harsh and challenging world of work: Implications for counselors. *Journal of Counseling and Development, 74,* 453–459.

Jones, R. N., Sheridan, S. M., & Binns, N. R. (1993). Schoolwide social skills training: Providing preventive services to students at-risk. *School Psychology Quarterly, 8*(1), 57–80.

Jones, T. S. (1998). Research supports effectiveness of peer mediation. *The Fourth R, 82,* 1–25.

Jordan K. M. (2000). Substance abuse among gay, lesbian, bisexual, transgender, and questioning adolescents. *School Psychology, 29,* 201–206.

Jorgensen, J. A., & Newlon, B. J. (1988). Life-style themes of unwed, pregnant adolescents who choose to keep their babies. *Individual Psychology, 44*(4), 466–471.

Juhnke, G. (1997). After school violence: An adapted critical incident stress debriefing model for student survivors and their parents. *Elementary School Guidance & Counseling, 31*(3), 163–170.

Kadel, S., & Follman, J. (1993). Reducing school violence. *SouthEastern Regional Vision for Education, March.*

Kagan, S. L., & Weissbourd, B. (Eds.). (1994). *Putting families first: America's family support movement and the challenge of change.* San Francisco: Jossey-Bass.

Kahn, D. J., Kazimi, M. M., & Mulvihill, M. N. (2001). Attitudes of New York City high school students regarding firearm violence. *Pediatrics, 107*(5), 1125–1132.

Kahn, J. S., Kehle, T. J., Jenson, W. R., & Clarke, E. (1990). Comparison of cognitive-behavioral, relaxation, and self-modeling intervention for depression among middle-school students. *School Psychology Review, 19,* 195–210.

Kalafat, J. (1994). On initiating school-based suicide response programs. *Special Services in the Schools, 8*(2), 21–31.

Kalichman, S. C. (1999). *Mandated reporting of suspect child abuse: Ethics, law, and policy* (2nd ed). Washington, DC: American Psychological Association.

Kalichman, S. C., & Brosig, C. L. (1993). Practicing psychologists' interpretations of compliance with child abuse reporting law. *Law and Human Behavior, 17,* 83–93.

Kaminer, Y. (1994). *Adolescent substance abuse: A comprehensive guide to theory and practice.* New York: Plenum Medical/Plenum.

Kamps, D., & Kay, P. (2001). Preventing problems through social skills instruction. In R. Algozzine & P. Kay (Eds.), *What works: How schools can prevent behavior problems.* Thousand Oaks, CA: Corwin Press.

Kandel, D. B., & Davies, M. (1996). High school students who use crack and other drugs. *Archives of General Psychiatry, 53,* 71–80.

Kann, L., Kinchen, S. A., Williams, B. I., Ross, J. G., Lowry, R., Hill, C. V., Grunbaum, J., Blumson, P. S., Collins, J. L., & Kolbe, L. J. (1998, August). *Youth risk behavior surveillance—United States, 1997* (Report No. SS-3). Washington, DC: U.S. Government Printing Office.

Kaplan, J. S. (1991). *Beyond behavior modification: A cognitive-behavioral approach to behavior management in the school.* Austin, TX: Pro-Ed.

Kashani, J. H., Daniel, A. E., Dandoy, A. C., & Holcomb, W. R. (1992). Family violence: Impact on children. *Journal of the American Academy of Child and Adolescent Psychiatry, 31*(2), 181–189.

Kaufman, P. Alt, M. N., & Chapman, C. (2001). Dropout rates in the United States: 2000. National Center for Education Statistics. Retrieved from *http://nces.ed.gov/pubsearch/pubsinfo.asp? pubid=2002114.*

Kaufman, P., Chen, X., Choy, S. P., Peter, K., Ruddy, S. A., Miller, A. K., Fleury, J. K., Planty, M. G., & Rand, M. R. (2001). *Indicators of school crime and safety: 2001.* U.S. Departments of Education and Justice. NCES 2002-113/NCJ-190075. Washington, DC: 2001.

Kay, P., Fitzgerald, M., & McConaughy, S. H. (2002). Building effective parent-teacher partnerships. In B. Algozzine & P. Kay (Eds.), *Preventing problem behaviors: A handbook of successful prevention strategies* (pp. 104–125). Thousand Oaks, CA: Corwin Press and Council for Exceptional Children.

Kazdin, A. E. (1994). Interventions for aggressive and antisocial children. In L. D. Eron, J. H. Gentry, & P. Schlegel (Eds.), *Reason to hope: A psychosocial perspective on violence and youth.* Washington: APA, 341–382.

Keane, S. P., & Conger, J. C. (1981). The implications of communication development for social skills training. *Journal of Pediatric Psychology, 6,* 369–381.

Keefe, C. H., & Keefe, D. R. (1993). Instruction for students with LD: A whole language model. *Intervention in School and Clinic, 28*(3), 172–177.

Kellam, S. G., Ling, X., Merisca, R., Brown, C. H., & Ialongo J. (1998). The effect of the level of aggression in the first grade classroom on the course and malleability of aggressive behavior into middle school. *Development and Psychopathology, 10,* 165–185.

Keller, C. L. (2002). A new twist on spelling instruction for elementary school teachers. *Intervention in School and Clinic, 38*(1), 3–7.

Kellogg, N. D., Hoffman, T. J., & Taylor, E. R. (1999). Early sexual experiences among pregnant and parenting adolescents. *Adolescence, 34*(134), 293–303.

Kelly, J. (1982). *Social skill training.* New York: Springer.

Kerr, M. E., & Bowen, M. (1988). *Family evaluation: An approach based on Bowen theory.* New York: W. W. Norton.

Key, J. D., Barbosa, G. A., & Owens, V. J. (2001). The second chance club: Repeat adolescent pregnancy prevention with a school-based intervention. *Journal of Adolescent Health, 28,* 167–169.

Kim, M., Ohls, J., & Cohen, R. (2001). *Hunger in America 2001: Local report prepared for Food for Survival, Inc. (3503).* Princeton, NJ: Mathematica Policy Research, Inc.

King, K. A., Price, J. H., Telljohann, S. K., & Wahl, J. (2000). Preventing adolescent suicide: Do high school counselors know the risk factors? *Professional School Counseling, 3,* 255–262.

King, S. M. (1991). Benign sabotage and Dreikurs' second goal of misbehavior. *Family Therapy, 18*(3), 265–268.

Kinnier, R. T., & Krumboltz, J. D. (1984). Procedures for successful career counseling. In N. Gysbers (Ed.), *Designing careers: Counseling to enhance education, work and leisure.* San Francisco: Jossey-Bass.

Kirby, D. (1985). *School-based health clinics: An emerging approach to improving adolescent health and addressing teenage pregnancy.* Washington, DC: Center for Population Options.

Kirby, D. (1999). Reducing adolescent pregnancy: Approaches that work. *Contemporary Pediatrics, 16,* 83–94.

Kirby, D. (2000). School-based interventions to prevent unprotected sex and HIV among adolescents. In J. L. Peterson & R. J. DiClemente (Eds.), *Handbook of HIV prevention* (pp. 83–101). New York: Kluwer Academic Press.

Kirby, D. (2001). *Emerging answers: Research findings on programs to reduce teen pregnancy.* National Campaign to Prevent Teen Pregnancy.

Kirby, D., Short, L., Collins, J., Rugg, D., Kolbe, L., Howard, M., Miller, B., Sonenstein, F., & Zabin, L. S. (1994). School-based programs to reduce sexual risk behaviors: A review of effectiveness. *Public Health Reports, 103*(3), 339–360.

Kiselica, M. S. (1995). *Multicultural counseling with teenage fathers.* Thousand Oaks, CA: Sage.

Klein, K., Forehand, R., & the Family Health Project Research Group. (2000). Family processes as resources for African American children exposed to a constellation of sociodemographic risk factors. *Journal of Clinical Child Psychology, 29*(1), 53–65.

Kliewer, W., & Sandler, I. N. (1992). Locus of control and self-esteem as moderators of stress-symptom relations in children and adolescents. *Journal of Abnormal Child Psychology, 20,* 393–413.

Knitzer, J., Steinberg, Z., & Fleisch, B. (1990). *At the schoolhouse door: An examination of programs and policies for children with behavioral and emotional problems.* New York: Bank Street College of Education.

Knowledge, response to suicidal statements, attitudes, and intention to help. *Suicide and Life-Threatening Behavior, 31*(3), 320–332.

Koch, M. (1988). Resolving disputes: Students can do it better. *NASSP Bulletin, 72*(504), 16–18.

Koeppen, A. S. (1974). Relaxation training for children. *Elementary School Guidance and Counseling, 9*(1), 14–21.

Koplow, L. (Ed.). (1996). *Unsmiling faces: How preschools can heal.* New York: Teachers College Press.

Korinek, L., Walther-Thomas, C., McLaughlin, V. L., & Williams, B. T. (1999). Creating classroom communities and networks for student support. *Intervention in School and Clinic, 35,* 3–8.

Kortering, L. J., & Braziel, P. M. (1999). School dropout from the perspective of former students. *Remedial and Special Education, 20*(2), 78–83.

Kosterman, R., Hawkins, J. D., Guo, J., Catalano, R. F., Abbott, R. D., Russell, S., & Joyner, K. (2000). Adolescent sexual orientation and suicide risk: Evidence from a natural study. *American Journal of Public Health, 91,* 1276–1282.

Kovacs, M. (1981). Rating scales to assess depression in school-aged children. *Acta Paedopsychiatrica, 46,* 305–315.

Kovacs, M., & Beck, A. T. (1977). An empirical-clinical approach toward a definition of childhood depression. In J. G. Schulterbrandt & A. Raskin (Eds.), *Depression in childhood: Diagnosis, treatment, and conceptual models* (pp. 1–25). New York: Raven.

Kovacs, M., & Devlin, B. (1998). Internalizing disorders in childhood. *Journal of Child Psychology and Psychiatry, 39,* 47–63.

Kozol, J. (1991) *Savage inequalities: Children in America's schools.* New York: Crown.

Krajewski, S. S., Rybarik, M. F., Dosch, M. F., & Gilmore, G. D. (1996). Results of a curriculum intervention with seventh graders regarding violence in relationships. *Journal of Family Violence, 11,* 93–112.

Kraut, R. Lundmark, V., Patterson, M., Kiesler, S., Mukopadhyay, T., & Scherlis, W. (1998). Internet paradox a social technology that reduces social involvement and psychological well-being? *American Psychologist, 53,* 1017–1031.

Kucinich, D. J. (2000). Providing for consideration of H.R. 3081, wage and employment growth act of 1999. *Congressional Record. Daily ed. 146*(26), H773–792.

Kumpfer, K. (1998). Selective prevention interventions: The strengthening families program. In R. Ashery, E. Robertson, & K. Kumpfer (Eds.), *Drug abuse prevention through family interventions.* Rockville, MD: National Institutes of Health, 160–207.

Kumpfer, K. L., & Alvarado, R. (1995). Strengthening families to prevent drug use in multiethnic youth. In

G. J. Botvin, S. Schinke, & M. A. Orlandi (Eds.), *Drug abuse prevention with multiethnic youth* (pp. 255–294). Thousand Oaks, CA: Sage.

Kumpfer, K. L., Molgaard, V., & Spoth, R. L. (1996). The strengthening families program for the prevention of delinquency and drug abuse. In R. D. Peters & R. J. McMahon (Eds.), *Preventing childhood disorders, substance abuse, and delinquency* (pp. 241–267). Newbury, CA: Sage.

Kumpfer, K. L., & Tait, C. M. (2000). Family skills training for parents and children. Washington, DC: U.S. Department of Justice, *Bulletin of the Office of Justice Programs, Office of Juvenile Justice and Delinquency Prevention,* 1–11.

Kupersmidt, J. B., Burchinaal, M., & Patterson, C. J. (1995). Developmental patterns of childhood peer relations as predictors of externalizing behavior problems. *Development & Psychopathology, 7,* 825–843.

Ladd, G. W., & Burgess K. B. (2001). Do relational risks and protective factors moderate the linkages between childhood aggression and early psychological and school adjustment? *Child Development, 72*(5), 1579–1601.

Ladd, G. W., Kochenderfer, B. J., & Coleman, C. C. (1996). Friendship quality as a predictor of young children's early school adjustment. *Child Development, 67,* 1103–1118.

LaFave, W. R. & Scott, A. W. (2002). *Substantive Criminal Law.* St. Paul, MN: West Publishing Co.

La Fromboise, T. D. (1988). American Indian mental health policy. *American Psychologist, 43*(5), 388–397.

Lal, S. R. (1991). *A study of strategies employed by junior high school administrators to overcome disruptive gang-related activities.* Unpublished doctoral dissertation, University of California, Los Angeles.

Lal, S. R., Lal, D., & Achilles, C. M. (1993). *Handbook on gangs in schools: Strategies to reduce gang-related activities.* Thousand Oaks, CA: Corwin Press, Inc.

LaMorte, M. W. (1993). *School law: Cases and concepts* (4th ed.). Needham Heights, MA: Allyn & Bacon.

Lanctot, N., & Smith, C. A. (2001). Sexual activity, pregnancy, and deviance in a representative urban sample of African-American girls. *Journal of Youth and Adolescence, 30,* 349–372.

Landers, S. (1989). Homelessness hinders academic performance. *APA Monitor, 20*(11), 5.

Lane, K. L., Gresham, F. M., & O'Shaughnessy, T. E. (Eds.). (2002). *Interventions for children with or at risk for emotional and behavioral disorders.* Boston: Allyn & Bacon.

Lane, P. S., & McWhirter, J. J. (1992). A peer mediation model: Conflict resolution for elementary and middle school children. *Elementary School Guidance and Counseling, 27*(1), 15–24.

Lane, P. S., & McWhirter, J. J. (1996). Creating a peaceful school community: Reconciliation operationalized. *Catholic School Studies, 69*(2), 31–34.

Lapan, R. T., Gysbers, N. C., & Petroski, G. F. (2001). Helping seventh graders be safe and successful: A statewide study of the impact of comprehensive guidance and counseling programs. *Journal of Counseling & Development, 79,* 320–330.

Lazarus, A. A. (1971). *Behavior therapy and beyond.* New York: McGraw-Hill.

Lebow, M. A. (1994). Contraceptive advertising in the United States. *Womens Health Issues, 4,* 196–208.

Lee, R. M., & Robbins, S. B. (1995). Measuring belongingness: The Social Connectedness and Social Assurance Scales. *Journal of Counseling Psychology, 42,* 232–241.

Lee, R. M., & Robbins, S. B. (1998). The relationship between social connectedness and anxiety, self-esteem, and social identity. *Journal of Counseling Psychology, 45,* 338–345.

Lee, R. M., & Robbins, S. B. (2000). Understanding social connectedness in college women and men. *Journal of Counseling and Development, 78,* 484–491.

Lee, R. M., Draper, M., & Lee, S. (2001). Social connectedness, dysfunctional interpersonal behaviors, and psychological distress: Testing a mediator model. *Journal of Counseling Psychology, 48,* 310–318.

Lee, R. M., Keough, K. A., & Sexton, J. D. (2002). Social connectedness, social appraisal, and perceived stress in college women and men. *Journal of Counseling and Development, 80,* 355–361.

Lenz, R. K. (1992). Self-managed learning strategy systems for children and youth. *School Psychology Review, 21,* 211–228.

Levin, H., Glass, G., & Meister, G. (1984). *Cost effectiveness of four educational interventions,* Project Report No 84-A11. Stanford, CA: Institute for Research on Educational Finance and Governance.

Levine, M. (1996). *Viewing violence: How media violence affects your child's and adolescent's development.* New York: Doubleday.

Levin, M. L., Whitaker, D. J., Miller, K. S., & May, D. C. (1999). Teenage partners' communication about sexual risk and condom use: The importance of the parent-teenager discussions. *Family Planning Perspectives, 31,* 117–121.

Levy, S. R., Jurkovic, G. L., & Spirito, A. (1995). A multisystems analysis of adolescent suicide attempters. *Journal of Abnormal Child Psychology, 23,* 221–234.

Lewinsohn, P., Rohde, P., & Seeley, J. K. (1993). Psychosocial characteristics of adolescents with a history of suicide attempts. *Journal of American Society of Child Adolescent Health Care, 4,* 106–108.

Lewinsohn, P., Rohde, P., Seeley, J., & Fischer, S. (1993). Age-cohort changes in the lifetime occurrence of depression and other mental disorders. *Journal of Abnormal Psychology, 102,* 110–120.

Lewinsohn, P. M., Hops, H., Roberts, R., Seeley, J. R., & Andrew, J. (1993). Adolescent psychopathology: I. Prevalence and incidence of depression and other DSM-III-R disorders in high school students. *Journal of Abnormal Psychology, 102*(4), 183–204.

Lewis, T. J., & Sugai, G. (1999). Effective behavior support: A systems approach to proactive schoolwide management. *Focus on Exceptional Children, 31*(6), 1–24.

Lickona, T. (1991). *Educating for character.* New York: Bantam.

Liddle, H. A., & Dakof, G. A. (1995). Efficacy of family therapy for drug abuse: Promising but not definitive. *Journal of Marital and Family Therapy, 21* (4), 511–543.

Lind, M. (2001). Thinking aloud: The case for a living wage. *New Leader, 84*(5), 12–14.

Lindblom, E. (1991). Towards a comprehensive homeless prevention policy. *Housing Policy Debate, 2*(3), 957–1025.

Linney, J. A., & Seidman, E. (1989). The future of schooling. *American Psychologist, 44,* 336–340.

Lipschitz, A. (1995). Suicide prevention in young adults. *Suicide and Life-Threatening Behavior, 25*(1), 155–169.

Lipsey, M. W., Wilson, D. B., & Cothern, L. 2000 (December). Effective intervention for serious juvenile offenders. Washington, DC: U.S. Department of Justice, Office of Justice Programs, *Bulletin of the Office of Juvenile Justice and Delinquency Prevention,* 1–8.

Littrell, J. M., Malia, J. A., & Vanderwood, M. (1995). Single-session brief counseling in a high school. *Journal of Counseling and Development, 73,* 451–458.

Lochman, J. E. (1987). Self and peer perceptions and attributional biases of aggressive and nonaggressive boys in dyadic interactions. *Journal of Consulting and Clinical Psychology, 55,* 404–410.

Lodge, J., Harte, D. K., & Tripp, G. (1998). Children's self-talk under conditions of mild anxiety. *Journal of Anxiety Disorders, 12,* 153–176.

Loeber, R., & Farrington, D. P. (1998). *Serious and violent juvenile offenders: Risk factors and successful interventions.* Thousand Oaks, CA: Sage.

Long, L. (1988). Providing assistance to latchkey families. *Pointer, 33*(1), 37–40.

Lord, M. (1999, October). The violent-kid profile. *U.S. News.* Retrieved from *www.usnews.com* on August 2001.

Lord, S. E., Eccles, J. S., & McCarthy, K. A. (1994). Surviving the junior high school transition: Family processes and self-perceptions as protective and risk factors. *Journal of Early Adolescence, 14*(2), 162–199.

Lorion, R., Price, R., & Eaton M. (1989). The prevention of child and adolescent disorders: From theory to research. In D. Shaffer, I. Philips, & N. B. Enzer (Eds.), *Prevention of mental disorders, alcohol and other drug use in children and adolescents* (pp. 55–95). Office of Substance Abuse Prevention and American Academy of Child and Adolescent Psychiatry, Prevention Monograph No. 2, (DHHS Publication No. ADM 89-1646). Rockville, MD: Office of Substance Abuse Prevention.

Lott, B. (2002). Cognitive and behavioral distancing from the poor. *American Psychologist, 57,* 100–110.

Lowe, G., Foxcroft, D. R., & Sibley, D. (1993). *Adolescent drinking and family life.* Langhorne, PA: Harwood Academic/Gordon & Breach Science.

Lowenthal, B. (1996). Integrated school services for children at risk: Rationale, models, barriers, and recommendations for implementation. *Intervention in School and Clinic, 31*(3), 154–157.

Lowry, D. T., & Shidler, J. A. (1993). Prime time TV portrayals of sex, safe sex and AIDS: A longitudinal analysis. *Journalism Quarterly, 70,* 628–637.

Lunenburg, F. C. (2000). America's hope: Making schools work for all children. *Journal of Instructional Psychology, 27*(1), 39–46.

Luthar, S. S. (1999). *Poverty and children's adjustment* (Vol. 41, Developmental Clinical Psychology and Psychiatry). Thousand Oaks, CA: Sage.

Lykken, D. T. (2001). Parental licensure. *American Psychologist, 56,* 885–894.

Lynskey, M., & Hall, W. (2000). The effects of adolescent cannabis use on educational attainment: A review. *Addiction, 95,* 1621–1630.

Lysynchuk, L. M., Pressley, M., & Vye, N. J. (1990). Reciprocal teaching improves standardized reading-comprehension performance in poor comprehenders. *Elementary School Journal, 90,* 469–484.

Maeroff, G. I. (1998). Altered destinies: Making life better for school children in need. *Phi Delta Kappan, 79*(6), 425–432.

Mahoney, J. L. (1998). The prediction and prevention of crime: Developmental antecedents and turning points. *Dissertation Abstracts International:* Section B: the Sciences & Engineering. 58(8-B), 4492.

Maine, S., Shute, R., & Martin, G. (2001). Educating parents about youth suicide: Responses to suicidal statements, attitudes, and intention to help. *Journal of Suicide and Life Threatening Behavior, 31,* 320–332.

Mallon, G. P. (1998). *We don't exactly get the welcome wagon: The experiences of gay and lesbian adolescents in child welfare systems.* New York: Columbia University Press.

Maltbia, G. (1991). Cultural diversity as a labor management issue. *Employee Assistance Program Exchange, 21*(5), 26.

Manaster, G. J. (1990). Unique people drop out: To educate all or each. *TACD Journal, 18*(1), 7–14.

Manlove, J. (1998). The influence of high school dropout and school disengagement on the risk of school-age pregnancy. *Journal of Research on Adolescence, 8,* 187–220.

Mannheim, C. I., Sancilio, M., Phipps-Yonas, S., Brunnquell, D., Somers, P., Farseth, G. & Ninonuevo, F. (2002). Ethical ambiguities in the practice of child clinical psychology. *Professional Psychology: Research and Practice, 33,* 24–29.

Marcus, G. F. (1996). Children's overregularization and its implications for cognition. In P. Broeder & J. M. J. Murre (Eds.), *Models of language acquisition: Inductive and deductive approaches.* Cambridge, MA: MIT Press.

Marris, S. Canetto, J. McIntosh, & M. Silverman (Eds.). (2000). *Review of suicidology, 2000* (pp. 3–33). New York: The Guilford Press.

Marttunen, M. J., Aro, H. M., & Lonnquist, J. K. (1993). Precipitant stressors in adolescent suicide. *Journal of the American Academy of Child and Adolescent Psychiatry, 32*(6), 1178–1183.

Marzen, T. J., O'Dowd, M. K., Crone, D., & Balch, T. J. (1985). Suicide: A constitutional right? *Duquesne Law Review 1,* 56–100.

Mash, J. M. (1989). *Adolescents' future orientation and goal-setting skills: Implications for conventional and problem behavior.* Master's thesis, Virginia Commonwealth University.

Massey, D. S., & Denton, N. A. (1993). *American apartheid: Segregation and the making of the underclass.* Cambridge, MA: Harvard University Press.

Mattison, R. E. (2000). School consultation: A review of research on issues unique to the school environment.

Journal of American Academy of Child and Adolescent Psychiatry, 39(4), 402–413.

Maxwell, J. (1989). Mediation in the schools. *Mediation Quarterly, 7,* 149–154.

Mayer, S. E. (1990). How much does a school's racial and economic mix affect graduation rates and teenage fertility rates? In C. Jencks & P. Peterson (Eds.), *The urban underclass.* Washington, DC: The Brookings Institution.

Maynard, R. A. (Ed.). (1996). *Kids having kids: A Robin Hood Foundation special report on the costs of adolescent childbearing.* New York: Robin Hood Foundation.

Mayou, R. A., Ehlers, A., & Hobbs, M. (2000). Psychological debriefing for road traffic accident victims: Three year follow-up of a randomized controlled trial. *British Journal of Psychiatry, 176,* 589–593.

Mazza, J. J., & Eggert, L. L (2001). Activity involvement among suicidal and non-suicidal high-risk and typical adolescents. *Suicide and Life-Threatening Behavior, 31*(3), 265–281.

McCormick, M. (1988). *Mediation in the schools: An evaluation of the Wakefield Pilot Peer Mediation Program in Tucson, Arizona.* Washington, DC: American Bar Association.

McCubbin, H. I., & McCubbin, M. A. (1988). Typologies of resilient families: Emerging roles of social class and ethnicity. *Family Relations, 37,* 247–254.

McDevitt, T. M. (1996). *Trends in adolescent fertility and contraceptive use in the developing world.* [IPC/95-1]. Washington, DC: U.S. Bureau of the Census.

McDowell, E. E., & Stillion, J. M. (1994). Suicide across the phases of life. In G. G. Noam & S. Borst (Eds.), *Children, youth, and suicide: Developmental perspectives* (pp. 7–22). San Francisco: Jossey-Bass.

McGee, J., & DeBernardo, C. R. (1999, May/June). The classroom avenger: A behavioral profile of school-based shootings. *The Forensic Examiner,* 16–18.

McGinnis, E., & Goldstein, A. P. (1984). *Skillstreaming in early childhood: Teaching prosocial skills to the preschool and kindergarten child.* Champaign, IL: Research Press.

McGinnis, E., & Goldstein, A. P. (1984). *Skillstreaming the elementary school child: A guide for teaching prosocial skills.* Champaign, IL: Research Press.

McGinnis, J. M., & Foege, W. H. (1993). Actual causes of death in the United States. *Journal of the American Medical Association, 270*(18), 2207–2212.

McGloin, J. M., & Widom, C. S. (2001). Resilience among abused and neglected children grown up. *Development and Psychopathology, 13,* 1021–1038.

McGoldrick, M., & Carter, B. (1999). *The expanded family life cycle: Individual, family, and social perspectives.* Boston: Allyn & Bacon.

McGowan, S. (1991, October). Confidentiality: Breaking a sacred trust. *Guidepost,* pp. 14–15.

McGuire, J. M., Parnell, T. F., Blau, B. I., & Abbott, D. W. (1994). Demands for privacy among adolescents in multimodal alcohol and other drug abuse treatment. *Journal of Counseling & Development, 73*(1), 74–78.

McIntosh, J. L. (2000). Epidemiology of adolescent suicide in the United States. In R. W. Maris, S. S. Canetto, J. L. McIntosh, & M. M. Silverman (Eds.), *Review of Suicidology,* 2000 (pp. 3–33). New York: Guilford.

McKee, P. W. (1993). *Suicide and the school: A practical guide to suicide prevention. Crisis intervention series.* Horsham, PA: LRP Publications.

McLaughlin, T. F., & Vacha, E. F. (1992). School programs for at-risk children and youth: A review. *Education and Treatment of Children, 15*(3), 255–267.

McLean, P., & Taylor, S. (1994). Family therapy for suicidal people. *Death Studies, 18*(4), 409–426.

McLloyd, V. C. (1989). Socialization and development in a changing economy: The effects of paternal job and income loss on children. *American Psychologist, 44*(2), 293–302.

McMillen, M. M., Kaufman, P., & Whitener, S. D. (1995). *Dropout rates in the United States: 1995.* Washington, DC: National Center for Education Statistics.

McNeely, C., Nonnemaker, J., & Blum, R. (2002). Improving the odds: The untapped power of schools to improve the health of teens. *Journal of School Health, 72*(4), or *www.allaboutkids.umn.edu.*

McReynolds, R. A., Morris, R. J., & Kratochwill, T. R. (1989). Cognitive-behavioral treatment of school-related fears and anxieties. In J. N. Hughes & Robert J. Hall (Eds.), *Cognitive-behavioral psychology in the schools* (pp. 434–465). New York: Guilford Press.

McWhirter, A. M. (1990). Whole language in the middle school. *Reading Teacher, 43,* 562–565.

McWhirter, B. T. (1990). Loneliness: A review of current literature, with implications for counseling and research. *Journal of Counseling and Development, 68*(4), 417–422.

McWhirter, B. T., & Burrow-Sanchez, J. J. (2004). Preventing and treating affective disorders in children and adolescents. In D. Capuzzi & D. Gross (Eds.), *Youth at risk: A prevention resource for counselors, teachers, & parents* (4th ed.). Alexandria, VA: ACA.

McWhirter, B. T., & Horan, J. J. (1996). Construct validity of cognitive-behavioral treatments for intimate and social loneliness. *Current Psychology, Developmental, Learning, Personality, Social, 15*(1), 42–52.

McWhirter, B. T., & McWhirter, J. J. (1990). University survival strategies and the learning disabled student. *Academic Therapy, 25*(3), 345–351.

McWhirter, B. T., McWhirter, E. H., & McWhirter, J. J. (1988). Groups in Latin America: Comunidades eclesial de base as mutual support groups. *Journal for Specialists in Group Work, 13*(2), 70–76.

McWhirter, B. T., & McWhirter, J. J. (1995). Youth at risk for violence and delinquency: A metaphor and a definition. *Monograph on Youth in the 1990s, 4,* 17–28.

McWhirter, B. T., McWhirter, J. J., Hart, R., & Gat, I. (2000). Preventing and treating depression in children and adolescents. In D. Capuzzi & D. Gross (Eds.), *Youth at risk: A prevention resource for counselors, teachers, & parents* (3rd ed., pp. 141–169). Alexandria, VA: ACA.

McWhirter, B. T., McWhirter, J. J., McWhirter, A. M., & McWhirter, E. H. (1993). Prevention of adolescent pregnancy: Self-understanding from an Adlerian perspective. *The Family Journal: Counseling and Therapy for Couples and Families, 1*(4), 324–330.

McWhirter, E. H. (1991). Empowerment in counseling. *Journal of Counseling and Development, 69*(3), 222–227.

McWhirter, E. H. (1994). *Counseling for empowerment.* Alexandria, VA: American Counseling Association.

McWhirter, E. H. (1998). An empowerment model of counsellor education. *Canadian Journal of Counselling, 32*(1), 12–26.

McWhirter, E. H. (2001, March). *Social action at the individual level: In pursuit of critical consciousness.* In P. Gore & J. Swanson (chairs), Counseling psychologists as agents of social change. Paper presented at the 4th National Conference on Counseling Psychology, Houston, TX.

McWhirter, J. J. (1988). *The learning disabled child: A school and family concern* (2nd ed.). Lanham, MD: University Press of America.

McWhirter, J. J. (1993). Will he live? A suicide assessment interview. In L. Golden & M. Norwood (Eds.), *Case studies in child counseling* (pp. 89–98). New York: Macmillan.

McWhirter, J. J. (2002). Will he choose life? In L. B. Golden (Ed.), *Case studies in child and adolescent counseling* (3rd ed.). New York: Merrill/Prentice Hall, pp. 81–89.

McWhirter, J. J. (1995). Emotional education for university students. *Journal of College Student Psychotherapy, 10*(2), 27–38.

McWhirter, J. J., Herrmann, D. S., Jefferys, K., & Quinn, M. M. (1997). Tools for violence prevention. *Catholic School Studies, 70*(1), 15–19.

McWhirter, J. J., & Kahn, S. E. (1974). A parent communication group. *Elementary School Guidance and Counseling, 9*(2).

McWhirter, J. J., & Kigin, T. J. (1988). Depression. In D. Capuzzi & L. Golden (Eds.), *Preventing adolescent suicide* (pp. 149–186). Muncie, IN: Accelerated Development.

McWhirter, J. J., & McWhirter, A. M. (1987). Family enrichment programs: Puppets as a pedagogical tool. *Guidance and Counseling, 2*(5), 77–84.

McWhirter, J. J., & McWhirter, E. H. (1989). Adolescents-at-risk: Poor soil yields damaged fruit. In D. Capuzzi & D. Gross (Eds.), *Working with at-risk youth: Issues and interventions.* Alexandria, VA: American Association for Counseling and Development.

McWhirter, J. J., & McWhirter, M. C. (1983). Increasing human potential: Relaxation and imagery training (RIT) with athletic and performing art teams. *Personnel and Guidance Journal, 62*(3), 135–138.

McWhirter, J. J., McWhirter, B. T., McWhirter, A. M., & McWhirter, E. H. (1994). High- and low-risk characteristics of youth: The five Cs of competency. *Elementary School Guidance & Counseling, 28*(3), 188–196.

McWhirter, J. J., McWhirter, B. T., McWhirter, A. M., & McWhirter, E. H. (1994). Who is at-risk? A continuum and a metaphor. *Kappa Delta Pi Record, 30*(3), 116–120.

McWhirter, J. J., McWhirter, B. T., McWhirter, A. M., & McWhirter, E. H. (1995). Youth at-risk: Another point of view. *Journal of Counseling and Development, 73*(5), 567–569.

McWhirter, J. J., & McWhirter, R. J. (1988). Legal considerations for the practitioner. In D. Capuzzi & L. B. Golden (Eds.), *Preventing adolescent suicide,* Muncie, IN: Accelerated Development.

McWhirter, J. J., & Santos de Barona, M. (1995). *The CAP program: Final Report* (#S184B 30225) *Cross-age peers: Reducing alcohol/tobacco through prevention.* Washington, DC: Drug Free Schools and Communities.

McWhirter, P. T. (1997). *Adolescents and substance use in Chile: Psychological and social risk factors.* Paper presented at the Annual Convention of the American Psychological Association, Chicago, IL.

McWhirter, P. T. (1998). Risk factors associated with adolescent alcohol, tobacco, marijuana, solvent inhalant, and cocaine use. *National Institute on Drug Abuse Research Monograph, 179,* 202.

McWhirter, P. T., & McWhirter, J. J. (1996). Transition-to-work group: University students with learning disabilities. *Journal for Specialists in Group Work, 21*(2), 144–148.

Meggert, S. S. (2000). Who cares what I think: Problems of low self-esteem. In D. Capuzzi & D. R. Gross (Eds.), *Youth risk: A prevention resource for counselors, teachers, and parents* (3rd ed., pp. 109–136). Alexandria, VA: American Counseling Association.

Meisels, S. J., & Liaw, F. R. (1993). Failure in grade: Do retained students catch up? *Journal of Educational Research, 87,* 69–77.

Melchert, T., & Burnett, K. F. (1990). Attitudes, knowledge, and sexual behavior of high-risk adolescents: Implications for counseling and sexuality education. *Journal of Counseling and Development, 68*(3), 293–298.

Metalsky, G. I., & Joiner, T. E. (1992). Vulnerability to depressive symptomatology: A prospective test of the diathesis-stress and causal mediation components of the hopelessness theory of depression. *Journal of Personality and Social Psychology, 63*(4), 667–675.

Metalsky, G. I., Joiner, T. E., Hardin, T. S., & Abramson, L. Y. (1993). Depressive reactions to failure in a naturalistic setting: A test of the hopelessness and self-esteem theories of depression. *Journal of Abnormal Psychology, 102*(1), 101–109.

Metcalf, L. (1995). *Counseling towards solutions: A practical solution-focused program for working with students, teachers, and parents.* New York: The Center for Applied Research in Education.

Metha, A., & Dunham, H. (1988). Behavioral indicators. In D. Capuzzi & L. Golden (Eds.), *Preventing adolescent suicide* (pp. 49–86). Muncie, IN: Accelerated Development.

Meyer, L. H., & Henry, L. A. (1993). Cooperative classroom management: Student needs and fairness in the regular classroom. In J. W. Putnum (Ed.), *Cooperative learning and strategies for inclusion: Celebrating diversity in the classroom* (p. 116). Baltimore: Paul H. Brookes Publishing Co.

Meyer, L. H., Williams, D. R., Harootunian, B., & Steinberg, A. (1995). An inclusion model to reduce at-risk status among middle school students: The Syracuse experience. In I. M. Evans, T. Cicchelli, M. Cohen, & N. P. Shapiro (Eds.), *Staying in school: Partnerships for educational change* (pp. 83–110). Baltimore: Paul H. Brookes.

Michaelis, K. L. (1993). *Reporting child abuse: A guide to mandatory requirements for school personnel.* Thousand Oaks, CA: Corwin Press.

Michenbaum, D. (1972). Clinical implications of modifying what clients say to themselves. *Research Reports in Psychology, 42.* Waterloo, Ontario, Canada: University of Waterloo.

Middlebrook, D. L., LeMaster, P. L., Beals, J., Novins, D. K., & Manson, S. M. (2001). Suicide prevention in American Indian and Alaska Native communities: a critical review of programs. *Suicide and Life Threatening Behavior, 31,* 32–49.

Milburn, N., & D'Ercole, A. (1991). Homeless women: Moving toward a comprehensive model. *American Psychologist, 46,* 1161–1169.

Miller, D. B., & MacIntosh, R. (1999). Promoting resilience in urban African American adolescents: Racial socialization and identity as protective factors. *Social Work Research, 23,* 159–169.

Miller, M., Azrael, D., & Hemenway, D. (2002). Firearm availability and unintentional firearm deaths, suicide, and homicide among 5–14 year olds. *Journal of Trauma, 52*(2), 267–275.

Miller, T. R., & Blincoe, L. J. (1994). Incidence and cost of alcohol-involved crashes in the United States. *Accident Analysis and Prevention, 26*(5), 583–591.

Miller, W. R., & Rollnick, S. (2002). *Motivational interviewing: Preparing people for change* (2nd ed.). New York: Guilford.

Miller-Kahn, L., & Smith, M. L. (2001, November 30). School choice policies in the political spectacle. *Education Policy Analysis Archives, 9*(50). Retrieved from *http://epaa.asu.edu/epaa/v9n50.html* on July 4, 2002.

Minuchin, S. (1974). *Families and family therapy.* Cambridge, MA: Harvard University Press.

Minuchin, S., & Nichols, M. (1993). *Family healing: Tales of hope and renewal from family therapy.* New York: The Free Press.

Mishel, L., & Bernstein, J. (1995). *State of working America, 1994–95.* Armonk, NY: EPI Publications.

Mitchell, J. J. (1996). *Adolescent vulnerability: A sympathetic look at the frailties and limitations of youth.* Calgary, Alberta: Detselig Enterprises Ltd.

Mize, J., & Pettit, G. S. (1997). Mothers' social coaching, mother-child relationship style, and children's peer competence: Is the medium the message? *Child Development, 68,* 291–311.

Moffitt, T. E. (1993). "Life-course-persistent" and "adolescent-limited" antisocial behavior: A developmental taxonomy. *Psychological Review, 100,* 674–701.

Moffitt, T. E., Caspi, A., Dickson, N., Silva, P., & Stanton, W. (1996). Childhood-onset versus adolescent onset antisocial conduct problems in males: Natural history from ages 3 to 18 years. *Development and Psychopathology, 8,* 399–424.

Monaco, V. C. (1982). Training manual for RIT groups. In V. C. Monaco, *Effects of relaxation/imagery training on children's anxiety, locus of control, and perception of classroom environment* (pp. 156–183). Ph.D. dissertation, Arizona State University, Tempe.

Montagne, M., & Scott, D. M. (1993). Prevention of substance use problems: Models, factors, and processes. *International Journal of the Addictions, 28,* 1177–1208.

Moon, J. R., & Eisler, R. M. (1983). Anger control: An experimental comparison of three behavioral treatments. *Behavior Therapy, 14,* 493–505.

Moon, M. W., McFarland, W., Kellogg, T., Baxter, M., Katz, M. H., MacKellar, D., & Valleroy, L. A. (2000). HIV risk behavior of runaway youth in San Francisco: Age of onset and relation to sexual orientation. *Youth & Society, 32*(2), 184–201.

Moore, D. D., & Forster, J. R. (1993). Student assistance programs: New approaches for reducing adolescent substance abuse. *Journal of Counseling and Development, 71,* 326–329.

Moore, J., & Hagedorn, J. (2001). *Female gangs: A focus on research.* Youth Gang Series Bulletin. Washington, DC: U.S. Department of Justice, Office of Justice Programs, Office of Juvenile Justice and Delinquency Prevention.

Moore, K. A. (1992). *Facts at a glance.* Washington, DC: Child Trends, Inc.

Moore, K. A. (1994). *Facts at a glance.* Washington, DC: Child Trends, Inc.

Moore, K. A. (1995). *Facts at a glance.* Washington, DC: Child Trends, Inc.

Moore, K. A., Morrison, D. R., & Greene, A. D. (1997). Effects on the children born to adolescent mothers. In R. A. Maynard (Ed.), *Kids having kids: Economic costs and social consequences of teen pregnancy* (pp. 145–180). Washington, DC: Urban Institute Press.

Morgan, D. P., & Jensen, W. R. (1988). *Teaching behavioral disordered students.* Columbus, OH: Merrill.

Morganett, (Smead) R. S. (1990). *Skills for living: Group counseling activities for elementary students.* Champaign, IL: Research Press.

Morganett, (Smead) R. S. (1995). *Skills for living: Group counseling activities for elementary students* (2nd ed.). Champaign, IL: Research Press.

Morris, L., Warren, C. W., & Aral, S. O. (1993). Measuring adolescent sexual behaviors and related health outcomes. *Public Health Report, 108*(suppl. 1), 31–36.

Mossman, D. (1994). Assessing predictions of violence: Being accurate about accuracy. *Journal of Consulting and Clinical Psychology, 62,* 783–792.

Mrazek, P. J., & Hagerty, R. J. (Eds.). (1994). *Reducing risks for mental disorders: Frontiers for preventive intervention research.* Washington, D.C.: National Academy Press.

Mruk, C. (1995). *Self-esteem: Research, theory, and practice.* Springer Publishing Co.

Mulhall, P. F., Stone, D., & Stone, B. (1996). Home alone: Is it a risk factor for middle school youth and drug use? *Journal of Drug Education, 26,* 39–48.

Mulroy, E. A. (1995). *The new uprooted: Single mothers in urban life.* Westport, CT: Auburn House/Greenwood.

Mulvey, E. P., & Cauffman, E. (2001). The inherent limits of predicting school violence. *American Psychologist, 56*(10), 797–802.

Murphy, J., & Duncan, B. (1997). *Brief interventions for school problems: Collaborating for practical solutions.* New York: Guilford.

Murphy, J. J. (1997). *Solution-focused counseling in middle and high schools.* Alexandria, VA: American Counseling Association.

Musick, J. S. (1993). *Young, poor, and pregnant.* New Haven, CT: Yale University Press.

Myers, H. F., & Taylor, S. (1998). Family contributions to risk and resilience in African American children. *Journal of Comparative Family Studies, 29,* 215–229.

Myrick, R. D., & Sorenson, D. L. (1985). *Peer pressure reversal: An adult guide to developing a responsible child.* Minneapolis: Educational Media Corporation.

Nansel, T. R., Overpeck, M., Pilla, R. S., Ruan, W. J., Simons-Morton, B., & Scheidt, P. (2001). Bullying behaviors among U.S. youth: Prevalence and association with psychosocial adjustment. *Journal of American Medical Association, 285*(16) 2094–2100.

National Campaign to Prevent Teen Pregnancy. (2001, May). *Emerging answers: Research findings on programs to reduce teen pregnancy.* Washington, DC: Author.

National Center for Children in Poverty. (2002). *Low-income children in the United States: A brief demographic profile.* Retrieved from *http://cpmcnet. columbia.edu/dept/nccp/ycpf.html* on May 9, 2002.

National Center for Chronic Disease Prevention and Health Promotion. (2000). *Adolescent and school* health: *Prevent alcohol and drug use.* Retrieved from *http://www.cdc.gov/nccdphp/dash/alcoholdrug. htm.*

National Center for Chronic Disease Prevention and Health Promotion, Centers for Disease Control and Prevention. (2000). *Youth risk behavior surveillance system.* Retrieved from *http://www.cdc.gov/nccdphp/ dash/yrbs /youth99online.htm* on May 10, 2002.

National Center for Chronic Disease Prevention and Health Promotion. (2002). *The burden of chronic diseases and their risk factors.* Retrieved from *http:// www.cdc.gov/nccdphp/burdenbook2002/03_ smokehs.htm.*

National Center for Education Statistics. (2000). *Indicators of school crime and safety.* Washington, D.C.: Author.

National Center for Education Statistics. (2001). *The condition of education 2001.* U.S. Department of Education (NCES 2001-072). Washington, DC: Government Printing Office.

National Center for Health Statistics. (1992). *Vital statistics of the United States: 1992, Volume I-Natality.* Washington, DC: U.S. Department of Health and Human Services.

National Center for Health Statistics. (1999). *Teen births.* Retrieved from *http://cdc.gov/nchs/fastats/ teenbrth.htm* on May 5, 2002.

National Center for Health Statistics. (2000). *Deaths: Final data for 1998.* Washington, DC: U.S. Department of Health and Human Services.

National Center for Vital Statistics. (2002). *Teenage births in the United States: State trends, 1991–2000, an update.* Volume 50(9), 1–4. (PHS) 2002-1120.

National Commission on Children. (1991). *Speaking of kids: A national survey of children and parents.* Washington, DC: Author.

National Commission on Excellence in Education. (1983). *A nation at risk: The imperative for educational reform.* Washington, DC: U.S. Government Printing Office.

National Gay and Lesbian Task Force Policy Institute. (1994). *Anti-gay/lesbian/bisexual violence fact sheet: April 1994 update.* Washington, DC: Author.

National Institute on Drug Abuse. (1995). *Drug use among racial/ethnic minorities.* Rockville, MD: National Institutes of Health.

National Institute on Drug Abuse. (1995). *National household survey of drug abuse: Population estimates, 1994.* Rockville, MD.

National Institute on Drug Abuse. (2002). *National household survey of drug abuse: Population estimates,* 2000. Rockville, MD: U.S. Department of Health and Human Services.

National Organization on Adolescent Pregnancy, Parenting, and Prevention. (1995). *Pregnancy, poverty, school, and employment.* Bethesda, MD: NOAPPP.

National Research Council. (1990). *Who cares for America's children?* Washington, DC: National Academy Press.

National School Safety Center (NSSC). (1999). *Checklist of characteristics of youth who have caused school-associated violent deaths.* Retrieved from *www.nssc1. org* on April 2001.

Newcomb, M. D., & Bentler, P. M. (1989). Substance use and abuse among children and teenagers. *American Psychologist, 44*(2), 242–248.

Newcomb, M. D., & Felix-Ortiz, M. (1992). Multiple protective and risk factors for drug use and abuse: Cross-sectional and prospective findings. *Journal of Personal and Social Psychology, 63,* 280–296.

Newcomb, M. D., & McGee, L. (1991). Influence of sensation seeking on general deviance and specific problem behaviors from adolescence to young adulthood. *Journal of Personality and Social Psychology, 61*(4), 614–628.

Nie, N. H., & Erbring, L. (2000). *Internet and society.* Stanford Institute for the Quantitative Study of Society. Retrieved from *http://www.stanford.edu/group/ siqss/Press_Release/Preliminary_Report.pdf* on July 26, 2002.

N.O.L. v. District of Columbia, 674 A.2d 498 (Dist. of Columbia, 1996).

Nock, S. L., & Kingston, P. W. (1991). Time with children: The impact of couples' work-time commitments. *Social Forces, 67,* 59–85.

Noell, J. W., & Ochs, L. M. (2001). Relationship of sexual orientation to substance use, suicidal ideation, suicide attempts, and other factors in a population of homeless adolescents. *Journal of Adolescent Health, 29*(1), 31–36.

Nolen-Hoeksema, S., Girgus, J. S., & Seligman, M. E. P. (1992). Predictors and consequences of childhood depressive symptoms: A 5-year longitudinal study. *Journal of Abnormal Psychology, 101,* 405–422.

Norton, A. J., & Glick, B. C. (1986). One-parent families: A social and economic profile. *Family Relations, 35,* 9–17.

Norton, D. G. (1994). Education for professionals in family support. In S. L. K. Kagan, & B. Weissbourd (Eds.), *Putting families first: America's family support movement and the challenge of change* (pp. 401–440). San Francisco: Jossey-Bass.

Norwood, P. M., Atkinson, S. E., Tellez, K., & Saldana, D. C. (1997). Contextualizing parent education programs in urban schools: The impact on minority parents and students. *Urban Education, 32*(3), 411–432.

Novoco, R. W. (1975). *Anger control: The development and evaluation of an experimental treatment.* Lexington, MA: Heath.

Novoco, R. W. (1979). The cognitive regulation of anger and stress. In P. C. Kendall & S. D. Hollan (Eds.), *Cognitive-behavioral interventions: Theory, research, and procedures* (pp. 241–285). New York: Academic Press.

Obiakor, F. E. (2001). *It even happens in "good" schools: Responding to cultural diversity in today's classrooms.* Thousand Oaks, CA: Sage.

O'Connor, M. F. (1992). Psychotherapy with gay and lesbian adolescents. In S. H. Dworkin & F. J. Gutierrez (Eds.), *Counseling gay men and lesbians: Journey to the end of the rainbow* (pp. 3–22). Alexandria, VA: AACD.

Oden, S., Schweinhart, L., & Weikart, D. P. (2000). *Into adulthood: A study of the effects of Head Start.* Michigan: High/Scope Educational Research Foundation.

Oetting, E. R., & Beauvais, F. (1986). Peer cluster theory: Drugs and the adolescent. *Journal of Counseling and Development, 65,* 17–22.

Oetting, E. R., & Beauvais, F. (1987). Peer cluster theory, socialization characteristics, and adolescent drug use: A path analysis. *Journal of Counseling Psychology, 34*(2), 205–213.

Oetting, E. R., & Beauvais, F. (1990). Adolescent drug use: Findings of national and local surveys. *Journal of Consulting and Clinical Psychology, 58,* 385–394.

Office of Elementary and Secondary Education. (2000). *Education for homeless children and youth program: Title VII, subtitle B of the McKinney-Vento homeless assistance act. Report to Congress, Fiscal Year 2000* (EDD00014). Washington, DC: U.S. Government Printing Office.

Office of Technology Assessment, U.S. Congress. (1991). *Adolescent health.* (Ota-H-468.) Washington, DC: U.S. Government Printing Office.

Office of the Surgeon General. (2001). *Youth violence: A report of the surgeon general.* Retrieved from http://www.surgeongeneral.gov/library/youthviolence/youvioreport.htm on May 10, 2002.

O'Hearn, T. C., & Gatz, M. (1996). The educational pyramid: A model for community intervention. *Applied and Preventive Psychology, 5,* 127–134.

Oldridge, O. A. (1982). Positive suggestion: It helps LD students learn. *Academic Therapy, 17,* 279–287.

Olrich, F. (1983). A whole person spelling class. *Academic Therapy, 19,* 73–78.

Olweus, D. (1993). Bully/victim problems among schoolchildren: Long term consequences and an effective intervention program. In S. Hodgins (Ed.), *Mental disorder and crime* (pp. 317–349). Thousand Oaks, CA: Sage.

Oregon Department of Education. (2002). *New century schools· Lessons learned.* Retrieved from http://www.ode.state.or.us/opte/New_Century_Schools/index.htm on July 3, 2002.

Orlinsky, D. E., Grawe, K., & Parks, B. K. (1994). Process and outcome in psychotherapy: *Noch einmal.* In A. E. Bergin & S. L. Garfield (Eds.), *Handbook of psychotherapy and behavior change* (4th ed., pp. 270–376). New York: Wiley.

O'Rourke, K., & Worzbyt, J. C. (1996). *Support groups for children.* Bristol, PA: Accelerated Development.

Orthner, D. K., & Randolph, K. A. (1999). Welfare reform and high school dropout patterns for children. *Children and Youth Services Review, 21*(9/10), 881–900.

O'Shaughnessy, T. E., Lane, K. L., Gresham, F. M., & Beebe-Frankenberger, M. E. (2002). Students with or at risk for emotional and behavioral difficulties: An integrated system of prevention and intervention. In K. L. Lane, F. M. Gresham, & T. E. O'Shaughnessy (Eds.), *Interventions for children with or at risk for emotional and behavioral disorders* (pp. 3–17). Boston: Allyn & Bacon.

Osofsky, J. D. (1997). *Children in a violent society.* New York: Guilford Press.

Otto, R. (1992). The prediction of dangerous behavior: A review and analysis of "second generation" research. *Forensic Reports, 5,* 103–133.

Overby, K. J., & Kegeles, S. M. (1994). The impact of AIDS on an urban population of high-risk female minority adolescents: Implications for intervention. *Journal of Adolescent Health, 15,* 216–227.

Oyserman, D., & Markus, H. R. (1990). Possible selves and delinquency. *Journal of Personality and Social Psychology, 59,* 112–125.

Pagliaro, A. M., & Pagliaro, L. (1996). *Substance use among children and adolescents: Its nature, extent, and effects from conception to adulthood.* Somerset, NJ: Wiley.

Papolos, D., & Papolos, J. (1999). *The bipolar child.* New York: Broadway Books.

Parham, T. (1991, April). *Effective counseling interventions for promoting wellness among African American males.* Paper presented at the American Association for Counseling and Development National Convention, Reno, NV.

Patterson, G. R. (1993). Orderly change in a stable world: The antisocial trait as a chimera. *Journal of Consulting and clinical Psychology, 61*, 911–919.

Patterson, G. R., Crosby, L., & Vuchinich, S. (1992). Predicting risk for early police arrest. *Journal of Quantitative Criminology, 8*(4), 335–355.

Patterson, G. R., De Baryshe, B. D., & Ramsey, E. (1989). A developmental perspective on antisocial behavior. *American Psychologist, 44*(2), 329–335.

Patterson, G. R., Reid, J. B., & Dishion, T. J. (1992). *Antisocial boys*. Eugene, OR: Castalia.

Patterson, G. R., Reid, J. B., & Dishion, T. J. (1998). Antisocial boys. In J. M. Jenkins & K. Oatley (Eds.), *Human emotions: A reader* (pp. 330–336). Malden, MA, US: Blackwell Publishers Inc.

Peck, P. (1989). The child at risk: Closing in on success. *Instructor, 98*(6), 30–32.

People v. Brac, 167 P.2d 535 (1946).

Perry, N. J. (1988, November). Saving the schools: How business can help. *Fortune*, pp. 42–56.

Peterson, A. C., & Mortimer, J. T. (Eds.). (1994). *Youth unemployment and society*. New York: Cambridge University Press.

Peterson, C., Maier, S., & Seligman, M. (1993). *Learned helplessness*. New York: Oxford.

Pettit, G. S., Bates, J. E., & Dodge, K. A. (1997). Supportive parenting, ecological context, and children's adjustment: A seven-year longitudinal study. *Child Development, 68*, 908–923.

Pfeffer, C. R., Hurt, S. W., Kakuma, T., Peskin, J. R., Siefker, C. A., & Nagabhairava, S. (1994). Suicidal children grow up: Suicidal episodes and effects of treatment during follow-up. *Journal of the American Academy of Child and Adolescent Psychiatry, 33*, 225–230.

Pfeffer, C. R., Normandin, L., & Kakuma, T. (1994). Suicidal children grow up: Suicidal behavior and psychiatric disorders among relatives. *Journal of the American Academy of Child and Adolescent Psychiatry, 33*, 1087–1097.

Phillips, K. (1990). *The politics of rich and poor: Wealth and the American electorate in the Regan aftermath*. New York: Random House.

Phillips, V., McCullough, L., Nelson, C. M., & Walker, H. M. (1992). Teamwork among teachers: Promoting a statewide agenda for students at risk for school failure. *Special Services in the Schools, 6*(3/4), 27–49.

Pierce, M. (2002). *No child left behind? A faculty response to President Bush's education bill*. Harvard Graduate School of Education News. Retrieved from *http://www.gse.harvard.edu/news/features/pierce0701 2002.html* on May 29, 2002.

Pierce, M. N., Stahlbrand, K., & Armstrong, S. B. (1984). *Increasing student productivity through peer tutoring programs*. Austin, TX: Pro-Ed.

Piers, E. V. (1984). *Piers-Harris children's self-concept scale—Revised edition*. Nashville, TN: Counselor Recordings and Tests.

Pines, D. (1991). *Parent training is prevention: Preventing alcohol and other drug problems among youth in the family*. Rockville, MD: Office for Substance Abuse Prevention.

Pinker, S. (1991). Rules of language. *Science, 253*, 530–555.

Pinnell, G. S., Lyons, C. A., DeFord, D. E., Bryk, A. S., & Seltzer, M. (1994). Comparing instructional models for the literacy education of high-risk first graders. *Reading Research Quarterly, 29*, 8–39.

Plunkett, K., & Marchman, V. (1993). From rote learning to system building: Acquiring verb morphology in children and connectionist nets. *Cognitive, 48*, 21–69.

Plunkett, M. (2000). Substance use rates among American Indian adolescents: Regional comparisons with monitoring the future high school seniors. *Journal of Drug Issues, 30*, 575–592.

Plunkett, M., & Mitchell, C. M. (2000). Substance use rates among American Indian adolescents: Regional comparisons with Monitoring the Future high school seniors. *Journal of Drug Issues, 30*, 575–592.

Pong, S., & Ju, D. (2000). The effects of change in family structure and income on dropping out of middle and high school. *Journal of Family Issues, 21*(2), 147–169.

Poulin, F., Dishion, T. J., & Burraston, B. (2001). 3-year iatrogenic effects associated with aggregating high-risk adolescents in cognitive-behavioral preventive interventions. *Applied Developmental Science, 5*(4), 214–224.

Premack, D. (1965). Reinforcement theory. In D. Levin (Ed.), *Nebraska Symposium on Motivation: 1965*. Lincoln: University of Nebraska Press.

Prilleltensky, I. (1989). Psychology and the status quo. *American Psychologist, 44*(5), 795–802.

Prilleltensky, I. (1997). Values, assumptions and practices: Assessing the moral implications of psychological discourse and action. *American Psychologist, 52*(5), 517–535.

Princeton Survey Research Associates. (1997, March). *National omnibus survey questions about teen pregnancy*. Association of Reproductive Health

Professionals and the National Campaign to Prevent Teen Pregnancy. Washington, DC: Author.

Princeton Survey Research Associates (2001). *Condom advertising on television.* Menlo Park, CA: Henry J. Kaiser Family Foundation. Retrieved 3-35-03 from *http://www.kff.org/content/2001/3135/SurveySnapshot. pdf.*

Prochaska, J., Velicer, W., DiClemente, C., & Fava, J. (1988). Measuring processes of change: Application to the cessation of smoking. *Journal of Consulting and Clinical Psychology, 56,* 520–528.

Prochaska, J. O., & DiClemente, C. C. (1983). Stages and processes of self-change of smoking: Toward an integrative model of change. *Journal of Consulting and Clinical Psychology, 51,* 390–395.

Prochaska, J. O., & DiClemente, C. C. (1986). Toward a comprehensive model for change. In W. R. Miller & N. Heather (Eds.), *Treating addictive behaviors.* New York: Plenum Press.

Prochaska, J. O., & DiClemente, C. C. (1992). Stages of change in the modification of problem behaviors. In J. O. Prochaska (Ed.). *Progress in Behavior Modification* (pp. 184–218). New York: Academic Press.

Proeger, C., & Myrick, R. (1980). Teaching children to relax. *Florida Educational Research and Development Council Research Bulletin, 14,* 51.

Prothrow-Stith, D. (2001). Youth, risk, and resilience: Community approaches to violence prevention. In J. M. Richmond & M. W. Fraser (Eds.), *The context of youth violence: Resilience, risk, and protection* (pp. 97–114). Westport, CT: Praeger.

Prothrow-Stith, D., & Weissman, M. (1991). *Deadly consequences: How violence is destroying our teenage population and a plan to begin solving the problem.* New York: Harper Perennial.

Pryor, D. B., & Tollerud, T. R. (1999). Applications of Adlerian principles in school settings. *Professional School Counseling, 2*(4), 299–304.

Queralt, M. (1993). Risk factors associated with completed suicide in Latino adolescents. *Adolescence, 28*(112), 831–850.

Quint, S. (1994). *Schooling homeless children.* New York: Teachers College Press.

Radke-Yarrow, M., Nottelmann, E., Belmont, B., & Welsh, J. D. (1993). Affective interactions of depressed and nondepressed mothers and their children. *Journal of Abnormal Child Psychology, 21,* 683–695.

Radkowsky, M., & Siegel, L. J. (1997). The gay adolescent: stressors, adaptations, and psychosocial interventions. *Journal of Clinical Psychology, 17,* 191–216.

Rafferty, Y., & Shinn, M. (1991). The impact of homelessness on children. *American Psychologist, 46,* 1170–1179.

Rak, C. F., & Patterson, L. E. (1996). Promoting resilience in at-risk children. *Journal of Counseling and Development, 74,* 368–373.

Randell, B., Eggert, L. L., & Pike, K. (2001). Immediate post intervention effects of two brief youth suicide prevention interventions. *Suicide and Life-Threatening Behavior, 31*(1), 41–61.

Randolph, S. M. (1995). African American children in single-mother families. In B. J. Dickerson (Ed.), *African American single mothers: Understanding their lives and families* (pp. 117–145). Thousand Oaks, CA: Sage.

Range, L. M., Leach, M. M., McIntyre, D., Posey-Deters, P. B., Marion, M. S., Kovac, S. H., et al. (1999). Multicultural perspectives on suicide. *Aggression and Violent Behavior, 4*(4), 413–430.

Ray, O., & Ksir, C. (1987). *Drugs, society, and human behavior.* St. Louis, MO: Times Mirror/Mosby.

Reasoner, R. W. (1992). *Teacher's manual: Building self-esteem in the elementary schools* (2nd ed.). Palo Alto: Consulting Psychologists Press.

Reddy, M., Borum, R., Berglund, J., Vossekuil, B., Fein, R., & Modzeleski, W. (2001). Evaluating risk for targeted violence in schools: Comparing risk assessment, threat assessment, and other approaches. *Psychology in the Schools, 38*(2), 157–172.

Reid, J. B., Patterson, G. R., & Snyder, J. (Eds.). (2002). *Antisocial behavior in children and adolescents: A developmental analysis and model for intervention.* Washington, DC: American Psychological Association.

Reid, J. B., Snyder, J. J., & Patterson, G. R. (Eds.). (2002). *Antisocial behavior in children and adolescents: A developmental analysis and the Oregon Model for Intervention.* Washington, DC: American Psychological Association.

Remafedi, G., Farrow, J. A., & Deisher, R. W. (1991). Risk factors for attempted suicide in gay and bisexual youth. *Pediatrics, 87,* 869–875.

Remafedi, G., French, S., Story, M., Resnick, M., & Blum, R. (1998). The relationship between suicide risk and sexual orientation: Results of a population-based study. *American Journal of Public Health, 88*(1), 57–60.

Reminger, K., Hidi, S., & Krapp, A. (Eds.). (1992). *The role of interest in learning and development.* Hillsdale, NJ: Erlbaum.

Renninger, S. M., Veach, P. M., & Bagdade, P. (2002). Psychologists' knowledge, opinions, and decision-making processes regarding child abuse and neglect reporting laws. *Professional Psychology: Research and Practice, 33,* 19–23.

Resnick, M. D., Bearman, P. S., Blum, R. W., Bauman, K. E., Harris, K. M., Jones, J., Tabor, J., Behring, T., Sieving, R. E., Shew, M., Ireland, M., Bearinger, L. H., & Uldry, J. R. (1997). Protecting adolescents from harm: Findings from the National Longitudinal Study on Adolescent Health. *Journal of the American Medical Association, 278* (10), 823–832.

Reville, P. (2002). No child left behind? A faculty response to President Bush's education bill. *Harvard Graduate School of Education News.* Retrieved from *http://www.gse.harvard.edu/news/features/reville 07012002.html* on May 29, 2002.

Rexroat, C., & Shehan, C. (1987). The family life cycle and spouses' time in housework. *Journal of Marriage and the Family, 49,* 737–750.

Reyes, O., & Hedeker, D. (1993). Identifying high-risk students during school transition. *Prevention in Human Services, 10*(2), 137–150.

Richardson, D., Hammock, G., Smith, S., Gardner, W., & Signo, M. (1994). Empathy as a cognitive inhibitor of interpersonal aggression. *Aggressive Behavior, 20,* 275–289.

Riche, M. F. (2000). America's diversity and growth: Signposts for the 21st century: Family life. *Population Bulletin, 55*(2), 26–28.

Rigby, K. (1999). Peer victimization at school and the health of secondary school students. *British Educational Psychology, 68,* 95–104.

Rigby, K. (2000). Effects of peer victimisation in schools and perceived social support on adolescent well-being. *Journal of Adolescence, 23,* 57–68.

Rigg, P. (1990). Whole language in adult ESL programs. *ERIC/CLL News Bulletin, 13* (2), 1–7.

Riley, P. L., & McDaniel, J. (2000). School violence prevention, intervention, and crisis response. *Professional School Counseling, 4*(2), 120–125.

Riley, R. W. (1986). Can we reduce the risk of failure? *Phi Delta Kappan, 68,* 214–219.

Rivera, E., & Omizo, M. M. (1980). The effects of relaxation and biofeedback on attention to task and impulsivity among male hyperactive children. *Exceptional Child, 27*(1), 41–51.

Rivers, I., & D'Augelli, A. R. (2001). The victimization of lesbian, gay, and bisexual youths. In A. R. D'Augelli & C. J. Patterson (Eds.), *Lesbian, gay, bisexual identities and youth: Psychological perspectives* (pp. 199–223). New York: Oxford University Press.

Roberts, S. (1994, December 24). Gap between rich and poor widens in New York. *New York Times.*

Robertson, D., & Mathews, B. (1989). Preventing adolescent suicide with group counseling. *Journal for Specialists in Group Work, 14*(1), 34–39.

Robin Hood Foundation. (1996). *Kids having kids.* Washington, DC: Author.

Robinson, R. B., & Frank, D. I. (1994). The relation between self-esteem, sexual activity, and pregnancy. *Adolescence, 29*(113), 27–35.

Robinson, W. L., Watkins-Ferrell, P., Davis-Scott, P., & Ruch-Ross, H. S. (1993). Preventing teenage pregnancy. In D. S. Glenwick, & L. A. Jason (Eds.), *Promoting health and mental health in children, youth, and families* (pp. 99–124). New York: Springer Publishing Co.

Roderick, M. (1994). Grade retention and school dropout: Investigating the association. *American Educational Research Journal, 31*(4), 729–759.

Roderick, T. (1988). Johnny can learn to negotiate. *Educational Leadership, 45*(4), 86–90.

Roe v. Wade, 410 U.S. 113 (1973).

Rogers, J. R. (1990). Female suicide: The trend toward increasing lethality in method of choice and its implications. *Journal of Counseling and Development, 69*(1), 37–38.

Romano, J. L., & Hage, S. M. (2000). Prevention and counseling psychology: Revitalizing commitments for the 21st century. *The Counseling Psychologist, 28,* 733–763.

Rose, S., Bisson, J., & Wessely, S. (2001). Psychological debriefing for preventing post traumatic stress disorder (PTSD) (Cochrane Review) [Abstract]. *Cochrane Library, 4.*

Rosenshine, B. V. (1986). Synthesis of research on explicit teaching. *Educational Leadership, 43*(7), 60–69.

Rosenshine, B., & Meister, C. (1991, April). *Reciprocal teaching: A review of nineteen experimental studies.* Paper presented at the annual meeting of the American Educational Research Association, Chicago.

Ross, J. G., Saavedra, P. J., Shur, G. H., Winters, F., & Felner, R. D. (1992). The effectiveness of an after-school program for primary grade latchkey students on precursors of substance abuse. *Journal of Community Psychology, OSAP Special Issue,* 22–38.

Roswal, G. M., Mims, A. A., Croce, R., Evans, M. D., Smith, B., Young, M., Bunch, M., Horvat, M. A., & Block, M. (1995). Effects of collaborative peer tutoring on urban seventh graders. *Journal of Educational Research, 88,* 275–279.

Rotheram-Borus, M. J., & Fernandez, I. (1995). Sexual orientation and developmental challenges experienced by gay and lesbian youths. *Suicide & Life-Threatening Behavior, 25,* 26–34.

Rotheram-Borus, M. J., & Langabeer, K. A. (2001). Developmental trajectories of gay, lesbian, and bisexual youths. In A. R. D'Augelli & C. J. Patterson (Eds.), *Lesbian, gay, and bisexual identities and youth* (pp. 97–128). New York: Oxford University Press.

Rotheram-Borus, M. J., Bradley, J., & Obolensky, N. (Eds.). (1990). *Planning to live: Evaluating and treating suicidal teens in community settings.* Tulsa: University of Oklahoma Press.

Rotheram-Borus, M. J., Rosario, M., & Koopman, C. (1991). Minority youths at high risk: Gay males and runaways. In M. E. Colten & S. Gore (Eds.), *Adolescent stress: Causes and consequences.* New York: Aldine de Gruyter, 181–200.

Rothstein, R. (1993). The myth of public school failure. *The American Prospect, 13*(Spring), 20–34.

Rowley, W. J., & MacDonald, D. (2001). Counseling and the Law: A cross-cultural perspective. *Journal of Counseling & Development, 79,* 422–429.

Roy, A. (1983). Family history of suicide. *Archives of General Psychiatry, 40,* 971–974.

Roy, A. (2001). Consumers of mental health services. *Suicide and Life-Threatening Behavior, 31*(1, Supplement), 60–83.

Rudolph, K. D., Lambert, S. F., Clark, A. G., & Kurlakowsky, K. D. (2001). Negotiating the transition to middle school: The role of self-regulatory processes. *Child Development, 72*(3), 929–946.

Rumberger, R. (1991). Chicano dropouts: A review of research and policy issues. In R. Valencia (Ed.), *Chicano school failure and success: Research and policy agendas for the 1990's* (pp. 64–89). New York: Falmer Press.

Rumberger, R. W. (1987). High school dropouts: A review of issues and evidence. *Review of Educational Research, 57,* 101–121.

Rumberger, R. W. (1990). Second chance for high school dropouts: The costs and benefits of dropout recovery programs in the United States. In D. Inbar (Ed.), *Second chance in education: An interdisciplinary and international perspective* (pp. 227–250). Basingstoke, England: Falmer Press.

Rumberger, R. W. (1995). Dropping out of middle school: A multilevel analysis of students and schools. *American Educational Research Journal, 32,* 583–625.

Russell, S. T., & Joyner, K. (2001). Adolescent sexual orientation and suicide risk: Evidence from a natural study. *American Journal of Public Health, 91,* 1276–1282.

Ryan, C. (2001). Counseling lesbian, gay, and bisexual youths. In A. R. D'Augelli & C. J. Patterson (Eds.), *Lesbian, gay, bisexual identities and youth: Psychological perspectives* (pp. 223–250). New York: Oxford University Press.

Ryan, C., & Futterman, D. (1998). *Lesbian & gay youth: Care & counseling.* New York: Columbia University Press.

Sadker, M. P., & Sadker, D. M. (1987). *Teachers, schools, and society.* New York: Random House.

Sadler, L., & Catrone, C. (1983). The adolescent parent: A dual developmental crisis. *Journal of Adolescent Health Care, 4,* 100–105.

San Francisco Community Board Program, Inc. (1982). *School initiatives* [video]. San Francisco: Author.

Sandau-Beckler, P. A., Salcido, R., & Ronnau, J. (1993). Culturally competent family preservation services: An approach for first-generation Hispanic families in an international border community. *The Family Journal: Counseling and Therapy for Couples and Families, 1*(4), 313–323.

Santa Rosa Health Care Corp. v. Garcia, 964 S.W.2d 940 (Tex. 1998).

Satir, V. (1967). *Conjoint family therapy: A guide to theory and technique* (Rev. Ed.). Palo Alto, CA: Science and Behavior.

Sautter, R. C. (1995). Standing up to violence. *Phi Delta Kappan, 76*(5), K1–K12.

Savin-Williams, R. C. (1994). Verbal and physical abuse as stressors in the lives of lesbian, gay male, and bisexual youths: Associations with school problems, running away, substance abuse, prostitution, and suicide. *Journal of Consulting and Clinical Psychology, 62*(2), 261–269.

Savin-Williams, R. C. (1995). Lesbian, gay male, and bisexual adolescents. In A. R. D'Augelli & C. J. Patterson (Eds.), *Lesbian, gay, and bisexual identities over the lifespan* (pp. 165–189). New York: Oxford University Press.

Savin-Williams, R. C., & Cohen, K. M. (Eds.). (1996a) *Developmental and clinical issues among lesbian, gay males, and bisexuals.* Fort Worth: Harcourt Brace.

Savin-Williams, R. C., & Cohen, K. M. (1996b). Psychosocial outcomes of verbal and physical abuse among lesbian, gay, and bisexual youths. In R. C. Savin-Williams & K. M. Cohen (Eds.), *The lives of lesbians, gays, and bisexuals: Children to adults* (pp. 181–200). Orlando, FL: Harcourt Brace College Publishers.

Savin-Williams, R. C., & Rodriguez, R. G. (1993). A developmental, clinical perspective on lesbian, gay male, and bisexual youths. In T. P. Gullotta, G. R. Adams, & R. Montemayor (Eds.), *Adolescent sexuality: Advances in adolescent development, 5* (pp. 77–101). Newbury Park, CA: Sage.

Sayger, T. V. (1996). Creating resilient children and empowering families using a multifamily group process. *The Journal for Specialists in Group Work, 21*(2), 81–89.

Scarr, S., Phillips, D., & McCartney, K. (1990). Facts, fantasies, and the future of child care in the United States. *Psychological Science, 1*(1), 26–35.

Scheier, L. (2001). Etiologic studies of adolescent drug use: A compendium of data resources and their implications for prevention. *Journal of Primary Prevention, 22*, 125–168.

Schliebner, C. T., & Peregoy, J. J. (1994). Unemployment effects on the family and the child: Interventions for counselors. *Journal of Counseling & Development, 72*(4), 368–372.

Schorr, L. B. (1988). *Within our reach: Breaking the cycle of disadvantage.* New York: Doubleday.

Schorr, L. B. (1997). *Common purpose: Strengthening families and neighborhoods to rebuild America.* New York: Doubleday.

Schultz, D., Izard, C. E., Ackerman, B. P., & Youngstrom, E. A. (2001). Emotion knowledge in economically disadvantaged children: Self-regulatory antecedents and relations to social difficulties and withdrawal. *Development and Psychopathology, 13*, 53–67.

Schwartz, D., McFadyen-Ketchum, S. A., Dodge, K. A., Pettit, G. S., & Bates, J. E. (1998). Peer group victimization as a predictor of children's behavior problems at home and in school. *Development and Psychopathology, 10*, 87–99.

Schwartz, J. A., Kaslow, N. J., Seeley, J., & Lewinsohn, P. (2000). Psychological, cognitive, and interpersonal correlates of attributional change in adolescents. *Journal of Clinical Child Psychology, 29*(2), 188–198.

Schweinhart, L. J., Weikart, B. P., & Larner, W. B. (1986). Consequences of three preschool curriculum models through age 15. *Early Childhood Research Quarterly, 1*(1), 15–45.

Schwendiman, J., & Fager, J. (1999, January). *After school programs: Good for kids, good for communities.* Northwest Regional Educational Laboratory. Retrieved from *http://www.nwrel.org* on January 10, 2002.

Scott, S. (1985). *Peer pressure reversal: An adult guide to developing a responsible child.* Amherst: Human Resource Development Press.

Scott, S. (1988). *Positive peer groups.* Amherst: Human Resource Development Press.

Seastrom, M. M., Gruber, K. J., Henke, R., McGrath, D. J., & Cohen, B. A. (2002). *Qualifications of the public school teacher workforce: Prevalence of out-of-field teaching, 1987–88 to 1999–2000.* (NCES Publication No. 2002-603). Washington, DC: U.S. Department of Education, National Center for Education Statistics.

Seidel, J. F., & Vaughn, S. (1991). Social alienation and the learning disabled school dropout. *Learning Disabilities Research and Practice, 6*(3), 152–157.

Seidman, E., & French, S. E. (1997). Normative school transitions among urban adolescents: When, where, and how to intervene. In H. J. Walberg & O. Reyes, et al. (Eds.), Children and youth: Interdisciplinary perspectives. *Issues in Children's and Families Lives, Vol. 7* (pp. 166–189). Thousand Oaks, CA: Sage.

Seligman, M. (1990). *Learned optimism.* New York: Knopf.

Seligman, M. (1993). *Helplessness: On depression, development, and death.* San Francisco: Freeman.

Seligman, M. (1994). *What you can change and what you can't.* New York: Knopf.

Seligman, M. E. P. (1995). *The optimistic child: A revolutionary program that safeguards children against depression and builds lifelong resilience.* New York: Houghton Mills.

Seligman, M. E. P., Schulman, B. S., DeRubeis, R. J., & Hollon, S. D. (1999). The prevention of depression and anxiety. *Prevention & Treatment, 2*, article 8. Retrieved from *http://journals.apa.org/prevention/volume2/pre0020008a.html* on June 15, 2002.

Sergiovanni, T. J. (1994). *Building community in schools.* San Francisco: Jossey-Bass.

Sergiovanni, T. J. (2001). *The principalship.* Needham Heights, MA: Allyn and Bacon.

Serna, I. A., & Hudelson, S. (1993). Emergent Spanish literacy in a whole language bilingual classroom. In R. Donmoyer & R. Kos (Eds.), *At-risk students: Portraits, policies, programs, and practices* (pp. 291–321). Albany, NY: State University of New York Press.

Sewell, K. W., & Mendelsohn, M. (2000). Profiling potentially violent youth: Statistical and conceptual problems. *Children's Services: Social Policy, Research, and Practice, 3*, 147–169.

Sexton, T. L., & Whiston, S. C. (1994). The status of the counseling relationship: An empirical review, theoretical implications, and research directions. *The Counseling Psychologist, 22*, 6–78.

Shakeshaft, C., Barber, E., Hergenrother, M. A., Johnson, Y. M., Mandel L. S., & Sawyer, J. (1995). Peer harassment in schools. *Journal for a Just and Caring Education, 1*(1), 30–44.

Shannon, P. (1989). The struggle for control of literacy lessons. *Language Arts, 66,* 625–633.

Shapiro, E. S., & Cole, C. L. (1992). Self-monitoring. In T. H. Ollendick & M. Hersen (Eds.), *Handbook of child and adolescent assessment* (pp. 124–139). New York: Pergamon Press.

Shapiro, E. S., & Cole, C. L. (1994). *Behavior change in the classroom: Self-management interventions.* New York: Guilford Publications.

Sharan, S. (Ed.). (1994). *Handbook of cooperative learning methods.* Westport, CT: Greenwood Publishing Group.

Sharan, S. (Ed.). (1999). *Handbook of cooperative learning methods* (2nd ed.). New York: Praeger.

Shearer, C. (1990, January 17). Bankrupt: Education reforms costly. *State Press* (Tempe, AZ), p. 3.

Shedler, J., & Block, J. (1990). Adolescent drug use and psychological health: A longitudinal inquiry. *American Psychologist, 45,* 612–630.

Sheley, J., McGee, A., & Wright, J. (1992). Gun-related violence in and around inner-city schools. *AJDC, 146,* 677–682.

Shepard, L. A., & Smith, M. L. (1987). Effects of kindergarten retention at the end of first grade. *Psychology in the Schools, 24,* 346–357.

Sherman, A. (1992). *Falling by the wayside: Children in rural America.* Washington, DC: Children's Defense Fund.

Sherman, A. (1995). *Wasting America's future: The Children's Defense Fund report on the costs of child poverty.* Washington, DC: Children's Defense Fund.

Sherraden, M. W. (1986). School dropouts in perspective. *Educational Forum, 51,* 15–31.

Shortt, A. L., Barrett, P. M., & Fox, T. L. (2001). Evaluating the FRIENDS program: A cognitive-behavioral group treatment for anxious children and their parents. *Journal of Clinical Child Psychology, 30*(4), 525–535.

Shubert, T. H., Bressette, S., Deeken, J., & Bender, W. N. (1999). Analysis of random school shootings. In W. N. Bender, G. Clinton, & R. L. Bender (Eds.), *Violence prevention and reduction in schools* (pp. 97–101). Austin, TX: PRO-ED.

Shure, M. B. (1992a). *I can problem solve (ICPS): An interpersonal cognitive problem solving program (preschool).* Champaign, IL: Research Press.

Shure, M. B. (1992b). *I can problem solve (ICPS): An interpersonal cognitive problem solving program (kindergarten/primary grades).* Champaign, IL: Research Press.

Shure, M. B. (1992c). *I can problem solve (ICPS): An interpersonal cognitive problem solving program (intermediate elementary grades).* Champaign, IL: Research Press.

Shure, M. B. (1993). I can problem solve (ICPS): Interpersonal cognitive problem solving for younger children. *Early Child Development and Care, 96,* 49–64.

Shure, M. B. (1996a). *Raising a thinking child: Help your young child to resolve everyday conflicts and get along with others.* New York: Pocketbooks.

Shure, M. B. (1996b). *Raising a thinking child workbook.* New York: Pocketbooks.

Shure, M. B. (1999, April). Preventing violence: The problem solving way. *Juvenile Justice Bulletin,* 1–11.

Shure, M. B., & Spivack, G. (1978). *Problem-solving techniques in child rearing.* San Francisco: Jossey-Bass.

Shure, M. B., & Spivack, G. (1988). Interpersonal cognitive problem solving. In R. H. Price, E. L. Cowen, R. P. Lorion, & J. Ramos-McKay (Eds.), *14 ounces of prevention: A casebook for practitioners* (pp. 69–82). Washington, DC: American Psychological Association.

Silbert, J., Carnine, D., & Stein, M. (1990). *Direct instruction mathematics* (2nd ed.). Columbus, OH: Merrill.

Simmons, R. (2002). *Odd girl out: The hidden culture of aggression in girls.* New York: Harcourt Books.

Simons, R. L., Whitbeck, L. B., Conger, R. D., & Melby, J. N. (1991). The effect of social skills, values, peers, and depression on adolescent substance use. *Journal of Early Adolescence, 11*(4), 466–481.

Sinclair, M. F., Hurley, C. M., Evelo, D. L., Christenson, S. L., & Thurlow, M. L. (2002). Making connections that keep students coming to school. In B. Algozzine & P. Kay (Eds.), *Preventing problem behaviors: A handbook of successful prevention strategies* (pp. 162–182). Thousand Oaks, CA: Sage.

Sitlington, P. L., & Frank, A. R. (1993). Dropouts with learning disabilities: What happens to them as young adults? *Learning Disabilities Research and Practice, 8*(4), 244–252.

Sklar, H. (1995). *Chaos or community? Seeking solutions, not scapegoats for bad economics.* Boston: South End Press.

Sklare, G. (1997). *Brief counseling works: A solution focused approach for school counselors.* Thousand Oaks, CA: Corwin Press, Inc.

Skolnick, A. (1991). *Embattled paradise: The American family in an age of uncertainty.* New York: Basic Books.

Slavin, R. (1983). *Cooperative learning.* New York: Longman.

Slavin, R., & Madden, N. (1989). What works for students at risk: A research synthesis. *Educational Leadership, 46*(5), 4–13.

Slavin, R. E. (1991). Cooperative learning and group contingencies. *Journal of Behavioral Education, 1*(1), 105–115.

Slavin, R. E. (1993). Ability grouping in the middle grades: Achievement effects and alternatives. *The Elementary School Journal, 93*(5), 535–552.

Slavin, R. E. (1994). Preventing early school failure: The challenge and the opportunity. In R. E. Slavin, N. L. Karweit, & B. A. Wasik (Eds.), *Preventing early school failure: Research, policy and practice* (pp. 1–12). Boston: Allyn & Bacon.

Slavin, R. E., Karweit, N. L., & Wasik, B. A. (Eds.). (1994). *Preventing early school failure: Research, policy, and practice.* Boston: Allyn & Bacon.

Small, M. A., Lyons, P. M., & Guy, L. S. (2002). Liability issues in child abuse and neglect reporting statutes. *Professional Psychology: Research and Practice, 33,* 13–18.

Smith, C. (1996). The link between childhood maltreatment and teenage pregnancy. *Social Work Research, 20*(3), 131–141.

Smith, D. J., Young, K. R., Nelson, J. R., & West, R. P. (1992). The effect of a self-management procedure on the classroom academic behavior of students with mild handicaps. *School Psychology Review, 21,* 59–72.

Smith, F. (1988). *Understanding reading: A psycholinguistic analysis of reading and learning to read* (Vol. 4). Hillsdale, NJ: Lawrence Erlbaum.

Smith, G. T. (1994). Psychological expentancy as mediator of vulnerability to alcoholism. *Annals of the New York Academy of Sciences, 70*(8), 165–171.

Smith, J. C., Mercer, J. A., & Rosenberg, M. L. (1989). Hispanic students in the Southwest, 1980–82. In *Alcohol, drug abuse, and mental health administration, Report of the secretary's task force on youth suicide, Volume 3: Prevention and interventions in youth suicide* (pp. 196–205). DHHS Pub. No. (ADM) 89-1623. Washington, DC: U.S. Government Printing Office.

Smith, K. (2002). *Who's minding the kids? Child care arrangements: Spring 1997.* Current Population Reports. Washington, DC: U.S. Census Bureau.

Smith, K. W., McGraw, S., Crawford, S. L., Costa, L. A., & McKinlay, J. B. (1993). HIV risk among Latino adolescents in two New England cities. *American Journal of Public Health, 83,* 1395–1399.

Smith, M. J. (1986). *Yes, I can say no.* New York: Arbor House.

Smith, R. C., & Lincoln, C. A. (1988). *America's shame, America's hope: Twelve million youth at risk.* Chapel Hill, NC: MDC.

Smith, S. W., & Daunic, A. P. (2002). Using conflict resolution and peer mediation to support positive behavior. In B. Algozzine & P. Kay (Eds.), *Preventing problem behaviors: A handbook of successful prevention strategies* (pp. 162–182). Thousand Oaks, CA: Sage.

Smith, T. (2000). *Data from the general social survey.* Chicago, IL: University of Chicago National Opinion Research Center.

Smylie, M. A., & Tuermer, U. (1992). *Hammond, Indiana: The politics of involvement v. the politics of confrontation.* Claremont, CA: Claremont Graduate School, Claremont Project VISION.

Snyder, C. R. (1994). *The psychology of hope: You can get there from here.* New York: Free Press.

Snyder, C. R., Sympson, S. C., Ybasco, F. C., Borders, T. F., Babyak, M. A., & Higgins, R. L. (1996). Development and validation of the State Hope Scale. *Journal of Personality and Social Psychology, 2,* 321–335.

Snyder, C. R., Wiklund, C., & Cheavens, J. (1998). *Hope and success in college: Making the grades, graduating, or dropping-out?* Unpublished manuscript, University of Kansas, Lawrence, Kansas.

Snyder, H. N. (2000, December). Juvenile arrests 1999. Washington, DC: U.S. Department of Justice, *Bulletin of the Office of Justice Programs, Office of Juvenile Justice and Delinquency Prevention,* 1–11.

Solow, R. M. (1994). *Wasting America's future: The Children's Defense Fund report on the costs of child poverty.* Washington, DC: Children's Defense Fund.

Sommers-Flanagan, J., & Sommers-Flanagan, R. (1998). Assessment and diagnosis of conduct disorder. *Journal of Counseling & Development, 76,* 189–197.

Southern Regional Project on Infant Mortality. (1997). *Investments and expenditures.* City: Author.

Spergel, I., Curry, D., Chance, R., Kane, C., Ross, R., Alexander, A., Simmons, E., & Oh, S. (1996). Gang suppression and intervention: Problem and response. Washington, DC: U.S. Department of Justice, *Research Summary, Office of Justice Programs, Office of Juvenile Justice and Delinquency Prevention.*

Spivack, G., & Shure, M. B. (1974). *Social adjustment of young children.* San Francisco: Jossey-Bass.

Spivack, G., Platt, J. J., & Shure, M. B. (1976). *The problem solving approach to adjustment.* San Francisco: Jossey-Bass.

SRI International. (1997, December 11) *Charter School Effectiveness.*

Starbuck, D., Howell, J. C., & Lindquist, D. (2001, December). Hybrid and other modern gangs. Washington, DC: U.S. Department of Justice, Office of Justice Programs, *Bulletin of the Office of Juvenile Justice and Delinquency Prevention.*

State v. Tritt, 23 Utah 365, 463 P.2d 806 (1970).

Stephens, S. (2001). The effectiveness of Motivational Enhancement Therapy in adolescent smoking cessation. *Dissertation Abstracts International, 62* (2-B). U.S. Department of Health and Human Services, Fact Sheet (2002). Substance Abuse—A National Challenge: Prevention, treatment and research at HHS. Retrieved from *http://www.cdc.gov/nccdphp/dash/alcoholdrug.htm.*

Stephens, T. M. (1992). *Social skills in the classroom* (2nd ed.). Odessa, FL: Psychological Assessment Resources.

Stevens, P., & Smith, R. (1996). *Substance abuse prevention and intervention: Theory and practice.* New York: Macmillan.

Stevens, R. J., & Slavin, R. E. (1995). The cooperative elementary school: Effects on students' achievement, attitudes, and social relations. *American Educational Research Journal, 32*(2), 321–351.

Stevens, R. J., Slavin, R. E., & Farnish, A. M. (1991). The effects of cooperative learning and direct instruction in reading comprehension strategies on main idea identification. *Journal of Educational Psychology, 83*(1), 8–16.

Stevenson, H. C. (1994). Racial socialization in African-American families: The art of balancing intolerance and survival. *Family Journal: Counseling and Therapy for Couples and Families, 2*(3), 190–198.

Stevens-Simon, C., & White, M. M. (1991). Adolescent pregnancy. *Pediatric Annals, 20,* 322–331.

Stivers, C. (1990). Promotion of self-esteem in the prevention of suicide. *Death Studies, 14,* 303–327.

Stormshak, E. A., Bierman, K. L., & The Conduct Problems Prevention Research Group. (1998). The implications of different developmental patterns of disruptive behavior problems for school adjustment. *Development and Psychopathology, 10,* 451–468.

Stormshak, E. A., & Dishion, T. J. (2002). An ecological approach to clinical and counseling psychology. *Clinical Child and Family Psychology Review, 5,* 197–215.

Straus, M. A. (1964). Power and support structure of the family in relation to socialization. *Journal of Marriage and Family, 26,* 318–326.

Straus, M. B. (1994). *Violence in the lives of adolescents.* New York: Norton.

Styron, T., Hanoff-Bulman, R., & Davidson, L. (2000). "Please ask me how I am": Experiences of family homelessness in the context of single mothers' lives. *Journal of Social Distress & the Homeless, 9*(2), 143–165.

Suarez, E. M., Mills, R. C., & Steward, D. (1987). *Sanity, insanity, and common sense: The missing link in understanding mental health* (2nd ed.). New York: Ballantine.

Sue, D. W., & Sue, D. (1999). *Counseling the culturally different: Theory and practice* (3rd ed.). New York: John Wiley & Sons, Inc.

Sue, D. W., & Sue, D. (2003). *Counseling the culturally diverse: Theory and practice* (4th ed.). New York: John Wiley & Sons.

Sugai, G. (1996). Providing effective behavior support to all students: Procedures and processes. *SAIL, 11*(1), 1–4.

Sugai, G., & Horner, R. H. (1999). Discipline and behavioral support: Preferred processes and practices. *Effective School Practices, 17*(4), 10–22.

Sugai, G., & Horner, R. H. (2001). Features of an effective behavior support at the school district level. *Beyond Behavior, 11*(1), 6–19.

Sullivan, M., & Wodarski, J. S. (2002). Social alienation in gay youth. *Journal of Human Behavior in the Social Environment, 5*(1), 1–17.

Summerville, M. B., Kaslow, N. J., & Doepke, K. J. (1996). Psychopathology and cognitive and family functioning in suicidal African-American adolescents. *Current Directions in Psychological Science, 5*(1), 7–11.

Sussman, S., Dent, C. W., Burton, D., Stacy, A. W., & Flay, B. R. (1995). *Developing school-based tobacco use prevention and cessation programs.* Thousand Oaks, CA: Sage.

Sutton, M., Brown, J. D., Wilson, K., & Klein, J. (2001). Shaking the tree of knowledge for forbidden fruit: Where adolescents learn about sexuality and contraception. In J. D. Brown, J. R. Steele, & K. W. Childers (Eds.), *Sexual teens, sexual media.* Hillsdale, NJ: Lawrence Erlbaum Associates.

Sutton, M. J., Brown, J. D., Wilson, K. M., & Klein, J. D. (2002). Shaking the tree of knowledge for forbidden fruit: Where adolescents learn about sexuality and contraception. In J. D. Brown, J. R. Steele, & K. Walsh-Childers (Eds.). *Sexual teens, sexual media.* Hillsdale: NJ: Lawrence Erlbaum Associates.

Swadener, B. B., & Lubeck, S. (Eds.). (1995). *Children and families at promise: Deconstructing the discourse of risk.* Albany: State University of New York Press.

Swaim, R. C., Oetting, E. R., Edwards, R. W., & Beauvais, F. (1989). Links from emotional distress to adolescent drug use: A path model. *Journal of Consulting and Clinical Psychology, 57,* 227–231.

Swanson, M. C. (1989). Advancement via individual determination: Project AVID. *Educational Leadership, 46*(5), 63–64.

Swearer, S., Song, S. Y., Cary, P. T., Eagle, J. W., & Mickelson, W. T. (2001). Psychosocial correlates in bullying and victimization: The relationship between depression, anxiety and bully/victim status. *Journal of Emotional Abuse, 2* (2/3), 95–122.

Sweeney, T. J. (1998). *Adlerian counseling: A practitioner's approach* (4th ed.). Philadelphia: Taylor & Francis.

Szapocznik, J., & Williams, R. A. (2000). Brief strategic family therapy: Twenty-five years of interplay among theory, research and practice in adolescent behavior problems and drug abuse. *Clinical Child and Family Psychology Review, 3*(2), 117–135.

Szapocznik, J., Santisteban, D., Kurtines, W. M., Perez-Vidal, A., & Hervis, O. (1984). Bicultural effectiveness training: A treatment intervention for enhancing intercultural adjustment in Cuban-American families. *Hispanic Journal of Behavioral Sciences, 6,* 317–344.

Szapocznik, J., Santisteban, D., Rio, A., Perez-Vidal, A., & Kurtines, W. M. (1986a). Family effectiveness training (FET) for Hispanic families. In H. P. Lefley & P. B. Pedersen (Eds.), *Cross-cultural training for mental health professionals.* Springfield, IL: Charles C Thomas.

Szapocznik, J., Santisteban, D., Rio, A., Perez-Vidal, A., & Kurtines, W. M. (1986b). Bicultural effectiveness training (BET): An experimental test of an intervention modality for families experiencing intergenerational/intercultural conflict. *Hispanic Journal of Behavioral Sciences, 8*(4), 303–330.

Szapocznik, J., Santisteban, D., Rio, A., Perez-Vidal, A., & Kurtines, W. M. (1989). Family effectiveness training: An intervention to prevent drug abuse and problem behaviors in Hispanic adolescents. *Hispanic Journal of Behavioral Sciences, 11*(1), 4–27.

Tang, M., & Cook, E. P. (2001). Understanding relationship and career concerns of middle school girls. In P. O'Reilly, E. M. Penn, & K. deMarrais (Eds.), *Educating young adolescent girls* (pp. 213–229). Mahwah, NJ: Lawrence Erlbaum Associates.

Tansy, M., Santos de Barona, M., McWhirter, J. J., & Herrmann, D. S. (1996). Peer and cross-age tutoring programs: Counsellor contribution to student achievement. *Guidance and Counselling, 12*(1), 21–24.

Taqi-Eddin, K., Macallair, D., & Schiraldi, V. (1998). *Class dismissed: Higher education vs. corrections during the Wilson years.* San Francisco, CA: The Justice Policy Institute.

Tarasoff v. Regents of the University of California, et.al., 17 Cal. 3d 425, 551 P2d 334 (1976).

Tarter, R. E., Blackson, T., Martin, C., Loeber, R., & Moss, H. B. (1993). Characteristics and correlates of child discipline practices in substance abuse and normal families. *American Journal on Addictions, 2,* 18–25.

Tate, D. C., Reppucci, N. D., & Mulvey, E. P. (1995). Violent juvenile delinquents: Treatment effectiveness and implications for future action. *American Psychologist, 50*(9), 777–781.

Taylor, B., Pressley, M., & Pearson, D. (2000). *Research-supported characteristics of teachers and schools that promote reading achievement.* Center for the Improvement of Early Reading Achievement.

Teacher Education Institute. (2002). *Bully prevention in schools: On-line course for teachers.* Retrieved from *http://www.teachereducation.com/course_outlines/ graduate_online/bully_gradon_outline.htm* on December 15, 2002.

Tell, C., & Conley, D. (1998). *Higher education's response to school reform in Oregon.* Council for Basic Education. Retrieved from *http://www.c-b-e.org/articles/oregon.htm* on July 5, 2002.

The dropout's perspective on leaving school. (1988). *CAPS Capsule,* 2–3.

The world almanac and book of facts. (1991). New York: World Almanac/Pharos.

Thomas, D. L., Gecas, V., Weigert, A., & Rooney, E. (1967). *Family socialization and the adolescent.* Lexington, MA: D. Heath.

Thompson, E. A., & Eggert, L. L. (1999). Using the suicide risk screen to identify suicidal adolescents among potential high school dropouts. *Journal of the American Academy of Child and Adolescent Psychiatry, 38*(12), 1506–1514.

Thomson, E., Hanson, T., & McLanahan, S. (1994). Family structure and child well-being: Economic resources vs. parental behaviors. *Sociological Forces, 73,* 221–242.

Tidwell, R., & Corona Garrett, S. (1994). Youth at risk: In search of a definition. *Journal of Counseling and Development, 72,* 444–446.

Tolan P. H., & Gorman-Smith, D. (1997). Families and the development of urban children. In H. J. Walberg & O. Reyes (Eds.), *Children and youth: interdisciplinary perspectives. Issues in children's and families' lives* (Vol. 7, pp. 67–91). Thousand Oaks, CA: Sage.

Tolan, P. H., & Guerra, N. G. (1994). Prevention of delinquency: Current status and issues. *Applied & Preventive Psychology, 3,* 251–273.

Tomlinson-Keasey, C., & Keasey, C. B. (1988). "Signatures" of suicide. In D. Capuzzi & L. Golden (Eds.), *Preventing adolescent suicide* (pp. 213–245). Muncie, IN: Accelerated Development.

Torres, A., & Forest, J. D. (1988). Why do women have abortions? *Family Planning Perspectives, 20,* 169–176.

Towberman, D. B., & McDonald, R. M. (1993). Dimensions of adolescent self-concept associated with substance use. *The Journal of Drug Issues, 23*(3), 525–533.

Townsend, K. C., & McWhirter, B. T. (2003). Connectedness: A review of current literature, with implications for counseling, assessment, and research. Unpublished manuscript, University of Oregon.

Triantafillou, N. (1997). A solution-focused approach to mental health supervision. *Journal of Systemic Therapies, 16,* 305–328.

Trimble, J. E., Bolek, C. S., & Niemcryk, S. J. (Eds.) (1992). *Ethnic and multicultural drug abuse: Perspectives on current research.* Binghamton, NY: Harrington Park Press.

United States v. Chase, 301 F.3d 1019 (9th Cir. 2002).

United States v. Glass, 133 F.3d 1356 (10th Cir. 1998).

United States v. Hayes, 227 F.3d 578 (6th Cir. 2000).

Upchurch, D. M., & McCarthy, J. (1990). The timing of first birth and high school completion. *American Sociological Review, 55,* 224–234.

U.S. Bureau of the Census. (1992). National data book and guide to sources. *Statistical abstracts of the United States, 1988.* Washington, DC: Government Printing Office.

U.S. Census Bureau. (2001). *Census 2000 Supplementary Survey.* Washington, DC: Demographic Surveys Division.

U.S. Census Bureau. (2001). *Historical poverty tables.* Retrieved from *http://www.census.gov/hhes/poverty/poverty00/table5.html* on August 9, 2002.

U.S. Census Bureau. (2002). *Mother's Day, 2002: May 12.* Retrieved from *http://www.census.gov/Press-Release/www/2002/cb02ff08.html* on August 9, 2002.

U.S. Conference of Mayors. (2001). A *status report on hunger and homelessness in America's cities: 2001.* Washington, DC: National League of Cities.

U.S. Department of Commerce. (1997). *March 1997 population survey.* U.S. Department of Commerce News (CB99-115). Washington, DC: Author.

U.S. Department of Commerce, Bureau of the Census. (1993). Washington, DC: Author.

U.S. Department of Education. (1998). *National educational goals panel report.* Washington, DC: Author.

U.S. Department of Education. (2000). *Safeguarding our children: An action guide.* Washington, DC: U.S. Government Printing Office.

U.S. Department of Education (2001). *Safe, disciplined, and drug-free schools programs.* Office of Special Educational Research and Improvement with Office of Reform Assistance and Dissemination. Washington, DC: Author.

U.S. Department of Education and Justice. (1999). *1999 annual report on school safety.* Washington, DC: U.S. Government Printing Office.

U.S. Department of Health & Human Services. (1998). *New tools for HIV care: STD treatment.* Rockville, MD: Health Resources & Services Administration.

Valleroy, L. A., MacKellar, D., & Jacobs, T. (1996). *HIV and risk behavior prevalence among young men who have sex with men sampled in six urban counties in the USA.* Presented to the 11th International Conference on AIDS, Vancouver, BC.

van Dalen, A., & Glasserman, M. (1997). My father, Frankenstein: A child's view of battering parents. *Journal of American Child and Adolescent Psychiatry, 36,* 1005–1007.

Vaughn, S., Hughes, M. T., Moody, S. W., & Elbaum, B. (2001). Instructional grouping for reading for students with LD: Implications for practice. *Intervention in School and Clinic, 36*(3), 131–137.

Velez, W., & Saenz, R. (2001). Toward a comprehensive model of the school leaving process among Latinos. *School Psychology Quarterly, 16*(4), 445–467.

Ventura, S., & Curtin, S. C. (1999). Recent trends in teen births in the United States. *Statistical Bulletin, 80*(1), 2–12.

Ventura, S. J., Martin, J. A., Curtin, S. C., Mathews, T. J., & Park, M. M. (2000). Births: Final data for 1998. *National Vital Statistics Reports, 48* (3). Hyattsville, MD: National Center for Health Statistics.

Ventura, S. J., Martin, J. A., Taffel, S. M., Matthews, T. J., & Clarke, S. C. (1992). Advance report of final natality statistics. *Monthly Vital Statistics Report, 43* (5 Suppl).

Ventura, S. J., Matthews T. J., & Hamilton, B. E. (2002). Teenage Births in the United States: State Trends, 1991–2000, an Update. *National Vital Statistics Reports, 50.* Atlanta, GA: Centers for Disease Control.

Vernon, A. (1983). Rational-emotive education. In A. Ellis & M. Bernards (Eds.), *Rational-emotive approaches to the problems of childhood.* New York: Plenum Press.

Vickers, H. S. (1994). Young children at risk: Differences in family functioning. *Journal of Educational Research, 87*(5), 262–270.

Vidal, J. A. (1989). *Student suicide: A guide for intervention.* Washington, DC: National Education Association.

Wachelka, D., & Katz, R. C. (1999). Reducing test anxiety and improving academic self-esteem in high school and college students with learning disabilities. *Journal of Behavior Therapy and Experimental Psychiatry, 30,* 191–198.

Wagner, E. F. (1993). Delay of gratification, coping with stress, and substance use in adolescence. *Experimental and Clinical Psychopharmacology, 1*(1–4), 27–43.

Wagner, W. G. (1996). Optimal development in adolescence: What is it and how can it be encouraged? *The Counseling Psychologist, 24*(3), 360–399.

Walker, H. M., Colvin, G., & Ramsey, E. (1995). *Antisocial behavior in school: Strategies and best practices.* Pacific Grove, CA: Brooks/Cole.

Walker, L. E. A. (1990). Psychological assessment of sexually abused children for legal evaluation and expert witness testimony. *Professional Psychology: Research and Practice, 21,* 344–353.

Walker, L. E. A. (1996). *Abused women and survivor therapy: A practical guide for the psychotherapist.* Washington, DC: American Psychological Association.

Wallace, S., & Estroff, T. (2001). In Estroff, T. (Ed.), *Manual of adolescent substance abuse treatment* (pp. 235–252). Washington, DC: American Psychiatric Publishing, Inc.

Walsh-Bowers, R. T. (1992). A creative drama prevention program for easing early adolescents' adjustment to school transitions. *Journal of Primary Prevention, 13*(2), 131–147.

Watkins, K. P., & Durant, L. (1996). *Working with children and families affected by substance abuse: A guide for early childhood education and human service staff.* West Nyack, NY: The Center for Applied Research Education.

Watt, D., & Roessingh, H. (1994). ESL dropout: The myth of educational equity. *Alberta Journal of Educational Research, 40*(3), 283–296.

Way, N., & Leadbeater, B. (1999). Pathways toward educational achievement among African American and Puerto Rican adolescent mothers: Reexamining the role of social support from families. *Development and Psychopathology, 11,* 349–361.

Wayne, A. (2002, June 13). Teacher inequality: New evidence on disparities in teachers' academic skills. *Education Policy Analysis Archives, 10*(30). Retrieved from *http://epaa.asu.edu/epaa/v10n30/* on July 4, 2002.

Webster-Stratton, C. (1997). From parent training to community building. *Families in Society: The Journal of Contemporary Human Services, 78,* 156–171.

Webster-Stratton, C., Reid, M. J., & Hammond, M. (2001). Preventing conduct problems, promoting social competence: A parent and teacher training partnership in Head Start. *Journal of Clinical Child Psychology, 30*(3), 283–302.

Weed, K., Keogh, D., & Borkowski, J. (2000). Predictors of resiliency in adolescent mothers. *Journal of Applied Developmental Psychology, 21,* 207–231.

Wehlege, G. C. (1991). School reform of at-risk students. *Equity and Excellence, 23*(1), 15–24.

Weinberg, N. Z., Dielman, T. E., Mandell, W., & Shope, J. T. (1994). Parental drinking and gender factors in the prediction of early adolescent alcohol use. *International Journal of the Addictions, 29*(1), 89–104.

Weinstein, B., Levine, M., Kogan, N., Harkavy-Friedman, J., Miller, J. M., (2000). Mental health professionals' experiences reporting suspected child abuse and maltreatment. *Child Abuse & Neglect, 24,* 1317–1328.

Weissman, M., Leaf, P., & Bruce, M. (1987). Single-parent women: A community study. *Social Psychiatry, 22,* 29–36.

Weisz, J. R., Sweeney, L., Proffitt, V., & Carr, T. (1993). Control-related beliefs and self-reported depressive symptoms in late childhood. *Journal of Abnormal Psychology, 102,* 411–418.

Wenz, K., & McWhirter, J. J. (1990). Enhancing the group experience: Creative writing exercise. *Journal for Specialists in Group Work, 15*(1), 37–42.

Werch, C. E., & DiClemente, C. C. (1994). A multicomponent stage model for matching drug prevention strategies and messages to youth stage of use. *Health Education Research: Theory & Practice, 9,* 37–46.

Werner, E. E. (1995). Resilience in development. *Current Directions in Psychological Science, 4*(3), 81–82.

Werner, E. E., & Smith, R. S. (1992). *Overcoming the odds: High risk children from birth to adulthood.* Ithica, NY: Cornell University Press.

West, P. (1992). Indians go on offensive to fight alcohol's effects. *Education Week, 11*(1), 12–13.

Whisman, M. A., & Kwon, P. (1993). Life stress and dysphoria: The role of self-esteem and hopelessness. *Journal of Personality and Social Psychology, 65*(5), 1054–1060.

White, R., Algozzine, B., Autette, B., Marr, M. B., & Ellis, E. (2001). Unified discipline: A school-wide approach for managing problem behavior. *Intervention in School and Clinic, 37,* 3–8.

Whiteman, T. L., Borkowski, J., Keogh, D., & Weed, K. (2001). *Interwoven lives: Adolescent mothers and their children.* Mahwah, NJ: Erlbaum.

Wiig, E. H. (1983). *Let's talk: Developing prosocial communication skills.* Columbus, OH: Merrill.

Wilcox, D., & Dowrick, P. W. (1992). Anger management with adolescents. *Residential Treatment for Children and Youth, 9*(3), 29–39.

Wilens, T. E., Biederman, J., Bredin, E., Hahesy, A. L., Abrantes, A., Neft, D., Millstein, R., & Spencer, T. J. (2002). A family study of high-risk children of opiod- and alcohol-dependent parents. *American Journal on Addictions, 11*(1), 41–51.

Wilke, M. (2001). *Changing standards: Condom advertising on American television a special report of the Kaiser Daily Reproductive Health Report* (Publication Number 3139). Menlo Park, CA: The Henry J. Kaiser Family Foundation.

Wilkinson, J., & Canter, S. (1982). *Social skills training manual: Assessment, program design, and management of training.* New York: Wiley.

Williams, B. F. (1992). Changing demographics: Challenges for educators. *Intervention in school and clinic, 27*(3), 157–163.

Williams, J. G., & Smith, J. P. (1993). Alcohol and other drug use among adolescents: Family and peer influences. *Journal of Substance Abuse, 5,* 289–294.

Williams, J. M., Bachman, J. G., O'Malley, P. M., & Johnston, L. D. (1995). Racial/ethnic differences in adolescent drug use. In G. J. Botvin, S. Schinke, & M. A. Orlandi (Eds.), *Drug abuse prevention with multiethnic youth* (pp. 59–80). Thousand Oaks, CA: Sage.

Williams, S. M. (1994). *Environment and mental health.* Chichester, England: John Wiley & Sons.

Wilson, J. Q. (1993). *The moral sense.* New York: Macmillan.

Winfield, L., & Millsap, M. A. (1994). Characteristics of programs and strategies. In S. Stringfield, L. Winfield, M. A. Millsap, M. J. Puma, B. Gamse, & B. Randall (Eds.), *Urban and suburban/rural special strategies for educating disadvantaged children: First year report.* Washington, DC: U.S. Government Printing Office.

Wohlstetter, P., & Smyer, R. (1994). Models of high-performance schools. In S. A. Mohrman & P. Wohlstetter (Eds.), *School-based management: Organizing for high performance* (pp. 81–107). San Francisco: Jossey-Bass.

Wolin, S., & Wolin, S. (1993). *The resilient self: How survivors of troubled families rise above adversity.* New York: Random House.

Wood, C., & Davidson, J. (1993). Conflict resolution in the family: A P.E.T. evaluation study. *Australian Psychologist, 28*(2), 100–104.

Workman, E. (1982). *Teaching behavioral self-control to students.* Austin, TX: Pro-Ed.

World Health Organization. (1999). *Partners in life skills education: Conclusions from a United Nations Inter-Agency meeting.* Geneva: Author.

Wright, D. M. (1975). Criminal aspects of suicide in the United States, *North Carolina Central Law Journal, 7,* 156–163.

Wu, L., & Martinson, B. (1993). Family structure and the risk of a premature birth. *American Sociological Review, 58,* 210–232.

Wubbolding, R. E. (2000). *Reality therapy for the 21st century.* Philadelphia: Brunner-Routledge.

Wycoff, S., Bacod-Gebhardt, M., Cameron, S., Brandt, M., & Armes, B. (2002). Have families fared well from welfare reform? Educating clinicians about policy, paradox, and change. *Family Journal: Counseling & Therapy for Couples & Families, 10*(3), 269–280.

Yokota, F., & Thompson, K. M. (2000, May 24/31). Violence in G-rated animated films. *Journal of the American Medical Association, 283,* 2716–2720.

Yondorf, B. A. (1992). *Adolescents and AIDS: Stopping the time bomb.* Denver, CO: State Legislative Report.

Younge, S. L., Oetting E. R., & Deffenbacher J. L. (1996). Correlations among maternal rejection, dropping out of school, and drug use in adolescence. *Journal of Clinical Psychology, 52*, 96–102.

Youngstrom, E., Wolpaw, J. M., Kogos, J. L., Schoff, K., Ackerman, B., & Izard, C. (2000). Interpersonal problem solving in preschool and first grade: developmental change and ecological validity. *Journal of Clinical Child Psychology, 29*(4) 589–602.

Zenker, E. (1984). In the dark about teaching spelling? Just relax! *Academic Therapy, 20*(2), 231–234.

Zenker, E., & Frey, D. (1985). Relaxation helps less capable students. *Journal of Reading, 28*(4), 242–244.

Ziedenberg, J., & Schiraldi, V. (1999). *The punishing decade: Prison and jail estimates at the millennium.* Center on Juvenile and Criminal Justice. Retrieved from *http://www.cjcj.org/pubs/punishing/punishing.html* on June 18, 2002.

Zigler, E. (1995). Reshaping early childhood intervention to be a more effective weapon against poverty.

American Journal of Community Psychology, 22(1), 37–47.

Zigler, E. F., & Lang, M. E. (1991). *Child care choices: Balancing the needs of children, families, and society.* New York: Free Press.

Zigler, E. F., & Muenchow, S. (1992). *Head Start: The inside story of America's most successful educational experiment.* New York: Basic Books.

Zigmond, N. (1990). Rethinking secondary school programs for students with learning disabilities. *Focus on Exceptional Children, 23*(1), 1–22.

Zill, N., Morrison, D., & Coiro, M. J. (1993). Long-term effects of parental divorce on parent-child relationships, adjustment, and achievement in young adulthood. *Journal of Family Psychology, 7*, 91–103.

Zorn, T. (2001). Article: Millennium dreams: 21st century EEO practices for federal employees. *Public Manager, 30*(2), 20–24.

NAME INDEX

SUBJECT INDEX

Abortion. *See also* Teen pregnancy
  legal and ethical issues, 314–315
  teen pregnancy, 136
Absolution, use of suicide to provide,
  205
Academic skills, 83
Acculturation, issues of, 13
Active listening, 298–299
Active participant, individual as an, 22
Addiction. *See* Substance use and
  addiction
Adoption and teen pregnancy, 136
Affirmations, use of positive, 256–257
Aftercare programs, 126
Aggression, role of, 8, 9, 83, 158,
  189–191, 201
Aging family stage, 40
AIDS, 142–144
Al-anon Family Groups, 301, 302
Alateen, 301, 302
Alcohol use, role of, 9, 13, 14. *See also*
  Substance use and addiction
Alderian Model
  assumed inadequacy, 150–151
  attention-getting mechanisms
    (AGMs), 147–148
  corrective procedures, 151–153
  encouragement, effective use of,
    154–155
  goals of misbehavior, 147–148
  natural and logical consequences,
    153–154
  power, misbehavior as, 148–149
  purpose of, 146–147
  purposiveness of behavior, 147
  revenge, misbehavior as, 149
Alienation, 85
Alternative education programs, 109
American with Disabilities Act (ADA), 99
Anger and aggression, role of, 201. *See
  also* Aggression, role of
Anger management programs, 189–191
  SCARE, 189–191, 251
Antisocial behavior. *See also*
  Delinquency, juvenile; Gang
  membership
  aggression and violence, family, 158
  authority conflict, 158
  community and neighborhoods, role
    of, 161, 163
  community prevention and
    intervention, 170
  conduct disorder (CD), 159

covert actions, 158
definition of, 157
developmental and ecological model,
  161, 162
family prevention and intervention,
  168–169
gay, lesbian, bisexual, and
    transgendered youth, in, 163
multisystemic therapy (MST), 169
oppositional defiant disorder, 159
origins, 161–168
overt actions, 158
peer environment, role of, 166
prevention and intervention
  strategies, 168–170
reality therapy, 170–176
risk factors, 163–166
school prevention and intervention,
  169–170
school problems, 158–159
societal influence, 161, 163
vandalism, 159
Anxiety, role of, 8, 88
Anxious, emotional involvement/calm
  detachment, 49
Approach continuum, 226–227
Asian American population, growth of,
  13
Assertiveness skills and training, 126,
  252–253
At-risk society
  category activity, 9
  causes and effects, 13
  contextual challenges, 9
  criticism and debate, 9
  definition of, 6
  facts of, 5
  high risk, 8
  imminent risk, 8–9
  improvement, signs of, 6
  influences of (*See* specific
    influences)
  metaphor for, 14–16
  minimal risk, 7–8
  remote risk, 8
  resiliency, role of, 79–82
  risk factors, 22–25, 28–32
Attention-getting mechanisms (AGMs),
  147–148
Authority conflict, 158

Barber v. State, 308–309
Beck Hopelessness Scale, 210

Behavioral changes, identification of,
  206
Bellotti v. Baird, 314
Beneficial relaxation, 254–255
Biased attributions, 85
Bicultural effectiveness training (BET),
  297
Bidirectionality, assumption of, 22
Bilingual education programs, 74, 75
Bipolar disorder, 8, 48, 209
Bisexual youth. *See* Gay, lesbian,
    bisexual, and transgendered youth
Blended families, 46, 200
Blue Shield of Virginia v. McCready,
  317
Bogust v. Iverson, 317
Booster sessions, 228
Boundaries, establishment of, 291
Brief therapy and skills training,
  211–212
Bullying, role and prevention of, 189,
  191–193

*Carey v. Population Services
    International*, 314
Charter schools, 73
Child abuse, 47–48, 306–309
Child care, role and access to
    affordable, 9, 23, 24, 32–33, 33
Child-rearing practices
  anxious, emotional involvement/calm
    detachment, 49
  consequence of, 52–53
  hostility/warmth dimension, 49
  parenting cube, 51–52
  permissiveness/restrictiveness
    dimension, 49
Chinese population, growth of, 13
Chizmar v. Mackie, 315
Chronosystem, 22
Cigarette use, 9
Civil law, 309–313
Classroom structure, 73–74. *See also*
    Educational systems
Cleveland school voucher program, 72
Closed-system families, 41–42
Cluster suicides, 200
Cognitive constriction, 203
Cognitive dissonance, 120
Cognitive distortion, 204
Cognitive restructuring, 261–262
Cognitive rigidity, 204
Cognitive therapy (CT), 261, 262–263

TO THE OWNER OF THIS BOOK:

I hope that you have found *At-Risk Youth: A Comprehensive Response for Counselors, Teachers, Psychologists and Human Service Professionals*, Third Edition useful. So that this book can be improved in a future edition, would you take the time to complete this sheet and return it? Thank you.

School and address: _____

_____

Department: _____

Instructor's name: _____

1. What I like most about this book is: _____

_____

_____

2. What I like least about this book is: _____

_____

_____

3. My general reaction to this book is: _____

_____

_____

4. The name of the course in which I used this book is: _____

_____

5. Were all of the chapters of the book assigned for you to read? _____

   If not, which ones weren't? _____

6. In the space below, or on a separate sheet of paper, please write specific suggestions for improving this book and anything else you'd care to share about your experience in using this book.

_____

_____

OPTIONAL:

Your name: _____ Date: _____

May we quote you, either in promotion for *At-Risk Youth: A Comprehensive Response for Counselors, Teachers, Psychologists and Human Service Professionals*, Third Edition, or in future publishing ventures?

Yes: _____ No: _____

Sincerely yours,

The McWhirters